The COMPLETE POETRY

and SELECTED PROSE *of*

J O H N   D O N N E

THE COMPLETE POETRY

and SELECTED PROSE OF

JOHN DONNE

EDITED, WITH AN INTRODUCTION BY

CHARLES M. COFFIN

THE MODERN LIBRARY · NEW YORK

821.3
D685c

THE MODERN LIBRARY
is published by RANDOM HOUSE, INC.

Manufactured in the United States of America

CONTENTS

ELEGIES AND HEROICALL EPISTLE

EPIGRAMS

SATYRES

INFINITATI SACRUM (Metempsychosis)

VERSE LETTERS TO SEVERALL PERSONAGES

EPITHALAMIONS, OR MARRIAGE SONGS

A FUNERALL ELEGIE AND THE FIRST AND SECOND ANNIVERSARIES

LATIN POEMS AND TRANSLATIONS

From ELEGIES UPON THE AUTHOR

PROSE

INTRODUCTION

BY CHARLES M. COFFIN

In 1880 Matthew Arnold was thinking about the future of poetry. It was "immense"—enough, probably, to shore up the modern spiritual life sagging from the decay of Christian orthodoxy.
He did not, I am sure, expect that the seventeenth-century poetry
of John Donne would figure in this future. Donne was not represented in the anthology that Arnold was introducing; moreover,
he was not classical in the sense that the "touchstones" and the
"high-seriousness" required. Yet, within fifty years Donne had
made an extraordinary place in the "immensity." In fact, in the
twentieth century he has been the poet to whom English and
American readers most often have turned—though not exclu-
sively—not for compensation for the lost religion, but for just
such an enlargement of our view of man and a sharpening of our
insight into his complication as the poet can give—in short, in
Arnold's phrase, for a "criticism of life."

Our concern with Donne's poetry has been pretty high for almost half a century. If a point were to be set to mark its beginning, I should say that 1912 would serve, the year when Professor Grierson published his great edition of the poems—though
that date is arbitrary, for already the Muses Library text was in
wide circulation, and in 1905 Charles Eliot Norton had made
his selection of the "love poems." Edmund Gosse's two volumes
of *The Life and Letters* had come out in 1899. It was obvious
that something was going on, and that it might go further than a
"revival" had been anticipated by George Saintsbury, who in
1896 had warned readers of Donne's genius for attracting the
coterie or for winning admirers "this side idolatry," and admitted that only a stiff critical resistance had moderated his own en-
thusiasms. By the twenties the interest had reached a pitch. The
"cult" of Donne was here. At the same time, a company of considerable poets put in their appearance—one could name most
of the important ones who came into prominence here and in
England after the First War—whose work clearly showed that
they had been reading Donne. Even those who had not yet made
his acquaintance—if their verses had the ruffled movement of
"spoken" music, a metaphor mingling objects of sense and in-

xvii

tellect, and an excitement of language generally—their critics
marked them with Donne's influence.

In 1921, Grierson's *Metaphysical Lyrics and Poems* added
further to Donne's prestige, and to that of the school of "metaphysical" poets with whom he had been associated since Dr.
Johnson's *Life of Cowley.* The appearance of this book occasioned the review by T. S. Eliot, which now has become a classic among the papers on the seventeenth-century poets. Eliot remarked their capacity for "direct sensuous apprehension of
thought," their possession of a "mechanism of sensibility which
could devour any kind of experience," indicative of the unified
sensibility which he regarded as a condition essential to their
peculiar accomplishment.[1] Thus, with a stroke, Eliot lightened
the burden of Johnson's long-standing judgment of the Meta-
physicals, that "the most heterogeneous ideas are yoked by violence together," by attributing to an accepted source of weak-
ness the cause of their special strength.

The prestige of Donne in these years could be measured not
only by the number of editions and reprints of his poetry which
were coming out, but also by the fact that its popularity had au-
thorized the recovery of his prose. In 1931, however, when the
three-hundredth anniversary of his death was being celebrated,
Eliot thought that the peak had been reached and that Donne's
poetry was a matter of current concern, not likely to enlist the
attentions of the future.[2] No doubt Donne had surrendered the
office of "poets' poet" which earlier he had filled. Yet, now, almost twenty years later, the scholars and critics are still busy with
him, as their numerous papers on his language, his rhetoric and
meter, and his biography show; and his poetry is still a discovery
for the young reader or for those who have heard his verse read
for the first time by a sensitive and experienced voice like that
of Austin Warren in his recent recordings. This discovery has
been summed up by F. R. Leavis, who, confident in his earlier
judgment, has but recently reissued the declaration that for us
Donne "obviously is a living poet in the most important sense."[3]

The impression possibly given that everyone has approved and
liked the kind of "living poet" that Donne is needs correction.
His reputation has been made too fast, some would say, and often

[1] "The Metaphysical Poets" (1921), in *Selected Essays 1917–1932*
(New York, 1932), pp. 246, 247.

[2] "Donne in Our Time," in *A Garland for John Donne 1631–1931,*
ed. Theodore Spencer (Cambridge, Mass., 1931), p. 5.

[3] "The Line of Wit," chap. 1, *Revaluation* (New York, 1947), p. 11.

at the expense of his betters. They have sensed something probably spurious about the whole affair, that we have "kidnapped" Donne rather than taken possession of him by the lawful means of sound literary judgment and a proper consideration of history. C. S. Lewis, for example, though sensible enough not to "deplore" history, has tried to ameliorate its ill effects by "explanation." Something has gone wrong with the modern world to make it especially hospitable to Donne: "an element of dandyism in Donne" has called to the "dandyism (largely of Franco-American importation) in the modern world"; or, it has lost its ear—"most modern readers do not know how to scan"—so that although "Donne may be metrically good or bad, in fact," it is "obvious that he might be bad without offending the great body of his modern admirers." [4]

The resistance to Donne centers upon his failure to square with "the tradition." Some years ago Eliot asked quite frankly if it was not time for us to regard Donne and his kind—the Herberts, King, Crashaw, Marvell, Vaughan, Cowley "at his best"—as being in the direct current of English poetry. [5] Answers have been given, affirmatively, like that of Cleanth Brooks in *Modern Poetry and the Tradition,* but there has been no consensus. Very likely the difficulty goes back pretty far, possibly to Ben Jonson, in whose ambiguous esteem his "true friend" was "the first poet in the world for some things," but "for not keeping of accent deserved hanging." Jonson reckoned that "for not being understood" Donne would perish, ironically aware that his own delight in his friend's learning and subtlety (he was "Longer a knowing, than most wits doe live") was not likely to be shared by everyone. "Obscure" and "difficult" are certainly words often used against Donne, and that he could be "harsh"—"My minde, neither with prides itch, nor yet hath been / Poyson'd with love to see, or to bee seene"—as well as harmonious, is well known, for he took pleasure in disturbing the composure of sound and sense which Spenser and Daniel had been teaching the poets. There are other "heresies": his distaste for the conventional Elizabethan love poetry—

> Rebell and Atheist too, why murmure I,
> As though I felt the worst that love could doe?

---

[4] "Donne and Love Poetry in the Seventeenth Century," in *Seventeenth Century Studies Presented to Sir Herbert Grierson* (Oxford, 1938), *esp.,* pp. 71–72.
[5] "The Metaphysical Poets," in *op. cit.,* p. 250.

> Love might make me leave loving, or might trie
> A deeper plague, to make her love mee too,

—and the irresponsibilities of taste and license of the youthful Elegies; and, above all, the bold analogues, or the "heterogeneity" of material which he coerced into his metaphors.

Yet, lines like these from *The Good-Morrow,* offered by Leavis in support of his judgment, can be submitted in reply to his critics:

> I wonder by my troth, what thou, and I
> Did, till we lov'd? were we not wean'd till then?
> But suck'd on countrey pleasures, childishly?
> Or snorted we in the seaven sleepers den?
> T'was so; But this, all pleasures fancies bee.
> If ever any beauty I did see,
> Which I desir'd, and got, t'was but a dreame of thee.

And the counter-statement could easily be extended.

Expectedly, the situation which I have summarized excites an interest in explanations—and many of them have been written. One important line which they have followed, though not the only one, remarks the fundamental compatibility—less cautious writers have said "similarity"—of Donne's time and our own. A matter of such scope and complication, obviously, cannot be arbitrated here; but the historical significance which Donne is felt to have is noteworthy, especially as he lived in a great period and, admittedly, expressed so complete an interest in it. He was born in London in 1571 or 1572, and he died near there in 1631. His life, then, was roughly coincident with Shakespeare's, Francis Bacon's, and Ben Jonson's; a little later than Spenser's, though overlapping nearly three decades. This was the age of the high Renaissance in England, and of its decline: Elizabethan England at its zenith and its setting and the shadowy years of the first two Stuart kings.

Comparing this period with the Greece of Pindar and Sophocles, Arnold remarks that then "the poet lived in a current of ideas in the highest degree animating and nourishing to the creative power; society was, in the fullest measure, permeated with fresh thought, intelligent and alive." The word "animating" or "animation"—the life in motion—which has the full connotation of his idea, might be taken as a suitable designation of possibly the most powerful quality of the Renaissance. There is the life and motion expressed outward, in the exploration of new lands and in the discovery of new facts in nature, in the earth and in the heavens; and, in the enlargement of the range of thought and sensation through the new association with the old classical literature and learning. There is also the reciprocal motion inward, increasing the sense of personal involvement in the world, and giving somehow a sense of responsibility for it, which placed man more nearly in the center of his own attentions and at the focus of all the animating forces.

There is at the same time the paradoxical "motion in corruption," as Donne puts it, the "breaking up" of history. Significantly, for example, there is the crumbling out "to his Atomies" of the old world-order, the massive body of moral and spiritual experience and natural learning which the logic of the Schoolmen and the Doctors of the Church had forged into a system of objective truth comprehending the totality of man's physical and metaphysical relations. The breakup of the feudal hierarchy and of the medieval Christian community are institutional aspects of the dissolution. Further, the movement toward the heightened individualism carried with it an inclination for self-analysis and introspection, ironically productive of anxiety and the feeling of personal isolation. Some time later Sir Thomas Browne, viewing the separation of the natural and the spiritual worlds which had come about, termed man that "great and true Amphibium," who was "disposed to live in divided and distinguished worlds." The extraordinary thing about the Renaissance is that then man could somehow inhabit the divided universe. For a brief period, at least, the power of old beliefs and values, surviving beyond the philosophical-theological structures in which earlier they were maintained, and a fine confidence in human worth—in the mind and in all of the "faculties of the soul"—collaborated to produce the sensibility which could apprehend significance in the total "heterogeneity" of the universe. And the fluid, unfixed state of the language of the period was the exact medium for the poets to present the complexity of the situation.

All this is reflected in Donne, in his writings and in his life, and a great deal is known about his life as well as about his texts. His own large correspondence in both verse and prose; the occasional pieces associated with identifiable persons and events; the explicitly autobiographical statements and allusions introduced into books and sermons; the memorial verses and other writings of friends, or such lively notes as William Drummond made of his conversations about Donne with Ben Jonson.

the official references in public documents; and, finally, the contemporary *Life* by Izaak Walton, constitute sources supplying a greater quantity of biographical information about Donne than exists for any other important English writer before John Milton.

The customary treatment of this material gives Donne three periods. The first shows us "Jack Donne" of the Town, prodigal of his fortune as well as of his affections, yet brilliantly ensconced in a courtly office until his secret marriage "above his class" to the niece of his employer lost him his post and all prospects of getting another. In the second period Donne is the distressed husband and father and the melancholy scholar, depending upon the generosity of friends and patrons, his fate oscillating between hope and disappointment until finally he accepted the invitation to take orders in the English Church. The last is the period of the divine, the Dean of Saint Paul's. His literary career is usually drawn into correspondence with his life, so that there is first the satirist and the cynical, rebellious love poet; then the poet of "sincere" love, sober verses, and scholarly books; and, at the end, the eloquent preacher and the author of holy sonnets and devotions. Both arrangements, however, are far too rigid and full of inaccuracies. The poetry especially has been forced into the formula by a zeal for biographical interpretation, which, in turn, has been made to argue the partitioning of his life.

Some particularization is in order. Donne came of a prosperous Roman Catholic family. His first teachers were Jesuits. He attended both Oxford and Cambridge, but received a degree from neither university because he could not take the oath required at graduation. He was admitted to the study of law, first at Thavies Inn and then at Lincoln's Inn. Early in the London years, having come into a considerable fortune, he became free to follow his native bent. He spent his money, at the theatre, on books and pleasures, and on travel on the Continent. In 1596 and 1597 he saw service under the popular Earl of Essex in the Cadiz expedition and the "Islands Voyage." Meanwhile, he had become the friend of the poet Christopher Brooke, his chamber-fellow at Lincoln's Inn, and of Ben Jonson, who was a member of Brooke's circle of literary associates.

Amidst all this activity Donne managed to remain a student and to cultivate an ambition for public life at Court. Looking back upon the earlier years, in *Pseudo-Martyr* (1610), Donne remarked his "naturall inclination not to digge painfully in deep, and stony, and sullen learnings," and an intellectual independence forbidding his attachment "to any one science, which should possess or denominate" him. Accordingly, in the same record, he admits having "survayed and digested the whole body of Divinity, controverted between ours and the Romane Church," and Walton says that he mastered "the grounds and use of Physicke." The remark on his divinity studies would imply that by 1610 he had broken with the family faith, though it would be incorrect to suppose that his "conversion" to Anglicanism came early, for the studious independence which was releasing him from the old ties did not easily let him establish new ones, and, as he goes on to say, "I used no inordinate hast, nor precipitation, in binding my conscience to any locall Religion." The poet of the Third Satyre expresses the same attitude. The state of his religious faith evidently was no obstacle to his public advancement, however, for after his return from service with Essex, he was appointed private secretary to Sir Thomas Egerton, Lord Keeper of the Privy Seal. Independently, or as a consequence of his new connection, he moved in a brilliant company, many of whom were to become his close friends, gentlemen like Sir Francis Wooley, Sir Henry Wotton, Rowland Woodward and George Gerrard and Sir Henry Goodyer, his special intimates in the coming years. The most important person he met, however, was Ann More, daughter of Sir George More and niece to Lady Egerton. They fell in love, carried on a secret courtship, and just before Christmas, 1601, were married, and, as Walton put it, "the remarkable error of his life" had been committed.

In these years Donne also had become a poet, and as well the author of many of the sportive prose exercises which go by the title *Paradoxes and Problemes (Juvenilia)*. Ben Jonson told Drummond as late as 1619 that Donne, in fact, had written his best poetry in these years, before he was twenty-five, a remark which, if taken literally, would exclude Ann More as the inspiration of what many suppose to be his finest pieces. If, however, we extend the period through the marriage year, 1601, we shall no doubt have the bulk of Donne's verse which later was classified as Songs and Sonets, Elegies ("Love elegies" in pentameter couplets), Satyres, Epigrams, and that strange, unfinished satirical "epistle" called *Metempsychosis: The Progresse of the Soule*, which carries the date "16 Augusti 1601." In addition, many of the Verse Letters will fall within this early period. A precise chronology of these poems cannot be offered. A very few of

Donne's poems were published in his lifetime *(The Baite, Breake of Day, Elegy on Prince Henry,* a couple of Latin pieces, and the notable *Funerall Elegie* on Elizabeth Drury and *The First and Second Anniversaries).* They got into wide circulation usually in manuscript, and, except where the person addressed or the occasion gives a clue, they are practically undatable. This fact, however, has not deterred interpreters from attempting the application of the biographical formula noted above, even after Grierson's warnings and his own practice of refraining from conjectures which could not be generously supported. How awkwardly the formula fits is evidenced, for example, by Grierson's discovery that *La Corona,* a group of religious sonnets, was probably written in 1609 instead of sometime after Donne had taken Holy Orders, or that Elegie XIV, with its joking conclusion about the wife's fidelity, if by Donne at all, came well along in the more sober years when he was supposed to have done with such matters. Again, although Walton sounds right in associating the famous *Valediction: Forbidding Mourning* with Donne's leave-taking from his wife when he went to the Continent in 1612, there is no such assurance for linking *The Canonization* with his uneasy courtship, nor for supposing that the "bracelet of bright haire about the bone" in *The Relique* was woven from Ann Donne's tresses. The inclination of many to attach the name of Lady Herbert to *The Autumnall* (Elegie IX) and *The Primrose,* or that of Lucy, Countess of Bedford, to *Twicknam Garden* and *A Nocturnall Upon S. Lucies Day* also raises considerable problems.

These early pieces assuredly bear Donne's stamp, and any estimate of his stature must take them fully into account. Their prominent subject is love, some aspect of the complex relation of man and woman, or some attitude of the lover toward this relation; but there are also the acrid portraits of flatterers and hypocrites or other creatures of the Court and London life of the Satyres. And there are some of the Verse Letters in this group which get the status of authentic poems because Donne understands how to mask the intimacies in the stiff permissive rhetoric of the form and at the same time to keep it in motion with the most direct kind of dramatic statement.

The thing in the love poems that is often talked about is their tonal range, from stark cynicism and disillusionment and reproach to the highest and gentlest celebration, but that way of speaking hardly brings one into contact with their most important qualities. One remembers the arresting opening lines:

——For Godsake hold your tongue, and let me **love**

—I am two-fooles, I know,

—If yet I have not all thy love,
    Deare, I shall never have it all,

—He is starke mad, who ever sayes,
    That he hath been in love an houre,

—I long to talke with some old lovers ghost,

——Goe, and catche a falling starre.

Lines like these command but do not halt the attention. They
open up a situation, and the attention enters fully. They are in
the rhetoric of address; yet it is not the poet addressing the
reader, nor addressing himself as poet, in the way, for instance,
that Shelley talks and declaims to himself. It is the poet as the
person *in* the poem speaking, and the voice is so precisely suited
to the meter that the phrasing and rhythm of real speech are
not only caught and retained, but emphasized. Donne is not, of
course, only a poet of brilliant introductions. The texts hold up.
There is the wonderful modulation in movement to fit the stress
and precision of the situations as they develop, effected by a
modification of diction, or by the calculated dislocation of the
phrase or word to give it the unexpected prominence and right-
ness which it requires—and yet the basic sense of an oral presen-
tation is maintained. The stanza from *The Good-Morrow* quoted
above illustrates this process.

Donne's lyric, further, is argumentative, dialectical, and thus
catches something of the tone of intellectualism of the late medieval Italian love poems, which likewise is in Wyatt who an-
ticipates Donne's speaking rhythms. This quality may be seen
if the conceptual language and the abstractions are taken into
account at the same time that the rhetorical structures of the
sentences are studied, wherein they present the question and
answer, the enumerative partitioning of the subjects, postulate
and inference, antithesis, and premise and conclusion. No doubt
the process reflects Donne's early acquaintance with the old dialectic, his native intellectual bent, and his familiarity with the
early poetry, but in Donne this is not "medievalism" once it is
naturalized within his animated rhythms and applied with dramatic directness to the personal situation. It is in some such
consideration of this, of Donne's sense for the animation of

language and of his delight in the play of mind upon the subjects, which Petrarch himself shows, that one comes to an understanding of his "revolt" from the popular love poetry of his day.
Actually Donne keeps to many of its words, like "sigh," "melt,"
"fair," "burn," "fuel," and "eyes"; but the Petrarchan psychology
("Fair is my love, and cruel as she is fair") had been frozen into
a reduction which his argumentative mind could not accept; and
the sensuous language of the sonneteers ("Whenas her hair,
more worth, more pale, than gold, / Like silver thread lies waft-
ing in the air," or "See where my love sits in the beds of
spices, / Beset all round with camphor, myrrh and roses") and
their smooth, distracting melody did not apprehend such an image of reality as he demanded. When one of his contemporaries
wrote, "My verse is the true image of my mind," he expressed
the kind of Platonic sentiment which kept much of this poetry
from connecting with experience in the way Donne's connects.
The reason is simply that such poetry reflects the formula, or
the doctrine in the mind, rather than the object in life and motion. Again, in comparing Donne's love poetry with the popular
kind, it is revealing to note the utterly different sense of the
personal pronouns, for example, in a line like "Burn on sweet
fire, for I live by that fuel," and in the first lines quoted above,
where the "living poet" articulates himself.

Another aspect of Donne's poetic, which has both historical
antecedents and use among his contemporaries, is the conceit, or
the metaphor compounded of disparate elements. In Donne's
poetry its use in conjunction with such features as those noted
above and its use in a way which makes it so completely expres-
sive of his sensibility and of his relation to so many facets of
his period make it almost the hallmark of his style. Examples
are abundant: phrases like "a naked thinking heart," "Bath'd in a
cold quicksilver sweat," "the spider love, which transubstantiates
all," or verses like

— As our blood labours to beget
    Spirits, as like soules as it can,
Because such fingers need to knit
    That subtile knot, which makes us man:

— Loves mysteries in soules doe grow,
    But yet the body is his booke,

— Who did the whole worlds soule contract, and drove
    Into the glasses of your eyes,

—   'Tis much that glasse should bee
        As all confessing, and through-shine as I,

— I, by loves limbecke, am the grave
        Of all, that's nothing,

—and one dare not omit reference to the classical example,
though written later, of the figure of the compasses in *A Valediction: Forbidding Mourning*, or, to the "cleare body" of the
lady of *A Funerall Elegie*, which was "so pure and thinne,"
" 'Twas but a through-light scarfe, her minde t'inroule."

So far in the description of Donne's poetry I have not used
the word "metaphysical," thinking it better to find the important
qualities in the texts than to appear to be deducing them from
a technical term. The word, it will be remembered, was first
linked to Donne's name by Dryden (He "affects the metaphys-
ics, not only in his satires, but in his amorous verses, where nature only should reign; and perplexes the minds of the fair sex
with nice speculations of philosophy, when he should engage
their hearts, and entertain them with the softnesses of love") and,
as noted, given wide application to seventeenth-century poetry
by Dr. Johnson. Some have wished to abandon the term, but the
word has managed to stick, and it remains a useful designation
for the combination of "passion and intellect" which one notes
in Donne's animated rendering of the dialectical and metaphorical features of his verse, and for the broad intellectual and
aesthetic implications of this process.

The passion which Donne shared with the Renaissance for
giving relation and organization to the multitudinous aspects
of this world is exhibited in the "heterogeneity" of the terms
comprising his metaphors; but there is also the passion for
relating the "divided and distinguished worlds" of matter and
spirit, and this gets expression through the significant juxtaposi-
tion of the secular terms with those whose referents are always
in some objective order of belief or big construct of reality. In
this way the certitudes of belief and value which received logical
endorsement in the medieval system are rendered symbolically
in Donne, to be grasped experientially as truths. Further, Donne
had a passion for the interior organization of the self, and this
also is realized in the metaphysical figure. The disparate elements
of human composition, for Donne, the Body and the Soul, are
never long allowed to go on their separate ways. To show this,
the treatment of the love experience is critical. There, the im-

pulse of both lover and beloved for the consummate joining of both flesh and spirit is strongest; and both as cause and as result of the perfection of their experience, the instinct of each is to achieve a completeness within himself. Nowhere in our poetry is this situation more suitably managed than in Donne's *Extasie*; and its significance is assumed in many other pieces, whether the local effect is honorific or cynical, for, paradoxically, the body and the soul are often at war as well as in rapport. Hence, the love experience in Donne's practice in these early poems is a kind of image of the persisting tension between Body and Soul, and between the secular and the divine. Yet, in dealing with the situation, Donne is not the mystic, for within the frame of the secular, human experience, which inevitably is his perspective, he acknowledges the dynamic of each of the principles in tension and does not admit the absorption of the energy of the one completely by the other.

The aesthetic implication of the metaphysical style is expressed by John Crowe Ransom when he says: "The impulse to metaphysical poetry . . . consists in committing the feelings in the case . . . to their determination within the elected figure." [6] The same impulse for relation and organization, for completeness, which operates in the situations already noted, operates within the poem itself and, in terms which the metaphor, the "elected figure," requires: as the body-soul image in *The Extasie,* the figures of annihilation in *A Nocturnall Upon S. Lucies Day,* the "hieroglyphical" importance of the *letter* in *A Valediction: of the Booke,* or, in the imagery clustered round "wonder" in *The Good-Morrow.* The texture of such pieces exploits the figure to display the argument so that all of the relevant possibilities are taken into account, and in an important order. Hence, the figure should not be taken to mean a single locution which is repeated many times, nor re-expressed as variously as ingenuity allows, as may be seen in shallow imitations. It is rather the vehicle of the basic thought-emotion situation, "elected" for its comprehension, or for its capacity to envelop the total meaning within its varied and appropriate manifestations.

Donne's successes, as expected, are not uniform. And to some, the levity so evident in pieces like *The Anagram* and *The Flea,* or the joking ambiguities and ugly language of *The Comparison,* or the calculated harshness of the Satyres suggest in several ways

---

[6] "Shakespeare at Sonnets," in *The World's Body* (New York, 1938). p. 286.

a cleverness or perversity which a poetry of seriousness and taste ought to avoid. It is extraordinary, however, to find him a good poet so much of the time, and often in the pieces where he is frowned upon. This simply means that we recognize that Donne, in fact, is an artist, quite responsible for what he is saying, and saying it in language, meter and stanza in a way which shows its importance. What he says, of course, in these early poems is nothing philosophical like the metaphysic which is structured in Dante's poem, nor is he throwing a poetical mask over a set of favorite concepts. Rather, he is realizing in language situations which may be referred to authentic human experiences, wherein ideas are in motion, that is, where both the mind and feelings are vigorously engaged.

In the first years of the seventeenth century, following the lively period of the early poems, when Donne was "out of favor" though still hoping for some preferment, he became, even if reluctantly, more and more the scholar, the "serious" poet and the contemplative. His correspondence multiplied; he attempted to put his learning to some public as well as private benefit; and he prepared himself, though unconsciously no doubt, not only for the composition of his most ambitious and most important poems, *The Anniversaries,* but as well for the profession which eventually he was going to follow. In the early phase of this period, until 1609, say, when Sir George More was induced to pay his daughter's dowry, or 1611, when he was generously assisted by the patronage of Sir Robert Drury, he was greatly helped along by friends like Sir Francis Wooley, or Lady Magdalene Herbert, George Herbert's mother, and Lucy, Countess of Bedford, the women who played such a prominent part in his life, as the literary and personal record shows.

In 1608 or thereabouts he wrote *Biathanatos,* a treatise on suicide. A book on such a subject at this time may expectedly show the "sickly inclination" to take his own life, which in the preface he confesses often to have felt. But there is little that is morbid in the text, and the personal note is kept far below the surface of the elaborate dialectic and show of learning which distinguish the composition. He did not, in fact, intend the "scandal" implicit in a defense of suicide, and if the nub of the argument can be isolated, it is that he wished to show the need for charitable interpretations of such an act whose motives are usually hidden and obscure, or, like Samson's, the evident desire to advance God's glory. The subtitle of the book, "a declaration of that paradoxe, or thesis, that selfe-homicide is not so naturally a sinne, that it may never be otherwise," suggests some formal relation with his *Paradoxes and Problemes*, and there is an ironical resemblance to these Juvenilia; but the real affinity is with those exercises in casuistry popular among the medieval theologians known as "cases of conscience," which examine particular points of conscience indeterminable by general principles. Walton says that Donne prepared many such exercises, and it is well known that the "cases of conscience" remained in fashion as a technique for alleviating troubled minds at least as late as Jeremy Taylor. Hence, as *Biathanatos* was not published by Donne, and as he continued to express an ambiguous regard for it ("Reserve it for me," he wrote to Sir Robert Carre, "and if I die, I only forbid it the Presse, and the Fire"), it seems reasonable to suppose that here Donne was instructing himself in a peculiarly personal case of conscience in order to relieve the "sickly inclination." Nor when one considers the therapeutic value of objectification does this interpretation seem inconsistent with the fact that the book was tricked out with all the academic paraphernalia and the many aspects of public address. *Biathanatos* was first published in 1646.

Donne's next extended effort was made as a consequence of his employment by Thomas Morton, afterward Bishop of Durham, whom he assisted in the preparation of some pamphlets in defense of the English Church against the Roman party. The collaboration led Morton to suggest that Donne ought to take Holy Orders, and it brought him into sufficient public attention as a champion of the English Church to persuade King James himself to invite him to enter the controversy directly. The dispute, it may be noted, concerned the Oath of Supremacy and Allegiance, imposed in 1605 because of the fears aroused by the allegedly Jesuit-incited Powder Treason or Gunpowder Plot. The result of the royal "order" was *Pseudo-Martyr*, which appeared in print in 1610 as his first published prose. The work is a "tract for the times," tedious in its legal learning and deployment of controversial tactics, though there are the interesting autobiographical references to his own Catholic background.

Pseudo-Martyr defends the proposition that "those which are of the Romane Religion in this Kingdome, may and ought to take the Oath of Allegiance," and condemns, as unwarranted self-persecution and "false martyrdom," the reward of martyrdom which the Jesuits promised to their followers who might suffer death for refusing to take the Oath. Donne's argument goes ahead with restraint and calm. As Englishman and Christian he respects the claims of both Church and State and sees no contradiction in the double loyalty. Further, there is the same independence of mind in matters of faith and religion that he expressed in the Third Satyre, and such a sense of charity in judgment as he proposed in *Biathanatos* for the treatment of true martyrdom, which there was instanced as a kind of self-homicide. The details exhibit an enormous learning, and the generalizations are quick insights into the nature of faith and patriotism. Had the occasion given him a wider scope, or if his method were not so directly apposite to the methods of the "scholastic men" whom he addresses, the book might have become something of a classic.

The next year, 1611, Donne "descended" to a different line towards the Jesuits, in a satire, *Ignatius his Conclave*, which was published anonymously in both Latin and English. The English title page reads "Translated out of Latine," and in a pseudonymous epistle, "The Printer to the Reader," Donne contrasts "his other booke," *Pseudo-Martyr*, testifying to the author's "ingenuity, and candor, and his disposition to labour for the reconciling of all parts," with this one, which "must teach what humane infirmity is," a condition sarcastically implied to have been learned from the Jesuits themselves. *Ignatius* is full of invention and ridicule, and there is something Swiftian in it, but the pedantry gets in the way and there is not the firmness of the irony throughout. He had the classical notion of what satire should attempt, and his overall strategy is right—anonymity, the affectation of translation, the "faked" epistle, and the great fiction of the journey of the soul and of the "dialogue in hell." The journey and the dialogue hold an interest not only for their satiric uses, but also for the connections they make with Renaissance history. Ignatius Loyola's rivals to the throne of Lucifer in hell, which is destined for the greatest "innovator" of the times, are Copernicus, Paracelsus, and Machiavelli. Both in the treatment accorded Copernicus and in the account of the "extasie" of Donne's "wandring sportful soule" surveying the planetary spaces while en route to hell, he shows that he knew the makers of the "new philosophy" with singular directness. In earlier works he had evidenced his acquaintance with Kepler, Copernicus, and Tycho; but here they reappear with such a sense of familiarity as the fiction requires, and in the company of Galileo, whose discoveries with the telescope, reported but the year before in *Sidereus Nuncius*, supply the appropriate cosmic geography.

No greater difficulty arises in connection with the interpreta-

tion of Donne's poetry than from attempting to deal literally
with his *Anniversaries,* the two most important poems of this
middle period. They are addressed to the memory of a lady
whom he did not know—Elizabeth Drury (died 1610), the fif-
teen-year old daughter of Sir Robert Drury of Hawstead. It was
really not out of the way for a poet to take account of the death
of some unknown, and there was a fine tradition of complimentary address for such occasions. The remarkable thing here is the
extravagance of Donne's hyperbole and Sir Robert's superlative
generosity. *A Funerall Elegie* won for Donne and his wife an
apartment in Drury House and much personal attention; the
bounty continued as Donne remembered the first anniversary of
E. D.'s death with *An Anatomie of the World*—"his first yeares
rent"—and the second, with *Of the Progresse of the Soule.* The
father's pleasure is further shown in the encouragement he gave
to their publication: *The First Anniversary* came out in 1611
with the original elegy, and both were reissued in 1612 with
The Progresse (The Second Anniversary). In 1612, also, Donne
accompanied Sir Robert to the Continent.

The praise accorded the young lady was presumably extrava-
gant even in an age of complimentary verse making: she is
"Fellow-Commissioner with Destinie" and the cause of the
world's "forme, and frame." Her death left the world "sicke,"
"yea, dead, yea, putrified," "corrupt and mortall in thy purest
part," and the example of her virtuous life and heavenly perfection are man's best guarantees of salvation. It is not hard to see
that on the surface this is preposterous, as some have thought, but
it is less easy to understand why readers who have admired
much of the text of the poems have been so hesitant about setting the hyperbole aside long enough to read them apart from
their local context for the discovery of the significance that was
intimated. Jonson had at least imputed a religious meaning to
The First Anniversary when he is said to have told Donne that
it was "profane and full of Blasphemies," and that "if it had been
written of ye Virgin Marie it had been something." Donne's reported answer, that "he described the Idea of Woman and not as
she was," is a kind of justification in a way acceptable to a generation when the Platonic idealization of woman was ironically as
popular as the attribution of all the world's ills to the conduct of
the daughters of Eve, but there is considerably more in the
poems than the Idea of Woman, or, for that matter, than the
evidence of Donne's skeptical concern for the new philosophy,
which our own age has liked to isolate for examination. Despite

the implication that the poems are fragmentary and inconclusive, from Donne's expression of a "chast ambition" to write an "anniversary" every year, one must conclude, I believe, that they are complete and complementary, and that Donne had said everything in them that he really had to say at this time in his life. Taken together, the *Anniversaries* present a brave attempt of the poet to set himself in full personal relation to his world, and we may be grateful to Elizabeth Drury for having provided the unique occasion.

In the years in which Donne wrote the *Anniversaries*, he was peculiarly fitted for attempting just such a thing. His learning of the past, which had become immense, had not isolated him from a sense of the importance of current books; and his experience in the world, though wide and intense, had not been so absorbing as to pre-empt a passion for spiritual things. To these conditions should be added the fact that his prospects for a career to which his increasingly complex and ambiguous equipment might be suited were exceedingly slight. The poems relate to all this; and insofar as the poet achieved within them a sense of location, first, in an existential order battered into incoherence by the forces of history and of private experience, and, second, a sense of location in a metaphysical economy where values are recognized and given permanence, he had achieved a critical insight into himself and into a great period of history, which is of first importance. Recently, Louis L. Martz has related the poems to the literature of the "religious exercises," and has remarked their expression of the poet "in meditation." The designation is further evidence of the seriousness of interpretation which they are capable of supporting.[7]

After the *Anniversaries,* it seems to me that his ordination to the Anglican priesthood was almost inevitable, and I think that a sympathetic study of *The Essayes in Divinity*, a writing belonging to this period, will give corroboration. *The Essayes*, according to Donne's son, who first published them in 1651, are "the voluntary sacrifices of severall hours, when he [Donne] had many debates betwixt God and himself" on his fitness to become a priest, and I have meant to suggest that the *Anniversaries* may be suitably associated with these "debates." Donne did not move directly, however; Drury's attentions were diverting, and his new state refreshed his hopes for secular preferment. In fact, in 1614 (April 5–June 7) it appears that actually he was again in Parlia-

---

[7] "John Donne in Meditation," *ELH*, XIV (1947), 247–73.

ment (he had served briefly once before late in the days of his service with Egerton), but the early dissolution of the session was not likely to encourage whatever political hopes his election may have raised. Again, in the same year he sought a diplomatic appointment, even though shortly before he had told Viscount Rochester, who had the disposition of the post, that he was "resolved to make my profession Divinity." Obviously such "hesitating on the threshold" will annoy those who think that a man should make up his mind and stick to it, but such a simplification will hardly apply to one of Donne's complexity. Precisely what the final "steps to the temple" were cannot be known for they are profoundly personal. One may conclude safely, however, that they were taken with entire sincerity and seriousness. Had he moved overconfidently and with ambition, he would have felt, if I follow his character correctly, that he had shown an unbecoming pride in his fitness for the office; on the other hand, had he acted as if in desperation after he was sure that every other line of advancement was closed to him, as many have concluded, he would, I am sure, have suffered an irrevocable sense of shame. In the strict sense of the word, the priesthood for Donne was a vocation, and his entry into it should be regarded, I think, not so much as a decision as a response to a totality of circumstance which had been accumulating over many years in both his private and public life. Early in January, 1615, he was ordained, and, as Walton remarks, "the English Church had gained a second St. Austin."

Donne did not disappoint those who saw which way the genius of his mature years lay. He became one of the distinguished preachers in a city and a period of great preaching. After the "apprenticeship" of a year, he became Rector of Sevenoaks in Kent, then Reader in Divinity to the Benchers of Lincoln's Inn, and in 1621, Dean of St. Paul's. While in that office, from 1624, he also enjoyed the vicarage of St. Dunstan's in the West. In addition to filling his regular pulpit assignments throughout these years, he very often preached "before the King," and "to the nobility," and on numerous special occasions.

In 1617 Donne's wife died. Twelve children had been born to them and seven survived their mother's death. So, under a heavy load of grief and domestic care, and in the words of the seventeenth Holy Sonnet, his mind "sett" "wholly on heavenly things," he entered upon the final phase of his career. It was in this period, after he had assumed the duties of St. Dunstan's, that his friendship with Walton began, and the record of these years given in the *Life* is full and unrivaled on the brilliance of his preaching and the details of his private and public life. In 1619 he was sent abroad by the King as member of Lord Doncaster's embassy which hoped to mediate a peace among the German princes, a mission which occasioned several sermons. In 1624 he published his *Devotions upon Emergent Occasions*, which since has been reprinted more often than any other of his prose works. The occasion most "emergent" was his nearly fatal illness of the year before, in the "vertiginous giddiness" of which he had composed the book. It is a strange writing, carrying furthest the line of self-examination which he so often takes in his poems and sermons. At the same time, the exercises of "meditation," "expostulation," and "prayer" present a sustained metaphorical texture which absorbs the intimacies into a symbolic argument of widest application. In 1623 presumably he also wrote *A Hymn to God the Father,* which Walton says Donne "caused to be set to a most grave and solemn tune" by the Choristers of St. Paul's. The Holy Sonnets and probably *The Lamentations of Jeremy* had followed soon upon his wife's death; his last piece was the *Hymne to God my God, In my Sicknesse,* written in 1631, just before his death.

Donne's sermons, with some exceptions, were published after his death, principally in the folios of 1640, 1649, and 1661, respectively entitled *LXXX Sermons, Fifty Sermons,* and *XXVI Sermons.* A proper consideration of the sermons should begin with the appreciation that the seventeenth-century sermon is a kind of oratory. It need not have been written out in advance of delivery; and in keeping with the best style, Donne's usually were not put down in manuscript before they were preached. That was done later, from notes and memory. Within the conditions which the rhetorical and exegetical formalities required, there was ample room for "originality" and difference, as T. S. Eliot has shown in distinguishing Donne and Lancelot Andrewes in his essay honoring the latter. Donne's special contribution is discoverable in his power of figurative language and in the tonality of his rhythms through which he relates his own private meditation dramatically to the persisting themes of Christianity: like the beauty and goodness of the world precariously set against its persisting evils; the human responsibility for the Fall of Man; the imperative of repentance; dying and death; and the infinite mercies of God. *Death's Duell*, his own "funeral sermon," will illustrate, though with a greater severity of limitation to the sense of dissolution and death than is habitual. The

sermon preached in 1626 at the funeral of Sir William Co-
kayne, the last of the *LXXX Sermons,* is, in my mind, exemplary
of Donne in the fulness of his powers. The line which he takes
in the pulpit and the elaboration of his art are foreign to modern preaching. The reader may find his learning tedious, but the
quotation and allusions are usually assimilated into the basic
spoken rhythms; or, he may find the language terrifying, or un-
expectedly personal, or argumentative. The sermons may shock
with their incisiveness and candor like the poems. In short, much
that has been said about the poetry has application to the sermons, for Donne accepted the pulpit discourse as a kind of art,
and much that he knew about the art which uses language he
had practiced years before in rhyme and verse.

A NOTE ON THE TEXT

DONNE'S PLACE in the twentieth century owes a great deal to the careful work of his editors. The establishment of a good text, of the poems especially, has been difficult, not only because Donne is not an easy poet, but also because of the considerable variation among the numerous manuscript copies and among the early printed editions. Except for the 1611 edition of the *First Anniversary*, which Donne probably saw through the press, he had no hand in the publication of any of his poems: they circulated in manuscript, subject to the vicissitudes which are inevitable to frequent transcription, and there was no collected edition until after his death. Professor Grierson was the first to surmount most of the difficulties presented by this situation, and his edition (1912) has become the foundation for all subsequent editorial work. So far, no substantial revision has been made, though important particular changes have been made, notably by John Hayward in his *Complete Poetry and Selected Prose* (London, 1929), and more recently—and more extensively—by Roger E. Bennett in his edition of *The Complete Poems* (Chicago, 1942).

With the exception of the *Paradoxes and Problemes*, which like the poems went round in manuscript, and the Letters, the prose has raised fewer editorial problems. The prose, however, has not been collected. Alford's incomplete and uncritical edition of the *Works* (1839) included a considerable bulk of it; and in our own time, Hayward's edition, just noted, made the fullest offering of the prose before the publication of the present volume. Until there is a complete and fully annotated text, Mrs. Simpson's *A Study of the Prose Works* (2nd ed., Oxford, 1948) will be the reader's indispensable guide to the complete performance of Donne as a prosewriter.

The text of the poetry and the prose given here, with some additions and rearrangement, reproduces John Hayward's text.[1]

---

[1] "The spelling of the original text, whether prose or poetry, has been retained, with the following exceptions: *Then* (indicating comparison) has been changed to *than* throughout; and *than* to *then* where the original text prints *than* for the sake of the rhyme. The long ∫ has become s, where necessary v has been changed to u, i to j, y to i, and all abbreviations . . . have been expanded to their full value

The prefatory material in the seventeenth-century editions of the poems is added, and two of the "elegies on the authors death" (Izaak Walton's and Thomas Carew's), which first appeared in the edition of 1633. The poems have been rearranged to bring similar "kinds" more closely together and to show the pieces within the several groupings in their approximate chronological order, so far as recent scholarship has helped to make such an undertaking feasible. For obvious reasons no attempt has been made to deal with the order of the Songs and Sonets, the Elegies, the Epigrams, and the Satyres; and it is emphasized that wherever a redistribution has been made (the *Anniversaries* and *A Funerall Elegie* excepted), a precise chronological order of the titles is not claimed.

Hayward's arrangement of the prose has been disturbed a great deal, although the Letters are left where they were (just before the works belonging to Donne's years in the priesthood), set in the order of the known dates of composition according to the latest determinations. The "source" of each letter is noted at the end of each text. The selections from the Sermons are regrouped, with the dates, exact or conjectural, shown in the headings. The undated pieces are assembled at the beginning of the sermon selection. Although the arrangement in this volume disregards one of Hayward's intentions, namely, of showing how Donne preached on similar occasions, it is expected that the present arrangement, so far as limited selection permits, will have the advantage of showing something of Donne's "development" as a preacher.

The following additions have been made to the prose: Problemes V, VIII (1633); selections from the prefatory matter of

---

throughout. In a few places where confusion was likely to occur, *hast* to *haste,* and *least* to *lest, to* to *too, of* to *off* have been silently altered. . . . The Elizabethan use of a mark of interrogation to denote an exclamation has been altered to conform with modern usage. In the prose works dropped, turned and inverted letters have been silently corrected, and proper names, where they are obviously incorrect, have been altered to the correct forms as they are printed elsewhere. As far as possible the punctuation of the early editions and manuscript collections has been retained. When, however, it is necessary to supplement or alter the punctuation of the text upon which a rescension is based, the punctuation of another edition or a manuscript often supplies the defect. . . ." From Hayward's "General Note on the Text" (1929). These principles have been generally applied to the additions that are made to the present selection.

Pseudo-Martyr, no part of which has been reprinted for its own sake since 1610; the *Epistle Dedicatorie* to the *Devotions* (1624); and the "Expostulation" and "Prayer" of the nineteenth "Devotion," an addition which gives the reader the whole of one of the exercises of that interesting book.

A SELECTED BIBLIOGRAPHY

IMPORTANT EDITIONS OF DONNE'S WORKS

1. *Poems, By J.D. with elegies on the authors death.* 4° London, 1633. Other seventeenth-century editions, with additions and modifications: 1635, 1639, 1649, 1650, 1654, 1669.
2. *The Poems, etc.,* ed. Herbert J. C. Grierson. 2 vols. Oxford, 1912. Also, for the "Oxford Standard Authors," London, 1929.
3. *Complete Poetry and Selected Prose,* ed. John Hayward, Bloomsbury, 1929; New York, 1930.
4. *The Complete Poems,* ed. Roger E. Bennett, Chicago, 1942.
5. *Juvenilia: or certaine paradoxes, and problemes, written by* J. Donne. 4° London, 1633. With additions and modifications, 1633, 1652 (including nos. 10, 11 below). *Paradoxes and Problemes, etc.,* from 1633 and 1652 (bibliographical preface by Geoffrey Keynes), London, 1923; edition of 1633, reproduced for The Facsimile Text Society (bibliographical note by R. E. Bennett), New York, 1936.
6. *The Courtier's Library, or Catalogus Librorum Aulicorum incomparabilium et non vendibilium,* ed. Evelyn Mary Simpson, with a translation (by Percy Simpson), London, 1930. Latin text first published with *Poems,* 1650.
7. *Letters to Severall Persons of Honour: written by* John Donne. 4° London, 1651. Reissued 1654. Published letters appear also in *A Collection of Letters,* made by Sir Tobie Mathews (1660); various editions of Walton's *Life of Donne* and *Life of Herbert; The Loseley Manuscripts* (ed. Alfred John Kempe, 1835); Edmund Gosse, *The Life and Letters* (1899); Evelyn M. Simpson, *A Study of the Prose Works*—letters from the Burley-on-the-Hill Manuscript—(Oxford, 1924; 2nd ed., 1948); Hayward's *Complete Poetry and Selected Prose* (no. 3 above); and elsewhere. *The Letters to Severall Persons* are included in Alford's edition of the *Works* (see no. 14 below); they were edited by C. S. Merrill, Jr. (1910).
8. *ΒΙΑΘΑΝΑΤΟΣ. A declaration of that paradoxe, or thesis, that Selfe-homicide is not so naturally a Sinne, that it may never be otherwise, etc.* 4° London, [1646]; reissued 1648. The first issue was reproduced by The Facsimile

Text Society (bibliographical note by J. William Hebel).
New York, 1930.

9. *Pseudo-Martyr.* 4° London, 1610.

10. *Ignatius his Conclave: Or His Inthronisation in a late Election in Hell, etc.* 12° London, 1611. Two editions of the Latin text, 1611; English editions appeared in 1626, 1634, 1635, 1653 (see no. 5 above); included in no. 3 above; and reproduced for The Facsimile Text Society (bibliographical note by Charles M. Coffin), New York, 1941.

11. *Essayes in Divinity: By the late Dr. Donne, etc.* 12° London, 1651. Edited by Augustus Jessopp, London, 1855. (See no. 5 above.)

12. *Devotions upon Emergent Occasions, and severall steps in my sicknes, etc.* 12° London, 1624. Many editions; see especially that by John Sparrow, Cambridge, 1923.

13. *Sermons* (collected). Several sermons were separately published in Donne's lifetime and shortly afterwards; some were gathered into small collections. The great collections are: *LXXX Sermons Preached by that Learned and Reverend Divine, etc.* (includes first edition of Walton's *Life*), F° London, 1640; *Fifty Sermons*, F° London, 1649; *XXVI Sermons*, F° London, 1660.

14. *The Works of John Donne, etc., with a memoir of his life.* By Henry Alford. 6 vols. London, 1839. Includes modernized texts of *Letters* (rearranged), *Devotions*, and of a selection of the *Poems*.

BIOGRAPHY

15. Izaak Walton, *Life of Dr. Donne, etc.* (in *LXXX Sermons*), London, 1640; enlarged, printed separately, 1658; in *Lives*, 1670, 1675 (with further addition).

16. Edmund Gosse, *The Life and Letters of John Donne.* 2 vols. London and New York, 1899.

BIBLIOGRAPHY AND CONCORDANCE

17. Geoffrey Keynes, *A Bibliography of Dr. John Donne*, 2nd ed. Cambridge, 1932.

18. Theodore Spencer (assisted by Evelyn Orr), "A Bibliography of Studies in Metaphysical Poetry, 1912–1938," in *Studies in Metaphysical Poetry* (with Mark Van Doren), New York, 1939.

19. Homer Carroll Combs and Zay Rusk Sullens, *A Concordance to the English Poetry of John Donne*, Chicago, 1940.

BOOKS AND ESSAYS ON DONNE

Note: The importance of much commentary on Donne in works in which he is not the primary subject warrants the offering of the titles of such pieces as well as the titles of special pieces.

20. Joan Bennett, *Four Metaphysical Poets*, Cambridge, 1934.
21. Louis I. Bredvold, "The Religious Thought of Donne in Relation to Medieval and Later Traditions," in *Studies in Shakespeare, Milton, and Donne. University of Michigan Publications. Language and Literature*, I, New York, 1925.
22. Cleanth Brooks, *Modern Poetry and the Tradition*, Chapel Hill, 1939; *The Well Wrought Urn*, New York, 1947.
23. Charles M. Coffin, *John Donne and the New Philosophy*, New York, 1937.
24. Thomas Stearns Eliot, "The Metaphysical Poets" (1921). In *Selected Essays*. New Edition, New York, 1950. (See no. 34 below.)
25. Herbert J. C. Grierson, "Introduction" to *Metaphysical Lyrics and Poems*, Oxford, 1921. (See no. 2 above.)
26. F. R. Leavis, "The Line of Wit," in *Revaluation*, New York, 1947. First published as "English Poetry in the Seventeenth Century," *Scrutiny*, IV, 1935.
27. James B. Leishman, *The Metaphysical Poets*, Oxford, 1934.
28. Josephine Miles, *The Primary Language of Poetry in the 1640's. University of California Publications in English*, 19, 1, Berkeley and Los Angeles, 1948. "The Language of the Donne Tradition," *Kenyon Review*, XIII, 1, 1951.
29. W. Fraser Mitchell, *English Pulpit Oratory from Andrewes to Tillotson*, London, 1932.
30. Mario Praz, *Secentismo e Marinismo in Inghilterra: John Donne—Richard Crashaw*, Florence, 1925. (See no. 34 below.)
31. Mary Paton Ramsay, *Les Doctrines Médiévales chez Donne*, London, 1917. (See no. 34 below.)
32. Milton Rugoff, *Donne's Imagery*, New York, 1939.
33. Evelyn M. Simpson, *A Study of the Prose Works of John Donne*, Oxford, 1924; 2nd ed., 1948. (See no. 34 below.)
34. Theodore Spencer, ed. *A Garland for John Donne 1631–1931*, Cambridge (Mass.), 1931. Includes essays by Eliot, Simpson, Praz, Hayward, Ramsay, Sparrow, Williamson, and Spencer.

35. Arnold Stein, "Donne's Prosody," *Publications of the Modern Language Association of America,* LIX, 1944; "Structures of Sound in Donne's Verse," *Kenyon Review,* XIII, 1, 1951.

36. Rosemond Tuve, *Elizabethan and Metaphysical Imagery,* Chicago, 1947. Reviewed by William Empson ("Donne and the Rhetorical Tradition"), *Kenyon Review,* XI, 4, 1949.

37. Leonard Unger, *Donne's Poetry and Modern Criticism,* Chicago, 1950.

38. Helen White, *The Metaphysical Poets,* New York, 1936.

39. George Williamson, *The Donne Tradition,* Cambridge (Mass.), 1930; "Textual Difficulties in the Interpretation of Donne's Poetry," *Modern Philology,* XXXVIII, 1940. (See no. 34 above.)

The COMPLETE POETRY

and SELECTED PROSE *of*

JOHN DONNE

POETRY

THE PRINTER TO THE UNDERSTANDERS

For this time I must speake only to you: at another, *Readers* may perchance serve my turne; and I thinke this a way very free from exception, in hope that very few will have a minde to confesse themselves ignorant.

If you looke for an Epistle, as you have before ordinary publications, I am sory that I must deceive you; but you will not lay it to my charge, when you shall consider that this is not ordinary, for if I should say it were the best in this kinde, that ever this Kingdome hath yet seene; he that would doubt of it must goe out of the Kingdome to enforme himselfe, for the best judgments, within it, take it for granted.

You may imagine (if it please you) that I could endeare it unto you, by saying, that importunity drew it on; that had it not beene presented here, it would have come to us from beyond the Seas; (which perhaps is true enough), That my charge and paines in procuring of it hath beene such, and such. I could adde hereto, a promise of more correctnesse, or enlargement in the next Edition, if you shall in the meane time content you with this. But these things are so common, as that I should profane this Peece by applying them to it; A Peece which who so takes not as he findes it, in what manner soever, he is unworthy of it, sith a scattered limbe of this Author, hath more amiablenesse in it, in the eye of a discerner, than a whole body of some other; Or (to expresse him best by himselfe),

> —A hand, or eye,
> By Hilyard drawne, is worth a history   *In the*
> By a worse Painter made;—   *Storme*

If any man (thinking I speake this to enflame him for the vent of the Impression) be of another opinion, I shall as willingly spare his money as his judgement. I cannot lose so much by him as hee will by himselfe. For I shall satisfie my selfe with the conscience of well doing, in making so much good common.

Howsoever it may appeare to you, it shall suffice mee to enforme you, that it hath the best warrant that can bee, publique authority, and private friends.

There is one thing more wherein I will make you of my counsell, and that is, That whereas it hath pleased some, who had studyed and did admire him, to offer to the memory of the Author, not long after his decease, I have thought I should do you service in presenting them unto you now: onely whereas, had I placed them in the beginning, they might have serv'd for so many Encomiums of the Author (as is usuall in other workes, where perhaps there is need of it, to prepare men to digest such stuffe as follows after), you shall here finde them in the end. for whosoever reades the rest so farre, shall perceive that there is no occasion to use them to that purpose; yet there they are, as an attestation for their sakes that knew not so much before, to let them see how much honour was attributed to this worthy man, by those that are capable to give it. *Farewell.*
[1633]

HEXASTICHON BIBLIOPOLAE

I see in his last preach'd, and printed Booke,
His Picture in a sheet; in *Pauls* I looke,
And see his Statue in a sheete of stone,
And sure his body in the grave hath one:
Those sheetes present him dead, these if you buy,
You have him living to Eternity.

                                      Jo[hn] Mar[riot]

[1633]

HEXASTICHON AD BIBLIOPOLAM
INCERTI

In thy Impression of Donnes *Poems rare,*
For his Eternitie thou hast ta'ne care:
'Twas well, and pious; And for ever may
He live: Yet shew I thee a better way;
Print but his Sermons, and if those we buy,
He, We, and Thou shall live t'Eternity.

[1635]

DEDICATION TO THE EDITION OF 1650

TO THE RIGHT HONOURABLE WILLIAM LORD CRAVEN BARON
OF HAMSTED-MARSHAM

My Lord,

MANY of these Poems have, for severall impressions, wandred up and down trusting (as well they might) upon the Authors reputation; neither do they now complain of any injury but what may proceed either from the kindnesse of the Printer, or the curtesie of the Reader; the one by adding something too much, lest any spark of this sacred fire might perish undiscerned, the other by putting such an estimation upon the wit & fancy they find here, that they are content to use it as their own: as if a man should dig out the stones of a royall Amphitheatre to build a stage for a countrey show. Amongst all the monsters this unlucky age has teemed with, I finde none so prodigious, as the Poets of these later times, wherein men as if they would level understandings too as well as estates, acknowledging no inequality of parts and Judgements, pretend as indifferently to the chaire of wit as to the Pulpit, & conceive themselves no lesse inspired with the spirit of Poetry than with that of Religion: so it is not onely the noise of Drums and Trumpets which have drowned the Muses harmony, or the feare that the Churches ruine wil destroy their Priests likewise, that now frights them from this Countrey, where they have been so ingenuously received, but these rude pretenders to excellencies they unjustly own who profanely rushing into *Minervaes* Temple, with noysome Ayres blast the lawrell which thunder cannot hurt. In this sad condition these learned sisters are fled over to beg your Lordships protection, who have been so certain a patron both to arts and armes, and who in this generall confusion have so intirely preserved your Honour, that in your Lordship we may still read a most perfect character of what *England* was in all her pompe and greatnesse, so that although these poems were formerly written upon severall occasions, and to severall persons, they now unite themselves, and are become one pyramid to set your Lordships statue upon, where you may stand like Armed *Apollo* the defendor of the Muses, encouraging the Poets now alive to celebrate your great Acts by affording your countenance to his poems that wanted onely so noble a subject.

     My Lord,

             Your most humble servant

                    John Donne [the Younger]

[1650]

TO JOHN DONNE

Donne, *the delight of Phoebus, and each Muse,*
   Who, to thy one, all other braines refuse;
Whose every work, of thy most early wit,
   Came forth example, and remaines so, yet:
Longer a knowing, than most wits doe live;
   And which no'n affection praise enough can give!
To it, thy language, letters, arts, best life,
   Which might with halfe mankind maintain a strife;
All which I mean[t] to praise, and, yet, I would;
   But leave, because I cannot as I should!

                    B[en] Jons[on]

[1650. From Jonson's *Works,* 1616]

TO LUCY, COUNTESSE OF BEDFORD, WITH M. DONNES SATYRES

Lucy, you brightnesse of our Spheare, who are
Life of the *Muses* day, their morning Starre!
If works (not th'Authors) their own grace should look
Whose poems would not wish to be your book?
But these, desir'd by you, the makers ends
Crown with their own. Rare Poems ask rare friends.
Yet, *Satyres,* since the most of mankind bee
Their unavoided subject, fewest see:
For none ere took that pleasure in sins sense,
But, when they heard it tax'd, took more offence.
They, then, that living where the matter is bred,
Dare for these Poems, yet, both ask, and read,
And like them too; must needfully, though few,
Be of the best: and 'mongst those best are you;

Lucy, you brightnesse of our Spheare, who are
The *Muses* evening, as their morning-Starre.

B[en] Jon[son]

[1650. From Jonson's *Works,* 1616]

TO JOHN DONNE

Who shall doubt, *Donne,* where I a *Poet* bee,
When I dare send my *Epigrammes* to thee?
That so alone canst judge, so'alone do'st make:
And, in thy censures, evenly, dost take
As free simplicity, to dis-avow,
As thou hast best authority, t'allow.
Read all I send: and, if I finde but one
Mark'd by thy hand, and with the better stone,
My title's seal'd. Those that for claps doe write,
Let pu[i']nees, porters, players praise delight,
And, till they burst, their backs, like asses load:
A man should seek great glory, and not broad.

B[en] Jon[son]

[1650. From Jonson's *Works,* 1616]

SONGS AND SONETS

THE GOOD-MORROW

I wonder by my troth, what thou, and I
Did, till we lov'd? were we not wean'd till then?
But suck'd on countrey pleasures, childishly?
Or snorted we in the seaven sleepers den?
T'was so; But this, all pleasures fancies bee.
If ever any beauty I did see,
Which I desir'd, and got, t'was but a dreame of thee.

And now good morrow to our waking soules,
Which watch not one another out of feare;
For love, all love of other sights controules,   **10**
And makes one little roome, an every where.
Let sea-discoverers to new worlds have gone,
Let Maps to other, worlds on worlds have showne,
Let us possesse one world, each hath one, and is one.

My face in thine eye, thine in mine appeares,
And true plaine hearts doe in the faces rest,
Where can we finde two better hemispheares
Without sharpe North, without declining West?
What ever dyes, was not mixt equally;
If our two loves be one, or, thou and I   **20**
Love so alike, that none doe slacken, none can die

SONG

Goe, and catche a falling starre,
  Get with child a mandrake roote,
Tell me, where all past yeares are,
  Or who cleft the Divels foot,

8

Teach me to heare Mermaides singing,
  Or to keep off envies stinging,
            And finde
            What winde
Serves to advance an honest minde.

If thou beest borne to strange sights,   10
  Things invisible to see,
Ride ten thousand daies and nights,
  Till age snow white haires on thee,
Thou, when thou retorn'st, wilt tell mee
All strange wonders that befell thee,
            And sweare
            No where
Lives a woman true, and faire.

If thou findst one, let mee know,
  Such a Pilgrimage were sweet;   20
Yet doe not, I would not goe,
  Though at next doore wee might meet,
Though shee were true, when you met her,
And last, till you write your letter,
            Yet shee
            Will bee
False, ere I come, to two, or three.

WOMANS CONSTANCY

Now thou hast lov'd me one whole day,
To morrow when thou leav'st, what wilt thou say?
Wilt thou then Antedate some new made vow?
            Or say that now
We are not just those persons, which we were?
Or, that oathes made in reverentiall feare
Of Love, and his wrath, any may forsweare?
Or, as true deaths, true maryages untie,
So lovers contracts, images of those,
Binde but till sleep, deaths image, them unloose?   10
            Or, your owne end to Justifie,
For having purpos'd change, and falsehood; you
Can have no way but falsehood to be true?

Vaine lunatique, against these scapes I could
           Dispute, and conquer, if I would,
           Which I abstaine to doe,
For by to morrow, I may thinke so too.

THE UNDERTAKING

I HAVE done one braver thing
    Than all the *Worthies* did,
And yet a braver thence doth spring,
    Which is, to keepe that hid.

It were but madnes now t'impart
    The skill of specular stone,
When he which can have learn'd the art
    To cut it, can finde none.

So, if I now should utter this,
    Others (because no more   **10**
Such stuffe to worke upon, there is,)
    Would love but as before.

But he who lovelinesse within
    Hath found, all outward loathes,
For he who colour loves, and skinne,
    Loves but their oldest clothes.

If, as I have, you also doe
    Vertue'attir'd in woman see,
And dare love that, and say so too,
    And forget the Hee and Shee;   **20**

And if this love, though placed so,
    From prophane men you hide,
Which will no faith on this bestow,
    Or, if they doe, deride:

Then you have done a braver thing
    Than all the *Worthies* did;
And a braver thence will spring,
    Which is, to keepe that hid.

THE SUNNE RISING

Busie old foole, unruly Sunne,
          Why dost thou thus,
Through windowes, and through curtaines call on us?
Must to thy motions lovers seasons run?
          Sawcy pedantique wretch, goe chide
          Late schoole boyes and sowre prentices,
      Goe tell Court-huntsmen, that the King will ride,
      Call countrey ants to harvest offices;
Love, all alike, no season knowes, nor clyme,
Nor houres, dayes, moneths, which are the rags of time.   10

          Thy beames, so reverend, and strong
          Why shouldst thou thinke?
I could eclipse and cloud them with a winke,
But that I would not lose her sight so long:
          If her eyes have not blinded thine,
          Looke, and to morrow late, tell mee,
      Whether both the'India's of spice and Myne
      Be where thou leftst them, or lie here with mee.
Aske for those Kings whom thou saw'st yesterday,
And thou shalt heare, All here in one bed lay.   20

          She'is all States, and all Princes, I,
          Nothing else is.
Princes doe but play us; compar'd to this,
All honor's mimique; All wealth alchimie.
          Thou sunne art halfe as happy'as wee,
          In that the world's contracted thus;
      Thine age askes ease, and since thy duties bee
      To warme the world, that's done in warming us.
Shine here to us, and thou art every where;
This bed thy center is, these walls, thy spheare.   30

THE INDIFFERENT

I can love both faire and browne,
Her whom abundance melts, and her whom want betraies,

Her who loves lonenesse best, and her who maskes and plaies,
Her whom the country form'd, and whom the town,
Her who beleeves, and her who tries,
Her who still weepes with spungie eyes,
And her who is dry corke, and never cries;
I can love her, and her, and you and you,
I can love any, so she be not true.

Will no other vice content you?   **10**
Wil it not serve your turn to do, as did your mothers?
Or have you all old vices spent, and now would finde out others?
Or doth a feare, that men are true, torment you?
Oh we are not, be not you so,
Let mee, and doe you, twenty know.
Rob mee, but binde me not, and let me goe.
Must I, who came to travaile thorow you,
Grow your fixt subject, because you are true?

Venus heard me sigh this song,
And by Loves sweetest Part, Variety, she swore,   **20**
She heard not this till now; and that it should be so no more.
She went, examin'd, and return'd ere long,
And said, alas, Some two or three
Poore Heretiques in love there bee,
Which thinke to stablish dangerous constancie.
But I have told them, since you will be true,
You shall be true to them, who'are false to you.

LOVES USURY

For every houre that thou wilt spare mee now,
     I will allow,
Usurious God of Love, twenty to thee,
When with my browne, my gray haires equall bee:
Till then, Love, let my body raigne, and let
Mee travell, sojourne, snatch, plot, have, forget,
Resume my last yeares relict: thinke that yet
     We'had never met.

Let mee thinke any rivalls letter mine,
     And at next nine   **10**

Keepe midnights promise; mistake by the way
The maid, and tell the Lady of that delay;
Onely let mee love none, no, not the sport;
From country grasse, to comfitures of Court,
Or cities quelque choses, let report
    My minde transport.

This bargaine's good; if when I'am old, I bee
    Inflam'd by thee,
If thine owne honour, or my shame, or paine,
Thou covet, most at that age thou shalt gaine.   **20**
Doe thy will then, then subject and degree,
And fruit of love, Love I submit to thee,
Spare mee till then, I'll beare it, though she bee
    One that loves mee.

THE CANONIZATION

FOR Godsake hold your tongue, and let me love,
    Or chide my palsie, or my gout,
My five gray haires, or ruin'd fortune flout,
    With wealth your state, your minde with Arts improve,
      Take you a course, get you a place,
      Observe his honour, or his grace,
Or the Kings reall, or his stamped face
    Contemplate, what you will, approve,
    So you will let me love.

Alas, alas, who's injur'd by my love?   **10**
    What merchants ships have my sighs drown'd?
Who saies my teares have overflow'd his ground?
    When did my colds a forward spring remove?
      When did the heats which my veines fill
      Adde one more to the plaguie Bill?
Soldiers finde warres, and Lawyers finde out still
    Litigious men, which quarrels move,
    Though she and I do love.

Call us what you will, wee are made such by love;
Call her one, mee another flye,   **20**
We'are Tapers too, and at our owne cost die.

And wee in us finde the'Eagle and the Dove.
The Phœnix ridle hath more wit
    By us, we two being one, are it.
So to one neutrall thing both sexes fit,
    Wee dye and rise the same, and prove
    Mysterious by this love.

Wee can dye by it, if not live by love,
    And if unfit for tombes and hearse
Our legend bee, it will be fit for verse;   **30**
    And if no peece of Chronicle wee prove,
    We'll build in sonnets pretty roomes;
    As well a well wrought urne becomes
The greatest ashes, as halfe-acre tombes,
    And by these hymnes, all shall approve
    Us *Canoniz'd* for Love:

And thus invoke us; You whom reverend love
    Made one anothers hermitage;
You, to whom love was peace, that now is rage;
    Who did the whole worlds soule contract, and drove   **40**
    Into the glasses of your eyes
    (So made such mirrors, and such spies,
That they did all to you epitomize,)
    Countries, Townes, Courts: Beg from above
    A patterne of your love!

THE TRIPLE FOOLE

    I AM two fooles, I know,
For loving, and for saying so
    In whining Poëtry;
But where's that wiseman, that would not be I,
    If she would not deny?
Then as th'earths inward narrow crooked lanes
Do purge sea waters fretfull salt away,
    I thought, if I could draw my paines,
Through Rimes vexation, I should them allay.
Griefe brought to numbers cannot be so fierce,   **10**
For, he tames it, that fetters it in verse.

But when I have done so,
Some man, his art and voice to show,
   Doth Set and sing my paine,
And, by delighting many, frees againe
   Griefe, which verse did restraine.
To Love, and Griefe tribute of Verse belongs,
But not of such as pleases when'tis read,
   Both are increased by such songs:
For both their triumphs so are published,   20
And I, which was two fooles, do so grow three;
Who are a little wise, the best fooles bee.

LOVERS INFINITENESSE

If yet I have not all thy love,
Deare, I shall never have it all,
I cannot breath one other sigh, to move,
Nor can intreat one other teare to fall,
And all my treasure, which should purchase thee,
Sighs, teares, and oathes, and letters I have spent.
Yet no more can be due to mee,
Than at the bargaine made was ment,
If then thy gift of love were partiall,
That some to mee, some should to others fall,   10
   Deare, I shall never have Thee All.

Or if then thou gavest mee all,
All was but All, which thou hadst then;
But if in thy heart, since, there be or shall,
New love created bee, by other men,
Which have their stocks intire, and can in teares,
In sighs, in oathes, and letters outbid mee,
This new love may beget new feares,
For, this love was not vowed by thee.
And yet it was, thy gift being generall,   20
The ground, thy heart is mine, what ever shall
   Grow there, deare, I should have it all.

Yet I would not have all yet,
Hee that hath all can have no more,
And since my love doth every day admit

New growth, thou shouldst have new rewards in store;
Thou canst not every day give me thy heart,
If thou canst give it, then thou never gavest it:
Loves riddles are, that though thy heart depart,
It stayes at home, and thou with losing savest it: **30**
But wee will have a way more liberall,
Than changing hearts, to joyne them, so wee shall
   Be one, and one anothers All.

SONG

SWEETEST love, I do not goe,
   For wearinesse of thee,
Nor in hope the world can show
   A fitter Love for mee;
     But since that I
Must dye at last, 'tis best,
To use my selfe in jest
   Thus by fain'd deaths to dye;

Yesternight the Sunne went hence,
   And yet is here to day,   **10**
He hath no desire nor sense,
   Nor halfe so short a way:
     Then feare not mee,
But beleeve that I shall make
Speedier journeyes, since I take
   More wings and spurres than hee.

O how feeble is mans power,
   That if good fortune fall,
Cannot adde another houre,
   Nor a lost houre recall!   **20**
     But come bad chance,
And wee joyne to'it our strength,
And wee teach it art and length,
   It selfe o'r us to'advance.

When thou sigh'st, thou sigh'st not winde,
   But sigh'st my soule away,

When thou weep'st, unkindly kinde,
  My lifes blood doth decay.
    It cannot bee
That thou lov'st mee, as thou say'st,   30
If in thine my life thou waste,
  That art the best of mee.

Let not thy divining heart
  Forethinke me any ill,
Destiny may take thy part,
  And may thy feares fulfill;
    But thinke that wee
Are but turn'd aside to sleepe;
They who one another keepe
  Alive, ne'r parted bee.   40

THE LEGACIE

WHEN I dyed last, and, Deare, I dye
  As often as from thee I goe,
  Though it be but an houre agoe,
And Lovers houres be full eternity,
I can remember yet, that I
  Something did say, and something did bestow;
Though I be dead, which sent mee, I should be
Mine owne executor and Legacie.

I heard mee say, Tell her anon,
  That my selfe, (that is you, not I,)   10
  Did kill me, and when I felt mee dye,
I bid mee send my heart, when I was gone,
But I alas could there finde none,
  When I had ripp'd me, 'and search'd where hearts did lye;
It kill'd mee againe, that I who still was true,
In life, in my last Will should cozen you.

Yet I found something like a heart,
  But colours it, and corners had,
  It was not good, it was not bad,
It was intire to none, and few had part.   20

As good as could be made by art
    It seem'd; and therefore for our losses sad,
I meant to send this heart in stead of mine,
    But oh, no man could hold it, for twas thine.

A FEVER

OH doe not die, for I shall hate
    All women so, when thou art gone,
That thee I shall not celebrate,
    When I remember, thou wast one.

But yet thou canst not die, I know,
    To leave this world behinde, is death,
But when thou from this world wilt goe,
    The whole world vapors with thy breath.

Or if, when thou, the worlds soule, goest,
    It stay, tis but thy carkasse then,   **10**
The fairest woman, but thy ghost,
    But corrupt wormes, the worthyest men.

O wrangling schooles, that search what fire
    Shall burne this world, had none the wit
Unto this knowledge to aspire,
    That this her feaver might be it?

And yet she cannot wast by this,
    Nor long beare this torturing wrong,
For such corruption needfull is   **20**
    To fuell such a feaver long.

These burning fits but meteors bee,
    Whose matter in thee is soone spent.
Thy beauty,'and all parts, which are thee,
    Are unchangeable firmament.

Yet t'was of my minde, seising thee,
    Though it in thee cannot persever.
For I had rather owner bee
    Of thee one houre, than all else ever.

AIRE AND ANGELS

Twice or thrice had I loved thee,
Before I knew thy face or name;
So in a voice, so in a shapeless flame,
Angells affect us oft, and worship'd bee;
 Still when, to where thou wert, I came,
Some lovely glorious nothing I did see.
 But since my soule, whose child love is,
Takes limmes of flesh, and else could nothing doe,
 More subtile than the parent is,
Love must not be, but take a body too,   10
 And therefore what thou wert, and who,
  I bid Love aske, and now
That it assume thy body, I allow,
And fixe it selfe in thy lip, eye, and brow.

Whilst thus to ballast love, I thought,
And so more steddily to have gone,
With wares which would sinke admiration,
I saw, I had loves pinnace overfraught,
 Ev'ry thy haire for love to worke upon
Is much too much, some fitter must be sought;   20
 For, nor in nothing, nor in things
Extreme, and scatt'ring bright, can love inhere;
 Then as an Angell, face, and wings
Of aire, not pure as it, yet pure doth weare,
 So thy love may be my loves spheare;
  Just such disparitie
As is twixt Aire and Angells puritie,
'Twixt womens love, and mens will ever bee

BREAKE OF DAY

'Tis true, 'tis day; what though it be?
O wilt thou therefore rise from me?
Why should we rise, because 'tis light?
Did we lie downe, because 'twas night?

Love which in spight of darknesse brought us hether,
Should in despight of light keepe us together.

Light hath no tongue, but is all eye;
If it could speake as well as spie,
This were the worst, that it could say,
That being well, I faine would stay,   10
And that I lov'd my heart and honor so,
That I would not from him, that had them, goe.

Must businesse thee from hence remove?
Oh, that's the worst disease of love,
The poore, the foule, the false, love can
Admit, but not the busied man.
He which hath businesse, and makes love, doth doe
Such wrong, as when a maryed man doth wooe.

THE ANNIVERSARIE

ALL Kings, and all their favorites,
    All glory of honors, beauties, wits,
The Sun it selfe, which makes times, as they passe,
Is elder by a yeare, now, than it was
When thou and I first one another saw:
All other things, to their destruction draw,
    Only our love hath no decay;
This, no to morrow hath, nor yesterday,
Running it never runs from us away,
But truly keepes his first, last, everlasting day.   10

Two graves must hide thine and my coarse,
    If one might, death were no divorce.
Alas, as well as other Princes, wee,
(Who Prince enough in one another bee,)
Must leave at last in death, these eyes, and eares,
Oft fed with true oathes, and with sweet salt teares;
    But soules where nothing dwells but love
(All other thoughts being inmates) then shall prove
This, or a love increased there above,
When bodies to their graves, soules from their graves remove. 20

And then wee shall be throughly blest,
But wee no more, than all the rest;
Here upon earth, we'are Kings, and none but wee
Can be such Kings, nor of such subjects bee.
Who is so safe as wee? where none can doe
Treason to us, except one of us two.
True and false feares let us refraine,
Let us love nobly, and live, and adde againe
Yeares and yeares unto yeares, till we attaine
To write threescore: this is the second of our raigne.   30

A VALEDICTION: OF MY NAME,
IN THE WINDOW

I

My name engrav'd herein,
Doth contribute my firmnesse to this glasse,
Which, ever since that charme, hath beene
As hard, as that which grav'd it, was;
Thine eye will give it price enough, to mock
The diamonds of either rock.

II

'Tis much that glasse should bee
As all confessing, and through-shine as I,
'Tis more, that it shewes thee to thee,
And cleare reflects thee to thine eye.   10
But all such rules, loves magique can undoe,
Here you see me, and I am you.

III

As no one point, nor dash,
Which are but accessaries to this name,
The showers and tempests can outwash,
So shall all times finde mee the same;
You this intirenesse better may fulfill,
Who have the patterne with you still.

IV

Or if too hard and deepe
This learning be, for a scratch'd name to teach,   20
   It, as a given deaths head keepe,
   Lovers mortalitie to preach,
Or thinke this ragged bony name to bee
     My ruinous Anatomie.

V

Then, as all my soules bee,
Emparadis'd in you, (in whom alone
   I understand, and grow and see,)
   The rafters of my body, bone
Being still with you, the Muscle, Sinew, and Veine,
     Which tile this house, will come againe.   30

VI

Till my returne, repaire
And recompact my scattered body so.
   As all the vertuous powers which are
   Fix'd in the starres, are said to flow
Into such characters, as graved bee
     When these starres have supremacie:

VII

So since this name was cut
When love and griefe their exaltation had,
   No doore 'gainst this names influence shut
   As much more loving, as more sad,   40
'Twill make thee; and thou shouldst, till I returne,
     Since I die daily, daily mourne.

VIII

When thy inconsiderate hand
Flings ope this casement, with my trembling name,
   To looke on one, whose wit or land,
   New battry to thy heart may frame.

Then thinke this name alive, and that thou thus
In it offendst my Genius.

IX

And when thy melted maid,
Corrupted by thy Lover's gold, and page,   50
His letter at thy pillow'hath laid,
Disputed it, and tam'd thy rage,
And thou begin'st to thaw towards him, for this,
May my name step in, and hide his.

X

And if this treason goe
To an overt act, and that thou write againe;
In superscribing, this name flow
Into thy fancy, from the pane.
So, in forgetting thou remembrest right,
And unaware to mee shalt write.   60

XI

But glasse, and lines must bee,
No meanes our firme substantiall love to keepe;
Neere death inflicts this lethargie,
And this I murmure in my sleepe;
Impute this idle talke, to that I goe,
For dying men talke often so.

TWICKNAM GARDEN

BLASTED with sighs, and surrounded with teares,
Hither I come to seeke the spring,
And at mine eyes, and at mine eares,
Receive such balmes, as else cure every thing;
But O, selfe traytor, I do bring
The spider love, which transubstantiates all,
And can convert Manna to gall,
And that this place may thoroughly be thought
True Paradise, I have the serpent brought.

'Twere wholsomer for mee, that winter did   **10**
   Benight the glory of this place,
   And that a grave frost did forbid
These trees to laugh, and mocke mee to my face;
   But that I may not this disgrace
Indure, nor yet leave loving, Love let mee
   Some senslesse peece of this place bee;
Make me a mandrake, so I may groane here,
   Or a stone fountaine weeping out my yeare.
Hither with christall vyals, lovers come,   **20**
   And take my teares, which are loves wine,
   And try your mistresse Teares at home,
For all are false, that tast not just like mine;
   Alas, hearts do not in eyes shine,
Nor can you more judge womans thoughts by teares,
   Than by her shadow, what she weares.
O perverse sexe, where none is true but shee,
   Who's therefore true, because her truth kills mee.

A VALEDICTION: OF THE BOOKE

I'LL tell thee now (deare Love) what thou shalt doe
   To anger destiny, as she doth us,
   How I shall stay, though she Esloygne me thus
And how posterity shall know it too;
    How thine may out-endure
     Sybills glory, and obscure
     Her who from Pindar could allure,
   And her, through whose helpe *Lucan* is not lame,
And her, whose booke (they say) *Homer* did finde, and name.

Study our manuscripts, those Myriades   **10**
   Of letters, which have past twixt thee and mee,
   Thence write our Annals, and in them will bee
To all whom loves subliming fire invades,
    Rule and example found;
    There, the faith of any ground
    No schismatique will dare to wound,
   That sees, how Love this grace to us affords,
To make, to keep, to use, to be these his Records.

This Booke, as long-liv'd as the elements,
   Or as the worlds forme, this all-graved tome   20
   In cypher writ, or new made Idiome,
Wee for loves clergie only'are instruments:
     When this booke is made thus,
     Should againe the ravenous
     Vandals and Goths inundate us,
   Learning were safe; in this our Universe
Schooles might learne Sciences, Spheares Musick, Angels Verse.

Here Loves Divines, (since all Divinity
   Is love or wonder) may finde all they seeke,
   Whether abstract spirituall love they like,   30
Their Soules exhal'd with what they do not see.
     Or, loth so to amuze
     Faiths infirmitie, they chuse
     Something which they may see and use.
   For, though minde be the heaven, where love doth sit,
Beauty a convenient type may be to figure it.

Here more than in their bookes may Lawyers finde,
   Both by what titles Mistresses are ours,
   And how prerogative these states devours,
Transferr'd from Love himselfe, to womankinde,   40
     Who though from heart, and eyes,
     They exact great subsidies,
   Forsake him who on them relies,
   And for the cause, honour, or conscience give,
Chimeraes, vaine as they, or their prerogative.

Here Statesmen, (or of them, they which can reade,)
   May of their occupation finde the grounds:
   Love and their art alike it deadly wounds,
If to consider what 'tis, one proceed,
     In both they doe excell   50
     Who the present governe well,
   Whose weaknesse none doth, or dares tell;
   In this thy booke, such will their nothing see,
As in the Bible some can finde out Alchimy.

Thus vent thy thoughts; abroad I'll studie thee,
   As he removes farre off, that great heights takes;
   How great love is, presence best tryall makes,

But absence tryes how long this love will bee;
   To take a latitude
    Sun, or starres, are fitliest view'd
    At their brightest, but to conclude
  Of longitudes, what other way have wee,
But to harke when, and where the darke eclipses bee?

COMMUNITIE

GOOD wee must love, and must hate ill,
For ill is ill, and good good still,
   But there are things indifferent,
Which wee may neither hate, nor love,
But one, and then another prove,
   As wee shall finde our fancy bent.

If then at first wise Nature had
Made women either good or bad,
   Then some wee might hate, and some chuse,
But since shee did them so create,
That we may neither love, nor hate,
   Onely this rests, All, all may use.

If they were good it would be seene,
Good is as visible as greene,
   And to all eyes it selfe betrayes:
If they were bad, they could not last,
Bad doth it selfe, and others wast,
   So, they deserve nor blame, nor praise.

But they are ours as fruits are ours,
He that but tasts, he that devours,
   And he that leaves all, doth as well:
Chang'd loves are but chang'd sorts of meat,
And when hee hath the kernell eate,
   Who doth not fling away the shell?

LOVES GROWTH

I scarce beleeve my love to be so pure
    As I had thought it was,
    Because it doth endure
Vicissitude, and season, as the grasse;
Me thinkes I lyed all winter, when I swore,
My love was infinite, if spring make'it more.
But if this medicine, love, which cures all sorrow
With more, not onely bee no quintessence,
But mixt of all stuffes, paining soule, or sense,
And of the Sunne his working vigour borrow,   10
Love's not so pure, and abstract, as they use
To say, which have no Mistresse but their Muse,
But as all else, being elemented too,
Love sometimes would contemplate, sometimes do.

And yet no greater, but more eminent,
    Love by the Spring is growne;
    As, in the firmament,
Starres by the Sunne are not inlarg'd, but showne.
Gentle love deeds, as blossomes on a bough,
From loves awakened root do bud out now.   20
If, as in water stir'd more circles bee
Produc'd by one, love such additions take,
Those like so many spheares, but one heaven make,
For, they are all concentrique unto thee.
And though each spring doe adde to love new heate,
As princes doe in times of action get
New taxes, and remit them not in peace,
No winter shall abate the springs encrease.

LOVES EXCHANGE

Love, any devill else but you,
Would for a given Soule give something too.
At Court your fellowes every day,
Give th'art of Riming, Huntsmanship, or Play,

For them which were their owne before;
Onely I have nothing which gave more,
But am, alas, by being lowly, lower.

I aske no dispensation now
To falsifie a teare, or sigh, or vow,
I dɔ not sue from thee to draw   10
A *non obstante* on natures law,
These are prerogatives, they inhere
In thee and thine; none should forsweare
Except that hee *Loves* minion were.

Give mee thy weaknesse, make mee blinde,
Both wayes, as thou and thine, in eies and minde;
Love, let me never know that this
Is love, or, that love childish is.
Let me not know that others know
That she knowes my paines, lest that so   20
A tender shame make me mine owne new woe.

If thou give nothing, yet thou'art just,
Because I would not thy first motions trust;
Small townes which stand stiffe, till great shot
Enforce them, by warres law *condition* not.
Such in loves warfare is my case,
I may not article for grace,
Having put Love at last to shew this face.

This face, by which he could command
And change the Idolatrie of any land,   30
This face, which wheresoe'r it comes,
Can call vow'd men from cloisters, dead from tombes,
And melt both Poles at once, and store
Deserts with cities, and make more
Mynes in the earth, than Quarries were before.

For this, Love is enrag'd with mee,
Yet kills not. If I must example bee
To future Rebells; If th'unborne
Must learne, by my being cut up, and torne:
Kill, and dissect me, Love; for this   40
Torture against thine owne end is,
Rack't carcasses make ill Anatomies.

CONFINED LOVE

SOME man unworthy to be possessor
Of old or new love, himselfe being false or weake.
  Thought his paine and shame would be lesser,
If on womankind he might his anger wreake,
        And thence a law did grow,
        One might but one man know;
        But are other creatures so?

  Are Sunne, Moone, or Starres by law forbidden,
To smile where they list, or lend away their light?
  Are birds divorc'd, or are they chidden   10
If they leave their mate, or lie abroad a-night?
        Beasts doe no joyntures lose
        Though they new lovers choose,
        But we are made worse than those.

  Who e'r rigg'd faire ship to lie in harbors,
And not to seeke new lands, or not to deale withall?
  Or built faire houses, set trees, and arbors,
Only to lock up, or else to let them fall?
        Good is not good, unlesse
        A thousand it possesse,   20
        But doth wast with greedinesse.

THE DREAME

DEARE love, for nothing lesse than thee
Would I have broke this happy dreame,
      It was a theame
For reason, much too strong for phantasie,
Therefore thou wakd'st me wisely; yet
My Dreame thou brok'st not, but continued'st it,
Thou art so truth, that thoughts of thee suffice,
To make dreames truths; and fables histories;
Enter these armes, for since thou thoughtst it best,
Not to dreame all my dreame, let's act the rest.   10

As lightning, or a Tapers light,
Thine eyes, and not thy noise wak'd mee;
      Yet I thought thee
(For thou lovest truth) an Angell, at first sight,
But when I saw thou sawest my heart,
And knew'st my thoughts, beyond an Angels art,
When thou knew'st what I dreamt, when thou knew'st when
Excesse of joy would wake me, and cam'st then,
I must confesse, it could not chuse but bee
Prophane, to thinke thee any thing but thee.   **20**

Comming and staying show'd thee, thee,
But rising makes me doubt, that now,
      Thou art not thou.
That love is weake, where feare's as strong as hee;
'Tis not all spirit, pure, and brave,
If mixture it of *Feare, Shame, Honor,* have.
Perchance as torches which must ready bee,
Men light and put out, so thou deal'st with mee,
Thou cam'st to kindle, goest to come; Then I
Will dreame that hope againe, but else would die.   **30**

A VALEDICTION: OF WEEPING

      LET me powre forth
My teares before thy face, whil'st I stay here,
For thy face coines them, and thy stampe they beare,
And by this Mintage they are something worth,
      For thus they bee
      Pregnant of thee;
Fruits of much griefe they are, emblemes of more,
When a teare falls, that thou falls which it bore,
So thou and I are nothing then, when on a divers shore.

      On a round ball   **10**
A workeman that hath copies by, can lay
An Europe, Afrique, and an Asia,
And quickly make that, which was nothing, *All*:
      So doth each teare,
      Which thee doth weare,

A globe, yea world by that impression grow,
Till thy teares mixt with mine doe overflow
This world, by waters sent from thee, my heaven dissolved so.

      O more than Moone,
Draw not up seas to drowne me in thy spheare,   **20**
Weepe me not dead, in thine armes, but forbeare
To teach the sea, what it may doe too soone;
      Let not the winde
      Example finde,
To doe me more harme, than it purposeth;
Since thou and I sigh one anothers breath,
Who e'r sighes most, is cruellest, and hastes the others death.

LOVES ALCHYMIE

SOME that have deeper digg'd loves Myne than I,
Say, where his centrique happinesse doth lie:
      I have lov'd, and got, and told,
But should I love, get, tell, till I were old,
I should not finde that hidden mysterie;
      Oh, 'tis imposture all:
And as no chymique yet th'Elixar got,
      But glorifies his pregnant pot,
      If by the way to him befall
Some odoriferous thing, or medicinall,   **10**
  So, lovers dreame a rich and long delight,
  But get a winter-seeming summers night.

Our ease, our thrift, our honor, and our day,
Shall we, for this vaine Bubles shadow pay?
      Ends love in this, that my man,
Can be as happy'as I can; If he can
Endure the short scorne of a Bridegroomes play?
      That loving wretch that sweares,
'Tis not the bodies marry, but the mindes,
      Which he in her Angelique findes,
      Would sweare as justly, that he heares,   **20**
In that dayes rude hoarse minstralsey, the spheares.
      Hope not for minde in women; at their best
      Sweetnesse and wit, they'are but *Mummy,* possest.

THE FLEA

MARKE but this flea, and marke in this,
How little that which thou deny'st me is;
It suck'd me first, and now sucks thee,
And in this flea, our two bloods mingled bee;
Thou know'st that this cannot be said
A sinne, nor shame, nor losse of maidenhead,
　Yet this enjoyes before it wooe,
　And pamper'd swells with one blood made of two,
　And this, alas, is more than wee would doe.

Oh stay, three lives in one flea spare,   **10**
Where wee almost, yea more than maryed are.
This flea is you and I, and this
Our mariage bed, and mariage temple is;
Though parents grudge, and you, w'are met,
And cloysterd in these living walls of Jet.
　Though use make you apt to kill mee,
　Let not to that, selfe murder added bee,
　And sacrilege, three sinnes in killing three.

Cruell and sodaine, hast thou since
Purpled thy naile, in blood of innocence?   **20**
Wherein could this flea guilty bee,
Except in that drop which it suckt from thee?
Yet thou triumph'st, and saist that thou
Find'st not thy selfe, nor mee the weaker now;
　'Tis true, then learne how false, feares bee;
　Just so much honor, when thou yeeld'st to mee,
　Will wast, as this flea's death tooke life from thee

THE CURSE

WHO ever guesses, thinks, or dreames he knowes
Who is my mistris, wither by this curse;
　　His only, and only his purse
　　May some dull heart to love dispose,
And shee yeeld then to all that are his foes;

May he be scorn'd by one, whom all else scorne,
Forsweare to others, what to her he'hath sworne,
With feare of missing, shame of getting, torne:

Madnesse his sorrow, gout his cramp, may hee
Make, by but thinking, who hath made him such: **10**
    And may he feele no touch
    Of conscience, but of fame, and bee
Anguish'd, not that'twas sinne, but that'twas shee:
  In early and long scarcenesse may he rot,
  For land which had been his, if he had not
Himselfe incestuously an heire begot:

May he dreame Treason, and beleeve, that hee
Meant to performe it, and confesse, and die,
    And no record tell why:
    His sonnes, which none of his may bee,   **20**
Inherite nothing but his infamie:
  Or may he so long Parasites have fed,
  That he would faine be theirs, whom he hath bred,
And at the last be circumcis'd for bread:

The venom of all stepdames, gamsters gall,
What Tyrans, and their subjects interwish,
    What Plants, Myne, Beasts, Foule, Fish,
    Can contribute, all ill which all
Prophets, or Poets spake; And all which shall
  Be annex'd in schedules unto this by mee,   **30**
  Fall on that man; For if it be a shee
Nature beforehand hath out-cursed mee.

THE MESSAGE

SEND home my long strayd eyes to mee,
Which (Oh) too long have dwelt on thee;
Yet since there they have learn'd such ill,
    Such forc'd fashions,
    And false passions,
      That they be
      Made by thee
Fit for no good sight, keep them still.

Send home my harmlesse heart againe,
Which no unworthy thought could staine;   **10**
But if it be taught by thine
    To make jestings
    Of protestings,
        And crosse both
        Word and oath,
Keepe it, for then 'tis none of mine.

Yet send me back my heart and eyes,
That I may know, and see thy lyes,
And may laugh and joy, when thou   **20**
    Art in anguish
    And dost languish
        For some one
        That will none,
Or prove as false as thou art now.

A NOCTURNALL UPON S. LUCIES DAY,

BEING THE SHORTEST DAY

Tis the yeares midnight, and it is the dayes,
Lucies, who scarce seaven houres herself unmaskes,
    The Sunne is spent, and now his flasks
    Send forth light squibs, no constant rayes;
        The worlds whole sap is sunke:
The generall balme th'hydroptique earth hath drunk,
Whither, as to the beds-feet, life is shrunke,
Dead and enterr'd; yet all these seeme to laugh,
Compar'd with mee, who am their Epitaph.

Study me then, you who shall lovers bee   **10**
At the next world, that is, at the next Spring:
    For I am every dead thing,
    In whom love wrought new Alchimie.
        For his art did expresse
A quintessence even from nothingnesse,
From dull privations, and leane emptinesse:
He ruin'd mee, and I am re-begot
Of absence, darknesse, death; things which are not.

All others, from all things, draw all that's good,
Life, soule, forme, spirit, whence they beeing have;   20
   I, by loves limbecke, am the grave
  Of all, that's nothing. Oft a flood
    Have wee two wept, and so
Drownd the whole world, us two; oft did we grow
To be two Chaosses, when we did show
Care to ought else; and often absences
Withdrew our soules, and made us carcasses.

But I am by her death, (which word wrongs her)
Of the first nothing, the Elixer grown;
   Were I a man, that I were one,   30
  I needs must know; I should preferre,
    If I were any beast,
Some ends, some means; Yea plants, yea stones detest,
And love; All, all some properties invest;
If I an ordinary nothing were,
As shadow, a light, and body must be here.

But I am None; nor will my Sunne renew.
You lovers, for whose sake, the lesser Sunne
   At this time to the Goat is runne
  To fetch new lust, and give it you,   40
    Enjoy your summer all;
Since shee enjoyes her long nights festivall,
Let mee prepare towards her, and let mee call
This houre her Vigill, and her Eve, since this
Both the yeares, and the dayes deep midnight is.

WITCHCRAFT BY A PICTURE

I FIXE mine eye on thine, and there
  Pitty my picture burning in thine eye,
My picture drown'd in a transparent teare,
  When I looke lower I espie;
   Hadst thou the wicked skill
By pictures made and mard, to kill,
How many wayes mightst thou performe thy will?

But now I have drunke thy sweet salt teares,
  And though thou poure more I'll depart;

My picture vanish'd, vanish feares, **10**
  That I can be endamag'd by that art;
    Though thou retaine of mee
One picture more, yet that will bee,
Being in thine owne heart, from all malice free.

THE BAITE

COME live with mee, and bee my love,
And wee will some new pleasures prove
Of golden sands, and christall brookes,
With silken lines, and silver hookes.

There will the river whispering runne
Warm'd by thy eyes, more than the Sunne.
And there the'inamor'd fish will stay,
Begging themselves they may betray.

When thou wilt swimme in that live bath,
Each fish, which every channell hath, **10**
Will amorously to thee swimme,
Gladder to catch thee, than thou him.

If thou, to be so seene, beest loath,
By Sunne, or Moone, thou darknest both,
And if my selfe have leave to see,
I need not their light, having thee.

Let others freeze with angling reeds,
And cut their legges, with shells and weeds,
Or treacherously poore fish beset,
With strangling snare, or windowie net: **20**

Let coarse bold hands, from slimy nest
The bedded fish in banks out-wrest,
Or curious traitors, sleavesilke flies
Bewitch poore fishes wandring eyes.

For thee, thou needst no such deceit,
For thou thy selfe art thine owne bait;
That fish, that is not catch'd thereby,
Alas, is wiser farre than I.

THE APPARITION

WHEN by thy scorne, O murdresse, I am dead,
And that thou thinkst thee free
From all solicitation from mee,
Then shall my ghost come to thy bed,
And thee, fain'd vestall, in worse armes shall see;
Then thy sicke taper will begin to winke,
And he, whose thou art then, being tyr'd before,
Will, if thou stirre, or pinch to wake him, thinke
    Thou call'st for more,
And in false sleepe will from thee shrinke,   **10**
And then poore Aspen wretch, neglected thou
Bath'd in a cold quicksilver sweat wilt lye
    A veryer ghost than I;
What I will say, I will not tell thee now,
Lest that preserve thee'; and since my love is spent,
I'had rather thou shouldst painfully repent,
Than by my threatnings rest still innocent.

THE BROKEN HEART

HE is starke mad, who ever sayes,
    That he hath been in love an houre,
Yet not that love so soone decayes,
    But that it can tenne in lesse space devour;
Who will beleeve mee, if I sweare
That I have had the plague a yeare?
    Who would not laugh at mee, if I should say,
    I saw a flaske of *powder burne a day?*

Ah, what a trifle is a heart,
    If once into loves hands it come!   **10**
All other griefes allow a part
    To other griefes, and aske themselves but some;
They come to us, but us Love draws,
Hee swallows us, and never chawes:
    By him, as by chain'd shot, whole rankes doe dye,
    He is the tyran Pike, our hearts the Frye.

If 'twere not so, what did become
   Of my heart, when I first saw thee?
I brought a heart into the roome,
   But from the roome, I carried none with mee: 20
If it had gone to thee, I know
Mine would have taught thine heart to show
   More pitty unto mee: but Love, alas,
   At one first blow did shiver it as glasse.

Yet nothing can to nothing fall,
   Nor any place be empty quite,
Therefore I thinke my breast hath all
   Those peeces still, though they be not unite;
And now as broken glasses show
A hundred lesser faces, so   30
   My ragges of heart can like, wish, and adore,
   But after one such love, can love no more.

A VALEDICTION: FORBIDDING MOURNING

As virtuous men passe mildly away,
   And whisper to their soules, to goe,
Whilst some of their sad friends doe say,
   The breath goes now, and some say, no:

So let us melt, and make no noise,
   No teare-floods, nor sigh-tempests move,
T'were prophanation of our joyes
   To tell the layetie our love.

Moving of th'earth brings harmes and feares,
   Men reckon what it did and meant,   10
But trepidation of the spheares,
   Though greater farre, is innocent.

Dull sublunary lovers love
   (Whose soule is sense) cannot admit
Absence, because it doth remove
   Those things which elemented it.

But we by a love, so much refin'd.
   That our selves know not what it is,

Inter-assured of the mind,
   Care lesse, eyes, lips, and hands to misse.   20

Our two soules therefore, which are one,
   Though I must goe, endure not yet
A breach, but an expansion,
   Like gold to ayery thinnesse beate.

If they be two, they are two so
   As stiffe twin compasses are two,
Thy soule the fixt foot, makes no show
   To move, but doth, if the'other doe.

And though it in the center sit,
   Yet when the other far doth rome,   30
It leanes, and hearkens after it,
   And growes erect, as that comes home.

Such wilt thou be to mee, who must
   Like th'other foot, obliquely runne;
Thy firmnes drawes my circle just,
   And makes me end, where I begunne.

THE EXTASIE

WHERE, like a pillow on a bed,
   A Pregnant banke swel'd up, to rest
The violets reclining head,
   Sat we two, one anothers best.
Our hands were firmely cimented
   With a fast balme, which thence did spring,
Our eye-beames twisted, and did thred
   Our eyes, upon one double string;
So to'entergraft our hands, as yet
   Was all the meanes to make us one,   10
And pictures in our eyes to get
   Was all our propagation.
As 'twixt two equall Armies, Fate
   Suspends uncertaine victorie,
Our soules, (which to advance their state,
   Were gone out,) hung 'twixt her, and mee.

And whil'st our soules negotiate there,
  Wee like sepulchrall statues lay;
All day, the same our postures were,
  And wee said nothing, all the day.   20
If any, so by love refin'd,
  That he soules language understood,
And by good love were growen all minde,
  Within convenient distance stood,
He (though he knew not which soul spake,
  Because both meant, both spake the same)
Might thence a new concoction take,
  And part farre purer than he came.
This Extasie doth unperplex
  (We said) and tell us what we love,   30
Wee see by this, it was not sexe,
  Wee see, we saw not what did move:
But as all severall soules containe
  Mixture of things, they know not what,
Love, these mixt soules, doth mixe againe,
  And makes both one, each this and that.
A single violet transplant,
  The strength, the colour, and the size,
(All which before was poore, and scant,)
  Redoubles still, and multiplies.   40
When love, with one another so
  Interinanimates two soules,
That abler soule, which thence doth flow,
  Defects of lonelinesse controules.
Wee then, who are this new soule, know,
  Of what we are compos'd, and made,
For, th'Atomies of which we grow,
  Are soules, whom no change can invade.
But O alas, so long, so farre
  Our bodies why doe wee forbeare?   50
They are ours, though they are not wee, Wee are
  The intelligences, they the spheares.
We owe them thankes, because they thus,
  Did us, to us, at first convay,
Yeelded their forces, sense, to us,
  Nor are drosse to us, but allay.
On man heavens influence workes not so,
  But that it first imprints the ayre,
Soe soule into the soule may flow,

Though it to body first repaire.   **60**
    our blood labours to beget
  Spirits, as like soules as it can,
Because such fingers need to knit
    That subtile knot, which makes us man:
So must pure lovers soules descend
    T'affections, and to faculties,
Which sense may reach and apprehend.
    Else a great Prince in prison lies.
To'our bodies turne wee then, that so
    Weake men on love reveal'd may looke;   **70**
Loves mysteries in soules doe grow,
    But yet the body is his booke.
And if some lover, such as wee,
    Have heard this dialogue of one,
Let him still marke us, he shall see
    Small change, when we'are to bodies gone.

LOVES DEITIE

I LONG to talke with some old lovers ghost,
    Who dyed before the god of Love was borne:
I cannot thinke that hee, who then lov'd most,
    Sunke so low, as to love one which did scorne.
But since this god produc'd a destinie,
And that vice-nature, custome, lets it be;
    I must love her, that loves not mee.

Sure, they which made him god, meant not so much,
    Nor he, in his young godhead practis'd it.
But when an even flame two hearts did touch,   **10**
    His office was indulgently to fit
Actives to passives. Correspondencie
Only his subject was; It cannot bee
    Love, till I love her, that loves mee.

But every moderne god will now extend
    His vast prerogative, as far as Jove.
To rage, to lust, to write to, to commend,
    All is the purlewe of the God of Love.
Oh were wee wak'ned by this Tyrannie

To ungod this child againe, it could not bee   **20**
    I should love her, who loves not mee.

Rebell and Atheist too, why murmure I,
    As though I felt the worst that love could doe?
Love might make me leave loving, or might trie
    A deeper plague, to make her love mee too,
Which, since she loves before, I'am loth to see;
Falshood is worse than hate; and that must bee,
    If shee whom I love, should love mee.

LOVES DIET

To what a combersome unwieldinesse
And burdenous corpulence my love had growne,
    But that I did, to make it lesse,
    And keepe it in proportion,
Give it a diet, made it feed upon
That which love worst endures, *discretion.*

Above one sigh a day I'allow'd him not,
Of which my fortune, and my faults had part;
    And if sometimes by stealth he got
    A she sigh from my mistresse heart,   **10**
And thought to feast on that, I let him see
'Twas neither very sound, nor meant to mee.

If he wroung from mee'a teare, I brin'd it so
With scorne or shame, that him it nourish'd not;
    If he suck'd hers, I let him know
    'Twas not a teare, which hee had got,
His drinke was counterfeit, as was his meat;
For, eyes which rowle towards all, weepe not, but sweat.

What ever he would dictate, I writ that,
But burnt my letters; When she writ to me,   **20**
    And that that favour made him fat,
    I said, if any title bee
Convey'd by this, Ah, what doth it availe,
To be the fortieth name in an entaile?

Thus I reclaim'd my buzard love, to flye
At what, and when, and how, and where I chuse;
   Now negligent of sport I lye,
   And now as other Fawkners use,
I spring a mistresse, sweare, write, sigh and weepe:
And the game kill'd, or lost, goe talke, and sleepe.   **30**

THE WILL

Before I sigh my last gaspe, let me breath,
Great love, some Legacies; Here I bequeath
Mine eyes to *Argus*, if mine eyes can see,
If they be blinde, then Love, I give them thee;
My tongue to Fame; to'Embassadours mine eares;
   To women or the sea, my teares.
Thou, Love, hast taught mee heretofore
By making mee serve her who'had twenty more,
That I should give to none, but such, as had too much before.

My constancie I to the planets give;   **10**
My truth to them, who at the Court doe live;
Mine ingenuity and opennesse,
To Jesuites; to Buffones my pensivenesse;
My silence to'any, who abroad hath beene;
   My mony to a Capuchin.
Thou Love taught'st me, by appointing mee
To love there, where no love receiv'd can be,
Onely to give to such as have an incapacitie.

My faith I give to Roman Catholiques;
All my good works unto the Schismaticks   **20**
Of Amsterdam: my best civility
And Courtship, to an Universitie;
My modesty I give to souldiers bare;
   My patience let gamesters share.
Thou Love taughtst mee, by making mee
Love her that holds my love disparity,
Onely to give to those that count my gifts indignity.

I give my reputation to those
Which were my friends; Mine industrie to foes;

To Schoolemen I bequeath my doubtfulnesse;   30
My sicknesse to Physitians, or excesse;
To Nature, all that I in Ryme have writ;
    And to my company my wit.
Thou Love, by making mee adore
Her, who begot this love in mee before,
Taughtst me to make, as though I gave, when I did but restore.

To him for whom the passing bell next tolls,
I give my physick bookes; my writen rowles
Of Morall counsels, I to Bedlam give;
My brazen medals, unto them which live   40
In want of bread; To them which passe among
    All forrainers, mine English tongue.
Thou, Love, by making mee love one
Who thinkes her friendship a fit portion
For yonger lovers, dost my gifts thus disproportion.

Therefore I'll give no more; But I'll undoe
The world by dying; because love dies too.
Then all your beauties will be no more worth
Than gold in Mines, where none doth draw it forth;
And all your graces no more use shall have   50
    Than a Sun dyall in a grave.
Thou Love taughtst mee, by making mee
Love her, who doth neglect both mee and thee,
To'invent, and practise this one way, to'annihilate all three.

THE FUNERALL

Who ever comes to shroud me, do not harme
    Nor question much
That subtile wreathe of haire, which crowns my arme;
The mystery, the signe you must not touch,
    For'tis my outward Soule,
Viceroy to that, which then to heaven being gone,
    Will leave this to controule,
And keep these limbes, her Provinces, from dissolution.

For if the sinewie thread my braine lets fall
    Through every part.   10

Can tye those parts, and make mee one of all;
These haires which upward grew, and strength and art
      Have from a better braine,
Can better do'it; Except she meant that I
      By this should know my pain,
As prisoners then are manacled, when they'are condemn'd to die.

What ere shee meant by'it, bury it with me,
      For since I am
Loves martyr, it might breed idolatrie,
If into others hands these Reliques came;   20
      As'twas humility
To afford to it all that a Soule can doe,
      So,'tis some bravery,
That since you would save none of mee, I bury some of you.

THE BLOSSOME

LITTLE think'st thou, poore flower,
  Whom I have watch'd sixe or seaven dayes,
And seene thy birth, and seene what every houre
Gave to thy growth, thee to this height to raise,
And now dost laugh and triumph on this bough,
      Little think'st thou
That it will freeze anon, and that I shall
To morrow finde thee falne, or not at all.

  Little think'st thou poore heart
  That labour'st yet to nestle thee,   10
And think'st by hovering here to get a part
In a forbidden or forbidding tree,
And hop'st her stiffenesse by long siege to bow:
      Little think'st thou,
That thou to morrow, ere that Sunne doth wake,
Must with this Sunne, and mee a journey take.

  But thou which lov'st to bee
  Subtile to plague thy selfe, wilt say,
Alas, if you must goe, what's that to me?
Here lyes my businesse, and here I will stay: 20

You goe to friends, whose love and meanes present
          Various content
To your eyes, eares, and tongue, and every part.
If then your body goe, what need you a heart?

  Well then, stay here; but know,
    When thou hast stayd and done thy most;
A naked thinking heart, that makes no show,
Is to a woman, but a kinde of Ghost;
How shall shee know my heart; or having none,
        Know thee for one?   **30**
Practise may make her know some other part,
But take my word, shee doth not know a Heart.

  Meet mee at London, then,
    Twenty dayes hence, and thou shalt see
Mee fresher, and more fat, by being with men,
Than if I had staid still with her and thee.
For Gods sake, if you can, be you so too:
        I would give you
There, to another friend, whom wee shall finde
Is glad to have my body, as my minde.   **40**

THE PRIMROSE, BEING AT MONTGOMERY CASTLE, UPON THE HILL, ON WHICH IT IS SITUATE

    UPON this Primrose hill,
      Where, if Heav'n would distill
A shoure of raine, each severall drop might goe
To his owne primrose, and grow Manna so;
And where their forme, and their infinitie
      Make a terrestriall Galaxie,
      As the small starres doe in the skie:
I walke to finde a true Love; and I see
That'tis not a mere woman, that is shee,
But must, or more, or lesse than woman bee.   **10**

    Yet know I not, which flower
      I wish; a sixe, or foure;
For should my true-Love lesse than woman bee,

She were scarce any thing; and then, should she
Be more than woman, shee would get above
     All thought of sexe, and thinke to move
     My heart to study her, and not to love;
Both these were monsters; Since there must reside
Falshood in woman, I could more abide,
She were by art, than Nature falsify'd.   **20**

     Live Primrose then, and thrive
     With thy true number five;
And women, whom this flower doth represent,
With this mysterious number be content;
Ten is the farthest number; if halfe ten
     Belonge unto each woman, then
     Each woman may take halfe us men;
Or if this will not serve their turne, Since all
Numbers are odde, or even, and they fall
First into this, five, women may take us all.   **30**

THE RELIQUE

     WHEN my grave is broke up againe
     Some second ghest to entertaine,
     (For graves have learn'd that woman-head
     To be to more than one a Bed)
     And he that digs it, spies
A bracelet of bright haire about the bone,
     Will he not let'us alone,
And thinke that there a loving couple lies,
Who thought that this device might be some way
To make their soules, at the last busie day,   **10**
Meet at this grave, and make a little stay?

     If this fall in a time, or land,
     Where mis-devotion doth command,
     Then, he that digges us up, will bring
     Us, to the Bishop, and the King,
     To make us Reliques; then
Thou shalt be a Mary Magdalen, and I
     A something else thereby;
All women shall adore us, and some men;

And since at such time, miracles are sought,   20
I would have that age by this paper taught
What miracles wee harmlesse lovers wrought.

First, we lov'd well and faithfully,
Yet knew not what wee lov'd, nor why,
Difference of sex no more wee knew,
Than our Guardian Angells doe;
          Comming and going, wce
Perchance might kisse, but not between those meales;
Our hands ne'r toucht the seales,
Which nature, injur'd by late law, sets free: 30
These miracles wee did; but now alas,
All measure, and all language, I should passe,
Should I tell what a miracle shee was.

THE DAMPE

When I am dead, and Doctors know not why,
          And my friends curiositie
Will have me cut up to survay each part,
When they shall finde your Picture in my heart,
          You thinke a sodaine dampe of love
          Will through all their senses move,
And worke on them as mee, and so preferre
Your murder, to the name of Massacre.

Poore victories! But if you dare be brave,
          And pleasure in your conquest have,   10
First kill th'enormous Gyant, your *Disdaine,*
And let th'enchantresse *Honor,* next be slaine,
          And like a Goth and Vandall rize,
          Deface Records, and Histories
Of your owne arts and triumphs over men,
And without such advantage kill me then.

For I could muster up as well as you
          My Gyants, and my Witches too,
Which are vast *Constancy,* and *Secretnesse,*
But these I neyther looke for, nor professe;   20
          Kill mee as Woman, let mee die
          As a meere man; doe you but trv

Your passive valor, and you shall finde then,
Naked you'have odds enough of any man.

THE DISSOLUTION

SHEE'is dead; And all which die
  To their first Elements resolve;
And wee were mutuall Elements to us,
    And made of one another.
My body then doth hers involve,
And those things whereof I consist, hereby
In me abundant grow, and burdenous,
    And nourish not, but smother.
My fire of Passion, sighes of ayre,
Water of teares, and earthly sad despaire,   **10**
    Which my materialls bee,
But neere worne out by loves securitie,
Shee, to my losse, doth by her death repaire,
  And I might live long wretched so
But that my fire doth with my fuell grow.
    Now as those Active Kings
  Whose foraine conquest treasure brings,
Receive more, and spend more, and soonest breake:
This (which I am amaz'd that I can speake)
    This death, hath with my store   **20**
    My use encreas'd.
And so my soule more earnestly releas'd,
Will outstrip hers; as bullets flowen before
A latter bullet may o'rtake, the pouder being more.

A JEAT RING SENT

  THOU art not so black, as my heart,
 Nor halfe so brittle, as her heart, thou art;
What would'st thou say? shall both our properties by thee bee
    spoke,
Nothing more endlesse, nothing sooner broke?

  Marriage rings are not of this stuffe;
Oh, why should ought lesse precious, or lesse tough

Figure our loves? Except in thy name thou have bid it say,
  I'am cheap, and nought but fashion, fling me'away.

     Yet stay with mee since thou art come,
  Circle this fingers top, which did'st her thombe.   **10**
Be justly proud, and gladly safe, that thou dost dwell with me,
  She that, Oh, broke her faith, would soon breake thee.

NEGATIVE LOVE

  I NEVER stoop'd so low, as they
  Which on an eye, cheeke, lip, can prey,
    Seldome to them, which soare no higher
    Than vertue or the minde to'admire,
  For sense, and understanding may
    Know, what gives fuell to their fire:
  My love, though silly, is more brave,
  For may I misse, when ere I crave,
  If I know yet, what I would have.

  If that be simply perfectest   **10**
  Which can by no way be exprest
    But *Negatives,* my love is so.
    To All, which all love, I say no.
  If any who deciphers best,
    What we know not, our selves, can know,
  Let him teach mee that nothing; This
  As yet my ease, and comfort is,
  Though I speed not, I cannot misse.

THE PROHIBITION

    TAKE heed of loving mee,
  At least remember, I forbade it thee;
  Not that I shall repaire my 'unthrifty wast
  Of Breath and Blood, upon thy sighes, and teares,
  By being to thee then what to me thou wast;
  But, so great Joy, our life at once outweares,
  Then, lest thy love, by my death, frustrate bee,
  If thou love mee, take heed of loving mee.

Take heed of hating mee,
Or too much triumph in the Victorie.   **10**
Not that I shall be mine owne officer,
And hate with hate againe retaliate;
But thou wilt lose the stile of conquerour,
If I, thy conquest, perish by thy hate.
Then, lest my being nothing lessen thee,
If thou hate mee, take heed of hating mee.

Yet, love and hate mee too,
So, these extreames shall neithers office doe;
Love mee, that I may die the gentler way;
Hate mee, because thy love is too great for mee;   **20**
Or let these two, themselves, not me decay;
So shall I, live, thy Stage, not triumph bee;
Lest thou thy love and hate and mee undoe,
To let mee live, O love and hate mee too.

THE EXPIRATION

So, so, breake off this last lamenting kisse,
    Which sucks two soules, and vapors Both away,
Turne thou ghost that way, and let mee turne this,
    And let our selves benight our happiest day,
We ask'd none leave to love; nor will we owe
    Any, so cheape a death, as saying, Goe;

Goe; and if that word have not quite kil'd thee,
    Ease mee with death, by bidding mee goe too.
Oh, if it have, let my word worke on mee,
    And a just office on a murderer doe.   **10**
Except it be too late, to kill me so,
    Being double dead, going, and bidding, goe.

THE COMPUTATION

For the first twenty yeares, since yesterday,
    I scarce beleev'd, thou could'st be gone away,
For forty more, I fed on favours past,
    And forty'on hopes, that thou would'st, they might last.

Teares drown'd one hundred, and sighes blew out two,
   A thousand, I did neither thinke, nor doe,
   Or not divide, all being one thought of you;
   Or in a thousand more, forgot that too.
Yet call not this long life; But thinke that I
Am, by being dead, Immortall; Can ghosts die?   **10**

THE PARADOX

No Lover saith, I love, nor any other
     Can judge a perfect Lover;
Hee thinkes that else none can, nor will agree
     That any loves but hee:
I cannot say I lov'd, for who can say
     Hee was kill'd yesterday?
Love with excesse of heat, more yong than old,
     Death kills with too much cold;
Wee dye but once, and who lov'd last did die,
     Hee that saith twice, doth lye: **10**
For though hee seeme to move, and stirre a while,
     It doth the sense beguile.
Such life is like the light which bideth yet
     When the lights life is set,
Or like the heat, which fire in solid matter
     Leaves behinde, two houres after.
Once I lov'd and dy'd; and am now become
     Mine Epitaph and Tombe.
Here dead men speake their last, and so do I;
     Love-slaine, loe, here I lye.   **20**

FAREWELL TO LOVE

     WHILST yet to prove,
I thought there was some Deitie in love
   So did I reverence, and gave
Worship; as Atheists at their dying houre
Call, what they cannot name, an unknowne power,
   As ignorantly did I crave:
       Thus when

Things not yet knowne are coveted by men,
  Our desires give them fashion, and so
As they waxe lesser, fall, as they sise, grow.   **10**

      But, from late faire
His highnesse sitting in a golden Chaire,
  Is not lesse cared for after three dayes
By children, than the thing which lovers so
Blindly admire, and with such worship wooe;
  Being had, enjoying it decayes:
        And thence,
What before pleas'd them all, takes but one sense,
  And that so lamely, as it leaves behinde
A kinde of sorrowing dulnesse to the minde.   **20**

      Ah cannot wee,
As well as Cocks and Lyons jocund be,
  After such pleasures? Unlesse wise
Nature decreed (since each such Act, they say,
Diminisheth the length of life a day)
  This, as shee would man should despise
        The sport,
Because that other curse of being short,
  And onely for a minute made to be
Eager, desires to raise posterity.   **30**

      Since so, my minde
Shall not desire what no man else can finde,
  I'll no more dote and runne
To pursue things which had indammag'd me.
And when I come where moving beauties be,
  As men doe when the summers Sunne
        Growes great,
Though I admire their greatnesse, shun their heat;
  Each place can afford shadowes. If all faile,
'Tis but applying worme-seed to the Taile.   **40**

A LECTURE UPON THE SHADOW

STAND still, and I will read to thee
A Lecture, love, in Loves philosophy.
    These three houres that we have spent,

Walking here, Two shadowes went
Along with us, which we our selves produc'd;
But, now the Sunne is just above our head,
    We doe those shadowes tread;
    And to brave clearnesse all things are reduc'd.
So whilst our infant loves did grow,
Disguises did, and shadowes, flow,   **10**
From us, and our cares; but, now 'tis not so.

That love hath not attain'd the high'st degree,
Which is still diligent lest others see.

Except our loves at this noone stay,
We shall new shadowes make the other way.
    As the first were made to blinde
    Others; these which come behinde
Will worke upon our selves, and blind our eyes.
If our loves faint, and westwardly decline;
    To me thou, falsly, thine,   **20**
    And I to thee mine actions shall disguise.
The morning shadowes weare away,
But these grow longer all the day,
But oh, loves day is short, if love decay.

Love is a growing, or full constant light;
And his first minute, after noone, is night.

SONNET. THE TOKEN

SEND me some token, that my hope may live,
    Or that my easelesse thoughts may sleep and rest;
Send me some honey to make sweet my hive,
    That in my passion I may hope the best.
I beg noe ribbond wrought with thine owne hands,
    To knit our loves in the fantastick straine
Of new-toucht youth; nor Ring to shew the stands
    Of our affection, that as that's round and plaine,
So should our loves meet in simplicity.
    No, nor the Coralls which thy wrist infold,   **10**
Lac'd up together in congruity,
    To shew our thoughts should rest in the same hold;

No, nor thy picture, though most gracious,
   And most desir'd, because best like the best;
Nor witty Lines, which are most copious,
   Within the Writings which thou hast addrest.

Send me nor this, nor that, t'increase my store,
But swear thou thinkst I love thee, and no more.

SELFE LOVE

He that cannot chuse but love,
And strives against it still,
Never shall my fancy move;
For he loves 'gaynst his will;
Nor he which is all his own,
And can att pleasure chuse,
When I am caught he can be gone,
And when he list refuse.
Nor he that loves none but faire,
For such by all are sought;   **10**
Nor he that can for foul ones care,
For his Judgement then is nought:
Nor he that hath wit, for he
Will make me his jest or slave;
Nor a fool, for when others . . .,
He can neither . . . . . .
Nor he that still his Mistresse payes,
For she is thrall'd therefore:
Nor he that payes not, for he sayes
Within, shee's worth no more.   **20**
Is there then no kinde of men
Whom I may freely prove?
I will vent that humour then
In mine own selfe love.

ELEGIES AND HEROICALL EPISTLE

ELEGIE I

JEALOSIE

FOND woman, which would'st have thy husband die,
And yet complain'st of his great jealousie;
If swolne with poyson, hee lay in'his last bed,
His body with a sere-barke covered,
Drawing his breath, as thick and short, as can
The nimblest crocheting Musitian,
Ready with loathsome vomiting to spue
His Soule out of one hell, into a new,
Made deafe with his poore kindreds howling cries,
Begging with few feign'd teares, great legacies,   10
Thou would'st not weepe, but jolly,'and frolicke bee,
As a slave, which to morrow should be free;
Yet weep'st thou, when thou seest him hungerly
Swallow his owne death, hearts-bane jealousie.
O give him many thanks, he'is courteous,
That in suspecting kindly warneth us.
Wee must not, as wee us'd, flout openly,
In scoffing ridles, his deformitie;
Nor at his boord together being satt,
With words, nor touch, scarce lookes adulterate.   20
Nor when he swolne, and pamper'd with great fare
Sits downe, and snorts, cag'd in his basket chaire,
Must wee usurpe his owne bed any more,
Nor kisse and play in his house, as before.
Now I see many dangers; for that is
His realme, his castle, and his diocesse.
But if, as envious men, which would revile
Their Prince, or coyne his gold, themselves exile
Into another countrie,'and doe it there,
Wee play'in another house, what should we feare?   30
There we will scorne his houshold policies,
His seely plots, and pensionary spies,
As the inhabitants of Thames right side
Do Londons Major; or Germans, the Popes pride.

ELEGIE II

THE ANAGRAM

MARRY, and love thy *Flavia,* for, shee
Hath all things, whereby others beautious bee,
For, though her eyes be small, her mouth is great,
Though they be Ivory, yet her teeth be jeat,
Though they be dimme, yet she is light enough,
And though her harsh haire fall, her skinne is rough;
What though her cheeks be yellow, her haire's red,
Give her thine, and she hath a maydenhead.
These things are beauties elements, where these
Meet in one, that one must, as perfect, please.   10
If red and white and each good quality
Be in thy wench, ne'r aske where it doth lye.
In buying things perfum'd, we aske; if there
Be muske and amber in it, but not where.
Though all her parts be not in th'usuall place,
She'hath yet an Anagram of a good face.
If we might put the letters but one way,
In the leane dearth of words, what could wee say?
When by the Gamut some Musitions make
A perfect song, others will undertake,   20
By the same Gamut chang'd, to equall it.
Things simply good, can never be unfit.
She's faire as any, if all be like her,
And if none bee, then she is singular.
All love is wonder; if wee justly doe
Account her wonderfull, why not lovely too?
Love built on beauty, soone as beauty, dies,
Chuse this face, chang'd by no deformities.
Women are all like Angels; the faire be
Like those which fell to worse; but such as thee,   30
Like to good Angels, nothing can impaire:
'Tis lesse griefe to be foule, than to'have beene faire.
For one nights revels, silke and gold we chuse,
But, in long journeyes, cloth, and leather use.
Beauty is barren oft; best husbands say,
There is best land, where there is foulest way.
Oh what a soveraigne Plaister will shee bee,

If thy past sinnes have taught thee jealousie!
Here needs no spies, nor eunuches; her commit
Safe to thy foes; yea, to a Marmosit.   40
When Belgiaes citties, the round countries drowne,
That durty foulenesse guards, and armes the towne:
So doth her face guard her; and so, for thee,
Which, forc'd by businesse, absent oft must bee,
Shee, whose face, like clouds, turnes the day to night,
Who, mightier than the sea, makes Moores seem white,
Who, though seaven yeares, she in the Stews had laid,
A Nunnery durst receive, and thinke a maid,
And though in childbeds labour she did lie,
Midwifes would sweare,'twere but a tympanie,   50
Whom, if shee accuse her selfe, I credit lesse
Than witches, which impossibles confesse,
Whom Dildoes, Bedstaves, and her Velvet Glasse
Would be as loath to touch as Joseph was:
One like none, and lik'd of none, fittest were,
For, things in fashion every man will weare.

ELEGIE III

CHANGE

ALTHOUGH thy hand and faith, and good workes too,
Have seal'd thy love which nothing should undoe,
Yea though thou fall backe, that apostasie
Confirme thy love; yet much, much I feare thee.
Women are like the Arts, forc'd unto none,
Open to'all searchers, unpriz'd, if unknowne.
If I have caught a bird, and let him flie,
Another fouler using these meanes, as I,
May catch the same bird; and, as these things bee,
Women are made for men, not him, nor mee.   10
Foxes and goats; all beasts change when they please,
Shall women, more hot, wily, wild than these,
Be bound to one man, and did Nature then
Idly make them apter to'endure than men?
They'are our clogges, not their owne; if a man bee
Chain'd to a galley, yet the galley'is free;
Who hath a plow-land, casts all his seed corne there,
And yet allowes his ground more corne should beare;

Though Danuby into the sea must flow,
The sea receives the Rhene, Volga, and Po.   20
By nature, which gave it, this liberty
Thou lov'st, but Oh! canst thou love it and mee?
Likenesse glues love: and if that thou so doe,
To make us like and love, must I change too?
More than thy hate, I hate'it, rather let mee
Allow her change, than change as oft as shee,
And soe not teach, but force my'opinion
To love not any one, nor every one.
To live in one land, is captivitie,
To runne all countries, a wild roguery;   30
Waters stincke soone, if in one place they bide
And in the vast sea are more putrifi'd:
But when they kisse one banke, and leaving this
Never looke backe, but the next banke doe kisse,
Then are they purest; Change'is the nursery
Of musicke, joy, life, and eternity.

ELEGIE IV

THE PERFUME

Once, and but once found in thy company,
All thy suppos'd escapes are laid on mee;
And as a thiefe at barre, is question'd there
By all the men, that have beene rob'd that yeare,
So am I, (by this traiterous meanes surpriz'd)
By thy Hydroptique father catechiz'd.
Though he had wont to search with glazed eyes,
As though he came to kill a Cockatrice,
Though hee hath oft sworne, that hee would remove
Thy beauties beautie, and food of our love,   10
Hope of his goods, if I with thee were seene,
Yet close and secret, as our soules, we'have beene.
Though thy immortall mother which doth lye
Still buried in her bed, yet will not dye,
Takes this advantage to sleepe out day-light,
And watch thy entries, and returnes all night,
And, when she takes thy hand, and would seeme kind.
Doth search what rings, and armelets she can finde,
And kissing notes the colour of thy face,

And fearing least thou'art swolne, doth thee embrace;   20
To trie if thou long, doth name strange meates,
And notes thy palenesse, blushing, sighs, and sweats;
And politiquely will to thee confesse
The sinnes of her owne youths ranke lustinesse;
Yet love these Sorceries did remove, and move
Thee to gull thine owne mother for my love.
Thy little brethren, which like Faiery Sprights
Oft skipt into our chamber, those sweet nights,
And kist, and ingled on thy fathers knee,
Were brib'd next day, to tell what they did see: 30
The grim eight-foot-high iron-bound serving-man,
That oft names God in oathes, and onely then,
He that to barre the first gate, doth as wide
As the great Rhodian Colossus stride,
Which, if in hell no other paines there were,
Makes mee feare hell, because he must be there:
Though by thy father he were hir'd to this,
Could never witnesse any touch or kisse.
But Oh, too common ill, I brought with mee
That, which betray'd mee to my enemie: 40
A loud perfume, which at my entrance cryed
Even at thy fathers nose, so were wee spied.
When, like a tyran King, that in his bed
Smelt gunpowder, the pale wretch shivered.
Had it beene some bad smell, he would have thought
That his owne feet, or breath, that smell had wrought.
But as wee in our Ile emprisoned,
Where cattell onely,'and diverse dogs are bred,
The pretious Unicornes, strange monsters call,
So thought he good, strange, that had none at all.   50
I taught my silkes, their whistling to forbeare,
Even my opprest shoes, dumbe and speechlesse were,
Onely, thou bitter sweet, whom I had laid
Next mee, mee traterously hast betraid,
And unsuspected hast invisibly
At once fled unto him, and staid with mee.
Base excrement of earth, which dost confound
Sense, from distinguishing the sicke from sound;
By thee the seely Amorous sucks his death
By drawing in a leprous harlots breath;   60
By thee, the greatest staine to mans estate
Falls on us, to be call'd effeminate;

Though you be much lov'd in the Princes hall,
There, things that seeme, exceed substantiall.
Gods, when yee fum'd on altars, were pleas'd well,
Because you'were burnt, not that they lik'd your smell;
You'are loathsome all, being taken simply alone,
Shall wee love ill things joyn'd, and hate each one?
If you were good, your good doth soone decay;
And you are rare, that takes the good away.   70
All my perfumes, I give most willingly
To'embalme thy fathers corse; What? will hee die?

ELEGIE V

HIS PICTURE

HERE take my Picture; though I bid farewell,
Thine, in my heart, where my soule dwels, shall dwell.
'Tis like me now, but I dead, 'twill be more
When wee are shadowes both, than'twas before.
When weather-beaten I come backe; my hand,
Perhaps with rude oares torne, or Sun beams tann'd,
My face and brest of hairecloth, and my head
With cares rash sodaine stormes, being o'rspread,
My body'a sack of bones, broken within,
And powders blew staines scatter'd on my skinne;   10
If rivall fooles taxe thee to'have lov'd a man,
So foule, and course, as, Oh, I may seeme then,
This shall say what I was: and thou shalt say,
Doe his hurts reach mee? doth my worth decay?
Or doe they reach his judging minde, that hee
Should now love lesse, what hee did love to see?
That which in him was faire and delicate,
Was but the milke, which in loves childish state
Did nurse it: who now is growne strong enough
To feed on that, which to disus'd tasts seemes tough.   20

ELEGIE VI

OH, let mee not serve so, as those men serve
Whom honours smoakes at once fatten and sterve;
Poorely enrich't with great mens words or lookes;

Nor so write my name in thy loving bookes
As those Idolatrous flatterers, which still
Their Princes stiles, with many Realmes fulfill
Whence they no tribute have, and where no sway.
Such services I offer as shall pay
Themselves, I hate dead names: O then let mee
Favorite in Ordinary, or no favorite bee.   **10**
When my Soule was in her owne body sheath'd,
Nor yet by oathes betroth'd, nor kisses breath'd
Into my Purgatory, faithlesse thee,
Thy heart seem'd waxe, and steele thy constancie:
So, carelesse flowers strow'd on the waters face,
The curled whirlepooles suck, smack, and embrace,
Yet drowne them; so, the tapers beamie eye
Amorously twinkling, beckens the giddie flie,
Yet burnes his wings; and such the devill is,
Scarce visiting them, who are intirely his.   **20**
When I behold a streame, which, from the spring,
Doth with doubtfull melodious murmuring,
Or in a speechlesse slumber, calmely ride
Her wedded channels bosome, and then chide
And bend her browes, and swell if any bough
Do but stoop downe, or kisse her upmost brow:
Yet, if her often gnawing kisses winne
The traiterous banke to gape, and let her in,
She rusheth violently, and doth divorce
Her from her native, and her long-kept course,   **30**
And rores, and braves it, and in gallant scorne,
In flattering eddies promising retorne,
She flouts the channell, who thenceforth is drie;
Then say I; that is shee, and this am I.
Yet let not thy deepe bitternesse beget
Carelesse despaire in mee, for that will whet
My minde to scorne; and Oh, love dull'd with paine
Was ne'r so wise, nor well arm'd as disdaine.
Then with new eyes I shall survay thee,'and spie
Death in thy cheekes, and darknesse in thine eye.   **40**
Though hope bred faith and love: thus taught, I shall
As nations do from Rome, from thy love fall.
My hate shall outgrow thine, and utterly
I will renounce thy dalliance: and when I
Am the Recusant, in that resolute state,
What hurts it mee to be'excommunicate?

ELEGIE VII

NATURES lay Ideot, I taught thee to love,
And in that sophistrie, Oh, thou dost prove
Too subtile: Foole, thou didst not understand
The mystique language of the eye nor hand:
Nor couldst thou judge the difference of the aire
Of sighes, and say, this lies, this sounds despaire:
Nor by the'eyes water call a maladie
Desperately hot, or changing feaverously.
I had not taught thee then, the Alphabet
Of flowers, how they devisefully being set   10
And bound up, might with speechlesse secrecie
Deliver arrands mutely, and mutually.
Remember since all thy words us'd to bee
To every suitor; *I, if my friends agree;*
Since, household charmes, thy husbands name to teach,
Were all the love trickes, that thy wit could reach;
And since, an houres discourse could scarce have made
One answer in thee, and that ill arraid
In broken proverbs, and torne sentences.
Thou art not by so many duties his,   20
That from the worlds Common having sever'd thee,
Inlaid thee, neither to be seene, nor see,
As mine: who have with amorous delicacies
Refin'd thee'into a blis-full Paradise.
Thy graces and good words my creatures bee;
I planted knowledge and lifes tree in thee,
Which Oh, shall strangers taste? Must I alas
Frame and enamell Plate, and drinke in Glasse?
Chafe waxe for others seales? breake a colts force
And leave him then, beeing made a ready horse?   30

ELEGIE VIII

THE COMPARISON

As the sweet sweat of Roses in a Still,
As that which from chaf'd muskats pores doth trill,
As the Almighty Balme of th'early East,

Such are the sweat drops of my Mistris breast,
And on her [brow] her skin such lustre sets,
They seeme no sweat drops, but pearle coronets.
Ranke sweaty froth thy Mistresse's brow defiles,
Like spermatique issue of ripe menstruous boiles,
Or like the skumme, which, by needs lawlesse law
Enforc'd, Sanserra's starved men did draw   10
From parboild shooes, and bootes, and all the rest
Which were with any soveraigne fatnes blest,
And like vile lying stones in saffrond tinne,
Or warts, or wheales, they hang upon her skinne.
Round as the world's her head, on every side,
Like to the fatall Ball which fell on Ide,
Or that whereof God had such jealousie,
As, for the ravishing thereof we die.
Thy *head* is like a rough-hewne statue of jeat,
Where marks for eyes, nose, mouth, are yet scarce set;   20
Like the first Chaos, or flat seeming face
Of Cynthia, when th'earths shadowes her embrace.
Like Proserpines white beauty-keeping chest,
Or Joves best fortunes urne, is her faire brest.
Thine's like worme eaten trunkes, cloth'd in seals skin,
Or grave, that's dust without, and stinke within.
And like that slender stalke, at whose end stands
The wood-bine quivering, are her armes and hands.
Like rough bark'd elmboughes, or the russet skin
Of men late scurg'd for madnes, or for sinne,   30
Like Sun-parch'd quarters on the citie gate,
Such is thy tann'd skins lamentable state.
And like a bunch of ragged carrets stand
The short swolne fingers of thy gouty hand.
Then like the Chymicks masculine equall fire,
Which in the Lymbecks warme wombe doth inspire
Into th'earths worthlesse durt a soule of gold,
Such cherishing heat her best lov'd part doth hold.
Thine's like the dread mouth of a fired gunne,
Or like hot liquid metalls newly runne   40
Into clay moulds, or like to that Ætna
Where round about the grasse is burnt away.
Are not your kisses then as filthy, and more,
As a worme sucking an invenom'd sore?
Doth not thy fearefull hand in feeling quake,
As one which gath'ring flowers, still feares a snake?

Is not your last act harsh, and violent,
As when a Plough a stony ground doth rent?
So kisse good Turtles, so devoutly nice
Are Priests in handling reverent sacrifice,   50
And such in searching wounds the Surgeon is
As wee, when wee embrace, or touch, or kisse.
Leave her, and I will leave comparing thus,
She, and comparisons are odious.

ELEGIE IX

THE AUTUMNALL

No *Spring*, nor *Summer* Beauty hath such grace,
  As I have seen in one *Autumnall* face.
Yong *Beauties* force our love, and that's a *Rape*,
  This doth but *counsaile*, yet you cannot scape.
If t'were a *shame* to love, here t'were no *shame*,
  Affection here takes *Reverences* name.
Were her first yeares the *Golden Age*; That's true,
  But now she's *gold* oft tried, and ever new.
That was her torrid and inflaming time;
  This is her tolerable *Tropique clyme*.   10
Faire eyes, who askes more heate than comes from hence,
  He in a fever wishes pestilence.
Call not these wrinkles, *graves*; If *graves* they were,
  They were *Loves graves*; for else he is no where.
Yet lies not Love *dead* here, but here doth sit
  Vow'd to this trench, like an *Anachorit*.
And here, till hers, which must be his *death*, come,
  He doth not digge a *Grave*, but build a *Tombe*.
Here dwells he, though he sojourne ev'ry where,
  In *Progresse*, yet his standing house is here.   20
Here, where still *Evening* is; not *noone*, nor *night*;
  Where no *voluptuousnesse*, yet all *delight*.
In all her words, unto all hearers fit,
  You may at *Revels*, you at *Counsaile*, sit.
This is loves timber, youth his under-wood;
  There he, as wine in *June*, enrages blood,
Which then comes seasonabliest, when our tast
  And appetite to other things, is past.

Xerxes strange *Lydian* love, the *Platane* tree,
  Was lov'd for age, none being so large as shee,   **30**
Or else because, being yong, nature did blesse
  Her youth with ages glory, *Barrennesse.*
If we love things long sought, *Age* is a thing
  Which we are fifty yeares in compassing.
If transitory things, which soone decay,
  Age must be lovelyest at the latest day.
But name not *Winter-faces,* whose skin's slacke;
  Lanke, as an unthrifts purse; but a soules sacke;
Whose *Eyes* seeke light within, for all here's shade;
  Whose *mouthes* are holes, rather worne out, than made, **40**
Whose every tooth to a severall place is gone,
  To vexe their soules at *Resurrection;*
Name not these living *Deaths-heads* unto mee,
  For these, not *Ancient,* but *Antique* be.
I hate extreames; yet I had rather stay
  With *Tombs* than *Cradles,* to weare out a day.
Since such loves naturall lation is, may still
  My love descend, and journey downe the hill,
Not panting after growing beauties, so,
  I shall ebbe out with them, who home-ward goe.   **50**

ELEGIE X

THE DREAME

IMAGE of her whom I love, more than she,
  Whose faire impression in my faithfull heart,
Makes mee her *Medall,* and makes her love mee,
  As Kings do coynes, to which their stamps impart
The value: goe, and take my heart from hence,
  Which now is growne too great and good for me:
Honours oppresse weake spirits, and our sense
  Strong objects dull; the more, the lesse wee see.

When you are gone, and *Reason* gone with you,
  Then *Fantasie* is Queene and Soule, and all;   **10**
She can present joyes meaner than you do;
  Convenient, and more proportionall.
So, if I dreame I have you, I have you,
  For, all our joyes are but fantasticall.

And so I scape the paine, for paine is true;
   And sleepe which locks up sense, doth lock out all.

After a such fruition I shall wake,
   And, but the waking, nothing shall repent;
And shall to love more thankfull Sonnets make,
   Than if more *honour, teares,* and *paines* were spent.   20
But dearest heart, and dearer image stay;
   Alas, true joyes at best are *dreame* enough;
Though you stay here you passe too fast away:
   For even at first lifes *Taper* is a snuffe.

Fill'd with her love, may I be rather grown
Mad with much *heart,* than *ideott* with none.

ELEGIE XI

THE BRACELET

UPON THE LOSSE OF HIS MISTRESSES CHAINE, FOR WHICH
HE MADE SATISFACTION

NOT that in colour it was like thy haire,
For Armelets of that thou maist let me weare:
Nor that thy hand it oft embrac'd and kist,
For so it had that good, which oft I mist:
Nor for that silly old moralitie,
That as these linkes were knit, our love should bee:
Mourne I that I thy seavenfold chaine have lost;
Nor for the luck sake; but the bitter cost.
O, shall twelve righteous Angels, which as yet
No leaven of vile soder did admit;   10
Nor yet by any way have straid or gone
From the first state of their Creation;
Angels, which heaven commanded to provide
All things to me, and be my faithfull guide;
To gaine new friends, t'appease great enemies;
To comfort my soule, when I lie or rise;
Shall these twelve innocents, by thy severe
Sentence (dread judge) my sins great burden beare?
Shall they be damn'd, and in the furnace throwne,
And punisht for offences not their owne?   20

They save not me, they doe not case my paines,
When in that hell they'are burnt and tyed in chains.
Were they but Crownes of France, I cared not,
For, most of these, their naturall Countreys rot
I think possesseth, they come here to us,
So pale, so lame, so leane, so ruinous;
And howsoe'r French Kings most Christian be,
Their Crownes are circumcis'd most Jewishly.
Or were they Spanish Stamps, still travelling.
That are become as Catholique as their King,   **30**
Those unlickt beare-whelps, unfil'd pistolets
That (more than Canon shot) availes or lets;
Which negligently left unrounded, looke
Like many angled figures, in the booke
Of some great Conjurer that would enforce
Nature, as these doe justice, from her course;
Which, as the soule quickens head, feet and heart,
As streames, like veines, run through th'earth's every part,
Visit all Countries, and have slily made
Gorgeous *France*, ruin'd, ragged and decay'd;   **40**
Scotland, which knew no State, proud in one day:
And mangled seventeen-headed *Belgia*.
Or were it such gold as that wherewithall
Almighty *Chymiques* from each minerall,
Having by subtle fire a soule out-pull'd;
Are dirtely and desperately gull'd:
I would not spit to quench the fire they'are in,
For, they are guilty of much hainous Sin.
But, shall my harmlesse angels perish? Shall
I lose my guard, my ease, my food, my all?   **50**
Much hope which they should nourish will be dead,
Much of my able youth, and lustyhead
Will vanish; if thou love let them alone,
For thou wilt love me lesse when they are gone;
And be content that some lowd squeaking Cryer
Well-pleas'd with one leane thred-bare groat, for hire,
May like a devill roare through every street;
And gall the finders conscience, if they meet.
Or let mee creepe to some dread Conjurer,
That with phantastique scheames fils full much paper;   **60**
Which hath divided heaven in tenements,
And with whores, theeves, and murderers stuft his rents,
So full, that though hee passe them all in sinne,

He leaves himselfe no roome to enter in.
But if, when all his art and time is spent,
Hee say 'twill ne'r be found; yet be content;
Receive from him that doome ungrudgingly,
Because he is the mouth of destiny.
  Thou say'st (alas) the gold doth still remaine,
Though it be chang'd, and put into a chaine;   70
So in the first falne angels, resteth still
Wisdome and knowledge; but,'tis turn'd to ill:
As these should doe good works; and should provide
Necessities; but now must nurse thy pride.
And they are still bad angels; Mine are none;
For, forme gives being, and their forme is gone:
Pitty these Angels; yet their dignities
Passe Vertues, Powers, and Principalities.
  But, thou art resolute; Thy will be done!
Yet with such anguish, as her onely sonne   80
The Mother in the hungry grave doth lay,
Unto the fire these Martyrs I betray.
Good soules, (for you give life to every thing)
Good Angels, (for good messages you bring)
Destin'd you might have beene to such an one,
As would have lov'd and worship'd you alone:
One that would suffer hunger, nakednesse,
Yea death, ere he would make your number lesse.
But, I am guilty of your sad decay;
May your few fellowes longer with me stay.   90
  But ô thou wretched finder whom I hate
So, that I almost pitty thy estate:
Gold being the heaviest metal amongst all,
May my most heavy curse upon thee fall:
Here fetter'd, manacled, and hang'd in chains,
First mayst thou bee; then chaind to hellish paines;
Or be with forraine gold brib'd to betray
Thy Countrey, and faile both of that and thy pay.
May the next thing thou stoop'st to reach, containe
Poyson, whose nimble fume rot thy moist braine;   100
Or libels, or some interdicted thing,
Which negligently kept, thy ruine bring.
Lust-bred diseases rot thee; and dwell with thee
Itchy desire, and no abilitie.
May all the evils that gold ever wrought;
All mischiefes that all devils ever thought;

Want after plenty; poore and gouty age;
The plagues of travellers; love; marriage
Afflict thee, and at thy lives last moment,
May thy swolne sinnes themselves to thee present.   110
    But, I forgive; repent thee honest man:
Gold is Restorative, restore it then:
But if from it thou beest loath to depart,
Because 'tis cordiall, would 'twere at thy heart.

ELEGIE XII

HIS PARTING FROM HER

SINCE she must go, and I must mourn, come Night,
Environ me with darkness, whilst I write:
Shadow that hell unto me, which alone
I am to suffer when my Love is gone.
Alas the darkest Magick cannot do it,
Thou and greate Hell to boot are shadows to it.
Should *Cinthia* quit thee, *Venus*, and each starre,
It would not forme one thought dark as mine are.
I could lend thee obscureness now, and say,
Out of my self, There should be no more Day,   10
Such is already my felt want of sight,
Did not the fires within me force a light.
Oh Love, that fire and darkness should be mixt,
Or to thy Triumphs soe strange torments fixt!
Is't because thou thy self art blind, that wee
Thy Martyrs must no more each other see?
Or tak'st thou pride to break us on the wheel,
And view old Chaos in the Pains we feel?
Or have we left undone some mutual Rite,
Through holy fear, that merits thy despight?   20
No, no. The falt was mine, impute it to me,
Or rather to conspiring destinie,
Which (since I lov'd for forme before) decreed,
That I should suffer when I lov'd indeed:
And therefore now, sooner than I can say,
I saw the golden fruit, 'tis rapt away.
Or as I had watcht one drop in a vast stream,
And I left wealthy only in a dream.
Yet Love, thou'rt blinder than thy self in this,

To vex my Dove-like friend for my amiss: 30
And, where my own sad truth may expiate
Thy wrath, to make her fortune run my fate:
So blinded Justice doth, when Favorites fall,
Strike them, their house, their friends, their followers all.
Was't not enough that thou didst dart thy fires
Into our blouds, inflaming our desires,
And made'st us sigh and glow, and pant, and burn,
And then thy self into our flame did'st turn?
Was't not enough, that thou didst hazard us
To paths in love so dark, so dangerous: 40
And those so ambush'd round with houshold spies,
And over all, thy husbands towring eyes
That flam'd with oylie sweat of jealousie:
Yet went we not still on with Constancie?
Have we not kept our guards, like spie on spie?
Had correspondence whilst the foe stood by?
Stoln (more to sweeten them) our many blisses
Of meetings, conference, embracements, kisses?
Shadow'd with negligence our most respects?
Varied our language through all dialects,   50
Of becks, winks, looks, and often under-boards
Spoak dialogues with our feet far from our words?
Have we prov'd all these secrets of our Art,
Yea, thy pale inwards, and thy panting heart?
And, after all this passed Purgatory,
Must sad divorce make us the vulgar story?
First let our eyes be rivited quite through
Our turning brains, and both our lips grow to
Let our armes clasp like Ivy, and our fear
Freese us together, that we may stick here,   60
Till Fortune, that would rive us, with the deed,
Strain her eyes open, and it make them bleed.
For Love it cannot be, whom hitherto
I have accus'd, should such a mischief doe.
Oh Fortune, thou'rt not worth my least exclame,
And plague enough thou hast in thy own shame.
Do thy great worst, my friend and I have armes,
Though not against thy strokes, against thy harmes.
Rend us in sunder, thou canst not divide
Our bodies so, but that our souls are ty'd,   70
And we can love by letters still and gifts,
And thoughts and dreams; Love never wanteth shifts.

I will not look upon the quickning Sun,
But straight her beauty to my sense shall run;
The ayre shall note her soft, the fire most pure;
Water suggest her clear, and the earth sure.
Time shall not lose our passages; the Spring
How fresh our love was in the beginning;
The Summer how it ripened in the eare;
And Autumn, what our golden harvests were.   80
The Winter I'll not think on to spite thee,
But count it a lost season, so shall shee.
And dearest Friend, since we must part, drown night
With hope of Day, burthens well born are light.
Though cold and darkness longer hang somewhere,
Yet *Phoebus* equally lights all the Sphere.
And what he cannot in like Portions pay,
The world enjoyes in Mass, and so we may.
Be then ever your self, and let no woe
Win on your health, your youth, your beauty: so   90
Declare your self base fortunes Enemy,
No less by your contempt than constancy:
That I may grow enamoured on your mind,
When my own thoughts I there reflected find.
For this to th'comfort of my Dear I vow,
My Deeds shall still be what my words are now;
The Poles shall move to teach me ere I start;
And when I change my Love, I'll change my heart;
Nay, if I wax but cold in my desire,
Think, heaven hath motion lost, and the world, fire: 100
Much more I could, but many words have made
That, oft, suspected which men would perswade;
Take therefore all in this: I love so true,
As I will never look for less in you.

ELEGIE XIII

JULIA

HARKE newes, ô envy, thou shalt heare descry'd
My *Julia*; who as yet was ne'r envy'd.
To vomit gall in slander, swell her vaines
With calumny, that hell it selfe disdaines,
Is her continuall practice; does her best,

To teare opinion even out of the brest
Of dearest friends, and (which is worse than vilde)
Sticks jealousie in wedlock; her owne childe
Scapes not the showres of envie, To repeate
The monstrous fashions, how, were, alive, to eate   10
Deare reputation. Would to God she were
But halfe so loath to act vice, as to heare
My milde reproofe. Liv'd *Mantuan* now againe,
That fœmall Mastix, to limme with his penne
This she *Chymera*, that hath eyes of fire,
Burning with anger, anger feeds desire,
Tongued like the night-crow, whose ill boding cries
Give out for nothing but new injuries,
Her breath like to the juice in *Tenarus*
That blasts the springs, though ne'r so prosperous,   20
Her hands, I know not how, us'd more to spill
The food of others, than her selfe to fill.
But oh her minde, that *Orcus,* which includes
Legions of mischiefs, countlesse multitudes
Of formlesse curses, projects unmade up,
Abuses yet unfashion'd, thoughts corrupt,
Mishapen Cavils, palpable untroths,
Inevitable errours, self-accusing oaths:
These, like those Atoms swarming in the Sunne,
Throng in her bosome for creation.   30
I blush to give her halfe her due; yet say,
No poyson's halfe so bad as *Julia*.

ELEGIE XIV

A TALE OF A CITIZEN AND HIS WIFE

I SING no harme good sooth to any wight,
To Lord or foole, Cuckold, begger or knight,
To peace-teaching Lawyer, Proctor, or brave
Reformed or reduced Captaine, Knave,
Officer, Jugler, or Justice of peace,
Juror or Judge; I touch no fat sowes grease,
I am no Libeller, nor will be any,
But (like a true man) say there are too many.
I feare not *ore tenus;* for my tale,
Nor Count nor Counsellour will redd or pale.   10

A citizen and his wife the other day
Both riding on one horse, upon the way
I overtooke, the wench a pretty peate,
And (by her eye) well fitting for the feate.
I saw the lecherous Citizen turne backe
His head, and on his wifes lip steale a smacke,
Whence apprehending that the man was kinde,
Riding before, to kisse his wife behinde,
To get acquaintance with him I began
To sort discourse fit for so fine a man: 20
I ask'd the number of the Plaguy Bill,
Ask'd if the Custome Farmers held out still,
Of the Virginian plot and whether Ward
The traffique of the I[n]land seas had marr'd.
Whether the Brittaine *Burse* did fill apace,
And likely were to give th'Exchange disgrace;
Of new-built *Algate*, and the *More-field* crosses,
Of store of Bankerouts, and poore Merchants losses
I urged him to speake; But he (as mute
As an old Courtier worne to his last suite)   30
Replies with onely yeas and nayes; At last
(To fit his element) my theame I cast
On Tradesmens gaines; that set his tongue agoing:
Alas, good sir (quoth he) *There is no doing
In Court nor City now;* she smil'd and I,
And (in my conscience) both gave him the lie
In one met thought: but he went on apace,
And at the present time with such a face
He rail'd, as fray'd me; for he gave no praise,
To any but my Lord of *Essex* dayes;   40
Call'd those the age of action; true (quoth Hee)
There's now as great an itch of bravery,
And heat of taking up, but cold lay downe,
For, put to push of pay, away they runne;
Our onely City trades of hope now are
Bawd, Tavern-keeper, Whore and Scrivener;
The much of priviledg'd kingsmen, and the store
Of fresh protections make the rest all poore;
In the first state of their Creation,
Though many stoutly stand, yet proves not one   50
A righteous pay-master. Thus ranne he on
In a continued rage: so void of reason
Seem'd his harsh talke, I sweat for feare of treason.

And (troth) how could I lesse? when in the prayer
For the protection of the wise Lord Major,
And his wise brethrens worships, when one prayeth,
He swore that none could say Amen with faith.
To get him off from what I glowed to heare,
(In happy time) an Angel did appeare,
The bright Signe of a lov'd and wel-try'd Inne,   60
Where many Citizens with their wives have bin
Well us'd and often; here I pray'd him stay,
To take some due refreshment by the way.
Looke how hee look'd that hid the gold (his hope)
And at's returne found nothing but a Rope,
So he on me, refus'd and made away,
Though willing she pleaded a weary day:
I found my misse, struck hands, and praid him tell
(To hold acquaintance still) where he did dwell;
He barely nam'd the street, promis'd the Wine,   70
But his kinde wife gave me the very Signe.

ELEGIE XV

THE EXPOSTULATION

To make the doubt cleare, that no woman's true,
    Was it my fate to prove it strong in you?
Thought I, but one had breathed purest aire,
    And must she needs be false because she's faire?
Is it your beauties marke, or of your youth,
    Or your perfection, not to study truth?
Or thinke you heaven is deafe, or hath no eyes?
    Or those it hath, smile at your perjuries?
Are vowes so cheape with women, or the matter
    Whereof they are made, that they are writ in water,   10
And blowne away with winde? Or doth their breath
    (Both hot and cold at once) make life and death?
Who could have thought so many accents sweet
    Form'd into words, so many sighs should meete
As from our hearts, so many oathes, and teares
    Sprinkled among, (all sweeter by our feares
And the divine impression of stolne kisses,
    That seal'd the rest) should now prove empty blisses?
Did you draw bonds to forfet? signe to breake?

Or must we reade you quite from what you speake,   20
And finde the truth out the wrong way? or must
  Hee first desire you false, would wish you just?
O I prophane, though most of women be
  This kinde of beast, my thought shall except thee;
My dearest love, though froward jealousie,
  With circumstance might urge thy'inconstancie.
Sooner I'll thinke the Sunne will cease to cheare
  The teeming earth, and *that* forget to beare,
Sooner that rivers will runne back, or Thames
  With ribs of Ice in June would bind his streames,   30
Or Nature, by whose strength the world endures,
  Would change her course, before you alter yours.
But O that treacherous breast to whom weake you
  Did trust our Counsells, and wee both may rue,
Having his falshood found too late, 'twas hee
  That made me *cast* you guilty, and you me,
Whilst he, black wretch, betray'd each simple word
  Wee spake, unto the cunning of a third.
Curst may hee be, that so our love hath slaine,
  And wander on the earth, wretched as *Cain,*   40
Wretched as hee, and not deserve least pitty;
  In plaguing him, let misery be witty;
Let all eyes shunne him, and hee shunne each eye,
  Till hee be noysome as his infamie;
May he without remorse deny God thrice,
  And not be trusted more on his Soules price;
And after all selfe torment, when hee dyes,
  May Wolves teare out his heart, Vultures his eyes,
Swine eate his bowels, and his falser tongue
  That utter'd all, be to some Raven flung,   50
And let his carrion coarse be a longer feast
  To the Kings dogges, than any other beast.
Now have I curst, let us our love revive;
  In mee the flame was never more alive;
I could beginne againe to court and praise,
  And in that pleasure lengthen the short dayes
Of my lifes lease; like Painters that do take
  Delight, not in made worke, but whiles they make;
I could renew those times, when first I saw
  Love in your eyes, that gave my tongue the law   60
To like what you lik'd; and at maskes and playes
  Commend the self same Actors, the same wayes;

Aske how you did, and often with intent
    Of being officious, be impertinent;
All which were such soft pastimes, as in these
    Love was as subtilly catch'd, as a disease;
But being got it is a treasure sweet,
    Which to defend is harder than to get:
And ought not be prophan'd on either part,
    For though'tis got by *chance*,'tis kept by *art*.   **70**

ELEGIE XVI

ON HIS MISTRIS

By our first strange and fatall interview,
By all desires which thereof did ensue,
By our long starving hopes, by that remorse
Which my words masculine perswasive force
Begot in thee, and by the memory
Of hurts, which spies and rivals threatned me,
I calmly beg: But by thy fathers wrath,
By all paines, which want and divorcement hath,
I conjure thee, and all the oathes which I
And thou have sworne to seale joynt constancy,   **10**
Here I unsweare, and overswear them thus,
Thou shalt not love by wayes so dangerous.
Temper, ô faire Love, loves impetuous rage,
Be my true Mistris still, not my faign'd Page;
I'll goe, and, by thy kinde leave, leave behinde
Thee, onely worthy to nurse in my minde,
Thirst to come backe; ô if thou die before,
My soule from other lands to thee shall soare.
Thy (else Almighty) beautie cannot move
Rage from the Seas, nor thy love teach them love,   **20**
Nor tame wilde Boreas harshnesse; Thou hast reade
How roughly hee in peeces shivered
Faire Orithea, whom he swore he lov'd.
Fall ill or good, 'tis madnesse to have prov'd
Dangers unurg'd; Feed on this flattery,
That absent Lovers one in th'other be.
Dissemble nothing, not a boy, nor change
Thy bodies habite, nor mindes; bee not strange
To thy selfe onely; All will spie in thy face

A blushing womanly discovering grace;   30
Richly cloath'd Apes, are call'd Apes, and as soone
Ecclips'd as bright we call the Moone the Moone.
Men of France, changeable Camelions,
Spittles of diseases, shops of fashions,
Loves fuellers, and the rightest company
Of Players, which upon the worlds stage be,
Will quickly know thee, and no lesse, alas!
Th'indifferent Italian, as we passe
His warme land, well content to thinke thee Page,
Will hunt thee with such lust, and hideous rage,   40
As *Lots* faire guests were vext. But none of these
Nor spungy hydroptique Dutch shall thee displease,
If thou stay here. O stay here, for, for thee
England is onely a worthy Gallerie,
To walke in expectation, till from thence
Our greatest King call thee to his presence.
When I am gone, dreame me some happinesse,
Nor let thy lookes our long hid love confesse,
Nor praise, nor dispraise me, nor blesse nor curse
Openly loves force, nor in bed fright thy Nurse   50
With midnights startings, crying out, oh, oh
Nurse, ô my love is slaine, I saw him goe
O'r the white Alpes alone; I saw him I,
Assail'd, fight, taken, stabb'd, bleed, fall, and die.
Augure me better chance, except dread *Jove*
Thinke it enough for me to'have had thy love.

ELEGIE XVII

VARIETY

THE heavens rejoyce in motion, why should I
Abjure my so much lov'd variety,
And not with many youth and love divide?
Pleasure is none, if not diversifi'd:
The sun that sitting in the chaire of light
Sheds flame into what else soever doth seem bright,
Is not contented at one Signe to Inne,
But ends his year and with a new beginnes.
All things doe willingly in change delight,
The fruitfull mother of our appetite: 10

Rivers the clearer and more pleasing are,
Where their fair spreading streames run wide and farr;
And a dead lake that no strange bark doth greet,
Corrupts it self and what doth live in it.
Let no man tell me such a one is faire,
And worthy all alone my love to share.
Nature in her hath done the liberall part
Of a kinde Mistresse, and imploy'd her art
To make her loveable, and I aver
Him not humane that would turn back from her: **20**
I love her well, and would, if need were, dye
To doe her service. But followes it that I
Must serve her onely, when I may have choice
Of other beauties, and in change rejoice?
The law is hard, and shall not have my voice.
The last I saw in all extreames is faire,
And holds me in the Sun-beames of her haire;
Her nymph-like features such agreements have
That I could venture with her to the grave:
Another's brown, I like her not the worse,   **30**
Her tongue is soft and takes me with discourse:
Others, for that they well descended are,
Do in my love obtain as large a share;
And though they be not fair, 'tis much with mee
To win their love onely for their degree.
And though I faile of my required ends,
The attempt is glorious and it selfe commends.
How happy were our Syres in ancient time,
Who held plurality of loves no crime!
With them it was accounted charity   **40**
To stirre up race of all indifferently;
Kindreds were not exempted from the bands:
Which with the Persian still in usage stands.
Women were then no sooner asked than won,
And what they did was honest and well done.
But since this title honour hath been us'd,
Our weake credulity hath been abus'd;
The golden laws of nature are repeald,
Which our first Fathers in such reverence held;
Our liberty's revers'd, our Charter's gone,   **50**
And we're made servants to opinion,
A monster in no certain shape attir'd,
And whose originall is much desir'd,

Formlesse at first, but growing on it fashions,
And doth prescribe manners and laws to nations.
Here love receiv'd immedicable harmes,
And was dispoiled of his daring armes.
A greater want than is his daring eyes,
He lost those awfull wings with which he flies;
His sinewy bow, and those immortall darts   60
Wherewith he'is wont to bruise resisting hearts.
Onely some few strong in themselves and free
Retain the seeds of antient liberty,
Following that part of Love although deprest,
And make a throne for him within their brest,
In spight of modern censures him avowing
Their Soveraigne, all service him allowing.
Amongst which troop although I am the least,
Yet equall in perfection with the best,
I glory in subjection of his hand,   70
Nor ever did decline his least command:
For in whatever forme the message came
My heart did open and receive the same.
But time will in his course a point discry
When I this loved service must deny,
For our allegiance temporary is,
With firmer age returnes our liberties.
What time in years and judgement we repos'd,
Shall not so easily be to change dispos'd,
Nor to the art of severall eyes obeying;   80
But beauty with true worth securely weighing,
Which being found assembled in some one,
Wee'l love her ever, and love her alone.

ELEGIE XVIII

LOVES PROGRESS

WHO ever loves, if he do not propose
The right true end of love, he's one that goes
To sea for nothing but to make him sick:
Love is a bear-whelp born, if we o're lick
Our love, and force it new strange shapes to take,
We erre, and of a lump a monster make.
Were not a Calf a monster that were grown

Fac'd like a man, though better than his own?
Perfection is in unitie: preferr
One woman first, and then one thing in her.   10
I, when I value gold, may think upon
The ductilness, the application,
The wholsomeness, the ingenuitie,
From rust, from soil, from fire ever free:
But if I love it, 'tis because 'tis made
By our new nature (Use) the soul of trade.
    All these in women we might think upon
(If women had them) and yet love but one.
Can men more injure women than to say
They love them for that, by which they're not they?   20
Makes virtue woman? must I cool my bloud
Till I both be, and find one wise and good?
May barren Angels love so. But if we
Make love to woman; virtue is not she:
As beauty'is not nor wealth: He that strayes thus
From her to hers, is more adulterous,
Than if he took her maid. Search every sphear
And firmament, our *Cupid* is not there:
He's an infernal god and under ground,
With *Pluto* dwells, where gold and fire abound: 30
Men to such Gods, their sacrificing Coles
Did not in Altars lay, but pits and holes.
Although we see Celestial bodies move
Above the earth, the earth we Till and love:
So we her ayres contemplate, words and heart,
And virtues; but we love the Centrique part.
    Nor is the soul more worthy, or more fit
For love, than this, as infinite as it.
But in attaining this desired place
How much they erre; that set out at the face?   40
The hair a Forest is of Ambushes,
Of springes, snares, fetters and manacles:
The brow becalms us when 'tis smooth and plain,
And when 'tis wrinckled, shipwracks us again.
Smooth, 'tis a Paradice, where we would have
Immortal stay, and wrinkled 'tis our grave.
The Nose (like to the first Meridian) runs
Not 'twixt an East and West, but 'twixt two suns;
It leaves a Cheek, a rosie Hemisphere
On either side, and then directs us where   50

Upon the Islands fortunate we fall,
(Not faynte *Canaries,* but *Ambrosiall*)
Her swelling lips; To which when wee are come,
We anchor there, and think our selves at home,
For they seem all: there Syrens songs, and there
Wise Delphick Oracles do fill the ear;
There in a Creek where chosen pearls do swell,
The Remora, her cleaving tongue doth dwell.
These, and the glorious Promontory, her Chin
Ore past; and the streight *Hellespont* betweene   60
The *Sestos* and *Abydos* of her breasts,
(Not of two Lovers, but two Loves the neasts)
Succeeds a boundless sea, but yet thine eye
Some Island moles may scattered there descry;
And Sailing towards her *India,* in that way
Shall at her fair Atlantick Navell stay;
Though thence the Current be thy Pilot made,
Yet ere thou be where thou wouldst be embay'd,
Thou shalt upon another Forest set,
Where many Shipwrack, and no further get.   70
When thou art there, consider what this chace
Mispent by thy beginning at the face.
      Rather set out below; practice my Art,
Some Symetry the foot hath with that part
Which thou dost seek, and is thy Map for that
Lovely enough to stop, but not stay at:
Least subject to disguise and change it is;
Men say the Devil never can change his.
It is the Emblem that hath figured
Firmness; 'tis the first part that comes to bed.   80
Civilitie we see refin'd: the kiss
Which at the face began, transplanted is,
Since to the hand, since to the Imperial knee,
Now at the Papal foot delights to be:
If Kings think that the nearer way, and do
Rise from the foot, Lovers may do so too;
For as free Spheres move faster far than can
Birds, whom the air resists, so may that man
Which goes this empty and Ætherial way,
Than if at beauties elements he stay.   90
Rich Nature hath in women wisely made
Two purses, and their mouths aversely laid:
They then, which to the lower tribute owe.

That way which that Exchequer looks, must go:
He which doth not, his error is as great,
As who by Clyster gave the Stomack meat.

ELEGIE XIX

TO HIS MISTRIS GOING TO BED

COME, Madam, come, all rest my powers defie,
Until I labour, I in labour lie.
The foe oft-times having the foe in sight,
Is tir'd with standing though he never fight.
Off with that girdle, like heavens Zone glistering,
But a far fairer world incompassing.
Unpin that spangled breastplate which you wear,
That th'eyes of busie fooles may be stopt there.
Unlace your self, for that harmonious chyme,
Tells me from you, that now it is bed time.   10
Off with that happy busk, which I envie,
That still can be, and still can stand so nigh.
Your gown going off, such beautious state reveals,
As when from flowry meads th'hills shadow steales.
Off with that wyerie Coronet and shew
The haiery Diademe which on you doth grow:
Now off with those shooes, and then safely tread
In this loves hallow'd temple, this soft bed.
In such white robes, heaven's Angels us'd to be
Receavd by men; Thou Angel bringst with thee   20
A heaven like Mahomets Paradice; and though
Ill spirits walk in white, we easly know,
By this these Angels from an evil sprite,
Those set our hairs, but these our flesh upright.
   Licence my roaving hands, and let them go,
Before, behind, between, above, below.
O my America! my new-found-land,
My kingdome, safeliest when with one man man'd,
My Myne of precious stones, My Emperie,
How blest am I in this discovering thee!   30
To enter in these bonds, is to be free;
Then where my hand is set, my seal shall be.
   Full nakedness! All joyes are due to thee,
As souls unbodied, bodies uncloth'd must be.

To taste whole joyes. Gems which you women use
Are like Atlanta's balls, cast in mens views,
That when a fools eye lighteth on a Gem,
His earthly soul may covet theirs, not them.
Like pictures, or like books gay coverings made
For lay-men, are all women thus array'd;   40
Themselves are mystick books, which only wee
(Whom their imputed grace will dignifie)
Must see reveal'd. Then since that I may know;
As liberally, as to a Midwife, shew
Thy self: cast all, yea, this white lynnen hence,
[Here] is no pennance, much less innocence.
    To teach thee, I am naked first; why then
What needst thou have more covering than a man.

ELEGIE XX

LOVES WARRE

TILL I have peace with thee, warr other Men,
And when I have peace, can I leave thee then?
All other Warrs are scrupulous; Only thou
O fayr free Citty, maist thyselfe allow
To any one: In Flanders, who can tell
Whether the Master presse; or men rebell?
Only we know, that which all Ideots say,
They beare most blows which come to part the fray.
France in her lunatique giddines did hate
Ever our men, yea and our God of late;   10
Yet she relyes upon our Angels well,
Which nere returne; no more than they which fell.
Sick Ireland is with a strange warr possest
Like to an Ague; now raging, now at rest;
Which time will cure: yet it must doe her good
If she were purg'd, and her head vayne let blood.
And Midas joyes our Spanish journeys give,
We touch all gold, but find no food to live.
And I should be in the hott parching clime,
To dust and ashes turn'd before my time.   20
To mew me in a Ship, is to inthrall
Mee in a prison, that weare like to fall;
Or in a Cloyster; save that there men dwell

In a calme heaven, here in a swaggering hell.
Long voyages are long consumptions,
And ships are carts for executions.
Yea they are Deaths; Is't not all one to flye
Into an other World, as t'is to dye?
Here let mee warr; in these armes lett mee lye;
Here lett mee parlee, batter, bleede, and dye.
Thyne armes imprison me, and myne armes thee,   30
Thy hart thy ransome is, take myne for mee.
Other men war that they their rest may gayne;
But wee will rest that wee may fight agayne.
Those warrs the ignorant, these th'experienc'd love,
There wee are alwayes under, here above.
There Engins farr off breed a just true feare,
Neere thrusts, pikes, stabs, yea bullets hurt not here.
There lyes are wrongs; here safe uprightly ly;
There men kil men, we'will make one by and by.   40
Thou nothing; I not halfe so much shall do
In these Warrs, as they may which from us two
Shall spring. Thousands wee see which travaile not
To warrs; But stay swords, armes, and shott
To make at home; And shall not I do then
More glorious service, staying to make men?

HEROICALL EPISTLE

SAPHO TO PHILÆNIS

WHERE is that holy fire, which *Verse* is said
   To have? is that inchanting force decai'd?
Verse that drawes *Natures* workes, from *Natures* law,
   Thee, her best worke, to her worke cannot draw.
Have my teares quench'd my old *Poetique* fire;
   Why quench'd they not as well, that of *desire?*
Thoughts, my mindes creatures, often are with thee,
   But I, their maker, want their libertie.
Onely thine image, in my heart, doth sit,
   But that is waxe, and fires environ it.   10
My fires have driven, thine have drawne it hence;
   And I am rob'd of *Picture, Heart*, and *Sense.*
Dwells with me still mine irksome *Memory,*
   Which, both to keepe, and lose, grieves equally.

That tells me'how faire thou art: Thou art so faire,
  As, *gods,* when *gods* to thee I doe compare,
Are grac'd thereby; And to make blinde men see,
  What things *gods* are, I say they'are like to thee.
For, if we justly call each silly *man*
  A *litle world,* What shall we call thee then?   **20**
Thou art not soft, and cleare, and strait, and faire,
  As *Down,* as *Stars, Cedars,* and *Lillies* are,
But thy right hand, and cheek, and eye, only
  Are like thy other hand, and cheek, and eye.
Such was my *Phao* awhile, but shall be never,
  As thou, wast, art, and, oh, maist be ever.
Here lovers sweare in their *Idolatrie,*
  That I am such; but *Griefe* discolors me.
And yet I grieve the lesse, lest *Griefe* remove
  My beauty, and make me'unworthy of thy love.   **30**
Plaies some soft boy with thee, oh there wants yet
  A mutuall feeling which should sweeten it.
His chinne, a thorny hairy unevennesse
  Doth threaten, and some daily change possesse.
Thy body is a naturall *Paradise,*
  In whose selfe, unmanur'd, all pleasure lies,
Nor needs *perfection;* why shouldst thou then
  Admit the tillage of a harsh rough man?
Men leave behinde them that which their sin showes,
  And are as theeves trac'd, which rob when it snows.   **40**
But of our dallyance no more signes there are,
  Than *fishes* leave in streames, or *Birds* in aire.
And betweene us all sweetnesse may be had;
  All, all that *Nature* yields, or *Art* can adde.
My two lips, eyes, thighs, differ from thy two,
  But so, as thine from one another doe;
And, oh, no more; the likenesse being such,
  Why should they not alike in all parts touch?
Hand to strange hand, lippe to lippe none denies;
  Why should they brest to brest, or thighs to thighs?   **50**
Likenesse begets such strange selfe flatterie,
  That touching my selfe, all seemes done to thee.
My selfe I embrace, and mine owne hands I kisse,
  And amorously thanke my selfe for this.
Me, in my glasse, I call thee; But alas,
  When I would kisse, teares dimme mine *eyes,* and *glasse.*
O cure this loving madnesse, and restore

Me to mee; thee, my *halfe,* my *all,* my *more.*
So may thy cheekes red outweare scarlet dye,
    And their white, whitenesse of the *Galaxy,*
So may thy mighty, amazing beauty move
    Envy'in all *women,* and in all *men, love,*
And so be *change,* and *sicknesse,* farre from thee,
    As thou by comming neere, keep'st them from me.

EPIGRAMS

HERO AND LEANDER

BOTH rob'd of aire, we both lye in one ground,
Both whom one fire had burnt, one water drownd.

PYRAMUS AND THISBE

'Two, by themselves, each other, love and feare
Slaine, cruell friends, by parting have joyn'd here.

NIOBE

BY childrens births, and death, I am become
So dry, that I am now mine owne sad tombe.

A BURNT SHIP

OUT of a fired ship, which, by no way
But drowning, could be rescued from the flame,
Some men leap'd forth, and ever as they came
Neere the foes ships, did by their shot decay;
So all were lost, which in the ship were found,
    They in the sea being burnt, they in the burnt ship drown'd.

FALL OF A WALL

UNDER an undermin'd, and shot-bruis'd wall
A too-bold Captaine perish'd by the fall,
Whose brave misfortune, happiest men envi'd,
That had a towne for tombe, his bones to hide.

A LAME BEGGER

I AM unable, yonder begger cries,
To stand, or move; if he say true, hee *lies*.

CALES AND GUYANA

IF you from spoyle of th'old worlds farthest **end**
To the new world your kindled valors bend,
What brave examples then do prove it trew
That one things end doth still beginne a new.

SIR JOHN WINGEFIELD

BEYOND th'old Pillers many have travailed
Towards the Suns cradle, and his throne, and bed.
A fitter Piller our Earle did bestow
In that late Island; for he well did know
Farther than Wingefield no man dares to goe.

A SELFE ACCUSER

YOUR mistris, that you follow whores, still taxeth you:
'Tis strange that she should thus confesse it, though'it be true.

A LICENTIOUS PERSON

THY sinnes and haires may no man equall call,
For, as thy sinnes increase, thy haires doe fall.

ANTIQUARY

IF in his Studie he hath so much care
To'hang all old strange things, let his wife beware.

DISINHERITED

THY father all from thee, by his last Will,
Gave to the poore; Thou hast good title still.

PHRYNE

THY flattering picture, *Phryne*, is like thee,
Onely in this, that you both painted be.

AN OBSCURE WRITER

PHILO, with twelve yeares study, hath beene griev'd
To be understood; when will hee be beleev'd?

KLOCKIUS

KLOCKIUS so deeply hath sworne, ne'r more to come
In bawdie house, that hee dares not goe home.

RADERUS

WHY this man gelded *Martiall* I muse,
Except himselfe alone his tricks would use,
As *Katherine*, for the Courts sake, put down Stewes.

MERCURIUS GALLO-BELGICUS

LIKE *Esops* fellow-slaves, O *Mercury*,
Which could do all things, thy faith is; and I

Like *Esops* selfe, which nothing; I confesse
I should have had more faith, if thou hadst lesse;
Thy credit lost thy credit: 'Tis sinne to doe,
In this case, as thou wouldst be done unto,
To beleeve all: Change thy name: thou art like
Mercury in stealing, but lyest like a *Greeke*.

RALPHIUS

COMPASSION in the world againe is bred:
Ralphius is sick, the broker keeps his bed.

THE LIER

THOU in the fields walkst out thy supping howers
    And yet thou swear'st thou hast supp'd like a king:
Like Nebuchadnezar perchance with grass and flowers,
    A sallet worse than Spanish dyeting.

SATYRES

SATYRE I

AWAY thou fondling motley humorist,
Leave mee, and in this standing woodden chest,
Consorted with these few bookes, let me lye
In prison, and here be coffin'd, when I dye;
Here are Gods conduits, grave Divines; and here
Natures Secretary, the Philosopher;
And jolly Statesmen, which teach how to tie
The sinewes of a cities mistique bodie;
Here gathering Chroniclers, and by them stand
Giddie fantastique Poëts of each land.   10
Shall I leave all this constant company,
And follow headlong, wild uncertaine thee?
First sweare by thy best love in earnest
(If thou which lov'st all, canst love any best)
Thou wilt not leave mee in the middle street,

Though some more spruce companion thou dost meet,
Not though a Captaine do come in thy way
Bright parcell gilt, with forty dead mens pay,
Not though a briske perfum'd piert Courtier
Deigne with a nod, thy courtesie to answer.   20
Nor come a velvet Justice with a long
Great traine of blew coats, twelve, or fourteen strong,
Wilt thou grin or fawne on him, or prepare
A speech to Court his beautious sonne and heire!
For better or worse take mee, or leave mee:
To take, and leave mee is adultery.
Oh monstrous, superstitious puritan,
Of refin'd manners, yet ceremoniall man,
That when thou meet'st one, with enquiring eyes
Dost search, and like a needy broker prize   30
The silke, and gold he weares, and to that rate
So high or low, dost raise thy formall hat:
That wilt comfort none, untill thou have knowne
What lands hee hath in hope, or of his owne,
As though all thy companions should make thee
Jointures, and marry thy deare company.
Why should'st thou (that dost not onely approve,
But in ranke itchie lust, desire, and love
The nakednesse and barenesse to enjoy,
Of thy plumpe muddy whore, or prostitute boy)   40
Hate vertue, though shee be naked, and bare?
At birth, and death, our bodies naked are;
And till our Soules be unapparrelled
Of bodies, they from blisse are banished.
Mans first blest state was naked, when by sinne
Hee lost that, yet hee was cloath'd but in beasts skin,
And in this course attire, which I now weare,
With God, and with the Muses I conferre.
But since thou like a contrite penitent,
Charitably warn'd of thy sinnes, dost repent   50
These vanities, and giddinesse, loe
I shut my chamber doore, and come, lets goe.
But sooner may a cheape whore, who hath beene
Worne by as many severall men in sinne,
As are black feathers, or musk-colour hose,
Name her childs right true father, 'mongst all those:
Sooner may one guesse, who shall beare away
The Infanta of London, Heire to an India;

And sooner may a gulling weather Spie
By drawing forth heavens Scheme tell certainly   60
What fashioned hats, or ruffes, or suits next yeare
Our subtile-witted antique youths will weare;
Than thou, when thou depart'st from mee, canst show
Whither, why, when, or with whom thou wouldst go.
But how shall I be pardon'd my offence
That thus have sinn'd against my conscience?
Now we are in the street; He first of all
Improvidently proud, creepes to the wall,
And so imprisoned, and hem'd in by mee
Sells for a little state his libertie;   70
Yet though he cannot skip forth now to greet
Every fine silken painted foole we meet,
He them to him with amorous smiles allures,
And grins, smacks, shrugs, and such an itch endures,
As prentises, or schoole-boyes which doe know
Of some gay sport abroad, yet dare not goe.
And as fidlers stop lowest, at highest sound,
So to the most brave, stoops hee nigh'st the ground.
But to a grave man, he doth move no more
Than the wise politique horse would heretofore,   80
Or thou O Elephant or Ape wilt doe,
When any names the King of Spaine to you.
Now leaps he upright, Joggs me, and cryes, Do you see
Yonder well favoured youth? Oh, 'tis hee
That dances so divinely; Oh, said I,
Stand still, must you dance here for company?
Hee droopt, wee went, till one (which did excell
Th'Indians, in drinking his Tobacco well)
Met us; they talk'd; I whispered, let'us goe,
'T may be you smell him not, truely I doe;   90
He heares not mee, but, on the other side
A many-coloured Peacock having spide,
Leaves him and mee; I for my lost sheep stay;
He followes, overtakes, goes on the way,
Saying, him whom I last left, all repute
For his device, in hansoming a sute,
To judge of lace, pinke, panes, print, cut, and pleate
Of all the Court, to have the best conceit;
Our dull Comedians want him, let him goe;
But Oh, God strengthen thee, why stoop'st thou so?   100
Why? he hath travayld; Long? No; but to me

(Which understand none,) he doth seeme to be
Perfect French, and Italian; I replyed,
So is the Poxe; He answered not, but spy'd
More men of sort, of parts, and qualities;
At last his Love he in a windowe spies,
And like light dew exhal'd, he flings from mee
Violently ravish'd to his lechery.
Many were there, he could command no more;
Hee quarrell'd, fought, bled; and turn'd out of dore   110
   Directly came to mee hanging the head,
    And constantly a while must keepe his bed.

SATYRE II

Sir; though (I thanke God for it) I do hate
Perfectly all this towne, yet there's one state
In all ill things so excellently best,
That hate, toward them, breeds pitty towards the rest.
Though Poëtry indeed be such a sinne
As I thinke that brings dearth, and Spaniards in,
Though like the Pestilence and old fashion'd love,
Ridlingly it catch men; and doth remove
Never, till it be sterv'd out; yet their state
Is poore, disarm'd, like Papists, not worth hate.   10
One, (like a wretch, which at Barre judg'd as dead,
Yet prompts him which stands next, and cannot reade,
And saves his life) gives ideot actors meanes
(Starving himselfe) to live by his labor'd sceanes;
As in some Organ, Puppits dance above
And bellows pant below, which them do move.
One would move Love by rithmes; but witchcrafts charms
Bring not now their old feares, nor their old harmes:
Rammes, and slings now are seely battery,
Pistolets are the best Artillerie.   20
And they who write to Lords, rewards to get,
Are they not like singers at doores for meat?
And they who write, because all write, have still
That excuse for writing, and for writing ill;
But hee is worst, who (beggarly) doth chaw
Others wits fruits, and in his ravenous maw

Rankly digested, doth those things out-spue,
As his owne things; and they are his owne, 'tis true,
For if one eate my meate, though it be knowne
The meate was mine, th'excrement is his owne: 30
But these do mee no harme, nor they which use
To out-swive Dildoes, and out-usure Jewes;
To out-drinke the sea, to out-sweare the Letanie;
Who with sinnes all kindes as familiar bee
As Confessors; and for whose sinfull sake,
Schoolemen new tenements in hell must make:
Whose strange sinnes, Canonists could hardly tell
In which Commandements large receit they dwell.
But these punish themselves; the insolence
Of Coscus onely breeds my just offence,   40
Whom time (which rots all, and makes botches poxe,
And plodding on, must make a calfe an oxe)
Hath made a Lawyer, which was (alas) of late
But a scarce Poët; jollier of this state,
Than are new benefic'd ministers, he throwes
Like nets, or lime-twigs, wheresoever he goes,
His title of Barrister, on every wench,
And wooes in language of the Pleas, and Bench:
A motion, Lady; Speake Coscus; I have beene
In love, ever since *tricesimo* of the Queene,   50
Continuall claimes I have made, injunctions got
To stay my rivals suit, that hee should not
Proceed; spare mee; In Hillary terme I went,
You said, If I return'd next size in Lent,
I should be in remitter of your grace;
In th'interim my letters should take place
Of affidavits: words, words, which would teare
The tender labyrinth of a soft maids eare,
More, more, than ten Sclavonians scolding, more
Than when winds in our ruin'd Abbeyes rore.   60
When sicke with Poëtrie, and possest with muse
Thou wast, and mad, I hop'd; but men which chuse
Law practise for meere gaine, bold soule, repute
Worse than imbrothel'd strumpets prostitute.
Now like an owlelike watchman, hee must walke
His hand still at a bill, now he must talke
Idly, like prisoners, which whole months will sweare
That onely suretiship hath brought them there,
And to every suitor lye in every thing,

Like a Kings favourite, yea like a King;   70
Like a wedge in a blocke, wring to the barre,
Bearing-like Asses; and more shamelesse farre
Than carted whores, lye, to the grave Judge; for
Bastardy abounds not in Kings titles, nor
Symonie and Sodomy in Churchmens lives,
As these things do in him; by these he thrives.
Shortly (as the sea) hee will compasse all our land,
From Scots, to Wight; from Mount, to Dover strand.
And spying heires melting with luxurie,
Satan will not joy at their sinnes, as hee.   80
For as a thrifty wench scrapes kitching-stuffe,
And barrelling the droppings, and the snuffe,
Of wasting candles, which in thirty yeare
(Relique-like kept) perchance buyes wedding geare;
Peecemeale he gets lands, and spends as much time
Wringing each Acre, as men pulling prime.
In parchments then, large as his fields, hee drawes
Assurances, bigge, as gloss'd civill lawes,
So huge, that men (in our times forwardnesse)
Are Fathers of the Church for writing lesse.
These hee writes not; nor for these written payes,   90
Therefore spares no length; as in those first dayes
When Luther was profest, He did desire
Short *Pater nosters*, saying as a Fryer
Each day his beads, but having left those lawes,
Addes to Christs prayer, the Power and glory clause.
But when he sells or changes land, he'impaires
His writings, and (unwatch'd) leaves out, *ses heires,*
As slily as any Commenter goes by
Hard words, or sense; or in Divinity   100
As controverters, in vouch'd Texts, leave out
Shrewd words, which might against them cleare the doubt.
Where are those spred woods which cloth'd hertofore
Those bought lands? not built, nor burnt within dore.
Where's th'old landlords troops, and almes? In great hals
Carthusian fasts, and fulsome Bachanalls
Equally I hate; meanes blesse; in rich mens homes
I bid kill some beasts, but no Hecatombs,
None starve, none surfet so; But (Oh) we allow,
Good workes as good, but out of fashion now,   110
Like old rich wardrops; but my words none drawes
Within the vast reach of th'huge statute lawes.

SATYRE III

KINDE pitty chokes my spleene; brave scorn forbids
Those teares to issue which swell my eye-lids;
I must not laugh, nor weepe sinnes, and be wise,
Can railing then cure these worne maladies?
Is not our Mistresse faire Religion,
As worthy of all our Soules devotion,
As vertue was to the first blinded age?
Are not heavens joyes as valiant to asswage
Lusts, as earths honour was to them? Alas,
As wee do them in meanes, shall they surpasse   10
Us in the end, and shall thy fathers spirit
Meete blinde Philosophers in heaven, whose merit
Of strict life may be imputed faith, and heare
Thee, whom hee taught so easie wayes and neare
To follow, damn'd? O if thou dar'st, feare this;
This feare great courage, and high valour is.
Dar'st thou ayd mutinous Dutch, and dar'st thou lay
Thee in ships woodden Sepulchers, a prey
To leaders rage, to stormes, to shot, to dearth?
Dar'st thou dive seas, and dungeons of the earth?   20
Hast thou couragious fire to thaw the ice
Of frozen North discoveries? and thrise
Colder than Salamanders, like divine
Children in th'oven, fires of Spaine, and the line,
Whose countries limbecks to our bodies bee,
Canst thou for gaine beare? and must every hee
Which cryes not, Goddesse, to thy Mistresse, draw,
Or eat thy poysonous words? courage of straw!
O desperate coward, wilt thou seeme bold, and
To thy foes and his (who made thee to stand   30
Sentinell in his worlds garrison) thus yeeld,
And for the forbidden warres, leave th'appointed field?
Know thy foes: The foule Devill (whom thou
Strivest to please,) for hate, not love, would allow
Thee faine, his whole Realme to be quit; and as
The worlds all parts wither away and passe,
So the worlds selfe, thy other lov'd foe, is
In her decrepit wayne, and thou loving this,

Dost love a withered and worne strumpet; last,
Flesh (it selfes death) and joyes which flesh can taste, 40
Thou lovest; and thy faire goodly soule, which doth
Give this flesh power to taste joy, thou dost loath.
Seeke true religion. O where? Mirreus
Thinking her unhous'd here, and fled from us,
Seekes her at Rome; there, because hee doth know
That shee was there a thousand yeares agoe,
He loves her ragges so, as wee here obey
The statecloth where the Prince sate yesterday,
Crantz to such brave Loves will not be inthrall'd,
But loves her onely, who at Geneva is call'd 50
Religion, plaine, simple, sullen, yong,
Contemptuous, yet unhansome; As among
Lecherous humors, there is one that judges
No wenches wholsome, but course country drudges.
Graius stayes still at home here, and because
Some Preachers, vile ambitious bauds, and lawes
Still new like fashions, bid him thinke that shee
Which dwels with us, is onely perfect, hee
Imbraceth her, whom his Godfathers will
Tender to him, being tender, as Wards still 60
Take such wives as their Guardians offer, or
Pay valewes. Carelesse Phrygius doth abhorre
All, because all cannot be good, as one
Knowing some women whores, dares marry none.
Graccus loves all as one, and thinkes that so
As women do in divers countries goe
In divers habits, yet are still one kinde,
So doth, so is Religion; and this blind-
nesse too much light breeds; but unmoved thou
Of force must one, and forc'd but one allow; 70
And the right; aske thy father which is shee,
Let him aske his; though truth and falshood bee
Neare twins, yet truth a little elder is;
Be busie to seeke her, beleeve mee this,
Hee's not of none, nor worst, that seekes the best.
To adore, or scorne an image, or protest,
May all be bad; doubt wisely; in strange way
To stand inquiring right, is not to stray;
To sleepe, or runne wrong, is. On a huge hill,
Cragged, and steep, Truth stands, and hee that will 80
Reach her, about must, and about must goe;

And what the hills suddennes resists, winne so;
Yet strive so, that before age, deaths twilight,
Thy Soule rest, for none can worke in that night.
To will, implyes delay, therefore now doe:
Hard deeds, the bodies paines; hard knowledge too
The mindes indeavours reach, and mysteries
Are like the Sunne, dazling, yet plaine to all eyes.
Keepe the truth which thou hast found; men do not stand
In so ill case here, that God hath with his hand   90
Sign'd Kings blanck-charters to kill whom they hate.
Nor are they Vicars, but hangmen to Fate.
Foole and wretch, wilt thou let thy Soule be tyed
To mans lawes, by which she shall not be tryed
At the last day? Oh, will it then boot thee
To say a Philip, or a Gregory,
A Harry, or a Martin taught thee this?
Is not this excuse for mere contraries,
Equally strong? cannot both sides say so?
That thou mayest rightly obey power, her bounds know;   100
Those past, her nature, and name is chang'd; to be
Then humble to her is idolatrie.
As streames are, Power is; those blest flowers that dwell
At the rough streames calme head, thrive and do well,
But having left their roots, and themselves given
To the streames tyrannous rage, alas are driven
Through mills, and rockes, and woods, and at last, almost
Consum'd in going, in the sea are lost:
So perish Soules, which more chuse mens unjust
Power from God claym'd, than God himselfe to trust.   110

SATYRE IV

WELL; I may now receive, and die; My sinne
Indeed is great, but I have beene in
A Purgatorie, such as fear'd hell is
A recreation to, and scarse map of this.
My minde, neither with prides itch, nor yet hath been
Poyson'd with love to see, or to bee seene,
I had no suit there, nor new suite to shew,
Yet went to Court; But as Glaze which did goe
To'a Masse in jest, catch'd, was faine to disburse

The hundred markes, which is the Statutes curse, 10
Before he scapt; So'it pleas'd my destinie
(Guilty of my sin of going), to thinke me
As prone to all ill, and of good as forget-
full, as proud, as lustfull, and as much in debt,
As vaine, as witlesse, and as false as they
Which dwell at Court, for once going that way.
Therefore I suffered this; Towards me did runne
A thing more strange, than on Niles slime, the Sunne
E'r bred; or all which into Noahs Arke came;
A thing, which would have pos'd Adam to name; 20
Stranger than seaven Antiquaries studies,
Than Africks Monsters, Guianaes rarities.
Stranger than strangers; One, who for a Dane,
In the Danes Massacre had sure beene slaine,
If he had liv'd then; And without helpe dies,
When next the Prentises 'gainst Strangers rise.
One, whom the watch at noone lets scarce goe by,
One, to whom, the examining Justice sure would cry,
Sir, by your priesthood tell me what you are.
His cloths were strange, though coarse; and black, though bare;30
Sleeveless his jerkin was, and it had beene
Velvet, but 'twas now (so much ground was seene)
Become Tufftaffatie; and our children shall
See it plaine Rashe awhile, then nought at all.
This thing hath travail'd, and saith, speakes all tongues
And only knoweth what to all States belongs.
Made of th'Accents, and best phrase of all these,
He speakes one language; If strange meats displease,
Art can deceive, or hunger force my tast,
But Pedants motley tongue, souldiers bumbast, 40
Mountebankes drugtongue, nor the termes of law
Are strong enough preparatives, to draw
Me to beare this: yet I must be content
With his tongue, in his tongue, call'd complement:
In which he can win widdowes, and pay scores,
Make men speake treason, cosen subtlest whores,
Out-flatter favorites, or outlie either
Jovius, or both together.
He names mee, and comes to mee; I whisper, God!
How have I sinn'd, that thy wraths furious rod, 50
This fellow chuseth me? He saith, Sir,
I love your judgement; Whom doe you prefer,

For the best linguist? And I seelily
Said, that I thought Calepines Dictionarie;
Nay, but of men, most sweet Sir; Beza then,
Some other Jesuites, and two reverend men
Of our two Academies, I named; There
He stopt mee, and said; Nay, your Apostles were
Good pretty linguists, and so Panurge was;
Yet a poore gentleman, all these may passe   60
By travaile. Then, as if he would have sold
His tongue, he prais'd it, and such wonders told
That I was faine to say, If you'had liv'd, Sir,
Time enough to have beene Interpreter
To Babells bricklayers, sure the Tower had stood.
He adds, If of court life you knew the good,
You would leave lonenesse. I said, not alone
My lonenesse is, but Spartanes fashion,
To teach by painting drunkards, doth not last
Now; Aretines pictures have made few chast;   70
No more can Princes courts, though there be few
Better pictures of vice, teach me vertue;
He, like to a high strecht lute string squeakt, O Sir,
'Tis sweet to talke of Kings. At Westminster,
Said I, The man that keepes the Abbey tombes,
And for his price doth with who ever comes,
Of all our Harries, and our Edwards talke,
From King to King and all their kin can walke:
Your eares shall heare nought, but Kings; your eyes meet
Kings only; The way to it, is Kingstreet.   80
He smack'd, and cry'd, He's base, Mechanique, coarse,
So are all your Englishmen in their discourse.
Are not your Frenchmen neate? Mine? as you see,
I have but one Frenchman, looke, hee followes mee.
Certes they are neatly cloth'd; I, of this minde am,
Your only wearing is your Grogaram.
Not so Sir, I have more. Under this pitch
He would not flie; I chaff'd him; But as Itch
Scratch'd into smart, and as blunt iron ground
Into an edge, hurts worse: So, I (foole) found,   90
Crossing hurt mee; To fit my sullennesse,
He to another key, his stile doth addresse,
And askes, what newes? I tell him of new playes.
He takes my hand, and as a Still, which staies
A Sembriefe, 'twixt each drop, he nigardly,

As loth to enrich mee, so tells many a lie.
More than ten Hollensheads, or Halls, or Stowes,
Of triviall houshold trash he knowes; He knowes
When the Queene frown'd, or smil'd, and he knowes what
A subtle States-man may gather of that;   100
He knowes who loves; whom; and who by poyson
Hasts to an Offices reversion;
He knowes who'hath sold his land, and now doth beg
A licence, old iron, bootes, shooes, and egge-
shels to transport; Shortly boyes shall not play
At span-counter, or blow-point, but they pay
Toll to some Courtier; And wiser than all us,
He knowes what Ladie is not painted; Thus
He with home-meats tries me; I belch, spue, spit,
Looke pale, and sickly, like a Patient; Yet   110
He thrusts on more; And as if he'd undertooke
To say Gallo-Belgicus without booke
Speakes of all States, and deeds, that have been since
The Spaniards came, to the losse of Amyens.
Like a bigge wife, at sight of loathed meat,
Readie to travaile: So I sigh, and sweat
To heare this Makeron talke: In vaine; for yet,
Either my humour, or his owne to fit,
He like a priviledg'd spie, whom nothing can
Discredit, Libells now 'gainst each great man.   120
He names a price for every office paid;
He saith, our warres thrive ill, because delai'd;
That offices are entail'd, and that there are
Perpetuities of them, lasting as farre
As the last day; And that great officers,
Doe with the Pirates share, and Dunkirkers.
Who wasts in meat, in clothes, in horse, he notes;
Who loves whores, who boyes, and who goats.
I more amas'd than Circes prisoners, when
They felt themselves turne beasts, felt my selfe then   130
Becomming Traytor, and mee thought I saw
One of our Giant Statutes ope his jaw
To sucke me in; for hearing him, I found
That as burnt venome Leachers do grow sound
By giving others their soares, I might growe
Guilty, and he free: Therefore I did shew
All signes of loathing; But since I am in,
I must pay mine, and my forefathers sinne

To the last farthing; Therefore to my power
Toughly and stubbornly I beare this crosse; But the'houre   140
Of mercy now was come; He tries to bring
Me to pay a fine to scape his torturing,
And saies, Sir, can you spare me; I said, willingly;
Nay, Sir, can you spare me a crowne? Thankfully I
Gave it, as Ransome; But as fidlers, still,
Though they be paid to be gone, yet needs will
Thrust one more jigge upon you: so did hee
With his long complementall thankes vexe me.
But he is gone, thankes to his needy want,
And the prerogative of my Crowne: Scant   150
His thankes were ended, when I, (which did see
All the court fill'd with more strange things than hee)
Ran from thence with such or more haste, than one
Who feares more actions, doth make from prison.
At home in wholesome solitarinesse
My precious soule began, the wretchednesse
Of suiters at court to mourne, and a trance
Like his, who dreamt he saw hell, did advance
It selfe on mee. Such men as he saw there,
I saw at court, and worse, and more; Low feare   160
Becomes the guiltie, not the accuser; Then,
Shall I, nones slave, of high borne, or rais'd men
Feare frownes? And, my Mistresse Truth, betray thee
To th'huffing braggart, puft Nobility?
No, no, Thou which since yesterday hast beene
Almost about the whole world, hast thou seene,
O Sunne, in all thy journey, Vanitie,
Such as swells the bladder of our court? I
Thinke he which made your waxen garden, and
Transported it from Italy to stand   170
With us, at London, flouts our Presence, for
Just such gay painted things, which no sappe, nor
Tast have in them, ours are; And naturall
Some of the stocks are, their fruits, bastard all.
'Tis ten a clock and past; All whom the Mews,
Baloune, Tennis, Dyet, or the stewes,
Had all the morning held, now the second
Time made ready, that day, in flocks, are found
In the Presence, and I, (God pardon mee.)
As fresh, and sweet their Apparrells be, as bee   180
The fields they sold to buy them; For a King

Those hose are, cry the flatterers; And bring
Them next weeke to the Theatre to sell;
Wants reach all states; Me seemes they doe as well
At stage, as court; All are players; who e'r lookes
(For themselves dare not goe) o'r Cheapside books,
Shall finde their wardrops Inventory. Now,
The Ladies come; As Pirats, which doe know
That there came weak ships fraught with Cutchannel,
The men board them; and praise, as they thinke, well,   190
Their beauties; they the mens wits; Both are bought.
Why good wits ne'r weare scarlet gownes, I thought
This cause, These men, mens wits for speeches buy,
And women buy all reds which scarlets die.
He call'd her beauty limetwigs, her haire net;
She feares her drugs ill laid, her haire loose set.
Would not Heraclitus laugh to see Macrine,
From hat to shooe, himselfe at doore refine,
As if the Presence were a Moschite, and lift
His skirts and hose, and call his clothes to shrift,   200
Making them confesse not only mortall
Great staines and holes in them; but veniall
Feathers and dust, wherewith they fornicate:
And then by *Durers* rules survay the state
Of his each limbe, and with strings the odds trye
Of his neck to his legge, and wast to thighe.
So in immaculate clothes, and Symetrie
Perfect as circles, with such nicetie
As a young Preacher at his first time goes
To preach, he enters, and a Lady which owes   210
Him not so much as good will, he arrests,
And unto her protests protests protests
So much as at Rome would serve to have throwne
Ten Cardinalls into the Inquisition;
And whisperd by Jesu, so often, that A
Pursevant would have ravish'd him away
For saying of our Ladies psalter; But 'tis fit
That they each other plague, they merit it.
But here comes Glorius that will plague them both,
Who, in the other extreme, only doth   220
Call a rough carelessenesse, good fashion;
Whose cloak his spurres teare; whom he spits on
He cares not, His ill words doe no harme
To him; he rusheth in, as if arme, arme,

He meant to crie; And though his face be as ill
As theirs which in old hangings whip Christ, still
He strives to looke worse, he keepes all in awe;
Jeasts like a licenc'd foole, commands like law.
Tyr'd, now I leave this place, and but pleas'd so
As men which from gaoles to'execution goe,   230
Goe through the great chamber (why is it hung
With the seaven deadly sinnes?). Being among
Those Askaparts, men big enough to throw
Charing Crosse for a barre, men that doe know
No token of worth, but Queenes man, and fine
Living, barrells of beefe, flaggons of wine,
I shooke like a spyed Spie. Preachers which are
Seas of Wit and Arts, you can, then dare,
Drowne the sinnes of this place, for, for mee
Which am but a scarce brooke, it enough shall bee   240
To wash the staines away; Although I yet
With *Macchabees* modestie, the knowne merit
Of my worke lessen: yet some wise man shall,
I hope, esteeme my writs Canonicall.

SATYRE V

THOU shalt not laugh in this leafe, Muse, nor they
Whom any pitty warmes; He which did lay
Rules to make Courtiers, (hee being understood
May make good Courtiers, but who Courtiers good?)
Frees from the sting of jests all who in extreme
Are wreched or wicked: of these two a theame
Charity and liberty give me. What is hee
Who Officers rage, and Suiters misery
Can write, and jest? If all things be in all,
As I thinke, since all, which were, are, and shall   10
Bee, be made of the same elements:
Each thing, each thing implyes or represents.
Then man is a world; in which, Officers
Are the vast ravishing seas; and Suiters,
Springs; now full, now shallow, now drye; which, to
That which drownes them, run: These selfe reasons do
Prove the world a man, in which, officers
Are the devouring stomacke, and Suiters

The excrements, which they voyd. All men are dust;
How much worse are Suiters, who to mens lust   20
Are made preyes? O worse than dust, or wormes meat,
For they do eate you now, whose selves wormes shall eate.
They are the mills which grinde you, yet you are
The winde which drives them; and a wastfull warre
Is fought against you, and you fight it; they
Adulterate lawe, and you prepare their way
Like wittals; th'issue your owne ruine is.
Greatest and fairest Empresse, know you this?
Alas, no more than Thames calme head doth know
Whose meades her armes drowne, or whose corne o'rflow: 30
You Sir, whose righteousnes she loves, whom I
By having leave to serve, am most richly
For service paid, authoriz'd, now beginne
To know and weed out this enormous sinne.
O Age of rusty iron! Some better wit
Call it some worse name, if ought equall it;
The iron Age *that* was, when justice was sold; now
Injustice is sold dearer farre. Allow
All demands, fees, and duties, gamsters, anon
The mony which you sweat, and sweare for, is gon   40
Into other hands: So controverted lands
Scape, like Angelica, the strivers hands.
If Law be the Judges heart, and hee
Have no heart to resist letter, or fee,
Where wilt thou appeale? powre of the Courts below
Flow from the first maine head, and these can throw
Thee, if they sucke thee in, to misery,
To fetters, halters; But if the injury
Steele thee to dare complaine, Alas, thou go'st
Against the stream, when upwards: when thou art most   50
Heavy and most faint; and in these labours they,
'Gainst whom thou should'st complaine, will in the way
Become great seas, o'r which, when thou shalt bee
Forc'd to make golden bridges, thou shalt see
That all thy gold was drown'd in them before;
All things follow their like, only who have may have more.
Judges are Gods; he who made and said them so,
Meant not that men should be forc'd to them to goe,
By meanes of Angels; When supplications
We send to God, to Dominations,   60
Powers, Cherubins, and all heavens Courts, if wee

Should pay fees as here, Daily bread would be
Scarce to Kings; so 'tis. Would it not anger
A Stoicke, a coward, yea a Martyr,
To see a Pursivant come in, and call
All his cloathes, Copes; Bookes, Primers; and all
His Plate, Challices; and mistake them away,
And aske a fee for comming? Oh, ne'r may
Faire lawes white reverend name be strumpeted,
To warrant thefts: she is established   70
Recorder to Destiny, on earth, and shee
Speakes Fates words, and but tells us who must bee
Rich, who poore, who in chaires, who in jayles:
Shee is all faire, but yet hath foule long nailes,
With which she scracheth Suiters; In bodies
Of men, so in law, nailes are th'extremities,
So Officers stretch to more than Law can doe,
As our nailes reach what no else part comes to.
Why barest thou to yon Officer? Foole, Hath hee
Got those goods, for which erst men bar'd to thee?   80
Foole, twice, thrice, thou hast bought wrong, and now hungerly
Beg'st right; But that dole comes not till these dye.
Thou had'st much, and lawes Urim and Thummim trie
Thou wouldst for more; and for all hast paper
Enough to cloath all the great Carricks Pepper.
Sell that, and by that thou much more shalt leese,
Than Haman, when he sold his Antiquities.
O wretch that thy fortunes should moralize
Esops fables, and make tales, prophesies.
Thou'art the swimming dog whom shadows cosened,   90
And div'st, neare drowning, for what's vanished.

UPON MR. THOMAS CORYATS CRUDITIES

Oh to what heighth will love of greatnesse drive
Thy leavened spirit, *Sesqui-superlative?*
Venice vast lake thou hadst seen, and wouldst seek then
Some vaster thing, and found'st a Curtizan.
That inland Sea having discovered well,
A Cellar gulfe, where one might saile to hell
From Heydelberg, thou longdst to see: And thou
This Booke, greater than all, producest now.

Infinite worke, which doth so far extend,
That none can study it to any end.   1&
'Tis no one thing, it is not fruit nor roote;
Nor poorely limited with head or foot.
If man be therefore man, because he can
Reason, and laugh, thy booke doth halfe make man.
One halfe being made, thy modestie was such,
That thou on th'other half wouldst never touch.
When wilt thou be at full, great Lunatique?
Not till thou exceed the world? Canst thou be like
A prosperous nose-borne wenne, which sometimes growes
To be farre greater than the Mother-nose?   **20**
Goe then; and as to thee, when thou didst go,
Munster did Townes, and *Gesner* Authors show,
Mount now to *Gallo-belgicus;* appear
As deepe a States-man, as a Gazettier.
Homely and familiarly, when thou com'st back,
Talke of *Will. Conquerour,* and *Prester Jack.*
Go bashfull man, lest here thou blush to looke
Upon the progresse of thy glorious booke,
To which both Indies sacrifices send;
The West sent gold, which thou didst freely spend,   **30**
(Meaning to see't no more) upon the presse.
The East sends hither her deliciousnesse;
And thy leaves must imbrace what comes from thence,
The Myrrhe, the Pepper, and the Frankincense.
This magnifies thy leaves; but if they stoope
To neighbour wares, when Merchants do unhoope
Voluminous barrels; if thy leaves do then
Convey these wares in parcels unto men;
If for vast Tons of Currans, and of Figs,
Of Medicinall and Aromatique twigs,   **40**
Thy leaves a better method do provide,
Divide to pounds, and ounces sub-divide;
If they stoope lower yet, and vent our wares,
Home-*manufactures,* to thick popular Faires,
If *omni-praegnant* there, upon warme stalls,
They hatch all wares for which the buyer calls;
Then thus thy leaves we justly may commend,
That they all kinde of matter comprehend.
Thus thou, by means which th'Ancients never took,
A Pandect makest, and Universall Booke.   **50**
The bravest Heroes, for publike good,

Scattered in divers Lands their limbs and blood.
Worst malefactors, to whom men are prize,
Do publike good, cut in Anatomies;
So will thy booke in peeces; for a Lord
Which casts at Protescues, and all the board,
Provide whole books; each leafe enough will be
For friends to passe time, and keep company.
Can all carouse up thee? no, thou must fit
Measures; and fill out for the half-pint wit: 60
Some shall wrap pils, and save a friends life so,
Some shall stop muskets, and so kill a foe.
Thou shalt not ease the Criticks of next age
So much, at once their hunger to asswage:
Nor shall wit-pirats hope to finde thee lye
All in one bottome, in one Librarie.
Some Leaves may paste strings there in other books,
And so one may, which on another looks,
Pilfer, alas, a little wit from you;
But hardly° much; and yet I think this true;   70
As *Sibyls* was, your booke is mysticall,
For every peece is as much worth as all.
Therefore mine impotency I confesse,
The healths which my braine bears must be far lesse:
Thy Gyant-wit 'orethrowes me, I am gone;
And rather than read all, I would reade none.

IN EUNDEM MACARONICON

Quot, dos haec, Linguists *perfetti, Disticha* fairont,
Tot cuerdos States-men. *hic* livre fara *tuus.*
Es *sat* a my l'honneur estre hic inteso; Car I leave
L'honra, de personne nestre creduto, *tibi.*

Explicit Joannes Donne.

° I meane from one page which shall paste strings in a booke.

INFINITATI SACRUM,
16. *Augusti* 1601.
METEMPSYCHOSIS.
POËMA SATYRICON.

EPISTLE.

OTHERS at the Porches and entries of their Buildings set their Armes; I, my picture; if any colours can deliver a minde so plaine, and flat, and through-light as mine. Naturally at a new Author, I doubt, and sticke, and doe not say quickly, good. I censure much and taxe; And this liberty costs mee more than others, by how much my owne things are worse than others. Yet I would not be so rebellious against my selfe, as not to doe it, since I love it; nor so unjust to others, to do it *sine talione*. As long as I give them as good hold upon mee, they must pardon mee my bitings. I forbid no reprehender, but him that like the Trent Councell forbids not bookes, but Authors, damning what ever such a name hath or shall write. None writes so ill, that he gives not some thing exemplary, to follow, or flie. Now when I beginne this booke, I have no purpose to come into any mans debt; how my stocke will hold out I know not; perchance waste, perchance increase in use; if I doe borrow any thing of Antiquitie, besides that I make account that I pay it to posterity, with as much and as good: You shall still finde mee to acknowledge it, and to thanke not him onely that hath digg'd out treasure for mee, but that hath lighted mee a candle to the place. All which I will bid you remember, (for I will have no such Readers as I can teach) is, that the Pithagorian doctrine doth not onely carry one soule from man to man, nor man to beast, but indifferently to plants also: and therefore you must not grudge to finde the same soule in an Emperour, in a Post-horse, and in a Mucheron, since no unreadinesse in the soule, but an indisposition in the organs workes this. And therefore though this soule could not move when it was a Melon, yet it may remember, and now tell mee, at what lascivious banquet it was serv'd. And though it could not speake, when it was a spider, yet it can remember, and now tell me, who used it for poyson to attaine dignitie. How

ever the bodies have dull'd her other faculties, her memory hath
ever been her owne, which makes me so seriously deliver you
by her relation all her passages from her first
making when shee was that apple which
Eve eate, to this time when shee is
hee, whose life you shall
finde in the end of
this booke

THE PROGRESSE OF THE SOULE

FIRST SONG

I

I sing the progresse of a deathlesse soule,
Whom Fate, which God made, but doth not controule,
Plac'd in most shapes; all times before the law
Yoak'd us, and when, and since, in this I sing.
And the great world to his aged evening;
From infant morne, through manly noone I draw.
What the gold Chaldee, or silver Persian saw,
Greeke brasse, or Roman iron, is in this one;
A worke t'outweare *Seths* pillars, bricke and stone,
    And (holy writt excepted) made to yeeld to none.   10

II

Thee, eye of heaven, this great Soule envies not,
By thy male force, is all wee have, begot.
In the first East, thou now beginst to shine,
Suck'st early balme, and Iland spices there,
And wilt anon in thy loose-rein'd careere
At Tagus, Po, Sene, Thames, and Danow dine,
And see at night thy Westerne land of Myne,
Yet hast thou not more nations seene than shee,
That before thee, one day beganne to bee,
    And thy fraile light being quench'd, shall long. long out
    live thee.   20

III

Nor, holy *Janus*, in whose soveraigne boate
The Church, and all the Monarchies did floate:

That swimming Colledge, and free Hospitall
Of all mankinde, that cage and vivarie
Of fowles, and beasts, in whose wombe, Destinie
Us, and our latest nephewes did install
(From thence are all deriv'd, that fill this All,)
Did'st thou in that great stewardship embarke
So diverse shapes into that floating parke,
    As have beene moved, and inform'd by this heavenly sparke.30

IV

Great Destiny the Commissary of God,
That hast mark'd out a path and period
For every thing; who, where wee of-spring tooke,
Our wayes and ends seest at one instant; Thou
Knot of all causes, thou whose changelesse brow
Ne'r smiles nor frownes, O vouch thou safe to looke
And shew my story, in thy eternall booke:
That (if my prayer be fit) I may'understand
So much my selfe, as to know with what hand,
    How scant, or liberall this my lifes race is spand.   40

V

To my six lustres almost now outwore,
Except thy booke owe mee so many more,
Except my legend be free from the letts
Of steepe ambition, sleepie povertie,
Spirit-quenching sicknesse, dull captivitie,
Distracting businesse, and from beauties nets,
And all that calls from this, and to others whets,
O let me not launch out, but let mee save
Th'expense of braine and spirit; that my grave
    His right and due, a whole unwasted man may have.   50

VI

But if my dayes be long, and good enough,
In vaine this sea shall enlarge, or enrough
It selfe; for I will through the wave, and fome,
And shall, in sad lone wayes a lively spright,
Make my darke heavy Poëm light, and light.
For though through many streights, and lands I roame,

I launch at paradise, and I saile towards home;
The course I there began, shall here be staid,
Sailes hoised there, stroke here, and anchors laid
    In Thames, which were at Tigrys, and Euphrates waide.   60

VII

For the great soule which here amongst us now
Doth dwell, and moves that hand, and tongue, and brow,
Which, as the Moone the sea, moves us; to heare
Whose story, with long patience you will long;
(For 'tis the crowne, and last straine of my song)
This soule to whom *Luther,* and *Mahomet* were
Prisons of flesh; this soule which oft did teare,
And mend the wracks of th'Empire, and late Rome,
And liv'd when every great change did come,
    Had first in paradise, a low, but fatall roome.   70

VIII

Yet no low roome, nor than the greatest, lesse,
If (as devout and sharpe men fitly guesse)
That Crosse, our joy, and griefe, where nailes did tye
That All, which alwayes was all, every where;
Which could not sinne, and yet all sinnes did beare;
Which could not die, yet could not chuse but die;
Stood in the selfe same roome in Calvarie,
Where first grew the forbidden learned tree,
For on that tree hung in security
    This Soule, made by the Makers will from pulling free.   80

IX

Prince of the orchard, faire as dawning morne,
Fenc'd with the law, and ripe as soone as borne
That apple grew, which this Soule did enlive,
Till the then climing serpent, that now creeps
For that offence, for which all mankinde weepes,
Tooke it, and t'her whom the first man did wive
(Whom and her race, only forbiddings drive)
He gave it, she, t'her husband, both did eate;
So perished the eaters, and the meate:
    And wee (for treason taints the blood) thence die and
        sweat.   90

X

Man all at once was there by woman slaine,
And one by one we'are here slaine o'er againe
By them. The mother poison'd the well-head,
The daughters here corrupt us, Rivolets;
No smalnesse scapes, no greatnesse breaks their nets;
She thrust us out, and by them we are led
Astray, from turning, to whence we are fled.
Were prisoners Judges, 'twould seeme rigorous,
Shee sinn'd, we beare; part of our paine is, thus
    To love them, whose fault to this painfull love yoak'd us.   100

XI

So fast in us doth this corruption grow,
That now wee dare aske why wee should be so.
Would God (disputes the curious Rebell) make
A law, and would not have it kept? Or can
His creatures will, crosse his? Of every man
For one, will God (and be just) vengeance take?
Who sinn'd? t'was not forbidden to the snake
Nor her, who was not then made; nor is't writ
That Adam cropt, or knew the apple; yet
    The worme and she, and he, and wee endure for it.   110

XII

But snatch mee heavenly Spirit from this vaine
Reckoning their vanities, lesse is their gaine
Than hazard still, to meditate on ill,
Though with good minde; their reasons, like those toyes
Of glassie bubbles, which the gamesome boyes
Stretch to so nice a thinnes through a quill
That they themselves breake, doe themselves spill:
Arguing is heretiques game, and Exercise
As wrastlers, perfects them; Not liberties
    Of speech, but silence; hands, not tongues, end heresies.   120

XIII

Just in that instant when the serpents gripe,
Broke the slight veines, and tender conduit-pipe,

Through which this soule from the trees root did draw
Life, and growth to this apple, fled away
This loose soule, old, one and another day.
As lightning, which one scarce dares say, he saw,
'Tis so soone gone, (and better proofe the law
Of sense, than faith requires) swiftly she flew
To a darke and foggie Plot; Her, her fates threw
  There through th'earths pores, and in a Plant hous'd her
    anew.   130

XIV

The plant thus abled, to it selfe did force
A place, where no place was; by natures course
As aire from water, water fleets away
From thicker bodies, by this root thronged so
His spungie confines gave him place to grow:
Just as in our streets, when the people stay
To see the Prince, and have so fill'd the way
That weesels scarce could passe; when she comes nere
They throng and cleave up, and a passage cleare,
  As if, for that time, their round bodies flatned were.   140

XV

His right arme he thrust out towards the East,
West-ward his left; th'ends did themselves digest
Into ten lesser strings, these fingers were:
And as a slumberer stretching on his bed,
This way he this, and that way scattered
His other legge, which feet with toes upbeare.
Grew on his middle parts, the first day, haire,
To show, that in loves businesse hee should still
A dealer bee, and be us'd well, or ill:
  His apples kindle, his leaves, force of conception kill.   150

XVI

A mouth, but dumbe, he hath; blinde eyes, deafe eares,
And to his shoulders dangle subtile haires;
A young *Colossus* there hee stands upright,
And as that ground by him were conquered
A leafie garland weares he on his head

Enchas'd with little fruits, so red and bright
That for them you would call your Loves lips white;
So, of a lone unhaunted place possest,
Did this soules second Inne, built by the guest,
  This living buried man, this quiet mandrake, rest.   160

XVII

No lustfull woman came this plant to grieve,
But 'twas because there was none yet but Eve:
And she (with other purpose) kill'd it quite;
Her sinne had now brought in infirmities,
And so her cradled child, the moist red eyes
Had never shut, nor slept since it saw light;
Poppie she knew, she knew the mandrakes might,
And tore up both, and so coold her childs blood;
Unvirtuous weeds might long unvex'd have stood;
  But hee's short liv'd, that with his death can doe most
     good.   170

XVIII

To an unfetterd soules quick nimble haste
Are falling stars, and hearts thoughts, but slow pac'd:
Thinner than burnt aire flies this soule, and she
Whom foure new comming, and foure parting Suns
Had found, and left the Mandrakes tenant, runnes
Thoughtlesse of change, when her firme destiny
Confin'd, and enjayld her, that seem'd so free,
Into a small blew shell, the which a poore
Warme bird orespread, and sat still evermore,
  Till her inclos'd child kickt, and pick'd it selfe a dore.   180

XIX

Outcrept a sparrow, this soules moving Inne,
On whose raw armes stiffe feathers now begin,
As childrens teeth through gummes, to breake with paine,
His flesh is jelly yet, and his bones threds,
All a new downy mantle overspreads,
A mouth he opes, which would as much containe
As his late house, and the first houre speaks plaine,
And chirps alowd for meat. Meat fit for men

His father steales for him, and so feeds then
  One, that within a moneth, will beate him from his hen.   **190**

XX

In this worlds youth wise nature did make haste,
Things ripened sooner, and did longer last;
Already this hot cocke, in bush and tree,
In field and tent oreflutters his next hen;
He asks her not, who did so last, nor when,
Nor if his sister, or his neece shee be;
Nor doth she pule for his inconstancie
If in her sight he change, nor doth refuse
The next that calls; both liberty doe use;
  Where store is of both kindes, both kindes may freely
    chuse.   **200**

XXI

Men, till they tooke laws which made freedome lesse,
Their daughters, and their sisters did ingresse;
Till now unlawfull, therefore ill, 'twas not.
So jolly, that it can move, this soule is,
The body so free of his kindnesses,
That selfe-preserving it hath now forgot,
And slackneth so the soules, and bodies knot,
Which temperance streightens; freely on his she friends
He blood, and spirit, pith, and marrow spends,
  Ill steward of himself, himselfe in three yeares ends.   **210**

XXII

Else might he long have liv'd; man did not know
Of gummie blood, which doth in holly grow,
How to make bird-lime, nor how to deceive
With faind calls, hid nets, or enwrapping snare,
The free inhabitants of the Plyant aire.
Man to beget, and woman to conceive
Askt not of rootes, nor of cock-sparrowes, leave:
Yet chuseth hee, though none of these he feares,
Pleasantly three, than streightned twenty yeares
  To live, and to encrease his race, himselfe outweares.   **220**

XXIII

This cole with overblowing quench'd and dead,
The Soule from her too active organs fled
T'a brooke. A female fishes sandie Roe
With the males jelly, newly lev'ned was,
For they had intertouch'd as they did passe,
And one of those small bodies, fitted so,
This soule inform'd, and abled it to rowe
It selfe with finnie oares, which she did fit:
Her scales seem'd yet of parchment, and as yet
    Perchance a fish, but by no name you could call it.   **230**

XXIV

When goodly, like a ship in her full trim,
A swan, so white that you may unto him
Compare all whitenesse, but himselfe to none,
Glided along, and as he glided watch'd,
And with his arched necke this poore fish catch'd.
It mov'd with state, as if to looke upon
Low things it scorn'd, and yet before that one
Could thinke he sought it, he had swallowed cleare
This, and much such, and unblam'd devour'd there
    All, but who too swift, too great, or well armed were.   **240**

XXV

Now swome a prison in a prison put,
And now this Soule in double walls was shut,
Till melted with the Swans digestive fire,
She left her house the fish, and vapour'd forth;
Fate not affording bodies of more worth
For her as yet, bids her againe retire
T'another fish, to any new desire
Made a new prey; For, he that can to none
Resistance make, nor complaint, sure is gone.
    Weaknesse invites, but silence feasts oppression.   **250**

XXVI

Pace with her native streame, this fish doth keepe,
And journeyes with her, towards the glassie deepe,

But oft retarded, once with a hidden net
Though with greate windowes, for when Need first taught
These tricks to catch food, then they were not wrought
As now, with curious greedinesse to let
None scape, but few, and fit for use, to get,
As, in this trap a ravenous pike was tane,
Who, though himselfe distrest, would faine have slain
    This wretch; So hardly are ill habits left again.   260

XXVII

Here by her smallnesse shee two deaths orepast,
Once innocence scap'd, and left the oppressor fast.
The net through-swome, she keepes the liquid path,
And whether she leape up sometimes to breath
And suck in aire, or finde it underneath,
Or working parts like mills or limbecks hath
To make the water thinne and airelike, faith
Cares not; but safe the Place she's come unto
Where fresh, with salt waves meet, and what to doe
    She knowes not, but betweene both makes a boord or
        two.   270

XXVIII

So farre from hiding her guests, water is,
That she showes them in bigger quantities
Than they are. Thus doubtfull of her way,
For game and not for hunger a sea Pie
Spied through this traiterous spectacle, from high,
The seely fish where it disputing lay,
And t'end her doubts and her, beares her away:
Exalted she'is, but to the exalters good,
As are by great ones, men which lowly stood.
    It's rais'd, to be the Raisers instrument and food.   280

XXIX

Is any kinde subject to rape like fish?
Ill unto man, they neither doe, nor wish:
Fishers they kill not, nor with noise awake,
They doe not hunt, nor strive to make a prey
Of beasts, nor their young sonnes to beare away;

Foules they pursue not, nor do undertake
To spoile the nests industrious birds do make;
Yet them all these unkinde kinds feed upon,
To kill them is an occupation,
    And lawes make Fasts, and Lents for their destruction.   290

XXX

A sudden stiffe land-winde in that selfe houre
To sea-ward forc'd this bird, that did devour
The fish; he cares not, for with ease he flies,
Fat gluttonies best orator: at last
So long hee hath flowen, and hath flowen so fast
That many leagues at sea, now tir'd hee lyes,
And with his prey, that till then languisht, dies;
The soules no longer foes, two wayes did erre,
The fish I follow, and keepe no calender
    Of the other; he lives yet in some great officer.   300

XXXI

Into an embrion fish, our Soule is throwne,
And in due time throwne out againe, and growne
To such vastness as, if unmanacled
From Greece, Morea were, and that by some
Earthquake unrooted, loose Morea swome,
Or seas from Africks body had severed
And torne the hopefull Promontories head,
This fish would seeme these, and, when all hopes faile,
A great ship overset, or without saile
    Hulling, might (when this was a whelp) be like this
      whale.   310

XXXII

At every stroake his brazen finnes do take,
More circles in the broken sea they make
Than cannons voices, when the aire they teare:
His ribs are pillars, and his high arch'd roofe
Of barke that blunts best steele, is thunder-proofe:
Swimme in him swallow'd Dolphins, without feare,
And feele no sides, as if his vast wombe were
Some inland sea, and ever as hee went

Hee spouted rivers up, as if he ment
  To joyne our seas, with seas above the firmament.   320

XXXIII

He hunts not fish, but as an officer,
Stayes in his court, at his owne net, and there
All suitors of all sorts themselves enthrall;
So on his backe lyes this whale wantoning,
And in his gulfe-like throat, sucks every thing
That passeth neare. Fish chaseth fish, and all,
Flyer and follower, in this whirlepoole fall;
O might not states of more equality
Consist? and is it of necessity
  That thousand guiltlesse smals, to make one great, must
    die?   330

XXXIV

Now drinkes he up seas, and he eates up flocks,
He justles Ilands, and he shakes firme rockes.
Now in a roomefull house this Soule doth float,
And like a Prince she sends her faculties
To all her limbes, distant as Provinces.
The Sunne hath twenty times both crab and goate
Parched, since first lanch'd forth this living boate;
'Tis greatest now, and to destruction
Nearest; There's no pause at perfection;
  Greatnesse a period hath, but hath no station.   340

XXXV

Two little fishes whom hee never harm'd,
Nor fed on their kinde, two not throughly arm'd
With hope that they could kill him, nor could doe
Good to themselves by his death (they did not eate
His flesh, nor suck those oyles, which thence outstreat)
Conspir'd against him, and it might undoe
The plot of all, that the plotters were two,
But that they fishes were, and could not speake.
How shall a Tyran wise strong projects breake,
  If wreches can on them the common anger wreake?   350

XXXVI

The flaile-finn'd Thresher, and steel-beak'd Sword-fish
Onely attempt to doe, what all doe wish.
The Thresher backs him, and to beate begins;
The sluggard Whale yeelds to oppression,
And t'hide himselfe from shame and danger, downe
Begins to sinke; the Swordfish upward spins,
And gores him with his beake; his staffe-like finnes,
So well the one, his sword the other plyes,
That now a scoffe, and prey, this tyran dyes,
    And (his owne dole) feeds with himselfe all companies. 360

XXXVII

Who will revenge his death? or who will call
Those to account, that thought, and wrought his fall?
The heires of slaine kings, wee see are often so
Transported with the joy of what they get,
That they, revenge and obsequies forget,
Nor will against such men the people goe,
Because h'is now dead, to whom they should show
Love in that act; Some kings by vice being growne
So needy of subjects love, that of their own
    They thinke they lose, if love be to the dead Prince
      shown.   370

XXXVIII

This Soule, now free from prison, and passion,
Hath yet a little indignation
That so small hammers should so soone downe beat
So great a castle. And having for her house
Got the streight cloyster of a wreched mouse
(As basest men that have not what to eate,
Nor enjoy ought, doe farre more hate the great
Than they, who good repos'd estates possesse)
This Soule, late taught that great things might by lesse
    Be slaine, to gallant mischiefe doth herselfe addresse. 380

XXXIX

Natures great master-peece, an Elephant,
The onely harmlesse great thing; the giant
Of beasts; who thought, no more had gone, to make one wise
But to be just, and thankfull, loth to offend,
(Yet nature hath given him no knees to bend)
Himselfe he up-props, on himselfe relies,
And foe to none, suspects no enemies,
Still sleeping stood; vex't not his fantasie
Blacke dreames; like an unbent bow, carelessly
   His sinewy Proboscis did remisly lie: 390

XL

In which as in a gallery this mouse
Walk'd, and surveid the roomes of this vast house,
And to the braine, the soules bedchamber, went,
And gnaw'd the life cords there; Like a whole towne
Cleane undermin'd, the slaine beast tumbled downe;
With him the murtherer dies, whom envy sent
To kill, not scape, (for, only hee that ment
To die, did ever kill a man of better roome,)
And thus he made his foe, his prey, and tombe:
   Who cares not to turn back, may any whither come.   400

XLI

Next, hous'd this Soule a Wolves yet unborne whelp,
Till the best midwife, Nature, gave it helpe,
To issue. It could kill, as soone as goe.
Abel, as white, and milde as his sheepe were,
(Who, in that trade, of Church, and kingdomes, there
Was the first type) was still infested soe,
With this wolfe, that it bred his losse and woe;
And yet his bitch, his sentinell attends
The flocke so neere, so well warnes and defends,
   That the wolfe, (hopelesse else) to corrupt her, intends. 410

XLII

Hee tooke a course, which since, successfully,
Great men have often taken, to espie

The counsels, or to breake the plots of foes.
To Abels tent he stealeth in the darke,
On whose skirts the bitch slept; ere she could barke,
Attach'd her with streight gripes, yet hee call'd those,
Embracements of love; to loves worke he goes,
Where deeds move more than words; nor doth she show,
Nor much resist, nor needs hee streighten so
    His prey, for, were shee loose, she would nor barke, nor
       goe.   420

XLIII

Hee hath engag'd her; his, she wholy bides;
Who not her owne, none others secrets hides.
If to the flocke he come, and Abell there,
She faines hoarse barkings, but she biteth not,
Her faith is quite, but not her love forgot.
At last a trap, of which some every where
Abell had plac'd, ends all his losse, and feare,
By the Wolves death; and now just time it was
That a quick soule should give life to that masse
    Of blood in Abels bitch, and thither this did passe.   430

XLIV

Some have their wives, their sisters some begot,
But in the lives of Emperours you shall not
Reade of a lust the which may equall this;
This wolfe begot himselfe, and finished
What he began alive, when hee was dead;
Sonne to himselfe, and father too, hee is
A ridling lust, for which Schoolemen would misse
A proper name. The whelpe of both these lay
In Abels tent, and with soft Moaba,
    His sister, being yong, it us'd to sport and play.   440

XLV

Hee soone for her too harsh, and churlish grew,
And Abell (the dam dead) would use this new
For the field. Being of two kindes thus made,
He, as his dam, from sheepe drove wolves away,
And as his Sire, he made them his owne prey.

Five yeares he liv'd, and cosened with his trade,
Then hopelesse that his faults were hid, betraid
Himselfe by flight, and by all followed,
From dogges, a wolfe; from wolves, a dogge he fled;
 And, like a spie to both sides false, he perished. **450**

XLVI

It quickned next a toyfull Ape, and so
Gamesome it was, that it might freely goe
From tent to tent, and with the children play.
His organs now so like theirs hee doth finde,
That why he cannot laugh, and speake his minde,
He wonders. Much with all, most he doth stay
With Adams fift daughter *Siphatecia*,
Doth gaze on her, and, where she passeth, passe,
Gathers her fruits, and tumbles on the grasse,
 And wisest of that kinde, the first true lover was. **460**

XLVII

He was the first that more desir'd to have
One than another; first that ere did crave
Love by mute signes, and had no power to speake;
First that could make love faces, or could doe
The valters sombersalts, or us'd to wooe
With hoiting gambolls, his owne bones to breake
To make his mistresse merry; or to wreake
Her anger on himselfe. Sinnes against kinde
They easily doe, that can let feed their minde
 With outward beauty; beauty they in boyes and beasts do
  find. **470**

XLVIII

By this misled, too low things men have prov'd,
And too high; beasts and angels have beene lov'd.
This Ape, though else through-vaine, in this was wise,
He reach'd at things too high, but open way
There was, and he knew not she would say nay;
His toyes prevaile not, likelier meanes he tries,
He gazeth on her face with teare-shot eyes,

And up lifts subtly with his russet pawe
Her kidskinne apron without feare or awe
   Of Nature; Nature hath no gaole, though shee hath law. 480

XLIX

First she was silly and knew not what he ment.
That vertue, by his touches, chaft and spent,
Succeeds an itchie warmth, that melts her quite;
She knew not first, nowe cares not what he doth,
And willing halfe and more, more than halfe loth,
She neither puls nor pushes, but outright
Now cries, and now repents; when *Tethlemite*
Her brother, enterd, and a great stone threw
After the Ape, who, thus prevented, flew.
   This house thus batter'd downe, the Soule possest a new. 490

L

And whether by this change she lose or win,
She comes out next, where the Ape would have gone in.
Adam and *Eve* had mingled bloods, and now
Like Chimiques equall fires, her temperate wombe
Had stew'd and form'd it: and part did become
A spungie liver, that did richly allow,
Like a free conduit, on a high hils brow,
Life-keeping moisture unto every part;
Part hardned it selfe to a thicker heart,
   Whose busie furnaces lifes spirits do impart.   500

LI

Another part became the well of sense,
The tender well-arm'd feeling braine, from whence,
Those sinowie strings which do our bodies tie,
Are raveld out; and fast there by one end,
Did this Soule limbes, these limbes a soule attend;
And now they joyn'd; keeping some quality
Of every past shape, she knew treachery,
Rapine, deceit, and lust, and ills enow
To be a woman. *Themech* she is now,
   Sister and wife to *Caine, Caine* that first did plow.   510

LII

Who ere thou beest that read'st this sullen Writ,
Which just so much courts thee, as thou dost it,
Let me arrest thy thoughts; wonder with mee,
Why plowing, building, ruling and the rest,
Or most of those arts, whence our lives are blest,
By cursed *Cains* race invented be,
And blest *Seth* vext us with Astronomie.
Ther's nothing simply good, nor ill alone,
Of every quality comparison,
  The onely measure is, and judge, opinion.   520

VERSE LETTERS TO SEVERALL PERSONAGES

THE STORME   [1597]

To MR. CHRISTOPHER BROOKE

THOU which art I, ('tis nothing to be soe)
Thou which art still thy selfe, by these shalt know
Part of our passage; And, a hand, or eye
By *Hilliard* drawne, is worth an history,
By a worse painter made; and (without pride)
When by thy judgment they are dignifi'd,
My lines are such: 'Tis the preheminence
Of friendship onely to'impute excellence.
England to whom we'owe, what we be, and have,
Sad that her sonnes did seeke a forraine grave   10
(For, Fates, or Fortunes drifts none can soothsay,
Honour and misery have one face and way.)
From out her pregnant intrailes sigh'd a winde
Which at th'ayres middle marble roome did finde
Such strong resistance, that it selfe it threw
Downeward againe; and so when it did view
How in the port, our fleet deare time did leese,
Withering like prisoners, which lye but for fees,
Mildly it kist our sailes, and, fresh and sweet,
As to a stomack sterv'd, whose insides meete,   20
Meate comes, it came; and swole our sailes, when wee

So joyd, as *Sara*'her swelling joy'd to see.
But 'twas but so kinde, as our countrimen,
Which bring friends one dayes way, and leave them then.
Then like two mighty Kings, which dwelling farre
Asunder, meet against a third to warre,
The South and West winds joyn'd, and, as they blew,
Waves like a rowling trench before them threw.
Sooner than you read this line, did the gale,
Like shot, not fear'd till felt, our sailes assaile;   30
And what at first was call'd a gust, the same
Hath now a stormes, anon a tempests name.
Jonas, I pitty thee, and curse those men,
Who when the storm rag'd most, did wake thee then;
Sleepe is paines easiest salve, and doth fulfill
All offices of death, except to kill.
But when I wakt, I saw, that I saw not;
Ay, and the Sunne, which should teach mee'had forgot
East, West, Day, Night, and I could onely say,
If'the world had lasted, now it had been day.   40
Thousands our noyses were, yet wee'mongst all
Could none by his right name, but thunder call:
Lightning was all our light, and it rain'd more
Than if the Sunne had drunke the sea before.
Some coffin'd in their cabbins lye,'equally
Griev'd that they are not dead, and yet must dye;
And as sin-burd'ned soules from graves will creepe,
At the last day, some forth their cabbins peepe:
And tremblingly'aske what newes, and doe heare so,
Like jealous husbands, what they would not know.   50
Some sitting on the hatches, would seeme there,
With hideous gazing to feare away feare.
Then note they the ships sicknesses, the Mast
Shak'd with this ague, and the Hold and Wast
With a salt dropsie clog'd, and all our tacklings
Snapping, like too-high-stretched treble strings.
And from our totterd sailes, ragges drop downe so,
As from one hang'd in chaines, a yeare agoe.
Even our Ordinance plac'd for our defence,
Strive to breake loose, and scape away from thence.   60
Pumping hath tir'd our men, and what's the gaine?
Seas into seas throwne, we suck in againe;
Hearing hath deaf'd our saylers; and if they
Knew how to heare, there's none knowes what to say.

Compar'd to these stormes, death is but a qualme,
Hell somewhat lightsome, and the'Bermuda calme.
Darknesse, lights elder brother, his birth-right
Claims o'er this world, and to heaven hath chas'd light.
All things are one, and that one none can be,
Since all formes, uniforme deformity   70
Doth cover, so that wee, except God say
Another *Fiat,* shall have no more day.
So violent, yet long these furies bee,
That though thine absence sterve me,'I wish not thee.

THE CALME   [1597]

OUR storme is past, and that storms tyrannous rage,
A stupid calme, but nothing it, doth swage.
The fable is inverted, and farre more
A blocke afflicts, now, than a storke before.
Stormes chafe, and soon weare out themselves, or us;
In calmes, Heaven laughs to see us languish thus.
As steady'as I can wish, that my thoughts were,
Smooth as thy mistresse glasse, or what shines there,
The sea is now. And, as the Iles which wee
Seeke, when wee can move, our ships rooted bee.   10
As water did in stormes, now pitch runs out:
As lead, when a fir'd Church becomes one spout.
And all our beauty, and our trimme, decayes,
Like courts removing, or like ended playes.
The fighting place now seamens ragges supply;
And all the tackling is a frippery.
No use of lanthornes; and in one place lay
Feathers and dust, to day and yesterday.
Earths hollownesses, which the worlds lungs are,
Have no more winde than the upper valt of aire.   20
We can nor lost friends, nor sought foes recover,
But meteorlike, save that wee move not, hover.
Onely the Calenture together drawes
Deare friends, which meet dead in great fishes jawes:
And on the hatches as on Altars lyes
Each one, his owne Priest, and owne Sacrifice.
Who live, that miracle do multiply
Where walkers in hot Ovens, doe not dye.

If in despite of these, wee swimme, that hath
No more refreshing, than our brimstone Bath,   30
But from the sea, into the ship we turne,
Like parboyl'd wretches, on the coales to burne.
Like *Bajazet* encag'd, the shepheards scoffe,
Or like slacke sinew'd *Sampson,* his haire off,
Languish our ships. Now, as a Miriade
Of Ants, durst th'Emperours lov'd snake invade,
The crawling Gallies, Sea-gaols, finny chips,
Might brave our Pinnaces, now bed-ridde ships.
Whether a rotten state, and hope of gaine,
Or to disuse mee from the queasie paine   40
Of being belov'd, and loving, or the thirst
Of honour, or faire death, out pusht mee first,
I lose my end: for here as well as I
A desperate may live, and a coward die.
Stagge, dogge, and all which from, or towards flies,
Is paid with life, or pray, or doing dyes.
Fate grudges us all, and doth subtly lay
A scourge,'gainst which wee all forget to pray,
He that at sea prayes for more winde, as well
Under the poles may begge cold, heat in hell.   50
What are wee then? How little more alas
Is man now, than before he was? he was
Nothing; for us, wee are for nothing fit;
Chance, or our selves still disproportion it.
Wee have no power, no will, no sense; I lye,
I should not then thus feele this miserie.

TO SIR HENRY WOTTON   [c. 1597–8]

SIR, more than kisses, letters mingle Soules;
For, thus friends absent speake. This ease controules
The tediousnesse of my life: But for these
I could ideate nothing, which could please,
But I should wither in one day, and passe
To'a bottle'of Hay, that am a locke of Grasse.
Life is a voyage, and in our lifes wayes
Countries, Courts, Towns are Rockes, or Remoraes;
They breake or stop all ships, yet our state's such,
'That though than pitch they staine worse, wee must touch.   10

If in the furnace of the even line,
Or under th'adverse icy poles thou pine,
Thou know'st two temperate Regions girded in,
Dwell there: But Oh, what refuge canst thou winne
Parch'd in the Court, and in the country frozen?
Shall cities, built of both extremes, be chosen?
Can dung and garlike be'a perfume? or can
A Scorpion and Torpedo cure a man?
Cities are worst of all three; of all three
(O knottie riddle) each is worst equally.   20
Cities are Sepulchers; they who dwell there
Are carcases, as if such there were.
And Courts are Theaters, where some men play
Princes, some slaves, all to one end, and of one clay.
The Country is a desert, where no good,
Gain'd (as habits, not borne,) is understood.
There men become beasts, and prone to more evils;
In cities blockes, and in a lewd court, devills.
As in the first Chaos confusedly
Each elements qualities were in the'other three;   30
So pride, lust, covetize, being severall
To these three places, yet all are in all,
And mingled thus, their issue incestuous.
Falshood is denizon'd. Virtue is barbarous.
Let no man say there, Virtues flintie wall
Shall locke vice in mee, I'll do none, but know all.
Men are spunges, which to poure out, receive,
Who know false play, rather than lose, deceive.
For in best understandings, sinne beganne,
Angels sinn'd first, then Devills, and then man.   40
Onely perchance beasts sinne not; wretched wee
Are beasts in all, but white integritie.
I thinke if men, which in these places live
Durst looke for themselves, and themselves retrive,
They would like strangers greet themselves, seeing then
Utopian youth, growne old Italian.
   Be thou thine owne home, and in thy selfe dwell;
Inne any where, continuance maketh hell.
And seeing the snaile, which every where doth rome,
Carrying his owne house still, still is at home,   50
Follow (for he is easie pac'd) this snaile,
Bee thine owne Palace, or the world's thy gaole.
And in the worlds sea, do not like corke sleepe

Upon the waters face; nor in the deepe
Sinke like a lead without a line: but as
Fishes glide, leaving no print where they passe,
Nor making sound; so closely thy course goe,
Let men dispute, whether thou breathe, or no.
Onely'in this one thing, be no Galenist: To make
Courts hot ambitions wholesome, do not take   60
A dramme of Countries dulnesse; do not adde
Correctives, but as chymiques, purge the bad.
But, Sir, I advise not you, I rather doe
Say o'er those lessons, which I learn'd of you:
Whom, free from German schismes, and lightnesse
Of France, and faire Italies faithlesnesse,
Having from these suck'd all they had of worth,
And brought home that faith, which you carried forth,
I throughly love. But if my selfe, I'have wonne
To know my rules, I have, and you have   70

DONNE.

TO SIR HENRY WOOTTON   [c. 1597–8]

HERE'S no more newes, than vertue,'I may as well
Tell you *Cales,* or *Saint Michaels* tale for newes, as tell
That vice doth here habitually dwell.

Yet, as to'get stomachs, we walke up and downe,
And toyle to sweeten rest, so, may God frowne,
If, but to loth both, I haunt Court, or Towne.

For here no one is from the'extremitie
Of vice, by any other reason free,
But that the next to'him, still, is worse than hee.

In this worlds warfare, they whom rugged Fate,   10
(Gods Commissary,) doth so throughly hate,
As in'the Courts Squadron to marshall their state:

If they stand arm'd with seely honesty,
With wishing prayers, and neat integritie,
Like Indians'gainst Spanish hosts they bee.

Suspitious boldnesse to this place belongs,
And to'have as many eares as all have tongues;
Tender to know, tough to acknowledge wrongs.

Beleeve mee Sir, in my youths giddiest dayes,
When to be like the Court, was a playes praise,   20
Playes were not so like Courts, as Courts'are like playes.

Then let us at these mimicke antiques jeast,
Whose deepest projects, and egregious gests
Are but dull Moralls of a game at Chests.

But now'tis incongruity to smile,
Therefore I end; and bid farewell a while,
At Court; though *From Court,* were the better stile.

HENRICO WOTTONI IN HIBERNIA
BELLIGERANTI   [1599]

WENT you to conquer? and have so much lost
Yourself, that what in you was best and most,
Respective friendship, should so quickly dye?
In publique gaine my share'is not such that I
Would lose your love for Ireland: better cheap
I pardon death (who though he do not reap
Yet gleanes hee many of our frends away)
Than that your waking mind should bee a prey
To lethargies. Lett shott, and boggs, and skeines
With bodies deale, as fate bids and restreynes;   10
Ere sicknesses attack, yong death is best,
Who payes before his death doth scape arrest.
Lett not your soule (at first with graces fill'd,
And since, and thorough crooked lymbecks, still'd
In many schools and courts, which quicken it,)
It self unto the Irish negligence submit.
I aske not labored letters which should weare
Long papers out: nor letters which should feare
Dishonest carriage: or a seers art:
Nor such as from the brayne come, but the hart.   20

TO MR. T. W. [THOMAS WOODWARD?]   [c. 1598–1608]

ALL haile sweet Poët, more full of more strong fire,
  Than hath or shall enkindle any spirit,
  I lov'd what nature gave thee, but this merit
Of wit and Art I love not but admire;
Who have before or shall write after thee,
Their workes, though toughly laboured, will bee
    Like infancie or age to mans firme stay,
    Or earely and late twilights to mid-day.

Men say, and truly, that they better be
  Which be envyed than pittied: therefore I,   10
  Because I wish thee best, doe thee envie:
O wouldst thou, by like reason, pitty mee!
But care not for mee: I, that ever was
In Natures, and in Fortunes gifts, (alas,
    Before thy grace got in the Muses Schoole)
    A monster and a begger, am now a foole.

Oh how I grieve, that late borne modesty
  Hath got such root in easie waxen hearts,
  That men may not themselves, their owne good parts
Extoll, without suspect of surquedrie,   20
For, but thy selfe, no subject can be found
Worthy thy quill, nor any quill resound
    Thy worth but thine: how good it were to see
    A Poëm in thy praise, and writ by thee.

Now if this song be too'harsh for rime, yet, as
  The Painters bad god made a good devill,
  'Twill be good prose, although the verse be evill,
If thou forget the rime as thou dost passe.
Then write, that I may follow, and so bee
Thy debter, thy'eccho, thy foyle, thy zanee.   30
    I shall be thought, if mine like thine I shape,
    All the worlds Lyon, though I be thy Ape.

TO MR. T. W. [THOMAS WOODWARD]   [c. 1598–1608]

HASTE thee harsh verse, as fast as thy lame measure
  Will give thee leave, to him, my pain and pleasure.
I have given thee, and yet thou art too weake,
  Feete, and a reasoning soule and tongue to speake.
Plead for me, and so by thine and my labour
  I am thy Creator, thou my Saviour.
Tell him, all questions, which men have defended
  Both of the place and paines of hell, are ended;
And 'tis decreed our hell is but privation
  Of him, at least in this earths habitation: 10
And 'tis where I am, where in every street
  Infections follow, overtake, and meete:
Live I or die, by you my love is sent,
  And you'are my pawnes, or else my Testament.

TO MR. T. W. [THOMAS WOODWARD]   [c. 1598–1608]

PREGNANT again with th'old twins Hope, and Feare,
Oft have I askt for thee, both how and where
Thou wert, and what my hopes of letters were;

As in the streets sly beggers narrowly
Watch motions of the givers hand and eye,
And evermore conceive some hope thereby.

And now thy Almes is given, thy letter'is read,
The body risen againe, the which was dead,
And thy poore starveling bountifully fed.

After this banquet my Soule doth say grace,   10
And praise thee for'it, and zealously imbrace
Thy love; though I thinke thy love in this case
  To be as gluttons, which say 'midst their meat,
  They love that best of which they most do eat.

TO MR. T. W. [THOMAS WOODWARD]   [c. 1598–1608]

AT once, from hence, my lines and I depart,
I to my soft still walks, they to my Heart;
I to the Nurse, they to the child of Art;

Yet as a firme house, though the Carpenter
Perish, doth stand: As an Embassadour
Lyes safe, how e'r his king be in danger:

So, though I languish, prest with Melancholy,
My verse, the strict Map of my misery,
Shall live to see that, for whose want I dye.

Therefore I envie them, and doe repent,   **10**
That from unhappy mee, things happy'are sent;
Yet as a Picture, or bare Sacrament,
   Accept these lines, and if in them there be
   Merit of love, bestow that love on mee.

TO MR. R. W. [ROWLAND WOODWARD]   [c. 1597–1608]

ZEALOUSLY my Muse doth salute all thee,
Enquiring of that mistique trinitee
Whereof thou'and all to whom heavens do infuse
Like fyer, are made; thy body, mind, and Muse.
Dost thou recover sicknes, or prevent?
Or is thy Mind travail'd with discontent?
Or art thou parted from the world and mee,
In a good skorn of the worlds vanitee?
Or is thy devout Muse retyr'd to sing
Upon her tender Elegiaque string?   **10**
Our Minds part not, joyne then thy Muse with myne,
For myne is barren thus devorc'd from thyne.

TO MR. R. W. [ROWLAND WOODWARD]   [c. 1597–1608]

Muse not that by thy Mind thy body is led:
For by thy Mind, my Mind's distempered.
So thy Care lives long, for I bearing part
It eates not only thyne, but my swolne hart.
And when it gives us intermission
We take new harts for it to feede upon.
But as a Lay Mans Genius doth controule
Body and mind; the Muse beeing the Soules Soule
Of Poets, that methinks should ease our anguish,
Although our bodyes wither and minds languish.   **10**
Wright then, that my griefes which thine got may bee
Cur'd by thy charming soveraigne melodee.

TO MR. C. B. [CHRISTOPHER BROOKE]   [c. 1597–1608]

Thy friend, whom thy deserts to thee enchaine,
    Urg'd by this unexcusable occasion,
    Thee and the Saint of his affection
Leaving behinde, doth of both wants complaine;
And let the love I beare to both sustaine
    No blott nor maime by this division,
    Strong is this love which ties our hearts in one,
And strong that love pursu'd with amorous paine;
But though besides thy selfe I leave behind
    Heavens liberall, and earths thrice-fairer Sunne,   **10**
    Going to where sterne winter aye doth wonne,
Yet, loves hot fires, which martyr my sad minde,
    Doe send forth scalding sighes, which have the Art
    To melt all Ice, but that which walls her heart.

TO MR. E. G. [EDWARD GUILPIN?]   [c. 1597–1608]

Even as lame things thirst their perfection, so
The slimy rimes bred in our vale below,
Bearing with them much of my love and hart,

Fly unto that Parnassus, where thou art.
There thou oreseest London: Here I have beene,
By staying in London, too much overseene.
Now pleasures dearth our City doth posses,
Our Theaters are fill'd with emptines;
As lancke and thin is every street and way
As a woman deliver'd yesterday.   10
Nothing whereat to laugh my spleen espyes
But bearbaitings or Law exercise.
Therefore I'le leave it, and in the Country strive
Pleasure, now fled from London, to retrive.
Do thou so too: and fill not like a Bee
Thy thighs with hony, but as plenteously
As Russian Marchants, thy selfes whole vessel load,
And then at Winter retaile it here abroad.
Blesse us with Suffolks Sweets; and as it is
Thy garden, make thy hive and warehouse this.   20

TO MR. R. W. [ROWLAND WOODWARD]   [c. 1597–1608]

IF, as mine is, thy life a slumber be,
  Seeme, when thou read'st these lines, to dreame of me,
Never did Morpheus nor his brother weare
  Shapes soe like those Shapes, whom they would appeare,
As this my letter is like me, for it
  Hath my name, words, hand, feet, heart, minde and wit;
It is my deed of gift of mee to thee,
  It is my Will, my selfe the Legacie.
So thy retyrings I love, yea envie,
  Bred in thee by a wise melancholy,   10
That I rejoyce, that unto where thou art,
  Though I stay here, I can thus send my heart,
As kindly'as any enamored Patient
  His Picture to his absent Love hath sent.

All newes I thinke sooner reach thee than mee;
  Havens are Heavens, and Ships wing'd Angels be,
The which both Gospell, and sterne threatnings bring;
  Guyanaes harvest is nip'd in the spring,
I feare; And with us (me thinkes) Fate deales so
  As with the Jewes guide God did; he did show   20

Him the rich land, but bar'd his entry in:
   Oh, slownes is our punishment and sinne.
Perchance, these Spanish businesse being done,
   Which as the Earth betweene the Moone and Sun
Eclipse the light which Guyana would give,
   Our discontinued hopes we shall retrive:
But if (as all th'All must) hopes smoake away,
   Is not Almightie Vertue 'an India?
If men be worlds, there is in every one
   Some thing to answere in some proportion   30
All the worlds riches: And in good men, this,
   Vertue, our formes forme and our soules soule, is.

TO MR. R. W. [ROWLAND WOODWARD]   [c. 1597–1608]

KINDLY I envy thy songs perfection
   Built of all th'elements as our bodyes are:
   That Litle of earth that is in it, is a faire
Delicious garden where all sweetes are sowne.
In it is cherishing fyer which dryes in mee
   Griefe which did drowne me: and halfe quench'd by it
   Are satirique fyres which urg'd me to have writt
In skorne of all: for now I admyre thee.
   And as Ayre doth fullfill the hollownes
   Of rotten walls; so it myne emptines,   10
Where tost and mov'd it did beget this sound
Which as a lame Eccho of thyne doth rebound.
   Oh, I was dead; but since thy song new Life did give,
I recreated, even by thy creature, live.

TO MR. S. B. [SAMUEL BROOKE]   [c. 1597–1608]

O THOU which to search out the secret parts
   Of the India, or rather Paradise
   Of knowledge, hast with courage and advise
Lately launch'd into the vast Sea of Arts,
Disdaine not in thy constant travailing
   To doe as other Voyagers, and make
   Some turnes into lesse Creekes, and wisely take

Fresh water at the Heliconian spring;
I sing not, Siren like, to tempt; for I
 Am harsh; nor as those Scismatiques with you,   10
 Which draw all wits of good hope to their crew;
But seeing in you bright sparkes of Poetry,
 I, though I brought noe fuell, had desire
With these Articulate blasts to blow the fire.

TO MR. I. L.   [c. 1597–1608]

OF that short Roll of friends writ in my heart
 Which with thy name begins, since their depart,
Whether in the English Provinces they be,
 Or drinke of Po, Sequan, or Danubie,
There's none that sometimes greets us not, and yet
 Your Trent is Lethe', that past, us you forget.
You doe not duties of Societies,
 If from the'embrace of a lov'd wife you rise,
View your fat Beasts, strech'd Barnes, and labour'd fields,
 Eate, play, ryde, take all joyes which all day yeelds,   10
And then againe to your embracements goe:
 Some houres on us your frends, and some bestow
Upon your Muse, else both wee shall repent,
 I that my love, she that her guifts on you are spent.

TO MR. I. L.   [c. 1597–1608]

BLEST are your North parts, for all this long time
 My Sun is with you, cold and darke'is our Clime;
Heavens Sun, which staid so long from us this yeare,
 Staid in your North (I thinke) for she was there,
And hether by kinde nature drawne from thence,
 Here rages, chafes, and threatens pestilence;
Yet I, as long as shee from hence doth staie,
 Thinke this no South, no Sommer, nor no day.
With thee my kinde and unkinde heart is run,
 There sacrifice it to that beauteous Sun: 10
And since thou art in Paradise and need'st crave
 No joyes addition, helpe thy friend to save.

So may thy pastures with their flowery feasts,
  As suddenly as Lard, fat thy leane beasts;
So may thy woods oft poll'd, yet ever weare
  A greene, and when thee list, a golden haire;
So may all thy sheepe bring forth Twins; and so
  In chace and race may thy horse all out goe;
So may thy love and courage ne'r be cold;
  Thy Sonne ne'r Ward; Thy lov'd wife ne'r seem old; **20**
But maist thou wish great things, and them attaine,
  As thou telst her, and none but her, my paine.

TO MR. B. B.

Is not thy sacred hunger of science
  Yet satisfy'd? Is not thy braines rich hive
  Fulfil'd with hony which thou dost derive
From the Arts spirits and their Quintessence?
Then weane thy selfe at last, and thee withdraw
  From Cambridge thy old nurse, and, as the rest,
  Here toughly chew, and sturdily digest
Th'immense vast volumes of our common law;
And begin soone, lest my griefe grieve thee too,
  Which is, that that which I should have begun   **10**
  In my youthes morning, now late must be done;
And I as Giddy Travellers must doe,
  Which stray or sleepe all day, and having lost
  Light and strength, darke and tir'd must then ride post.

If thou unto thy Muse be marryed,
  Embrace her ever, ever multiply,
  Be far from me that strange Adulterie
To tempt thee and procure her widowhed.
My Muse, (for I had one,) because I'am cold,
  Divorc'd her selfe: the cause being in me,   **20**
  That I can take no new in Bigamye,
Not my will only but power doth withhold.
Hence comes it, that these Rymes which never had
  Mother, want matter, and they only have
  A little forme, the which their Father gave;
They are prophane, imperfect, oh, too bad
  To be counted Children of Poetry
  Except confirm'd and Bishoped by thee.

TO THE COUNTESSE OF HUNTINGDON

THAT unripe side of earth, that heavy clime
That gives us man up now, like *Adams* time
Before he ate; mans shape, that would yet bee
(Knew they not it, and fear'd beasts companie)
So naked at this day, as though man there
From Paradise so great a distance were,
As yet the newes could not arrived bee
Of *Adams* tasting the forbidden tree;
Depriv'd of that free state which they were in,
And wanting the reward, yet beare the sinne.   10
  But, as from extreme hights who downward looks,
Sees men at childrens shapes, Rivers at brookes,
And loseth younger formes; so, to your eye,
These (Madame) that without your distance lie,
Must either mist, or nothing seeme to be,
Who are at home but wits mere *Atomi*.
But, I who can behold them move, and stay,
Have found my selfe to you, just their midway;
And now must pitty them; for, as they doe
Seeme sick to me, just so must I to you.   20
Yet neither will I vexe your eyes to see
A sighing Ode, nor crosse-arm'd Elegie.
I come not to call pitty from your heart,
Like some white-liver'd dotard that would part
Else from his slipperie soule with a faint groane,
And faithfully, (without you smil'd) were gone.
I cannot feele the tempest of a frowne,
I may be rais'd by love, but not throwne down.
Though I can pittie those sigh twice a day,
I hate that thing whispers it selfe away.
Yet since all love is fever, who to trees
Doth talke, doth yet in loves cold ague freeze.
'Tis love, but, with such fatall weaknesse made,
That it destroyes it selfe with its owne shade.
Who first look'd sad, griev'd, pin'd, and shew'd his pain
Was he that first taught women, to disdaine.
  As all things were one nothing, dull and weake,
Untill this raw disordered heape did breake,

And severall desires led parts away,
Water declin'd with earth, the ayre did stay,   40
Fire rose, and each from other but unty'd,
Themselves unprison'd were and purify'd:
So was love, first in vast confusion hid,
An unripe willingnesse which nothing did,
A thirst, an Appetite which had no ease,
That found a want, but knew not what would please.
What pretty innocence in those dayes mov'd!
Man ignorantly walk'd by her he lov'd;
Both sigh'd and enterchang'd a speaking eye,
Both trembled and were sick, both knew not why.   50
That naturall fearefulnesse that struck man dumbe,
Might well (those times consider'd) man become,
As all discoverers whose first assay
Findes but the place, after, the nearest way:
So passion is to womans love, about,
Nay, farther off, than when we first set out.
It is not love that sueth, or doth contend;
Love either conquers, or but meets a friend.
Man's better part consists of purer fire,
And findes it selfe allow'd, ere it desire.   60
Love is wise here, keepes home, gives reason sway,
And journeys not till it finde summer-way.
A weather-beaten Lover but once knowne,
Is sport for every girle to practise on.
Who strives through womans scornes, women to know,
Is lost, and seekes his shadow to outgoe;
It must be sicknesse, after one disdaine,
Though he be call'd aloud, to looke againe.
Let others sigh, and grieve; one cunning sleight
Shall freeze my Love to Christall in a night.   70
I can love first, and (if I winne) love still;
And cannot be remov'd, unlesse she will.
It is her fault if I unsure remaine,
Shee onely can untie, and binde againe.
The honesties of love with ease I doe,
But am no porter for a tedious woo.
    But (madame) I now thinke on you; and here
Where we are at our hights, you but appeare,
We are but clouds you rise from, our noone-ray
But a foule shadow, not your breake of day.   80
You are at first hand all that's faire and right,

And others good reflects but backe your light.
You are a perfectnesse, so curious hit,
That youngest flatteries doe scandall it.
For, what is more doth what you are restraine,
And though beyond, is downe the hill againe.
We'have no next way to you, we crosse to it:
You are the straight line, thing prais'd, attribute;
Each good in you's a light; so many a shade
You make, and in them are your motions made.   90
These are your pictures to the life. From farre
We see you move, and here your *Zani's* are:
So that no fountaine good there is, doth grow
In you, but our dimme actions faintly shew.

  Then finde I, if mans noblest part be love,
Your purest luster must that shadow move.
The soule with body, is a heaven combin'd
With earth, and for mans ease, but nearer joyn'd.
Where thoughts the starres of soule we understand,
We guesse not their large natures, but command.   100
And love in you, that bountie is of light,
That gives to all, and yet hath infinite.
Whose heat doth force us thither to intend,
But soule we finde too earthly to ascend,
'Till slow accesse hath made it wholly pure,
Able immortall clearnesse to endure.
Who dare aspire this journey with a staine,
Hath waight will force him headlong backe againe.
No more can impure man retaine and move
In that pure region of a worthy love,   110
Than earthly substance can unforc'd aspire,
And leave his nature to converse with fire:
Such may have eye, and hand; may sigh, may speak;
But like swoln bubles, when they are high'st they break.

  Though far removed Northerne fleets scarce finde
The Sunnes comfort; others thinke him too kinde.
There is an equall distance from her eye,
Men perish too farre off, and burne too nigh.
But as ayre takes the Sunne-beames equall bright
From the first Rayes, to his last opposite: 120
So able men, blest with a vertuous Love,
Remote or neare, or howsoe'r they move;
Their vertue breakes all clouds that might annoy,
There is no Emptinesse, but all is Joy.

He much profanes whom violent heats do move
To stile his wandring rage of passion, *Love*.
Love that imparts in every thing delight,
Is fain'd, which only tempts mans appetite.
Why love among the vertues is not knowne
Is, that love is them all contract in one.   **130**

TO SIR H[ENRY] W[OTTON] AT HIS GOING AMBASSADOR TO VENICE   [1604]

AFTER those reverend papers, whose soule is
    Our good and great Kings lov'd hand and fear'd name,
By which to you he derives much of his,
    And (how he may) makes you almost the same,

A Taper of his Torch, a copie writ
    From his Originall, and a faire beame
Of the same warme, and dazeling Sun, though it
    Must in another Sphere his vertue streame:

After those learned papers which your hand
    Hath stor'd with notes of use and pleasure too,   **10**
From which rich treasury you may command
    Fit matter whether you will write or doe:

After those loving papers, where friends send
    With glad griefe, to your Sea-ward steps, farewel,
Which thicken on you now, as prayers ascend
    To heaven in troupes at'a good mans passing bell:

Admit this honest paper, and allow
    It such an audience as your selfe would aske;
What you must say at Venice this meanes now,
    And hath for nature, what you have for taske: **20**

To sweare much love, not to be chang'd before
    Honour alone will to your fortune fit;
Nor shall I then honour your fortune, more
    Than I have done your honour wanting it.

But'tis an easier load (though both oppresse)
  To want, than governe greatnesse, for wee are
In that, our owne and onely businesse,
  In this, wee must for others vices care;

'Tis therefore well your spirits now are plac'd
  In their last Furnace, in activity;   **30**
Which fits them (Schooles and Courts and Warres o'rpast)
  To touch and test in any best degree.

For mee, (if there be such a thing as I)
  Fortune (if there be such a thing as shee)
Spies that I beare so well her tyranny,
  That she thinks nothing else so fit for mee;

But though she part us, to heare my oft prayers
  For your increase, God is as neere mee here;
And to send you what I shall begge, his staires
  In length and ease are alike every where.   **40**

TO MRS. M. H. [MAGDALEN HERBERT]   [c. 1604]

MAD paper stay, and grudge not here to burne
  With all those sonnes whom my braine did create,
At least lye hid with mee, till thou returne
  To rags againe, which is thy native state.

What though thou have enough unworthinesse
  To come unto great place as others doe,
That's much; emboldens, pulls, thrusts I confesse,
  But'tis not all; Thou should'st be wicked too.

And, that thou canst not learne, or not of mee;
  Yet thou wilt goe? Goe, since thou goest to her   **10**
Who lacks but faults to be a Prince, for shee,
  Truth, whom they dare not pardon, dares preferre.

But when thou com'st to that perplexing eye
  Which equally claimes *love* and *reverence,*
Thou wilt not long dispute it, thou wilt die;
  And having little now, have then no sense.

Yet when her warme redeeming hand, which is
    A miracle; and made such to worke more,
Doth touch thee (saples leafe) thou grow'st by this
    Her creature; glorify'd more than before.   **20**

Then as a mother which delights to heare
    Her early child mis-speake halfe uttered words,
Or, because majesty doth never feare
    Ill or bold speech, she Audience affords.

And then, cold speechlesse wretch, thou diest againe,
    And wisely; what discourse is left for thee?
For, speech of ill, and her, thou most abstaine,
    And is there any good which is not shee?

Yet maist thou praise her servants, though not her,
    And wit, and vertue,'and honour her attend,   **30**
And since they'are but her cloathes, thou shalt not erre,
    If thou her shape and beauty'and grace commend.

Who knowes thy destiny? when thou hast done,
    Perchance her Cabinet may harbour thee,
Whither all noble ambitious wits doe runne,
    A nest almost as full of Good as shee.

When thou art there, if any, whom wee know,
    Were sav'd before, and did that heaven partake,
When she revolves his papers, marke what show
    Of favour, she alone, to them doth make.   **40**

Marke, if to get them, she o'r skip the rest,
    Marke, if she read them twice, or kisse the name;
Marke, if she doe the same that they protest,
    Marke, if she marke whether her woman came.

Marke, if slight things be'objected, and o'r blowne,
    Marke, if her oathes against him be not still
Reserv'd, and that shee grieves she's not her owne,
    And chides the doctrine that denies Freewill.

I bid thee not doe this to be my spie;
    Nor to make my selfe her familiar;   **50**
But so much I doe love her choyce, that I
    Would faine love him that shall be lov'd of her.

TO SIR HENRY GOODYERE   [c. 1605–8]

WHO makes the Past, a patterne for next yeare,
  Turnes no new leafe, but still the same things reads,
Seene things, he sees againe, heard things doth heare,
  And makes his life, but like a paire of beads.

A Palace, when'tis that, which it should be,
  Leaves growing, and stands such, or else decayes:
But hee which dwels there, is not so; for hee
  Strives to urge upward, and his fortune raise;

So had your body'her morning, hath her noone,
  And shall not better; her next change is night: 10
But her faire larger guest, to'whom Sun and Moone
  Are sparkes, and short liv'd, claimes another right.

The noble Soule by age growes lustier,
  Her appetite, and her digestion mend,
Wee must not sterve, nor hope to pamper her
  With womens milke, and pappe unto the end.

Provide you manlyer dyet; you have seene
  All libraries, which are Schools, Camps, and Courts:
But aske your Garners if you have not beene
  In harvests, too indulgent to your sports.   20

Would you redeeme it? then your selfe transplant
  A while from hence. Perchance outlandish ground
Beares no more wit, than ours, but yet more scant
  Are those diversions there, which here abound.

To be a stranger hath that benefit,
  Wee can beginnings, but not habits choke.
Goe; whither? Hence; you get, if you forget;
  New faults, till they prescribe in us, are smoake.

Our Soule, whose country'is heaven, and God her father,
  Into this world, corruptions sinke, is sent,   30
Yet, so much in her travaile she doth gather,
  That she returnes home, wiser than she went;

It payes you well, if it teach you to spare,
    And make you,'asham'd, to make your hawks praise, yours,
Which when herselfe she lessens in the aire,
    You then first say, that high enough she toures.

However, keepe the lively tast you hold
    Of God, love him as now, but feare him more,
And in your afternoones thinke what you told
    And promis'd him, at morning prayer before.   **40**

Let falshood like a discord anger you,
    Else be not froward. But why doe I touch
Things, of which none is in your practise new,
    And Tables, or fruit-trenchers teach as much;

But thus I make you keepe your promise Sir,
    Riding I had you, though you still staid there,
And in these thoughts, although you never stirre,
    You came with mee to Micham, and are here.

TO MR. ROWLAND WOODWARD

LIKE one who'in her third widdowhood doth professe
Her selfe a Nunne, tyed to retirednesse,
So'affects my muse now, a chast fallownesse;

Since shee to few, yet to too many'hath showne
How love-song weeds, and Satyrique thornes are growne
Where seeds of better Arts, were early sown.

Though to use, and love Poëtrie, to mee,
Betroth'd to no'one Art, be no'adulterie;
Omissions of good, ill, as ill deeds bee.

For though to us it seeme, 'and be light and thinne,   **10**
Yet in those faithfull scales, where God throwes in
Mens workes, vanity weighs as much as sinne.

If our Soules have stain'd their first white, yet wee
May cloth them with faith, and deare honestie,
Which God Imputes, as native puritie.

There is no Vertue, but Religion:
Wise, valiant, sober, just, are names, which none
Want, which want not Vice-covering discretion.

Seeke wee then our selves in our selves; for as
Men force the Sunne with much more force to passe,   20
By gathering his beames with a christall glasse;

So wee, If wee into our selves will turne,
Blowing our sparkes of vertue, may outburne
The straw, which doth about our hearts sojourne.

You know, Physitians, when they would infuse
Into any'oyle, the Soules of Simples, use
Places, where they may lie still warme, to chuse.

So workes retirednesse in us; To rome
Giddily, and be every where, but at home,
Such freedome doth a banishment become.   30

Wee are but farmers of our selves, yet may,
If we can stocke our selves, and thrive, uplay
Much, much deare treasure for the great rent day.

Manure thy selfe then, to thy selfe be'approv'd,
And with vaine outward things be no more mov'd,
But to know, that I love thee'and would be lov'd.

TO THE COUNTESSE OF BEDFORD   [c. 1607–8]

MADAME,
REASON is our Soules left hand, Faith her right,
By these wee reach divinity, that's you;
Their loves, who have the blessings of your light,
Grew from their reason, mine from faire faith grew.

But as, although a squint lefthandednesse
Be'ungracious, yet we cannot want that hand,
So would I, not to encrease, but to expresse
My faith, as I beleeve, so understand.

Therefore I study you first in your Saints,
Those friends, whom your election glorifies,   10
Then in your deeds, accesses, and restraints,
And what you reade, and what your selfe devize.

But soone, the reasons why you'are lov'd by all,
Grow infinite, and so passe reasons reach,
Then backe againe to'implicite faith I fall,
And rest on what the Catholique voice doth teach;

That you are good: and not one Heretique
Denies it: if he did, yet you are so.
For, rockes, which high top'd and deep rooted sticke,
Waves wash, not undermine, nor overthrow.   20

In every thing there naturally growes
A *Balsamum* to keepe it fresh, and new,
If'twere not injur'd by extrinsique blowes:
Your birth and beauty are this Balme in you.

But you of learning and religion,
And vertue,'and such ingredients, have made
A methridate, whose operation
Keepes off, or cures what can be done or said.

Yet, this is not your physicke, but your food,
A dyet fit for you; for you are here   30
The first good Angell, since the worlds frame stood,
That ever did in womans shape appeare.

Since you are then Gods masterpeece, and so
His Factor for our loves; do as you doe,
Make your returne home gracious; and bestow
This life on that; so make one life of two.
   For so God helpe mee,'I would not misse you there
   For all the good which you can do me here.

TO THE COUNTESSE OF BEDFORD   [c. 1607–8]

MADAME,
You have refin'd mee, and to worthyest things
(Vertue, Art, Beauty, Fortune,) now I see

Rarenesse, or use, not nature value brings;
And such, as they are circumstanc'd, they bee.
  Two ills can ne're perplexe us, sinne to'excuse;
  But of two good things, we may leave and chuse.

Therefore at Court, which is not vertues clime,
(Where a transcendent height, (as, lownesse mee)
Makes her not be, or not show) all my rime
Your vertues challenge, which there rarest bee;   10
  For, as darke texts need notes: there some must bee
  To usher vertue, and say, *This is shee.*

So in the country'is beauty; to this place
You are the season (Madame) you the day,
'Tis but a grave of spices, till your face
Exhale them, and a thick close bud display.
  Widow'd and reclus'd else, her sweets she'enshrines;
  As China, when the Sunne at Brasill dines.

Out from your chariot, morning breaks at night,
And falsifies both computations so;   20
Since a new world doth rise here from your light,
We your new creatures, by new recknings goe.
  This showes that you from nature lothly stray,
  That suffer not an artificiall day.

In this you'have made the Court the Antipodes,
And will'd your Delegate, the vulgar Sunne,
To doe profane autumnall offices,
Whilst here to you, wee sacrificers runne;
  And whether Priests, or Organs, you wee'obey,
  We sound your influence, and your Dictates say.   30

Yet to that Deity which dwels in you,
Your vertuous Soule, I now not sacrifice;
These are *Petitions,* and not *Hymnes;* they sue
But that I may survay the edifice.
  In all Religions as much care hath bin
  Of Temples frames, and beauty,'as Rites within.

As all which goe to Rome, doe not thereby
Esteeme religions, and hold fast the best,
But serve discourse, and curiosity,

With that which doth religion but invest,   **40**
   And shunne th'entangling laborinths of Schooles,
   And make it wit, to thinke the wiser fooles:

So in this pilgrimage I would behold
You as you'are vertues temple, not as shee,
What walls of tender christall her enfold,
What eyes, hands, bosome, her pure Altars bee;
   And after this survay, oppose to all
   Bablers of Chappels, you th'Escuriall.

Yet not as consecrate, but merely'as faire,
On these I cast a lay and country eye.   **50**
Of past and future stories, which are rare
I finde you all record, and prophecie.
   Purge but the booke of Fate, that it admit
   No sad nor guilty legends, you are it.

If good and lovely were not one, of both
You were the transcript, and originall,
The Elements, the Parent, and the Growth,
And every peece of you, is both their All:
   So'intire are all your deeds, and you, that you
   Must do the same thinge still; you cannot two.   **60**

But these (as nice thinne Schoole divinity
Serves heresie to furder or represse)
Tast of Poëtique rage, or flattery,
And need not, where all hearts one truth professe;
   Oft from new proofes, and new phrase, new doubts grow,
   As strange attire aliens the men wee know.

Leaving then busie praise, and all appeale
To higher Courts, senses decree is true,
The Mine, the Magazine, the Commonweale,
The story of beauty,'in Twicknam is, and you.   **70**
   Who hath seene one, would both; As, who had bin
   In Paradise, would seeke the Cherubin.

TO SIR EDWARD HERBERT AT JULYERS   [1610]

MAN is a lumpe, where all beasts kneaded bee,
    Wisdome makes him an Arke where all agree;
The foole, in whom these beasts do live at jarre,
    Is sport to others, and a Theater;
Nor scapes hee so, but is himselfe their prey,
    All which was man in him, is eate away,
And now his beasts on one another feed,
    Yet couple'in anger, and new monsters breed.
How happy'is hee, which hath due place assign'd
    To'his beasts, and disaforested his minde!   10
Empail'd himselfe to keepe them out, not in;
    Can sow, and dares trust corne, where they have bin;
Can use his horse, goate, wolfe, and every beast,
    And is not Asse himselfe to all the rest.
Else, man not onely is the heard of swine,
    But he's those devills too, which did incline
Them to a headlong rage, and made them worse:
    For man can adde weight to heavens heaviest curse.
As Soules (they say) by our first touch, take in
    The poysonous tincture of Originall sinne,   20
So, to the punishments which God doth fling,
    Our apprehension contributes the sting.
To us, as to his chickins, he doth cast
    Hemlocke, and wee as men, his hemlocke taste;
We do infuse to what he meant for meat,
    Corrosivenesse, or intense cold or heat.
For, God no such specifique poyson hath
    As kills we know not how; his fiercest wrath
Hath no antipathy, but may be good
    At least for physicke, if not for our food.   30
Thus man, that might be'his pleasure, is his rod,
    And is his devill, that might be his God.
Since then our businesse is, to rectifie
    Nature, to what she was, wee'are led awry
By them, who man to us in little show;
    Greater than due, no forme we can bestow
On him; for Man into himselfe can draw
    All; All his faith can swallow,'or reason chaw.

All that is fill'd, and all that which doth fill,
  All the round world, to man is but a pill,   **40**
In all it workes not, but it is in all
  Poysonous, or purgative, or cordiall,
For, knowledge kindles Calentures in some,
  And is to others icy *Opium*.
As brave as true, is that profession then
  Which you doe use to make; that you know man.
This makes it credible; you have dwelt upon
  All worthy bookes, and now are such an one.
Actions are authors, and of those in you
  Your friends finde every day a mart of new.   **50**

TO THE COUNTESSE OF BEDFORD [AFTER 1609]

T'HAVE written then, when you writ, seem'd to mee
  Worst of spirituall vices, Simony,
And not t'have written then, seemes little lesse
  Than worst of civill vices, thanklessenesse.
In this, my debt I seem'd loath to confesse,
  In that, I seem'd to shunne beholdingnesse.
But 'tis not soe; *nothings,* as I am, may
  Pay all they have, and yet have all to pay.
Such borrow in their payments, and owe more
  By having leave to write so, than before.   **10**
Yet since rich mines in barren grounds are showne,
  May not I yeeld (not gold) but coale or stone?
Temples were not demolish'd, though prophane:
  Here *Peter Joves*, there *Paul* hath *Dian's* Fane.
So whether my hymnes you admit or chuse,
  In me you'have hallowed a Pagan Muse,
And denizend a stranger, who mistaught
  By blamers of the times they mard, hath sought
Vertues in corners, which now bravely doe
  Shine in the worlds best part, or all It; You.   **20**
I have beene told, that vertue'in Courtiers hearts
  Suffers an Ostracisme, and departs.
Profit, ease, fitnesse, plenty, bid it goe,
  But whither, only knowing you, I know;
Your (or you) vertue two vast uses serves,
  It ransomes one sex, and one Court preserves.

There's nothing but your worth, which being true,
  Is knowne to any other, not to you:
And you can never know it; To admit
  No knowledge of your worth, is some of it.   30
But since to you, your praises discords bee,
  Stoop, others ills to meditate with mee.
Oh! to confesse wee know not what we should,
  Is halfe excuse; wee know not what we would:
Lightnesse depresseth us, emptinesse fills,
  We sweat and faint, yet still goe downe the hills.
As new Philosophy arrests the Sunne,
  And bids the passive earth about it runne,
So wee have dull'd our minde, it hath no ends;
  Onely the bodie's busie, and pretends;   40
As dead low earth ecclipses and controules
  The quick high Moone: so doth the body, Soules.
In none but us, are such mixt engines found,
  As hands of double office: For, the ground
We till with them; and them to heav'n wee raise;
  Who prayer-lesse labours, or, without this, prayes,
Doth but one halfe, that's none; He which said, *Plough
  And looke not back*, to looke up doth allow.
Good seed degenerates, and oft obeyes
  The soyles disease, and into cockle strayes;   50
Let the minds thoughts be but transplanted so,
  Into the body,'and bastardly they grow.
What hate could hurt our bodies like our love?
  Wee (but no forraine tyrants could) remove
These not ingrav'd, but inborne dignities,
  Caskets of soules; Temples, and Palaces:
For, bodies shall from death redeemed bee,
  Soules but preserv'd, not naturally free.
As men to'our prisons, new soules to us are sent,
  Which learne vice there, and come in innocent.   60
First seeds of every creature are in us,
  What ere the world hath bad, or pretious,
Mans body can produce, hence hath it beene
  That stones, wormes, frogges, and snakes in man are seene:
But who ere saw, though nature can worke soe,
  That pearle, or gold, or corne in man did grow?
We'have added to the world Virginia,'and sent
  Two new starres lately to the firmament;
Why grudge wee us (not heaven) the dignity

T'increase with ours, those faire soules company.   70
But I must end this letter, though it doe
   Stand on two truths, neither is true to you.
Vertue hath some perversenesse; For she will
   Neither beleeve her good, nor others ill.
Even in you, vertues best paradise,
   Vertue hath some, but wise degrees of vice.
Too many vertues, or too much of one
   Begets in you unjust suspition;
And ignorance of vice, makes vertuelesse,
   Quenching compassion of our wretchednesse.   80
But these are riddles; Some aspersion
   Of vice becomes well some complexion.
Statesmen purge vice with vice, and may corrode
   The bad with bad, a spider with a toad:
For so, ill thralls not them, but they tame ill
   And make her do much good against her will,
But in your Commonwealth, or world in you,
   Vice hath no office, or good worke to doe.
Take then no vitious purge, but be content
   With cordiall vertue, your knowne nourishment.   90

TO THE COUNTESSE OF BEDFORD

ON NEW-YEARES DAY

THIS twilight of two yeares, not past nor next,
   Some embleme is of mee, or I of this,
Who Meteor-like, of stuffe and forme perplext,
   Whose *what*, and *where*, in disputation is,
   If I should call mee *any thing*, should misse.

I summe the yeares, and mee, and finde mee not
   Debtor to th'old, nor Creditor to th'new,
That cannot say, My thankes I have forgot,
   Nor trust I this with hopes, and yet scarce true
   This bravery is, since these times shew'd mee you.   10

In recompence I would show future times
   What you were, and teach them to'urge towards such.
Verse embalmes vertue;'and Tombs, or Thrones of rimes,

Preserve fraile transitory fame, as much
As spice doth bodies from corrupt aires touch.

Mine are short-liv'd; the tincture of your name
    Creates in them, but dissipates as fast.
New spirits: for, strong agents with the same
    Force that doth warme and cherish, us doe wast;
    Kept hot with strong extracts, no bodies last: **20**

So, my verse built of your just praise, might want
    Reason and likelihood, the firmest Base,
And made of miracle, now faith is scant,
    Will vanish soone, and so possesse no place,
    And you, and it, too much grace might disgrace.

When all (as truth commands assent) confesse
    All truth of you, yet they will doubt how I,
One corne of one low anthills dust, and lesse,
    Should name, know, or expresse a thing so high,
    And not an inch, measure infinity.   **30**

I cannot tell them, nor my selfe, nor you,
    But leave, lest truth b'endanger'd by my praise,
And turne to God, who knowes I thinke this true,
    And useth oft, when such a heart mis-sayes,
    To make it good, for, such a praiser prayes.

Hee will best teach you, how you should lay out
    His stock of *beauty, learning, favour, blood;*
He will perplex security with doubt,
    And cleare those doubts; hide from you,'and shew you good,
    And so increase your appetite and food;   **40**

Hee will teach you, that good and bad have not
    One latitude in cloysters, and in Court;
Indifferent there the greatest space hath got;
    Some pitty'is not good there, some vaine disport,
    On this side sinne, with that place may comport.

Yet he, as hee bounds seas, will fixe your houres,
    Which pleasure, and delight may not ingresse,
And though what none else lost, be truliest yours,

Hee will make you, what you did not, possesse,
By using others, not vice, but weakenesse.   50

He will make you speake truths, and credibly,
    And make you doubt, that others doe not so:
Hee will provide you keyes, and locks, to spie,
    And scape spies, to good ends, and hee will show
    What you may not acknowledge, what not know.

For your owne conscience, he gives innocence,
    But for your fame, a discreet warinesse,
And though to scape, than to revenge offence
    Be better, he showes both, and to represse
    Joy, when your state swells, *sadnesse* when'tis lesse.   60

From need of teares he will defend your soule,
    Or make a rebaptizing of one teare;
Hee cannot, (that's, he will not) dis-inroule
    Your name; and when with active joy we heare
    This private Ghospell, then'tis our New Yeare.

TO THE LADY BEDFORD   [c. 1609]

You that are she and you, that's double shee,
    In her dead face, halfe of your selfe shall see;
Shee was the other part, for so they doe
    Which build them friendships, become one of two;
So two, that but themselves no third can fit,
    Which were to be so, when they were not yet;
Twinnes, though their birth *Cusco*, and *Musco* take,
    As divers starres one Constellation make,
Pair'd like two eyes, have equall motion, so
    Both but one meanes to see, one way to goe.   10
Had you dy'd first, a carcasse shee had beene;
    And wee your rich Tombe in her face had seene;
She like the Soule is gone, and you here stay,
    Not a live friend; but th'other halfe of clay;
And since you act that part, As men say, here
    Lies such a Prince, when but one part is there,
And do all honour and devotion due
    Unto the whole, so wee all reverence you;

For, such a friendship who would not adore
  In you, who are all what both were before,   20
Not all, as if some perished by this,
  But so, as all in you contracted is.
As of this all, though many parts decay,
  The pure which elemented them shall stay;
And though diffus'd, and spread in infinite,
  Shall recollect, and in one All unite:
So madame, as her Soule to heaven is fled,
  Her flesh rests in the earth, as in the bed;
Her vertues do, as to their proper spheare,
  Returne to dwell with you, of whom they were;   30
As perfect motions are all circular,
  So they to you, their sea, whence lesse streames are.
Shee was all spices, you all metalls; so
  In you two wee did both rich Indies know;
And as no fire, nor rust can spend or waste
  One dramme of gold, but what was first shall last,
Though it bee forc'd in water, earth, salt, aire,
  Expans'd in infinite, none will impaire;
So, to your selfe you may additions take,
  But nothing can you lesse, or changed make.   40
Seeke not in seeking new, to seeme to doubt,
  That you can match her, or not be without;
But let some faithfull booke in her roome be,
  Yet but of *Judith* no such booke as shee.

TO THE COUNTESSE OF BEDFORD   [c. 1611–12]

HONOUR is so sublime perfection,
And so refinde; that when God was alone
And creaturelesse at first, himselfe had none;

But as of the elements, these which wee tread,
Produce all things with which wee'are joy'd or fed,
And, those are barren both above our head:

So from low persons doth all honour flow;
Kings, whom they would have honoured, to us show,
And but *direct* our honour, not *bestow*.

For when from herbs the pure part must be wonne   10
From grosse, by Stilling, this is better done
By despis'd dung, than by the fire or Sunne.

Care not then, Madame,'how low your praysers lye;
In labourers balads oft more piety
God findes, than in *Te Deums* melodie.

And, ordinance rais'd on Towers, so many mile
Send not their voice, nor last so long a while
As fires from th'earths low vaults in *Sicil* Isle.

Should I say I liv'd darker than were true,
Your radiation can all clouds subdue;   20
But one,'tis best light to contemplate you.

You, for whose body God made better clay,
Or tooke Soules stuffe such as shall late decay,
Or such as needs small change at the last day.

This, as an Amber drop enwraps a Bee,
Covering discovers your quicke Soule; that we
May in your through-shine front your hearts thoughts see.

You teach (though wee learne not) a thing unknowne
To our late times, the use of specular stone,
Through which all things within without were shown.   30

Of such were Temples; so and of such you are;
Beeing and *seeming* is your equall care,
And *vertues* whole *summe* is but *know* and *dare*.

But as our Soules of growth and Soules of sense
Have birthright of our reasons Soule, yet hence
They fly not from that, nor seeke presidence:

Natures first lesson, so, discretion,
Must not grudge zeale a place, nor yet keepe none,
Not banish it selfe, nor religion.

Discretion is a wisemans Soule, and so   40
Religion is a Christians, and you know
How these are one; her *yea,* is not her *no.*

Nor may we hope to sodder still and knit
These two, and dare to breake them; nor must wit
Be colleague to religion, but be it.

In those poor types of God (round circles) so
Religious tipes, the peecelesse centers flow,
And are in all the lines which all waves goe.

If either ever wrought in you alone
Or principally, then religion   **50**
Wrought your ends, and your wayes discretion.

Goe thither stil, goe the same way you went,
Who so would change, do covet or repent;
Neither can reach you, great and innocent.

TO THE COUNTESSE OF BEDFORD   [c. 1611–12]

BEGUN IN FRANCE BUT NEVER PERFECTED

THOUGH I be *dead*, and buried, yet I have
    (Living in you,) Court enough in my grave,
As oft as there I thinke my selfe to bee,
    So many resurrections waken mee.
That thankfullnesse your favours have begot
    In mee, embalmes mee, that I doe not rot.
This season as 'tis Easter, as 'tis spring,
    Must both to growth and to confession bring
My thoughts dispos'd unto your influence; so,
    These verses bud, so these confessions grow.   **10**
First I confesse I have to others lent
    Your stock, and over prodigally spent
Your treasure, for since I had never knowne
    Vertue or beautie, but as they are growne
In you, I should not thinke or say they shine,
    (So as I have) in any other Mine.
Next I confesse this my confession,
    For, 'tis some fault thus much to touch upon
Your praise to you, where half rights seeme too much,
    And make your minds sincere complexion blush.   **20**
Next I confesse my'impenitence, for I
    Can scarce repent my first fault, since thereby

Remote low Spirits, which shall ne'r read you,
   May in lesse lessons finde enough to doe,
By studying copies, not Originals,
       Desunt cætera.

A LETTER TO THE LADY CAREY AND
MRS. ESSEX RICHE, FROM AMYENS
[c. 1611–12]

MADAME,
HERE where by All All Saints invoked are,
'Twere too much schisme to be singular,
And 'gainst a practise generall to warre.

Yet turning to Saincts, should my'humility
To other Sainct than you directed bee,
That were to make my schisme, heresie.

Nor would I be a Convertite so cold,
As not to tell it; If this be too bold,
Pardons are in this market cheaply sold.

Where, because Faith is in too low degree,   **10**
I thought it some Apostleship in mee
To speake things which by faith alone I see.

That is, of you, who are a firmament
Of virtues, where no one is growne, or spent,
They'are your materials, not your ornament.

Others whom wee call vertuous, are not so
In their whole substance, but, their vertues grow
But in their humours, and at seasons show.

For when through tastlesse flat humilitie
In dow bak'd men some harmlessenes we see,   **20**
'Tis but his *flegme* that's *Vertuous,* and not Hee·

Soe is the Blood sometimes; who ever ran
To danger unimportun'd, he was then
No better than a *sanguine* Vertuous man.

So cloysterall men, who, in pretence of feare
All contributions to this life forbeare,
Have Vertue in *Melancholy,* and only there.

Spirituall *Cholerique* Crytiques, which in all
Religions find faults, and forgive no fall,
Have, through this zeale, Vertue but in their Gall.   30

We'are thus but parcel guilt; to Gold we'are growne
When Vertue is our Soules complexion;
Who knowes his Vertues name or place, hath none.

Vertue'is but anguish, when 'tis severall,
By occasion wak'd, and circumstantiall.
True vertue is Soule, Alwaies in all deeds *All.*

This Vertue thinking to give dignitie
To your soule, found there no infirmitie,
For, your soule was as good Vertue, as shee;

Shee therefore wrought upon that part of you   40
Which is scarce lesse than soule, as she could do,
And so hath made your beauty, Vertue too.

Hence comes it, that your Beauty wounds not hearts,
As Others, with prophane and sensuall Darts,
But as an influence, vertuous thoughts imparts.

But if such friends by the honor of your sight
Grow capable of this so great a light,
As to partake your vertues, and their might,

What must I thinke that influence must doe,
Where it findes sympathie and matter too,   50
Vertue, and beauty of the same stuffe, as you?

Which is, your noble worthie sister, shee
Of whom, if what in this my Extasie
And revelation of you both I see,

I should write here, as in short Galleries
The Master at the end large glasses ties,
So to present the roome twice to our eyes,

So I should give this letter length, and say
That which I said of you; there is no way
From either, but by the other, not to stray.   **60**

May therefore this be enough to testifie
My true devotion, free from flattery;
He that beleeves himselfe, doth never lie.

TO THE COUNTESSE OF HUNTINGDON   [c. 1614–15]

MADAME,

MAN to Gods image, *Eve*, to mans was made,
   Nor finde wee that God breath'd a soule in her,
Canons will not Church functions you invade,
   Nor lawes to civill office you preferre.

Who vagrant transitory Comets sees,
   Wonders, because they'are rare; But a new starre
Whose motion with the firmament agrees,
   Is miracle; for, there no new things are;

In woman so perchance milde innocence
   A seldome comet is, but active good   **10**
A miracle, which reason scapes, and sense;
   For, Art and Nature this in them withstood.

As such a starre, the *Magi* led to view
   The manger-cradled infant, God below:
By vertues beames by fame deriv'd from you,
   May apt soules, and the worst may, vertue know.

If the worlds age, and death be argued well
   By the Sunnes fal, which now towards earth doth bend,
Then we might feare that vertue, since she fell
   So low as woman, should be neare her end.   **20**

But she's not stoop'd, but rais'd; exil'd by men
   She fled to heaven, that's heavenly things, that's you;
She was in all men, thinly scatter'd then,
   But now amass'd, contracted in a few.

She guilded us: But you are gold, and Shee;
  Us she inform'd, but transubstantiates you;
Soft dispositions which diectile bee,
  Elixarlike, she makes not cleane, but new.

Though you a wifes and mothers name retaine,
  'Tis not a woman, for all are not soe,   30
But vertue having made you vertue,'is faine
  T'adhere in these names, her and you to show,

Else, being alike pure, wee should neither see;
  As, water being into ayre rarify'd,
Neither appeare, till in one cloud they bee,
  So, for our sakes you do low names abide;

Taught by great constellations, which being fram'd,
  Of the most starres, take low names, *Crab,* and *Bull,*
When single planets by the *Gods* are nam'd,
  You covet not great names, of great things full.   40

So you, as woman, one doth comprehend,
  And in the vaile of kindred others see;
To some ye are reveal'd, as in a friend,
  And as a vertuous Prince farre off, to mee.

To whom, because from you all vertues flow,
  And 'tis not none, to dare contemplate you,
I, which doe so, as your true subject owe
  Some tribute for that, so these lines are due.

If you can thinke these flatteries, they are,
  For then your judgement is below my praise,   50
If they were so, oft, flatteries worke as farre,
  As Counsels, and as farre th'endeavour raise.

So my ill reaching you might there grow good,
  But I remaine a poyson'd fountaine still;
But not your beauty, vertue, knowledge, blood
  Are more above all flattery, than my will.

And if I flatter any,'tis not you
  But my owne judgement, who did long agoe

Pronounce, that all these praises should be true,
   And vertue should your beauty,'and birth outgrow.   60

Now that my prophesies are all fulfill'd,
   Rather than God should not be honour'd too,
And all these gifts confess'd, which hee instill'd,
   Your selfe were bound to say that which I doe.

So I, but your Recorder am in this,
   Or mouth, or Speaker of the universe,
A ministeriall Notary, for'tis
   Not I, but you and fame, that makes this verse;

I was your Prophet in your yonger dayes,
And now your Chaplaine, God in you to praise.   70

TO THE COUNTESSE OF SALISBURY

[AUGUST 1614]

FAIRE, great, and good, since seeing you, wee see
What Heaven can doe, and what any Earth can be:
Since now your beauty shines, now when the Sunne
Growne stale, is to so low a value runne,
That his disshevel'd beames and scattered fires
Serve but for Ladies Periwigs and Tyres
In lovers Sonnets: you come to repaire
Gods booke of creatures, teaching what is faire.
Since now, when all is withered, shrunke, and dri'd,
All Vertues ebb'd out to a dead low tyde,   10
All the worlds frame being crumbled into sand,
Where every man thinks by himselfe to stand,
Integritie, friendship, and confidence,
(Ciments of greatnes) being vapor'd hence,
And narrow man being fill'd with little shares,
Court, Citie, Church, are all shops of small-wares,
All having blowne to sparkes their noble fire,
And drawne their sound gold-ingot into wyre;
All trying by a love of littlenesse
To make abridgments, and to draw to lesse,   20
Even that nothing, which at first we were;
Since in these times, your greatnesse doth appeare,

And that we learne by it, that man to get
Towards him that's infinite, must first be great.
Since in an age so ill, as none is fit
So much as to accuse, much lesse mend it,
(For who can judge, or witnesse of those times
Where all alike are guiltie of the crimes?)
Where he that would be good, is thought by all
A monster, or at best fantasticall: 30
Since now you durst be good, and that I doe
Discerne, by daring to contemplate you,
That there may be degrees of faire, great, good,
Through your light, largenesse, vertue understood:
If in this sacrifice of mine, be showne
Any small sparke of these, call it your owne.
And if things like these, have been said by mee
Of others; call not that Idolatrie.
For had God made man first, and man had seene
The third daies fruits, and flowers, and various greene, **40**
He might have said the best that he could say
Of those faire creatures, which were made that day;
And when next day he had admir'd the birth
Of Sun, Moone, Stars, fairer than late-prais'd earth,
Hee might have said the best that he could say,
And not be chid for praising yesterday:
So though some things are not together true,
As, that another is worthiest, and, that you:
Yet, to say so, doth not condemne a man,
If when he spoke them, they were both true then.   50
How faire a proofe of this, in our soule growes?
Wee first have soules of growth, and sense, and those,
When our last soule, our soule immortall came,
Were swallowed into it, and have no name.
Nor doth he injure those soules, which doth cast
The power and praise of both them, on the last;
No more doe I wrong any; I adore
The same things now, which I ador'd before,
The subject chang'd, and measure; the same thing
In a low constable, and in the King   60
I reverence; His power to work on mee:
So did I humbly reverence each degree
Of faire, great, good; but more, now I am come
From having found their *walkes*, to find their *home*
And as I owe my first soules thankes, that they

For my last soule did fit and mould my clay,
So am I debtor unto them, whose worth,
Enabled me to profit, and take forth
This new great lesson, thus to study you;
Which none, not reading others, first, could doe.   70
Nor lacke I light to read this booke, though I
In a dark Cave, yea in a Grave doe lie;
For as your fellow Angells, so you doe
Illustrate them who come to study you.
The first whom we in Histories doe finde
To have profest all Arts, was one borne blinde:
He lackt those eyes beasts have as well as wee,
Not those, by which Angels are seene and see;
So, though I'am borne without those eyes to live,
Which fortune, who hath none her selfe, doth give,   80
Which are, fit meanes to see bright courts and you,
Yet may I see you thus, as now I doe;
I shall by that, all goodnesse have discern'd,
And though I burne my librarie, be learn'd.

EPITHALAMIONS, OR MARRIAGE SONGS

EPITHALAMION MADE AT
LINCOLNES INNE

THE Sun-beames in the East are spred,
Leave, leave, faire Bride, your solitary bed,
No more shall you returne to it alone,
It nourseth sadnesse, and your bodies print,
Like to a grave, the yielding downe doth dint;
You and your other you meet there anon;
Put forth, put forth that warme balme-breathing thigh,
Which when next time you in these sheets wil smother,
There it must meet another,
Which never was, but must be, oft, more
nigh;   10
Come glad from thence, goe gladder than you came,
To day put on perfection, and a womans name.

Daughters of London, you which bee
Our Golden Mines, and furnish'd Treasurie,
You which are Angels, yet still bring with you

Thousands of Angels on your mariage daies,
Help with your presence and devise to praise
     These rites, which also unto you grow due;
     Conceitedly dresse her, and be assign'd,
By you, fit place for every flower and jewell,   20
   Make her for love fit fewell
      As gay as Flora, and as rich as Inde;
So may shee faire, rich, glad, and in nothing lame,
To day put on perfection, and a womans name.

And you frolique Patricians,
Sonnes of these Senators, wealths deep oceans,
   Ye painted courtiers, barrels of others wits,
Yee country men, who but your beasts love none,
Yee of those fellowships whereof hee's one,
     Of study and play made strange Hermaphrodits,   30
   Here shine; This Bridegroom to the Temple bring.
Loe, in yon path which store of straw'd flowers graceth,
     The sober virgin paceth;
      Except my sight faile, 'tis no other thing;
Weep not nor blush, here is no griefe nor shame,
To day put on perfection, and a womans name.

Thy two-leav'd gates faire Temple unfold,
And these two in thy sacred bosome hold,
   Till, mystically joyn'd, but one they bee;
Then may thy leane and hunger-starved wombe   40
Long time expect their bodies and their tombe,
   Long after their owne parents fatten thee.
   All elder claimes, and all cold barrennesse,
All yeelding to new loves bee far for ever,
     Which might these two dissever,
      All wayes all th'other may each one possesse;
For, the best Bride, best worthy of praise and fame,
Today puts on perfection, and a womans name.

Oh winter dayes bring much delight,
Not for themselves, but for they soon bring night;   50
   Other sweets wait thee than these diverse meats,
Other disports than dancing jollities,
Other love tricks than glancing with the eyes,
   But that the Sun still in our halfe Spheare sweates;
     Hee flies in winter, but he now stands still.

Yet shadowes turne; Noone point he hath attain'd,
  His steeds nill bee restrain'd,
    But gallop lively downe the Westerne hill;
Thou shalt, when he hath runne the worlds half frame,
To night put on a perfection, and a womans name.   60

The amorous evening starre is rose,
Why then should not our amorous starre inclose
  Her selfe in her wish'd bed? Release your strings
Musicians, and dancers take some truce
With these your pleasing labours, for great use
  As much wearinesse as perfection brings;
    You, and not only you, but all toyl'd beasts
Rest duly; at night all their toyles are dispensed;
But in their beds commenced
  Are other labours, and more dainty feasts;   70
She goes a maid, who, lest she turne the same
To night puts on perfection, and a womans name.

Thy virgins girdle now untie,
And in thy nuptiall bed (loves altar) lye
  A pleasing sacrifice; now dispossesse
Thee of these chaines and robes which were put on
T'adorne the day, not thee; for thou, alone,
  Like vertue'and truth, art best in nakednesse;
    This bed is onely to virginitie
A grave, but, to a better state, a cradle;   80
Till now thou wast but able
  To be what now thou art; then that by thee
No more be said, *I may bee,* but, *I am,*
To night put on perfection, and a womans name.

Even like a faithfull man content,
That this life for a better should be spent,
  So, shee a mothers rich stile doth preferre,
And at the Bridegroomes wish'd approach doth lye,
Like an appointed lambe, when tenderly
  The priest comes on his knees t'embowell her;   90
    Now sleep or watch with more joy; and O light
Of heaven, to morrow rise thou hot, and early;
This Sun will love so dearely
  Her rest, that long, long we shall want her sight;

Wonders are wrought, for shee which had no maime,
To night puts on perfection, and a womans name.

AN EPITHALAMION, OR MARIAGE SONG

ON THE LADY ELIZABETH, AND COUNT PALATINE BEING MARRIED ON ST. VALENTINES DAY

I

HAILE Bishop Valentine, whose day this is,
    All the Aire is thy Diocis,
    And all the chirping Choristers
And other birds are thy Parishioners,
       Thou marryest every yeare
The Lirique Larke, and the grave whispering Dove,
The Sparrow that neglects his life for love,
The household Bird, with the red stomacher,
       Thou mak'st the black bird speed as soone,
As doth the Goldfinch, or the Halcyon;   **10**
The husband cocke lookes out, and straight is sped,
And meets his wife, which brings her feather-bed.
This day more cheerfully than ever shine,
This day, which might enflame thy self, Old Valentine.

II

Till now, Thou warmd'st with multiplying loves
    Two larkes, two sparrowes, or two Doves,
    All that is nothing unto this.
For thou this day couplest two Phœnixes;
       Thou mak'st a Taper see
What the sunne never saw, and what the Arke   **20**
(Which was of foules, and beasts, the cage, and park,)
Did not containe, one bed containes, through Thee,
       Two Phœnixes, whose joyned breasts
Are unto one another mutuall nests,
Where motion kindles such fires, as shall give
Yong Phœnixes, and yet the old shall live.
Whose love and courage never shall decline,
But make the whole year through, thy day, O Valentine.

III

Up then faire Phœnix Bride, frustrate the Sunne,
  Thy selfe from thine affection   **30**
  Takest warmth enough, and from thine eye
All lesser birds will take their Jollitie.
  Up, up, faire Bride, and call,
Thy starres, from out their severall boxes, take
Thy Rubies, Pearles, and Diamonds forth, and make
Thy selfe a constellation, of them All,
  And by their blazing, signifie,
That a Great Princess falls, but doth not die;
Bee thou a new starre, that to us portends
Ends of much wonder; And be Thou those ends. **40**
Since thou dost this day in new glory shine,
May all men date Records, from this thy Valentine.

IV

Come forth, come forth, and as one glorious flame
  Meeting Another, growes the same,
  So meet thy Fredericke, and so
To an unseparable union growe.
  Since separation
Falls not on such things as are infinite,
Nor things which are but one, can disunite,
You'are twice inseparable, great, and one; **50**
  Goe then to where the Bishop staies,
To make you one, his way, which divers waies
Must be effected; and when all is past,
And that you'are one, by hearts and hands made fast,
You two have one way left, your selves to'entwine,
Besides this Bishops knot, or Bishop Valentine.

V

But oh, what ailes the Sunne, that here he staies,
  Longer to day, than other daies?
  Staies he new light from these to get?
And finding here such store, is loth to set? **60**
  And why doe you two walke,
So slowly pac'd in this procession?

Is all your care but to be look'd upon,
And be to others spectacle, and talke?
　　　The feast, with gluttonous delaies,
Is eaten, and too long their meat they praise,
The masquers come too late, and'I thinke, will stay,
Like Fairies, till the Cock crow them away.
Alas, did not Antiquity assigne
A night, as well as day, to thee, O Valentine?   **70**

VI

They did, and night is come; and yet wee see
　　　　Formalities retarding thee.
　　　What meane these Ladies, which (as though
They were to take a clock in peeces,) goe
　　　　So nicely about the Bride;
A Bride, before a good night could be said,
Should vanish from her cloathes, into her bed,
As Soules from bodies steale, and are not spy'd.
　　　But now she is laid; What though shee bee?
Yet there are more delayes, For, where is he?   **80**
He comes, and passes through Spheare after Spheare,
First her sheetes, then her Armes, then any where.
Let not this day, then, but this night be thine,
Thy day was but the eve to this, O Valentine.

VII

Here lyes a shee Sunne, and a hee Moone here,
　　　She gives the best light to his Spheare,
　　　Or each is both, and all, and so
They unto one another nothing owe,
　　　And yet they doe, but are
So just and rich in that coyne which they pay,   **90**
That neither would, nor needs forbeare nor stay;
Neither desires to be spar'd, nor to spare,
　　　They quickly pay their debt, and then
Take no acquittances, but pay again;
They pay, they give, they lend, and so let fall
No such occasion to be liberall.
More truth, more courage in these two do shine,
Than all thy turtles have, and sparrows, Valentine.

VIII

And by this act of these two Phenixes
    Nature againe restored is,   100
    For since these two are two no more,
Ther's but one Phenix still, as was before.
    Rest now at last, and wee
As Satyres watch the Sunnes uprise, will stay
Waiting, when your eyes opened, let out day,
Onely desir'd, because your face wee see;
    Others neare you shall whispering speake,
And wagers lay, at which side day will breake,
And win by'observing, then, whose hand it is
That opens first a curtaine, hers or his;   110
This will be tryed to morrow after nine,
Till which houre, wee thy day enlarge, O Valentine.

ECCLOGUE

1613. DECEMBER 26

Allophanes *finding* Idios *in the country in Christmas time, reprehends his absence from court, at the mariage of the Earle of Sommerset,* Idios *gives an account of his purpose therein, and of his absence thence.*
Allophanes.

UNSEASONABLE man, statue of ice,
    What could to countries solitude entice
Thee, in this yeares cold and decrepit time?
    Natures instinct drawes to the warmer clime
Even small birds, who by that courage dare,
    In numerous fleets, saile through their Sea, the aire.
What delicacie can in fields appeare,
    Whil'st Flora'herselfe doth a freeze jerkin weare?
Whil'st windes do all the trees and hedges strip
    Of leafes, to furnish roddes enough to whip   10
Thy madnesse from thee; and all springs by frost
    Have taken cold, and their sweet murmure lost;
If thou thy faults or fortunes would'st lament
    With just solemnity, do it in Lent;

At Court the spring already advanced is,
  The Sunne stayes longer up; and yet not his
The glory is, farre other, other fires.
  First, zeale to Prince and State; then loves desires
Burne in one brest, and like heavens two great lights,
  The first doth governe dayes, the other nights.   20
And then that early light, which did appeare
  Before the Sunne and Moone created were,
The Princes favour is defus'd o'r all,
  From which all Fortunes, Names, and Natures fall;
Then from those wombes of starres, the Brides bright eyes,
  At every glance, a constellation flyes,
And sowes the Court with starres, and doth prevent
  In light and power, the all-ey'd firmament;
First her eyes kindle other Ladies eyes,
  Then from their beames their jewels lusters rise,   30
And from their jewels torches do take fire,
  And all is warmth, and light, and good desire;
Most other Courts, alas, are like to hell,
  Where in darke plotts, fire without light doth dwell;
Or but like Stoves, for lust and envy get
  Continuall, but artificiall heat;
Here zeale and love growne one, all clouds disgest,
  And make our Court an everlasting East.
And can'st thou be from thence?

Idios.   No, I am there.
As heaven, to men dispos'd, is every where,   40
So are those Courts, whose Princes animate,
  Not onely all their house, but all their State.
Let no man thinke, because he is full, he hath all,
  Kings (as their patterne, God) are liberall
Not onely in fulnesse, but capacitie,
  Enlarging narrow men, to feele and see,
And comprehend the blessings they bestow.
  So, reclus'd hermits often times do know
More of heavens glory, than a worldling can.
  As man is of the world, the heart of man,   50
Is an epitome of Gods great booke
  Of creatures, and man need no farther looke;
So is the Country of Courts, where sweet peace doth,
  As their one common soule, give life to both,
I am not then from Court.

Allophanes.   Dreamer, thou art.
  Think'st thou fantastique that thou hast a part
In the East-Indian fleet, because thou hast
    A little spice, or Amber in thy taste?
Because thou art not frozen, art thou warme?
    Seest thou all good because thou seest no harme?   60
The earth doth in her inward bowels hold
    Stuffe well dispos'd, and which would faine be gold,
But never shall, except it chance to lye,
    So upward, that heaven gild it with his eye;
As, for divine things, faith comes from above,
    So, for best civill use, all tinctures move
From higher powers; From God religion springs,
    Wisdome, and honour from the use of Kings.
Then unbeguile thy selfe, and know with mee,
    That Angels, though on earth employd they bee,   70
Are still in heav'n, so is hee still at home
    That doth, abroad, to honest actions come.
Chide thy selfe then, O foole, which yesterday
    Might'st have read more than all thy books bewray;
Hast thou a history, which doth present
    A Court, where all affections do assent
Unto the Kings, and that, that Kings are just?
    And where it is no levity to trust?
Where there is no ambition, but to'obey,
    Where men need whisper nothing, and yet may;   80
Where the Kings favours are so plac'd, that all
    Finde that the King therein is liberall
To them, in him, because his favours bend
    To vertue, to the which they all pretend?
Thou hast no such; yet here was this, and more,
    An earnest lover, wise then, and before.
Our little Cupid hath sued Livery,
    And is no more in his minority,
Hee is admitted now into that brest
    Where the Kings Counsells and his secrets rest.   90
What hast thou lost, O ignorant man?

Idios.   I knew
  All this, and onely therefore I withdrew.
To know and feele all this, and not to have
    Words to expresse it, makes a man a grave
Of his owne thoughts; I would not therefore stay

At a great feast, having no grace to say.
And yet I scap'd not here; for being come
  Full of the common joy, I utter'd some;
Reade then this nuptiall song, which was not made
  Either the Court or mens hearts to invade,   **100**
But since I'am dead, and buried, I could frame
  No Epitaph, which might advance my fame
So much as this poor song, which testifies
  I did unto that day some sacrifice.

EPITHALAMION

I

THE TIME OF THE MARIAGE

THOU art repriv'd old yeare, thou shalt not die,
Though thou upon thy death bed lye,
  And should'st within five dayes expire,
Yet thou art rescu'd by a mightier fire,
  Than thy old Soule, the Sunne,
When he doth in his largest circle runne.   **110**
The passage of the West or East would thaw,
And open wide their easie liquid jawe
To all our ships, could a Promethean art
Either unto the Northerne Pole impart
The fire of these inflaming eyes, or of this loving heart.

II

EQUALITY OF PERSONS

BUT undiscerning Muse, which heart, which eyes,
  In this new couple, dost thou prize,
  When his eye as inflaming is
As hers, and her heart loves as well as his?
  Be tryed by beauty, and then   **120**
The bridegroome is a maid, and not a man.
If by that manly courage they be tryed,
Which scornes unjust opinion; then the bride
Becomes a man. Should chance or envies Art
Divide these two, whom nature scarce did part?
Since both have both th'enflaming eyes, and both the loving heart.

III

RAISING OF THE BRIDEGROOM

THOUGH it be some divorce to thinke of you
    Singly, so much one are you two,
    Yet let me here contemplate thee,
First cheerfull Bridegroome, and first let mee see,   130
    How thou prevent'st the Sunne,
And his red foming horses dost outrunne,
How, having laid downe in thy Soveraignes brest
All businesses, from thence to reinvest
Them, when these triumphs cease, thou forward art
To shew to her, who doth the like impart,
The fire of thy inflaming eyes, and of thy loving heart.

IV

RAISING OF THE BRIDE

BUT now, to Thee, faire Bride, it is some wrong,
    To thinke thou wert in Bed so long,
    Since Soone thou lyest downe first, tis fit   140
Thou in first rising should'st allow for it.
    Pouder thy Radiant haire,
Which if without such ashes thou would'st weare,
Thou, which to all which come to looke upon,
Art meant for Phœbus, would'st be Phaëton.
For our ease, give thine eyes th'unusual part
Of joy, a Teare; so quencht, thou maist impart,
To us that come, thy inflaming eyes, to him, thy loving heart.

V

HER APPARRELLING

THUS thou descend'st to our infirmitie,
    Who can the Sun in water see.   150
    Soe dost thou, when in silke and gold,

Thou cloudst thy selfe; since wee which doe behold,
    Are dust, and wormes, 'tis just
Our objects be the fruits of wormes and dust;
Let every Jewell be a glorious starre,
Yet starres are not so pure, as their spheares are.
And though thou stoope, to'appeare to us in part,
Still in that Picture thou intirely art,
Which thy inflaming eyes have made within his loving heart.

VI

GOING TO THE CHAPPELL

Now from your Easts you issue forth, and wee,   160
    As men which through a Cipres see
    The rising sun, doe thinke it two,
Soe, as you goe to Church, doe thinke of you,
    But that vaile being gone,
By the Church rites you are from thenceforth one.
The Church Triumphant made this match before,
And now the Militant doth strive no more;
Then, reverend Priest, who Gods Recorder art,
Doe, from his Dictates, to these two impart
All blessings, which are seene, or thought, by Angels eye or
    heart.   170

VII

THE BENEDICTION

BLEST payre of Swans, Oh may you interbring
    Daily new joyes, and never sing;
    Live, till all grounds of wishes faile,
Till honor, yea till wisedome grow so stale,
    That, new great heights to trie,
It must serve your ambition, to die;
Raise heires, and may here, to the worlds end, live
Heires from this King, to take thankes, you, to give,
Nature and grace doe all, and nothing Art.
May never age, or error overthwart   180
With any West, these radiant eyes, with any North, this heart.

VIII

FEASTS AND REVELLS

But you are over-blest. Plenty this day
    Injures; it causeth time to stay;
    The tables groane, as though this feast
Would, as the flood, destroy all fowle and beast.
    And were the doctrine new
That the earth mov'd, this day would make it true;
For every part to dance and revell goes.
They tread the ayre, and fal not where they rose.
Though six houres since, the Sunne to bed did part,   **190**
The masks and banquets will not yet impart
A sunset to these weary eyes, A Center to this heart.

IX

THE BRIDES GOING TO BED

What mean'st thou Bride, this companie to keep?
    To sit up, till thou faine wouldst sleep?
    Thou maist not, when thou art laid, doe so.
Thy selfe must to him a new banquet grow,
    And you must entertaine
And doe all this daies dances o'er againe.
Know that if Sun and Moone together doe
Rise in one point, they doe not set so too;   **200**
Therefore thou maist, faire Bride, to bed depart,
Thou art not gone, being gone; where e'r thou art,
Thou leav'st in him thy watchfull eyes, in him thy loving heart.

X

THE BRIDEGROOMES COMMING

As he that sees a starre fall, runs apace,
    And findes a gellie in the place,
    So doth the Bridegroome haste as much,

Being told this starre is falne, and findes her such.
    And as friends may looke strange,
By a new fashion, or apparrells change,
Their soules, though long acquainted they had beene,   210
These clothes, their bodies, never yet had seene;
Therefore at first shee modestly might start,
But must forthwith surrender every part,
As freely, as each to each before, gave either eye or heart.

XI

THE GOOD-NIGHT

Now, as in Tullias tombe, one lampe burnt cleare,
    Unchang'd for fifteene hundred yeare,
    May these love-lamps we here enshrine,
In warmth, light, lasting, equall the divine.
    Fire ever doth aspire,
And makes all like it selfe, turnes all to fire,   220
But ends in ashes, which these cannot doe,
For none of these is fuell, but fire too.
This is joyes bonfire, then, where loves strong Arts
Make of so noble individuall parts
One fire of foure inflaming eyes, and of two loving hearts.

Idios.
As I have brought this song, that I may doe
    A perfect sacrifice, I'll burne it too.

Allophanes.
No Sir. This paper I have justly got,
    For, in burnt incense, the perfume is not
His only that presents it, but of all;   230
    What ever celebrates this Festivall
Is common, since the joy thereof is so.
    Nor may your selfe be Priest: But let me goe,
Backe to the Court, and I will lay'it upon
    Such Altars, as prize your devotion.

A FUNERALL ELEGIE AND
THE FIRST AND SECOND ANNIVERSARIES

A FUNERALL ELEGIE
[ON ELIZABETH DRURY. 1610?]

'TIS lost, to trust a Tombe with such a guest,
Or to confine her in a marble chest.
Alas, what's Marble, Jeat, or Porphyrie,
Priz'd with the Chrysolite of either eye,
Or with those Pearles, and Rubies, which she was?
Joyne the two Indies in one Tombe, 'tis glasse;
And so is all to her materials,
Though every inch were ten Escurials,
Yet she's demolish'd: can wee keepe her then
In works of hands, or of the wits of men?   **10**
Can these memorials, ragges of paper, give
Life to that name, by which name they must live?
Sickly, alas, short-liv'd, aborted bee
Those carcasse verses, whose soule is not shee.
And can shee, who no longer would be shee,
Being such a Tabernacle, stoop to be
In paper wrapt; or, when shee would not lie
In such a house, dwell in an Elegie?
But 'tis no matter; wee may well allow
Verse to live so long as the world will now,   **20**
For her death wounded it. The world containes
Princes for armes, and Counsellors for braines,
Lawyers for tongues, Divines for hearts, and more,
The Rich for stomackes, and for backes, the Poore;
The Officers for hands, Merchants for feet,
By which, remote and distant Countries meet.
But those fine spirits which do tune, and set
This Organ, are those peeces which beget
Wonder and love; and these were shee; and shee
Being spent, the world must needs decrepit bee;   **30**
For since death will proceed to triumph still,
He can finde nothing, after her, to kill,
Except the world it selfe, so great as shee.
Thus brave and confident may Nature bee,
Death cannot give her such another blow,

Because shee cannot such another show.
But must wee say she's dead? may't not be said
That as a sundred clocke is peecemeale laid,
Not to be lost, but by the makers hand
Repollish'd, without errour then to stand,   **40**
Or as the Affrique Niger streame enwombs
It selfe into the earth, and after comes
(Having first made a naturall bridge, to passe
For many leagues) farre greater than it was,
May't not be said, that her grave shall restore
Her, greater, purer, firmer, than before?
Heaven may say this, and joy in't, but can wee
Who live, and lacke her, here this vantage see?
What is't to us, alas, if there have beene
An Angell made a Throne, or Cherubin?   **50**
Wee lose by't: and as aged men are glad
Being tastlesse growne, to joy in joyes they had,
So now the sick starv'd world must feed upon
This joy, that we had her, who now is gone.
Rejoyce then Nature, and this World, that you,
Fearing the last fires hastning to subdue
Your force and vigour, ere it were neere gone,
Wisely bestow'd and laid it all on one.
One, whose cleare body was so pure and thinne,
Because it need disguise no thought within.   **60**
'Twas but a through-light scarfe, her minde t'inroule;
Or exhalation breath'd out from her Soule.
One, whom all men who durst no more, admir'd:
And whom, who ere had worth enough, desir'd;
As when a Temple's built, Saints emulate
To which of them, it shall be consecrate.
But, as when heaven lookes on us with new eyes,
Those new starres every Artist exercise,
What place they should assigne to them they doubt,
Argue, and agree not, till those starres goe out: **70**
So the world studied whose this peece should be,
Till shee can be no bodies else, nor shee:
But like a Lampe of Balsamum, desir'd
Rather t'adorne, than last, she soone expir'd,
Cloath'd in her virgin white integritie,
For marriage, though it doe not staine, doth dye.
To scape th'infirmities which wait upon
Woman, she went away, before sh'was one:

And the worlds busie noyse to overcome,
Tooke so much death, as serv'd for *opium;*   80
For though she could not, nor could chuse to dye,
She'ath yeelded to too long an extasie:
Hee which not knowing her said History,
Should come to reade the booke of destiny,
How faire, and chast, humble, and high she'ad been
Much promis'd, much perform'd, at not fifteene,
And measuring future things, by things before,
Should turne the leafe.to reade, and reade no more,
Would thinke that either destiny mistooke,
Or that some leaves were torne out of the booke.   90
But 'tis not so; Fate did but usher her
To yeares of reasons use, and then inferre
Her destiny to her selfe, which liberty
She tooke but for thus much, thus much to die.
Her modestie not suffering her to bee
Fellow-Commissioner with Destinie,
She did no more but die; if after her
Any shall live, which dare true good prefer,
Every such person is her deligate,
T'accomplish that which should have beene her Fate.   100
They shall make up that Booke and shall have thanks
Of Fate, and her, for filling up their blankes.
For future vertuous deeds are Legacies,
Which from the gift of her example rise;
And 'tis in heav'n part of spirituall mirth,
To see how well the good play her, on earth.

AN ANATOMIE OF THE WORLD
THE FIRST ANNIVERSARY

WHEREIN,
BY OCCASION OF THE UNTIMELY DEATH OF
MISTRESS ELIZABETH DRURY, THE FRAILTY AND THE
DECAY OF THIS WHOLE WORLD IS REPRESENTED

[1611]

THE FIRST ANNIVERSARY

TO THE PRAISE OF THE DEAD,
AND THE ANATOMIE [By Joseph Hall?]

WELL *dy'd the World, that we might live to see*
This world of wit, in his Anatomie:
No evill wants his good; so wilder heires
Bedew their Fathers Tombes, with forced teares,
Whose state requites their losse: whiles thus we gain,
Well may wee walke in blacks, but not complaine.
Yet how can I consent the world is dead
While this Muse lives? which in his spirits stead
Seemes to informe a World; and bids it bee,
In spight of losse or fraile mortalitie?   10
And thou the subject of this welborne thought,
Thrice noble maid, couldst not have found nor sought
A fitter time to yeeld to thy sad Fate,
Than whiles this spirit lives, that can relate
Thy worth so well to our last Nephews eyne,
That they shall wonder both at his and thine:
Admired match! where strives in mutuall grace
The cunning pencill, and the comely face:
A taske which thy faire goodnesse made too much
For the bold pride of vulgar pens to touch;   20
Enough is us to praise them that praise thee,
And say, that but enough those prayses bee,
Which hadst thou liv'd, had hid their fearfull head
From th'angry checkings of thy modest red:
Death barres reward and shame: when envy's gone,
And gaine, 'tis safe to give the dead their owne.

As then the wise Egyptians wont to lay
More on their Tombes than houses: these of clay,
But those of brasse, or marble were: so wee
Give more unto thy Ghost, than unto thee.   30
Yet what wee give to thee, thou gav'st to us,
And may'st but thanke thy selfe, for being thus:
Yet what thou gav'st, and wert, O happy maid,
Thy grace profest all due, where 'tis repayd.
So these high songs that to thee suited bin
Serve but to sound thy Makers praise, in thine,
Which thy deare soule as sweetly sings to him
Amid the Quire of Saints, and Seraphim,
As any Angels tongue can sing of thee;
The subjects differ, though the skill agree: 40
For as by infant-yeares men judge of age,
Thy early love, thy vertues, did presage
What an high part thou bear'st in those best songs,
Whereto no burden, nor no end belongs.
Sing on thou virgin Soule, whose lossfull gaine
Thy lovesick parents have bewail'd in vaine;
Never may thy Name be in our songs forgot,
Till wee shall sing thy ditty and thy note.

AN ANATOMY OF THE WORLD

THE FIRST ANNIVERSARY

The entrie
into the
worke.

WHEN that rich Soule which to her heaven is gone,
Whom all do celebrate, who know they have one,
(For who is sure he hath a Soule, unlesse
It see, and judge, and follow worthinesse,
And by Deedes praise it? hee who doth not this,
May lodge an In-mate soule, but 'tis not his.)
When that Queene ended here her progresse time,
And, as t'her standing house to heaven did climbe,
Where loath to make the Saints attend her long,
She's now a part both of the Quire, and Song,   10
This World, in that great earthquake languished;
For in a common bath of teares it bled,
Which drew the strongest vitall spirits out:
But succour'd then with a perplexed doubt,

Whether the world did lose, or gaine in this,
(Because since now no other way there is,
But goodnesse, to see her, whom all would see,
All must endeavour to be good as shee,)
This great consumption to a fever turn'd,
And so the world had fits; it joy'd, it mourn'd;   20
And, as men thinke, that Agues physick are,
And th'Ague being spent, give over care,
So thou sicke World, mistak'st thy selfe to bee
Well, when alas, thou'rt in a Lethargie.
Her death did wound and tame thee then, and then
Thou might'st have better spar'd the Sunne, or Man.
That wound was deep, but 'tis more misery,
That thou hast lost thy sense and memory.
'Twas heavy then to heare thy voyce of mone,
But this is worse, that thou art speechlesse growne.   30
Thou hast forgot thy name, thou hadst; thou wast
Nothing but shee, and her thou hast o'rpast.
For as a child kept from the Font, untill
A prince, expected long, come to fulfill
The ceremonies, thou unnam'd had'st laid,
Had not her comming, thee her Palace made:
Her name defin'd thee, gave thee forme, and frame,
And thou forgett'st to celebrate thy name.
Some moneths she hath beene dead (but being dead,
Measures of times are all determined)   40
But long she'ath beene away, long, long, yet none
Offers to tell us who it is that's gone.
But as in states doubtfull of future heires,
When sicknesse without remedie empares
The present Prince, they're loth it should be said,
The Prince doth languish, or the Prince is dead:
So mankinde feeling now a generall thaw,
A strong example gone, equall to law,
The Cyment which did faithfully compact,
And glue all vertues, now resolv'd, and slack'd,   50
Thought it some blasphemy to say sh'was dead,
Or that our weakenesse was discovered
In that confession; therefore spoke no more
Than tongues, the Soule being gone, the losse deplore.
But though it be too late to succour thee,
Sicke World, yea, dead, yea putrified, since shee
Thy'intrinsique balme, and thy preservative,

Can never be renew'd, thou never live,
I (since no man can make thee live) will try
What wee may gaine by thy Anatomy.   60
Her death hath taught us dearely, that thou art
Corrupt and mortall in thy purest part.
Let no man say, the world it selfe being dead,
'Tis labour lost to have discovered
The worlds infirmities, since there is none
Alive to study this dissection;

What life
the world
hath stil
For there's a kinde of World remaining still,
Though shee which did inanimate and fill
The world, be gone, yet in this last long night,
Her Ghost doth walke; that is, a glimmering light,   70
A faint weake love of vertue, and of good,
Reflects from her, on them which understood
Her worth; and though she have shut in all day,
The twilight of her memory doth stay;
Which, from the carcasse of the old world, free,
Creates a new world, and new creatures bee
Produc'd: the matter and the stuffe of this,
Her vertue, and the forme our practice is:
And though to be thus elemented, arme
These creatures, from home-borne intrinsique harme,   80
(For all assum'd unto this dignitie,
So many weedlesse Paradises bee,
Which of themselves produce no venemous sinne,
Except some forraine Serpent bring it in)
Yet, because outward stormes the strongest breake,
And strength it selfe by confidence growes weake,

The sick
nesses
of the
World.
This new world may be safer, being told
The dangers and diseases of the old:
For with due temper men doe then forgoe,
Or covet things, when they their true worth know.   90

Impossi-
bility of
health.
There is no health; Physitians say that wee,
At best, enjoy but a neutralitie.
And can there bee worse sicknesse, than to know
That we are never well, nor can be so?
Wee are borne ruinous: poore mothers cry,
That children come not right, nor orderly;
Except they headlong come and fall upon
An ominous precipitation.
How witty's ruine! how importunate
Upon mankinde! it labour'd to frustrate   100

Even Gods purpose; and made woman, sent
For mans reliefe, cause of his languishment.
They were to good ends, and they are so still,
But accessory, and principall in ill;
For that first marriage was our funerall:
One woman at one blow, then kill'd us all,
And singly, one by one, they kill us now.
We doe delightfully our selves allow
To that consumption; and profusely blinde,
We kill our selves to propagate our kinde.   110
And yet we do not that; we are not men:
There is not now that mankinde, which was then,
When as, the Sunne and man did seeme to strive,
(Joynt tenants of the world) who should survive;   Shortnesse
When, Stagge, and Raven, and the long-liv'd tree,   of life.
Compar'd with man, dy'd in minoritie;
When, if a slow pac'd starre had stolne away
From the observers marking, he might stay
Two or three hundred yeares to see't againe,
And then make up his observation plaine;   120
When, as the age was long, the sise was great:
Mans growth confess'd, and recompenc'd the meat;
So spacious and large, that every Soule
Did a faire Kingdome, and large Realme controule:
And when the very stature, thus erect,
Did that soule a good way towards heaven direct.
Where is this mankinde now? who lives to age,
Fit to be made *Methusalem* his page?
Alas, we scarce live long enough to try
Whether a true made clocke run right, or lie.   130
Old Grandsires talke of yesterday with sorrow,
And for our children wee reserve to morrow.
So short is life, that every peasant strives,
In a torne house, or field, to have three lives.
And as in lasting, so in length is man
Contracted to an inch, who was a spanne;   Smalnesse
For had a man at first in forrests stray'd,   of stature.
Or shipwrack'd in the Sea, one would have laid
A wager, that an Elephant, or Whale,
That met him, would not hastily assaile   140
A thing so equall to him: now alas,
The Fairies, and the Pigmies well may passe
As credible; mankinde decayes so soone,

We'are scarce our Fathers shadowes cast at noone:
Onely death addes t'our length: nor are wee growne
In stature to be men, till we are none.
But this were light, did our lesse volume hold
All the old Text; or had wee chang'd to gold
Their silver; or dispos'd into lesse glasse
Spirits of vertue, which then scatter'd was.   **150**
But 'tis not so: w'are not retir'd, but dampt;
And as our bodies, so our mindes are crampt:
'Tis shrinking, not close weaving that hath thus,
In minde, and body both bedwarfed us.
Wee seeme ambitious, Gods whole worke t'undoe;
Of nothing hee made us, and we strive too,
To bring our selves to nothing backe; and wee
Doe what wee can, to do't so soone as hee.
With new diseases on our selves we warre,
And with new Physicke, a worse Engin farre.   **160**
Thus man, this worlds Vice-Emperour, in whom
All faculties, all graces are at home;
And if in other creatures they appeare,
They're but mans Ministers, and Legats there,
To worke on their rebellions, and reduce
Them to Civility, and to mans use:
This man, whom God did wooe, and loth t'attend
Till man came up, did downe to man descend,
This man, so great, that all that is, is his,
Oh what a trifle, and poore thing he is!   **170**
If man were any thing, he's nothing now:
Helpe, or at least some time to wast, allow
T'his other wants, yet when he did depart
With her whom we lament, hee lost his heart.
She, of whom th'Ancients seem'd to prophesie,
When they call'd vertues by the name of *shee;*
Shee in whom vertue was so much refin'd,
That for Allay unto so pure a minde
Shee tooke the weaker Sex; shee that could drive
The poysonous tincture, and the staine of *Eve,*   **180**
Out of her thoughts, and deeds; and purifie
All, by a true religious Alchymie;
Shee, shee is dead; shee's dead: when thou knowest this,
Thou knowest how poore a trifling thing man is.
And learn'st thus much by our Anatomie,
The heart being perish'd, no part can be free.

And that except thou feed (not banquet) on
The supernaturall food, Religion,
Thy better Growth growes withered, and scant;
Be more than man, or thou'rt lesse than an Ant.   190
Then, as mankinde, so is the worlds whole frame
Quite out of joynt, almost created lame:
For, before God had made up all the rest,
Corruption entred, and deprav'd the best:
It seis'd the Angels, and then first of all
The world did in her cradle take a fall,
And turn'd her braines, and tooke a generall maime,
Wronging each joynt of th'universall frame.
The noblest part, man, felt it first; and then
Both beasts and plants, curst in the curse of man.   200
So did the world from the first houre decay,   Decay of
That evening was beginning of the day,   nature in
And now the Springs and Sommers which we see,   other
Like sonnes of women after fiftie bee.   parts.
And new Philosophy calls all in doubt,
The Element of fire is quite put out;
The Sun is lost, and th'earth, and no mans wit
Can well direct him where to looke for it.
And freely men confesse that this world's spent,
When in the Planets, and the Firmament   210
They seeke so many new; then see that this
Is crumbled out againe to his Atomies.
'Tis all in peeces, all cohaerence gone;
All just supply, and all Relation:
Prince, Subject, Father, Sonne, are things forgot,
For every man alone thinkes he hath got
To be a Phœnix, and that then can bee
None of that kinde, of which he is, but hee.
This is the worlds condition now, and now
She that should all parts to reunion bow,   220
She that had all Magnetique force alone,
To draw, and fasten sundred parts in one;
She whom wise nature had invented then
When she observ'd that every sort of men
Did in their voyage in this worlds Sea stray,
And needed a new compasse for their way;
She that was best, and first originall
Of all faire copies, and the generall
Steward to Fate; she whose rich eyes, and breast

Guilt the West Indies, and perfum'd the East;　230
Whose having breath'd in this world, did bestow
Spice on those Iles, and bad them still smell so,
And that rich Indie which doth gold interre,
Is but as single money, coyn'd from her:
She to whom this world must it selfe refer,
As Suburbs, or the Microcosme of her,
Shee, shee is dead; shee's dead: when thou knowst this,
Thou knowst how lame a cripple this world is.
And learn'st thus much by our Anatomy,
That this worlds generall sickenesse doth not lie　240
In any humour, or one certaine part;
But as thou sawest it rotten at the heart,
Thou seest a Hectique feaver hath got hold
Of the whole substance, not to be contrould,
And that thou hast but one way, not t'admit
The worlds infection, to be none of it.
For the worlds subtilst immateriall parts

Disform-　Feele this consuming wound, and ages darts.
ity of　For the worlds beauty is decai'd, or gone,
parts.　Beauty, that's colour, and proportion.　250
We thinke the heavens enjoy their Sphericall,
Their round proportion embracing all.
But yet their various and perplexed course,
Observ'd in divers ages, doth enforce
Men to finde out so many Eccentrique parts,
Such divers downe-right lines, such overthwarts,
As disproportion that pure forme: It teares
The Firmament in eight and forty sheires,
And in these Constellations then arise
New starres, and old doe vanish from our eyes:　260
As though heav'n suffered earthquakes, peace or war,
When new Towers rise, and old demolish't are.
They have impal'd within a Zodiake
The free-borne Sun, and keepe twelve Signes awake
To watch his steps; the Goat and Crab controule,
And fright him backe, who else to either Pole
(Did not these Tropiques fetter him) might runne:
For his course is not round; nor can the Sunne
Perfit a Circle, or maintaine his way
One inch direct; but where he rose to-day　270
He comes no more, but with a couzening line,
Steales by that point, and so is Serpentine:

And seeming weary with his reeling thus,
He means to sleepe, being now falne nearer us.
So, of the Starres which boast that they doe runne
In Circle still, none ends where he begun.
All their proportion's lame, it sinkes, it swels.
For of Meridians, and Parallels,
Man hath weav'd out a net, and this net throwne
Upon the Heavens, and now they are his owne.   280
Loth to goe up the hill, or labour thus
To goe to heaven, we make heaven come to us.
We spur, we reine the starres, and in their race
They're diversly content t'obey our pace.
But keepes the earth her round proportion still?
Doth not a Tenarif, or higher Hill
Rise so high like a Rocke, that one might thinke
The floating Moone would shipwrack there, and sinke?
Seas are so deepe, that Whales being strooke to day,
Perchance to morrow, scarse at middle way   290
Of their wish'd journies end, the bottome, die.
And men, to sound depths, so much line untie,
As one might justly thinke, that there would rise
At end thereof, one of th'Antipodies:
If under all, a Vault infernall bee,
(Which sure is spacious, except that we
Invent another torment, that there must
Millions into a straight hot roome be thrust)
Then solidnesse, and roundnesse have no place.
Are these but warts, and pock-holes in the face   300
Of th'earth? Thinke so: but yet confesse, in this
The worlds proportion disfigured is;
That those two legges whereon it doth rely,   Disorder
Reward and punishment are bent awry.   in the
And, Oh, it can no more be questioned,   world.
That beauties best, proportion, is dead,
Since even griefe it selfe, which now alone
Is left us, is without proportion.
Shee by whose lines proportion should bee
Examin'd, measure of all Symmetree,   310
Whom had that Ancient seen, who thought soules made
Of Harmony, he would at next have said
That Harmony was shee, and thence infer,
That soules were but Resultances from her,
And did from her into our bodies goe,

As to our eyes, the formes from objects flow:
Shee, who if those great Doctors truly said
That the Arke to mans proportions was made,
Had been a type for that, as that might be
A type of her in this, that contrary   320
Both Elements, and Passions liv'd at peace
In her, who caus'd all Civill war to cease.
Shee, after whom, what forme soe'r we see,
Is discord, and rude incongruitie;
Shee, shee is dead, shee's dead; when thou knowst this,
Thou knowst how ugly a monster this world is:
And learn'st thus much by our Anatomie,
That here is nothing to enamour thee:
And that, not only faults in inward parts,
Corruptions in our braines, or in our hearts,   330
Poysoning the fountaines, whence our actions spring,
Endanger us: but that if every thing
Be not done fitly'and in proportion,
To satisfie wise, and good lookers on,
(Since most men be such as most thinke they bee)
They're lothsome too, by this Deformitee.
For good, and well, must in our actions meete;
Wicked is not much worse than indiscreet.
But beauties other second Element,
Colour, and lustre now, is as neere spent.   340
And had the world his just proportion,
Were it a ring still, yet the stone is gone.
As a compassionate Turcoyse which doth tell
By looking pale, the wearer is not well,
As gold falls sicke being stung with Mercury,
All the worlds parts of such complexion bee.
When nature was most busie, the first weeke,
Swadling the new born earth, God seem'd to like
That she should sport her selfe sometimes, and play,
To mingle, and vary colours every day: 350
And then, as though shee could not make inow,
Himselfe his various Rainbow did allow.
Sight is the noblest sense of any one,
Yet sight hath only colour to feed on,
And colour is decai'd: summers robe growes
Duskie, and like an oft dyed garment showes.
Our blushing red, which us'd in cheekes to spred,
Is inward sunke, and only our soules are red.

Perchance the world might have recovered,
If she whom we lament had not beene dead: 360
But shee, in whom all white, and red, and blew
(Beauties ingredients) voluntary grew,
As in an unvext Paradise; from whom
Did all things verdure, and their lustre come,
Whose composition was miraculous,
Being all colour, all Diaphanous,
(For Ayre, and Fire but thick grosse bodies were,
And liveliest stones but drowsie, and pale to her,)
Shee, shee, is dead; shee's dead: when thou know'st this,
Thou knowst how wan a Ghost this our world is: 370
And learn'st thus much by our Anatomie,
That it should more affright, than pleasure thee.
And that, since all faire colour then did sinke,
'Tis now but wicked vanitie, to thinke
To colour vicious deeds with good pretence,
Or with bought colors to illude mens sense.
Nor in ought more this worlds decay appeares,
Than that her influence the heav'n forbeares,
Or that the Elements doe not feele this,
The father, or the mother barren is.   380
The cloudes conceive not raine, or doe not powre,
In the due birth time, downe the balmy showre;
Th'Ayre doth not motherly sit on the earth,
To hatch her seasons, and give all things birth;
Spring-times were common cradles, but are tombes;
And false-conceptions fill the generall wombes;
Th'Ayre showes such Meteors, as none can see,
Not only what they meane, but what they bee;
Earth such new wormes, as would have troubled much
Th'Ægyptian *Mages* to have made more such.   390
What Artist now dares boast that he can bring
Heaven hither, or constellate any thing,
So as the influence of those starres may bee
Imprison'd in an Hearbe, or Charme, or Tree,
And doe by touch, all which those stars could doe?
The art is lost, and correspondence too.
For heaven gives little, and the earth takes lesse,
And man least knowes their trade and purposes.
If this commerce twixt heaven and earth were not
Embarr'd, and all this traffique quite forgot,   400
She, for whose losse we have lamented thus,

Weak-
nesse in
the want
of corre-
spond-
ence of
heaven
and
earth.

Would worke more fully, and pow'rfully on us:
Since herbes, and roots, by dying lose not all,
But they, yea Ashes too, are medicinall,
Death could not quench her vertue so, but that
It would be (if not follow'd) wondred at:
And all the world would be one dying Swan,
To sing her funerall praise, and vanish then.
But as some Serpents poyson hurteth not,
Except it be from the live Serpent shot,   410
So doth her vertue need her here, to fit
That unto us; shee working more than it.
But shee, in whom to such maturity
Vertue was growne, past growth, that it must die;
She, from whose influence all Impressions came,
But, by Receivers impotencies, lame,
Who, though she could not transubstantiate
All states to gold, yet guilded every state,
So that some Princes have some temperance;
Some Counsellers some purpose to advance   420
The common profit; and some people have
Some stay, no more than Kings should give, to crave;
Some women have some taciturnity,
Some nunneries some graines of chastitie.
She that did thus much, and much more could doe,
But that our age was Iron, and rustie too,
Shee, shee is dead; shee's dead; when thou knowst this
Thou knowst how drie a Cinder this world is.
And learn'st thus much by our Anatomy,
That 'tis in vaine to dew, or mollifie   430
It with thy teares, or sweat, or blood: nothing
Is worth our travaile, griefe, or perishing,
But those rich joyes, which did possesse her heart,
Of which she's now partaker, and a part.
Conclusion But as in cutting up a man that's dead,
The body will not last out, to have read
On every part, and therefore men direct
Their speech to parts, that are of most effect;
So the worlds carcasse would not last, if I
Were punctuall in this Anatomy;   440
Nor smels it well to hearers, if one tell
Them their disease, who faine would think they're well.
Here therefore be the end: And, blessed maid,
Of whom is meant what ever hath been said,

Or shall be spoken well by any tongue,
Whose name refines course lines, and makes prose song,
Accept this tribute, and his first yeares rent,
Who till his darke short tapers end be spent,
As oft as thy feast sees this widowed earth,
Will yearely celebrate thy second birth,   450
That is, thy death; for though the soule of man
Be got when man is made, 'tis borne but then
When man doth die; our body's as the wombe,
And, as a Midwife, death directs it home.
And you her creatures, whom she workes upon,
And have your last, and best concoction
From her example, and her vertue, if you
In reverence to her, do thinke it due,
That no one should her praises thus rehearse,
As matter fit for Chronicle, not verse;   460
Vouchsafe to call to minde that God did make
At last, and lasting'st peece, a song. He spake
To *Moses* to deliver unto all,
That song, because hee knew they would let fall
The Law, the Prophets, and the History,
But keepe the song still in their memory:
Such an opinion (in due measure) made
Me this great Office boldly to invade:
Nor could incomprehensiblenesse deterre
Mee, from thus trying to emprison her,   470
Which when I saw that a strict grave could doe,
I saw not why verse might not do so too.
Verse hath a middle nature: heaven keepes Soules,
The Grave keepes bodies, Verse the Fame enroules.

AN ANATOMIE OF THE WORLD

THE PROGRESSE OF THE SOULE

WHEREIN,

BY OCCASION OF THE RELIGIOUS DEATH OF MISTRESS ELIZABETH DRURY, THE INCOMMODITIES OF THE SOULE IN THIS LIFE, AND HER EXALTATION IN THE NEXT, ARE CONTEMPLATED

THE SECOND ANNIVERSARY [1612]

THE HARBINGER TO THE PROGRESSE
[BY JOSEPH HALL]

Two *Soules move here, and mine (a third) must move*
Paces of admiration and of love;
Thy Soule (deare virgin) whose this tribute is,
Mov'd from this mortall Spheare to lively blisse;
And yet moves still, and still aspires to see
The worlds last day, thy glories full degree:
Like as those starres which thou o'r-lookest farre,
Are in their place, and yet still moved are:
No soule (whiles with the luggage of this clay
It clogged is) can follow thee halfe way; 10
Or see thy flight, which doth our thoughts outgoe
So fast, that now the lightning moves but slow:
But now thou are as high in heaven flowne
As heaven's from us; what soule besides thine owne
Can tell thy joyes, or say he can relate
Thy glorious Journals in that blessed state?
I envie thee (Rich soule) I envy thee,
Although I cannot yet thy glory see:
And thou (great spirit) which hers follow'd hast
So fast, as none can follow thine so fast; 20
So far, as none can follow thine so farre,
(And if this flesh did not the passage barre
Hadst caught her) let me wonder at thy flight
Which long agone hadst lost the vulgar sight,
And now mak'st proud the better eyes, that they

Can see thee less'ned in thine ayery way;
So while thou mak'st her soule by progresse knowne
Thou mak'st a noble progresse of thine owne,
From this worlds carkasse having mounted high
To that pure life of immortalitie;   30
Since thine aspiring thoughts themselves so raise
That more may not beseeme a creatures praise,
Yet still thou vow'st her more; and every yeare
Mak'st a new progresse, while thou wandrest here;
Still upward mount; and let thy Makers praise
Honor thy Laura, and adorne thy laies.
And since thy Muse her head in heaven shrouds,
Oh let her never stoope below the clouds:
And if those glorious sainted soules may know
Or what wee doe, or what wee sing below,   40
Those acts, those songs, shall still content them best
Which praise those awfull Powers that make them blest.

OF THE PROGRESSE OF THE SOULE

THE SECOND ANNIVERSARIE

NOTHING could make me sooner to confesse   **The**
That this world had an everlastingnesse,   **entrance.**
Than to consider, that a yeare is runne,
Since both this lower world's, and the Sunnes Sunne,
The Lustre, and the vigor of this All,
Did set; 'twere blasphemie to say, did fall.
But as a ship which hath strooke saile, doth runne
By force of that force which before, it wonne:
Or as sometimes in a beheaded man,
Though at those two Red seas, which freely ranne,   **10**
One from the Trunke, another from the Head,
His soule be sail'd, to her eternall bed,
His eyes will twinckle, and his tongue will roll,
As though he beckned, and cal'd backe his soule,
He graspes his hands, and he pulls up his feet,
And seemes to reach, and to step forth to meet
His soule; when all these motions which we saw,
Are but as Ice, which crackles at a thaw:
Or as a Lute, which in moist weather, rings
Her knell alone, by cracking of her strings: **20**

So struggles this dead world, now shee is gvne;
For there is motion in corruption.
As some daies are at the Creation nam'd,
Before the Sunne, the which fram'd daies, was fram'd,
So after this Sunne's set, some shew appeares,
And orderly vicissitude of yeares.
Yet a new Deluge, and of *Lethe* flood,
Hath drown'd us all, All have forgot all good,
Forgetting her, the maine reserve of all.
Yet in this deluge, grosse and generall,   30
Thou seest me strive for life; my life shall bee,
To be hereafter prais'd, for praysing thee;
Immortall Maid, who though thou would'st refuse
The name of Mother, be unto my Muse
A Father, since her chast Ambition is,
Yearely to bring forth such a child as this.
These Hymnes may worke on future wits, and so
May great Grand children of thy prayses grow.
And so, though not revive, embalme and spice
The world, which else would putrifie with vice.   40
For thus, Man may extend thy progeny,
Untill man doe but vanish, and not die.
These Hymnes thy issue, may encrease so long,
As till Gods great *Venite* change the song.
Thirst for that time, O my insatiate soule,

A just
disesti-
mation of
the
world.

And serve thy thirst, with Gods safe-sealing **Bowle.**
Be thirstie still, and drinke still till thou goe
To th'only Health, to be Hydroptique so.
Forget this rotten world; And unto thee
Let thine owne times as an old storie bee.   50
Be not concern'd: studie not why, nor when;
Doe not so much as not beleeve a man.
For though to erre, be worst, to try truths forth,
Is far more businesse, than this world is worth.
The world is but a carkasse; thou art fed
By it, but as a worme, that carkasse bred;
And why should'st thou, poore worme, consider more,
When this world will grow better than before,
Than those thy fellow wormes doe thinke upon
That carkasses last resurrection.   60
Forget this world, and scarce thinke of it so,
As of old clothes, cast off a yeare agoe.
To be thus stupid is Alacritie:

Men thus Lethargique have best Memory.
Look upward; that's towards her, whose happy state
We now lament not, but congratulate.
Shee, to whom all this world was but a stage,
Where all sat harkning how her youthfull age
Should be emploi'd, because in all shee did,
Some Figure of the Golden times was hid.   70
Who could not lacke, what e'r this world could give,
Because shee was the forme, that made it live;
Nor could complaine, that this world was unfit
To be staid in, then when shee was in it;
Shee that first tried indifferent desires
By vertue, and vertue by religious fires,
Shee to whose person Paradise adher'd,
As Courts to Princes, shee whose eyes ensphear'd
Star-light enough, t'have made the South controule,
(Had shee beene there) the Star-full Northerne Pole,   80
Shee, shee is gone; she is gone; when thou knowest this,
What fragmentary rubbidge this world is
Thou knowest, and that it is not worth a thought;
He honors it too much that thinkes it nought.
Thinke then, my soule, that death is but a Groome,
Which brings a Taper to the outward roome,
Whence thou spiest first a little glimmering light,
And after brings it nearer to thy sight:
For such approaches doth heaven make in death.
Thinke thy selfe labouring now with broken breath,   90
And thinke those broken and soft Notes to bee
Division, and thy happyest Harmonie.
Thinke thee laid on thy death-bed, loose and slacke
And thinke that, but unbinding of a packe,
To take one precious thing, thy soule from thence.
Thinke thy selfe parch'd with fevers violence,
Anger thine ague more, by calling it
Thy Physicke; chide the slacknesse of the fit.
Thinke that thou hear'st thy knell, and think no more,
But that, as Bels cal'd thee to Church before,   100
So this, to the Triumphant Church, calls thee.
Thinke Satans Sergeants round about thee bee,
And thinke that but for Legacies they thrust;
Give one thy Pride, to'another give thy Lust:
Give them those sinnes which they gave thee before,
And trust th'immaculate blood to wash thy score.

Contem-
plation of
our state
in our
death-
bed.

Thinke, thy friends weeping round, and thinke that they
Weepe but because they goe not yet thy way.
Thinke that they close thine eyes, and thinke in this,
That they confesse much in the world, amisse,   **110**
Who dare not trust a dead mans eye with that,
Which they from God, and Angels cover not.
Thinke that they shroud thee up, and think from thence
They reinvest thee in white innocence.
Thinke that thy body rots, and (if so low,
Thy soule exalted so, thy thoughts can goe,)
Think thee a Prince, who of themselves create
Wormes which insensibly devoure their State.
Thinke that they bury thee, and thinke that right
Laies thee to sleepe but a Saint Lucies night.   **120**
Thinke these things cheerefully: and if thou bee
Drowsie or slacke, remember then that shee,
Shee whose Complexion was so even made,
That which of her Ingredients should invade
The other three, no Feare, no Art could guesse:
So far were all remov'd from more or lesse.
But as in Mithridate, or just perfumes,
Where all good things being met, no one presumes
To governe, or to triumph on the rest,
Only because all were, no part was best.   **130**
And as, though all doe know, that quantities
Are made of lines, and lines from Points arise,
None can these lines or quantities unjoynt,
And say this is a line, or this a point,
So though the Elements and Humors were
In her, one could not say, this governes there.
Whose even constitution might have wonne
Any disease to venter on the Sunne,
Rather than her: and make a spirit feare,
That hee to disuniting subject were.   **140**
To whose proportions if we would compare
Cubes, th'are unstable; Circles, Angular;
She who was such a chaine as Fate employes
To bring mankinde all Fortunes it enjoyes;
So fast, so even wrought, as one would thinke,
No Accident could threaten any linke;
Shee, shee embrac'd a sicknesse, gave it meat,
The purest blood, and breath, that e'r it eate;
And hath taught us, that though a good man hath

Title to heaven, and plead it by his Faith, 150
And though he may pretend a conquest, since
Heaven was content to suffer violence,
Yea though hee plead a long possession too,
(For they're in heaven on earth who heavens workes do)
Though hee had right and power and place, before,

Incom-
modities
of the
Soule in
the Body.

Yet Death must usher, and unlocke the doore.
Thinke further on thy selfe, my Soule, and thinke
How thou at first wast made but in a sinke;
Thinke that it argued some infirmitie,
That those two soules, which then thou foundst in me, 160
Thou fedst upon, and drewst into thee, both
My second soule of sense, and first of growth.
Thinke but how poore thou wast, how obnoxious;
Whom a small lumpe of flesh could poyson thus.
This curded milke, this poore unlittered whelpe
My body, could, beyond escape or helpe,
Infect thee with Originall sinne, and thou
Couldst neither then refuse, nor leave it now.
Thinke that no stubborne sullen Anchorit,
Which fixt to a pillar, or a grave, doth sit 170
Bedded, and bath'd in all his ordures, dwels
So fowly as our Soules in their first-built Cels.
Thinke in how poore a prison thou didst lie
After, enabled but to suck and crie.
Thinke, when'twas growne to most,'twas a poore Inne,
A Province pack'd up in two yards of skinne,
And that usurp'd or threatned with the rage
Of sicknesses, or their true mother, Age.
But thinke that Death hath now enfranchis'd thee,
Thou hast thy'expansion now, and libertie; 180

Her lib-
erty by
death.

Thinke that a rustie Peece, discharg'd, is flowne
In peeces, and the bullet is his owne,
And freely flies: This to thy Soule allow,
Thinke thy shell broke, thinke thy Soule hatch'd but now.
And think this slow-pac'd soule, which late did cleave
To'a body, and went but by the bodies leave,
Twenty, perchance, or thirty mile a day,
Dispatches in a minute all the way
Twixt heaven, and earth; she stayes not in the ayre,
To looke what Meteors there themselves prepare; 190
She carries no desire to know, nor sense,
Whether th'ayres middle region be intense;

For th'Element of fire, she doth not know,
Whether she past by such a place or no;
She baits not at the Moone, nor cares to trie
Whether in that new world, men live, and die.
Venus retards her not, to'enquire, how shee
Can, (being one starre) *Hesper,* and *Vesper* bee;
Hee that charm'd *Argus* eyes, sweet *Mercury,*
Workes not on her, who now is growne all eye;   200
Who, if she meet the body of the Sunne,
Goes through, not staying till his course be runne;
Who findes in *Mars* his Campe no corps of Guard;
Nor is by *Jove,* nor by his father barr'd;
But ere she can consider how she went,
At once is at, and through the Firmament.
And as these starres were but so many beads
Strung on one string, speed undistinguish'd leads
Her through those Spheares, as through the beads, a string,
Whose quick succession makes it still one thing: 210
As doth the pith, which, lest our bodies slacke,
Strings fast the little bones of necke, and backe;
So by the Soule doth death string Heaven and Earth;
For when our Soule enjoyes this her third birth,
(Creation gave her one, a second, grace,)
Heaven is as neare, and present to her face,
As colours are, and objects, in a roome
Where darknesse was before, when Tapers come.
This must, my Soule, thy long-short Progresse bee;
To'advance these thoughts, remember then, that she,   220
She, whose faire body no such prison was,
But that a Soule might well be pleas'd to passe
An age in her; she whose rich beauty lent
Mintage to other beauties, for they went
But for so much as they were like to her;
Shee, in whose body (if we dare preferre
This low world, to so high a marke as shee,)
The Westerne treasure, Easterne spicerie,
Europe, and Afrique, and the unknowne rest
Were easily found, or what in them was best;   230
And when w'have made this large discoverie
Of all, in her some one part then will bee
Twenty such parts, whose plenty and riches is
Enough to make twenty such worlds as this;
Shee, whom had they knowne who did first betroth

The Tutelar Angels, and assign'd one, both
To Nations, Cities, and to Companies,
To Functions, Offices, and Dignities,
And to each severall man, to him, and him,
They would have given her one for every limbe;   **240**
She, of whose soule, if we may say, 'twas Gold,
Her body was th'Electrum, and did hold
Many degrees of that; wee understood
Her by her sight; her pure, and eloquent blood
Spoke in her cheekes, and so distinctly wrought,
That one might almost say, her body thought;
Shee, shee, thus richly and largely hous'd, is gone:
And chides us slow-pac'd snailes who crawle upon
Our prisons prison, earth, nor thinke us well,
Longer, than whil'st wee beare our brittle shell.   **250**
But 'twere but little to have chang'd our roome,   Her igno-
If, as we were in this our living Tombe   rance in
Oppress'd with ignorance, wee still were so.   this life
Poore soule, in this thy flesh what dost thou know?   and
Thou know'st thy selfe so little, as thou know'st not,   knowl-
How thou didst die, nor how thou wast begot.   edge in
Thou neither know'st how thou at first cam'st in,   the next.
Nor how thou took'st the poyson of mans sinne.
Nor dost thou, (though thou know'st, that thou art so)
By what way thou art made immortall, know.   **260**
Thou art too narrow, wretch, to comprehend
Even thy selfe: yea though thou wouldst but bend
To know thy body. Have not all soules thought
For many ages, that our body'is wrought
Of Ayre, and Fire, and other Elements?
And now they thinke of new ingredients,
And one Soule thinkes one, and another way
Another thinkes, and 'tis an even lay.
Knowst thou but how the stone doth enter in
The bladders cave, and never breake the skinne?   **270**
Know'st thou how blood, which to the heart doth flow,
Doth from one ventricle to th'other goe?
And for the putrid stuffe, which thou dost spit,
Know'st thou how thy lungs have attracted it?
There are no passages, so that there is
(For ought thou know'st) piercing of substances.
And of those many opinions which men raise
Of Nailes and Haires, dost thou know which to praise?

What hope have wee to know our selves, when wee
Know not the least things, which for our use be?   280
Wee see in Authors, too stiffe to recant,
A hundred controversies of an Ant;
And yet one watches, starves, freeses, and sweats,
To know but Catechismes and Alphabets
Of unconcerning things, matters of fact;
How others on our stage their parts did Act;
What *Cæsar* did, yea, and what *Cicero* said.
Why grasse is greene, or why our blood is red,
Are mysteries which none have reach'd unto.
In this low forme, poore soule, what wilt thou doe?   290
When wilt thou shake off this Pedantery,
Of being taught by sense, and Fantasie?
Thou look'st through spectacles; small things seeme great
Below; But up unto the watch-towre get,
And see all things despoyl'd of fallacies:
Thou shalt not peepe through lattices of eyes,
Nor heare through Labyrinths of eares, nor learne
By circuit, or collections to discerne.
In heaven thou straight know'st all, concerning it,
And what concernes it not, shalt straight forget.   300
There thou (but in no other schoole) maist bee
Perchance, as learned, and as full, as shee,
Shee who all libraries had throughly read
At home in her owne thoughts, and practised
So much good as would make as many more:
Shee whose example they must all implore,
Who would or doe, or thinke well, and confesse
That all the vertuous Actions they expresse,
Are but a new, and worse edition
Of her some one thought, or one action: 310
She who in th'art of knowing Heaven, was growne
Here upon earth, to such perfection,
That she hath, ever since to Heaven she came,
(In a far fairer print,) but read the same:
Shee, shee not satisfied with all this waight,
(For so much knowledge, as would over-fraight
Another, did but ballast her) is gone
As well t'enjoy, as get perfection.
And cals us after her, in that shee tooke,
(Taking her selfe) our best, and worthiest booke.   320

Returne not, my Soule, from this extasie,
And meditation of what thou shalt bee,
To earthly thoughts, till it to thee appeare,
With whom thy conversation must be there.
With whom wilt thou converse? what station
Canst thou choose out, free from infection,
That will not give thee theirs, nor drinke in thine?
Shalt thou not finde a spungie slacke Divine
Drinke and sucke in th'instructions of Great men,
And for the word of God, vent them agen?
Are there not some Courts (and then, no things bee
So like as Courts) which, in this let us see,
That wits and tongues of Libellers are weake,
Because they do more ill, than these can speake?
The poyson's gone through all, poysons affect
Chiefly the chiefest parts, but some effect
In nailes, and haires, yea excrements, will show;
So lyes the poyson of sinne in the most low.
Up, up, my drowsie Soule, where thy new eare
Shall in the Angels songs no discord heare;
Where thou shalt see the blessed Mother-maid
Joy in not being that, which men have said.
Where she is exalted more for being good,
Than for her interest of Mother-hood.
Up to those Patriarchs, which did longer sit
Expecting Christ, than they'have enjoy'd him yet.
Up to those Prophets, which now gladly see
Their Prophesies growne to be Historie.
Up to th'Apostles, who did bravely runne
All the Suns course, with more light than the Sunne.
Up to those Martyrs, who did calmly bleed
Oyle to th'Apostles Lamps, dew to their seed.
Up to those Virgins, who thought, that almost
They made joyntenants with the Holy Ghost,
If they to any should his Temple give.
Up, up, for in that squadron there doth live
She, who hath carried thither new degrees
(As to their number) to their dignities.
Shee, who being to her selfe a State, injoy'd
All royalties which any State employ'd;
For shee made warres, and triumph'd; reason still
Did not o'rthrow, but rectifie her will:

Of our
company
in this
life, and
in the
next.

330

340

350

360

And she made peace, for no peace is like this,
That beauty, and chastity together kisse:
She did high justice, for she crucified
Every first motion of rebellious pride:
And she gave pardons, and was liberall,
For, onely her selfe except, she pardon'd all:
Shee coy'nd, in this, that her impressions gave
To all our actions all the worth they have: 370
She gave protections; the thoughts of her brest
Satans rude Officers could ne'r arrest.
As these prerogatives being met in one,
Made her a soveraigne State; religion
Made her a Church; and these two made her all.
She who was all this All, and could not fall
To worse, by company, (for she was still
More Antidote, than all the world was ill,)
Shee, shee doth leave it, and by Death, survive
All this, in Heaven; whither who doth not strive   380
The more, because shees there, he doth not know
That accidentall joyes in Heaven doe grow.
But pause, my soule; And study, ere thou fall
Of essen-   On accidentall joyes, th'essentiall.
tiall joy   Still before Accessories doe abide
in this   A triall, must the principall be tride.
life and   And what essentiall joy can'st thou expect
in the   Here upon earth? what permanent effect
next.   Of transitory causes? Dost thou love
Beauty? (And beauty worthy'st is to move)   390
Poore cousened cousenor, *that* she, and *that* thou,
Which did begin to love, are neither now;
You are both fluid, chang'd since yesterday;
Next day repaires, (but ill) last dayes decay.
Nor are, (although the river keepe the name)
Yesterdaies waters, and to daies the same.
So flowes her face, and thine eyes, neither now
That Saint, nor Pilgrime, which your loving vow
Concern'd, remaines; but whil'st you thinke you bee
Constant, you'are hourely in inconstancie.   400
Honour may have pretence unto our love,
Because that God did live so long above
Without this Honour, and then lov'd it so,
That he at last made Creatures to bestow
Honour on him: not that he needed it.

But that, to his hands, man might grow more fit.
But since all Honours from inferiours flow,
(For they doe give it; Princes doe but shew
Whom they would have so honor'd) and that this
On such opinions, and capacities   410
Is built, as rise and fall, to more and lesse:
Alas, 'tis but a casuall happinesse.
Hath ever any man to'himselfe assign'd
This or that happinesse to'arrest his minde,
But that another man which takes a worse
Thinks him a foole for having tane that course?
They who did labour Babels tower to'erect,
Might have considered, that for that effect,
All this whole solid Earth could not allow
Nor furnish forth materialls enow;   420
And that this Center, to raise such a place,
Was farre too little, to have beene the Base;
No more affords this world, foundation
To erect true joy, were all the meanes in one.
But as the Heathen made them severall gods,
Of all Gods Benefits, and all his Rods,
(For as the Wine, and Corne, and Onions are
)Gods unto them, so Agues bee, and Warre)
And as by changing that whole precious Gold
To such small Copper coynes, they lost the old,   430
And lost their only God, who ever must
Be sought alone, and not in such a thrust:
So much mankinde true happinesse mistakes;
No Joy enjoyes that man, than many makes.
Then, Soule, to thy first pitch worke up againe;
Know that all lines which circles doe containe,
For once that they the Center touch, doe touch
Twice the circumference; and be thou such;
Double on heaven thy thoughts on earth emploid;
All will not serve; Only who have enjoy'd   440
The sight of God, in fulnesse, can thinke it;
For it is both the object, and the wit.
This is essentiall joy, where neither hee
Can suffer diminution, nor wee;
'Tis such a full, and such a filling good;
Had th'Angels once look'd on him, they had stood.
To fill the place of one of them, or more,
Shee whom wee celebrate, is gone before.

She, who had Here so much essentiall joy,
As no chance could distract, much lesse destroy;   450
Who with Gods presence was acquainted so,
(Hearing, and speaking to him) as to know
His face in any naturall Stone, or Tree,
Better than when in Images they bee:
Who kept by diligent devotion,
Gods Image, in such reparation,
Within her heart, that what decay was growne,
Was her first Parents fault, and not her owne:
Who being solicited to any act,
Still heard God pleading his safe precontract;   460
Who by a faithfull confidence, was here
Betroth'd to God, and now is married there;
Whose twilights were more cleare, than our mid-day;
Who dreamt devoutlier, than most use to pray;
Who being here fil'd with grace, yet strove to bee,
Both where more grace, and more capacitie
At once is given: she to Heaven is gone,
Who made this world in some proportion
A heaven, and here, became unto us all,
Joy, (as our joyes admit) essentiall.   470
But could this low world joyes essentiall touch,
Heavens accidentall joyes would passe them much.
How poor and lame, must then our casuall bee?
If thy Prince will his subjects to call thee
My Lord, and this doe swell thee, thou art then,
By being greater, growne to bee lesse Man.
When no Physitian of redresse can speake,
A joyfull casuall violence may breake
A dangerous Apostem in thy breast;
And whil'st thou joyest in this, the dangerous rest,   480
The bag may rise up, and so strangle thee.
What e'r was casuall, may ever bee.
What should the nature change? Or make the same
Certaine, which was but casuall, when it came?
All casuall joy doth loud and plainly say,
Only by comming, that it can away.
Only in Heaven joyes strength is never spent;
And accidentall things are permanent.
Joy of a soules arrivall ne'r decaies;
For that soule ever joyes and ever staies.   490
Joy that their last great Consummation

Of accidentall joys in both places

Approaches in the resurrection;
When earthly bodies more celestiall
Shall be, than Angels were, for they could fall;
This kinde of joy doth every day admit
Degrees of growth, but none of losing it.
In this fresh joy, 'tis no small part, that shee,
Shee, in whose goodnesse, he that names degree,
Doth injure her; ('Tis losse to be cal'd best,
There where the stuffe is not such as the rest)　　　500
Shee, who left such a bodie, as even shee
Only in Heaven could learne, how it can bee
Made better; for shee rather was two soules,
Or like to full on both sides written Rols,
Where eyes might reade upon the outward skin,
As strong Records for God, as mindes within;
Shee, who by making full perfection grow,
Peeces a Circle, and still keepes it so,
Long'd for, and longing for it, to heaven is gone,
Where shee receives, and gives addition.　　　510
Here in a place, where mis-devotion frames　　　Conclu-
A thousand Prayers to Saints, whose very names　　　sion.
The ancient Church knew not, Heaven knows not yet:
And where, what lawes of Poetry admit,
Lawes of Religion have at least the same,
Immortall Maide, I might invoke thy name.
Could any Saint provoke that appetite,
Thou here should'st make me a French convertite.
But thou would'st not; nor would'st thou be content,
To take this, for my second yeares true Rent,　　　520
Did this Coine beare any other stampe, than his,
That gave thee power to doe, me, to say this.
Since his will is, that to posteritie,
Thou should'st for life, and death, a patterne bee,
And that the world should notice have of this,
The purpose, and th'authoritie is his;
Thou art the Proclamation; and I am
The Trumpet, at whose voyce the people came.

EPICEDES AND OBSEQUIES UPON THE DEATHS OF SUNDRY PERSONAGES AND EPITAPHS

ELEGIE ON THE L. C. [LORD CHAMBERLAIN] [1596]

SORROW, who to this house scarce knew the way:
Is, Oh, heire of it, our All is his prey.
This strange chance claimes strange wonder, and to us
Nothing can be so strange, as to weepe thus.
'Tis well his lifes loud speaking workes deserve,
And give praise too, our cold tongues could not serve·
'Tis well, hee kept teares from our eyes before,
That to fit this deepe ill, we might have store.
Oh, if a sweet briar, climbe up by'a tree,
If to a paradise that transplanted bee,   10
Or fell'd, and burnt for holy sacrifice,
Yet, that must wither, which by it did rise,
As wee for him dead: though no familie
Ere rigg'd a soule for heavens discoverie
With whom more Venturers more boldly dare
Venture their states, with him in joy to share.
Wee lose what all friends lov'd, him; he gaines now·
But life by death, which worst foes would allow,
If hee could have foes, in whose practise grew
All vertues, whose names subtile Schoolmen knew.   20
What ease, can hope that wee shall see'him, beget,
When wee must die first, and cannot dye yet?
His children are his pictures, Oh they bee
Pictures of him dead, senselesse, cold as he.
Here needs no marble Tombe, since hee is gone,
He, and about him, his, are turn'd to stone.

ELEGIE ON THE LADY MARCKHAM   [d. 1609]

MAN is the World, and death th'Ocean,
    To which God gives the lower parts of man.
This Sea invirons all, and though as yet

God hath set markes, and bounds, twixt us and it,
Yet doth it rore, and gnaw, and still pretend,
   And breaks our bankes, when ere it takes a friend.
Then our land waters (teares of passion) vent;
   Our waters, then, above our firmament,
(Teares which our Soule doth for her sins let fall);
   Take all a brackish tast, and Funerall,   10
And even these teares, which should wash sin, are sin.
   We, after Gods *Noe,* drowne our world againe.
Nothing but man of all invenom'd things
   Doth worke upon itselfe, with inborne stings.
Teares are false Spectacles, we cannot see
   Through passions mist, what wee are, or what shee.
In her this sea of death hath made no breach,
   But as the tide doth wash the slimie beach,
And leaves embroder'd workes upon the sand,
   So is her flesh refin'd by deaths cold hand.   20
As men of China,'after an ages stay,
   Do take up Porcelane, where they buried Clay;
So at this grave, her limbecke, which refines
   The Diamonds, Rubies, Saphires, Pearles, and Mines,
Of which this flesh was, her soule shall inspire
   Flesh of such stuffe, as God, when his last fire
Annuls this world, to recompence it, shall,
   Make and name then, th'Elixar of this All.
They say, the sea, when it gaines, loseth too;
   If carnall Death (the yonger brother) doe   30
Usurpe the body,'our soule, which subject is
   To th'elder death, by sinne, is freed by this;
They perish both, when they attempt the just;
   For, graves our trophies are, and both deaths' dust.
So, unobnoxious now, she'hath buried both;
   For, none to death sinnes, that to sinne is loth,
Nor doe they die, which are not loth to die;
   So hath she this, and that virginity.
Grace was in her extremely diligent,
   That kept her from sinne, yet made her repent.   40
Of what small spots pure white complaines! Alas,
   How little poyson cracks a christall glasse!
She sinn'd, but just enough to let us see
   That God's word must be true, All, sinners be.
Soe much did zeale her conscience rarefie,
   That, extreme truth lack'd little of a lye,

Making omissions, acts; laying the touch
  Of sinne, on things that sometimes may be such.
As *Moses* Cherubines, whose natures doe
  Surpasse all speed, by him are winged too: **50**
So would her soule, already'in heaven, seeme then,
  To clyme by teares, the common staires of men.
How fit she was for God, I am content
  To speake, that Death his vaine haste may repent.
How fit for us, how even and how sweet,
  How good in all her titles, and how meet,
To have reform'd this forward heresie,
  That women can no parts of friendship bee;
How Morall, how Divine shall not be told,
  Lest they that heare her vertues, thinke her old: **60**
And lest we take Deaths part, and make him glad
  Of such a prey, and to his tryumph adde.

ELEGIE ON MISTRIS BOULSTRED   [d. 1609]

DEATH I recant, and say, unsaid by mee
  What ere hath slip'd, that might diminish thee.
Spirituall treason, atheisme 'tis, to say,
  That any can thy Summons disobey.
Th'earths face is but thy Table; there are set
  Plants, cattell, men, dishes for Death to eate.
In a rude hunger now hee millions drawes
  Into his bloody, or plaguy, or sterv'd jawes.
Now hee will seeme to spare, and doth more wast,
  Eating the best first, well preserv'd to last.   **10**
Now wantonly he spoiles, and eates us not,
  But breakes off friends, and lets us peecemeale rot.
Nor will this earth serve him; he sinkes the deepe
  Where harmlesse fish monastique silence keepe,
Who (were Death dead) by Roes of living sand,
  Might spunge that element, and make it land.
He rounds the aire, and breakes the hymnique notes
  In birds (Heavens choristers,) organique throats,
Which (if they did not dye) might seeme to bee
  A tenth ranke in the heavenly hierarchie.   **20**
O strong and long-liv'd death, how cam'st thou in?
  And how without Creation didst begin?
Thou hast, and shalt see dead, before thou dyest.

All the foure Monarchies, and Antichrist.
How could I thinke thee nothing, that see now
  In all this All, nothing else is, but thou.
Our births and lives, vices, and vertues, bee
  Wastfull consumptions, and degrees of thee.
For, wee to live, our bellowes weare, and breath,
  Nor are wee mortall, dying, dead, but death.   30
And though thou beest, O mighty bird of prey,
  So much reclaim'd by God, that thou must lay
All that thou kill'st at his feet, yet doth hee
  Reserve but few, and leaves the most to thee.
And of those few, now thou hast overthrowne
  One whom thy blow makes, not ours, nor thine own.
She was more stories high: hopelesse to come
  To her Soule, thou'hast offer'd at her lower roome.
Her Soule and body was a King and Court:
  But thou hast both of Captaine mist and fort.   40
As houses fall not, though the King remove,
  Bodies of Saints rest for their soules above.
Death gets 'twixt soules and bodies such a place
  As sinne insinuates 'twixt just men and grace,
Both worke a separation, no divorce.
  Her Soule is gone to usher up her corse,
Which shall be'almost another soule, for there
  Bodies are purer, than best Soules are here.
Because in her, her virtues did outgoe
  Her yeares, would'st thou, O emulous death, do so?   50
And kill her young to thy losse? must the cost
  Of beauty,'and wit, apt to doe harme, be lost?
What though thou found'st her proofe 'gainst sins of youth?
  Oh, every age a diverse sinne pursueth.
Thou should'st have stay'd, and taken better hold,
  Shortly, ambitious; covetous, when old,
She might have prov'd: and such devotion
  Might once have stray'd to superstition.
If all her vertues must have growne, yet might
  Abundant virtue'have bred a proud delight.   60
Had she persever'd just, there would have bin
  Some that would sinne, mis-thinking she did sinne.
Such as would call her friendship, love, and faine
  To sociablenesse, a name profane;
Or sinne, by tempting, or, not daring that,
  By wishing, though they never told her what.

Thus might'st thou'have slain more soules, had'st thou not crost
    Thy selfe, and to triumph, thine army lost.
Yet though these wayes be lost, thou hast left one,
    Which is, immoderate griefe that she is gone.   **70**
But we may scape that sinne, yet weepe as much,
    Our teares are due, because we are not such.
Some teares, that knot of friends, her death must cost,
    Because the chaine is broke, though no linke lost.

ELEGIE

DEATH

LANGUAGE thou art too narrow, and too weake
    To ease us now; great sorrow cannot speake;
If we could sigh out accents, and weepe words,
    Griefe weares, and lessens, that tears breath affords.
Sad hearts, the lesse they seeme the more they are,
    (So guiltiest men stand mutest at the barre)
Not that they know not, feele not their estate,
    But extreme sense hath made them desperate.
Sorrow, to whom we owe all that we bee;
    Tyrant, in the fift and greatest Monarchy,   **10**
Was't, that she did possesse all hearts before,
    Thou hast kil'd her, to make thy Empire more?
Knew'st thou some would, that knew her not, lament,
    As in a deluge perish th'innocent?
Was't not enough to have that palace wonne,
    But thou must raze it too, that was undone?
Had'st thou staid there, and look'd out at her eyes,
    All had ador'd thee that now from thee flies,
For they let out more light, than they tooke in,
    They told not when, but did the day beginne.   **20**
She was too Saphirine, and cleare for thee;
    Clay, flint, and jeat now thy fit dwellings be;
Alas, shee was too pure, but not too weake;
    Who e'r saw Christall Ordinance but would break?
And if wee be thy conquest, by her fall
    Th'hast lost thy end, for in her perish all;
Or if we live, we live but to rebell,
    They know her better now, that knew her well.
If we should vapour out, and pine, and die;

Since, shee first went, that were not miserie. 30
Shee chang'd our world with hers; now she is gone,
   Mirth and prosperity is oppression;
For of all morall vertues she was all,
   The Ethicks speake of vertues Cardinall.
Her soule was Paradise; the Cherubin
   Set to keepe it was grace, that kept out sinne.
Shee had no more than let in death, for wee
   All reape consumption from one fruitfull tree.
God tooke her hence, lest some of us should love
   Her, like that plant, him and his lawes above, 40
And when wee teares, hee mercy shed in this,
   To raise our mindes to heaven where now she is;
Who if her vertues would have let her stay
   Wee'had had a Saint, have now a holiday.
Her heart was that strange bush, where, sacred fire,
   Religion, did not consume, but'inspire
Such piety, so chast use of Gods day,
   That what we turne to *feast*, she turn'd to *pray*,
And did prefigure here, in devout tast,
   The rest of her high Sabaoth, which shall last. 50
Angels did hand her up, who next God dwell,
   (For she was of that order whence most fell)
Her body left with us, lest some had said,
   Shee could not die, except they saw her dead;
For from lesse vertue, and lesse beautiousnesse,
   The Gentiles fram'd them Gods and Goddesses.
The ravenous earth that now wooes her to be
   Earth too, will be a *Lemnia;* and the tree
That wraps that christall in a wooden Tombe,
   Shall be tooke up spruce, fill'd with diamond; 60
And we her sad glad friends all beare a part
   Of griefe, for all would waste a Stoicks heart.

ELEGIE ON THE UNTIMELY DEATH

OF THE

INCOMPARABLE PRINCE HENRY   [d. 1612]

Look to me, *Faith;* and look to my *Faith*, God:
For, both my *Centres* feel This *Period*.
Of *Waight,* one *Centre;* one of *Greatness* is:

And REASON is That *Centre;* FAITH is This.
For into our *Reason* flowe, and there doe end,
All that this naturall World doth comprehend;
Quotidian things, and Equi-distant hence,
Shut-in for Men in one *Circumference:*
But, for th'enormous *Greatnesses,* which are
So disproportion'd and so angulare,   **10**
As is GOD's *Essence, Place,* and *Providence,*
Where, How, When, What, Soules do, departed hence:
These *Things* (*Eccentrique* else) on Faith do strike;
Yet neither All, nor upon all alike:
For, *Reason,* put t'her best *Extension,*
Almost meetes *Faith,* and makes both *Centres* one:
And nothing ever came so neer to This,
As *Contemplation* of the PRINCE wee misse.
For, All that *Faith* could credit Mankinde *could,*
Reason still seconded that This PRINCE *would.*   **20**
If then, least Movings of the *Centre* make
(More than if whole Hell belcht) the World to shake,
What must This doo, *Centres* distracted so,
That Wee see not what to beleeve or knowe?
Was it not well believ'd, till now, that *Hee,*
Whose *Reputation* was an *Extasie*
On neighbour States; which knew not Why to wake
Till *Hee* discoverd what wayes *Hee* would take:
For *Whom* what *Princes* angled (when they tryed)
Mett a *Torpedo,* and were stupefied: **30**
And Others studies, how *Hee* would be bent;
Was His great *Father's* greatest Instrument,
And activ'st spirit to convey and tye
This soule of *Peace* through CHRISTIANITIE?
Was it not well believ'd, that *Hee* would make
This *general Peace* th'eternall overtake?
And that *His* Times might have stretcht out so far
As to touch Those of which they *Emblems* are?
For, to confirm this just Belief, that Now
The *last Dayes* came, wee saw Heaven did allow   **40**
That but from *His* aspect and Exercise,
In *Peace*-full times, Rumors of *Warrs* should rise.
But *now* This *Faith* is *Heresie:* wee must
Still stay, and vexe our *Great-Grand-Mother,* DUST.
Oh! Is GOD prodigall? Hath he spent his store
Of Plagues on us? and only now, when more

Would ease us much, doth he grudge *Miserie,*
And will not lett's enjoy our *Curse,* to *Dye?*
As, for the Earth throw'n lowest downe of all,
'Twere an *Ambition* to desire to fall: 50
So God, in our *desire* to *dye,* dooth know
Our Plot for *Ease,* in beeing *Wretched* so.
Therefore *Wee live:* though such a Life we have
As but so manie *Mandrakes* on his Grave.

What had *His growth* and *generation* donne?
When what wee are, his *putrefaction*
Sustains in us, Earth, which *Griefs* animate?
Nor hath our World now other *soule* than That.
And could *Grief* gett so high as Heav'n, that *Quire*
Forgetting This, their new Joy, would desire   60
(With grief to see him) *Hee* had staid belowe,
To rectifie Our *Errors* They foreknowe.

Is th'other *Centre,* REASON, faster, then?
Where should wee look for That, now w'are not Men:
For, if our *Reason* be our *Connexion*
Of *Causes,* now to us there can be none.
For, as, if all the *Substances* were spent,
'Twere madnes to enquire of *Accident:*
So is't to looke for *Reason,* HEE being gone,
The only *subject* REASON wrought upon.   70

If *Faith* have such a *chaine,* whose divers Links
Industrious Man discerneth, as he thinks,
When Miracle dooth joine, and so steal-in
A new link Man knowes not where to begin:
At a much deader Fault must *Reason* bee,
Death having broke-off such a Link as *Hee.*
But, now, for us with busie *Proofs* to come
That w'have no *Reason,* would prove we had some:
So would just *Lamentations.* Therefore Wee
May safelier say, that Wee are dead, than *Hee.*   80
So, if our *Griefs* wee doo not well declare,
W'have double Excuse; *Hee* is not *dead,* We are.
Yet would not I dye yet; for though I bee
Too narrow, to think HIM, as *Hee* is HEE
(Our *Soule's* best Bayting and Mid-*period*
In her long *journey* of *Considering* GOD)
Yet (no Dishonor) I can reach Him *thus;*
As *Hee* embrac't the *Fires* of *Love* with us.
Oh! May I (*since* I live) but see or hear

That *Shee-Intelligence* which mov'd This *Sphear*,　　　90
I pardon Fate my Life. Who-e'r thou bee
Which hast the noble *Conscience*, Thou art *Shee*.
I conjure Thee by all the *Charmes Hee* spoke,
By th'Oathes which only you *Two* never broke,
By all the *Soules* you sigh'd; that if you see
These Lines, you wish I knew *Your Historie:*
So, much as *You Two mutual Heavens* were *here*,
I were an *Angel singing* what *You* were.

TO THE COUNTESSE OF BEDFORD

MADAME,

I HAVE *learn'd by those lawes wherein I am a little conversant,
that hee which bestowes any cost upon the dead, obliges him
which is dead, but not the heire; I do not therefore send this
paper to your Ladyship, that you should thanke mee for it, or
thinke that I thanke you in it; your favours and benefits to mee
are so much above my merits, that they are even above my gratitude, if that were to be judged by words which must expresse it:
But, Madame, since your noble brothers fortune being yours, the
evidences also concerning it are yours, so his vertue being yours,
the evidences concerning it, belong also to you, of which by
your acceptance this may be one peece, in which quality I humbly present it, and as a testimony how intirely your familie possesseth*

Your Ladiships most humble
and thankfull servant

JOHN DONNE

OBSEQUIES TO THE LORD HARRINGTON,

BROTHER TO THE LADY LUCY, COUNTESSE OF BEDFORD

[d. 1614]

FAIRE soule, which wast, not onely, as all soules bee,
Then when thou wast infused, harmony,
But did'st continue so; and now dost beare
A part in Gods great organ, this whole Spheare:
If looking up to God; or downe to us,

Thou finde that any way is pervious,
Twixt heav'n and earth, and that mans actions doe
Come to your knowledge, and affections too,
See, and with joy, mee to that good degree
Of goodnesse growne, that I can studie thee,   10
And, by these meditations refin'd,
Can unapparell and enlarge my minde,
And so can make by this soft extasie,
This place a map of heav'n, my selfe of thee.
Thou seest mee here at midnight, now all rest;
Times dead-low water; when all mindes devest
To morrows businesse, when the labourers have
Such rest in bed, that their last Church-yard grave,
Subject to change, will scarce be'a type of this,
Now when the clyent, whose last hearing is   20
To morrow, sleeps, when the condemned man,
(Who when hee opes his eyes, must shut them then
Againe by death,) although sad watch hee keepe,
Doth practice dying by a little sleepe,
Thou at this midnight seest mee, and as soone
As that Sunne rises to mee, midnight's noone,
All the world growes transparent, and I see
Through all, both Church and State, in seeing thee;
And I discerne by favour of this light,
My selfe, the hardest object of the sight.   30
God is the glasse; as thou when thou dost see
Him who sees all, seest all concerning thee,
So, yet unglorified, I comprehend
All, in these mirrors of thy wayes, and end.
Though God be our true glasse, through which we see
All, since the beeing of all things is hee,
Yet are the trunkes which doe to us derive
Things, in proportion fit, by perspective,
Deeds of good men; for by their living here,
Vertues, indeed remote, seeme to be neare.   40
But where can I affirme, or where arrest
My thoughts on his deeds? which shall I call best?
For fluid vertue cannot be look'd on,
Nor can endure a contemplation.
As bodies change, and as I do not weare
Those Spirits, humors, blood I did last yeare,
And, as if on a streame I fixe mine eye,
That drop, which I looked on, is presently

Pusht with more waters from my sight, and gone,
So in this sea of vertues, can no one   50
Bee'insisted on; vertues, as rivers, passe,
Yet still remaines that vertuous man there was;
And as if man feed on mans flesh, and so
Part of his body to another owe,
Yet at the last two perfect bodies rise,
Because God knowes where every Atome lyes;
So, if one knowledge were made of all those,
Who knew his minutes well, hee might dispose
His vertues into names, and ranks; but I
Should injure Nature, Vertue, and Destinie,   60
Should I divide and discontinue so,
Vertue, which did in one intirenesse grow.
For as, hee that would say, spirits are fram'd
Of all the purest parts that can be nam'd,
Honours not spirits halfe so much, as hee
Which sayes, they have no parts, but simple bee;
So is't of vertue; for a point and one
Are much entirer than a million.
And had Fate meant to have his vertues told,
It would have let him live to have beene old;   70
So, then that vertue in season, and then this,
We might have seene, and said, that now he is
Witty, now wise, now temperate, now just:
In good short lives, vertues are faine to thrust,
And to be sure betimes to get a place,
When they would exercise, lacke time, and space.
So was it in this person, forc'd to bee
For lack of time, his owne epitome:
So to exhibit in few yeares as much,
As all the long breath'd Chronicles can touch.   80
As when an Angell down from heav'n doth flye,
Our quick thought cannot keepe him company,
Wee cannot thinke now hee is at the Sunne,
Now through the Moon, now he through th'aire doth run,
Yet when he's come, we know he did repaire
To all twixt Heav'n and Earth, Sunne, Moon, and Aire;
And as this Angell in an instant knowes,
And yet wee know, this sodaine knowledge growes
By quick amassing severall formes of things,
Which he successively to order brings;   90
When they, whose slow-pac'd lame thoughts cannot goe

So fast as hee, thinke that he doth not so;
Just as a perfect reader doth not dwell,
On every syllable, nor stay to spell,
Yet without doubt, hee doth distinctly see
And lay together every A, and B;
So, in short liv'd good men, is'not understood
Each severall vertue, but the compound good;
For, they all vertues paths in that pace tread,
As Angells goe, and know, and as men read.   **100**
O why should then these men, these lumps of Balme
Sent hither, this worlds tempests to becalme,
Before by deeds they are diffus'd and spread,
And so make us alive, themselves be dead?
O Soule, O circle, why so quickly bee
Thy ends, thy birth and death, clos'd up in thee?
Since one foot of thy compasse still was plac'd
In heav'n, the other might securely'have pac'd
In the most large extent, through every path,
Which the whole world, or man the abridgment hath. **110**
Thou knowst, that though the tropique circles have
(Yea and those small ones which the Poles engrave,)
All the same roundnesse, evennesse, and all
The endlesnesse of the equinoctiall;
Yet, when we come to measure distances,
How here, how there, the Sunne affected is,
When he doth faintly worke, and when prevaile,
Onely great circles, then can be our scale:
So, though thy circle to thy selfe expresse
All, tending to thy endlesse happinesse,   **120**
And wee, by our good use of it may trye,
Both how to live well young, and how to die,
Yet, since we must be old, and age endures
His Torrid Zone at Court, and calentures
Of hot ambitions, irrelegions ice,
Zeales agues, and hydroptique avarice,
Infirmities which need the scale of truth,
As well as lust, and ignorance of youth,
Why did'st thou not for these give medicines too,
And by thy doing tell us what to doe?   **130**
Though as small pocket-clocks, whose every wheele
Doth each mismotion and distemper feele,
Whose *hand* gets shaking palsies, and whose *string*
(His sinews) slackens, and whose *Soule*, the spring,

Expires, or languishes, whose pulse, the flye,
Either beates not, or beates unevenly,
Whose voice, the *Bell*, doth rattle, or grow dumbe,
Or idle,'as men, which to their last houres come,
If these clockes be not wound, or be wound still,
Or be not set, or set at every will;   140
So, youth is easiest to destruction,
If then wee follow all, or follow none.
Yet, as in great clocks, which in steeples chime,
Plac'd to informe whole towns, to'imploy their time,
An error doth more harme, being generall,
When, small clocks faults, only'on the wearer fall;
So worke the faults of age, on which the eye
Of children, servants, or the State relie.
Why wouldst not thou then, which hadst such a soule,
A clock so true, as might the Sunne controule,   150
And daily hadst from him, who gave it thee,
Instructions, such as it could never be
Disordered, stay here, as a generall
And great Sun-dyall, to have set us All?
O why wouldst thou be any instrument
To this unnaturall course, or why consent
To this, not miracle, but Prodigie,
That when the ebbs, longer than flowings be,
Vertue, whose flood did with thy youth begin,
Should so much faster ebb out, than flow in?   160
Though her flood was blowne in, by thy first breath,
All is at once sunke in the whirle-poole death.
Which word I would not name, but that I see
Death, else a desert, growne a Court by thee.
Now I grow sure, that if a man would have
Good companie, his entry is a grave.
Mee thinkes all Cities now, but Anthills bee,
Where, when the severall labourers I see,
For children, house, Provision, taking paine,
They'are all but Ants, carrying eggs, straw, and grain; 170
And Church-yards are our cities, unto which
The most repaire, that are in goodnesse rich.
There is the best concourse, and confluence,
There are the holy suburbs, and from thence
Begins Gods City, New Jerusalem,
Which doth extend her utmost gates to them.
At that gate then Triumphant soule, dost thou

Begin thy Triumph; But since lawes allow
That at the Triumph day, the people may,
All that they will, 'gainst the Triumpher say,   180
Let me here use that freedome, and expresse
My griefe, though not to make thy Triumph lesse.
By law, to Triumphs none admitted bee,
Till they as Magistrates get victorie;
Though then to thy force, all youthes foes did yield,
Yet till fit time had brought thee to that field,
To which thy ranke in this state destin'd thee,
That there thy counsailes might get victorie,
And so in that capacitie remove
All jealousies 'twixt Prince and subjects love,   190
Thou could'st no title, to this triumph have,
Thou didst intrude on death, usurp'dst a grave.
Then (though victoriously) thou hadst fought as yet
But with thine owne affections, with the heate
Of youths desires, and colds of ignorance,
But till thou should'st successefully advance
Thine armes 'gainst forraine enemies, which are
Both Envy, and acclamations popular,
(For, both these engines equally defeate,
Though by a divers Mine, those which are great,)   200
Till then thy War was but a civill War,
For which to Triumph, none admitted are.
No more are they, who though with good successe,
In a defensive war, their power expresse;
Before men triumph, the dominion
Must be *enlarg'd* and not *preserv'd* alone;
Why should'st thou then, whose battailes were to win
Thy selfe, from those straits nature put thee in,
And to deliver up to God that state,
Of which he gave thee the vicariate,   210
(Which is thy soule and body) as intire
As he, who takes endeavours, doth require.
But didst not stay, t'enlarge his kingdome too,
By making others, what thou didst, to doe;
Why shouldst thou Triumph now, when Heav'n no more
Hath got, by getting thee, than't had before?
For, Heav'n and thou, even when thou livedst here,
Of one another in possession were.
But this from Triumph most disables thee,
That, that place which is conquered, must bee   220

Left safe from present warre, and likely doubt
Of imminent commotions to breake out:
And hath he left us so? or can it bee
His territory was no more than Hee?
No, we were all his charge, the Diocis
Of ev'ry exemplar man, the whole world is,
And he was joyned in commission
With Tutelar Angels, sent to every one.
But though his freedome to upbraid, and chide
Him who Triumph'd, were lawfull, it was ty'd   230
With this, that it might never reference have
Unto the Senate, who this triumph gave;
Men might at Pompey jeast, but they might not
At that authoritie, by which he got
Leave to Triumph, before, by age, he might;
So, though, triumphant soule, I dare to write,
Mov'd with a reverentiall anger, thus,
That thou so earely wouldst abandon us;
Yet I am farre from daring to dispute
With that great soveraigntie, whose absolute   240
Prerogative hath thus dispens'd with thee,
'Gainst natures lawes, which just impugners bee
Of early triumphs; And I (though with paine)
Lessen our losse, to magnifie thy gaine
Of triumph, when I say, It was more fit,
That all men should lacke thee, than thou lack it.
Though then in our time, be not suffered
That testimonie of love, unto the dead,
To die with them, and in their graves be hid,
As Saxon wives, and French soldurii did;   250
And though in no degree I can expresse
Griefe in great Alexanders great excesse,
Who at his friends death, made whole townes devest
Their walls and bullwarks which became them best:
Doe not, faire soule, this sacrifice refuse,
That in thy grave I doe interre my Muse,
Who, by my griefe, great as thy worth, being cast
Behind hand, yet hath spoke, and spoke her last.

AN HYMNE TO THE SAINTS, AND TO MARQUESSE HAMYLTON

TO SIR ROBERT CARR [MARCH 22, 1625]

SIR,

I PRESUME *you rather try what you can doe in me, than what I can doe in verse; you know my uttermost when it was best, and even then I did best when I had least truth for my subjects. In this present case there is so much truth as it defeats all Poetry. Call therefore this paper by what name you will, and, if it bee not worthy of him, nor of you, nor of mee, smother it, and bee that the sacrifice. If you had commanded mee to have waited on his body to Scotland and preached there, I would have embraced the obligation with more alacrity; But, I thanke you that you would command me that which I was loath to doe, for, even that hath given a tincture of merit to the obedience of*

Your poore friend and servant in Christ Jesus

J. D.

WHETHER that soule which now comes up to you
Fill any former ranke or make a new,
Whether it take a name nam'd there before,
Or be a name it selfe, and *order* more
Than was in heaven till now; (for may not hee
Bee so, if every severall Angell bee
A *kind* alone?) What ever order grow
Greater by him in heaven, wee doe not so.
One of your orders growes by his accesse;
But, by his losse grow all our *orders* lesse;   **10**
The name of *Father, Master, Friend,* the name
Of *Subject* and of *Prince,* in one are lame;
Faire mirth is dampt, and conversation black,
The *household* widdow'd, and the *garter* slack;
The *Chappell* wants an eare, *Councell* a tongue;
Story, a theame; and *Musicke* lacks a song;
Blest *order* that hath him! the losse of him
Gangred all *Orders* here; all lost a limbe.
Never made body such haste to confesse
What a soule was; All former comelinesse   **20**
Fled, in a minute, when the soule was gone,
And, having lost that beauty, would have none;

So fell our *Monasteries,* in one instant growne
Not to lesse houses, but, to heapes of stone;
So sent this body that faire forme it wore,
Unto the spheare of formes, and doth (before
His soule shall fill up his sepulchrall stone,)
Anticipate a Resurrection;
For, as in his fame, now, his soule is here,
So, in the forme thereof his bodie's there;   **30**
And if, faire soule, not with first *Innocents*
Thy station be, but with the *Pænitents,*
(And, who shall dare to aske then when I am
Dy'd scarlet in the blood of that pure Lambe,
Whether that colour, which is scarlet then,
Were black or white before in eyes of men?)
When thou rememb'rest what sins thou didst finde
Amongst those many friends now left behinde,
And seest such sinners as they are, with thee
Got thither by repentance, Let it bee   **40**
Thy wish to wish all there, to wish them cleane;
Wish *him* a *David, her* a *Magdalen.*

EPITAPHS

EPITAPH ON HIMSELFE

TO THE COUNTESSE OF BEDFORD

Madame,
  That I might make your Cabinet my tombe,
    And for my fame which I love next my soule,
Next to my soule provide the happiest roome,
    Admit to that place this last funerall Scrowle.
      Others by Wills give Legacies, but I
      Dying, of you doe beg a Legacie.

My fortune and my will this custome breake,
When we are senselesse grown to make stones speak,
Though no stone tell thee what I was, yet thou
In my graves inside see what thou art now: **10**
Yet th'art not yet so good; till us death lay
To ripe and mellow there, w'are stubborne clay,

Parents make us earth, and soules dignifie
Us to be glasse, here to grow gold we lie;
Whilst in our soules sinne bred and pampered is,
Our soules become worme-eaten Carkasses.

OMNIBUS

My Fortune and my choice this custome break,
When we are speechlesse grown, to make stones speak,
Though no stone tell thee what I was, yet thou
In my graves inside seest what thou art now:
Yet thou'art not yet so good, till death us lay
To ripe and mellow here, we are stubborne Clay.
Parents make us earth, and soules dignifie
Us to be glasse; here to grow gold we lie.
Whilst in our soules sinne bred and pamper'd is,
Our soules become wormeaten carkases;   10
So we our selves miraculously destroy.
Here bodies with lesse miracle enjoy
Such priviledges, enabled here to scale
Heaven, when the Trumpets ayre shall them exhale.
Heare this, and mend thy selfe, and thou mendst me,
By making me, being dead, doe good to thee,
    And thinke me well compos'd, that I could now
    A last-sicke houre to syllables allow.

DIVINE POEMS

TO E. OF D. [THE EARL OF DORSET?] WITH SIX HOLY SONNETS

See Sir, how as the Suns hot Masculine flame
  Begets strange creatures on Niles durty slime,
  In me, your fatherly yet lusty Ryme
(For, these songs are their fruits) have wrought the same;
But though the ingendring force from whence they came
  Bee strong enough, and nature doe admit
  Seaven to be borne at once, I send as yet

But six; they say, the seaventh hath still some maime.
  I choose your judgement, which the same degree
  Doth with her sister, your invention, hold,   **10**
As fire these drossie Rymes to purifie,
  Or as Elixar, to change them to gold;
You are that Alchimist which alwaies had
Wit, whose one spark could make good things of bad.

TO THE LADY MAGDALEN HERBERT:
OF ST. MARY MAGDALEN

HER of your name, whose fair inheritance
  Bethina was, and jointure Magdalo:
An active faith so highly did advance,
  That she once knew, more than the Church did know,
The Resurrection; so much good there is
  Deliver'd of her, that some Fathers be
Loth to believe one Woman could do this;
  But, think these Magdalens were two or three.
Increase their number, Lady, and their fame:
  To their Devotion, add your Innocence;   **10**
Take so much of th'example, as of the name;
  The latter half; and in some recompence
That they did harbour Christ himself, a Guest,
  Harbour these Hymns, to his dear name addrest.

HOLY SONNETS

LA CORONA

1

DEIGNE *at my hands this crown of prayer and praise,*
Weav'd in my low devout melancholie,
Thou which of good, hast, yea art treasury,
All changing unchang'd Antient of dayes;
But doe not, with a vile crowne of fraile bayes,
Reward my muses white sincerity,
But what thy thorny crowne gain'd, that give mee,
A crowne of Glory, which doth flower alwayes;

The ends crowne our workes, but thou crown'st our ends,
For, at our end begins our endlesse rest;   10
The first last end, now zealously possest,
With a strong sober thirst, my soule attends.
'Tis time that heart and voice be lifted high,
Salvation to all that will is nigh.

2

ANNUNCIATION

Salvation to all that will is nigh;
That All, which alwayes is All every where,
Which cannot sinne, and yet all sinnes must beare,
Which cannot die, yet cannot chuse but die,
Loe, faithfull Virgin, yeelds himselfe to lye
In prison, in thy wombe; and though he there
Can take no sinne, nor thou give, yet he'will weare
Taken from thence, flesh, which deaths force may trie.
Ere by the spheares time was created, thou
Wast in his minde, who is thy Sonne, and Brother;   10
Whom thou conceiv'st, conceiv'd; yea thou art now
Thy Makers maker, and thy Fathers mother;
Thou'hast light in darke; and shutst in little roome,
Immensity cloystered in thy deare wombe.

3

NATIVITIE

Immensity cloystered in thy deare wombe,
Now leaves his welbelov'd imprisonment,
There he hath made himselfe to his intent
Weake enough, now into our world to come;
But Oh, for thee, for him, hath th' Inne no roome?
Yet lay him in this stall, and from the Orient,
Starres, and wisemen will travell to prevent
Th'effect of *Herods* jealous generall doome.
Seest thou, my Soule, with thy faiths eyes, how he
Which fils all place, yet none holds him, doth lye?   10
Was not his pity towards thee wondrous high,

That would have need to be pittied by thee?
Kisse him, and with him into Egypt goe,
With his kinde mother, who partakes thy woe.

4

TEMPLE

With his kinde mother who partakes thy woe,
Joseph turne backe; see where your child doth sit,
Blowing, yea blowing out those sparks of wit,
Which himselfe on the Doctors did bestow;
The Word but lately could not speake, and loe
It sodenly speakes wonders, whence comes it,
That all which was, and all which should be writ,
A shallow seeming child, should deeply know?
His Godhead was not soule to his manhood,
Nor had time mellowed him to this ripenesse,   **10**
But as for one which hath a long taske, 'tis good,
With the Sunne to beginne his businesse,
He in his ages morning thus began
By miracles exceeding power of man.

5

CRUCIFYING

By miracles exceeding power of man,
Hee faith in some, envie in some begat,
For, what weake spirits admire, ambitious, hate;
In both affections many to him ran,
But Oh! the worst are most, they will and can,
Alas, and do, unto the immaculate,
Whose creature Fate is, now prescribe a Fate,
Measuring selfe-lifes infinity to'a span,
Nay to an inch. Loe, where condemned hee
Beares his owne crosse, with paine, yet by and by   **10**
When it beares him, he must beare more and die.
Now thou art lifted up, draw mee to thee,
And at thy death giving such liberall dole,
Moyst, with one drop of thy blood, my dry soule.

6

RESURRECTION

Moyst with one drop of thy blood, my dry soule
Shall (though she now be in extreme degree
Too stony hard, and yet too fleshly,) bee
Freed by that drop, from being starv'd, hard, or foule,
And life, by this death abled, shall controule
Death, whom thy death slue; nor shall to mee
Feare of first or last death, bring miserie,
If in thy little booke my name thou enroule,
Flesh in that long sleep is not putrified,
But made that there, of which, and for which 'twas;   **10**
Nor can by other meanes be glorified.
May then sinnes sleep, and deaths soone from me passe,
That wak't from both, I againe risen may
Salute the last, and everlasting day.

7

ASCENTION

Salute the last and everlasting day,
Joy at the uprising of this Sunne, and Sonne,
Yee whose just teares, or tribulation
Have purely washt, or burnt your drossie clay;
Behold the Highest, parting hence away,
Lightens the darke clouds, which hee treads upon,
Nor doth hee by ascending, show alone,
But first hee, and hee first enters the way.
O strong Ramme, which hast batter'd heaven for mee,
Mild Lambe, which with thy blood, hast mark'd the
        path;   **19**
Bright Torch, which shin'st, that I the way may see,
Oh, with thy owne blood quench thy owne just wrath,
And if thy holy Spirit, my Muse did raise,
Deigne at my hands this crown of prayer and praise.

THE CROSSE

SINCE Christ embrac'd the Crosse it selfe, dare I
His image, th'image of his Crosse deny?

Would I have profit by the sacrifice,
And dare the chosen Altar to despise?
It bore all other sinnes, but is it fit
That it should beare the sinne of scorning it?
Who from the picture would avert his eye,
How would he flye his paines, who there did dye?
From mee, no Pulpit, nor misgrounded law,
Nor scandall taken, shall this Crosse withdraw,   **10**
It shall not, for it cannot; for, the losse
Of this Crosse, were to mee another Crosse;
Better were worse, for, no affliction,
No Crosse is so extreme, as to have none.
Who can blot out the Crosse, which th'instrument
Of God, dew'd on mee in the Sacrament?
Who can deny mee power, and liberty
To stretch mine armes, and mine owne Crosse to be?
Swimme, and at every stroake, thou art thy Crosse;
The Mast and yard make one, where seas do tosse;   **20**
Looke downe, thou spiest out Crosses in small things;
Looke up, thou seest birds rais'd on crossed wings;
All the Globes frame, and spheares, is nothing else
But the Meridians crossing Parallels.
Material Crosses then, good physicke bee,
But yet spirituall have chiefe dignity.
These for extracted chimique medicine serve,
And cure much better, and as well preserve;
Then are you your own physicke, or need none,
When Still'd, or purg'd by tribulation.   **30**
For when that Crosse ungrudg'd, unto you stickes,
Then are you to your selfe, a Crucifixe.
As perchance, Carvers do not faces make,
But that away, which hid them there, do take.
Let Crosses, soe, take what hid Christ in thee,
And be his image, or not his, but hee.
But, as oft Alchimists doe coyners prove,
So may a selfe-dispising, get selfe-love;
And then as worst surfets, of best meates bee,
Soe is pride, issued from humility,   **40**
For, 'tis no child, but monster; therefore Crosse
Your joy in crosses, else, 'tis double losse,
And crosse thy senses, else, both they, and thou
Must perish soone, and to destruction bowe.
For if the'eye seeke good objects, and will take

No crosse from bad, wee cannot scape a snake.
So with harsh, hard, sowre, stinking, crosse the rest,
Make them indifferent all; call nothing best.
But most the eye needs crossing, that can rome,
And move; To th'other th'objects must come home.   **50**
And crosse thy heart: for that in man alone
Points downewards, and hath palpitation.
Crosse those dejections, when it downeward tends,
And when it to forbidden heights pretends.
And as the braine through bony walls doth vent
By sutures, which a Crosses forme present,
So when thy braine workes, ere thou utter it,
Crosse and correct concupiscence of witt.
Be covetous of Crosses, let none fall.
Crosse no man else, but crosse thy selfe in all.   **60**
Then doth the Crosse of Christ worke fruitfully
Within our hearts, when wee love harmlessly
That Crosses pictures much, and with more care
That Crosses children, which our Crosses are.

RESURRECTION, IMPERFECT

SLEEP sleep old Sun, thou canst not have repast
As yet, the wound thou took'st on friday last;
Sleepe then, and rest; The world may beare thy stay,
A better Sun rose before thee to day,
Who, not content to'enlighten all that dwell
On the earths face, as thou, enlightned hell,
And made the darke fires languish in that vale,
As, at thy presence here, our fires grow pale.
Whose body having walk'd on earth, and now
Hasting to Heaven, would, that he might allow   **10**
Himselfe unto all stations, and fill all,
For these three daies become a minerall;
Hee was all gold when he lay downe, but rose
All tincture, and doth not alone dispose
Leaden and iron wills to good, but is
Of power to make even sinfull flesh like his.
Had one of those, whose credulous pietie
Thought, that a Soule one might discerne and see
Goe from a body,'at this sepulcher been,

And, issuing from the sheet, this body seen,   **20**
He would have justly thought this body a soule,
If not of any man, yet of the whole.

Desunt cætera

UPON THE ANNUNTIATION AND PASSION

FALLING UPON ONE DAY. 1608[MARCH 25, 1608/9]

TAMELY, fraile body,'abstaine to day; to day
My soule eates twice, Christ hither and away.
She sees him man, so like God made in this,
That of them both a circle embleme is,
Whose first and last concurre; this doubtfull day
Of feast or fast, Christ came, and went away.
Shee sees him nothing twice at once, who'is all;
Shee sees a Cedar plant it selfe, and fall,
Her Maker put to making, and the head
Of life, at once, not yet alive, yet dead.   **10**
She sees at once the virgin mother stay
Reclus'd at home, Publique at Golgotha;
Sad and rejoyc'd shee's seen at once, and seen
At almost fiftie, and at scarce fifteene.
At once a Sonne is promis'd her, and gone,
Gabriell gives Christ to her, He her to John;
Not fully a mother, Shee's in Orbitie,
At once receiver and the legacie.
All this, and all betweene, this day hath showne,
Th'Abridgement of Christs story, which makes one   **20**
(As in plaine Maps, the furthest West is East)
Of the'Angels *Ave*,'and *Consummatum est*.
How well the Church, Gods Court of faculties
Deales, in some times, and seldome joyning these!
As by the selfe-fix'd Pole wee never doe
Direct our course, but the next starre thereto,
Which showes where the'other is, and which we say
(Because it strayes not farre) doth never stray;
So God by his Church, neerest to him, wee know
And stand firme, if wee by her motion goe;   **30**
His Spirit, as his fiery Pillar doth
Leade, and his Church, as cloud; to one end both.
This Church, by letting these daies joyne, hath shown

Death and conception in mankinde is one;
Or'twas in him the same humility,
That he would be a man, and leave to be:
Or as creation he hath made, as God,
With the last judgement, but one period,
His imitating Spouse would joyne in one
Manhoods extremes: He shall come, he is gone: **40**
Or as though one blood drop, which thence did fall,
Accepted, would have serv'd, he yet shed all;
So though the least of his paines, deeds, or words,
Would busie a life, she all this day affords;
This treasure then, in grosse, my Soule uplay,
And in my life retaile it every day.

THE LITANIE

I

THE FATHER

FATHER of Heaven, and him, by whom
It, and us for it, and all else, for us
    Thou madest, and govern'st ever, come
And re-create mee, now growne ruinous:
        My heart is by dejection, clay,
        And by selfe-murder, red.
From this red earth, O Father, purge away
All vicious tinctures, that new fashioned
I may rise up from death, before I'm dead.

II

THE SONNE

O Sonne of God, who seeing two things,   **10**
Sinne, and death crept in, which were never made,
    By bearing one, tryed'st with what stings
The other could thine heritage invade;
        O be thou nail'd unto my heart,
        And crucified againe,
Part not from it, though it from thee would part,
But let it be, by applying so thy paine,
Drown'd in thy blood, and in thy passion slaine.

III

THE HOLY GHOST

O Holy Ghost, whose temple I
Am, but of mudde walls, and condensed dust, **20**
  And being sacrilegiously
Halfe wasted with youths fires, of pride and lust,
    Must with new stormes be weatherbeat;
    Double in my heart thy flame,
Which let devout sad teares intend; and let
(Though this glasse lanthorne, flesh, do suffer maime)
Fire, Sacrifice, Priest, Altar be the same.

IV

THE TRINITY

O Blessed glorious Trinity,
Bones to Philosophy, but milke to faith,
  Which, as wise serpents, diversly **30**
Most slipperinesse, yet most entanglings hath,
    As you distinguish'd undistinct
    By power, love, knowledge bee,
Give mee a such selfe different instinct
Of these; let all mee elemented bee,
Of power, to love, to know, you unnumbred three.

V

THE VIRGIN MARY

For that faire blessed Mother-maid,
Whose flesh redeem'd us; That she-Cherubin,
  Which unlock'd Paradise, and made
One claime for innocence, and disseiz'd sinne, **40**
    Whose wombe was a strange heav'n for there
    God cloath'd himselfe, and grew,
Our zealous thankes wee poure. As her deeds were
Our helpes, so are her prayers; nor can she sue
In vaine, who hath such titles unto you.

VI

THE ANGELS

And since this life our nonage is,
And wee in Wardship to thine Angels be,
   Native in heavens faire Palaces,
Where we shall be but denizen'd by thee,
      As th'earth conceiving by the Sunne,   **50**
      Yeelds faire diversitie,
Yet never knowes which course that light doth run,
So let mee study, that mine actions bee
Worthy their sight, though blinde in how they see.

VII

THE PATRIARCHES

And let thy Patriarches Desire
(Those great Grandfathers of thy Church, which saw
   More in the cloud, than wee in fire,
Whom Nature clear'd more, than us Grace and Law,
      And now in Heaven still pray, that wee
      May use our new helpes right,)   **60**
Be satisfy'd, and fructifie in mee;
Let not my minde be blinder by more light
Nor Faith, by Reason added, lose her sight.

VIII

THE PROPHETS

Thy Eagle-sighted Prophets too,
Which were thy Churches Organs, and did sound
   That harmony, which made of two
One law, and did unite, but not confound;
      Those heavenly Poëts which did see
      Thy will, and it expresse
In rythmique feet, in common pray for mee,   **70**
That I by them excuse not my excesse
In seeking secrets, or Poëtiquenesse.

IX

THE APOSTLES

And thy illustrious Zodiacke
Of twelve Apostles, which ingirt this All,
    (From whom whosoever do not take
Their light, to darke pits, throw downe, and fall,)
        As through their prayers, thou'hast let mee know
        That their bookes are divine;
May they pray still, and be heard, that I goe
Th'old broad way in applying; O decline   80
Mee, when my comment would make thy word mine.

X

THE MARTYRS

And since thou so desirously
Did'st long to die, that long before thou could'st,
    And long since thou no more couldst dye,
Thou in thy scatter'd mystique body wouldst
        In Abel dye, and ever since
        In thine; let their blood come
To begge for us, a discreet patience
Of death, or of worse life: for Oh, to some   90
Not to be Martyrs, is a martyrdome.

XI

THE CONFESSORS

Therefore with thee triumpheth there
A Virgin Squadron of white Confessors,
    Whose bloods betroth'd, not marryed were,
Tender'd, not taken by those Ravishers:
        They know, and pray, that wee may know,
        In every Christian
Hourly tempestuous persecutions grow;
Tentations martyr us alive; A man
Is to himselfe a Dioclesian.

XII

THE VIRGINS

The cold white snowie Nunnery,   **100**
Which, as thy mother, their high Abbesse, sent
    Their bodies backe againe to thee,
As thou hadst lent them, cleane and innocent,
        Though they have not obtain'd of thee,
        That or thy Church, or I,
Should keep, as they, our first integrity;
Divorce thou sinne in us, or bid it die,
And call chast widowhead Virginitie.

XIII

THE DOCTORS

Thy sacred Academie above
Of Doctors, whose paines have unclasp'd, and taught   **110**
    Both bookes of life to us (for love
To know thy Scriptures tells us, we are wrote
        In thy other booke) pray for us there
        That what they have misdone
Or mis-said, wee to that may not adhere;
Their zeale may be our sinne. Lord let us runne
Meane waies, and call them stars, but not the Sunne.

XIV

And whil'st this universall Quire,
That Church in triumph, this in warfare here,
    Warm'd with one all-partaking fire   **120**
Of love, that none be lost, which cost thee deare,
        Prayes ceaslesly,'and thou hearken too,
        (Since to be gratious
Our taske is treble, to pray, beare, and doe)
Heare this prayer Lord: O Lord deliver us
From trusting in those prayers, though powr'd out thus.

XV

From being anxious, or secure,
Dead clods of sadnesse, or light squibs of mirth,
From thinking, that great courts immure
All, or no happinesse, or that this earth   **130**
    Is only for our prison fram'd,
    Or that thou art covetous
To them thou lovest, or that they are maim'd
From reaching this worlds sweet, who seek thee thus,
With all their might, Good Lord deliver us.

XVI

From needing danger, to bee good,
From owing thee yesterdaies teares to day,
    From trusting so much to thy blood,
That in that hope, wee wound our soule away,
    From bribing thee with Almes, to excuse   **140**
    Some sinne more burdenous,
From light affecting, in religion, newes,
From thinking us all soule, neglecting thus
Our mutuall duties, Lord deliver us.

XVII

From tempting Satan to tempt us,
By our connivence, or slack companie,
    From measuring ill by vitious,
Neglecting to choake sins spawne, Vanitie,
    From indiscreet humilitie,
    Which might be scandalous,   **150**
And cast reproach on Christianitie,
From being spies, or to spies pervious,
From thirst, or scorne of fame, deliver us.

XVIII

Deliver us for thy descent
Into the Virgin, whose wombe was a place
    Of middle kind; and thou being sent

To'ungratious us, staid'st at her full of grace;
      And through thy poore birth, where first thou
      Glorifiedst Povertie,
And yet soone after riches didst allow,   **160**
By accepting Kings gifts in the Epiphanie,
Deliver, and make us, to both waies free.

XIX

And through that bitter agonie,
Which is still the agonie of pious wits,
   Disputing what distorted thee,
And interrupted evennesse, with fits;
      And through thy free confession
      Though thereby they were then
Made blind, so that thou might'st from them have gone,
Good Lord deliver us, and teach us when   **170**
Wee may not, and we may blinde unjust men.

XX

Through thy submitting all, to blowes
Thy face, thy clothes to spoile; thy fame to scorne,
   All waies, which rage, or Justice knowes,
And by which thou could'st shew, that thou wast born
      And through thy gallant humblenesse
      Which thou in death did'st shew,
Dying before thy soule they could expresse,
Deliver us from death, by dying so,
To this world, ere this world doe bid us goe.   **180**

XXI

When senses, which thy souldiers are,
Wee arme against thee, and they fight for sinne,
   When want, sent but to tame, doth warre
And worke despaire a breach to enter in,
      When plenty, Gods image, and seale
      Makes us Idolatrous,
And love it, not him, whom it should reveale,
When wee are mov'd to seeme religious
Only to vent wit, Lord deliver us.

XXII

In Churches, when the'infirmitie   **190**
Of him which speakes, diminishes the Word,
    When Magistrates doe mis-apply
To us, as we judge, lay or ghostly sword,
       When plague, which is thine Angell, raignes,
       Or wars, thy Champions, swaie,
When Heresie, thy second deluge, gaines;
In th'houre of death, the'Eve of last judgement day,
Deliver us from the sinister way.

XXIII

Heare us, O heare us Lord; to thee
A sinner is more musique, when he prayes,   **200**
    Than spheares, or Angels praises bee,
In Panegyrique Allelujaes;
       Heare us, for till thou heare us, Lord
       We know not what to say;
Thine eare to'our sighes, teares, thoughts gives voice
     and word.
O Thou who Satan heard'st in Jobs sicke day,
Heare thy selfe now, for thou in us dost pray.

XXIV

That wee may change to evennesse
This intermitting aguish Pietie;
    That snatching cramps of wickednesse   **210**
And Apoplexies of fast sin, may die;
       That musique of thy promises,
       Not threats in Thunder may
Awaken us to our just offices;
What in thy booke, thou dost, or creatures say,
That we may heare, Lord heare us, when wee pray.

XXV

That our eares sicknesse wee may cure,
And rectifie those Labyrinths aright,
    That wee, by harkning, not procure

Our praise, nor others dispraise so invite,   **220**
　　That wee get not a slipperinesse,
　　And senslesly decline,
From hearing bold wits jeast at Kings excesse,
To'admit the like of majestie divine,
That we may locke our eares, Lord open thine.

XXVI

　　That living law, the Magistrate,
Which to give us, and make us physicke, doth
　　Our vices often aggravate,
That Preachers taxing sinne, before her growth,
　　That Satan, and invenom'd men   **230**
　　Which well, if we starve, dine,
When they doe most accuse us, may see then
Us, to amendment, heare them; thee decline:
That we may open our eares, Lord lock thine.

XXVII

　　That learning, thine Ambassador,
From thine allegeance wee never tempt,
　　That beauty, paradises flower
For physicke made, from poyson be exempt,
　　That wit, borne apt high good to doe,
　　By dwelling lazily   **240**
On Natures nothing, be not nothing too,
That our affections kill us not, nor dye,
Heare us, weake ecchoes, O thou eare, and cry.

XXVIII

　　Sonne of God heare us, and since thou
By taking our blood, owest it us againe,
　　Gaine to thy self, or us allow;
And let not both us and thy selfe be slaine;
　　O Lambe of God, which took'st our sinne
　　Which could not stick to thee,
O let it not returne to us againe,   **250**
But Patient and Physition being free,
As sinne is nothing, let it no where be.

GOODFRIDAY, 1613. RIDING WESTWARD

LET mans Soule be a Spheare, and then, in this,
The intelligence that moves, devotion is,
And as the other Spheares, by being growne
Subject to forraigne motions, lose their owne,
And being by others hurried every day,
Scarce in a yeare their naturall forme obey:
Pleasure or businesse, so, our Soules admit
For their first mover, and are whirld by it.
Hence is't, that I am carryed towards the West
This day, when my Soules forme bends towards the East.   10
There I should see a Sunne, by rising set,
And by that setting endlesse day beget;
But that Christ on this Crosse, did rise and fall,
Sinne had eternally benighted all.
Yet dare I'almost be glad, I do not see
That spectacle of too much weight for mee.
Who sees Gods face, that is selfe life, must dye;
What a death were it then to see God dye?
It made his owne Lieutenant Nature shrinke,
It made his footstoole crack, and the Sunne winke.   20
Could I behold those hands which span the Poles,
And tune all spheares at once, peirc'd with those holes?
Could I behold that endlesse height which is
Zenith to us, and our Antipodes,
Humbled below us? or that blood which is
The seat of all our Soules, if not of his,
Made durt of dust, or that flesh which was worne
By God, for his apparell, rag'd, and torne?
If on these things I durst not looke, durst I
Upon his miserable mother cast mine eye,   30
Who was Gods partner here, and furnish'd thus
Halfe of that Sacrifice, which ransom'd us?
Though these things, as I ride, be from mine eye,
They'are present yet unto my memory,
For that looks towards them; and thou look'st towards mee,
O Saviour, as thou hang'st upon the tree;
I turne my backe to thee, but to receive

Corrections, till thy mercies bid thee leave.
O thinke mee worth thine anger, punish mee,
Burne off my rusts, and my deformity,   40
Restore thine Image, so much, by thy grace,
That thou may'st know mee, and I'll turne my face.

HOLY SONNETS

I

THOU hast made me, And shall thy worke decay?
Repaire me now, for now mine end doth haste,
I runne to death, and death meets me as fast,
And all my pleasures are like yesterday;
I dare not move my dimme eyes any way,
Despaire behind, and death before doth cast
Such terrour, and my feeble flesh doth waste
By sinne in it, which it t'wards hell doth weigh;
Onely thou art above, and when towards thee
By thy leave I can looke, I rise againe;   10
But our old subtle foe so tempteth me,
That not one houre my selfe I can sustaine;
Thy Grace may wing me to prevent his art,
And thou like Adamant draw mine iron heart.

II

As due by many titles I resigne
My selfe to thee, O God, first I was made
By thee, and for thee, and when I was decay'd
Thy blood bought that, the which before was thine;
I am thy sonne, made with thy selfe to shine,
Thy servant, whose paines thou hast still repaid,
Thy sheepe, thine Image, and, till I betray'd
My selfe, a temple of thy Spirit divine;
Why doth the devill then usurpe on mee?
Why doth he steale, nay ravish that's thy right?   10
Except thou rise and for thine owne worke fight,
Oh I shall soone despaire, when I doe see
That thou lov'st mankind well, yet wilt'not chuse me,
And Satan hates mee, yet is loth to lose mee.

III

O MIGHT those sighes and teares returne againe
Into my breast and eyes, which I have spent,
That I might in this holy discontent
Mourne with some fruit, as I have mourn'd in vaine;
In mine Idolatry what showres of raine
Mine eyes did waste? what griefs my heart did rent?
That sufferance was my sinne; now I repent;
'Cause I did suffer I must suffer paine.
Th'hydroptique drunkard, and night-scouting thiefe,
The itchy Lecher, and selfe tickling proud   10
Have the remembrance of past joyes, for reliefe
Of comming ills. To (poore) me is allow'd
No ease; for, long, yet vehement griefe hath beene
Th'effect and cause, the punishment and sinne.

IV

OH my blacke Soule! now thou art summoned
By sicknesse, deaths herald, and champion;
Thou art like a pilgrim, which abroad hath done
Treason, and durst not turne to whence hee is fled,
Or like a thiefe, which till deaths doome be read,
Wisheth himselfe delivered from prison;
But damn'd and hal'd to execution,
Wisheth that still he might be imprisoned.
Yet grace, if thou repent, thou canst not lacke;
But who shall give thee that grace to beginne?   10
Oh make thy selfe with holy mourning blacke,
And red with blushing, as thou art with sinne;
Or wash thee in Christs blood, which hath this might
That being red, it dyes red soules to white.

V

I AM a little world made cunningly
Of Elements, and an Angelike spright,
But black sinne hath betraid to endlesse night
My worlds both parts, and (oh) both parts must die.
You which beyond that heaven which was most high
Have found new sphears, and of new lands can write,

Powre new seas in mine eyes, that so I might
Drowne my world with my weeping earnestly,
Or wash it if it must be drown'd no more:
But oh it must be burnt! alas the fire   **10**
Of lust and envie have burnt it heretofore,
And made it fouler; Let their flames retire,
And burne me ô Lord, with a fiery zeale
Of thee and thy house, which doth in eating heale.

VI

THIS is my playes last scene, here heavens appoint
My pilgrimages last mile; and my race
Idly, yet quickly runne, hath this last pace,
My spans last inch, my minutes latest point,
And gluttonous death, will instantly unjoynt
My body, and soule, and I shall sleepe a space,
But my'ever-waking part shall see that face,
Whose feare already shakes my every joynt:
Then, as my soule, to'heaven her first seate, takes flight,
And earth-borne body, in the earth shall dwell,   **10**
So, fall my sinnes, that all may have their right,
To where they'are bred, and would presse me, to hell.
Impute me righteous, thus purg'd of evill,
For thus I leave the world, the flesh, the devill.

VII

AT the round earths imagin'd corners, blow
Your trumpets, Angells, and arise, arise
From death, you numberlesse infinities
Of soules, and to your scattred bodies goe,
All whom the flood did, and fire shall o'erthrow,
All whom warre, dearth, age, agues, tyrannies,
Despaire, law, chance, hath slaine, and you whose eyes,
Shall behold God, and never tast deaths woe.
But let them sleepe, Lord, and mee mourne a space,
For, if above all these, my sinnes abound,   **10**
'Tis late to aske abundance of thy grace,
When wee are there; here on this lowly ground,
Teach mee how to repent; for that's as good
As if thou'hadst seal'd my pardon, with thy blood.

VIII

If faithfull soules be alike glorifi'd
As Angels, then my fathers soul doth see,
And adds this even to full felicitie,
That valiantly I hels wide mouth o'rstride:
But if our mindes to these soules be descry'd
By circumstances, and by signes that be
Apparent in us, not immediately,
How shall my mindes white truth by them be try'd?
They see idolatrous lovers weepe and mourne,
And vile blasphemous Conjurers to call   10
On Jesus name, and Pharisaicall
Dissemblers feigne devotion. Then turne
O pensive soule, to God, for he knowes best
Thy true griefe, for he put it in my breast.

IX

If poysonous mineralls, and if that tree,
Whose fruit threw death on else immortall us,
If lecherous goats, if serpents envious
Cannot be damn'd; Alas; why should I bee?
Why should intent or reason, borne in mee,
Make sinnes, else equall, in mee more heinous?
And mercy being easie, and glorious
To God; in his sterne wrath, why threatens hee?
But who am I, that dare dispute with thee
O God? Oh! of thine onely worthy blood,   10
And my teares, make a heavenly Lethean flood,
And drowne in it my sinnes blacke memorie;
That thou remember them, some claime as debt,
I thinke it mercy, if thou wilt forget.

X

Death be not proud, though some have called thee
Mighty and dreadfull, for, thou art not soe,
For, those, whom thou think'st, thou dost overthrow,
Die not, poore death, nor yet canst thou kill mee.
From rest and sleepe, which but thy pictures bee,
Much pleasure, then from thee, much more must flow,

And soonest our best men with thee doe goe,
Rest of their bones, and soules deliverie.
Thou art slave to Fate, Chance, kings, and desperate men,
And dost with poyson, warre, and sicknesse dwell,   10
And poppie, or charmes can make us sleepe as well,
And better than thy stroake; why swell'st thou then?
One short sleepe past, wee wake eternally,
And death shall be no more; death, thou shalt die.

XI

SPIT in my face you Jewes, and pierce my side,
Buffet, and scoffe, scourge, and crucifie mee,
For I have sinn'd, and sinn'd, and onely hee,
Who could do no iniquitie, hath dyed:
But by my death can not be satisfied
My sinnes, which passe the Jewes impiety:
They kill'd once an inglorious man, but I
Crucifie him daily, being now glorified.
Oh let mee then, his strange love still admire:
Kings pardon, but he bore our punishment.   10
And *Jacob* came cloth'd in vile harsh attire
But to supplant, and with gainfull intent:
God cloth'd himselfe in vile mans flesh, that so
Hee might be weake enough to suffer woe.

XII

WHY are wee by all creatures waited on?
Why doe the prodigall elements supply
Life and food to mee, being more pure than I,
Simple, and further from corruption?
Why brook'st thou, ignorant horse, subjection?
Why dost thou bull, and bore so seelily
Dissemble weaknesse, and by'one mans stroke die,
Whose whole kinde, you might swallow and feed upon?
Weaker I am, woe is mee, and worse than you,
You have not sinn'd, nor need be timorous.   10
But wonder at a greater wonder, for to us
Created nature doth these things subdue,
But their Creator, whom sin, nor nature tyed,
For us, his Creatures, and his foes, hath dyed.

XIII

WHAT if this present were the worlds last night?
Marke in my heart, O Soule, where thou dost dwell,
The picture of Christ crucified, and tell
Whether that countenance can thee affright,
Teares in his eyes quench the amazing light,
Blood fills his frownes, which from his pierc'd head fell.
And can that tongue adjudge thee unto hell,
Which pray'd forgivenesse for his foes fierce spight?
No, no; but as in my idolatrie   10
I said to all my profane mistresses,
Beauty, of pitty, foulnesse onely is
A signe of rigour: so I say to thee,
To wicked spirits are horrid shapes assign'd,
This beauteous forme assures a pitious minde.

XIV

BATTER my heart, three person'd God; for, you
As yet but knocke, breathe, shine, and seeke to mend;
That I may rise, and stand, o'erthrow mee,'and bend
Your force, to breake, blowe, burn and make me new.
I, like an usurpt towne, to'another due,
Labour to'admit you, but Oh, to no end,
Reason your viceroy in mee, mee should defend,
But is captiv'd, and proves weake or untrue.
Yet dearely'I love you,'and would be loved faine,
But am betroth'd unto your enemie: 10
Divorce mee,'untie, or breake that knot againe,
Take mee to you, imprison mee, for I
Except you'enthrall mee, never shall be free,
Nor ever chast, except you ravish mee.

XV

WILT thou love God, as he thee? then digest,
My Soule, this wholsome meditation,
How God the Spirit, by Angels waited on
In heaven, doth make his Temple in thy brest
The Father having begot a Sonne most blest,
And still begetting, (for he ne'r begonne)

Hath deign'd to chuse thee by adoption,
Coheire to'his glory,'and Sabbaths endlesse rest;
And as a robb'd man, which by search doth finde
His stolne stuffe sold, must lose or buy'it againe: **10**
The Sonne of glory came downe, and was slaine,
Us whom he'had made, and Satan stolne, to unbinde.
'Twas much, that man was made like God before,
But, that God should be made like man, much more.

XVI

FATHER, part of his double interest
Unto thy kingdome, thy Sonne gives to mee,
His joynture in the knottie Trinitie
Hee keepes, and gives to me his deaths conquest.
This Lambe, whose death, with life the world hath blest,
Was from the worlds beginning slaine, and he
Hath made two Wills, which with the Legacie
Of his and thy kingdome, doe thy Sonnes invest.
Yet such are thy laws, that men argue yet
Whether a man those statutes can fulfill;   **10**
None doth; but all-healing grace and spirit
Revive againe what law and letter kill.
Thy lawes abridgement, and thy last command
Is all but love; Oh let this last Will stand!

XVII

SINCE she whom I lov'd hath payd her last debt
To Nature, and to hers, and my good is dead,
And her Soule early into heaven ravished,
Wholly on heavenly things my mind is sett.
Here the admyring her my mind did whett
To seeke thee God; so streames do shew their head;
But though I have found thee, and thou my thirst hast fed,
A holy thirsty dropsy melts mee yett.
But why should I begg more Love, when as thou
Dost wooe my soule for hers; offring all thine: **10**
And dost not only feare least I allow
My Love to Saints and Angels things divine,
But in thy tender jealosy dost doubt
Least the World, Fleshe, yea Devill putt thee out.

XVIII

SHOW me deare Christ, thy Spouse, so bright and clear.
What! is it She, which on the other shore
Goes richly painted? or which rob'd and tore
Laments and mournes in Germany and here?
Sleepes she a thousand, then peepes up one yeare?
Is she selfe truth and errs? now new, now outwore?
Doth she, and did she, and shall she evermore
On one, on seaven, or on no hill appeare?
Dwells she with us, or like adventuring knights
First travaile we to seeke and then make Love?   **10**
Betray kind husband thy spouse to our sights,
And let myne amorous soule court thy mild Dove,
Who is most trew, and pleasing to thee, then
When she'is embrac'd and open to most men.

XIX

OH, to vex me, contraryes meet in one:
Inconstancy unnaturally hath begott
A constant habit; that when I would not
I change in vowes, and in devotione.
As humorous is my contritione
As my prophane Love, and as soone forgott:
As ridlingly distemper'd, cold and hott,
As praying, as mute; as infinite, as none.
I durst not view heaven yesterday; and to day
In prayers, and flattering speaches I court God: **10**
To morrow I quake with true feare of his rod.
So my devout fitts come and go away
Like a fantastique Ague: save that here
Those are my best dayes, when I shake with feare.

UPON THE TRANSLATION OF THE PSALMES

BY SIR PHILIP SYDNEY,
AND THE COUNTESSE OF PEMBROKE HIS SISTER

ETERNALL God, (for whom who ever dare
Seeke new expressions, doe the Circle square,
And thrust into strait corners of poore wit

Thee, who art cornerlesse and infinite)
I would but blesse thy Name, not name thee now;
(And thy gifts are as infinite as thou:)
Fixe we our prayses therefore on this one,
That, as thy blessed Spirit fell upon
These Psalmes first Author in a cloven tongue;
(For 'twas a double power by which he sung   10
The highest matter in the noblest forme;)
So thou hast cleft that spirit, to performe
That worke againe, and shed it, here, upon
Two, by their bloods, and by thy Spirit one;
A Brother and a Sister, made by thee
The Organ, where thou art the Harmony.
Two that make one *John Baptists* holy voyce,
And who that Psalme, *Now let the Iles rejoyce,*
Have both translated, and apply'd it too,
But told us what, and taught us how to doe.   20
They shew us Ilanders our joy, our King,
They tell us *why,* and teach us *how* to sing;
Make all this All, three Quires, heaven, earth, and sphears;
The first, Heaven, hath a song, but no man heares,
The Spheares have Musick, but they have no tongue,
Their harmony is rather danc'd than sung;
But our third Quire, to which the first gives eare,
(For, Angels learne by what the Church does here)
This Quire hath all. The Organist is hee
Who hath tun'd God and Man, the Organ we: 30
The songs are these, which heavens high holy Muse
Whisper'd to *David, David* to the Jewes:
And *Davids* Successors, in holy zeale,
In formes of joy and art doe re-reveale
To us so sweetly and sincerely too,
That I must not rejoyce as I would doe
When I behold that these Psalmes are become
So well attyr'd abroad, so ill at home,
So well in Chambers, in thy Church so ill,
As I can scarce call that reform'd untill   40
This be reform'd; Would a whole State present
A lesser gift than some one man hath sent?
And shall our Church, unto our Spouse and King
More hoarse, more harsh than any other, sing?
For *that* we pray, we praise thy name for *this.*
Which, by this *Moses* and this *Miriam,* is

Already done; and as those Psalmes we call
(Though some have other Authors) *Davids* all:
So though some have, some may some Psalmes translate,
We thy Sydnean Psalmes shall celebrate,   50
And, till we come th'Extemporall song to sing,
(Learn'd the first hower, that we see the King,
Who hath translated those translators) may
These their sweet learned labours, all the way
Be as our tuning, that, when hence we part,
We may fall in with them, and sing our part.

TO MR. TILMAN AFTER HE HAD
TAKEN ORDERS

THOU, whose diviner soule hath caus'd thee now
To put thy hand unto the holy Plough,
Making Lay-scornings of the Ministry,
Not an impediment, but victory;
What bringst thou home with thee? how is thy mind
Affected since the vintage? Dost thou finde
New thoughts and stirrings in thee? and as Steele
Toucht with a Loadstone, dost new motions feele?
Or, as a Ship after much paine and care,
For Iron and Cloth brings home rich Indian ware,   10
Hast thou thus traffiqu'd, but with farre more gaine
Of noble goods, and with lesse time and paine?
Thou art the same materials, as before,
Onely the stampe is changed; but no more.
And as new crowned Kings alter the face,
But not the monies substance; so hath grace
Chang'd onely Gods old Image by Creation,
To Christs new stampe, at this thy Coronation;
Or, as we paint Angels with wings, because
They beare Gods message, and proclaime his lawes,   20
Since thou must doe the like, and so must move,
Art thou new feather'd with cœlestiall love?
Deare, tell me where thy purchase lies, and shew
What thy advantage is above, below.
But if thy gainings doe surmount expression,
Why doth the foolish world scorne that profession,
Whose joyes passe speech? Why do they think unfit

That Gentry should joyne families with it?
As if their day were onely to be spent
In dressing, Mistressing and complement;   30
Alas poore joyes, but poorer men, whose trust
Seemes richly placed in refined dust;
(For, such are cloathes and beauty, which though gay,
Are, at the best, but of sublimed clay.)
Let then the world thy calling disrespect,
But goe thou on, and pitty their neglect.
What function is so noble, as to bee
Embassadour to God and destinie?
To open life, to give kingdomes to more
Than Kings give dignities; to keepe heavens doore?   40
Maries prerogative was to beare Christ, so
'Tis preachers to convey him, for they doe
As Angels out of clouds, from Pulpits speake;
And blesse the poore beneath, the lame, the weake.
If then th'Astronomers, whereas they spie
A new-found Starre, their Opticks magnifie,
How brave are those, who with their Engine, can
Bring man to heaven, and heaven againe to man?
These are thy titles and preheminences,
In whom must meet Gods graces, mens offences,   50
And so the heavens which beget all things here,
And the earth our mother, which these things doth beare,
Both these in thee, are in thy Calling knit,
And make thee now a blest Hermaphrodite.

A HYMNE TO CHRIST,

AT THE AUTHORS LAST GOING INTO GERMANY

In what torne ship soever I embarke,
That ship shall be my embleme of thy Arke;
What sea soever swallow mee, that flood
Shall be to mee an embleme of thy blood;
Though thou with clouds of anger do disguise
Thy face; yet through that maske I know those eyes,
    Which, though they turne away sometimes,
        They never will despise.

I sacrifice this Iland unto thee,
And all whom I lov'd there, and who lov'd mee;   10

When I have put our seas twixt them and mee,
Put thou thy sea betwixt my sinnes and thee.
As the trees sap doth seeke the root below
In winter, in my winter now I goe,
　　Where none but thee, th'Eternall root
　　　Of true Love I may know.

Nor thou nor thy religion dost controule,
The amorousnesse of an harmonious Soule,
But thou would'st have that love thy selfe: As thou
Art jealous, Lord, so I am jealous now,　　　　　　　20
Thou lov'st not, till from loving more, thou free
My soule: Who ever gives, takes libertie:
　　O, if thou car'st not whom I love
　　　Alas, thou lov'st not mee.

Seale then this bill of my Divorce to All,
On whom those fainter beames of love did fall;
Marry those loves, which in youth scattered bee
On Fame, Wit, Hopes (false mistresses) to thee
Churches are best for Prayer, that have least light:
To see God only, I goe out of sight:　　　　　　　30
　　And to scape stormy dayes, I chuse
　　　An Everlasting night.

THE LAMENTATIONS OF JEREMY,

FOR THE MOST PART ACCORDING TO TREMELIUS

CHAP. I

1 How sits this citie, late most populous,
　　Thus solitary, and like a widdow thus!
Amplest of Nations, Queene of Provinces
　　She was, who now thus tributary is!

2 Still in the night shee weepes, and her teares fall
　　Downe by her cheeks along, and none of all
Her lovers comfort her; Perfidiously
　　Her friends have dealt, and now are enemie.

3 Unto great bondage, and afflictions
　　Juda is captive led; Those nations　　　　　　　10

With whom shee dwells, no place of rest afford,
   In streights shee meets her Persecutors sword.

4 Emptie are the gates of Sion, and her waies
   Mourne, because none come to her solemne dayes.
Her Priests doe groane, her maides are comfortlesse,
   And shee's unto her selfe a bitternesse.

5 Her foes are growne her head, and live at Peace,
   Because when her transgressions did increase,
The Lord strooke her with sadnesse: Th'enemie
   Doth drive her children to captivite.   **20**

6 From Sions daughter is all beauty gone,
   Like Harts, which seeke for Pasture, and find none,
Her Princes are, and now before the foe
   Which still pursues them, without strength they go.

7 Now in her daies of Teares, Jerusalem
   (Her men slaine by the foe, none succouring them)
Remembers what of old, shee esteemed most,
   Whilest her foes laugh at her, for what she hath lost.

8 Jerusalem hath sinn'd, therefore is shee
   Remov'd, as women in uncleannesse bee;   **30**
Who honor'd, scorne her, for her foulnesse they
   Have seene; her selfe doth groane, and turne away.

9 Her foulnesse in her skirts was seene, yet she
   Remembred not her end; Miraculously
Therefore she fell, none comforting: Behold
   O Lord my affliction, for the Foe growes bold.

10 Upon all things where her delight hath beene,
   The foe hath stretch'd his hand, for shee hath seene
Heathen, whom thou command'st, should not doe so,
   Into her holy Sanctuary goe.   **40**

11 And all her people groane, and seeke for bread;
   And they have given, only to be fed,
All precious things, wherein their pleasure lay:
   How cheape I'am growne, O Lord, behold, and weigh.

12 All this concernes not you, who passe by mee,
  O see, and marke if any sorrow bee
Like to my sorrow, which Jehova hath
  Done to mee in the day of his fierce wrath?

13 That fire, which by himselfe is governed
  He hath cast from heaven on my bones, and spred   50
A net before my feet, and mee o'rthrowne,
  And made me languish all the day alone.

14 His hand hath of my sinnes framed a yoake
  Which wreath'd, and cast upon my neck, hath broke
My strength. The Lord unto those enemies
  Hath given mee, from whom I cannot rise.

15 He under foot hath troden in my sight
  My strong men; He did company invite
To breake my young men; he the winepresse hath
  Trod upon Juda's daughter in his wrath.   60

16 For these things doe I weepe, mine eye, mine eye
  Casts water out; For he which should be nigh
To comfort mee, is now departed farre;
  The foe prevailes, forlorne my children are.

17 There's none, though *Sion* do stretch out her hand,
  To comfort her, it is the Lords command
That *Jacobs* foes girt him. *Jerusalem*
  Is as an uncleane woman amongst them.

18 But yet the Lord is just, and righteous still,
  I have rebell'd against his holy will;   70
O heare all people, and my sorrow see,
  My maides, my young men in captivitie.

19 I called for my *lovers* then, but they
  Deceiv'd mee, and my Priests, and Elders lay
Dead in the citie; for they sought for meat
  Which should refresh their soules, they could not get.

20 Because I am in streights, *Jehova* see
  My heart o'rturn'd, my bowells muddy bee,

Because I have rebell'd so much, as fast
  The sword without, as death within, doth wast.   80

21 Of all which heare I mourne, none comforts mee,
  My foes have heard my griefe, and glad they be,
That thou hast done it; But thy promis'd day
  Will come, when, as I suffer, so shall they.

22 Let all their wickednesse appeare to thee,
  Doe unto them, as thou hast done to mee,
For all my sinnes: The sighs which I have had
  Are very many, and my heart is sad.

CHAP. II

1 How over Sions daughter hath God hung
  His wraths thicke cloud! and from heaven hath flung   90
To earth the beauty of *Israel*, and hath
  Forgot his foot-stoole in the day of wrath!

2 The Lord unsparingly hath swallowed
  All Jacobs dwellings, and demolished
To ground the strengths of *Juda*, and prophan'd
  The Princes of the Kingdome, and the land.

3 In heat of wrath, the horne of *Israel* hee
  Hath cleane cut off, and lest the enemie
Be hindred, his right hand he doth retire,
  But is towards *Jacob,* All-devouring fire.   100

4 Like to an enemie he bent his bow,
  His right hand was in posture of a foe,
To kill what *Sions* daughter did desire,
  'Gainst whom his wrath, he poured forth, like fire.

5 For like an enemie *Jehova* is,
  Devouring *Israel*, and his Palaces,
Destroying holds, giving additions
  To *Juda's* daughters lamentations.

6 Like to a garden hedge he hath cast downe
  The place where was his congregation,   110

And *Sions* feasts and sabbaths are forgot;
　　Her King, her Priest, his wrath regardeth not.

7 The Lord forsakes his Altar, and detests
　　His Sanctuary, and in the foes hand rests
His Palace, and the walls, in which their cries
　　Are heard, as in the true solemnities.

8 The Lord hath cast a line, so to confound
　　And levell *Sions* walls unto the ground;
He drawes not back his hand, which doth oreturne
　　The wall, and Rampart, which together mourne.   **120**

9 Their gates are sunke into the grounde, and hee
　　Hath broke the barres; their King and Princes bee
Amongst the heathen, without law, nor there
　　Unto their Prophets doth the Lord appeare.

10 There *Sions Elders* on the ground are plac'd,
　　And silence keepe; Dust on their heads they cast,
In sackcloth have they girt themselves, and low
　　The Virgins towards ground, their heads do throw.

11 My bowells are growne muddy, and mine eyes
　　Are faint with weeping: and my liver lies   **130**
Pour'd out upon the ground, for miserie
　　That sucking children in the streets doe die.

12 When they had cryed unto their Mothers, where
　　Shall we have bread, and drinke? they fainted there
And in the streets like wounded persons lay
　　Till 'twixt their mothers breasts they went away.

13 *Daughter Jerusalem,* Oh what may bee
　　A witnesse, or comparison for thee?
Sion, to ease thee, what shall I name like thee?
　　Thy breach is like the sea, what help can bee?   **140**

14 For thee vaine foolish things thy Prophets sought,
　　Thee, thine iniquities they have not taught,
Which might disturne thy bondage: but for thee
　　False burthens, and false causes they would see.

15 The passengers doe clap their hands, and hisse,
   And wag their head at thee, and say, Is this
That citie, which so many men did call
   Joy of the earth, and perfectest of all?

16 Thy foes doe gape upon thee, and they hisse,
   And gnash their teeth, and say, Devoure wee this,   150
For this is certainly the day which wee
   Expected, and which now we finde, and see.

17 The Lord hath done that which he purposed,
   Fulfill'd his word of old determined;
He hath throwne downe, and not spar'd, and thy foe
   Made glad above thee, and advanc'd him so.

18 But now, their hearts against the Lord do call,
   Therefore, O walls of *Sion*, let teares fall
Downe like a river, day and night; take thee
   No rest, but let thine eye incessant be.   160

19 Arise, cry in the night, poure, for thy sinnes,
   Thy heart, like water, when the watch begins;
Lift up thy hands to God, lest children dye,
   Which, faint for hunger, in the streets doe lye.

20 Behold O Lord, consider unto whom
   Thou hast done this; what, shall the women come
To eate their children of a spanne? shall thy
   Prophet and Priest be slaine in Sanctuary?

21 On ground in streets, the yong and old do lye,
   My virgins and yong men by sword do dye;   170
Them in the day of thy wrath thou hast slaine,
   Nothing did thee from killing them containe.

22 As to a solemne feast, all whom I fear'd
   Thou call'st about mee; when his wrath appear'd,
None did remaine or scape, for those which I
   Brought up, did perish by mine enemie.

CHAP. III

1 I AM the man which have affliction seene,
　Under the rod of Gods wrath having beene,
2 He hath led mee to darknesse, not to light,
　3 And against mee all day, his hand doth fight.　　　　180

4 Hee hath broke my bones, worne out my flesh and skinne,
　5 Built up against mee; and hath girt mee in
With hemlocke, and with labour; 6 and set mee
　In darke, as they who dead for ever bee.

7 Hee hath hedg'd me lest I scape, and added more
　To my steele fetters, heavier than before.
8 When I crie out, he out shuts my prayer: 9 And hath
　Stop'd with hewn stone my way, and turn'd my path.

10 And like a Lion hid in secrecie,
　Or Beare which lyes in wait, he was to mee.　　　　190
11 He stops my way, teares me, made desolate,
　12 And hee makes mee the marke he shooteth at.

13 Hee made the children of his quiver passe
　Into my reines, 14 I with my people was
All the day long, a song and mockery.
　15 Hee hath fill'd mee with bitternesse, and he

Hath made me drunke with wormewood. 16 He hath burst
　My teeth with stones, and covered mee with dust;
17 And thus my Soule farre off from peace was set,
　And my prosperity I did forget.　　　　200

18 My strength, my hope (unto my selfe I said)
　Which from the Lord should come, is perished.
19 But when my mournings I do thinke upon,
　My wormwood, hemlocke, and affliction,

20 My Soule is humbled in remembring this;
　21 My heart considers, therefore, hope there is.
22 'Tis Gods great mercy we'are not utterly
　Consum'd, for his compassions do not die:

23 For every morning they renewed bee,
   For great, O Lord, is thy fidelity.   210
24 The Lord is, saith my Soule, my portion,
   And therefore in him will I hope alone.

25 The Lord is good to them, who on him relie,
   And to the Soule that seeks him earnestly.
26 It is both good to trust, and to attend
   (The Lords salvation) unto the end:

27 'Tis good for one his yoake in youth to beare;
28 He sits alone, and doth all speech forbeare,
Because he hath borne it. 29 And his mouth he layes
   Deepe in the dust, yet then in hope he stayes.   220

30 He gives his cheekes to whosoever will
   Strike him, and so he is reproched still.
31 For, not for ever doth the Lord forsake,
   32 But when he'hath strucke with sadnes, hee doth take

Compassion, as his mercy'is infinite;
   33 Nor is it with his heart, that he doth smite;
34 That underfoot the prisoners stamped bee,
   35 That a mans right the Judge himselfe doth see

To be wrung from him, 36 That he subverted is
   In his just cause; the Lord allowes not this.   230
37 Who then will say, that ought doth come to passe,
   But that which by the Lord commanded was?

38 Both good and evill from his mouth proceeds;
   39 Why then grieves any man for his misdeeds?
40 Turne wee to God, by trying out our wayes;
   41 To him in heaven, our hands with hearts upraise.

42 Wee have rebell'd, and falne away from thee,
   Thou pardon'st not; 43 Usest no clemencie;
Pursuest us, kill'st us, coverest us with wrath,
   44 Cover'st thy selfe with clouds, that our prayer hath   240

No power to passe. 45 And thou hast made us fall
   As refuse, and off-scouring to them all.

46 All our foes gape at us. 47 Feare and a snare
  With ruine, and with waste, upon us are.

48 With watry rivers doth mine eye oreflow
  For ruine of my peoples daughter so;
49 Mine eye doth drop downe teares incessantly,
  50 Untill the Lord looke downe from heaven to see.

51 And for my citys daughters sake, mine eye
  Doth breake mine heart. 52 Causles mine enemy,   **250**
Like a bird chac'd me. 53 In a dungeon
  They have shut my life, and cast on me a stone.

54 Waters flow'd o'r my head, then thought I, I am
  Destroy'd; 55 I called Lord, upon thy name
Out of the pit. 56 And thou my voice didst heare;
  Oh from my sigh, and crye, stop not thine eare.

57 Then when I call'd upon thee, thou drew'st nere
  Unto mee, and said'st unto mee, do you feare.
58 Thou Lord my Soules cause handled hast, and thou
  Rescud'st my life. 59 O Lord do thou judge now,   **260**

Thou heardst my wrong. 60 Their vengeance all they
    have wrought;
  61 How they reproach'd, thou hast heard, and what
    they thought,
62 What their lips uttered, which against me rose,
  And what was ever whisper'd by my foes.

63 I am their song, whether they rise or sit,
  64 Give them rewards Lord, for their working fit,
65 Sorrow of heart, thy curse. 66 And with thy might
  Follow, and from under heaven destroy them quite.

CHAP. IV

1 How is the gold become so dimme? How is
  Purest and finest gold thus chang'd to this?   **270**
The stones which were stones of the Sanctuary,
  Scattered in corners of each street do lye.

2 The pretious sonnes of Sion, which should bee
  Valued at purest gold, how do wee see
Low rated now, as earthen Pitchers, stand,
  Which are the worke of a poore Potters hand.

3 Even the Sea-calfes draw their brests, and give
  Sucke to their young; my peoples daughters live,
By reason of the foes great cruelnesse,
  As do the Owles in the vast Wildernesse.   280

4 And when the sucking child doth strive to draw,
  His tongue for thirst cleaves to his upper jaw.
And when for bread the little children crye,
  There is no man that doth them satisfie.

5 They which before were delicately fed,
  Now in the streets forlorne have perished,
And they which ever were in scarlet cloath'd,
  Sit and embrace the dunghills which they loath'd.

6 The daughters of my people have sinned more,
  Than did the towne of *Sodome* sinne before;   290
Which being at once destroy'd, there did remaine
  No hands amongst them, to vexe them againe.

7 But heretofore purer her Nazarite
  Was than the snow, and milke was not so white;
As carbuncles did their pure bodies shine,
  And all their polish'dnesse was Saphirine.

8 They are darker now than blacknes, none can know
  Them by the face, as through the streets they goe,
For now their skin doth cleave unto the bone,
  And withered, is like to dry wood growne.   300

9 Better by sword than famine 'tis to dye;
  And better through pierc'd, than through penury.
10 Women by nature pitifull have eate
  Their children drest with their owne hand for meat

11 *Jehova* here fully accomplish'd hath
  His indignation, and powr'd forth his wrath,

Kindled a fire in *Sion*, which hath power
   To eate, and her foundations to devour.

12 Nor would the Kings of the earth, nor all which live   310
   In the inhabitable world beleeve,
That any adversary, any foe
   Into *Jerusalem* should enter so.

13 For the Priests sins, and Prophets, which have shed
   Blood in the streets, and the just murthered:
14 Which when those men, whom they made blinde, did
      stray
   Thorough the streets, defiled by the way

With blood, the which impossible it was
   Their garments should scape touching, as they passe,
15 Would cry aloud, depart defiled men,
   Depart, depart, and touch us not: and then   320

They fled, and strayd, and with the *Gentiles* were,
   Yet told their friends, they should not long dwell there;
16 For this they are scattered by Jehovahs face
   Who never will regard them more; No grace

Unto their old men shall the foe afford,
   Nor, that they are Priests, redeeme them from the
      sword.
17 And wee as yet, for all these miseries
   Desiring our vaine helpe, consume our eyes:

And such a nation as cannot save,
   We in desire and speculation have.   330
18 They hunt our steps, that in the streets wee feare
   To goe: our end is now approached neere,

Our dayes accomplish'd are, this the last day.
   19 Eagles of heaven are not so swift as they
Which follow us, o'r mountaine tops they flye
   At us, and for us in the desart lye.

20 The annointed Lord, breath of our nostrils, hee
   Of whom we said, under his shadow, wee

Shall with more ease under the Heathen dwell,
   Into the pit which these men digged, fell. 340

21 Rejoyce O *Edoms daughter*, joyfull bee
   Thou which inhabitst *Huz*, for unto thee
This cup shall passe, and thou with drunkennesse
   Shalt fill thy selfe, and shew thy nakednesse.

22 And then thy sinnes O *Sion*, shall be spent,
   The Lord will not leave thee in banishment.
Thy sinnes O *Edoms daughter*, hee will see,
   And for them, pay thee with captivitie.

CHAP. V

1 REMEMBER, O Lord, what is fallen on us;
   See, and marke how we are reproached thus, 350
2 For unto strangers our possession
   Is turn'd, our houses unto Aliens gone,

3 Our mothers are become as widowes, wee
   As Orphans all, and without father be;
4 Waters which are our owne, wee drunke, and pay,
   And upon our owne wood a price they lay.

5 Our persecutors on our necks do sit,
   They make us travaile, and not intermit,
6 We stretch our hands unto th'*Egyptians*
   To get us bread; and to the *Assyrians*. 360

7 Our Fathers did these sinnes, and are no more,
   But wee do beare the sinnes they did before.
8 They are but servants, which do rule us thus,
   Yet from their hands none would deliver us.

9 With danger of our life our bread wee gat;
   For in the wildernesse, the sword did wait.
10 The tempests of this famine wee liv'd in,
   Black as an Oven colour'd had our skinne:

11 In *Judaes* cities they the maids abus'd
   By force, and so women in *Sion* us'd. 370

12 The Princes with their hands they hung; no grace
   Nor honour gave they to the Elders face.

13 Unto the mill our yong men carried are,
   And children fell under the wood they bare.
14 Elders, the gates; youth did their songs forbeare,
15 Gone was our joy; our dancings, mournings were.

16 Now is the crowne falne from our head; and woe
   Be unto us, because we'have sinned so.
17 For this our hearts do languish, and for this
   Over our eyes a cloudy dimnesse is.   **380**

18 Because mount *Sion* desolate doth lye,
   And foxes there do goe at libertie:
19 But thou O Lord art ever, and thy throne
   From generation, to generation.

20 Why should'st thou forget us eternally?
   Or leave us thus long in this misery?
21 Restore us Lord to thee, that so we may
   Returne, and as of old, renew our day.

22 For oughtest thou, O Lord, despise us thus,
   And to be utterly enrag'd at us?   **390**

A HYMNE TO GOD THE FATHER

I

WILT thou forgive that sinne where I begunne,
   Which is my sin, though it were done before?
Wilt thou forgive those sinnes, through which I runne,
   And do run still: though still I do deplore?
     When thou hast done, thou hast not done,
        For, I have more.

II

Wilt thou forgive that sinne by which I'have wonne
   Others to sinne? and, made my sinne their doore?
Wilt thou forgive that sinne which I did shunne

A yeare, or two: but wallowed in, a score?   **10**
  When thou hast done, thou hast not done,
      For I have more.

III

I have a sinne of feare, that when I have spunne
  My last thred, I shall perish on the shore;
Sweare by thy selfe, that at my death thy sonne
  Shall shine as he shines now, and heretofore;
    And, having done that, Thou haste done,
      I feare no more

HYMNE TO GOD MY GOD, IN MY SICKNESSE

SINCE I am comming to that Holy roome,
  Where, with thy Quire of Saints for evermore,
I shall be made thy Musique; As I come
  I tune the Instrument here at the dore,
  And what I must doe then, thinke here before.

Whilst my Physitians by their love are growne
  Cosmographers, and I their Mapp, who lie
Flat on this bed, that by them may be showne
  That this is my South-west discoverie
  Per fretum febris, by these streights to die,   **10**

I joy, that in these straits, I see my West;
  For, though theire currants yeeld returne to none,
What shall my West hurt me? As West and East
  In all flatt Maps (and I am one) are one,
  So death doth touch the Resurrection.

Is the Pacifique Sea my home? Or are
  The Easterne riches? Is *Jerusalem*?
Anyan, and *Magellan*, and *Gibraltare*,
  All streights, and none but streights, are wayes to them,
  Whether where *Japhet* dwelt, or *Cham*, or *Sem*.   **20**

We thinke that *Paradise* and *Calvarie*,
  Christs Crosse, and *Adams* tree, stood in one place;
Looke Lord, and finde both *Adams* met in me;

As the first *Adams* sweat surrounds my face,
May the last *Adams* blood my soule embrace.

So, in his purple wrapp'd receive mee Lord,
  By these his thornes give me his other Crowne;
And as to others soules I preach'd thy word,
  Be this my Text, my Sermon to mine owne,
  Therefore that he may raise the Lord throws down.   **30**

LATIN POEMS & TRANSLATIONS

DE LIBRO CUM MUTUARETUR IMPRESSO; DOMI À PUERIS FRUSTATIM LACERATO; ET POST REDDITO MANUSCRIPTO

DOCTISSIMO AMICISSIMOQUE V.
D. D. ANDREWS

PARTURIUNT madido quae nixu praela, recepta,
  Sed quae scripta manu, sunt veneranda magis.
Qui liber in pluteos, blattis cinerique relictos,
  Si modo sit praeli sanguine tinctus, abit;
Accedat calamo scriptus, reverenter habetur,
  Involat et veterum scrinia summa Patrum.
Dicat Apollo modum; Pueros infudere libro
  Nempe vetustatem canitiemque novo.
Nil mirum, medico pueros de semine natos,
  Haec nova fata libro posse dedisse novo.   **10**
Si veterem faciunt pueri, qui nuperus, Annon
  Ipse Pater Juvenem me dabit arte senem?
Hei miseris senibus! nos vertit dura senectus
  Omnes in pueros, neminem at in Juvenem.
Hoc tibi servasti praestandum, Antique Dierum,
  Quo viso, et vivit, et juvenescit Adam.
Interea, infirmae fallamus taedia vitae,
  Libris, et Coelorum aemulâ amicitiâ.
Hos inter, qui a te mihi redditus iste libellus,
  Non mihi tam charus, tam meus, ante fuit.   **20**

EPIGRAMMA

Transiit in Sequanam Moenus; Victoris in aedes;
  Et Francofurtum te revehente, meat.

AMICISSIMO, ET MERITISSIMO
BEN. JONSON

IN VULPONEM

QUOD arte ausus es hic tuâ, Poeta,
Si auderent hominum Deique juris
Consulti, veteres sequi aemularierque,
O omnes saperemus ad salutem.
His sed sunt veteres araneosi;
Tam nemo veterum est sequutor, ut tu
Illos quod sequeris novator audis.
Fac tamen quod agis; tuique primâ
Libri canitie induantur horâ:
Nam chartis pueritia est neganda,   **10**
Nascanturque senes, oportet, illi
Libri, queis dare vis perennitatem.
Priscis, ingenium facit, laborque
Te parem; hos superes, ut et futuros,
Ex nostrâ vitiositate sumas,
Quâ priscos superamus, et futuros.

TO MR. GEORGE HERBERT,

WITH ONE OF MY SEALS, OF THE ANCHOR AND CHRIST

QUI prius assuetus Serpentum fasce Tabellas
    Signare, (haec nostrae symbola parva Domus)
Adscitus domui Domini, patrioque relicto
    Stemmate, nanciscor stemmata jure nova.
Hinc mihi Crux primo quae fronti impressa lavacro,
    Finibus extensis, anchora facta patet.
Anchorae in effigiem Crux tandem desinit ipsam,
    Anchora fit tandem Crux tolerata diu.
Hoc tamen ut fiat, Christo vegetatur ab ipso
    Crux, et ab Affixo, est Anchora facta, Jesu.   **10**
Nec Natalitiis penitus serpentibus orbor,
    Non ita dat Deus, ut auferat ante data.
Quâ sapiens, Dos est; Quâ terram lambit et ambit.
    Pestis; At in nostra fit Medicina Cruce,

Serpens; fixa Cruci si sit Natura; Crucique
  A fixo, nobis, Gratia tota fluat.
Omnia cum Crux sint, Crux Anchora facta, sigillum
  Non tam dicendum hoc quam Catechismus erit.
Mitto nec exigua, exiguâ sub imagine, dona,
  Pignora amicitiae, et munera; Vota, preces.   20
Plura tibi accumulet, sanctus cognominis, Ille
  Regia qui flavo Dona sigillat Equo.

A SHEAFE of Snakes used heretofore to be
My Seal, The Crest of our poore Family.
Adopted in Gods Family, and so
Our old Coat lost, unto new armes I go.
The Crosse (my seal at Baptism) spred below,
Does, by that form, into an Anchor grow.
Crosses grow Anchors; Bear, as thou shouldst do
Thy Crosse, and that Crosse grows an Anchor too.
But he that makes our Crosses Anchors thus,
Is Christ, who there is crucifi'd for us.   10
Yet may I, with this, my first Serpents hold,
God gives new blessings, and yet leaves the old;
The Serpent, may, as wise, my pattern be;
My poison, as he feeds on dust, that's me.
And as he rounds the Earth to murder sure,
My death he is, but on the Crosse, my cure.
Crucifie nature then, and then implore
All Grace from him, crucified there before;
When all is Crosse, and that Crosse Anchor grown,
This Seal's a Catechism, not a Seal alone.   20
Under that little Seal great gifts I send,
[Wishes,] and prayers, pawns, and fruits of a friend.
And may that Saint which rides in our great Seal,
To you, who bear his name, great bounties deal.

TRANSLATED OUT OF GAZÆUS, *VOTA AMICO FACTA*. Fol. 160

GOD grant thee thine own wish, and grant thee mine,
Thou, who dost, best friend, in best things outshine,
May thy soul, ever chearfull, nere know cares,
Nor thy life, ever lively, know gray haires.

Nor thy hand, ever open, know base holds,
Nor thy purse, ever plump, know pleits, or folds.
Nor thy tongue, ever true, know a false thing,
Nor thy word, ever mild, know quarrelling.
Nor thy works, ever equall, know disguise,
Nor thy fame, ever pure, know contumelies.   10
Nor thy prayers, know low objects, still Divine;
God grant thee thine own wish, and grant thee mine.

From ELEGIES UPON THE AUTHOR

AN ELEGIE UPON DR. DONNE

Is *Donne*, great *Donne* deceas'd? then England say
Thou'hast lost a man where language chose to stay
And shew it's gracefull power. I would not praise
That and his vast wit (which in these vaine dayes
Make many proud) but as they serv'd to unlock
That Cabinet, his minde: where such a stock
Of knowledge was repos'd, as all lament
(Or should) this generall cause of discontent.
    And I rejoyce I am not so severe,
But (as I write a line) to weepe a teare   10
For his decease; Such sad extremities
May make such men as I write *Elegies*.
    And wonder not; for, when a generall losse
Falls on a nation, and they slight the crosse,
God hath rais'd *Prophets* to awaken them
From stupifaction; witnesse my milde pen,
Not us'd to upraid the world, though now it must
Freely and boldly, for, the cause is just.
    Dull age, Oh I would spare thee, but th'art worse,
Thou art not onely dull, but hast a curse   20
Of black ingratitude; if not, couldst thou
Part with *miraculous Donne*, and make no vow
For thee and thine, successively to pay
A sad remembrance to his dying day?
    Did his youth scatter *Poetrie*, wherein
Was all Philosophie? Was every sinne
Character'd in his *Satyres*? made so foule

That some have fear'd their shapes, and kept their soule
Freer by reading verse? Did he give *dayes*
Past marble monuments, to those, whose praise   30
He would perpetuate? Did hee (I feare
The dull will doubt:) these at his twentieth yeare?
   But, more matur'd: Did his full soule conceive,
And in harmonious-holy-numbers weave
A *Crowne of sacred sonets*, fit to adorne   *La Corona*
A dying Martyrs brow: or, to be worne
On that blest head of *Mary Magdalen*:
After she wip'd Christs feet, but not till then?
Did hee (fit for such penitents as shee
And hee to use) leave us a *Litany*?   40
Which all devout men love, and sure, it shall,
As times grow better, grow more classicall.
Did he write *Hymnes,* for piety and wit
Equall to those great grave *Prudentius* writ?
Spake he all *Languages*? knew he all *Lawes*?
The grounds and use of *Physicke;* but because
'Twas mercenary wav'd it? Went to see
That blessed place of *Christs nativity*?
Did he returne and preach him? preach him so
As none but hee did, or could do? They know   50
(Such as were blest to heare him know) 'tis truth.
Did he confirme thy age? [ag'd?] convert thy youth?
Did he these wonders? And is this deare losse
Mourn'd by so few? (few for so great a crosse.)
   But sure the silent are ambitious all
To be *Close Mourners* at his Funerall;
If not; In common pitty they forbare
By repetitions to renew our care;
Or, knowing, griefe conceiv'd, conceal'd, consumes
Man irreparably, (as poyson'd fumes   60
Do waste the braine) make silence a safe way
To'inlarge the Soule from these walls, mud and clay,
(Materialls of this body) to remaine
With *Donne* in heaven, where no promiscuous paine
Lessens the joy wee have, for, with *him*, all
Are satisfyed with *joyes essentiall*.
   My thoughts, Dwell on this *Joy*, and do not call
Griefe backe, by thinking of his Funerall;
Forget he lov'd mee; Waste not my sad yeares;
(Which haste to *Davids* seventy, fill'd with feares   70

And sorrow for his death;) Forget his parts,
Which finde a living grave in good mens hearts;
And, (for, my first is daily paid for sinne)
Forget to pay my second sigh for him:
Forget his powerfull preaching; and forget
I am his *Convert.* Oh my frailtie! let
My flesh be no more heard, it will obtrude
This lethargie: so should my gratitude,
My vowes of gratitude should so be broke;
Which can no more be, than *Donnes* vertues ~~spoke~~   80
By any but himselfe; for which cause, I
   Write no *Encomium,* but an *Elegie.*

IZ [aak] WA [lton]

AN ELEGIE UPON THE DEATH OF THE DEANE OF PAULS, DR. JOHN DONNE:

BY MR. THO[MAS] CARIE. [CAREW]

CAN we not force from widdowed Poetry,
Now thou art dead (Great Donne) one Elegie
To crowne thy Hearse? Why yet dare we not trust
Though with unkneaded dowe-bak't prose thy dust,
Such as the uncisor'd Churchman from the flower
Of fading Rhetorique, short liv'd as his houre,
Dry as the sand that measures it, should lay
Upon thy Ashes, on the funerall day?
Have we no voice, no tune? Did'st thou dispense
Through all our language, both the words and sense?   10
'Tis a sad truth; The Pulpit may her plaine,
And sober Christian precepts still retaine,
Doctrines it may, and wholesome Uses frame,
Grave Homilies, and Lectures, But the flame
Of thy brave Soule, that shot such heat and light,
As burnt our earth, and made our darknesse bright,
Committed holy Rapes upon our Will,
Did through the eye the melting heart distill:
And the deepe knowledge of darke truths so teach,
As sense might judge, what phansie could not reach;   20
Must be desir'd for ever. So the fire,
That fills with spirit and heat the Delphique quire,
Which kindled first by thy Promethean breath,

Glow'd here a while, lies quench't now in thy death;
The Muses garden with Pedantique weedes
O'rspred, was purg'd by thee; The lazie seeds
Of servile imitation throwne away;
And fresh invention planted, Thou didst pay
The debts of our penurious bankrupt age;
Licentious thefts, that make poëtique rage   30
A Mimique fury, when our soules must bee
Possest, or with Anacreons Extasie,
Or Pindars, not their owne; The subtle cheat
Of slie Exchanges, and the jugling feat
Of two-edg'd words, or whatsoever wrong
By ours was done the Greeke, or Latine tongue,
Thou hast redeem'd, and open'd Us a Mine
Of rich and pregnant phansie, drawne a line
Of masculine expression, which had good
Old Orpheus seene, Or all the ancient Brood   40
Our superstitious fooles admire, and hold
Their lead more precious, than thy burnish't Gold,
Thou hadst beene their Exchequer, and no more
They each in others dust, had rak'd for Ore.
Thou shalt yield no precedence, but of time,
And the binde fate of language, whose tun'd chime
More charmes the outward sense; Yet thou maist claime
From so great disadvantage greater fame,
Since to the awe of thy imperious wit
Our stubborne language bends, made only fit   50
With her tough-thick-rib'd hoopes to gird about
Thy Giant phansie, which had prov'd too stout
For their soft melting Phrases. As in time
They had the start, so did they cull the prime
Buds of invention many a hundred yeare,
And left the rifled fields, besides the feare
To touch their Harvest, yet from those bare lands
Of what is purely thine, thy only hands
(And that thy smallest worke) have gleaned more
Than all those times, and tongues could reape before;   60
But thou art gone, and thy strict lawes will be
Too hard for Libertines in Poetrie.
They will repeale the goodly exil'd traine
Of gods and goddesses, which in thy just raigne
Were banish'd nobler Poems, now, with these
The silenc'd tales o'th'Metamorphoses

Shall stuffe their lines, and swell the windy Page,
Till Verse refin'd by thee, in this last Age,
Turne ballad rime, Or those old Idolls bee
Ador'd againe, with new apostasie;   70
Oh, pardon mee, that breake with untun'd verse
The reverend silence that attends thy herse,
Whose awfull solemne murmures were to thee
More than these faint lines, A loud Elegie,
That did proclaime in a dumbe eloquence
The death of all the Arts, whose influence
Growne feeble, in these panting numbers lies
Gasping short winded Accents, and so dies:
So doth the swiftly turning wheele not stand
In th'instant we withdraw the moving hand,   80
But some small time maintaine a faint weake course
By vertue of the first impulsive force:
And so whil'st I cast on thy funerall pile
Thy crowne of Bayes, Oh, let it crack a while,
And spit disdaine, till the devouring flashes
Suck all the moysture up, then turne to ashes.
I will not draw the envy to engrosse
All thy perfections, or weepe all our losse;
Those are too numerous for an Elegie,
And this too great, to be express'd by mee.   90
Though every pen should share a distinct part,
Yet art thou Theme enough to tyre all Art;
Let others carve the rest, it shall suffice
I on thy Tombe this Epitaph incise.

   Here lies a King, that rul'd as hee thought fit
   The universall Monarchy of wit;
   Here lie two Flamens, and both those, the best,
   Apollo's first, at last, the true Gods Priest.

PROSE

From JUVENILIA: OR CERTAINE PARADOXES, AND PROBLEMES

PARADOXES

I

A DEFENCE OF WOMENS INCONSTANCY

THAT Women are *Inconstant*, I with any man confess, but that *Inconstancy* is a bad quality, I against any man will maintain: For every thing as it is one better than another, so is it fuller of *change*; The *Heavens* themselves continually turn, the *Stars* move, the *Moon* changeth; *Fire* whirleth, *Aire* flyeth, *Water* ebbs and flowes, the face of the *Earth* altereth her looks, *time* staies not; the Colour that is most light, will take most dyes: so in Men, they that have the most reason are the most alterable in their designes, and the darkest or most ignorant, do seldomest change; therefore Women changing more than Men, have also more *Reason*. They cannot be immutable like stocks, like stones, like the Earths dull Center; Gold that lyeth still, rusteth; Water, corrupteth; Aire that moveth not, poysoneth; then why should that which is the perfection of other things, be imputed to Women as greatest imperfection? Because thereby they deceive Men. Are not your wits pleased with those jests, which cozen your expectation? You can call it pleasure to be beguil'd in troubles, and in the most excellent toy in the world, you call it Treachery: I would you had your *Mistresses* so constant, that they would never change, no not so much as their *smocks,* then should you see what sluttish vertue, *Constancy* were. *Inconstancy* is a most commendable and cleanly quality, and Women in this quality are far more absolute than the Heavens, than the Stars, Moon, or any thing beneath it; for long observation hath pickt certainty out of their mutability. The Learned are so well acquainted with the Stars, Signes and Planets, that they make them but Characters, to read the meaning of the Heaven in his own forehead. Every simple fellow can bespeak the change of the *Moon* a great while beforehand: but I would fain have the learnedst man so skilfull, as to tell when the simplest Woman meaneth to vary. Learning affords no rules to know, much less knowledge to rule the minde of a Woman: For as *Philosophy* teacheth us, that *Light things do always tend upwards,* and *heavy things decline downward;* Experience teacheth us otherwise, that the disposition of a *Light* Woman, is to fall down, the nature of women being contrary to all Art and Nature. Women are like *Flies,* which feed among us at our Table, or *Fleas* sucking our very blood, who leave not our most retired places free from their familiarity, yet for all their fellowship will they never be tamed nor commanded by us. Women are like the *Sun,* which is violently carried one way, yet hath a proper course contrary: so though they, by the mastery of some over-ruling churlish husbands, are forced to his Byas, yet have they a motion of their own, which their husbands never know of: It is the nature of nice and fastidious mindes to know things only to be weary of them: Women by their slye *changeableness,* and pleasing doubleness, prevent even the mislike of those, for they can never be so well known, but that there is still more unknown. Every woman is a *Science;* for he that plods upon a woman all his life long, shall at length finde himself short of the knowledge of her: they are born to take down the pride of wit, and ambition of wisdom, making *fools* wise in the adventuring to win them, *wisemen* fools in conceit of losing their labours; *witty* men stark mad, being confounded with their uncertainties. *Philosophers* write against them for spight, not desert, that having attained to some knowledge in all other things, in them only they know nothing, but are meerly ignorant: *Active* and *Experienced* men rail against them, because they love in their liveless and decrepit age, when all goodness leaves them. These envious *Libellers* ballad against them, because having nothing in themselves able to deserve their love, they maliciously discommend all they cannot obtain, thinking to make men believe they know much, because they are able to dispraise much, and rage against *Inconstancy,* when they were never admitted into so much favour as to be forsaken. In mine opinion such men are happie that women are *Inconstant,* for so may they chance to be beloved of some excellent woman (when it comes to their turn) out of their *Inconstancy* and mutability, though not out of their own desert. And what reason is there to clog any woman with one man, be he never so singular? Women had rather, and it is far better and more Judicial to enjoy all the vertues in several men, than but some of them in one, for other-

wise they lose their taste, like divers sorts of meat minced together in one dish: and to have all excellencies in one man (if
it were possible) is *Confusion* and *Diversity*. Now who can
deny, but such as are obstinately bent to undervalue their worth,
are those that have not soul enough to comprehend their excellency, Women being the most excellent Creatures, in that Man
is able to subject all things else, and to grow wise in every
thing, but still persists a fool in Woman? The greatest *Scholler,*
if he once take a wife, is found so unlearned, that he must begin
his *Horn-book*, and all is by *Inconstancy*. To conclude therefore;
this name of *Inconstancy*, which hath so much been poysoned
with slanders, ought to be changed into *variety*, for the which
the world is so delightfull, *and a Woman for that the most delightfull thing in this world.*

II

THAT WOMEN OUGHT TO PAINT

Foulness is *Lothsome:* can that be so which helps it? who forbids
his beloved to gird in her waste? to mend by shooing her un-
even lameness? to burnish her teeth? or to perfume her breath?
yet that the *Face* be more precisely regarded, it concerns more:
For as open confessing sinners are always punished, but the wary
and concealing offenders without witness do it also without punishment; so the secret parts needs the less respect; but of the
Face, discovered to all Examinations and surveys, there is not too
nice a Jealousie. Nor doth it only draw the busie Eyes, but it is
subject to the divinest touch of all, to *kissing,* the strange and
mystical union of souls. If she should prostitute her self to a
more unworthy man than thy self, how earnestly and justly
wouldst thou exclaim, that for want of this easier and ready way
of repairing, to betray her body to ruine and deformity (the
tyrannous *Ravishers,* and sodain *Deflourers* of all women) what
a hainous adultery is it! What thou lovest in her *face* is *colour,*
and *painting* gives that, but thou hatest it, not because it is, but
because thou knowest it. Fool, whom Ignorance makes happy,
the Stars, the Sun, the Skye whom thou admirest, alas, have no
colour, but are fair, because they seem to be coloured: If this
seeming will not satisfie thee in her, thou hast good assurance of
her *colour,* when thou seest her *lay* it on. If her *face* be *painted*
on a Board or Wall, thou wilt love it, and the Board, and the

Wall: Canst thou loath it then when it speaks, smiles, and kisses, because it is *painted?* Are we not more delighted with seeing Birds, Fruits, and Beasts *painted* than we are with Naturals? And do we not with pleasure behold the *painted* shape of Monsters and Devils, whom true, we durst not regard? We repair the ruines of our houses, but first cold tempests warn us of it, and bites us through it; we mend the wrack and stains of our Apparell, but first our eyes, and other bodies are offended; but by this providence of Women, this is prevented. If in *Kissing* or *breathing* upon her, the *painting* fall off, thou art angry; wilt thou be so, if it stick on? Thou didst love her; if thou beginnest to hate her, then 'tis because she is not *painted.* If thou wilt say now, thou didst hate her before, thou didst hate her and love her together. Be constant in something, and love her who shews her great *love* to thee, in taking this pains to seem *lovely* to thee.

IV

THAT GOOD IS MORE COMMON THAN EVIL

I HAVE not been so pittifully tired with any *vanity,* as with silly *Old Mens* exclaiming against these times, and extolling their own: Alas! they betray themselves, for if the *times* be *changed,* their manners have changed them. But their senses are to *pleasures,* as *sick mens* tastes are to *Liquors;* for indeed no *new thing* is done in the *world,* all things are what, and as they were, and *Good* is as ever it was, more plenteous, and must of necessity be *more common than Evil,* because it hath this for *nature* and *perfection* to be *common.* It makes *Love* to all *Natures,* all, all affect it. So that in the *Worlds* early *Infancy,* there was a time when nothing was *Evill,* but if this World shall suffer *dotage,* in the extreamest *Crookednesse* thereof, there shall be no time when nothing shall be *good.* It dares appear and spread, and glister in the *World,* but *Evill* buries it self in night and darkness, and is chastised and suppressed when *Good* is cherished and rewarded. And as *Imbroderers, Lapidaries,* and other *Artisans,* can by all things adorn their works; for by adding better things, the better they shew in [*Lustre*] and in *Eminency;* so *Good* doth not only prostrate her *Amiablenesse* to all, but refuses no end, no not of her utter contrary *Evill,* that she may be the more *common* to us. For *Evill Manners* are *Parents* of *good Lawes;* and in every *Evill* there is an *excellency,* which (in common speech) we call *good*. For the fashions of *habits*, for our moving in *gestures*, for phrases in our *speech*, we say they are *good* as long as they were used, that is, as long as they were *common;* and we eat, we walk, only when it is, or seems *good* to do so. All *fair*, all *profitable*, all *vertuous*, is, *good*, and these three things I think embrace all things, but their utter *contraries;* of which also *fair* may be *rich* and *vertuous; poor*, may be *vertuous* and *fair; vitious*, may be *fair* and *rich;* so that *Good* hath this good means to be *common*, that some subjects she can possess entirely; and in subjects poysoned with *Evill*, she can humbly stoop to accompany the *Evill*. And of *Indifferent* things many things are become perfectly good by being *Common*, as *Customs* by use are made binding *Lawes*. But I remember nothing that is therefore *ill*, because it is *Common*, but *Women*, of whom also: *They that are most Common, are the best of that Occupation they profess.*

VI

THAT IT IS POSSIBLE TO FINDE SOME VERTUE IN SOME WOMEN

I AM not of that seard *Impudence* that I dare defend *Women*, or pronounce them good; yet we see *Physitians* allow some *vertue* in every *poyson*. Alas! why should we except *Women?* since certainly, they are good for *Physicke* at least, so as some *wine* is good for a *feaver*. And though they be the *Occasioners* of many sins, they are also the *Punishers* and *Revengers* of the same sins: For I have seldom seen one which consumes his *substance* and *body* upon them, escape *diseases*, or *beggery;* and this is their *Justice*. And if *suum cuique dare*, be the fulfilling of all *Civil Justice*, they are *most just;* for they deny that which is theirs to no man.

Tanquam non liceat nulla puella negat.

And who may doubt of great wisdome in them, that doth but observe with how much labour and cunning our *Justicers* and other *dispensers* of the *Laws* studie to imbrace them: and how zealously our *Preachers* dehort men from them, only by urging their *subtilties* and *policies*, and *wisdom*, which are in them? Or who can deny them a good measure of *Fortitude*, if he consider how *valiant men* they have overthrown, and being themselves overthrown, how much and how patiently they *bear?* And though they be most *intemperate*, I care not, for I undertook to furnish them with *some vertue*, not with *all. Necessity*, which makes even bad things good, prevails also for them, for we must say of them, as of some sharp pinching *Laws:* If men were free from *infirmities*, they were needless. These or none must serve for *reasons*, and it is my great happiness that *Examples* prove not *Rules*, for to confirm this *Opinion*, the World yields not *one Example.*

VIII

THAT NATURE IS OUR WORST GUIDE

SHALL she be *guide* to all *Creatures*, which is her self one? Or if she also have a *guide*, shall any *Creature* have a better guide than we? The affections of *lust* and *anger*, yea even to *erre* is natural, shall we follow these? Can she be a good *guide* to us, which hath *corrupted* not us only but her self? was not the first *Man*, by the desire of *knowledge*, corrupted even in the *whitest integrity* of *Nature?* And did not *Nature*, (if *Nature* did any thing) infuse into him this desire of *knowledge*, and so this *Corruption* in him, into us? If by *Nature* we shall understand our *essence*, our *definition* [*our reasonableness*], then this being alike common to all (the *Idiot* and the *Wizard* being equally *reasonable*) why should not all men having equally all one *nature*, follow one course? Or if we shall understand our *inclinations;* alas! how unable a guide is that which follows the *temperature* of our slimie *bodies!* For we cannot say that we derive our *inclinations*, our *mindes*, or *soules* from our *Parents* by any way: to say that it is *all from all*, is *errour* in *reason*, for then with the first nothing remains; or is a *part from all*, is *errour* in *experience*, for then this *part* equally imparted to many children, would like *Gavell-kind lands*, in few generations become nothing: or to say it by *communication*, is *errour* in *Divinity*, for to communicate the *ability* of communicating *whole essence* with any but God, is utterly *blasphemy*. And if thou hit thy *Fathers nature* and *inclination*, he also had his *Fathers*, and so climbing up, all comes of one man, and have one *nature*, all shall imbrace one course; but that cannot be, therefore our *Complexions* and whole *Bodies*, we inherit from *Parents;* our *inclinations* and minds follow that: For our *mind* is heavy in our *bodies afflictions*, and rejoyceth in our *bodies pleasure*: how then shall this *nature* governe us, that is governed by the worst part of us? *Nature though oft chased away, it will return;* 'tis true, but those *good motions* and *inspirations* which be our guides must be *wooed, courted,* and *welcomed,* or else they abandon us. And that old *Axiome, nihil invita, &c.* must not be said thou *shalt,* but thou *wilt* doe nothing against *Nature;* so *unwilling* he notes us to curbe our *naturall appetites.* Wee call our *bastards* alwayes our *naturall issue,* and we define a *Foole* by nothing so ordinary, as by the name of *naturall.* And that poore knowledge whereby we conceive what *rain* is, what *wind,* what *thunder,* we call *Metaphysicke, supernaturall;* such *small* things, such *no* things do we allow to our pliant *Natures,* apprehension. Lastly, by following her, we lose the pleasant, and lawfull *Commodities* of this *life,* for we shall drinke water and eate rootes, and those not sweet and delicate, as now by Mans *art* and *industry* they are made: we shall lose all the necessities of *societies, lawes, arts,* and *sciences,* which are all the workemanship of *Man*: yea we shall lack the last *best refuge* of misery, *death,* because *no death is naturall*: for if yee will not dare to call all *death violent* (though I see not why *sicknesses* be not *violences*) yet *causes* of all *deaths* proceed of the *defect* of that which *nature* made perfect, and would preserve, and therefore all against *nature.*

x

THAT A WISE MAN IS KNOWN BY MUCH LAUGHING

Ride, si sapis, ô puella ride; If thou beest *wise, laugh*: for since the *powers* of *discourse,* and *Reason,* and *laughter,* be equally *proper* unto Man only, why shall not he be only most *wise,* which hath most use of *laughing,* as well as he which hath most of *reasoning* and *discoursing?* I always did, and shall understand that *Adage;*

Per risum multum possis cognoscere stultum,

That by much *laughing* thou maist know there is a *fool,* not, that the *laughers* are *fools,* but that among them there is some *fool,* at whom *wise men* laugh: which moved *Erasmus* to put this as his first *Argument* in the mouth of his *Folly,* that *she made Beholders laugh*: for *fools* are the most laughed at, and laugh the least themselves of any. And *Nature* saw this *faculty* to be so necessary in man, that she hath been content that by *more causes* we should be importuned to *laugh*, than to the *exercise* of any other *power;* for things in themselves utterly *contrary,* beget this effect; for we *laugh* both at *witty* and *absurd* things: At both which sorts I have seen men *laugh so long,* and *so earnestly,* that at last they have *wept* that they could laugh no more. And therefore the *Poet* having described the *quietnesse* of a *wise retired man,* saith in one, what we have said before in many lines; *Quid facit Canius tuus? ridet.* We have received that even the *extremity* of *laughing,* yea of *weeping* also, hath been accounted *wisdom*: and that *Democritus* and *Heraclitus,* the *lovers* of these *Extreams,* have been called *lovers of Wisdom.* Now among our *wise men,* I doubt not but many would be found, who would laugh at *Heraclitus* weeping, none which weep at *Democritus* laughing. At the hearing of *Comedies* or other *witty* reports, I have noted some, which not understanding *jests,* &c. have yet chosen this as the best means to seem *wise* and *understanding,* to *laugh* when their *Companions laugh;* and I have presumed them *ignorant,* whom I have seen *unmoved.* A *fool* if he come into a *Princes Court,* and see a *gay* man leaning at the wall, so *glistering,* and so *painted* in many *colours* that he is hardly discerned from one of the *Pictures* in the *Arras* hanging, his *body* like an *Ironbound chest,* girt in and thick *ribb'd* with *broad gold laces,* may (and commonly doth) envy him. But alas! shall a *wise man,* which may not only not *envy,* but not *pitty* this *Monster,* do nothing? Yes, let him *laugh.* And if one of these *hot cholerick firebrands,* which nourish themselves by *quarrelling,* and kindling others, spit upon a *fool* one *sparke* of *disgrace,* he, like a *thatcht house* quickly burning, may be *angry;* but the *wise man,* as *cold* as the *Salamander,* may not only not be *angry* with him, but not be *sorry* for him; therefore let him *laugh*: so he shall be known a Man, because he can *laugh,* a *wise Man* that he knows at *what* to *laugh,* and a *valiant Man* that he *dares* laugh: for he that *laughs* is justly reputed more *wise,* than at whom it is *laughed.* And hence I think proceeds that which in these later *formal* times I have much noted; that now when our *superstitious civilitie* of *manners* is become a mutuall *tickling flattery* of one another, almost every man affecteth an *humour* of *jesting,* and is content to be *deject,* and to *deform* himself, yea become *fool* to no other *end* that I can spie, but to give his *wise Companion* occasion to *laugh;* and to shew themselves in *promptness* of *laughing* is so great in *wise men,* that I think all *wise men,* if any *wise men* do read this *Paradox,* will *laugh* both at it and me.

XI

THAT THE GIFTS OF THE BODY ARE BETTER THAN THOSE OF THE MINDE

I say again, that the *body* makes the *minde,* not that it created it a *minde,* but *forms* it a *good* or a *bad minde;* and this *minde* may be confounded with *soul* without any violence or injustice to *Reason* or *Philosophy*: then the *soul* it seems is enabled by our *Body,* not this by it. My *Body* licenseth my *soul* to *see* the worlds *beauties* through mine *eyes:* to *hear* pleasant things through mine *ears;* and affords it apt *Organs* for the conveiance of all perceivable *delight.* But alas! my *soul* cannot make any *part,* that is not of it self disposed to *see* or *hear,* though without doubt she be as able and as willing to see *behinde as before.* Now if my *soule* would say, that she enables any part to taste these *pleasures,* but is her selfe only delighted with those rich *sweetnesses* which her *inward eyes* and *senses* apprehend, shee should dissemble; for I see her often solaced with *beauties,* which shee sees through mine *eyes,* and with *musicke* which through mine *eares* she heares. This *perfection* then my *body* hath, that it can impart to my *minde* all his *pleasures;* and my *mind* hath still many, that she can neither teach my *indisposed* part her *faculties,* nor to the best *espoused* parts shew it *beauty* of *Angels,* of *Musicke,* of *Spheres,* whereof she boasts the *contemplation.* Are *Chastity, Temperance,* and *Fortitude* gifts of the *minde?* I appeale to *Physitians* whether the *cause* of these be not in the *body; health* is the gift of the *body,* and *patience* in sicknesse the gift of the *minde:* then who will say that *patience* is as good a happinesse, as *health,* when wee must be extremely *miserable* to purchase this *happinesse.* And for nourishing of *civill societies* and *mutuall love* amongst men, which is our *chief end* while we are men; I say, this *beauty, presence,* and *proportion* of the *body,* hath a more *masculine* force in begetting this *love,* than the *vertues* of the *minde:* for it strikes us *suddenly,* and possesseth us *immoderately;* when to know those *vertues* requires some *Judgement* in him which shall discerne, a *long time* and *conversation* between them. And even at last how much of our *faith* and *beleefe* shall we be driven to bestow, to assure our selves that these *vertues* are not *counterfeited:* for it is the same to *be*, and *seem vertuous*, because that he that hath *no vertue*, can *dissemble* none, but he which hath a *little*, may *gild* and *enamell*, yea and transforme much *vice* into *vertue:* For allow a man to be *discreet* and *flexible* to *complaints,* which are great *vertuous* gifts of the *minde*, this *discretion* will be to him the *soule* and *Elixir* of all *vertues,* so that touched with this, even *pride* shall be made *humility;* and *Cowardice,* honourable and wise *valour.* But in things seen there is not this danger, for the *body* which thou lovest and esteemest *faire,* is *faire:* certainly if it be not *faire* in *perfection,* yet it is *faire* in the same *degree* that thy *Judgment* is good. And in a *faire body,* I do seldom suspect a *disproportioned minde,* and as seldome hope for a *good,* in a *deformed.* When I see a *goodly house,* I assure my selfe of a *worthy possessour,* from a *ruinous weather-beaten building* I turn away, because it seems either stuffed with *varlets* as a *Prison,* or handled by an *unworthy* and *negligent tenant,* that so suffers the *wast* thereof. And truly the gifts of *Fortune,* which are *riches,* are only *handmaids,* yea *Pandars* of the *bodies pleasure;* with their service we nourish *health,* and preserve *dainty,* and wee buy *delights;* so that *vertue* which must be loved for *it selfe,* and respects no further *end,* is indeed *nothing:* And *riches,* whose *end* is the *good* of the *body,* cannot be so *perfectly good,* as the *end* whereto it levels.

XII

THAT VIRGINITY IS A VERTUE

I CALL not that *Virginity a vertue,* which resideth onely in the *Bodies integrity;* much lesse if it be with a purpose of perpetuall keeping it: for then it is a most inhumane vice—But I call that *Virginity a vertue* which is willing and desirous to yeeld it selfe upon honest and lawfull terms, when just reason requireth; and until then, is kept with a modest chastity of Body and Mind. Some perchance will say that *Virginity* is in us by *Nature,* and therefore no *vertue.* True, as it is in us by *Nature,* it is neither a *Vertue* nor *Vice,* and is onely in the body: (as in Infants, Children, and such as are incapable of parting from it) But that *Virginity* which is in Man or Woman of perfect age, is not in them by *Nature: Nature* is the greatest enemy to it, and with most subtile allurements seeks the overthrow of it, continually beating against it with her *Engines,* and giving such forcible assaults to it, that it is a strong and more than ordinary *vertue* to hold out till marriage. *Ethick* Philosophy saith, *That no Vertue is corrupted, or is taken away by that which is good:* Hereupon some may say, that *Virginity* is therfore, no *vertue,* being taken away by marriage. *Virginity* is no otherwise taken away by marriage, than is the light of the starres by a greater light (the light of the Sun:) or as a lesse Title is taken away by a greater (an Esquire by being created an Earle:) yet *Virginity* is a *vertue,* and hath her Throne in the middle: The extreams are, in *Excesse,* to violate it before marriage; in *Defect,* not to marry. In ripe years as soon as reason perswades and opportunity admits, These extreams are equally removed from the mean: The excesse proceeds from *Lust,* the defect from *Peevishnesse, Pride* and *Stupidity.* There is an old Proverb, That, *they that dy maids, must lead Apes in Hell.* An Ape is a ridiculous and an unprofitable Beast, whose flesh is not good for meat, nor its back for burden, nor is it commodious to keep an house: and perchance for the unprofitablenesse of this Beast did this proverb come up: For surely nothing is more unprofitable in the Commonwealth of *Nature,* than they that dy old maids, because they refuse to be used to that end for which they were only made. The Ape bringeth forth her young, for the most part by twins; that which she loves best, she killeth by pressing it too hard: so foolish maids soothing themselves with a false conceit of *vertue,* in fond obstinacie, live and die maids; and so not onely kill in themselves the *vertue* of *Virginity,* and of a *Vertue* make it a *Vice,* but they also accuse their parents in condemning marriage. If this application hold not touch, yet there may be an excellent one gathered from an Apes tender love to Conies in keeping them from the Weasel and Ferret. From this similitude of an Ape and an old Maid did the foresaid proverb first arise. But alas, there are some old Maids that are *Virgins* much against their wills, and fain would change their *Virginlife* for a *Married:* such if they never have had any offer of fit Husbands, are in some sort excusable, and their willingnesse, their desire to marry, and their forbearance from all dishonest, and unlawfull copulation, may be a kind of inclination to *vertue,* although not *Vertue* it selfe. This *Vertue* of *Virginity* (though it be small and fruitlesse) it is an extraordinary, and no common *Vertue*. All other *Vertues* lodge in the *Will* (it is the *Will* that makes them vertues.) But it is the unwillingnesse to keep it, the desire to forsake it, that makes this a *vertue*. As in the naturall generation and formation made of the seed in the womb of a woman, the body is joynted and organized about the 28 day, and so it begins to be no more an *Embrion*, but capable as a matter prepared to its form to receive the soule, which faileth not to insinuate and innest it selfe into the body about the fortieth day; about the third month it hath motion and sense: Even so *Virginity* is an *Embrion*, an unfashioned lump, till it attain to a certain time, which is about twelve years of age in women, fourteen in men, and then it beginneth to have the soule of *Love* infused into it, and to become a *vertue:* There is also a certain limited time when it ceaseth to be a *vertue*, which in men is about fourty, in women about thirty years of age: yea, the losse of so much time makes their *Virginity* a *Vice*, were not their endeavour wholly bent, and their desires altogether fixt upon marriage: In Harvest time do we not account it a great vice of sloath and negligence in a Husbandman, to overslip a week or ten dayes after his fruits are fully ripe; May we not much more account it a more heynous vice, for a *Virgin* to let her Fruit (*in potentia*) consume and rot to nothing, and to let the *vertue* of her *Virginity* degenerate into *Vice*, (for *Virginity* ever kept is ever lost.) Avarice is the greatest deadly sin next Pride: it takes more pleasure in hoording Treasure than in making use of it, and will neither let the possessor nor others take benefit by it during the Misers life; yet it remains intire, and when the Miser dies must come to som body. *Virginity* ever kept, is a vice far worse than Avarice, it will neither let the possessor nor others take benefit by it, nor can it be bequeathed to any: with long keeping it decayes and withers, and becomes corrupt and nothing worth. Thus seeing that *Virginity* becomes a vice in defect, by exceeding a limited time; I counsell all female *Virgins* to make choyce of some *Paracelsian* for their Physitian, to prevent the death of that *Vertue*: The *Paracelsians* (curing like by like) say, That if the lives of living Creatures could be taken down, they would make us immortall. By this Rule, female *Virgins* by a discreet marriage should swallow down into their *Virginity* another *Virginity*, and devour such a life and spirit into their womb, that it might make them, as it were, immortall here on earth, besides their perfect immortality in heaven: And that *Vertue* which otherwise would putrifie and corrupt, shall then be compleat; and shall be

recorded in Heaven, and enrolled here on Earth; and the name
of *Virgin* shal be exchanged for a farre more honorable name,
A Wife.

PROBLEMES

II

WHY PURITANS MAKE LONG SERMONS?

IT needs not for *perspicuousnes,* for God knows they are plain
enough: nor do all of them use *Sem-brief-Accents,* for some of
them have *Crotchets* enough. It may be they intend not to rise
like *glorious Tapers* and *Torches,* but like *Thin-wretched-sick-
watching-Candles,* which *languish* and are in a Divine **Consumption** from the first minute, yea in their *snuff,* and *stink,*
when others are in their more profitable *glory.* I have thought
sometimes, that out of conscience, they allow *long measure* to
course ware. And sometimes, that *usurping* in that *place* a *liberty* to *speak freely* of *Kings,* they would *reigne* as long as they
could. But now I think they do it out of a *zealous* imagination,
that, *It is their duty to Preach on till their Auditory wake.*

V

WHY DOE YOUNG LAY-MEN SO MUCH STUDIE DIVINITY

Is it because others tending busily *Churches preferment* neglect
studie? Or had the *Church* of *Rome* shut up all our wayes,
till the *Lutherans* broke downe their *uttermost stubborne dores,*
and the *Calvinists* picked their *inwardest* and *subtlest lockes?*
Surely the *Divell* cannot bee such a *Foole* to hope that hee shall
make this study *contemptible,* by making it *common.* Nor that
as the *Dwellers* by the river *Origus* are said (by drawing infinite
ditches to sprinckle their *barren Countrey*) to have exhausted
and intercepted their *maine channell,* and so lost their more
profitable course to the *Sea;* so wee, by providing every *ones
selfe, divinity* enough for his *owne use,* should neglect our
Teachers and *Fathers.* Hee cannot hope for better *heresies* than
he hath had, nor was his *Kingdome* ever so much advanced by

debating Religion (though with some *aspersions* of *Error*) as by a *Dull* and *stupid security*, in which many *grosse things* are swallowed. Possible out of such an *Ambition* as we have now, to speake *plainely* and *fellow-like* with *Lords* and *Kings*, wee thinke also to acquaint our selves with *Gods secrets:* Or perchance when wee study it by *mingling humane* respects, *It is not Divinity.*

VI

WHY HATH THE COMMON OPINION AFFORDED WOMEN SOULES?

IT is agreed that we have not so much from them as any *part* of either our *mortal soules* of *sense* or *growth;* and we deny *soules* to others equall to them in all but in *speech* for which they are beholding to their *bodily instruments:* For perchance an *Oxes* heart, or a *Goates*, or a *Foxes*, or a *Serpents* would speake just so, if it were in the *breast*, and could move that *tongue* and *jawes.* Have they so many *advantages* and *means* to hurt us (for, ever their *loving* destroyed us) that we dare not *displease* them, but give them what they will? And so when some call them *Angels*, some *Goddesses*, and the [*Peputian*] *Hereticks* made them *Bishops*, we descend so much with the stream, to allow them *Soules?* Or do we somewhat (in this dignifying of them) flatter *Princes* and *great Personages* that are so much governed by them? Or do we in that *easiness* and *prodigality*, wherein we daily lose our own *souls* to we care not whom, so labour to perswade our selves, that sith a *woman* hath a *soul*, a *soul* is no great matter? Or do we lend them *souls* but for use, since they for our sakes, give their *souls* again, and their *bodies* to boot? Or perchance because the *Devil* (who is all *soul*) doth most *mischief*, and for convenience and proportion, because they would come *nearer* him, we allow them some souls: and so as the *Romans* naturalized some *Provinces* in revenge, and made them *Romans*, only for the *burthen* of the *Common-wealth;* so we have given *women* souls only to make them capable of *Damnation?*

WHY VENUS-STARRE ONELY DOTH CAST A SHADOW?

Is it because it is *neerer* the *earth*? But they whose *profession* it is to see that nothing be done in *heaven* without their *consent* (as *Re-[Kepler]* saies in himselfe of *Astrologers*) have bid *Mercury* to bee *neerer*. Is it because the *workes* of *Venus* want *shadowing, covering,* and *disguising*? But those of *Mercury* needs it more; for *Eloquence*, his *Occupation,* is all *shadow* and *colours*; let our *life* be a *sea,* and then our *reason* and *Even passions* are *wind* enough to carry us whether we should go, but *Eloquence* is a *storme* and *tempest* that miscarries: and who doubts that *Eloquence* which must perswade *people* to take a *yoke* of *soveraignty* (and then beg and make lawes to tye them *faster,* and then give money to the *Invention,* repaire and strengthen it) needs more *shadowes* and *colouring,* than to perswade any Man or Woman to that which is *naturall.* And *Venus markets* are so *naturall,* that when we solicite the best way (which is by *marriage*) our perswasions worke not so much to *draw* a woman *to us,* as against her *Nature* to draw her *from all other* besides. And so when we goe against *Nature,* and from *Venus-worke* (for *marriage* is *chastity*) we need *shadowes* and *colours,* but not else. In *Seneca's* time it was a course, an *unromane* and a *contemptible* thing even in a *Matrone,* not to have had a *love* beside her *husband,* which though the *Law* required not at their hands, yet they did it *zealously* out of the counsell of *Custome* and *fashion,* which was *venery* of *Supererogation:*

Et te spectator plusquam delectat Adulter, saith *Martial*: And *Horace,* because many *lights* would not shew him enough, created many *images* of the same *Object* by *wainscoting* his *chamber* with *looking-glasses:* so that *Venus flyes not light,* so much as *Mercury,* who creeping into our *understanding,* our *darknesse* would bee defeated, if hee were perceived. Then either this *shaddow* confesseth that same darke *Melancholy Repentance,* which accompanies; or that so *violent fires,* needes some *shadowy* refreshing, and *Intermission:* Or else *light* signifying both *day* and *youth,* and *shadow* both *night* and *Age,* shee pronounceth by this that shee professeth both all *persons* and *times.*

IX

WHY IS VENUS-STAR MULTINOMINOUS, CALLED BOTH *HESPERUS* AND *VESPER?*

THE *Moone* hath as many *names*, but not as she is a *starre*, but as she hath divers *governments;* but *Venus* is *multinominous* to give example to her *prostitute disciples*, who so often, either to *renew* or *refresh* them selves towards *lovers*, or to *disguise* themselves from *Magistrates*, are to take *new names*. It may be she takes *new names* after her many *functions*, for as she is *Supreme* Monarch of all *Love* at large (which is *lust*) so is she joyned in Commission with all *Mythologicks*, with *Juno*, *Diana*, and all others for *Marriage*. It may be because of the divers *names* to her self, for her *Affections* have more *names* than any *vice; scilicet: Pollution, Fornication, Adultery, Lay-Incest, Church-Incest, Rape, Sodomy, Mastupration, Masturbation*, and a thousand others. Perchance her divers *names* shewed her appliableness to divers men, for *Neptune* distilled and wet her in *Love*, the *Sunne* warms and melts her, *Mercury* perswaded and swore her, *Jupiters* authority secured, and *Vulcan* hammer'd her. As *Hesperus* she presents you with her *bonum utile*, because it is *wholesomest* in the *Morning:* As *Vesper* with her *bonum delectabile*, because it is *pleasantest* in the *Evening*. And because *industrious* men rise and endure with the *Sunne* in their *civill* businesses, this *starre* cals them up a little before, and remembers them again a little after for her business; for certainly,

Venit Hesperus, ite capellae:

was spoken to *lovers* in the persons of *Goats*.

XI

WHY DOTH THE POXE SOE MUCH AFFECT TO UNDERMINE THE NOSE?

Paracelsus perchance saith true, That every Disease hath his Exaltation in some part certaine. But why this in the Nose? Is there so much mercy in this desease, that it provides that one

should not smell his own stinck? Or hath it but the common
fortune, that being begot and bred in obscurest and secretest
places, because therefore his serpentine crawling and insinua-
tion should not be suspected, nor seen, he comes soonest into
great place, and is more able to destroy the worthiest member,
than a Disease better born? Perchance as mice defeat Elephants
by knawing their *Proboscis,* which is their Nose, this wretched
Indian Vermine practiseth to doe the same upon us. Or as the
ancient furious Custome and Connivency of some Lawes, that
one might cut off their Nose whome he deprehended in Adulterie, was but a Tipe of this; And that now more charitable
lawes having taken away all Revenge from particular hands, this
common Magistrate and Executioner is come to doe the same
Office invisibly? Or by withdrawing this conspicuous part, the
Nose, it warnes us from all adventuring upon that Coast; for it
is as good a marke to take in a flag, as to hang one out. Possibly
heate, which is more potent and active than cold, thought her
selfe injured, and the Harmony of the world out of tune, when
cold was able to shew the high-way to Noses in *Muscovia,* except she found the meanes to doe the same in other Countries.
Or because by the consent of all, there is an Analogy, Proportion
and affection between the Nose and that part where this disease
is first contracted, and therefore *Heliogabalus* chose not his
Minions in the Bath but by the Nose; And *Albertus* had a
knavish meaning when he prefered great Noses; And the licentious Poet was *Naso Poeta.* I think this reason is nearest truth,
That the Nose is most compassionate with this part: Except this
be nearer, that it is reasonable that this Disease in particular
should affect the most eminent and perspicuous part, which in
general doth affect to take hold of the most eminent and conspicuous men.

XVI

WHY ARE COURTIERS SOONER ATHEISTS
THAN MEN OF OTHER CONDITIONS?

Is it because as *Physitians* contemplating Nature, and finding
many abstruse things subject to the search of Reason, think therfore that all is so; so they (seeing mens destinies, mad[e] at
Court, neck[s] [put] out and [in] joynt there, *War, Peace,*
Life and *Death* derived from thence) climb no higher? Or

doth a familiarity with greatness, and daily conversation and acquaintance with it breed a contempt of all greatness? Or because that they see that opinion or need of one another, and fear makes the degrees of servants, Lords and Kings, do they think that God likewise for such Reason hath been mans Creator? Perchance it is because they see Vice prosper best there, and, burthened with sinne, doe they not, for their ease, endeavour to put off the feare and Knowledge of God, as facinorous men deny Magistracy? Or are the most Atheists in that place, because it is the foole that said in his heart, There is no God.

CHARACTERS, ESSAY, AND *CONCEITED NEWES*

THE CHARACTER OF A SCOT AT THE FIRST SIGHT

AT his first appearing in the *Charterhouse*, an Olive coloured Velvet suit owned him, which since became mous-colour, A pair of unskour'd stockings-gules, One indifferent shooe, his band of *Edenburgh*, and cuffs of *London*, both strangers to his shirt, a white feather in a hat that had bin sod, one onely cloak for the rain, which yet he made serve him for all weathers: A Barren-half-acre of Face, amidst whereof an eminent Nose advanced himself, like the new Mount at *Wansted*, over-looking his Beard, and all the wilde Countrey thereabouts; He was tended enough, but not well; for they were certain dumb creeping Followers, yet they made way for their Master, the Laird. At the first presentment his Breeches were his Sumpter, and his Packets, Trunks, Cloak-bags, Portmanteaus and all; He then grew a Knight-wright, and there is extant of his ware at 100 1. 150 1. and 200 1. price. Immediately after this, he shifteth his suit, so did his Whore, and to a Bear-baiting they went, whither I followed them not, but *Tom. Thorney* did.

THE TRUE CHARACTER OF A DUNCE

HE hath a soule drownd in a lumpe of flesh, or is a peece of earth that *Prometheus* put not halfe his proportion of fire into. A thing that hath neither edge of desire, nor feeling of affection in it; the most dangerous creature for confirming an Atheist,

who would sweare his soule were nothing but the bare temperature of his body. He sleepes as hee goes, and his thoughts seldome reach an inch further than his eies. The most part of the
faculties of his soule lie fallow, or are like the restive Jades,
that no spur can drive forwards towards the pursuit of any
worthy designes. One of the most unprofitable of Gods creatures being as he is, a thing put cleane besides the right use,
made fit for the cart and the flayle; and by mischance intangled
amongst books and papers. A man cannot tell possibly what hee
is now good for, save to move up and downe and fill roome, or
to serve as *animatum instrumentum* for others to worke withall
in base imployments, or to be foile for better wits, or to serve
(as they say Monsters doe) to set out the varietie of nature,
and ornament of the universe. Hee is meere nothing of himselfe, neither eats, nor drinkes, nor goes, nor spits, but by Imitation, for all which he hath set-formes and fashions, which he
never varies, but stickes to with the like plodding constancie,
that a mill-horse followes his trace. But the Muses and the
Graces are his hard Mistresses, though he daily invocate them,
though he sacrifice *Hecatombs*, they still look asquint. You shall
note him oft (besides his dull eye, and a lowering head, and a
certain clammy benummed pace) by a faire displaied beard, a
night cap, and a gowne, whose very wrinckles proclaime him the
true *Genius* of formalitie. But of all others, his discourse, and
compositions best speake him, both of them are much of one
stuffe and fashion. He speakes just what his bookes or last company said unto him, without varying one whit, and very seldome understands himselfe. You may know by his discourse
where he was last: for what he heard or read yesterday, hee now
dischargeth his memory or Note-booke of, not his understanding,
for it never came there. What hee hath, he flings abroad at all
adventures without accomodating it to time, place, persons, or
occasions. He commonly loseth himselfe in his tale, and flutters
up and downe windlesse without recovery, and whatsoever next
presents it selfe, his heavy conceit seizeth upon, and goeth along
with, how ever *Heterogeneall* to his matter in hand. His Jests
are either old flead *Proverbs,* or leane-sterv'd-hackney-*Apoph-
thegmes,* or poore verball quips, outworne by Servingmen, Tap-
sters, and Milkemaids, even laid aside by Balladers. He assents
to all men that bring any shadow of reason, and you may make
him when he speakes most Dogmatically, even with one breath,
to averre poore contradictions. His compositions differ onely
terminorum positione, from dreames; nothing but rude heaps of

immaterial, incoherent, drossie, rubbish stuffe, promiscuously thrust up together. Enough to infuse dulnesse and barrennesse of conceit into him that is so prodigall of his eares as to give the hearing. Enough to make a mans memory ake with suffering such durty stuffe cast into it. As unwelcome to any true conceit, as sluttish morsels, or wallowish potions to a nice stomacke, which whiles he empties himselfe of, it stickes in his teeth, nor can hee bee delivered without sweat, and sighes, and hems, and coughs, enough to shake his Grandams teeth out of her head. He spits, and scratches, and spawles, and turnes like sick men from one elbow to another, and deserves as much pitty during his torture, as men in fits of *Tertian fevers* or selfe-lashing Penitentiaries. In a word, rippe him quite asunder, and examine every shred of him, you shall find him to bee just nothing, but the subject of nothing; the object of contempt; yet such as hee is you must take him, for there is no hope he should ever become better.

AN ESSAY OF VALOUR

I AM of opinion, that nothing is so potent either to procure, or merit Love, as Valour, and I am glad I am so, for thereby I shall doe my selfe much ease. Because valour never needs much wit to maintain it. To speak of it in it selfe, It is a quality which he that hath, shall have least need of: so the best league betweene Princes, is a mutuall feare of each other. It teacheth a man to value his reputation as his life, and chiefely to hold the lie insufferable, though being alone hee findes no hurt it doth him. It leaves it selfe to others censures. For he that brags of his owne, disswades others from beleeving it. It feareth a Sword no more than an Ague, It alwaies makes good the owner, for though he be generally held a foole, hee shall seldome heare so much by word of mouth; and that inlargeth him more than any spectacles, for it maketh a little fellow be called a *Tall-man*. It yeelds the wall to none but a woman, whose weaknesse is her prerogative; or a man seconded with a woman, as an Usher which alwaies goes before his betters. It makes a man become the witnesse of his owne wordes, and stand to what ever he hath said, and thinketh it a reproach to commit his liveing unto the Law. It furnisheth youth with action, and age with discourse, and both by futures; for a man must ever boast himself in the present tense. And to come neerer home, nothing drawes a

woman like to it, for valour towards men, is an Embleme of an
Ability towards women, a good quality signifies a better: Nothing is more behoovefull for that Sexe; for from it they receive
protection, and we free from the danger of it: Nothing makes a
shorter cut to obteyning, for a man of armes is alwaies void of
ceremonie, which is the wall that stands betwixt *Piramus* and
Thisbe, that is, Man and Woman, for there is no pride in
women but that which rebounds from our owne basenesse (as
cowards grow valiant upon those that are more cowards) so that
onely by our pale asking, we teach them to deny. And by our
shamefac'tnesse, wee put them in minde to bee modest: whereas
indeed it is cunning Rhetoricke to perswade the hearers that
they are that already, which he would have them to be. This
kinde of bashfulnesse is far from men of valour, and especially
from souldiers, for such are ever men (without doubt) forward,
and confident, losing no time lest they should lose opportunity,
which is the best Factor for a Lover. And because they know
women are given to dissemble; they will never beleeve them
when they deny. Whilome before this age of wit, and wearing
black broke in upon us, there was no way knowne to win a
Lady, but by Tilting, Tournying, and Riding through Forrests,
in which time these slender striplings with little legs, were
held but of strength enough to marie their widowes. And even
in our daies there can be given no reason of the inundation of
servingmen upon their mistresses, but onely that usually they
carry their Masters weapons, and his valour. To bee counted
handsome, just, learned, or well favoured; all this carries no
danger with it, but it is to bee admitted to the title of valiant
Acts, at least the venturing of his mortality, and al women take
delight to hold him safe in their armes, who hath escaped
thither through many dangers. To speak at once, man hath a
priviledge in valour; In clothes and good faces we but imitate
women, and many of that sexe will not thinke much (as far
as an answer goes) to dissemble wit too. So then these
neat youths, these women in mens apparell, are too neere a
woman to bee beloved of her, they bee both of a Trade, but
be of grim aspect, and such a one a Glass dares take, and she
will desire him for newnesse and variety. A skar in a mans face
is the same that a mole in a womans, and a mole in a womans,
is a Jewell set in white to make it seeme more white; For a skar
in a man is a marke of honour, and no blemish; for 'tis a skarre
and a blemish in a Souldier to be without one. Now as for all
things else, which are to procure Love, as a good face,

wit, cloathes, or a good body; each of them I confesse may worke somewhat for want of a better, that is, *if valour be not their Ryvall.* A good face availes nothing if it be in a coward that is bashfull, the utmost of it is to be kissed, which rather increaseth than quencheth Appetite. Hee that sendes her guifts, sends her word also that he is a man of small guifts otherwise: for wooing by signes and tokens, implies the author dumbe. And if *Ovid* who writ the Law of Love, were alive (as hee is extant) would allow it as good a diversitie, that gifts should bee sent as gratuities, not as bribes. Wit getteth rather promise than Love. Wit is not to bee seene: and no woman takes advice of any in her loving; but of her own eies, and her wayting womans: Nay which is worse, wit is not to be felt, and so no good Bed fellow: Wit applied to a woman makes her dissolve her sympering, and discover her teeth with laughter, and this is surely a purge for love; for the beginning of love is a kind of foolish melancholly. As for the man that makes his Taylor his Bawd, and hopes to inveagle his love with such a coloured suite, surely the same deepely hazards the losse of her favour upon every change of his cloathes. So likewise for the other that courts her silently with a good Body, let me certifie him that his cloathes depend upon the comlinesse of his body, and so both upon opinion. Shee that hath beene seduced by apparell, let me give her to wit, that men alwaies put off their cloathes before they goe to bed. And let her that hath beene enamoured of her servants body, understand, that if she saw him in a skinne of cloath, that is, in a Suit made to the patterne of his body, she would see slender cause to love him ever after. There is no cloathes sit so well in a womans eye, as a Suit of steele, though not of the fashion, and no man so soone surpriseth a womans affections, as he that is the subject of all whispering, and hath alwaies twenty stories of his owne deedes depending upon him. Mistake me not, I understand not by valour, one that never fights, but when he is backed with drinke or anger, or hissed on with beholders, nor one that is desperate, nor one that takes away a Servingmans weapons, when perchance it cost him his Quarters wages, nor yet one that weares a privie coat of defence and therein is confident for then such as made Bucklers would bee counted the Catalines of the Commonwealth. I intend one of an even Resolution grounded upon reason: which is alwaies even, having his power restrained by the Law of not doing wrong. But now I remember I am for valour, and therefore must bee a man of few words.

NEWES FROM THE VERY COUNTREY

THAT it is a fripery of Courtiers, Merchants and others, which have been in fashion, and are very neere worne out. That Justices of peace have the felling of underwoods, but the Lords have the great falls.

That Jesuits are like Apricocks, heretofore here and there one succour'd in a great man's house, and cost deare, now you may have them for nothing in every cottage.

That every great vice is a Pike in a pond, that devoures vertues and lesse vices.

That it is wholsomest getting a stomacke, by walking on your own ground: and the thriftiest laying of it at another's table.

That debtors are in *London* close prisoners, and here have the libertie of the house.

That *Atheists* in affliction, like blind beggers, are forced to aske though they know not of whom.

That there are (God be thanked) not two such acres in all the country, as the *Exchange* and *Westminster-hall.*

That only Christmas Lords know their ends.

That weomen are not so tender fruit, but that they doe as well and beare as well upon beds, as plashed against walls.

That our carts are never worse employed, than when they are wayted on by coaches.

That sentences in Authors, like haires in an horse-taile, concurre in one root of beauty and strength, but being pluckt out one by one, serve onely for springes and snares.

That both want and abundance equally advance a rectified man from the world, as cotton and stones are both good casting for an hawke.

That I am sure there is none of the forbidden fruit left, because we doe not all eat thereof.

That our best three pilde mischiefe comes from beyond the sea, and rides post through the country, but his errand is to Court.

That next to no wife and children, your owne wife and children are best pastime, anothers wife and your children worse, your wife and anothers children worst.

That Statesmen hunt their fortunes, and are often at default: Favorites course her and are ever in view.

That intemperance is not so unwholesome heere, for none ever saw Sparrow sicke of the pox.

That here is no trechery nor fidelity, but it is because here are
no secrets.

That Court motions are up and down, ours circular; theirs like
squibs cannot stay at the highest, nor return to the place which
they rose from, but vanish and weare out in the way, Ours are
like mill-wheels busie without changing place; they have per-
emptorie fortunes, we vicissitudes.

FROM *ΒΙΑΘΑΝΑΤΟΣ*

A

DECLARATION
OF THAT
PARADOXE,
OR
THESIS, THAT
SELFE-HOMICIDE IS NOT SO NATURALLY
SINNE, THAT IT MAY NEVER
BE OTHERWISE

[1608?]

PREFACE TO *ΒΙΑΘΑΝΑΤΟΣ*

DECLARING THE REASONS, THE PURPOSE, THE WAY, AND THE END OF THE AUTHOR.

BEZA, a man as eminent and illustrious, in the full glory and
Noone of Learning, as others were in the dawning, and Morning, when any, the least sparkle was notorious, confesseth of
himself, that only for the anguish of a Scurffe, which over-ranne
his head, he had once drown'd himselfe from the Miller's bridge
in Paris, if his Uncle by chance had not then come that way; I
have often such a sickly inclination. And, whether it be, because
I had my first breeding and conversation with men of supressed
and afflicted Religion, accustomed to the despite of death, and
hungry of an imagin'd Martyrdome; Or that the common Enemie find that doore worst locked against him in mee; Or that
there bee a perplexitie and flexibility in the doctrine it selfe;
Or because my Conscience ever assures me, that no rebellious
grudging at Gods gifts, nor other sinfull concurrence accompanies these thoughts in me, or that a brave scorn, or that a

faint cowardlinesse beget it, whensoever any affliction assails me, mee thinks I have the keyes of my prison in mine owne hand, and no remedy presents it selfe so soone to my heart, as mine own sword. Often Meditation of this hath wonne me to a charitable interpretation of their action, who dy so: and provoked me a little to watch and exagitate their reasons, which pronounce so peremptory judgements upon them.

A devout and godly man, hath guided us well, and rectified our uncharitablenesse in such cases, by this remembrace, [Scis lapsum etc. *Thou knowest this mans fall, but thou knowest not his wrastling; which perchance was such, that almost his very fall is justified and accepted of God.*] For, to this end, saith one, [*God hath appointed us tentations, that we might have some excuse for our sinnes, when he calls us to account.*]

An uncharitable mis-interpreter unthriftily demolishes his own house, and repaires not another. He loseth without any gaine or profit to any. And, as Tertullian comparing and making equall, him which provokes another, and him who will be provoked by another, sayes,[*There is no difference, but that the provoker offended first, And that is nothing, because in evill there is no respect of Order or Prioritie.*] So wee may soone become as ill as any offendor, if we offend in a severe increpation of the fact. For, Climachus in his Ladder of Paradise, places these two steps very neere one another, when hee sayes, [*Though in the world it were possible for thee, to escape all defiling by actuall sinne, yet by judging and condemning those who are defiled, thou art defiled.*] In this thou art defiled, as *Basil* notes, [*That in comparing others sinnes, thou canst not avoid excusing thine owne*] Especially this is done, if thy zeale be too fervent in the reprehension of others: For, as in most other Accidents, so in this also, Sinne hath the nature of Poyson, that [*It enters easiest, and works fastest upon cholerique constitutions.*] It is good counsell of the Pharises stiled, [*Ne judices proximum, donec ad ejus locum pertingas.*] Feele and wrastle with such tentations as he hath done, and thy zeale will be tamer. For, [*Therefore* (saith the Apostle) *it became Christ to be like us, that he might be mercifull.*] If therefore after a Christian protestation of an innocent purpose herein, And after a submission of all which is said, not only to every Christian Church, but to every Christian man, and after an entreaty, that the Reader will follow this advice of Tabaeus, [*Qui litigant, sint ambo in conspectu tuo mali et rei,*] and trust neither me, nor the adverse part, but the Reasons, there be any scandall in this enterprise of mine, it is Taken, not Given. And though I know, that the malitious prejudged man, and the lazy affectors of ignorance, will use the same calumnies and obtrectations toward me, (for the voyce and sound of the Snake and Goose is all one) yet because I thought, that as in the poole of *Bethsaida*, there was no health till the water was troubled, so the best way to finde the truth in this matter, was to debate and vexe it, (for [We must as well dispute de veritate, *as* pro veritate,]) I abstained not for feare of mis-interpretation from this undertaking. Our stomachs are not now so tender, and queasie, after so long feeding upon solid Divinity, nor we so umbragious and startling, having been so long enlightened in Gods pathes, that wee should thinke any truth strange to us, or relapse into that childish age, in which a Councell in France forbad *Aristotles Metaphysiques*, and punished with Excommunication the excribing, reading, or having that booke.

Contemplative and bookish men, must of necessitie be more quarrelsome than others, because they contend not about matter of fact, nor can determine their controversies by any certaine witnesses, nor judges. But as long as they goe towards peace, that is Truth, it is no matter which way. The tutelare Angels resisted one another in *Persia*, but neither resisted Gods revealed purpose. *Hierome* and *Gregorie* seem to be of opinion, that *Solomon* is damned; *Ambrose* and *Augustine*, that he is saved: All Fathers, all zealous of Gods glory. At the same time when the *Romane* Church canonized *Becket*, the Schooles of *Paris* disputed whether hee could be saved; both Catholique Judges, and of reverend authoritie. And after so many Ages of a devout and religious celebrating the memory of Saint *Hierome*, *Causaeus* hath spoken so dangerously, that *Campian* saies, hee pronounceth him to be as deepe in hell as the Devill. But in all such intricacies, where both opinions seem equally to conduce to the honor of God, his Justice being as much advanced in the one, as his Mercie in the other, it seemes reasonable to me, that this turne the scales, if on either side there appeare charity towards the poore soul departed. The Church in her Hymnes and Antiphones, doth often salute the Nayles and the Crosse, with Epithets of sweetnesse, and thanks; But the Speare which pierced Christ when he was dead, it ever calles *dirum Mucronem*.

This pietie, I protest againe, urges me in this discourse; and what infirmity soever my reasons may have, yet I have comfort in Trismegistus Axiome, [*Qui pius est, summe Philosophatur.*]

And therefore without any disguising, or curious and libellous concealing, I present and object it, to all of candour, and indifferencie, to escape that just taxation, [*Novum malitiæ genus est, et intemperantis, scribere quod occultes.*] For as, when *Ladislaus* tooke occasion of the great schisme, to corrupt the nobility in Rome, and hoped thereby to possesse the towne, to their seven Governours whom they called *Sapientes* they added three more, whom they called *Bonos*, and confided in them; So doe I wish, and as much as I can, effect, that to those many learned and subtile men which have travelled in this point, some charitable and compassionate men might be added.

If therefore, of Readers, which *Gorionides* observes to be of foure sorts, [Spunges which attract all without distinguishing; Howre-glasses, which receive and powre out as fast; Bagges which retaine onely the dregges of the Spices, and let the Wine escape; And Sives, which retaine the best onely], I finde some of the last sort, I doubt not but they may bee hereby enlightened. And as the eyes of *Eve*, were opened by the taste of the Apple, though it bee said before that shee saw the beauty of the tree, So the digesting of this may, though not present faire objects, yet bring them to see the nakednesse and deformity of their owne reasons, founded upon a rigorous suspition, and winne them to be of that temper, which *Chrisostome* commends, [*He which suspects benignly would faine be deceived, and bee overcome, and is piously glad, when he findes it to be false, which he did uncharitably suspect.*] And it may have as much vigour (as one observes of another Author) as the Sunne in March; it may stirre and dissolve humors, though not expell them; for that must bee the worke of a stronger power.

Every branch which is excerpted from other authors, and engrafted here, is not written for the readers faith, but for illustration and comparison. Because I undertooke the declaration of such a proposition as was controverted by many, and therefore was drawne to the citation of many authorities, I was willing to goe all the way with company, and to take light from others, as well in the journey as at the journeys end. If therefore in multiplicity of not necessary citations there appeare vanity, or ostentation, or digression my honesty must make my excuse and compensation, who acknowledge as Pliny doth [*That to chuse rather to be taken in a theft, than to give every man due, is obnoxii animi, et infelicis ingenii.*] I did it the rather because scholastique and artificiall men use this way of instructing; and I made account that I was to deal with such, because I presume

that naturall men are at least enough inclinable of themselves
to this doctrine.

This my way; and my end is to remove scandall. For certainly
God often punisheth a sinner much more severely, because others have taken occasion of sinning by his fact. If therefore wee
did correct in our selves this easines of being scandalized, how
much easier and lighter might we make the punishment of
many transgressors! for God in his judgement hath almost made
us his assistants, and counsellers, how far he shall punish; and
our interpretation of anothers sinne doth often give the measure to Gods Justice or Mercy.

If therefore, since [*disorderly long haire which was pride
and wantonnesse in* Absolon, *and squallor and horridnes in* Neb-
uchodonozor *was vertue and strength in* Samson, *and sanctification in* Samuel,] these severe men will not allow to indifferent
things the best construction they are capable of, nor pardon my
inclination to do so, they shall pardon me this opinion, that
their severity proceeds from a self-guiltines, and give me leave
to apply that of *Ennodius,* [*That it is the nature of stiffe
wickednesse, to think that of others, which themselves deserve
and it is all the comfort the guilty have, not to find any innocent.*]

THE THIRD PART
OF THE
LAW OF GOD.
DISTINCTION I SECT. I.

THAT light which issues from the Moone, doth best represent
and expresse that which in our selves we call the light of Nature; for as that in the Moone is permanent and ever there, and
yet it is unequal, various, pale, and languishing, So is our light
of Nature changeable. For being at the first kindling at full, it
wayned presently, and by departing farther and farther from
God, declined by generall sinne, to almost a totall Eclipse: till
God comming neerer to us, first by the Law, and then by
Grace, enlightned and repayred it againe, conveniently to his
ends, and further exercise of his Mercy and Justice. And then
those Artificiall Lights, which our selves make for our use and
service here, as Fires, Tapers, and such, resemble the light of
Reason, as wee have in our Second part accepted that Word.

For though the light of these Fires and Tapers be not so naturall, as the Moone, yet because they are more domestique,
and obedient to us, wee distinguish particular objects better by
them, than by the Moone; So by the Arguments, and Deductions, and Conclusions, which our selves beget and produce, as
being more serviceable and under us, because they are our creatures, particular cases are made more cleare and evident to us;
for these we can behold withall, and put them to any office, and
examine, and prove their truth, or likelihood, and make them
answere as long as wee will aske; whereas the light of Nature,
with a solemne and supercilious Majestie, will speake but once,
and give no Reason, nor endure Examination.

But because of these two kindes of light, the first is too
weake, and the other false, (for onely colour is the object of
sight, and we not trust candlelight to discerne Colours) we have
therefore the Sunne, which is the Fountaine and Treasure of all
created light, for an Embleme of that third best light of our
understanding, which is the Word of God. [*Mandatum lucerna,
et Lex Lux*] sayes *Solomon.* But yet as weake credulous men
thinke sometimes they see two or three Sunnes, when they see
none but Meteors, or other apparances; so are many transported
with like facilitie or dazeling, that for some opinions which
they maintaine, they think they have the light and authority of
Scripture, when, God knowes, truth, which is the light of Scriptures, is Diametrally under them, and removed in the farthest
distance that can bee. If any small place of Scripture mis-
appeare to them to bee of use for justifying any opinion of
theirs; then (as the Word of God hath that precious nature of
gold, that a little quantity thereof, by reason of a faithfull ten-
acity and ductilenesse, will be brought to cover 10000 times as
much of any other metall,) they extend it so farre, and labour,
and beat it, to such a thinnesse, as it is scarce any longer the
Word of God, only to give their other reasons a little tincture
and colour of gold, though they have lost all their waight and
estimation.

But since the Scripture it self teaches, [*That no Prophecie in
the Scripture, is of private interpretation,*] the whole Church
may not be bound and concluded by the fancie of one, or of a
few, who being content to enslumber themselves in an opinion, and lazy prejudice, dreame arguments to establish, and
authorize that.

A professed interpreter of Dreames, tells us, [*That no
Dreame of a private man may be interpreted to signifie a pub-*

lique businesse.] This I say because of those places of Scriptures, which are aledged for the Doctrine which we now examine, scarce any one, (except the Precept, *Thou shalt not kill*) is offered by any two Authors. But to one, one place, to another, another seemes directly to governe in the point, and to me, (to allow Truth her naturall and comely boldnesse) no place, but that seemes to looke towards it.

And therefore in going over all those sentences, which I have gathered from many Authors, and presenting convenient answers and interpretations thereof, I will forbeare the names of those Authors, who produced them so impertinently, least I should seeme to discover their nakednesse, or insimulate them even of prevarication.

If any Divine shall thinke the cause, or persons injured herein, and esteeme me so much worth reducing to the other opinion, as to apply an answer hereunto, with the same Charitie which provoked me, and which, I thanke God hath accompanied me from the beginning, I beseech him, to take thus much advantage from me and my instruction, that he will doe it without bitternesse. He shall see the way the better, and shew it the better and saile through it the better, if he raise no stormes.

Such men, as they are [*Fishers of meal*], so may they also hunt us into their nets, for our good. But there is perchance, some mystique interpretation belonging to that Canon which allowes Clergy men to hunt; for they may doe it by Nets and Snares, but not by Dogges; for clamour and biting are forbidden them.

And I have been sorry to see, that even *Beza* himselfe, writing against an Adversary, and a cause equally and extreamly obnoxious, onely by allowing too much fuell to his zeale, enraged against the man, and neglecting, or but prescribing in the cause, hath with lesse thoroughnesse and satisfaction, than either became his learning and watchfulnesse, or answered his use and custome, given an answer to *Ochius* booke of *Polygamy*.

From PSEUDO–MARTYR

Wherein out of Certaine Propositions and Gradations, **This Con-**
clusion is evicted. That those which are of the Romane
Religion in this Kingdome, may and ought to take the Oath
of Allegeance. 1610

From AN ADVERTISEMENT TO THE READER

AND for my selfe, (because I have already received some light,
that some of the Romane profession, having onely seene the
Heads and Grounds handled in this Booke, have traduced me, as
an impious and profane under-valewer of Martyrdome,) I most
humbly beseech him, (till the reading of the Booke, may guide
his Reason) to beleeve, that I have a just and Christianly estimation, and reverence, of that devout and acceptable Sacrifice
of our lifes, for the glory of our blessed Saviour. For, as my fortune hath never beene so flattering nor abundant, as should
make this present life sweet and precious to me, as I am a
Moral man: so, as I am a Christian, I have beene ever kept
awake in a meditation of Martyrdome, by being derived from
such a stocke and race, as, I beleeve, no family, (which is not
of farre larger extent, and greater branches,) hath endured and
suffered more in their persons and fortunes, for obeying the
Teachers of Romane Doctrine, than it hath done. I did not
therefore enter into this, as a carnall or over-indulgent favourer
of this life, but out of such reasons, as may arise to his knowledge, who shall be pleased to read the whole worke.

And in those places which are cited from other Authors (which
hee shall know by the Margine) I doe not alwayes precisely and
superstitiously binde myselfe to the words of the Authors; which
was impossible to me, both because sometimes I collect their
sense, and expresse their Arguments or their opinions, and the
Resultance of a whole leafe, in two or three lines, and some few
times, I cite some of their Catholique Authors, out of their owne
fellowes, who had used the same fashion of collecting their sense,
without precise binding themselves to All, or onely their words.
This is the comfort which my conscience hath, and the assurance
which I can give the Reader, that I have no where made any
Author, speake more or lesse, in sense, than hee intended, to that
purpose, for which I cite him. If any of their owne fellowes from
whom I cite them, have dealt otherwise, I cannot be wounded

but through their sides. So that I hope either mine Innocence, or their own fellowes guiltinesse, shall defend me, from the curious malice of those men, who in this sickly decay, and declining of their cause, can spy out falsifyings in every citation: as in a jealous, and obnoxious state, a Decipherer can pick out Plots, and Treason, in any familiar letter which is intercepted.

And thus much it seemed necessary to mee, to let the Reader
know, to whose charitable and favourable
opinion I commit the booke, and my
selfe to his Christianly and
devout Prayers.

TO THE HIGH AND MIGHTIE PRINCE JAMES,
BY THE GRACE OF GOD, KING OF GREAT BRITAINE,
FRANCE AND IRELAND, DEFENDER OF THE FAITH.

Most mightie and sacred Soveraigne

As Temporall armies consist of Press'd men, and voluntaries, so doe they also in this warfare, in which your Majestie hath appear'd by your Bookes. And not only your strong and full Garisons, which are your Cleargie, and your Universities, but also obscure Villages can minister Souldiours. For, the equall interest, which all your Subjects have in the cause (all being equally endanger'd in your dangers) gives every one of us a Title to the Dignitie of this warfare; And so makes those, whom the Civill Lawes made opposite, all one, Paganos, Milites. Besides, since in this Battaile, your Majestie, by your Bookes, is gone in Person out of the Kingdome, who can bee exempt from waiting upon you in such an expedition. For this Oath must worke upon us all; and as it must draw from the Papists a profession, so it must from us, a Confirmation of our Obedience; They must testifie an Alleageance by the Oath, we, an Alleageance to it. For, since in providing for your Majesties securitie, the Oath defends us, it is reason, that wee defend it. The strongest Castle that is, cannot defend the Inhabitants, if they sleepe, or neglect the defence of that, which defends them; No more can this Oath, though framed with all advantagious Christianly wisedome, secure your Majestie, and us in you, if by our negligence wee should open it, either to the adversaries Batteries, or to his underminings.

The influence of those your Majesties Bookes, as the Sunne,

which penetrates all corners, hath wrought uppon me, and drawen up, and exhaled from my poore Meditations, these discourses: Which, with all reverence and devotion, I present to your Majestie, who in this also have the power and office of the Sunne, that those things which you exhale, you may at your pleasure dissipate, and annull; or suffer them to fall downe againe, as a wholesome and fruitfull dew, upon your Church & Commonwealth. Of my boldnesse in this addresse, I most humbly beseech your Majestie, to admit this excuse, that having observed, how much your Majestie had vouchsafed to descend to a conversation with your Subjects, by way of your Bookes, I also conceiv'd an ambition, of ascending to your presence, by the same way, and of participating, by this meanes, their happinesse, of whome, that saying of the Queene of *Sheba*, may bee usurp'd: Happie are thy men, and happie are those thy Servants, which stand before thee alwayes, and heare thy wisedome. For, in this, I make account, that I have performed a duetie, by expressing
in an exterior, and (by your Majesties permission) a
publicke Act, the same desire, which God heares
in my daily prayers, That your Majestie
may very long governe us in
your Person, and ever,
in your Race and
Progenie.

> *Your Majesties most*
> *humble and loyall*
> *Subject:*
> JOHN DONNE

From A PREFACE TO THE PRIESTES AND JESUITS, AND TO THEIR DISCIPLES IN THIS KINGDOME.

AND if they will be content to impute to me all humane infirmities, they shall neede to faine nothing: I am, I confesse, obnoxious enough. My naturall impatience not to digge painefully in deepe, and stony, and sullen learnings: My Indulgence to my freedome and libertie, as in all other indifferent things, so in my studies also, not to betroth or enthral myselfe, to any one science, which should possesse or denominate me: My easines, to affoord a sweete and gentle Interpretation, to all professors of Christian Religion, if they shake not the Foundation, wherein I have in my ordinary Communication and familiar writings, often expressed and declared my selfe: hath opened me enough to their malice, and put me into their danger, and given them advantage to impute to me, whatsoever such degrees of lazines, of liberty, of irresolution, can produce.

3 But if either they will transferre my personall weakenesses upon the cause, or extend the faults of my person to my minde, or to her purest part, my conscience: If they will calumniate this poore and innocent worke of mine, as if it were written, either for *Ostentation* of any ability or faculty in my selfe; or for *Provocation*, to draw them to an awnswere, and so continue a Booke-warre; or for *Flattery* to the present State; which, thogh my services be by many just titles due to it, needs it not; or for *exasperation*, to draw out the civill sword in causes, which have some pretence and colour of being spirituall; or to get *Occasion* hereby to uncover the nakednes, and lay open the incommodious and undefensible sentences and opinions, of divers severall Authors in that Church; or to maintaine and further a scisme and division amongst you, in this point of the Popes pretence to temporall jurisdiction: I have no other shelter against these imputations, but an appeale to our blessed Saviour, and a protestation before his face, that my principall and direct scope and purpose herein, is the unity and peace of his Church. For as when the roofe of the Temple rent asunder, not long after followed the ruine of the foundation it selfe: So if these two principall beames and Toppe-rafters, *the Prince* and *the Priest,* rent asunder, the whole frame and Foundation of Christian Religion will be shaked. And if we distinguish not between Articles of faith & jurisdiction, but account all those superedifications and furnitures, and ornaments which God hath affoorded to his Church, for exteriour government, to be equally the Foundation it selfe, there can bee no Church; as there could be no body of a man, if it were all eye.

4 They who have descended so lowe, as to take knowledge of me, and to admit me into their consideration, know well that I used no inordinate hast, nor precipitation in binding my conscience to any locall Religion. I had a longer worke to doe than many other men; for I was first to blot out, certain impressions of the Romane religion, and to wrastle both against the examples and against the reasons, by which some hold was taken; and some anticipations early layde upon my conscience, both by Persons who by nature had a power and superiority over my will, and others who by their learning and good life, seem'd to me justly to claime an interest for the guiding, and rectifying

of mine understanding in these matters. And although I apprehended well enough, that this irresolution not onely retarded my
fortune, but also bred some scandall, and endangered my spirituall reputation, by laying me open to many mis-interpretations;
yet all these respects did not transport me to any violent and
sudden determination, till I had, to the measure of my poore wit
and judgement, survayed and digested the whole body of
Divinity, controverted betweene ours and the Romane Church.
In which search and disquisition, that God, which awakened me
then, and hath never forsaken me in that industry, as he is the
Authour of that purpose, so is he a witnes of this protestation;
that I behaved my selfe, and proceeded therin with humility,
and diffidence in my selfe; and by that, which by his grace, I
tooke to be the ordinary meanes, which is frequent prayer,
and equall and indifferent affections.

5 And this course held in rectifying and reducing mine understanding and judgment, might justifie & excuse my forward-
nes; if I shold seeme to any to have intruded and usurped the office of others, in writing of Divinity and spirituall points, having
no ordinary calling to that function. For, to have alwayes abstained from this declaration of my selfe, had beene to betray and
to abandon, and prostitute my good name to their misconceivings
and imputations; who thinke presently, that hee hath no Religion, which dares not call his Religion by some newer name
than *Christian*. And then, for my writing in Divinity, though no
professed Divine; all Ages, all Nations, all Religions, even
yours, which is the most covetous and lothest to divide, or communicate with the Layety, any of the honours reserved to the
Clergie, affoord me abundantly examples, and authorities for such
an undertaking.

6 But for this poore worke of mine, I need no such *Advocates*, nor *Apologizers;* for it is not of Divinity, but meerely of
temporall matters, that I write. And you may as justly accuse
Vitruvius, who writ of the fashion of building Churches, or
those Authors which have written of the nature of Bees and use
of Waxe, or of Painting, or of Musique, to have usurped upon
the office of Divines, and to have written of Divinity, because
all these are ingredients into your propitiatory medicine, the
Masse, and conduce to spirituall and divine worship: as you may
impute to any, which writes of civil obedience to the Prince,
that he meddles with Divinity: not that this obedience is not
safely grounded in Divinity, or that it is not an act of Religion,
but that it is so well engravd in our hearts, and naturally ob•

vious to every understanding, that men of all conditions have a sense and apprehension, and assurednes of that obligation.

7 The cause therefore is reduced to a narrow issue, and contracted to a strict point, when the differences betweene us are brought to this; Whether a Subject may not obey his Prince, if the Turk or any other man forbid it? And as his Majestie in his Kingdomes, is Religiously and prudently watchfull, to preserve that Crowne, which his Predecessors had redeemed from the rust, and drosse, wherewith forraine usurpation had infected it; so is it easie to be observed, that all the other Princes of Christendome, beginne to shake off those fetters, which insensibly and drowsily they had admitted; and labour by all wayes, which are as yet possible to them, to returne to their naturall Supremacy and Jurisdiction.

.   .   .   .

28 But my purpose is not to exasperate, and aggrieve you, by traducing or drawing into suspition the bodie of your Religion, otherwise than as it conduces to this vicious and inordinate affectation of danger: Yet your charitie may give me leave to note, that as *Physitians*, when to judge of a disease, they must observe *Decubitum*, that is, the time of the Patients lying downe, and yeelding himselfe to his bedde; because that is not alike in all sicke men, but that some walke longer before they yeelde than others doe; therefore they remoove that marke, and reckon *ab Actionibus lexis:* that is when their appetite, and digestion, and other faculties fail'd in doing their functions and offices: so, if we will judge of the diseases of the Romane Church, though because they crept in insensiblie, and the good state of health, which her provident Nources indued her withall, made her hold out long; we cannot well pitch a certaine time of her lying downe and sickning, yet we may wel discern *Actiones læsas,* by her practise, and by her disusing her stomach from spirituall foode, and surfetting upon this temporall jurisdiction: For then she appeared to be lame and impotent, when she tooke this staffe and crouch to sustaine her selfe, having lost the abilitie of those two legges, whereon shee should stand, *The Word* and *Censures.*

29 And if the suspicious and quarrelsome title and claime to this temporall jurisdiction; If Gods often and strange protection of this Kingdome against it, by which he hath almost made Miracles ordinarie and familiar, If your owne just and due preservation, worke nothing upon you, yet have some pitie and compassion towards your Countrey, whose reputation is defaced

Examen.
Edicti.
Anglica.
Stanislaus
Christian-
onicus.
Paris,
1607

and scandalized by this occasion, when one of your owne Authors, being anguished and perplexed, how to answere these often Rebellions and Treasons, to put it off from that Religion, layes it upon the nature of an Englishman, whom, in all professions he accuses to be naturally disloyall and trecherous to his Prince.

30 And have some pitie and compassion (though you neglect your particulars) upon that cause, which you call the Catholicke cause: Since, as we say of Agues, that no man dies by an Ague, nor without an Ague: So at Executions for Treasons, we may justly say, No man dies for the Romane Religion, nor without it. Such a naturall consequence, or at least unluckie concomitance they have together, that so many examples will at last build up a Rule, which a few exceptions, and instances to the contrarie will not destroy.

31 I call to witnesse against you, those whose testimonie God himselfe hath accepted. Speake then and testifie, O you glorious and triumphant Army of Martyrs, who enjoy now a permanent triumph in heaven, which knew the voice of your Shepheard, and staid till he cald, and went then with all alacritie: Is there any man received into your blessed Legion, by title of such a Death, as sedition, scandall, or any humane respect occasioned? O no, for they which are in possession of that Laurell, are such as have washed their garments, not in their owne blood onely (for so they might still remaine redde and staind) but in the *blood of the Lambe which changes them to white. Saint Chrisostome* writes well, that the *Sinner* in the *Gospel bath'd and wash'd her selfe in her teares, not in her blood:* And of Saint *Peter,* hee askes this question; *When he had denied Christ, Numquid sanguinem sudit?* No, sayes he, *but hee pourd foorth teares, and washed away his transgression.*

Revel. 7.
15.

Homil. 2.
i. Psal. 50.

32 That which Christian Religion hath added to old Philosophie, which was, *To doe no wrong,* is in this point, no more but this, *To keepe our mind in an habituall preparation of suffering wrong*: but not to urge and provoke, and importune affliction so

much, as to make those punishments just, which otherwise had beene wrongfully inflicted upon us. Wee are not sent into this world, to *Suffer*, but to *Doe*, and to performe the Offices of societie, required by our severall callings. The way to triumph in secular Armies, was not to be slaine in the Battell, but to have kept the station, and done all Militarie dueties. And as it was in the Romane Armies, so it ought to be taught in the Romane Church, *Ius legionis facile: Non sequi, non fugere.* For we must neither pursue persecution so forwardly, that our naturall preservation be neglected, nor runne away from it so farre, that Gods cause be scandaliz'd, and his Honour diminished.

Vegetius. l. 2. c. 17

33 Thus much I was willing to premit, to awaken you, if it please you to heare it, to a just love of your owne safetie, of the peace of your Countrey, of the honour and reputation of your Countreymen, and of the integritie of that, which you call the Catholicke cause; and to acquaint you so farre, with my disposition and temper, as that you neede not be afraid to reade my poore writings, who joyne you with mine owne Soule in my Prayers, that your Obedience here, may prepare your admission into the heavenly *Jerusalem*, and that by the same Obedience, *Your dayes may bee long in the land, which the Lord your God hath given you.*
Amen.

Exod. 20.

IGNATIUS HIS CONCLAVE

OR

HIS INTHRONISATION IN A LATE ELECTION
IN HELL:

WHEREIN MANY THINGS ARE MINGLED BY
WAY OF SATYR;

Concerning
The Disposition of Jesuits,
The Creation of a new Hell,
The establishing of a Church in the Moone.
There is also added an Apology
for Jesuites.

All dedicated to the two Adversary
Angels, which are protectors of
the Papall Consistory, and of
the Colledge of Sorbon.
Translated out of Latine.   [1611]

THE PRINTER TO THE READER

DOEST thou seeke after the Author? It is in vaine; for hee is
harder to be found than the parents of Popes were in the old
times: yet if thou have an itch of gessing, receive from me so
much, as a friend of his, to whom he sent his booke to bee read,
writ to me. "The Author was unwilling to have this booke published, thinking it unfit both for the matter which in it selfe is
weighty and serious, and for that gravity which himselfe had proposed and observed in an other booke formerly published, to descend to this kinde of writing. But I on the other side, mustered
my forces against him, and produced reasons and examples. I proposed to him the great *Erasmus* (whom though *Scribanius* the
Jesuit cal him *one of our Preachers*: yet their great *Coccius* is well
content to number him amongst his Authors). And to his bitter
jestings and skirmishings in this kinde, our enemies confesse,
that our Church is as much beholden, as to *Luther* himselfe, who
fought so valiantly in the maine battell. I remembred him also
how familiar a fashion this was among the *Papists* themselves;
and how much *Rebullus* that *Run-away* had done in this kinde, as
well in those bookes, which he cals *Salmonees,* as in his other,
which he entitles *The Cabal of the Reformed Churches,* of which
booke, if he were not the Author, hee was certainly the *Apolo-*
gist, and defender. Neither was that man, whosoever hee bee,
which cals himselfe *Macer,* inferiour to *Reboul* in this kinde,
when hee dedicated to *Laughter* and to *Pleasure,* his disputation
of that horrible Excommunication of *Paulus* 5. against the *Vene-*
tians, and of other matters concerning the salvation of soules.
Both which, not contenting themselves, as this Author doth, to
sport and obey their naturall disposition in a busnesse (if you
consider the persons) light inough (for what can bee vainer than
a *Jesuit*?) have saucily risen up against *Princes,* and the *Lords*
Anointed. I added moreover, that the things delivered in this
booke, were by many degrees more modest, than those which
themselves in their owne civill warres, do daily vomit forth, when
they butcher and mangle the fame and reputation of their *Popes*
and *Cardinals* by their revived *Lucian, Pasquil.* At last he

yeelded, and made mee owner of his booke, which I send to you to be delivered over to forraine nations, (a) farre from the father: and (as his desire is) (b) his last in this kinde. Hee chooses and desires, that his other book should testifie his ingenuity, and candor, and his disposition to labour for the reconciling of all parts. This Booke must teach what humane infirmity is, and how hard a matter it is for a man much conversant in the bookes and Acts of *Jesuites*, so thoroughly to cast off the *Jesuits*, as that he contract nothing of their naturall drosses, which are *Petulancy*, and *Lightnesse*. Vale."

TO THE TWO TUTELAR ANGELS,

PROTECTORS OF THE POPES CONSISTORY, AND OF THE COLLEDGE OF SORBON

MOST noble couple of *Angels*, lest it should be sayd that you did never agree, and never meet, but that you did ever abhorre one another, and ever

> *Resemble* Janus *with a diverse face,*

I attempted to bring and joyne you together once in these papers; not that I might compose your differences, for you have not chosen me for *Arbitrator;* but that you might beware of an enemy common to you both, I will relate what I saw. I was in an *Extasie*, and

> *My little wandring sportful Soule,*
> *Ghest, and Companion of my body*

had liberty to wander through all places, and to survey and reckon all the roomes, and all the volumes of the heavens, and to comprehend the situation, the dimensions, the nature, the people, and the policy, both of the swimming Ilands, the *Planets*, and of all those which are fixed in the firmament. Of which, I thinke it an honester part as yet to be silent, than to do *Galileo* wrong by speaking of it, who of late hath summoned the other worlds, the Stars to come neerer to him, and give him an account of themselves. Or to *Keppler*, who (as himselfe testifies of himselfe) *ever since* Tycho Braches *death hath received it into his care, that no new thing should be done in heaven without his knowledge.* For by the law, *Prevention* must take place; and therefore what they have found and discovred first, I am content they speake and utter first. Yet this they may vouchsafe to take from me, that they shall hardly find *Enoch*, or *Elias* any where in their circuit. When I had surveid al the Heavens, then *as*

The Larke by busie and laborious wayes,
Having climb'd up th' etheriall hill, doth raise
His Hymnes to Phœbus *Harpe, And striking then*
His sailes, his wings, doth fall downe backe agen
So suddenly, that one may safely say
A stone came lazily, that came that way,

In the twinckling of an eye, I saw all the roomes in Hell open to
my sight. And by the benefit of certaine spectacles, I know not of
what making, but, I thinke, of the same, by which *Gregory* the
great, and *Beda* did discerne so distinctly the soules of their
friends, when they were discharged from their bodies, and sometimes the soules of such men as they knew not by sight, and of
some that were never in the world, and yet they could distinguish
them flying into Heaven, or conversing with living men, I saw
all the channels in the bowels of the Earth; and all the inhabitants of all nations, and of all ages were suddenly made familiar
to me. I thinke truely, *Robert Aquinas* when he tooke *Christs* long
Oration, as he hung upon the Crosse, did use some such instrument as this, but applied to the eare: And so I thinke did he,
which dedicated to *Adrian* 6, that Sermon which *Christ* made in
prayse of his father *Joseph*: for else how did they heare that,
which none but they ever heard? As for the *Suburbs* of Hel (I
meane both *Limbo* and *Purgatory*) I must confesse I passed them
over so negligently, that I saw them not: and I was hungerly
caried, to find new places, never discovered before. For *Purgatory*
did not seeme worthy to me of much diligence, because it may
seeme already to have beene beleeved by some persons, in some
corners of the *Romane Church*, for about 50 yeares; that is, ever
since the Councell of *Trent* had a minde to fulfill the prophecies
of *Homer, Virgil,* and the other *Patriarkes* of the *Papists;* and beeing not satisfied with making one *Transubstantiation,* purposed to
bring in another: which is, to change *fables* into *Articles* of faith.
Proceeding therefore to more inward places, I saw a secret place,
where there were not many, beside Lucifer himselfe; to which,
onely they had title, which had so attempted any innovation in
this life, that they gave an affront to all antiquitie, and induced
doubts, and anxieties, and scruples, and after, a libertie of beleeving what they would; at length established opinions, directly contrary to all established before. Of which place in *Hell, Lucifer*
affoarded us heretofore some little knowledge, when more than
200 yeares since, in an *Epistle* written to the *Cardinall* S. *Sexti,*
hee promised him a roome *in his palace, in the remotest part of*

his eternall Chaos, which I take to bee this place. And here Pope *Boniface* 3, and *Mahomet,* seemed to contend about the highest roome. Hee gloried of having expelled an old Religion, and *Mahomet* of having brought in a new: each of them a great deluge to the world. But it is to be feared, that *Mahomet* will faile therein, both because hee attributed something to the old *Testament,* and because he used *Sergius* as his fellow-bishop, in making the *Alcoran;* whereas it was evident to the supreme Judge *Lucifer,* (for how could he be ignorant of that, which himselfe had put into the Popes mind?) that *Boniface* had not onely neglected, but destroyed the policy of the State of *Israel* established in the old *Testament,* when he prepared *Popes* a way, to tread upon the neckes of *Princes,* but that he also abstained from all Example and Coadjutor, when he took upon him that newe Name, which *Gregorie* himselfe (a Pope neither very foolish nor over-modest) ever abhord. Besides that, every day affoords new Advocates to *Boniface* his side. For since the *Franciscans* were almost worne out (of whome their General, *Francis,* had seene 6000 souldiers in one army, that is, in one chapter which, because they were then but fresh souldiers, he saw assisted with 18000 Divels), the *Jesuits* have much recompenced those decayes and damages, who sometimes have maintained in their Tents 200000 schollers. For though the order of *Benedict* have ever bene so fruitfull, that they say of it, *That all the new Orders, which in later times have broken out, are but little springs, or drops, and that Order the Ocean, which hath sent out 52 Popes, 200 Cardinals, 1600 Archbishops, 4000 Bishops, and 50000 Saints approved by the Church,* and therefore it cannot be denied, but that *Boniface* his part is much releeved by that Order; yet if they be compared to the *Jesuits,* or to the weake and unperfect Types of them, the *Franciscans,* it is no great matter that they have done. Though therefore they esteeme *Mahomet* worthy of the name of an *Innovator,* and therein, perchance not much inferiour to *Boniface,* yet since his time, to ours, almost all which have followed his sect, have lived barren in an unanimity, and idle concord, and cannot boast that they have produced any new matter: whereas *Boniface* his successors, awakened by him, have ever beene fruitfull in bringing forth new sinnes, and new pardons, and idolatries and King-killings. Though therefore it may religiously, and piously be beleeved, that *Turkes,* as well as *Papists,* come daily in troupes to the ordinary and common places of *Hell;* yet certainly to this more honourable roome reserved for especiall *Innovators,* the *Papists* have more frequent accesse; and therefore *Mahomet* is out of hope to prevaile, and must imitate the *Christian Emperours,* and be content to sit (as yet hee doth) at the Popes feet. Now to this place, not onely such endeavour to come, as have innovated in matters, directly concerning the soule, but they also which have done so, either in the Arts, or in conversation, or in any thing that exerciseth the faculties of the soule, and may so provoke to quarrelsome and brawling controversies: For so the truth be lost, it is no matter how. But the gates are seldome opened, nor scarce oftner than once in an Age. But my destiny favoured mee so much, that I was present then, and saw all the pretenders and all that affected an entrance, and *Lucifer* himselfe, who then came out into the outward chamber, to heare them pleade their owne Causes. As soone as the doore creekt, I spied a certaine *Mathematitian*, which till then had bene busied to finde, to deride, to detrude *Ptolomey;* and now with an erect countenance, and setled pace, came to the gates, and with hands and feet (scarce respecting *Lucifer* himselfe) beat the dores, and cried; "Are these shut against me, to whom all the Heavens were ever open, who was a Soule to the Earth, and gave it motion?"

By this I knew it was *Copernicus:* For though I had never heard ill of his life, and therefore might wonder to find him there; yet when I remembred, that the *Papists* have extended the name, and the punishment of Heresie, almost to every thing, and that as yet I used *Gregories* and *Bedes* spectacles, by which one saw *Origen*, who deserved so well of the *Christian Church, burning in Hell*, I doubted no longer, but assured my selfe that it was *Copernicus* which I saw. To whom *Lucifer* sayd; "Who are you? For though even by this boldnesse you seeme worthy to enter, and have attempted a new faction even in *Hell*, yet you must first satisfie those, which stand about you, and which expect the same fortune as you do." "Except, O *Lucifer*," answered *Copernicus*, "I thought thee of the race of the starre *Lucifer,* with which I am so well acquainted, I should not vouchsafe thee this discourse. I am he, which pitying thee who wert thrust into the Center of the world, raysed both thee, and thy prison, the Earth, up into the Heavens; so as by my meanes *God* doth not enjoy his revenge upon thee. The Sunne, which was an officious spy, and a betrayer of faults, and so thine enemy, I have appointed to go into the lowest part of the world. Shall these gates be open to such as have innovated in small matters? and shall they be shut against me, who have turned the whole frame of the world, and am thereby almost a new Creator?" More than this he spoke not. *Lucifer* stuck in a meditation. For what should he do? It seemed unjust to deny entry to him which had deserved so well, and dangerous to graunt it, to one of so great ambitions, and undertakings: nor did he thinke that himselfe had attempted greater matters before his fall. Something he had which he might have conveniently opposed, but he was loath to utter it, least he should confesse his feare. But *Ignatius Loyola* which was got neere his chaire, a subtile fellow, and so indued with the Divell, that he was able to tempt, and not onely that, but (as they say) even to possesse the Divell, apprehended this perplexity in *Lucifer*. And making himselfe sure of his owne entrance, and knowing well, that many thousands of his family aspired to that place, he opposed himselfe against all others. He was content they should be damned, but not that they should governe. And though when hee died he was utterly ignorant in all great learning, and knew not so much as *Ptolomeys*, or *Copernicus* name, but might have beene perswaded, that the words *Almagest*, *Zenith*, and *Nadir*, were Saints names, and fit to bee put into the *Litanie*, and *Ora pro nobis* joyned to them; yet after hee had spent some time in hell, he had learnt somewhat of his *Jesuites*, which daily came thither. And whilst he staied at the threshold of *Hell;* that is, from the time when he delivered himselfe over to the Popes will, hee tooke a little taste of learning. Thus furnished, thus hee undertakes *Copernicus*. "Do you thinke to winne our *Lucifer* to your part, by allowing him the honour of being of the race of that starre? who was not onely made before all the starres, but being glutted with the glory of shining there, transferred his dwelling and Colonies unto this Monarchy, and thereby gave our Order a noble example, to spy, to invade, and to possesse forraine kingdomes. Can our *Lucifer*, or his followers have any honour from that starre *Lucifer*, which is but *Venus?* whose face how much wee scorne, appeares by this, that, for the most part we use her aversly and preposterously. Rather let our *Lucifer* glory in *Lucifer* the *Calaritan Bishop*; not therefore because he is placed amongst Heretiques, onely for affirming the propagation of the soule; but especially for this, that he was the first that opposed the dignity of Princes, and imprinted the names of *Antichrist*, *Judas*, and other stigmatique markes upon the *Emperour;* But for you, what new thing have you invented, by which our *Lucifer* gets any thing? What cares hee whether the earth travell, or stand still? Hath your raising up of the earth into heaven, brought men to that confidence, that they build new towers or threaten God againe? Or do they out of this motion of

the earth conclude, that there is no hell, or deny the punishment
of sin? Do not men beleeve? do they not live just, as they did
before? Besides, this detracts from the dignity of your learning,
and derogates from your right and title of comming to this place,
that those opinions of yours may very well be true. If therfore
any man have honour or title to this place in this matter, it
belongs wholly to our *Clavius*, who opposed himselfe opportunely
against you, and the truth, which at that time was creeping into
every mans minde. Hee only can be called the Author of all
contentions, and schoole-combats in this cause; and no greater
profit can bee hoped for heerein, but that for such brabbles,
more necessarie matters bee neglected. And yet not onely for
this is our *Clavius* to bee honoured, but for the great paines also
which hee tooke in the *Gregorian Calender*, by which both the
peace of the Church, and Civill businesses have beene egre-
giously troubled: nor hath heaven it selfe escaped his violence,
but hath ever since obeied his apointments: so that S. *Stephen*,
John Baptist, and all the rest, which have bin commanded
to worke miracles at certain appointed daies, where their Reliques are preserved, do not now attend till the day come, as
they were accustomed, but are awaked ten daies sooner, and
constrained by him to come downe from heaven to do that
businesse; But your inventions can scarce bee called yours,
since long before you, *Heraclides*, *Ecphantus*, and *Aristarchus*
thrust them into the world: who notwithstanding content themselves with lower roomes amongst the other Philosophers, and
aspire not to this place, reserved onely for *Antichristian Heroes*:
neither do you agree so wel amongst your selves, as that you
can be said to have made a *Sect*, since, as you have perverted
and changed the order and *Scheme* of others: so *Tycho Brache*
hath done by yours, and others by his. Let therefore this little
Mathematitian (dread Emperour) withdraw himselfe to his
owne company. And if hereafter the fathers of our Order can
draw a *Cathedral Decree* from the Pope, by which it may be
defined as a matter of faith: *That the earth doth not move;*
and an *Anathema* inflicted upon all which hold the contrary: then perchance both the Pope which shall decree that, and
Copernicus his followers, (if they be Papists) may have the dignity of this place." *Lucifer* signified his assent; and *Copernicus*,
without muttering a word, was as quiet, as he thinks the sunne,
when he which stood next him, entred into his place. To whom
Lucifer said: "And who are you?" Hee answered, "*Philippus Aureolus Theophrastus Paracelsus Bombast of Hohenheim.*" At this

Lucifer trembled, as if it were a new *Exorcisme*, and he thought it might well be the first verse of Saint *John*, which is alwaies imployed in *Exorcismes*, and might now bee taken out of the *Welsh*, or *Irish Bibles*. But when hee understood that it was but the webbe of his name, hee recollected himselfe, and raising himselfe upright, asked what he had to say to the great *Emperour Sathan, Lucifer, Belzebub, Leviathan, Abaddon. Paracelsus* replyed, "It were an injurie to thee, ô glorious *Emperour*, if I should deliver before thee, what I have done, as thogh al those things had not proceeded from thee, which seemed to have bin done by me, thy organe and conduit: yet since I shal rather be thy trumpet herein, than mine own, some things may be uttered by me. Besides therfore that I broght all *Methodicall Phisitians*, and the art it selfe into so much contempt, that that kind of phisick is almost lost; This also was ever my principal purpose, that no certaine new Art, nor fixed rules might be established, but that al remedies might be dangerously drawne from my uncertaine, ragged, and unperfect experiments, in triall whereof, how many men have beene made carkases? And falling upon those times which did abound with paradoxicall, and unusuall diseases, of all which, the pox, which then began to rage, was almost the center and sinke; I ever professed an assured and an easy cure thereof, least I should deterre any from their licentiousnesse, And whereas almost all poysons are so disposed and conditioned by nature, that they offend some of the senses, and so are easily discerned and avoided, I brought it to passe, that that trecherous quality of theirs might bee removed, and so they might safely bee given without suspicion, and yet performe their office as strongly. All this I must confesse, I wrought by thy minerals and by thy fires, but yet I cannot dispaire of my reward, because I was thy first Minister and instrument, in these innovations." By this time *Ignatius* had observed a tempest risen in *Lucifers* countenance: for he was just of the same temper as *Lucifer,* and therefore suffered with him in every thing and felt al his alterations. That therefore he might deliver him from *Paracelsus*, hee said; "You must not thinke sir, that you may heere draw out an oration to the proportion of your name. It must be confessed, that you attempted great matters, and well becomming a great officer of *Lucifer,* when you undertook not onely to make a man, in your *Alimbicks,* but also to preserve him immortall. And it cannot be doubted, but that out of your *Commentaries* upon the *Scriptures* in which you were utterly ignorant, many men have taken occasion of erring, and thereby this kingdome much indebted to you. But must you therefore have accesse to this secret place? what have you compassed, even in *Phisicke* it selfe, of which wee *Jesuits* are ignorant? For though our *Ribadenegra* have reckoned none of our *Order*, which hath written in *Physicke*, yet how able and sufficient wee are in that faculty, I will bee tryed by that Pope, who hath given a *priveledge* to *Jesuites* to practise *Phisicke*, and to be present at *Death-beds*, which is denyed to other *Orders:* for why should hee deny us their bodies, whose soules he delivers to us? and since he hath transferd upon us the power to practise *Physick*, he may justly be thought to have transferd upon us the Art it selfe, by the same *Omnipotent Bul*; since hee which graunts the end, is by our *Rules* of *law* presumed to have graunted all meanes necessary to that end. Let me (dread *Emperour*,) have leave to speake truth before thee; These men abuse and profane too much thy mettals, which are the bowels, and treasure of thy kingdome: For what doth *Physicke* profit thee? *Physicke* is a soft, and womanish thing. For since *no medicine doth naturally draw bloud*, that science is not fit nor worthy of our study, Besides why should those things, which belong to you, bee employed to preserve from deiseases, or to procure long life? were it not fitter, that your *brother*, and *colleague*, the Bishop of *Rome*, which governes upon the face of your earth, and gives dayly increase to your kingdome, should receive from you these helps and subsidies? To him belonges all the Gold, to him all the pretious stones, conceal'd in your entrailes, wherby hee might baite and ensnare the *Princes* of the earth, through their Lord, and counsellours meanes to his obedience, and to receive his commandements, especially in these times, when almost everywhere his auncient rights and tributes are denied unto him. To him belongs your Iron, and the ignobler mettals, to make engines; To him belong your Minerals apt for poyson; To him, the Saltpeter, and all the Elements of Gun-powder, by which he may demolish and overthrow Kings and Kingdomes, and Courts, and seates of Justice. Neither doth *Paracelsus* truly deserve the name of an *Innovator*, whose doctrine, *Severinus* and his other followers do referre to the most ancient times. Thinke therefore your selfe well satisfied, if you be admitted to governe in chiefe that Legion of homicide-Phisitians, and of Princes which shall be made away by poyson in the midst of their sins, and of woemen tempting by paintings and face-phisicke. Of all which sorts great numbers will daily come hither out of your *Academy*."

Content with this sentence, *Paracelsus* departed; and *Machia-*

vel succeeded, who having observed *Ignatius* his forwardness, and saucinesse, and how, uncal'd, he had thrust himselfe into the office of *kings Atturney,* thought this stupid patience of *Copernicus,* and *Paracelsus* (men which tasted too much of their *Germany*) unfit for a *Florentine:* and therefore had provided some venemous darts, out of his *Italian Arsenal,* to cast against this worne souldier of *Pampelune,* this *French-spanish* mungrell, *Ignatius.* But when he thought better upon it, and observed that *Lucifer* ever approved whatsoever *Ignatius* sayd, he suddenly changed his purpose; and putting on another resolution, he determined to direct his speech to *Ignatius,* as to the principall person next to *Lucifer,* as well by this meanes to sweeten and mollifie him, as to make *Lucifer* suspect, that by these honors and specious titles offered to *Ignatius,* and entertained by him, his owne dignity might bee eclipsed, or clouded; and that *Ignatius* by winning to his side, politique men, exercised in civill businesses, might attempt some innovation in that kingdome. Thus therefore he began to speake. "Dread *Emperour,* and you, his watchfull and diligent *Genius,* father *Ignatius, Archchancellor* of this *Court,* and highest *Priest* of this highest *Synagogue* (except the primacy of the *Romane Church* reach also unto this place) let me before I descend to my selfe, a little consider, speake, and admire your stupendious wisedome, and the government of this state. You may vouchsafe to remember (great *Emperour*) how long after the *Nazarens* death, you were forced to live a solitarie, a barren, and an Eremiticall life: till at last (as it was ever your fashion to imitate heaven) out of your aboundant love, you begot this deerely beloved sonne of yours, *Ignatius,* which stands at your right hand. And from both of you proceedes a spirit, whom you have sent into the world, who triumphing both with *Mitre* and *Crowne,* governes your Militant Church there. As for those sonnes of *Ignatius,* who either he left alive, or were borne after his death, and your spirit, the Bishop of *Rome;* how justly and properly may they be called *Equivocal* men? And not only *Equivocall in* that sence, in which the *Popes Legates,* at your *Nicene Councel* were called *Equivocal,* because *they did agree in all their opinions, and in all their words:* but especially because they have brought into the world a new art of *Equivocation.* O wonderfull, and incredible *Hypercritiques,* who, not out of marble fragments, but out of the secretest Records of Hell itselfe: that is, out of the minds of *Lucifer,* the *Pope,* and *Ignatius,* (persons truly equivocall) have raised to life againe

the language of the Tower of *Babel,* so long concealed, and
brought us againe from understanding one an other. For my
part (ô noble paire of *Emperours*) that I may freely confesse
the truth, all which I have done, wheresoever there shall be
mention made of the Jesuites, can be reputed but childish;
for this honor I hope will not be denied me, that I brought
in an *Alphabet,* and provided certaine Elements, and was
some kind of schoolmaister in preparing them a way to higher
undertakings; yet it grieves me, and makes me ashamed, that
I should be ranked with this idle and Chymaericall *Copernicus,* or this cadaverous vulture, *Paracelsus,* I scorne that those
gates, into which such men could conceive any hope of entrance, should not voluntarily flie open to mee: yet I can better endure the rashnesse and fellowship of *Paracelsus,* than
the other: because hee having beene conveniently practised in
the butcheries, and mangling of men, hee had the reason to
hope for favour of the Jesuites: For I my selfe went alwaies
that way of bloud, and therefore I did ever preferre the sacrifices of the *Gentiles,* and of the *Jewes,* which were performed with effusion of bloud (whereby not only the people,
but the Priests also were animated to bold enterprises) before
the soft and wanton sacrifices of *Christians.* If I might have
had my choyce, I should rather have wished, that the *Romane
Church* had taken the *Bread,* than the *Wine,* from the people,
since in the wine there is some colour, to imagine and represent blood. Neither did you, (most Reverend *Bishop* of this
Dioces, Ignatius) abhorre from this way of blood. For having
consecrated your first age to the wars, and growne somewhat
unable to follow that course, by reason of a wound; you did
presently begin to thinke seriously of a spirituall warre,
against the *Church,* and found meanes to open waies, even
into Kings chambers, for your executioners. Which dignitie,
you did not reserve onely to your own *Order,* but (though I
must confesse, that the foundation, and the nourishment of
this Doctrine remaines with you, and is peculiar to you,) out
of your infinite liberalitie you have vouchsafed sometime, to
use the hands of other men in these imploiments. And therefore as well as they, who have so often in vaine attempted it
in *England,* as they which have brought their great purposes
to effect in *Fraunce,* are indebted only to you for their courage and resolution. But yet although the entrance into this
place may be decreed to none, but the Innovators, and onely
such of them as have dealt in *Christian* businesse; and of

them also, to those only which have had the fortune to doe
much harme, I cannot see but that next to the Jesuites, I
must bee invited to enter, since I did not onely teach those
wayes, by which, thorough *perfidiousnesse* and *dissembling of
Religion*, a man might possesse, and usurpe upon the liberty
of free *Commonwealths;* but also did arme and furnish the
people with my instructions, how when they were under this
oppression, they might safeliest conspire, and remove a *tyrant*,
or revenge themselves of their *Prince*, and redeeme their former losses; so that from both sides, both from *Prince* and *People*,
I brought an aboundant harvest, and a noble encrease to this
kingdome." By this time I perceived *Lucifer* to bee much moved
with this Oration, and to incline much towards *Machiavel*. For
he did acknowledge him to bee a kind of Patriarke, of those
whom they call *Laymen*. And he had long observed, that the
Clergie of *Rome* tumbled downe to *Hell* daily, easily, voluntarily, and by troupes, because they were accustomed to sinne
against their conscience, and knowledge; but that the *Layitie*
sinning out of a slouthfulnesse, and negligence of finding the
truth, did rather offend by ignorance, and omission. And therefore he thought himselfe bound to reward *Machiavel*, which
had awakened this drowsie and implicite *Layitie* to greater,
and more bloody undertakings. Besides this, since *Ignatius*
could not bee denied the place, whose ambitions and turbu-
lencies *Lucifer* understood very wel, he thought *Machiavel* a fit
and necessarie instrument to oppose against him; that so the
skales beeing kept even by their factions, hee might governe
in peace, and two poysons mingled might do no harme. But
hee could not hide this intention from *Ignatius*, more subtil
than the *Devill*, and the verier *Lucifer* of the two: Therefore
Ignatius rushed out, threw himselfe downe at *Lucifers* feet,
and groveling on the ground adored him. Yet certainly, *Vasques*
would not cal this *idolatry*, because in the shape of the *Devil*
hee worshipped him, whom hee accounted the true *God*. Here
Ignatius cried, and thundred out,

> *With so great noise and horror,*
> *That had that powder taken fire, by which*
> *All the Isle of Britaine had flowne to the Moone,*
> *It had not equalled this noise and horror.*

And when he was able to speak distinctly, thus hee spoke. "It
cannot be said (unspeakable *Emperour*) how much this obscure *Florentine* hath transgressed against thee, and against

the *Pope* thy *image-bearer*, (whether the word bee accepted, as *Gratian* takes it, when he calles the *Scriptures*, Imaginarie Bookes; or as they take it, which give that style to them who carrie the *Emperours* image in the field;) and last of all against our Order. Durst any man before him, thinke upon this kinde of injurie and calumnie, as to hope that he should be able to flatter, to catch, to entrap *Lucifer* himselfe? Certainely whosoever flatters any man, and presents him those praises, which in his owne opinion are not due to him, thinkes him inferiour to himselfe and makes account, that he hath taken him prisoner, and triumphs over him. Who ever flatters, either he derides, or (at the best) instructs. For there may bee, even in flattery, an honest kind of teaching, if Princes, by being told that they are already indued with all vertues necessary for their functions, be thereby taught what those vertues are, and by a facile exhortation excited to endeavour to gaine them. But was it fit that this fellow, should dare either to deride you, or (which is the greater injury) to teach you? Can it be beleeved, that he delivers your praises from his heart, and doth not rather herein follow *Gratians* levity; who saies, *That you are called Prince of the world, as a king at Chests, or as the Cardinall of Ravenna, onely by derision?* This man, whilst he lived, attributed so much to his own wit, that hee never thought himselfe beholden to your helps, and insinuations; and was so farre from invoking you, or sacrificing to you, that he did not so much as acknowledge your kingdome, nor beleeve that there was any such thing in nature as you. I must confesse, that hee had the same opinion of God also, and therefore deserves a place here, and a better than any of the *Pagan* or *Gentile* idolaters: for, in every idolatrie, and false worship, there is some Religion, and some perverse simplicitie, which tastes of humilitie; from all which, this man was very free, when in his heart he utterly denyed that there was any God. Yet since he thoght so in earnest, and beleeved that those things which hee affirmed were true, hee must not be rancked with them, which having beene sufficiently instructed of the true God, and beleeving him to be so, doe yet fight against him in his enemies armie. Neither ought it to be imputed to us as a fault, that sometimes in our *exorcismes* wee speake ill of you, and call you *Hereticke*, and *Drunkard*, and *Whisperer*, and *scabbed Beast*, and *Conjure the elements that they should not receive you*, and threaten you with *Indissoluble Damnation, and torments a thousand thousand times worse than you suffer yet.* For these things, you know, are done out of a secret covenant and contract betweene us, and out of *Mysteries,* which must not bee opened to this *Neophite,* who in our *Synagogue* is yet but amongst the *Cathecumeni.* Which also we acknowledge of *Holy Water,* and our *Agnus Dei,* of which you doe so wisely dissemble a feare, when they are presented to you: For certainly, if there were any true force in them, *to deliver Bodies from Diseases, soules from sinnes, and the Elements from Spirits, and malignant impressions,* (as in the verses which *Urban* the fift sent with his *Agnus Dei* to the Emperour it is pretended); it had beene reason, that they should first have exercised their force upon those verses, and so have purged and delivered them, if not from Heresie, yet from Barbarousnesse, and *solaecismes;* that Heretiques might not justly say, there was no truth in any of them, but onely the last; which is,

> *That the least peece which thence doth fall,*
> *Will doe one as much good as all.*

And though our *Order* have adventured further in *Exorcismes* than the rest, yet that must be attributed to a speciall priviledge, by which wee have leave to question any possessed person, of what matters we will; whereas all other Orders are miserably bound to the present matter, and the businesse then in hand. For, though I do not beleeve, that either from your selfe, or from your *vicar* the *Pope,* any such priviledge is issued; yet our *Cotton* deserves to be praised, who being questioned, how he durst propose certaine seditious Interrogatories to a possessed person, to deliver himselfe, fained such a priviledge; and with an un-heard-of boldnesse, and a new kind of falsifying, did (in a manner) counterfeit *Lucifers* hand and seale, since none but he onely could give this priviledge; But, if you consider us out of this liberty in *Exorcismes,* how humble and servile we are towards you, the Relations of *Peru* testifie inough, where it is recorded, that when one of your angels at midnight appeared to our *Barcena* alone in his chamber, hee presently rose out of his chaire, and gave him the place, whom he professed to bee farre worthier thereof, than he was. But to proceede now to the injuries, which this fellow hath done to the *Bishop* of *Rome,* although very much might be spoken, yet by this alone, his disposition may bee sufficiently discerned, that he imputes to the *Pope,* vulgar and popular sinnes, farre unworthy of his greatnesse. Weake praising, is a

kind of Accusing, and wee detract from a mans honour, if when
wee praise him for small things, and would seeme to have said
all, we conceale greater. Perchance this man had seen some of
the *Catalogues* of *Reserv'd Cases*, which every yeare the *Popes*
encrease, and he might thinke, that the *Popes* did therefore
reserve these sinnes to themselves, that they only might commit them. But either hee is ignorant, or injurious to them. For,
can they bee thought to have taken away the libertie of sinning
from the people, who do not onely suffer men to keepe *Concu-
bines,* but sometimes doe commaund them? who make S. *Peter*
beholden to the *stewes,* for part of his revenue: and who excuse
women from the infamous name of whore, till they have delivered
themselves over to 23000 men? The Professors of which Religion teach, *that Universitie men, which keep whores in their
chambers, may not be expeld for that, because it ought to be
presumed before hand, that schollers will not live without
them.* Shal he be thought to have a purpose of deterring others
from sinne, which provides so well for their security, that he
teaches, that he *may dispense in all the commaundements of
the second Table, and in all moral law, and that those commandements of the second table can neither be called Principles,
nor Conclusions, necessarily deduced from Principles?* And
therefore, (as they ever love that manner of teaching) hee did
illustrate his *Rule* with an Example, and dispensed in a mariage
between *Brother* and *Sister,* and hath hoorded up so many *Indul-
gencies* in one barne, the citie of *Rome,* that it is easie for any man
in an houre, or two, to draw out Pardons inough for 100000
yeares. How cleare a witnesse of this liberality is *Leo* 10,
who only for rehearsing once the *Lords* praier, and thrise repeat-
ing the name of *Jesu* (bee it spoken heere without horrour)
hath given 3000 yeares indulgence! How profuse a *Steward*
or *Auditor* was *Boniface,* who acknowledges so many *Indulgences* to be in that one *Church* of *Lateran, that none but God
can number them!* Besides these, plenary Indulgences are given,
not only to the *Franciscans* themselves, but to their *Parents* also:
and to any which dies in their habit; and to any which desire that
they may do so; and to those who are wrapped in it after death,
though they did not desire it; and five yeares *Indulgence* to
those who doe but kisse it. And at last, *Clement* 7, by a
priviledge first given to one Order, (which since is communi-
cated to our Order, as the priviledge of all other Orders are)
gave to any who should but visite a place belonging to them,
or any other place, if hee could not come thither: or if he

could come to no such place, yet if he had but a desire to it, *All indulgences which had beene graunted, or heereafter should be graunted in the universal world.* And though it be true, that if in any of these Indulgences a certaine sum of money were limited to bee given (as for the most part it is;) a poore man, which could not give that money, though he were never so contrite for his sins, could have no benefit thereby: and though *Gerson* durst call those Indulgences foolish, and superstitious, which gave 20000 yeares pardon for rehearsing one praier, yet they do aboundantly testifie the *Popes* liberall disposition, and that he is not so covetous in reserving sinnes to himselfe; But if perchance once in an hundred yeares, some one of the scumme of the people be put to death for *Sodomy;* and that, not so much for the offence, as for usurping the right of the *Ecclesiastique* Princes, wee must not much lament nor grudge at that, since it is onely done to discontinue, and interrupt a praescription, to gaine which Title, the *Layety* hath ever beene very forward against the *Clergie:* for even in this kinde of his delicacies, the *Pope* is not so reserved and covetous, but that he allowes a taste thereof to his *Cardinals,* whom you once called *Carpidineros,* (by an elegancy proper onely to your *Secritaries,* the *Monkes*) in an *Epistle* which you writ to one of that Colledge: For since, the *Cardinals* are so compacted into the Pope, and so made his owne body: *That it is not lawfull for them, without licence first obtained from him, to be let bloud in a Fever,* what may be denied unto them? Or what kind of sin is likely to be left out of their glorious priviledges, which are at least 200? *Which Order the Pope can no more remove out of the Ecclesiastique Hierarchy, than hee can Bishops; both because Cardinals were instituted by God, and because the Apostles themselves were Cardinals before they were Bishops.* Whom also in their creation he stiles *his brothers, and Princes of the world, and Co-judges of the whole earth:* and to perfect all: *That there are so many Kings as there are Cardinals.* O fearefull body; and as in many other things, so in this especialy monstrous, that they are not able to propagate their species: *For all the Cardinals in a vacancy are not able to make one Cardinal more.* To these men certainly the Pope doth no more grudge the plurality of sins, than he doth of Benefices. And he hath beene content, that even *Borgia* shoud enjoy this dignity, if hee hath heaped up, by his ingenious wickednesse, more sorts of sins in one Act, than (as far as I know) as any the *Popes* themselves have attempted: For he did not only give the full reine to his licentiousnesse, but raging with a second ambition, hee would also change the Sex. Therein also his stomacke was not towardes young beardlesse boyes, nor such greene fruit: for hee did not thinke, that hee went farre inough from the right Sex, except hee had a manly, a reverend and a bearded *Venus*. Neither staied he there; but his witty lust proceeded further: yet he sollicited not the *Minions* of the *Popes;* but striving to equall the licentiousnesse of *Sodomits*, which would have had the *Angels;* to come as neare them as hee could, hee tooke a *Cleargy-man*, one of the portion, and lot of the *Lord:* and so made the maker of *God*, a *Priest* subject to his lust; nor did hee seeke him out in a Cloyster, or Quire; but that his *Venus* might bee the more monstrous, hee would have her in a *Mitre*. And yet his prodigious lust was not at the height; as much as he could he added: and having found a *Man* a *Cleargy-man*, a *Bishop*, he did not solicite him with entreaties, and rewards, but ravished him by force. Since then the Popes doe, out of the fulnesse of their power, come to those kindes of sinne, which have neither *Example* nor *Name*, insomuch that Pope *Paulus Venetus*, which used to paint himselfe, and desired to seeme a woman, was called the *Goddesse Cibele* (which was not without mysterie, since, prostitute boyes are sacred to that *Goddesse*,) and since they do not graunt ordinarily that liberty of practising sinnes, till they have used their owne right and priviledge of *Prevention* and *Anticipation*, This pratling fellow *Machiavell* doth but treacherously, and dishonestly prevaricate, and betraie the cause, if hee thinke hee hath done inough for the dignity of the *Popes*, when he hath affoorded to them sins common to all the world. The transferring of Empires, the ruine of Kingdomes, the Excommunications, and depositions of Kings, and devastations by fire and sword, should have bene produced as their marks and characters: for though the examples of the *Popes* transferring the *Empire*, which our men so much stand upon, bee not indeede true, nor that the ancient *Popes* practised any such thing; yet since the states-men of our Order, wiser than the rest, have found how much this *Temporal jurisdiction* over *Princes*, conduces to the growth of the Church, they have perswaded the *Popes* that this is not only lawfull for them, but often practised heeretofore: And therefore they provide, that the *Canons* and *Histories* bee detorted to that opinion: for though one of our *Order* doe weaken that famous *Canon, Nos sanctorum*, which was used still to bee produced for this doctrine, yet hee did it then, when the *King of Great Britaine* was to bee mollified and sweetned towardes us, and the lawes to bee mitigated, and when him-selfe had put on the name *Eudaemon.* But let him returne to his true state, and professe himselfe a *Cacodaemon,* and he will bee of our opinion. In which respect also wee may pardon our *Cudsemius* his rashnesse, when he denies the *English nation to be heretiques, because they remaine in a perpetuall succession of Bishops:* for herein these men have thought it fit, to follow, in their practise, that *Translation,* which reades the words of *Paul: Serve the time,* and not that which saies: *Serve the Lord.* As for the injury which this petty companion hath offered to our *Order,* since in our wrongs, both yours, and the *Popes* Maj-esty is wounded; since to us, as to your *Dictators,* both you have given that large and auncient Commission: *That wee should take care that the state take no harme,* we cannot doubt of our revenge: yet this above all the rest, doth especially vexe me, that when he calls me *Prelate,* and *Bishop,* (names which wee so much abhorre and detest) I know well, that out of his inward malignity, hee hath a relation to *Bellarmines,* and *Tolets* sacrilegious Vow-breaking ambitions, by which they imbraced the *Cardinalship,* and other Church-dignities: but herein this poore fellow, unacquainted with our affaires, is deceived, being ignorant, that these men, by this act of beeing thus incorporated into the Pope are so much the neerer to their *Center* and finall happinesse, this chamber of *Lucifer,* and that by the breach of a vow, which themselves thought just, they have got a new title therunto: For the *Cardinalship* is our *Martyrdome:* and though not many of our *Order,* have had that strength, that they have beene such *Martyrs,* and that the Popes themselves have beene pleased to transferre this persecution into the other *Orders,* who have had more *Cardinals* than wee; yet without doubt, for such of ours which have had so much courage, new Crownes, and new Garlands, appropriate to our *Martyrs,* are prepared for them in this their *Heaven;* because, being inabled by greater meanes, they are fitter for greater mischiefes. Wee therefore la-ment the weakenesse of our *Laynez,* and our *Borgia,* who re-fused the *Cardinalship* offered by *Paulus* 4. and *Julius* 3; (for in this place and this meeting it is not unfit to say they did so) even amongst the auncient *Romans,* when they sacrified to you those sacrifices, which offered any resistance, were ever reputed unaccepted: And therefore our *Bellarmine* deserves much praise, who finding a new *Genius* and courage in his new *Cardinalship,* set out his Retractations, and corrected all those places in his workes, which might any way bee interpreted in the favour of

Princes. But let us pass over all these things: for wee understand one another well inough; and let us more particularly consider those things, which this man, who pretends to exceed all Auncient and Moderne *States-men,* boasts to have beene done by him. Though truly no man will easily beleeve, that hee hath gone farre in any thing, which did so tire at the beginning, or mid-way, that having seene the *Pope,* and knowne him, yet could never come to the knowledge of the *Devill.* I know what his excuse and escape wil be: that things must not be extended infinitly; that wee must consist and arrest somewhere, and that more meanes and instruments ought not to be admitted, where the matter may be dispatched by fewer. When therefore he was sure that the *Bishop* of *Rome* was the cause of all mischiefe, and the first mover therof, he chose rather to settle and determine in him, than by acknowledging a *Divel,* to induce a new *tyrany,* and to be driven to confesse, that the *Pope* had usurped upon the *divels* right, which opinion, if any man bee pleased to maintaine, we do not forbid him: but yet it must be an argument to us of no very nimble wit, if a man do so admire the *Pope,* that he leave out the *Divell,* and so worship the Image, without relation to the prototype and first patterne. But besides this, how idle, and how very nothings they are, which he hath shoveld together in his bookes, this makes it manifest, that some of every *Religion,* and of every profession, have risen up against him, and no man attempted to defend him: neither doe I say this, because I think his doctrine the worse for that, but it is therefore the lesse artificially caried, and the lesse able to worke those endes to which it is directed. For our parts wee have not proceeded so: For wee have dished and dressed our precepts in these affaires, with such cunning, that when our owne men produce them to ensnare and establish our puples, then we put upon them the majesty and reverence of the *Doctrine of the Church,* and of *the common opinion:* But when our adversaries alleadge then, either to cast envy upon us, or to deterre the weaker sort, then they are content with a lower roome, and vouchsafe to step aside into the ranck of *private opinions.* And the *Canons* themselves are with us sometimes glorious, in their mitres and pontificall habits, and sound nothing but meere *Divine resolutions* out of the Chaire it selfe, and so have the force of *Oracles;* somtimes we say they are ragged and lame, and do but whisper with a doubtfull and uncertaine murmure, a hollow cloistral, or an eremitical voice, and so have no more authority, than those poore men which writ them: sometimes we say they were but rashly thrown into the peoples ears out of pulpits, in the Homilies of fathers; sometimes that they were derived out of such *Councels* as suffered *abortion,* and were delivered of their children, which are their *Canons,* before inanimation, which is the Popes assent, or out of such *Councels,* as are now discontinued and dead, (howsoever they remained, long time in use and lively and in good state of health) and therefore cannot be thought fit to be used now, or applyed in civil businesses; sometimes wee say the Popes voyce is in them by this approbation; sometimes that onely the voyce of those authors, from whom they are taken, speakes in them. And accordingly we deliver divers and various *Phylosophy* upon our *Gratian,* who compiled them; sometimes we allow him the honour and dignity of *Diamonds* and the nobler sort of stones, which have both their cleerenesse, and their firmenesse from this, that they are compacted of lesse parts, and atomes, than others are: and so is *Gratian;* whom for the same cause, sometimes we account but a hil of many sands cast together, and very unfit to receive any foundation. I must confesse, that the *fathers* of our *Order,* out of a youthfull fiercenesse, which made them dare and undertake any thing (for our *order* was scarce at yeares at that time) did amisse in inducing the *Councell* of *Trent* to establish certaine *Rules* and *Definitions,* from which it might not be lawfull to depart: for indeed there is no remedy, but that sometimes wee must depart from them: nor can it be dissembled, that both the writers of our *Order,* and the *Dominicans* have departed from them in that great war and *Tragedy* lately raised at *Rome,* about *Grace* and *Free-wil.* For it is not our purpose, that the writings of our men should be so ratified, that they may not be changed, so that they bee of our *Order* which change them: so by the same liberty, which Dæmon-Joannes hath taken in delivering the *King* of *Britaine* from the danger of *Deposition; (because as yet no sentence is given against him)* and also from many other *Canons,* which others thinke may justly bee discharged against him, it will be as lawfull for us, when that *kingdome* shal be inough stupified with this our *Opium,* to restore those *Canons* to their former vigor, and to awake that state out of her *Lethargy,* either with her owne heat, intestine warre, or by some *Medicine* drawne from other places: for *Princes* have all their securities from our indulgence, and from the slacke and gentle interpretation of the *Canons:* they are but privileges, which since they are derived, and receive life from us, they may be by us diminished, revoked, and anulled: for as it was lawfull for *Mariana* to depart from the doctrine of the *Councel* of *Constance*, so it was lawfull for *Cotton* to depart from *Mariana:* which, notwithstanding, wee would have onely lawfull for our *Order*, to whom it is given to know times, and secrets of state: for we see the *Sorbonists* themselves, (which may seeme to have an *Aristocratical Papacie* amongst themselves) though they laboured to destroy the doctrine of *Mariana*, did yet wisely forbeare to name him, or any other *Jesuit*, which was a modesty that I did not hope for at their hands; since, before I dyed, they made one *Decree* against me: but yet therein, I thinke somewhat may bee attributed to my patience, and providence; who knowing their strength, and our owne infancy, forbad all of my *Order* to make any answere to that *Decree* of theirs: neither were we so *Herculean* as to offer to strangle Serpents in our cradle. But yet since after that time, they have beene often provoked by our men: (for I gave not so iron a *Rule* and *Precepts* to my *Disciples*, as *Francis* did to his who would have not his Rule applyed to times and to new occasions) certainly they might have bin excused, if they had beene at this time sharper against us. And if the *Parliament* of *Paris* thought it not fit to carry the matter so modestly in their *Arrest* against *Mariana*, but made both the *Booke*, and the *Doctrine*, and the *Man*, infamous: What should wee say more of it, but that it is a *Gyant*, and a wilde beast, which our men could never tame: for still it cryes and howles, *The Pope is bound to proceede lawfully* and *Canonically;* and this they malitiously interprete of their owne lawes, and of *auncient Canons*, which they hope to bring into use againe, by an insensible way of *Arrest*, and *Sentences* in that *Court.* This then is the point of which wee accuse Machiavell, that he carried not his Mine so safely, but that the enemy perceived it still. But wee, who have received the *Church* to be as a ship, do freely saile in the deep sea; we have an *anchor*, but wee have not cast it yet, but keepe it ever in our power, to cast it, and weigh it at our pleasure. And we know well enough, that as to sailing shippes, so to our sailing Church, all rocks, all promontories, all firme and fast places are dangerous, and threaten shipwracke, and therefore to be avoyded, and liberty and sea-roome to bee affected; yet I doe not obstinately say, that there is nothing in *Machiavels commentary*, which may be of use to this Church. Certainely there is very much; but wee are not men of that poverty, that wee neede begge from others, nor dignify those things with our prayses, which proceede not from oui

selves. The Senate of *Rome* gave us heeretofore a noble example
of this temperance and abstinence, which therefore refused to
place *Christ* amongst their *gods*, because the matter was proposed by the *Emperour*, and begunne not in themselves. As for
that particular, wherein Machiavel useth especially to glory;
which is, that he brought in the liberty of dissembling, and lying,
it hath neither foundation nor colour: For not onely *Plato*, and
other fashioners of *Common-wealths*, allowed the libertie of lying, to Magistrates, and to Physicians; but we also considering the
fathers of the *Church, Origen, Chrysostome, Hierome,* have not
onely found that doctrine in them, but wee have also delivered
them from all imputation, and reprehension by this evasion: *That
it was lawfull for them to maintaine that opinion, till some definition of the Church had established the contrarie.* Which certainely, (though this should not be openly spoken of) as yet
was never done. But yet wee have departed from this doctrine
of free lying, though it were received in practise, excused by the
Fathers, strengthened by examples of Prophets and Angels, in
the Scriptures, and so almost established by the law of *Nations,*
and *Nature;* onely for this reason, because we were not the
first *Authors* of it. But wee have supplied this losse with another doctrine, lesse suspitious; and yet of as much use for our
Church; which is *Mentall Reservation,* and *Mixt propositions.*
The libertie therefore of lying, is neither new, nor safe, as almost all Machiavells precepts are so stale and obsolete, that our
Serarius using, I must confesse, his *Jesuiticall* liberty of wilde
anticipation, did not doubt to call *Herod,* who lived so long before Machiavell, a Machiavellian. But that at one blow wee may
cut off all his reasons, and all his hopes, this I affirme, this I pronounce; that all his bookes, and all his deedes, tend onely to
this, that thereby a way may be prepared to the ruine and destruction of that part of this Kingdome, which is established at
Rome: for what else doth hee endeavour or go about, but to
change the forme of common-wealth, and so to deprive the people (who are a soft, a liquid and ductile mettall, and apter for
our impressions) of all their liberty: and having so destroyed
all civility and re-publique, to reduce all states to *Monarchies;* a
name which in secular states, wee doe so much abhor, (I cannot
say it without teares,) but I must say it, that not any one *Monarch* is to be found, which either hath not withdrawne himselfe
wholy from our kingdome, or wounded and endamadged in some
weighty point: hereupon our *Cotton* confesses, that the authority
of the Pope is incomparably lesse than it was, and that now the

Christian Church, (which can agree to none but the *Romanes,*)
is but a diminutive. And hereupon also it is, that the Cardinals,
who were wont to meete oftner, meete now but once in a weeke,
because the businesses of the *Court* of *Rome* growe fewer. To
forbeare therefore mentioning of the Kings of *Britaine,* and *Den-
marke,* and the other Monarkes of the first sort, which have
utterly cast off *Rome;* even in *France,* our enemies are so much
encreased, that they equal us almost in number: and for their
strength, they have this advantage above us, that they agree
within themselves, and are at unity with their neighbour Re-
fourmed *Churches;* whereas our men, which call themselves
Catholick there, doe so much differ from the Romane Catholick,
that they do not onely preferre Councels, but even the *king,* before the *Pope,* and evermore oppose those their two great *Gyants, Gog* and *Magog,* their Parliament of *Paris,* and their *Colledge* of *Sorbon,* against all our endeavours. Besides all this, we
languish also miserably in *Spaine,* where *Cleargy men, if they
breake their fealty to their Lord, are accused of treason;* where
Ecclesiasticall persons are subject to secular judgement, and, *if
they be sacreligious, are burnt by the Ordinarie Magistrate:* which
are doctrines and practises, contrary, and dangerous to us. And
though they will seeme to have given almost halfe the kingdome
to the *church,* and so to have divided equally; yet those Graunts
are so infected, with pensions, and other burdens, by which
the kings servants, and the yonger sons of great persons are
maintained, that this greatnesse of the Church there is rather
a dropsie, than a sound state of health, established by wel-
concocted nourishment, and is rather done, to cast an Envy upon
the Church, than to give any true Majestie to it. And even in
usurping *Ecclesiasticall* Jurisdiction, the kings of *Spaine* have
not onely exceeded the kings of *Fraunce,* but also of *Britany.*
For (*says Baronius* of that king) *there is now risen up a new
Head, a monster, and a wonder.* He Excommunicates, *and he Ab-
solves: And he practiseth this power even against Bishops, and
Cardinals: He stops Appeales, and he acknowledges no superiority in the sea of Rome, but onely in case of Prevention:* And
therefore, the name Monarch, is a hatefull and execrable name to
us. Against which, *Baronius* hath thundred with such violence,
such fiercenesse, and such bitternesse, that I could hardly adde
any thing thereunto, if I should speake (unspeakable *Emperour*)
with thine owne tongue: for he cals it an *Adulterine name,* and
a *Tower of Babel,* and threatens destruction to that king (though
himselfe were his subject) except he forbeare the name. In the

meane time, he resolves him to be a *Tyrant,* and pronounces him
to stand yearely Excommunicate by the *Bulla Cœnae.* Neither
doth he offer to defend himselfe with any other excuse, when a
Cardinall reprehended his fiercenes towards the king, than this;
An Imperious zeale, hath no power to spare God himselfe. And
yet he confesseth, that this zeale was kindled by the *Popes
speciall command,* and by his *Oath* taken, as Cardinall. Neither
hath our *Bellarmine* almost any other cause of advauncing *Mo-
narchicall* government so much as he doth, than thereby to remove all secular men from so great a dignitie, and to reserve it
only to the Church. It was therefore well done of that Rebellus
(who now begins to bee knowne in this state) when having sur-
feited with Calumnies against the *French* Church, and her Ministers, he hath dared of late to draw his pen, and to joyne battell
against a most puissant forraine Prince: hee did well (I say) and
fitly, when hee called *Bellarmine* and *Baronius, The sword and
buckler of the Romane Church.* And I cannot choose but thanke
him for affoording the Title of *Sword* to our *Order:* as well, because after so many expositions of those words, (*Behold, here are
two swords*) which our side hath gathered, to establish a temporall Jurisdiction in the *Pope,* and which our Adversaries have
removed, worne out, or scorned, this man hath relieved us with
a new, and may seeme to intend by the *two swords, the Popes
Excommunications,* and the *Jesuites Assassinates,* and *King-killings;* as also because he hath reserved to our *Order* that soveraigne dignity, that as God himselfe was pleased to defend his
Paradice with fire and sword, so we stand watchfull upon the
borders of our *Church,* not onely provided, as that *Cherubin* was
with fire and sword, but with the later invention of *Gun-powder;*
about the first inventour whereof I wonder, why *Antiquaries*
should contend, whether it were the *Divell* or a *Frier,* since that
may be all one. But as (O unspeakable *Emperour*) you have almost in all things endevoured to imitate *God:* so have you most
throughly performed it in us: For when *God* attempted the *Reformation* of his *Church,* it became you also to reforme yours.
And accordingly by your *Capuchins,* you did reforme your *Franciscans;* which, before we arose, were your chiefest labourers, and
workemen: and after, you Reformed your *Capuchins,* by your
Recolets. And when you perceived that in the *Church* of *God,*
some men proceeded so farre in that *Reformation,* that they endevoured to draw out, not onely all the peccant and dangerous
humours, but all her beautie, and exteriour grace and Ornament,
and even her vitall spirits, with her corrupt bloud, and so induce

a leannesse, and il-favourednes upon her, and thought to cure a rigid coldnesse with a fever, you also were pleased to follow that Example, and so, in us, did Reforme, and awaken to higher enterprises, the dispositions as well of the *Circumcellions,* as of the *Assassins:* for we do not limit our selves in that lowe degree of the *Circumcellions,* when we urge and provoke others to put us to death; nor of the *Assassins* which were hired to kill some Kings, which passed through their quarter: for we exceed them both, because wee doe these things voluntarily, for nothing, and every where. And as wee will bee exceeded by none, in the thinge itselfe: so to such things as may seeme mysticall and significant, wee oppose mysticall things. And so, lest that *Canon; That no Cleargy-man should weare a knife with a point,* might seeme to concerne us, by some prophetical relation, we in our *Rules* have opposed this precept: *That our knife be often whetted,* and so kept in an apt readines for all uses: for our divination lies in the contemplation of entrails; in which art we are thus much more subtile than those amongst the old *Romans,* that wee consider not the entrails of *Beasts,* but the entrails of souls, in confessions, and the entrails of *Princes,* in treasons; whose hearts wee do not believe to be with us, till we see them: let therefore this pratling *Secretary* hold his tongue, and be content that his booke be had in such reputation, as the world affoords to an *Ephemerides,* or yearely *Almanack,* which being accommodated to certaine places, and certaine times, may be of some short use in some certaine place: and let the *Rules* and precepts of his disciples, like the *Canons* of *provincial Councels* bee of force there, where they were made, but onely ours which pierce, and passe through all the world, retaine the strength and vigour of *Universall Councels.* Let him enjoy some honourable place amongst the *Gentiles;* but abstaine from all of our sides: neither when I say, *Our side,* doe I only meane Moderne man: for in all times in the *Romane* Church, there have bene *Friers* which have farr exceeded *Machiavel.*" Truely I thought this Oration of *Ignatius* very long: and I began to thinke of my body which I had so long abandoned, least it should putrifie, or grow mouldy, or bee buried; yet I was loath to leave the stage, till I saw the play ended: And I was in hope, that if any such thing should befall my body, the Jesuits, who work *Miracles* so familiarly, and whose reputation I was so careful of in this matter, would take compassion upon me, and restore me againe. But as I had sometimes observed

Feathers or strawes swimme on the waters face,
Brought to the bridge, where through a narrow place
The water passes, throwne backe, and delai'd;
And having daunced a while, and nimbly plai'd
Upon the watry circles, Then have bin
By the streames liquid snares, and jawes suck'd in
And suncke into the wombe of that swolne bourne,
Leave the beholder desperate of returne:

So I saw *Machiavel* often put forward, and often thrust back, and at last vanish. And looking earnestly upon *Lucifers* counte-nance, I perceived him to bee affected towardes *Ignatius*, as Princes, who though they envy and grudge, that their great Of-ficers should have such immoderate meanes to get wealth; yet they dare not complaine of it, lest thereby they should make them odious and comtemptible to the people; so that *Lucifer* now suf-fered a new *Hell:* that is, the danger of a *Popular Divell,* vaine-glorious, and inclined to innovations there. Therefore he deter-mined to withdraw himselfe into his inward chamber, and to ad-mit none but *Ignatius:* for he could not exclude him, who had deserved so well; neither did hee thinke it safe to stay without, and give him more occasions to amplifie his owne worth, and undervalue all them there in publique, and before so many vul-gar *Divels.* But as hee rose, a whole army of soules besieged him. And all which had invented any new thing, even in the smallest matters, thronged about him, and importuned an admission. Even those which had but invented new attire for woemen, and those whom *Pancirollo* hath recorded in his *Commentaries* for invention of *Porcellan dishes,* of *Spectacles,* of *Quintans,* of *stirrups,* and of *Caviari,* thrust themselves into the troupe. And of those, which pretended that they had *squared the circle,* the number was infinite. But *Ignatius* scattered all this cloud quickly, by commaunding, by chiding, by deriding, and by force and vio-lence. Amongst the rest, I was sory to see him use *Peter Aretine* so ill as he did: For though *Ignatius* told him true when he boasted of his licentious pictures, that because he was not much learned, hee had left out many things of that kind, with which the ancient histories and poëmes abound; and that therefore *Are-tine* had not onely not added any new invention, but had also taken away all courage and spurres from youth, which would rashly trust, and relie upon his diligence, and seeke no further, and so lose that infinite and precious treasure of Antiquitie. He added moreover, that though *Raderus,* and others of his *Order,* did use to gelde *Poets,* and other *Authors:* (and heere I could not choose but wonder, why they have not gelded their *Vulgar Edition,* which in some places hath such obscene words as the *Hebrew* tongue, which is therefore called *Holy,* doth so much abhorre, that no obscene things can be uttered in it) insomuch, that (as one of them very subtilly notes) the starre of *Venus* is very seldome called by that name in the Scripture: for how could it be, the word being not *Hebrew?* yet (said hee) our men doe not geld them to that purpose, that the memory thereof should bee abolished; but that when themselves had first tried, whether *Tiberius* his *Spintria* and *Martialis symplegma,* and others of that kinde, were not rather *Chimeraes,* and speculations of luxuriant wits, than things certaine and constant, and such as might bee reduced to an Art and methode in licentiousnes (for Jesuits never content themselves with the *Theory* in anything, but straight proceed to *practise*) they might after communicate them to their owne *Disciples* and *Novitiates:* for this Church is fruitfull in producing *Sacraments;* and being now loaded with *Divine sacraments,* it produces Morall sacraments. In which, as in the divine, it bindes the *Layety* to one species; but they reserve to themselves the divers formes, and the secrets and mysteries in this matter, which they finde in the *Authors* whom they geld. Of which kind I thinke they give a liitle glimmering and intimation, when in the life of their last made *Goddesse Francisca Romana,* they say: *that the bed where shee lay with her husband, was a perpetuall Martyrdome to her, and a shop of miracles.* But for all this, since *Aretine* was one, who by a long custome of libellous and contumelious speaking against Princes, had got such a habit, that at last he came to diminish and dis-esteeme *God* himselfe, I wonder truly, that this *Arch-Jesuite,* though hee would not admit him to any eminent place in his *Triumphant Church,* should deny him an office of lower estimation: For truly to my thinking, he might have beene fit, either to serve *Ignatius,* as *maister of his pleasures,* or *Lucifer* as his *Crier:* for whatsoever *Lucifer* durst think, this man durst speake. But *Ignatius,* who thought himselfe sufficient for all uses, thrust him away, and when he offered upward, offered his staffe at him: Nor did he use *Christopher Columbus* with any better respect; who having found all waies in the earth, and sea open to him, did not feare any difficulty in *Hell,* but when hee offered to enter, *Ignatius* staid him, and said: "You must remember, sir, that if this kingdome have got any thing by the discovery of the *West Indies,* al that must be attributed to our *Order:* for if the opinion of the *Dominicans* had prevailed, *That the inhabitants should be reduced, onely by preaching and without violence,* certainely their 200000 of men would scarce in so many ages have beene brought to a 150 which by our meanes was so soone performed. And if the law, made by *Ferdinando,* onely against *Canibals: That all which would not bee Christians should bee bond-slaves,* had not beene extended into other Provinces, wee should have lacked men, to digg us out that benefite, which their countries affoord. Except we when wee tooke away their old Idolatrie, had recompenced them with a new one of ours; except we had obtruded to those ignorant and barbarous people sometimes naturall things, sometimes artificiall, and counterfeit, in steed of *Miracles;* and except we had been alwaies ready to convey, and to apply this *medicine* made of this pretious *American* dung, unto the Princes of *Europe,* and their Lords, and *Counsellours,* the profite by the onely discovery of these places (which must of necessity bee referred to fortune) would have been very little; yet I praise your perseverance, and your patience; which since that seemes to be your principall vertue, you shall have good occasion to exercise heere, when you remaine in a lower and remoter place, than you thinke belongs to your merits." But although *Lucifer* being put into a heate, and almost smothered with this troupe and deluge of pretenders, seemed to have admitted *Ignatius,* as his *Lieutenant,* or *Legat a latere,* and trusted him with an absolute power of doing what hee would, yet he quickly spied his owne errour, and danger thereby. He began to remember how forcibly they use to urge the *Canon Alius;* by which the king of *Fraunce* is sayd to have beene deposed, not for his wickednesse, but for his infirmity, and unfitnesse to governe: And that kings do forfeit their dignity, if they give themselves to other matters, and leave the government of the State to their officers. Therefore *Lucifer* thought it time for him to enter into the businesse, least at last *Ignatius* should prescribe therein; by which title of prescription he well knew, how much the *Church* of *Rome* doth advaunce and defend it selfe against other *Princes.* And though he seemed very thankfull to *Ignatius,* for his delivery from this importunate company, yet when he perceived, that his scope and purpose was, to keepe all others out, he thought the case needed greater consideration; For though he had a confidence in his owne *Patriarkes,* which had long before possest that place, and in whose company (as an *Abbot* said to the *Divell,* who after long intermission now tempted him) *hee*

was growne old, and doubted not but that they would defend
their right, and oppose themselves against any innovation, which
Ignatius should practise, yet if none but hee in a whole age
should bee brought in, hee was afraid, that this singularity would
both increase his courage and spirit, and their reverence, and respect towards him. Casting therefore his eyes into every corner,
at last a great way off, hee spied *Philip Nerius:* who acknowledging in his owne particular no especiall merit towardes this
kingdome, forbore to presse neere the gate; But *Lucifer* called
to his remembrance, that *Nerius* and all that *Order,* of which
hee was the *Author,* which is called *congregatio Oratorii,* were
erected, advaunced, and dignifyed by the *Pope,* principally to
this end, that, by their incessant Sermons to the people, of the
lives of *Saints* and other *Ecclesiatique Antiquities,* they might
get a new reputation, and so the torrent, and generall superstition towards the Jesuits, might grow a little remisser, and luke-
warme: for at that time the Pope himselfe beganne to bee
afraid of the Jesuites, for they beganne to publish their *Paradox
of Confession and absolution to bee given by letters, and Messengers,* and by that meanes to draw the secrets of all Princes
onely to themselves; And they had tried and sollicited a great
Monarch, who hath manie designes upon *Italy,* against the *Pope,*
and delivered to that prince diverse articles, for the reforming of
him. Now the *Pope* and *Lucifer* love ever to follow one anothers example: And therefore that which the one had done in
the middle world, the other attempted in the lower. Hereupon
he called for *Philip Nerius,* and gave him many evidences of a
good inclination towards him. But *Nerius* was too stupid, to interprete them aright. Yet *Ignatius* spied them, and before *Lucifer* should declare himselfe any further, or proceed too farre
herein, lest after he were farre engaged, there should be no way,
to avert or withdraw him from his owne propositions (for he
saw there must be respect had of his honour and constancy) hee
thought it fittest to oppose now at the beginning. He sayd therfore, "that he now perceived, that *Lucifer* had not bene altogether so much conversant with *Philip* as with the *Jesuits,* since
he knew not, how much *Philip* had ever professed himselfe an
enemy to him. For he did not onely deny all visions, and apparitions, And commaunded one to spit in *Maries* face, when
she appeared againe, because he thought it was the *Divell;* And
drove away an other that came to tempt a sicke man, in the
shape of a Phisition: And was hardly drawne to beleeve any pos-
sessings: but when three *Divels* did meete him in the way, to

afright him, he neither thought them worthy of any *Exorcisme,* nor so much as the signe of the Crosse, but meerely went by them, as though he scorned to look at them, and so de- spighted them with that negligence. It may be that hee hath drawne others into *Religion,* but himselfe remained then in the *Layety:* in so much as I remember, that I used to call him, *The Saints Bell,* that hangs without, and cals others into the *Church.* Neither doe they which follow this *Order,* bind them- selves with any *vow* or *oath;* Neither do I know any thing for which this kingdome is beholding to him, but that *he moved Baronius to write his Annals.*"

To all this *Nerius* sayde nothing, as though it had beene spoken of some body else. Without doubt, either he never knew, or had forgot that he had done those things which they write of him. But *Lucifer* himselfe tooke the boldnesse (having with some difficultie got *Ignatius* leave) to take *Nerius* his part: and proceeded so farre, that he adventured to say, that *Baronius, Bozius,* and others, which proceeded out of the *Hyve* of *Nerius,* had used a more free, open, and hard fashion against *Princes,* and better provided for the Popes *Direct Jurisdiction* upon all Kingdomes, and more stoutly defended it, than they; which un- dertaking the cause more tremblingly, than becomes the Majestie of so great a businesse, adhered to *Bellarmines* sect, and devised such crooked wayes, and such perplexed intanglings, as by reason of the various, and uncertaine circumstances, were of no use: And that whatsoever *Nerius* his *schollers* had performed, must be attributed to him, as the fruit to the roote." *Ignatius* per- ceiving that *Lucifer* undertooke all offices for *Nerius,* and be- came Judge, Advocate, and witnesse, pursuing his former reso- lution, determined to interrupt him, lest when hee had enlarged himselfe in *Nerius* commendation, hee should thereby bee bound to a reward. He therefore cried out, "What hath *Nerius* done? what hath he, or his followers put in execution? have they not ever bene onely exercised in speculations, and in preparatory doctrines? Are these bookes which are written of the *Jurisdiction* of the *Pope,* to any better use than *Phisitians Lectures* of dis- eases, and of Medicines? whilest these *Receits* lie hid in *Phisi- tians* bookes, and no body goes to the *Patient:* no body applies the medicine to the disease, what good, what profit comes by all this? what part; what member of this languishing body have they undertaken? In what *Kingdome* have they corrected these humours, which offend the *Pope,* either by their *Incision* or *cauterising?* what state have they cut up into an *Anatomy?*

what *Sceleton* have they provided for the instruction of Posterity? Do they hope to cure their diseases, by talking and preaching, as it were with charmes and enchantments? If *Nerius* shall bee thought worthy of this Honour, and this place, because out of his *schollers* writings something may be gleaned, which may be applied to this purpose, why should we not have *Beza* and *Calvin*, and the rest of that sort here in Hell, since in their bookes there may be some things found, which may be wrested to this purpose? But, since their scope was not to extirpate *Monarchies*, since they published no such *Canons* and *Aphorismes* as might be applied to all cases, and so brought into certaine use and consequence, but limited theirs to circumstances which seldome fall out, since they delivered nothing dangerous to Princes, but where, in their opinion, the *Sovereignty* resided in the *People*, or in certaine *Ephori*, since they never said, that this power to violate the person of a prince, might either be taken by any private man, or committed to him, and that, therefore, none of their disciples hath ever boasted of having done any thing upon the person of his soveraigne: we see that this place hath ever bene shut against them: there have bene some few of them (though I can scarce affoord those men the honour to number them with *Knox*, and *Goodman*, and *Buchanan*) which following our examples have troubled the peace of some states, and beene injurious to some princes, and have beene admitted to some place in this Kingdome; but since they have performed nothing with their hands, nor can excuse themselves by saying, they were not able: (for wherein was *Clement*, or *Ravillac* more able than they: or what is not he able to doe in the middest of an Army, who despiseth his owne life? they scarce ever aspire, or offer at this secret and sacred *Chamber*." *Lucifer* had a purpose to have replied to this: that perchaunce all their hands which had bin imbrued in the bowels of Princes, were not so immediatly armed by the Jesuits, as that they were ever present at all consultations and resolutions: (and yet he meant to say this, not as a sworne witnesse, but as *Lucifer* himselfe, and the father of lies, in which capacitie he might say any thing). But that it was inough that *Confessours* do so possesse them with that doctrine, that it is not now proposed to them as *Phisicke*, but as naturall food, and ordinarie diet: and that therefore for the performance of these things a Jesuits person is no more requisite, than the heart of a man, because it sends forth spirits into every limbe, should therefore bee present in every limbe: that when it was in use for the *Consuls* of *Rome* for the safety of their country and army, to devote themselves over to the infernall *god*, it was lawfull for themselves to absteine and forbeare the act, and they might appoint any Souldier for that *Sacrifice:* and that so the Jesuites for the performance of their resolutions, might stirre up any amongst the people: (for now they enjoy all the priviledges, of the *Franciscans*, who say: *That the name of people comprehends all which are not of their Order:*) And that if this be granted, *Nerius* his scollers are inferiour to none; with those bookes (if all the *Jesuites* should perish) the Church might content herselfe, and never feare dearth or leanesse." This *Lucifer* would have spoken; but hee thought it better and easier to forbeare: for hee observed, that *Ignatius* had given a signe, and that all his troupes which were many, subtile, and busie, set up their bristles, grumbled, and compacted themselves into one body, gathered, produced and urged all their evidence, whatsoever they had done, or suffered. There the *English Legion*, which was called *Capistrata*, which *Campian* led, and (as I thinke) *Garnet* concluded, was fiercer than all the rest. And as though there had beene such a second *martyrdome* to have beene suffered or as though they might have put off their *Immortalitie*, they offered themselves to any imploiment. Therefore *Lucifer* gave *Nerius* a secret warning to withdraw himselfe, and spoke no more of him; and despairing of bringing in an other, began earnestly to thinke, how he might leave *Ignatius* out. This therefore he said to him: "I am sorry my *Ignatius*, that I can neither find in others, deserts worthy of this place, nor any roome in this place worthy of your deserts. If I might die, I see there would be no longe strife for a successour: For if you have not yet done that act which I did at first in *Heaven*, and thereby got this Empire, this may excuse you, that no man hath beene able to tell you what it was: For if any of the *Auncients* say true, when they call it *Pride*, or *Licentiousnesse*, or *Lying:* or if it be in any of the Casuists which professe the Art of sinning, you cannot be accused of having omitted it. But since I may neither forsake this *kingdome*, nor divide it, this onely remedy is left: I will write to the Bishop of *Rome:* he shall call *Galilæo* the *Florentine* to him; who by this time hath throughly instructed himselfe of all the hills, woods, and Cities in the new world, the *Moone*. And since he effected so much with his first *Glasses*, that he saw the *Moone*, in so neere a distance that hee gave himselfe satisfaction of all, and the least parts in her, when now being growne to more perfection in his Art, he shall have made new *Glasses*, and they received a hallowing from the *Pope*, he may draw the *Moone*, like

a boate floating upon the water, as neere the earth as he will.
And thither (because they ever claime that those imployments
of discovery belong to them) shall all the Jesuites bee transferred,
and easily unite and reconcile the *Lunatique Church* to the *Romane Church;* without doubt, after the Jesuites have been there a
little while, there will soone grow naturally a *Hell* in that world
also: over which, you *Ignatius* shall have dominion, and establish
your kingdome and dwelling there. And with the same ease as
you passe from the earth to the *Moone,* you may passe from the
Moone to the other *starrs,* which are also thought to be worlds,
and so you may beget and propagate many *Hells,* and enlarge
your *Empire,* and come nearer unto that high seate which I left
at first." *Ignatius* had not the patience to stay till *Lucifer* had
made an end; but as soone as hee saw him pause, and take
breath, and looke, first upon his face, to observe what changes
were there, and after to cast his eye to an other place in *Hell*
where a great noyse was suddenly raysed: hee apprehended this
intermission, and as though *Lucifer* had ended, he said: "That of
Lucifers affection to the *Romane Church,* and to their *Order,* every day produced new Testimonies: and that this last was to bee
accounted as one of the greatest. That he knew well with how
great devotion the Bishop of *Rome* did ever embrace and execute all counsels proceeding from him: And that therefore he
hoped, that hee would reserve that imployment for the *Jesuits,*
and that *Empire* for him their founder: and that he beleeved
the *Pope* had thought of this before; and at that time when he
put *Parsons* the *English* Jesuitè in hope of a *Cardinalship,* hee
had certainly a reference to this place, and to this *Church:* That
it would fall out shortly, that all the damages, which the *Romane
Church* hath lately suffered upon the earth, shall bee recompenced onely there. And that, now this refuge was opened, if
she should be reduced into greater streights, or if she should be
utterly exterminated, the world would not much lament and
mourne for it. And for the entertainment of the Jesuites there,
there can be no doubt made at this time, when, (although their
profession bee to enter whether Princes will or no) all the
Princes of the world will not onely graciously affoord them leave
to goe, but willingly and cheerfully accompany them with Cer-
tificates, and Dimissory letters. Nor would they much resist it, if
the *Pope* himselfe would vouchsafe to go with them, and so
fulfill in some small measure, that prophecy of his *Gerson, De
Auferibilitate Papae.* Besides this a woman governes there; of
which Sex they have ever made their profite, which have at-

tempted any *Innovation* in religion; with how much diligence were the two *Empresses Pulcheria* and *Eudoxia* sollicited by the *Pope* for the establishing of *Easter?* how earnestly did both *Pelagius* and the *Pope* strive by their letters to draw the *Empresse* to their side? For since *Julia* had that honour given to her in publique coines, that she was called *the mother of the Armie, the Mother of the Gods, and of the Senate, and the Mother of her Countrie;* Why may not woemen instructed by us, be called *Mothers of the Church?* Why may not wee relie upon the wit of woemen, when, once, the Church delivered over her selfe to a woman-*Bishop?* And since wee are reputed so fortunate in obtaining the favour of woemen, *that woemen are forbid to come into our houses;* and we are forbid, *to take the charge of any Nunnes;* since we have had so good experience of their favour in all the *Indies,* or at least have thought it fit, that they which have the charge to write our anniversary letters from thence should make that boast, and adde something to the Truth, both because the Auncient *Heretiques* helde that course in insinuating their opinions, and because they which are acquainted with our practises will think any thing credible, which is written of us in that behalfe, why should wee doubt of our fortune in this *Queene* which is so much subject to alterations, and passions? She languishes often in the absence of the Sunne, and often in *Ecclipses* falles into swounes, and is at the point of death. In these advantages we must play our parts, and put our devises in practise: for at these times any thing may be drawne from her. Nor must we forbeare to try, what verses, and incantations may worke upon her: For in those things which the *Poets* writ, though they themselves did not beleeve them, we have since found many truths, and many deep mysteries: nor can I call to minde any woman, which either deceived our hope, or scaped our cunning, but *Elizabeth* of *England;* who might the rather be pardoned that, because she had put off all affections of woemen. The Principall Dignity of which sex, (which is, to be a *Mother*) what reason had she to wish, or affect, since without those *womanish* titles, unworthy of her, of wife, and mother, such an heire was otherwise provided for her, as was not fit to be kept any longer from the inheritance. But when I, who hate them, speake thus much in the honour of these two *Princes,* I finde myselfe caried with the same fury, as those *Beasts* were, which our men say, did sometimes adore the *Host* in the *Masse.* For it is against my will, that I pay thus much to the *Manes* of *Elizabeth;* from scorning of which word *Manes,* when the king of great *Brittaine* writ it, I would our *Parsons* had forborne, since one of our owne *Jesuits* useth the same word, when reprehending our Adversaries, he says, *That they do insult upon Garnets Manes*. And yet this *Elizabeth* was not free from all *Innovation:* For the ancient *Religion* was so much worne out, that to reduce that to the former dignity, and so to renew it, was a kinde of *Innovation:* and by this way of innovating shee satisfied the infirmity of her Sex, if shee suffered any: for a little *Innovation* might serve her, who was but a little a woman. Neither dare I say, that this was properly an *Innovation*, lest thereby I should confesse that *Luther* and many others which live in banishment in *Heaven* farre from us, might have a title to this place, as such *Innovators.* But we cannot doubt, but that this *lunatique Queen* will be more inclinable to our Innovations: for our *Clavius* hath beene long familiarly conversant with her, what she hath done from the beginning, what she wil do hereafter, how she behaves herselfe towardes her neighbour kingdoms, the rest of the starrs, and all the planetary, and firmamentary worlds; with whom she is in league, and amity, and with whom at difference, he is perfectly instructed, so he have his *Ephemerides* about him. But *Clavius* is too great a personage to be bestowed upon this *Lunatique Queene*, either as her Counsellour, or (which were more to our profit) as her Confessor. So great a man must not bee cast away upon so small a matter. Nor have we any other besides, whom upon any occasion we may send to the Sunne, or to the other worlds, beyond the world. Therefore wee must reserve *Clavius* for greater uses. Our *Herbestus*, or *Busaeus*, or *Voellus* (and these bee all which have given any proofe of their knowledge in *Mathematiques*) although they bee but tastelesse, and childish, may serve to observe her aspects, and motions, and to make *Catechismes* fit for this *Lunatique Church;* for though *Garnet* had *Clavius* for his *Maister*, yet he profited little in the Arts, but being filled with *Bellarmines Dictates*, (who was also his *Maister*) his minde was all upon *Politiques*. When wee are established there, this will adde much to our dignity, that in our letters which wee send downe to the earth, (except perchaunce the whole *Romane Church* come up to us into the *Moone*) we may write of what miracles wee list: which we offered to doe out of the *Indies*, and with good successe, till one of our *Order*, in a simplicity, and ingenuity fitter for a *Christian*, than a Jesuite, acknowledged and lamented that there were no *miracles* done there. Truly it had bin better for us to have spit all those five *Brothers, Acostas*, out of our *Order*, than that any one of them should have vomited this reproach against us. It is of such men as these in our *Order*, that our *Gretzer* saies: *There is no body without his Excrements,* because though they speake truth, yet they speake it too rawly. But as for this contemplation, and the establishing of that government, (though it be a pleasant consideration) we may neither pamper our selves longer with it now, nor detaine you longer therein. Let your *Greatnesse* write; let the *Pope* execute your counsell; let the *Moone* approach when you two think fit. In the meane time let me use this Chamber, as a resting place: For though *Pope Gregory* were strucken by the Angell with a perpetuall paine in his stomach and feet, because hee compelled *God* by his praiers, to deliver *Trajan* out of *Hell,* and transferre him to *Heaven;* and therefore *God,* by the mouth of *Gregorie,* tooke an assurance for all his *Successours,* that they should never dare to request the like againe: yet when the *Pope* shall call mee backe from hence, hee can be in no danger, both because in this contract, *God* cannot bee presumed to have thought of me, since I never thought of him, and so the contract therein void; and because the Condition is not broken, if I bee not removed into *Heaven,* but transferred from an Earthly *Hell,* to a *Lunatique Hell.*" More than this he could not be heard to speake: For that noise, of which I spoke before, increased exceedingly, and when *Lucifer* asked the cause, it was told him, that there was a soule newly arrived in *Hell,* which said that the *Pope* was at last entreated to make *Ignatius* a *Saint,* and that hee hastened his Canonization, as thinking it an unjust thing, that when all artificers, and prophane Butchers had particular *Saints* to invocate, only these spirituall Butchers, and *King-killers,* should have none: for when the Jesuite *Cotton* in those questions which by vertue of his invisible priviledge he had provided for a possest person, amongst others, dangerous both to *England* and *France,* had inserted this question: *What shall I do for* Ignatius *his Canonizing?* and found out at last, that *Philip, King of Spaine,* and *Henry, King of Fraunce,* contended by their Ambassadors at *Rome,* which of them should have the honour of obtaining his Canonizing (for both pretending to be King of *Navarre,* both pretended that this right and honour belonged to him: and so both deluded the Jesuits:) For *D'Alcala* a *Franciscan,* and *Penafort* a *Jacobite,* were by *Philips* meanes canonized, and the Jesuite left out. At last hee despaired of having any assistance from these Princes: nor did he thinke it convenient, that a Jesuite should be so much beholden to a King, since *Baronius* was already come to that heighth and constancy, that being accused of some wronges done to his King, hee did not vouchsafe to write in his owne excuse to the King, till the *Conclave* which was then held, was fully ended, lest (as himselfe gives the reason) if hee had then beene chosen *Pope,* it should bee thought hee had beene beholden to the King therein. For these reasons therefore they labour the *Pope* themselves. They confesse, that if they might choose, they had rather hee should restore them into all which they had lost in *Fraunce,* and *Venice,* than that *Ignatius* should be sent up into *Heaven;* and that the *Pope* was rather bound to do so, by the Order which *God himselfe* seemes to have observed in the *Creation,* where he first furnished the *Earth,* and then the *Heavens,* and confirmed himselfe to be the *Israelites God* by the *Argument,* that he had given them the land of *Canaan,* and other temporall blessings. But since this exceeded the Popes omnipotence in Earth, it was fit he should try, what he could do in *Heaven.* Now the *Pope* would faine have satisfied them with the title of *Beatus,* which formerly upon the intreaty of the Princes of that *Family,* he had affoorded to *Aloisius Gonzaga* of that *Order.* He would also have given this title of *Saint* rather to *Xaverius,* who had the reputation of having done *Miracles.* Indeed he would have done anything, so hee might have slipped over *Ignatius.* But at last hee is overcome; and so against the will of *Heaven,* and of the *Pope, Lucifer* himselfe being not very forward in it, *Ignatius* must bee thrust in amongst the *Saints.* All this discourse, I, beeing growne cunninger than that Doctor, *Gabriell Nele* (of whom *Bartolus* speaketh) that by the only motion of his lippes, without any utterance, understood all men, perceived and read in every mans countenance there. These things, as soone as *Lucifer* apprehended them, gave an end to the contention; for now hee thought he might no longer doubt nor dispute of *Ignatius* his admission, who besides his former pretences, had now gotten a new right and title to the place, by his *Canonization;* and he feared that the *Pope* would take all delay ill at his handes, because *Canonization* is now growne a kinde of *Declaration,* by which all men may take knowledge, that such a one, to whom the Church of *Rome* is much beholden, is now made partaker of the principall dignities, and places in *Hell:* For these men ever make as though they would follow *Augustine* in all things, and therefore they provide that that also shall bee true which he said in this point: *That the Reliques of many are honoured upon earth whose soules are tormented in Hell.* Therefore he took *Ignatius* by the hand, and led him to the gate. In the meane time, I, which doubted of the truth of this report of his Canonizing, went a little out for further instruction: for I thought it scarce credible, that *Paulus 5.* who had but lately burdened both the *Citie* of *Rome,* and the *Church,* with so great expences, when he canonized *Francisca Romana,* would so easily proceed to canonize *Ignatius* now, when neither any Prince offered to beare the charge, nor so much as sollicited it: for so he must bee forced to waste both the *Treasures* of the Church at once. And from *Leo* 3. who 800 yeares after Christ, is the first Pope which Canonized any, I had not observed that this had ever beene done: Neither do I think that *Paulus 5.* was drawne to the Canonizing of this woman by any other respect, than because that Rule which shee appointed to her *Order, was Dictated and written by Saint Paul:* For though *Peter,* and *Magdalene,* and others, were present at the writing thereof, as witnesses, yet *Paul* was the *Author* thereof. And since Saint Pauls old Epistles trouble and disadvantage this Church, they were glad to apprehend any thing of his new writing, which might be for them, that so this new worke of his might beare witnesse of his second conversion to *Papistry,* since by his first conversion to *Christianity,* they got nothing: for to say, that in this business *Paulus 5. could not choose but be God, God himselfe,* to say, *that hee must needes have lived familiarly with the God-head*: and must have heard *Predestination it selfe whispering to him: And must have had a place to sit in Councell with the most Divine Trinitie,* (all which *Valladerius* sayes of him) is not necessary in this matter, wherein the Popes, for the most part, proceed as humane affections leade them. But at last, after some enquiry, I found that a certaine idle *Gazettier,* which used to scrape up Newes, and Rumours at *Rome,* and so to make up sale letters, vainer, and falser, than the Jesuites Letters of *Japan,* and the *Indies,* had brought this newes to *Hell,* and a little Jesuiticall *Novice,* a credulous soule, received it by his implicit faith, and published it. I laughed at *Lucifers* easinesse to beleeve, and I saw no reason ever after, to accuse him of infidelity. Upon this I came backe againe, to spie (if the gates were stil open) with what affection *Ignatius,* and they who were in auncient possession of that place, behaved themselves towardes one an other. And I found him yet in the porch, and there beginning a new contention: for having presently cast his eyes to the principall place, next to *Lucifers* owne *Throne,* and finding it possest, he stopt *Lucifer,* and asked him, who it was that sate there. It was

answered, that it was *Pope Boniface;* to whome, as to a principall Innovator, for having first chalenged the name of *Univer-*
sall Bishop, that honour was affoorded. Is he an Innovator thundred *Ignatius?* Shall I suffer this, when all my Disciples have
laboured all this while to prove to the world, that all the *Popes*
before his time did use that name? And that *Gregory* did not
reprehend the *Patriarch John* for taking to himselfe an Antichristian name, but for usurping a name which was due to none
but the *Pope.* And could it be fit for you, *Lucifer,* (who in this
were either unmindfull of the *Romane Church,* or else too
weake and incapable of her secrets and mysteries) to give way
to any sentence in *Hell,* which (though it were according to
truth,) yet differed from the Jesuites *Oracles?* With this *Igna-*
tius flyes upwardes, and rushes upon *Boniface,* and throwes him
out of his Seate: And *Lucifer* went up with him as fast, and
gave him assistance, lest, if hee should forsake him, his owne
seate might bee endangered. And I returned to my body; which

> As a flower wet with last nights dew, and then
> Warm'd with the new Sunne, doth shake off agen
> All drowsinesse and raise his trembling Crowne,
> Which crookedly did languish, and stoope downe
> To kisse the earth, and panted now to finde
> Those beames return'd, which had not long time shin'd,

was with this returne of my soule sufficiently refreshed. And
when I had seene all this, and considered how fitly and pro-
portionally *Rome* and *Hell* answered one another, after I had
seene a Jesuit turne the *Pope* out of his *Chaire* in *Hell,* I suspected that that *Order* would attempt as much at *Rome.*

AN APOLOGY FOR JESUITES

Now is it time to come to the *Apology* for *Jesuites:* that is, it
is time to leave speaking of them, for hee favours them most,
which saies least of them; Nor can any man, though hee had
declaimed against them till all the sand of the sea were run
through his houre-glasse, lacke matter to adde of their practises.
If any man have a mind to adde any thing to this *Apology,*
hee hath my leave; and I have therefore left roome for three
or foure lines: which is enough for such a paradox: and more
than *Jungius, Scribanius, Gretzerus, Richeonius, Cydonius,* and

all the rest which are used to *Apologies,* and almost tyred with
a defensive warre, are able to employ, if they will write onely
good things, and *true,* of the *Jesuites.* Neither can they comfort
themselves with this, That *Cato* was called to his answere foure
and forty times: for hee was so many times acquitted, which
both the *Parliaments* of *England,* and *France* deny of the *Jesuites.* But if any man thinke this *Apology* too short, he may
thinke the whole booke an *Apology,* by this *rule* of their owne.
*That it is their greatest argument of innocency to be accused
by us.* At this time, whilst they are yet somewhat able to do
some harme, in some places, let them make much of this *Apology.* It will come to passe shortly, when as they have bene dis-
poyled and expelled at *Venice,* and shaked and fanned in
France, so they will bee forsaken of other *Princes,* and then
their owne weakenesse will bee their *Apology,* and they will
grow harmelesse out of necessity, and that which *Vegetius* sayd
of chariots armed with sithes and hookes, will be applied to the
Jesuites, *at first they were a terror, and after a scorne.*

From ESSAYES IN DIVINITY   [1614?]

FIVE PRAYERS
FROM
ESSAYES IN DIVINITY

I

O ETERNALL and Almighty power, which being infinite, hast
enabled a limited creature, Faith, to comprehend thee; And being, even to Angels but a passive Mirror and looking-glasse, art
to us an Active guest and domestick, (for thou hast said, *I
stand at the door and knock, if any man hear me, and open the
doore, I will come in unto him, and sup with him, and he with
me*), and so thou dwellst in our hearts; And not there only,
but even in our mouths; for though thou beest greater and
more remov'd, yet humbler and more communicable than the
Kings of *Egypt,* or *Roman* Emperours, which disdain'd their
particular distinguishing Names, for *Pharaoh* and *Caesar,* names
of confusion; hast contracted thine immensity, and shut thy
selfe within Syllables, and accepted a Name from us; O keep

and defend my tongue from misusing that Name in lightnesse, passion, or falshood; and my heart, from mistaking thy Nature, by an inordinate preferring thy Justice before thy Mercy, or advancing this before that. And as, though thy self hadst no beginning thou gavest a beginning to all things in which thou wouldst be served and glorified; so, though this soul of mine, by which I partake thee, begin not now, yet let this minute, O God, this happy minute of thy visitation, be the beginning of her conversion, and shaking away confusion, darknesse, and barrennesse; and let her now produce Creatures, thoughts, words, and deeds agreeable to thee. And let her not produce them, O God, out of any contemplation, or (I cannot say, *Idœa*) but *Chimera* of my worthinesse, either because I am a man and no worme, and within the pale of thy Church, and not in the wild forrest, and enlightned with some glimmerings of Naturall knowledge; but meerely out of Nothing: Nothing pre-existent in her selfe, but by power of thy Divine will and word. By which, as thou didst so make Heaven, as thou didst not neglect Earth, and madest them answerable and agreeable to one another, so let my Soul's Creatures have that temper and Harmony, that they be not by a mis-devout consideration of the next life, stupidly and trecherously negligent of the offices and duties which thou enjoynest amongst us in this life; nor so anxious in these, that the other (which is our better business, though this also must be attended) be the less endeavoured. Thou hast, O God, denyed even to Angells, the ability of arriving from one Extreme to another, without passing the mean way between. Nor can we pass from the prison of our Mothers womb, to thy palace, but we must walk (in that pace whereto thou hast enabled us) through the street of this life, and not sleep at the first corner, nor in the midst. Yet since my soul is sent immediately from thee, let me (for her return) rely, not principally, but wholly upon thee and thy word: and for this body, made of preordained matter, and instruments, let me so use the materiall means of her sustaining, that I neither neglect the seeking, nor grudge the missing of the Conveniences of this life: And that for fame, which is a mean Nature between them, I so esteem opinion, that I despise not other thoughts of me, since most men are such, as most men think they be: nor so reverence it, that I make it alwayes the rule of my Actions. And because in this world my Body was first made, and then my Soul, but in the next my soul shall be first, and then my body, In my Exterior and morall conversation let my first and

presentest care be to give them satisfaction with whom I am
mingled, because they may be scandaliz'd, but thou, which seest
hearts, canst not: But for my faith, let my first relation be to
thee, because of that thou art justly jealous, which they cannot
be. Grant these requests, O God, if I have asked fit things fitly,
and as many more, under the same limitations, as are within
that prayer which (as thy *Manna*, which was meat for all tasts,
and served to the appetite of him which took it, and was that
which every man would) includes all which all can aske, *Our
Father which art, etc.*

II

O ETERNALL God, as thou didst admit thy faithfull serv·
ant *Abraham*, to make the granting of one petition an incour·
agement and rise to another, and gavest him leave to gather
upon thee from fifty to ten; so I beseech thee, that since by
thy grace, I have thus long meditated upon thee, and spoken of
thee, I may now speak to thee. As thou hast enlightened and
enlarged me to contemplate thy greatness, so, O God, descend
thou and stoop down to see my infirmities and the Egypt in
which I live; and (If thy good pleasure be such) hasten mine
Exodus and deliverance, for I desire to be disolved, and be with
thee. O Lord, I most humbly acknowledge and confess thine infinite Mercy, that when thou hadst almost broke the staff of
bread, and called a famine of thy word almost upon all the
world, then thou broughtest me into this Egypt, where thou
hadst appointed thy stewards to husband thy blessings, and to
feed thy flock. Here also, O God, thou hast multiplied thy
children in me, by begetting and cherishing in me reverent devotions, and pious affections towards thee, but that mine own
corruption, mine own *Pharaoh* hath ever smothered and strangled them. And thou hast put me in my way towards thy land
of promise, thy Heavenly *Canaan*, by removing me from the
Egypt of frequented and populous, glorious places, to a more
solitary and desart retiredness, where I may more safely feed
upon both thy Mannaes, thy self in thy Sacrament, and that other,
which is true Angells food, contemplation of thee. O Lord, I
most humbly acknowledge and confess, that I feel in me so
many strong effects of thy Power, as only for the Ordinariness
and frequency thereof, they are not Miracles. For hourly thou
rectifiest my lameness, hourly thou restorest my sight, and
hourly not only deliverest me from the Egypt, but raisest me

from the death of sin. My sin, O God, hath not only caused thy descent hither, and passion here; but by it I am become that hell into which thou descendedst after thy Passion; yea, after thy glorification: for hourly thou in thy Spirit descendest into my heart, to overthrow there Legions of spirits of Disobedience, and Incredulity, and Murmuring. O Lord, I most humbly acknowledge and confesse, that by thy Mercy I have a sense of thy Justice; for not onely those afflictions with which it pleaseth thee to exercise mee, awaken me to consider how terrible thy severe justice is; but even the rest and security which thou affordest mee, puts me often into fear, that thou reservest and sparest me for a greater measure of punishment. O Lord, I most humbly acknowledge and confesse, that I have understood sin, by understanding thy laws and judgments; but have done against thy known and revealed will. Thou hast set up many candlesticks, and kindled many lamps in mee; but I have either blown them out, or carried them to guide me in by and forbidden ways. Thou hast given mee a desire of knowledge, and some meanes to it, and some possession of it; and I have armed my self with thy weapons against thee: Yet, O God, have mercy upon me, for thine own sake have mercy upon me. Let not sin and me be able to exceed thee, nor to defraud thee, nor to frustrate thy purposes: But let me, in despite of Me, be of so much use to thy glory, that by thy mercy to my sin, other sinners may see how much sin thou canst pardon. Thus show mercy to many in one: And shew thy power and al-mightinesse upon thy self, by casting manacles upon thine own hands, and calling back those Thunder-bolts which thou hadst thrown against me. Show thy Justice upon the common Seducer and Devourer of us all: and show us so much of thy Judgments, as may instruct, not condemn us. Hear us, O God, hear us, for this contrition which thou hast put into us, who come to thee with that watch-word, by which thy Son hath assured us of access. *Our Father which art in Heaven, &c.*

III

O ETERNALL God, who art not only first and last, but in whom, first and last is all one, who art not only all Mercy, and all Justice, but in whom Mercy and Justice is all one; who in the height of thy Justice, wouldst not spare thine own, and only most innocent Son; and yet in the depth of thy mercy, would'st not have the wretched'st liver come to destruction; Behold us,

O God, here gathered together in thy fear, according to thine ordinance, and in confidence of thy promise, that when two or three are gathered together in thy name, thou wilt be in the midst of them, and grant them their petitions. We confess O God, that we are not worthy so much as to confess: less to be heard, least of all to be pardoned our manifold sins and transgressions against thee. We have betrayed thy Temples to prophaness, our bodies to sensuality, thy fortresses to thine enemy, our soules to Satan. We have armed him with thy munition to fight against thee, by surrendring our eyes, and eares, all our senses, all our faculties to be exercised and wrought upon, and tyrannized by him. Vanities and disguises have covered us, and thereby we are naked; licenciousness hath inflam'd us, and thereby we are frozen; voluptuousness hath fed us, and thereby we are sterved, the fancies and traditions of men have taught and instructed us, and thereby we are ignorant. These distempers, thou only, O God, who art true, and perfect harmonie, canst tune, and rectify, and set in order again. Doe so then, O most Merciful Father, for thy most innocent Sons sake: and since he hath spread his armes upon the cross, to receive the whole world, O Lord, shut out none of us (who are now fallen before the throne of thy Majesty and thy Mercy) from the benefit of his merits; but with as many of us, as begin their conversion and newness of life, this minute, this minute, O God, begin thou thy account with them, and put all that is past out of thy remembrance. Accept our humble thanks for all thy Mercies; and, continue and enlarge them upon the whole Church, etc.

IV

O most glorious and most gracious God, into whose presence our own consciences make us afraid to come, and from whose presence we cannot hide our selves, hide us in the wounds of thy Son, our Saviour Christ Jesus; And though our sins be as red as scarlet, give them there another redness, which may be acceptable in thy sight. We renounce, O Lord, all our confidence in this world; for this world passeth away, and the lusts thereof: Wee renounce all our confidence in our own merits for we have done nothing in respect of that which we might have done; neither could we ever have done any such thing, but that still we must have remained unprofitable servants to thee: we renounce all confidence, even in our own confessions.

and accusations of our self; for our sins are above number, if we would reckon them; above weight and measure, if we would weigh and measure them; and past finding out, if we would seek them in those dark corners, in which we have multiplied them against thee: yea we renounce all confidence even in our repentances; for we have found by many lamentable experiences that we never perform our promises to thee, never perfect our purposes in our selves, but relapse again and again into those sins which again and again we have repented. We have no confidence in this world, but in him who hath taken possession of the next world for us, by sitting down at thy right hand. We have no confidence in our merits, but in him, whose merits thou hast been pleased to accept for us, and to apply to us, we have: no confidence in our own confessions and repentances, but in that blessed Spirit, who is the Author of them, and loves to perfect his own works and build upon his own foundations, we have: Accept them therefore, O Lord, for their sakes whose they are; our poor endeavours, for thy glorious Sons sake, who gives them their root, and so they are his; our poor beginnings of sanctification, for thy blessed Spirits sake, who gives their growth, and so they are his: and for thy Sons sake, in whom only our prayers are acceptable to thee: and for thy Spirits sake which is now in us, and must be so whensoever we do pray acceptably to thee; accept our humble prayers for, etc.

v

O ETERNAL and most merciful God, against whom, as we know and acknowledge that we have multiplied contemptuous and rebellious sins, so we know and acknowledge too, that it were a more sinfull contempt and rebellion, than all those, to doubt of thy mercy for them; have mercy upon us: In the merits and mediation of thy Son, our Saviour Christ Jesus, be mercifull unto us. Suffer not, O Lord, so great a waste, as the effusion of his blood, without any return to thee; suffer not the expence of so rich a treasure, as the spending of his life, without any purchace to thee; but as thou didst empty and evacuate his glory here upon earth, glorify us with that glory which his humiliation purchased for us in the kingdom of Heaven. And as thou didst empty that Kingdome of thine, in a great part, by the banishment of those Angels, whose pride threw them into everlasting ruine, be pleased to repair that Kingdom, which their fall did so far depopulate, by assuming us into their places, and making us rich with their confiscations. And to that purpose, O Lord, make us capable of that succession to thine Angels there; begin in us here in this life an angelicall purity, an angelicall chastity, an angelicall integrity to thy service, an Angelical acknowledgment that we alwaies stand in thy presence, and should direct all our actions to thy glory. Rebuke us not, O Lord, in thine anger, that we have not done so till now; but enable us now to begin that great work; and imprint in us an assurance that thou receivest us now graciously, as reconciled, though enemies; and fatherly, as children, though prodigals; and powerfully, as the God of our Salvation, though our own consciences testifie against us. Continue and enlarge thy blessings upon the whole Church, etc.

LETTERS

[TO———?]

[August 1597]

THE first act of that play which I sayd I would go over the water to see is done and yet the people hisse. How it will end I know not ast ego vicissim (Cicero). It is true that Jonas was in a whales belly three dayes but hee came not voluntary as I did nor was troubled with the stinke of 150 land soldiers as wee; and I was there 20 dayes of so very very bad wether that even some of the marriners have beene drawen to thinke it were not altogether amisse to pray, and my self heard one of them say god help us. For all our paynes wee have seene the land of promise Spaine; whether wee shall enter or no I guess not; I think there is a blott in their tables but perchaunce tis not on our dice to hitt it. Wee are now againe at Plymouth quasi ply-mouth; for wee do nothing but eate and scarce that: I think when wee came in the burghers tooke us for the spanish fleet for they have either hid or convayd all there mony. Never was extreame beggery so extreamely brave except when a company of mummers had lost theire box. I do not think that 77 Kelleys could distill 10 1. out of all the towne. He that hath supt and hath 2 or 3s is a king; for none hath a crowne fayth; lands, jerkins, knighthoods, are reprobate pawnes and but for the much gay cloathes (which yet are much melted) I should thinke wee were in utopia: all are so utterly coyneles. In one bad bare word the want is so generall that the lord general wants, and till this day wee wanted the lord generall: you will pardone me if I write nothing ernest. Salute all whome thou lovest in my name and love me as I would deserve.

Written from Plymouth.

[Burley MS.]

[TO SIR HENRY WOTTON?]

SIR,   [1600?]

ONLY in obedience I send you some of my paradoxes: I love you and myself and them too well to send them willingly for they carry with them a confession of there lightnes, and your trouble and my shame. But indeed they were made rather to deceave tyme than her daughther truth: although they have beene written in an age when any thing is strong enough to overthrow her. If they make you to find better reasons against them they do there office: for they are but swaggerers: quiet enough if you resist them. If perchaunce they be pretyly guilt, that is there best for they are not hatcht: they are rather alarums to truth to arme her than enemies: and they have only this advantadge to scape from being caled ill things that they are nothings. Therefore take heed of allowing any of them least you make another. Yet Sir though I know there low price, except I receive by your next letter an assurance upon the religion of your friendship that no coppy shall bee taken for any respect of these or any other my compositions sent to you, I shall sinn against my conscience if I send you any more. I speake that in playnes which becomes (methinkes) our honest-yes; and therefore call not this a distrustfull but a free spirit: I meane to acquaint you with all mine: and to my satyrs there belongs some feare and to some elegies and these perhaps, shame. Against both which affections although I be tough enough, yet I have a ridling disposition to bee ashamed of feare and afrayd of shame. Therefore I am desirous to hyde them with out any over reconing of them or there maker. But they are not worth thus much words in theyre disprayse. I will step to a better subject, your last letter, to which I need not tell I made no answere but I had need excuse it. All your letter I embrace and beleeve it when it speakes of your self and when of me too, if the good words which you speake of me bee ment of my intentions to goodnes: for else alas! no man is more beggerly in actuall vertue than I. I am sory you should (with any great earnestnes) desyre any thing of P. Aretinus, not that he could infect; but

that it seemes you are alredy infected with the common opinion of him: beleeve me he is much lesse than his fame and
was too well payd by the Roman church in that coyne which he
coveted most where his bookes were by the counsell of Trent
forbidden which if they had beene permitted to have beene
worne by all long ere this had beene worne out: his divinyty
was but a sirrope to enwrapp his prophane bookes to get them
passage, yet in these bookes which have devine titles there is
least harme as in his letters most good: his others have no other
singularyty in them but that they are forbidden. The psalmes
(which you aske) If I cannot shortly procure you one to poses
I can and will at any tyme borrow for you: In the meane tyme
Sir have the honor of forgiving two faults togeather: my not
writing last tyme and my abrupt ending now.

[Burley MS.]

[TO SIR HENRY WOTTON?]

SIR,   [c. 1600?]

I AM no great voyager in other mens works: no swallower
nor devourer of volumes nor pursuant of authors. Perchaunce it
is because I find borne in my self knowledge or apprehension
enough, for (without forfeiture or impeachment of modesty) I
think I am bond to God thankfully to acknowledge it) to con-
syder him and my self: as when I have at home a convenient
garden I covet not to walk in others broad medows or woods,
especially because it falls not within that short reach which my
foresight embraceth, to see how I should employ that which I
already know; to travayle for inquiry of more were to labor to
gett a stomach and then find no meat at home. To know how
to live by the booke is a pedantery, and to do it is a bondage.
For both hearers and players are more delighted with voluntary than with sett musike. And he that will live by precept
shall be long without the habite of honesty: as he that would
every day gather one or two feathers might become brawne
with hard lying before he make a feather bed of his gettings.
That Erle of Arundell that last dyed (that tennis ball whome
fortune after tossing and banding brikwald into the hazard) in
his imprisonment used more than much reading, and to him
that asked him why he did so he answered he read so much
lest he should remember something. I am as far from following
his counsell as hee was from Petruccios: but I find it true that
after long reading I can only tell you how many leaves I have

read. I do therfore more willingly blow and keep awake that
smale coale which God hath pleased to kindle in mee than farr
off to gather a faggott of greene sticks which consume without
flame or heat in a black smoother: yet I read something. But
indeed not so much to avoyd as to enjoy idlenes. Even when I
begun to write these I flung away Dant the Italian, a man pert
enough to bee beloved and too much to bee beeleeved: it
angred me that Celestine a pope [so] far from the manners of
other popes, that he left even their seat, should by the court of
Dants witt bee attacked and by him throwne into his purgatory.
And it angred me as much, that in the life of a pope he should
spy no greater fault, than that in the affectation of a cowardly
securyty he slipt from the great burthen layd upon him. Alas!
what would Dant have him do? Thus wee find the story related: he that thought himself next in succession, by a trunke
thorough a wall whispered in Celestines eare counsell to remove
the papacy: why should not Dant be content to thinke that
Celestine tooke this for as imediate a salutacion and discourse of
the holy ghost as Abraham did the commandment of killing his
sonn? If he will needs punish retyrednes thus, what hell can his
witt devise for ambition? And if white integryty merit this,
what shall Male or Malum which Seneca condems most, deserve? But as the chancellor Hatton being told after a decree
made, that his predecessors was of another opinion, he answered
hee had his genius and I had myne. So say I of authors that
they thinke and I thinke both reasonably yet posibly both er-
roniously; that is manly: for I am so far from perswading yea
conselling you to beleeve others that I care not that you beleeve
not mee when I say that others are not to bee beleeved: only
beleeve that I love you and I have enough.

I have studied philosophy, therefore marvayle not if I make
such accompt of arguments qui trahuntur ab effectibus.

[Burley MS.]

TO SIR GEORGE MORE

Sir,

If a very respective feare of your displeasure, and a doubt
that my Lord whom I know owt of your worthiness to love you
much, would be so compassionate with you as to add his anger
to yours, did not so much increase my sicknes as that I cannot
stir, I had taken the boldnes to have donne the office of this
letter by wayting upon you myself to have given you truthe

and clearnes of this matter between your daughter and me, and
to show you plainly the limits of our fault, by which I know
your wisdome will proportion the punishment. So long since as
her being at York House this had foundacion, and so much
then of promise and contract built upon it withowt violence to
conscience might not be shaken. At her lyeing in town this
last Parliament, I found meanes to see her twice or thrice. We
both knew the obligacions that lay upon us, and we adventured
equally, and about three weeks before Christmas we married.
And as at the doinge, there were not usd above fyve persons,
of which I protest to you by my salvation, there was not one
that had any dependence or relation to you, so in all the
passage of it did I forbear to use any suche person, who by
furtheringe of it might violate any trust or duty towards you.
The reasons why I did not foreacquaint you with it (to deale
with the same plainnes that I have usd) were these. I knew
my present estate lesse than fitt for her, I knew (yet I knew
not why) that I stood not right in your opinion. I knew that to
have given any intimacion of it had been to impossibilitate
the whole matter. And then having these honest purposes in
our harts, and those fetters in our consciences, me thinks we
should be pardoned, if our fault be but this, that wee did not,
by fore-revealinge of it, consent to our hindrance and torment.
Sir, I acknowledge my fault to be so great, as I dare scarse
offer any other prayer to you in mine own behalf than this, to
beleeve this truthe, that I neyther had dishonest end nor
meanes. But for her whom I tender much more than my fortunes or lyfe (els I woould I might neyther joy in this lyfe, nor
enjoy the next), I humbly beg of you that she may not to her
danger feele the terror of your sodaine anger. I know this
letter shall find you full of passioñ; but I know no passion can
alter your reason and wisdome, to which I adventure to commend these particulers; that it is irremediably donne; that if
you incense my Lord you destroy her and me; that it is easye to
give us happines, and that my endevors and industrie, if it please
you to prosper them, may soone make me somewhat worthyer of
her. If any take the advantage of your displeasure against me,
and fill you with ill thoughts of me, my comfort is, that you
know that fayth and thanks are due to them onely, that speak
when theyr informacions might do good; which now it cannot
work towards any party. For my excuse I can say nothing, except I knew what were sayd to you. Sir, I have truly told you
this matter, and I humbly beseeche you so to deale in it as the

persuasions of Nature, Reason, Wisdome, and Christianity shall inform you; and to accept the vowes of one whom you may now rayse or scatter, which are that as my love is directed unchangeably upon her, so all my labors shall concur to her contentment, and to show my humble obedience to your self.

Yours in all duty and humblenes,

J. DONNE.

From my lodginge by the Savoy,
    2 Februa: 1601 [/2].
To the right wor. Sir George
    More, kt.

[Loseley MSS.–Kempe]

TO SIR GEORGE MORE

SIR,   [Feb. 1601]

THE inward accusacions in my conscience, that I have offended you beyond any ability of redeeming it by me, and the feeling of my Lord's heavy displeasure following it, forceth me to wright, though I know my faults make my letters very ungracious to you. Allmighty God, whom I call to witnesse that all my griefe is that I have in this manner offended you and him, direct you to beleeve that which owt of an humble and afflicted hart I now wright to you. And since we have no meanes to move God, when he will not hear our prayers, to hear them, but by prayeng, I humbly beseech you to allow by his gracious example, my penitence so good entertainment, as it may have a beeliefe and a pittie. Of nothinge in this one fault that I hear sayd to me, can I disculpe myselfe, but of the contemptuous and despightfull purpose towards you, which I hear is surmised against me. But for my dutifull regard to my late lady, for my religion, and for my lyfe, I refer my selfe to them that may have observed them. I humbly beseech you to take off these waytes, and to put my fault into the balance alone, as it was donne with out the addicon of these ill reports, and though then it wyll be too heavy for me, yett then it will less grieve you to pardon it. How litle and how short the comfort and pleasure of destroyeng is, I know your wisdome and religion informs you. And though perchance you intend not utter destruction, yett the way through which I fall towards it is so headlong, that beeing thus pushed, I shall soone be at bottome, for it pleaseth God, from whom I acknowledge the punishment to be just, to accompany my other ills with so much sicknes as I have no refuge but that of mercy, which I beg of him, my Lord, and you, which I hope you will not repent to have afforded me, since all my endevors, and the whole course of my lyfe shal be bent, to make my selfe worthy of your favor and her love, whose peace of conscience and quiett I know must be much wounded and violenced if your displeasure sever us. I can present nothing to your thoughts which you knew not before, but my submission, my repentance, and my harty desire to do any thing satisfactory to your just displeasure. Of which I beseech you to make a charitable use and construction. From the Fleete, 11 Febr. 1601.

> Yours in all faythfull duty and obedience,
>
> J. DONNE

To the right wor. Sir Geo.
    More, kt.

[Loseley MSS.–Kempe]

TO SIR THOMAS EGERTON

[1601]

THE honorable favor that your Lordship hath afforded me, in allowinge me the liberty of mine own chamber, hath given me leave so much to respect and love myself, that now I can desire to be well. And therfore health, not pleasure (of which your Lordships displeasure hath dulld in me all tast and apprehension), I humbly beseeche your Lordship so much more to slacken my fetters, that as I ame by your Lordships favor mine own keeper, and surety, so I may be mine owne phisician and apothecary, which your Lordship shall worke, if you graunt me liberty to take the ayre about this towne. The whole world is a streight imprisonment to me, whilst I ame barrd your Lordships sight; but this favor may lengthen and better my lyfe, which I desire to preserve, onely in hope to redeeme by my sorrowe and desire to do your Lordship service, my offence past. Allmighty God dwell ever in your Lordships hart, and fill it with good desires, and graunt them.

> Your Lordships poorest servant,
>
> J. DONNE

To the right honorable my very
good Lord and Master Sir Thomas
Egerton, knight, Lord Keeper of
the Great Seale of England.

[Loseley MSS.–Kempe]

TO SIR [HENRY GOODYER]

[c. 1604?]

IF you were here, you would not think me importune, if I
bid you good morrow every day; and such a patience will excuse my often Letters. No other kinde of conveyance is better
for knowledge, or love: What treasures of Morall knowledge
are in *Senecaes* Letters to onely one *Lucilius?* And what of
Naturall in *Plinies?* How much of the storie of the time, is in
Ciceroes Letters? And how of all these times, in the Jesuites
Eastern and Western Epistles? Where can we finde so perfect
a Character of *Phalaris,* as in his own Letters, which are almost
so many writs of Execution? Or of *Brutus,* as in his privie seals
for monie? The Evangiles and Acts, teach us what to beleeve,
but the Epistles of the Apostles what to do. And those who
have endevoured to dignifie *Seneca* above his worth, have no
way fitter, than to imagine Letters between him and S. *Paul.*
As they think also that they have expressed an excellent person,
in that Letter which they obtrude, from our B. Saviour to
King *Agabarus.* The Italians, which are most discursive, and
think the world owes them all wisdome, abound so much in
this kinde of expressing, that *Michel Montaig[n]e* saies, he
hath seen, (as I remember) 400 volumes of Italian Letters. But
it is the other capacity which must make mine acceptable, that
they are also the best conveyers of love. But, though all knowledge be in those Authors already, yet, as some poisons, and
some medicines, hurt not, nor profit, except the creature in
which they reside, contribute their lively activitie, and vigor; so,
much of the knowledge buried in Books perisheth, and becomes
ineffectuall, if it be not applied, and refreshed by a companion,
or friend. Much of their goodnesse, hath the same period, which
some Physicians of *Italy* have observed to be in the biting of
their *Tarentola,* that it affects no longer, than the flie lives. For
with how much desire we read the papers of any living now,
(especially friends) which we would scarce allow a boxe in our
cabinet, or shelf in our Library, if they were dead! And we do
justly in it, for the writings and words of men present, we
may examine, controll, and expostulate, and receive satisfaction
from the authors; but the other we must beleeve, or discredit;
they present no mean. Since then at this time, I am upon the
stage, you may be content to hear me. And now that perchance

I have brought you to it, (as *Thom. Badger* did the King) now I have nothing to say. And it is well, for the Letter is already long enough, else let this probleme supply, which was occasioned by you, of women wearing stones; which, it seems, you were afraid women should read, because you avert them at the beginning, with a protestation of cleanlinesse. *Martiall* found no way fitter to draw the Romane Matrons to read one of his Books, which he thinks most morall and cleanly, than to counsell them by the first Epigram to skip the Book, because it was obscene. But either you write not at all for women, or for those of sincerer palates. Though their unworthinesse, and your own ease be advocates for me with you, yet I must adde my entreaty, that you let goe no copy of my Problems, till I review them. If it be too late, at least be able to tell me who hath them.

Yours,

J. DONNE
[*Letters,* 1651]

TO SIR H[ENRY]. G[OODYER].

Sir,   [Mitcham, c. 1608]

BECAUSE I am in a place and season where I see every thing bud forth, I must do so too, and vent some of my meditations to you; the rather because all other buds being yet without taste or virtue, my Letters may be like them. The pleasantnesse of the season displeases me. Every thing refreshes, and I wither, and I grow older and not better, my strength diminishes, and my load growes, and being to passe more and more stormes, I finde that I have not only cast out all my ballast which nature and time gives, Reason and discretion, and so am as empty and light as Vanity can make me; but I have over fraught my self with Vice, and so am ridd[l]ingly subject to two contrary wrackes, Sinking and Oversetting, and under the iniquity of such a disease as inforces the patient when he is almost starved, not only to fast, but to purge. For I have much to take in, and much to cast out; sometimes I thinke it easier to discharge my self of vice than of vanity, as one may sooner carry the fire out of a room than the smoake: and then I see it was a new vanity to think so. And when I think sometimes that vanity, because it is thinne and airie, may be expelled with vertue or businesse, or substantiall vice; I find that I give entrance thereby to new vices. Certainly as the earth and water, one sad, the other fluid, make but one bodie: so to aire and Vanity, there is but one *Centrum morbi*. And that which later Physicians say of our bodies, is fitter for our mindes: for that which they call Destruction, which is a corruption and want of those fundamentall parts whereof we consist, is Vice: and that *Collectio stercorum*, which is but the excrement of that corruption, is our Vanity and indiscretion: both these have but one root in me, and must be pulled out at once, or never. But I am so farre from digging to it, that I know not where it is, for it is not in mine eyes only, but in every sense, nor in my concupiscence only, but in every power and affection. Sir, I was willing to let you see how impotent a man you love, not to dishearten you from doing so still (for my vices are not infectious, nor wandring, they came not yesterday, nor mean to go away to day: they Inne not, but dwell in me, and see themselves so welcome, and find in me so good bad company of one another, that they will not change, especially to one not apprehensive, nor easily accessible) but I do it, that your counsell might cure me, and if you deny that, your example shal, for I will as much strive to be like you as I will wish you to continue good.

[Letters, 1651]

TO SIR H[ENRY]. G[OODYER].

SIR,   [c. 1608]
    THIS letter hath no more merit, than one of more diligence, for I wrote it in my bed, and with much pain. I have occasion to sit late some nights in my study, (which your books make a pretty library) and now I finde that that room hath a wholesome emblematique use: for having under it a vault, I make that promise me, that I shall die reading, since my book and a grave are so near. But it hath another as unwholesome, that by raw vapors rising from thence, (for I can impute it to nothing else) I have contracted a sicknesse which I cannot name nor describe. For it hath so much of a continuall Cramp, that it wrests the sinews, so much of a Tetane, that it withdraws and puls the mouth, and so much of the Gout, (which they whose counsell I use, say it is) that it is not like to be cured, though I am too hasty in three days to pronounce it. If it be the Gout, I am miserable; for that affects dangerous parts, as my neck

and brest, and (I think fearfully) my stomach, but it will not
kill me yet; I shall be in this world, like a porter in a great
house, ever nearest the door, but seldomest abroad: I shall have
many things to make me weary, and yet not get leave to be
gone. If I go, I will provide by my best means that you suffer
not for me, in your bonds. The estate which I should leave behinde me of any estimation, is my poor fame, in the memory
of my friends, and therefore I would be curious of it, and provide that they repent not, to have loved me. Since my imprisonment in my bed, I have made a meditation in verse, which I
call a Litany; the word you know imports no other than supplication, but all Churches have one forme of supplication, by
that name. Amongst ancient annals, I mean some 800 years, I
have met two Letanies in Latin verse, which gave me not the
reason of my meditations, for in good faith I thought not upon
them then, but they give me a defence, if any man; to a Lay
man, and a private, impute it as a fault, to take such divine
and publique names, to his own little thoughts. The first of
these was made by *Ratpertus,* a monk of *Suevia;* and the other
by S. *Notker,* of whom I will give you this note by the way,
that he is a private Saint, for a few Parishes; they were both
but Monks, and the Letanies poor and barbarous enough; yet
Pope *Nicolas* the 5, valued their devotion so much, that he canonized both their Poems, and commanded them for publike
service in their Churches: mine is for lesser Chappels, which are
my friends, and though a copy of it were due to you, now, yet
I am so unable to serve my self with writing it for you at this
time, (being some 30 staves of 9 lines) that I must intreat you
to take a promise that you shall have the first, for a testimony
of that duty which I owe to your love, and to my self, who am
bound to cherish it by my best offices. That by which it will
deserve best acceptation, is, That neither the Roman Church
need call it defective, because it abhors not the particular mention of the blessed Triumphers in heaven; nor the Reformed
can discreetly accuse it, of attributing more than a rectified devotion ought to doe. The day before I lay down, I was at *London,* where I delivered your Letter for *Sir Edward Conway,* and
received another for you, with the copy of my Book, of which
it is impossible for me to give you a copy so soon, for it is not
of much lesse than 300 pages. If I die, it shall come to you in
that fashion that your Letter desires it. If I warm again, (as I
have often seen such beggers as my indisposition is, end themselves soon, and the patient as soon) you and I shal speak to

gether of that, before it be too late to serve you in that commandment. At this time I onely assure you, that I have not appointed it upon any person, nor ever purposed to print it:
which latter perchance you thought, and grounded your request
thereupon. A Gent. that visited me yesterday told me that our
Church hath lost Mr. *Hugh Broughton,* who is gone to the Roman side. I have known before, that *Serarius* the Jesuit was an
instrument from Cardinall *Baronius* to draw him to Rome, to
accept a stipend, onely to serve the Christian Churches in controversies with the Jews, without indangering himself to
change of his perswasion in particular deductions between these
Christian Churches, or being enquired of, or tempted thereunto.
And I hope he is not otherwise departed from us. If he be, we
shall not escape scandall in it; because, though he be a man of
many distempers, yet when he shall come to eat assured bread,
and to be removed from partialities, to which want drove him,
to make himself a reputation and raise up favourers; you shall
see in that course of opposing the Jews, he will produce worthy
things: and our Church will perchance blush to have lost a
Souldier fit for that great battell; and to cherish onely those
single Duellisms, between *Rome* and *England,* or that more
single, and almost self-homicide, between the unconformed
Ministers, and Bishops. I writ to you last week that the plague
increased; by which you may see that my Letters [*blank space
in text*] opinion of the song, not that I make such trifles for
praise, but because as long as you speak comparatively of it
with mine own, and not absolutely, so long I am of your opinion even at this time; when I humbly thank God, I ask and
have, his comfort of sadder meditations; I doe not condemn in
my self, that I have given my wit such evaporations, as those, if
they be free from prophaneness, or obscene provocations. Sir
you would pity me if you saw me write, and therefore will pardon me if I write no more: my pain hath drawn my head so
much awry, and holds it so, that mine eye cannot follow mine
hand: I receive you therefore into my prayers, with mine own
weary soul, and commend my self to yours. I doubt not but
next week I shall be good news to you, for I have mending or
dying on my side, which is two to one. If I continue thus, I
shall have comfort in this, that my B. Saviour exercising his
Justice upon my two worldly parts, my fortune, and body, reserves all his mercy for that which best tasts it, and most needs
it, my soul. I professe to you truly, that my lothnesse to give

over now, seems to my self an ill sign, that I shall write no
more.

Your poor friend, and Gods poor patient,

Jo. Donne
[Letters, 1651]

TO SIR. H[ENRY]. GOODERE

Sir,   [Mitcham, Sept. 1608]
    Every tuesday I make account that I turn a great hourglass,
and consider that a weeks life is run out since I writ. But if I
ask myself what I have done in the last watch, or would do in
the next, I can say nothing; if I say that I have passed it without hurting any, so may the Spider in my window. The primitive Monkes were excusable in their retirings and enclosures of
themselves: for even of them every one cultivated his own garden and orchard, that is, his soul and body, by meditation, and
manufactures; and they ought the world no more since they
consumed none of her sweetnesse, nor begot others to burden
her. But for me, if I were able to husband all my time
so thriftily, as not onely not to wound my soul in any minute
by actuall sinne, but not to rob and cousen her by giving any
part to pleasure or businesse, but bestow it all upon her in
meditation, yet even in that I should wound her more, and contract another guiltinesse: As the Eagle were very unnaturall if
because she is able to do it, she should pearch a whole day
upon a tree, staring in contemplation of the majestie and glory
of the Sun, and let her young Eglets starve in the nest. Two of
the most precious things which God hath afforded us here, for
the agony and exercise of our sense and spirit, which are a
thirst and inhiation after the next life, and a frequency of
prayer and meditation in this, are often envenomed, and putre-
fied, and stray into a corrupt disease: for as God doth thus occasion, and positively concurre to evill, that when a man is purposed to do a great sin, God infuses some good thoughts which
make him choose a lesse sin, or leave out some circumstance
which aggravated that; so the devill doth not only suffer but
provoke us to some things naturally good, upon condition that
we shall omit some other more necessary and more obligatory.
And this is his greatest subtilty; because herein we have the
deceitfull comfort of having done well, and can very hardly spie

our errour because it is but an insensible omission, and no accusing act. With the first of these I have often suspected my self to be overtaken; which is, with a desire of the next life: which though I know it is not meerly out of a wearinesse of this, because I had the same desires when I went with the tyde, and enjoyed fairer hopes than now: yet I doubt worldly encombrances have encreased it. I would not that death should take me asleep. I would not have him meerly seise me, and onely declare me to be dead, but win me, and overcome me. When I must shipwrack, I would do it in a Sea, where mine impotencie might have some excuse; not in a sullen weedy lake, where I could not have so much as exercise for my swimming. Therefore I would fain do something; but that I cannot tell what, is no wonder. For to chuse, is to do: but to be no part of any body, is to be nothing. At most, the greatest persons, are but great wens, and excrescences; men of wit and delightfull conversation, but as moales for ornament, except they be so incorporated into the body of the world, that they contribute something to the sustentation of the whole. This I made account that I begun early, when I understood the study of our laws: but was diverted by the worst voluptuousness, which is an Hydroptique immoderate desire of humane learning and languages: beautifull ornaments to great fortunes; but mine needed an occupation, and a course which I thought I entred well into, when I submitted my self to such a service, as I thought might imploy those poor advantages, which I had. And there I stumbled too, yet I would try again: for to this hour I am nothing, or so little, that I am scarce subject and argument good enough for one of mine own letters: yet I fear, that doth not ever proceed from a good root, that I am so well content to be lesse, that is dead. You, Sir, are farre enough from these descents, your vertue keeps you secure, and your naturall disposition to mirth will preserve you; but lose none of these holds, a slip is often as dangerous as a bruise, and though you cannot fall to my lownesse, yet in a much lesse distraction you may meet my sadnesse; for he is no safer which falls from an high tower into the leads, than he which falls from thence to the ground: make therefore to your self some mark, and go towards it alegrement. Though I be in such a planetary and erratique fortune, that I can do nothing constantly, yet you may finde some constancy in my constant advising you to it.

Your hearty true friend

J. DONNE

I came this evening from Mr. Jones *his house in* Essex, *where Mr.* Martin *hath been, and left a relation of Captain* Whitcocks *death, perchance it is no news to you, but it was to me; without doubt want broke him; for when Mr.* Hollands *company by reason of the plague broke, the Captain sought to be at Mistress* Jones *house, who in her husbands absence declining it, he went in the night, his boy carrying his cloak-bag, on foot to the Lord of* Sussex, *who going next day to hunt, the Captain not then sick, told him he would see him no more. A Chaplain came up to him, to whom he delivered an account of his understanding, and I hope, of his beliefe, and soon after dyed; and my Lord hath buryed him with his own Ancestors. Perchance his life needed a longer sicknesse, but a man may go faster and safer, when he enjoyes that day light of a clear and sound understanding, than in the night or twilight of an ague or other disease. And the grace of Almighty God doth every thing suddenly and hastily, but depart from us; it inlightens us, warms us, heats us, ravishes us, at once. Such a medicin, I fear, his inconsideration needed; and I hope as confidently that he had it. As our soul is infused when it is created, and created when it is infused, so at her going out, Gods mercy is had by asking, and that is asked by having. Lest your* Polesworth *carrier should cousen me, I send my man with this letter early to* London, *whither this Tuesday all the Court come to a Christening at* Arondell *house, and stay in town so that I will sup with the good Lady, and write again to morrow to you, if any thing be occasioned there, which concerns you, and I will tell her so; next day they are to return to* Hampton, *and upon Friday the King to* Royston.

[*Letters,* 1651]

A V[UESTRA] MERCED
[TO YOUR WORSHIP; SIR HENRY GOODYER?]

Sir,   [c. 1609]

I write not to you out of my poor Library, where to cast mine eye upon good Authors kindles or refreshes sometimes meditations not unfit to communicate to near friends; nor from the high way, where I am contracted, and inverted into my self; which are my two ordinary forges of Letters to you. But I write from the fire side in my Parler, and in the noise of three gamesome children; and by the side of her, whom because I have transplanted into a wretched fortune, I must labour to disguise that from her by all such honest devices, as giving her my company, and discourse, therefore I steal from her, all the time which I give this Letter, and it is therefore that I take so short a list, and gallop so fast over it; I have not been out of my house since I received your pacquet. As I have much quenched my senses, and disused my body from pleasure, and so tried how I can indure to be mine own grave, so I try now how I can suffer a prison. And since it is but to build one wall more about our soul, she is still in her own Center, how many circumferences soever fortune or our own perversnesse cast about her. I would I could as well intreat her to go out, as she knows whither to go. But if I melt into a melancholy whilest I write, I shall be taken in the manner: and I sit by one too tender towards these impressions, and it is so much our duty, to avoid all occasions of giving them sad apprehensions, as S. *Hierome* accuses *Adam* of no other fault in eating the Apple, but that he did it *Ne contristaretur delicias suas*. I am not carefull what I write, because the inclosed Letters may dignifie this ill-favoured bark, and they need not grudge so coarse a countenance, because they are now to accompany themselves, my man fetched them, and therefore I can say no more of them than themselves say. Mistress *Meauly* intreated me by her Letter to hasten hers; as I think, for by my troth I cannot read it. My Lady was dispatching in so much haste for *Twicknam*, as she gave no word to a Letter which I sent with yours; of Sir *Tho. Bartlet*, I can say nothing, nor of the plague, though your Letter bid me: but that he diminishes, the other increases, but in what proportion I am not clear. To them at *Hammersmith*, and Mistress *Herbert* I will do your command. If I have been good in hope, or can promise any little offices in the future probably, it is comfortable, for I am the worst present man in the world; yet the instant, though it be nothing, joynes times together, and therefore this unprofitableness, since I have been, and will still indevour to be so, shall not interrupt me now from being

Your servant and lover

J. DONNE

[*Letters,* 1651]

TO SIR H[ENRY]. G[OODYER].

SIR, [c. 1609]

IT should be no interruption to your pleasures, to hear me often say that I love you, and that you are as much my meditations as my self: I often compare not you and me, but the sphear in which your resolutions are, and my wheel; both I hope concentrique to God: for me thinks the new Astronomie is thus appliable well, that we which are a little earth, should rather move towards God, than that he which is fulfilling, and can come no whither, should move towards us. To your life full of variety, nothing is old, nor new to mine; and as to that life, all stickings and hesitations seem stupid and stony, so to this, all fluid slipperinesses, and transitory migrations seem giddie and featherie. In that life one is ever in the porch or postern, going in or out, never within his house himself: It is a garment made of remnants, a life raveld out into ends, a line discontinued, and a number of small wretched points, uselesse, because they concurre not: A life built of past and future, not proposing any constant present; they have more pleasures than we, but not more pleasure; they joy oftener, we longer; and no man but of so much understanding as may deliver him from being a fool, would change with a mad-man, which had a better proportion of wit in his often *Lucidis*. You know, they which dwell farthest from the Sun, if in any convenient distance, have longer daies, better appetites, better digestion, better growth, and longer life: And all these advantages have their mindes who are well removed from the scorchings, and dazlings, and exhalings of the worlds glory: but neither of our lives are in such extremes; for you living at Court without ambition, which would burn you, or envy, which would devest others, live in the Sun, not in the fire: And I which live in the Country without stupefying, am not in darknesse, but in shadow, which is not no light, but a pallid, waterish, and diluted one. As all shadows are of one colour, if you respect the body from which they are cast, (for our shadows upon clay will be dirty, and in a garden green, and flowery) so all retirings into a shadowy life are alike from all causes, and alike subject to the barbarousnesse and insipid dulnesse of the Country: onely the emploiments, and that upon which you cast and bestow your pleasure, businesse, or books, gives it the tincture, and beauty. But truly wheresoever we are, if we can but tell our selves truly what and where we would be, we may make any state and place such; for we are so composed, that if abundance, or glory scorch and melt us, we have an earthly cave, our bodies, to go into by consideration, and cool our selves: and if we be frozen, and contracted with lower and dark fortunes, we have within us a torch, a soul, lighter and warmer than any without: we are therefore our

own umbrellas, and our own suns. These, Sir, are the sallads
and onions of *Micham,* sent to you with as wholesome affection
as your other friends send Melons and Quelque-choses from
Court and *London.* If I present you not as good diet as they, I
would yet say grace to theirs, and bid much good do it you. I
send you, with this, a Letter which I sent to the Countesse. It
is not my use nor duty to doe so, but for your having of it,
there were but two consents, and I am sure you have mine, and
you are sure you have hers. I also writ to her Ladyship for the
verses she shewed in the garden, which I did, not onely to extort them, nor onely to keep my promise of writing, for that I
had done in the other Letter, and perchance she hath forgotten
the promise; nor onely because I think my Letters just good
enough for a progresse, but because I would write apace to her,
whilest it is possible to expresse that which I yet know of her,
for by this growth I see how soon she will be ineffable.

[*Letters,* 1651]

[TO THE COUNTESS OF BEDFORD?]

[1608?–1614?]

THE Tyrrany of a suddaine raging sicknes (comfortable in
nothing but the violence of itt) assures that either itt or I are
short lived, having found either vertue or stubbernes inough
in me to disdaine all bitternes that itt can make against my
body, now assayles my mind and shews me that (by imprison-
ing me in my chamber) itt is able to deprive me of that happines which by your grace was allowed me when you gave me
the priviledge of having leave to visit you. I confesse that this
is my sicknes worst fitt and as fearefully ominous as Tamerlins
last dayes black ensignes whose threatnings none scaped. Let
not your charity therefore desdayne to [j]oyne with me, in an
honest deceit, to breake this tempest of my sicknes, and since
this letter hath my name, and hand, and words, and thoughts,
bee content to thinke itt me, and to give itt leave thus
to speake to you, though you vouchsafe not to speake to itt
againe. It shall tell you truly (for from me itt sucked no levin
of flattery) with what height or rather lownes of devotion I
reverence you: who besides the commandment of a noble birth,
and your perswasive eloquence of beauty, have the advantage of
the furniture of arts and languages, and such other vertues as
might serve to justify a reprobate fortune and the lowest con-

dition: soe that if these things whereby some few other are named are made worthy, are to you but ornaments, such might be left without leaving you unperfect. To that treasure of your vertues whereof your fayre eyes curtesy is not the least jewell I present this paper: and if itt be not too much boldnes in itt my excuse of not visiting you. And so kindly kissing your fayre hand that vouchsafes the receipt of these lines I take leave.

[Burley MS.]

TO THE PRINCE [OF WALES]

[1610]

NEXT to that boldness of having dedicated this booke to our soveraigne lord your Highnes father, it were the greatest boldnes that I could committ not to present to your Highnes a copy thereof, who are so perfitt a copy of him. For though this booke be none of those things which devolve upon you because they are his (for by so great a title as that, onely kingdomes and vertues belong to you) yett itt belongs to your Highnes because itt endevors to prepare and dispose some irresolved and undetermined persons to an obedience of our lawes, and so it respects and relates to future tymes which are yours. Though therefore some extreme contemplative philosophers have thought itt to be the highest degree of reverence which man could use towards God to abstaine from outward sacrifices and from verball prayer, because nothinge but our purest thoughts, before they are mingled with any affections or passions, can have any proportion to God or gett within any distance of him, yett they errd, because they thought we went to God in these actions when indeed God comes to us. So also do princes descend to receive the offices of such men as cannot reach up to them; for therefore hath God allowed them so many of his own attributes, that they might not take a measure of their greatnes by the lownes of others but by their conforminge themselves to him and doinge as he doth. And therefore though I might have performed some part of my duty by continuinge in my private prayers in my study for your Highnes and this state, yett I cannot fear but that you will also descend to this and accept the same duty as it is thus uttered and apparelled in this booke. For since as well as the whole body of this state I also felt the benefitt and sweetnes which we enjoy in this government, itt became mee to contrib-

ute some thinge in testimony of my thankfullnes and onely in
wishinge your Highnes happines and in this matter of express-
inge itt, am I a subsidy man.

[Bath MSS.]

TO MY HONOURED FRIEND G[EORGE].
G[ARRARD]. ESQUIRE

Sir,

NEITHER your Letters, nor silence, needs excuse; your friendship is to me an abundant possession, though you remember me
but twice in a year: He that could have two harvests in that
time, might justly value his land at a high rate; but, Sir, as we
doe not onely then thank our land, when we gather the fruit,
but acknowledge that all the year she doth many motherly offices in preparing it: so is not friendship then onely to be esteemed, when she is delivered of a Letter, or any other reall
office, but in her continuall propensnesse and inclination to do
it. This hath made me easie in pardoning my long silences, and
in promising my self your forgivenesse for not answering your
Letter sooner. For my purpose of proceeding in the profession
of the law, so farre as to a title you may be pleased to correct
that imagination, wheresoever you finde it. I ever thought the
study of it my best entertainment, and pastime, but I have no
ambition, nor designe upon the style. Of my Anniversaries, the
fault that I acknowledge in my self, is to have descended to
print any thing in verse, which though it have excuse even in
our times, by men who professe, and practise much gravitie;
yet I confesse I wonder how I declined to it, and do not pardon my self: But for the other part of the imputation of having said too much, my defence is, that my purpose was to say
as well as I could: for since I never saw the Gentlewoman, I
cannot be understood to have bound my self to have spoken
just truths, but I would not be thought to have gone about to
praise her, or any other in rime: except I took such a person,
as might be capable of all that I could say. If any of those
Ladies think that Mistris *Drewry* was not so, let that Lady make
her self fit for all those praises in the book, and they shall be
hers. Sir, this messenger makes so much haste that I cry you
mercy for spending any time of this letter in other imployment
than thanking you for yours. I hope before *Christmas* to see
England, and kisse your hand, which shall ever, (if it disdain

not that office) hold all the keyes of the libertie and affection,
and all the faculties of

Your most affectionate servant,

J. D.

Paris the 14th of
Aprill, here, 1612.

[*Letters,* 1651]

IN KINDNESSE SENT TO AN ABSENT FRIEND
[GEORGE GARRARD?]

SIR,   [c. 1613?]
    YOUR long silence, could never bring me to any doubt of
having lost my Title to your friendship. It shall not be in
your power, to be able, so to prescribe, even in your self,
against me, but that still I will be making my continuall claim
to your love. For Friendship hath so much of Soveraignty, yea
and of Religion too, that no prescription can be admitted
against it. And as for losing you by any forfeit, or demerit on
my part, I have been very carefull, and shall be watchfull still,
to blesse my self from such a curse, as that. And indeed, such
care is all the merit, which can be hoped for, at the hands of a
person, so uselesse as my self. And from this care now proceeds
my haste, to thank you for your last Letter; and to begge a
preservation of that love, which though, at first, it fell not directly, and immediately upon my self, but by way of reflection
or Briccole, through your other Friends (to use the Metaphor of
a Game, wherein I congratulate that excellencie, to which my
Lord *Clifford* tells me, you have arrived) yet now I dare conceive, that your love belongs to me, even as a kind of due;
since I see, you now discern that I am so much in earnest in
loving you.

[Sir Tobie Mathews Collection, 1660]

TO THE HONORABLE KT. SIR EDWARD
HERBERT

SIR,
    BECAUSE since I had the honor to see you, or hear from you,
I have receyved such a change, as, if my unworthynes did not
avile it, were an addition, I ame bold to present to you the
knowledge thereof: because therby your power, and jurisdiction,

which is entirely over mee, is somewhat enlardged. For, as if I should put any other stampe upon a peece of your gold, the gold were not the lesse yours, so (if there be not too much taken by mee, in that comparison) by havinge, by the orders of our churche, receyved a new character, I ame not departed from your title, and possession of mee. But, as I was ever, by my devotion, and your acceptance, your humble servant, so I ame become, by this addition, capable of the dignity, of beeinge

Your very humble
chapleyn

23 Jan. 1614 [/5] which was   J. DONNE
the very day wherein I
took orders.

[Herbert MSS.]

WITH A KIND OF LABOUR'D COMPLEMENT
TO A FRIEND OF HIS

SIR,   [c. 1614?]

THERE is a dangerous Rule in Law, *Socius socii mei, non est socius meus*. If it extend to Friendship, as well as to Familiaritie, I who can pretend no other title to your friendship, than that I am allowed some little interest in them, who have more in you, may well account my self to be within the danger of it. But, as in Divine, so in Morall things, where the beginning is from others, the assistance, and co-operation, is in our selves. I therefore, who could do nothing towards the begetting, would fain do somewhat towards the breeding and cherishing of such degrees of friendship, as formerly I had the honour to hold with you. If Letters be not able to do that office, they are yet able, at least, to testifie, that he, who sends them, would be glad to do more, if he could. I have a great desire, not without some hope, to see you this Summer there; and I have more hope and more desire, to see you this next Winter here; and I have abundantly more of both, that, at least, we shall meet in Heaven. That we differ in our wayes, I hope we pardon one another. Men go to *China*, both by the Straights, and by the *Cape*. I never mis-interpreted your way; nor suffered it to be so, wheresoever I found it in discourse. For I was sure, you took not up your Religion upon trust, but payed ready money for it, and at a high Rate. And this taste of mine towards you, makes me hope for, and claime the same disposition in you towards me. I am sure, this messenger beares so many Letters to you, as if this of mine (which is written upon the first day of my comming to Town) should offer at any thing of the Times, it might perhaps shake your beliefe from somewhat, expressed in some of your other Letters, by my relating them diverselie. For it is but earlie daies with me here; and I see not things so distinctlie yet, as to lay them under such eyes as yours. This Letter doth therefore onely aske your safe conduct, for those others of mine, which are to follow, as the most constant testimonies of my love, etc.

[Sir Tobie Mathews Collection, 1660]

TO MY VERY TRUE AND VERY GOOD FRIEND
SIR HENRY GOODERE

Sir,   [April 1615?]
At some later reading, I was more affected with that part of your Letter, which is of the book, and the namelesse Letters, than at first. I am not sorry, for that affection were for a jealousie or suspicion of a flexibility in you. But I am angry, that any should think, you had in your Religion peccant humours, defective, or abundant, or that such a booke, (if I mistake it not) should be able to work upon you; my comfort is, that their judgment is too weak to endanger you, since by this it confesses, that it mistakes you, in thinking you irresolved or various: yet let me be bold to fear, that that sound true opinion, that in all Christian professions there is way to salvation (which I think you think) may have been so incommodiously or intempestively sometimes uttered by you; or else your having friends equally near you of all the impressions of Religion, may have testified such an indifferency, as hath occasioned some to further such inclinations, as they have mistaken to be in you. This I have feared, because hertofore the inobedient Puritans, and now the over-obedient Papists attempt you. It hath hurt very many, not in their conscience, nor ends, but in their reputation, and ways, that others have thought them fit to be wrought upon. As some bodies are as wholesomly nourished as ours, with Akornes, and endure nakednesse, both which would be dangerous to us, if we for them should leave our former habits, though theirs were the Primitive diet and custome: so are many souls well fed with such formes, and dressings of Religion, as would distemper and misbecome us, and

make us corrupt towards God, if any humane circumstance
moved it, and in the opinion of men, though none. You shall
seldome see a Coyne, upon which the stamp were removed,
though to imprint it better, but it looks awry and squint. And
so, for the most part, do mindes which have received divers
impressions. I will not, nor need to you, compare the Religions. The channels of Gods mercies run through both fields;
and they are sister teats of his graces, yet both diseased and infected, but not both alike. And I think, that as *Copernicisme*
in the Mathematiques hath carried earth farther up, from the
stupid Center; and yet not honoured it, nor advantaged it, because for the necessity of appearances, it hath carried heaven
so much higher from it: so the *Roman* profession seems to exhale, and refine our wills from earthly Dr[e]gs, and Lees, more
than the Reformed, and so seems to bring us nearer heaven;
but then that carries heaven farther from us, by making us
pass so many Courts, and Offices of Saints in this life, in all
our petitions and lying in a painfull prison in the next, during
the pleasure not of him to whom we go, and who must be our
Judge, but of them from whom we come, who know not our case.
Sir, as I said last time, labour to keep your alacrity and dignity,
in an even temper: for in a dark sadnesse, indifferent things
seem abominable, or necessary, being neither; as trees, and
sheep to melancholique night-walkers have unproper shapes.
And when you descend to satisfie all men in your own religion,
or to excuse others to al; you prostitute your self and your understanding, though not a prey, yet a mark, and a hope, and
a subject, for every sophister in Religion to work on. For the
other part of your Letter, spent in the praise of the Countesse,
I am always very apt to beleeve it of her, and can never beleeve it so well, and so reasonably, as now, when it is averred
by you; but for the expressing it to her, in that sort as you
seem to counsaile, I have these two reasons to decline it. That
that knowledge which she hath of me, was in the beginning of
a graver course, than of a Poet, into which (that I may also keep
my dignity) I would not seem to relapse. The Spanish proverb
informes me, that he is a fool which cannot make one Sonnet,
and he is mad which makes two. The other stronger reason, is
my integrity to the other Countesse, of whose worthinesse
though I swallowed your opinion at first upon your words, yet
I have had since an explicit faith, and now a knowledge: and
for her delight (since she descends to them) I had reserved
not only all the verses, which I should make, but all the

thoughts of womens worthinesse. But because I hope she will not disdain, that I should write well of her Picture, I have obeyed you thus far, as to write: but intreat you by your friendship, that by this occasion of versifying, I be not traduced, nor esteemed light in that Tribe, and that house where I have lived. If those reasons which moved you to bid me write be not constant in you still, or if you meant not that I should write verses; or if these verses be too bad, or too good, over or under her understanding, and not fit; I pray receive them, as a companion and supplement of this Letter to you; and as such a token as I use to send, which use, because I wish rather they should serve (except you wish otherwise) I send no other; but after I have told you, that here at a Christning at *Peckam*, you are remembered by divers of ours, and I commanded to tell you so, I kisse your hands, and so seal to you my pure love, which I would not refuse to do by any labour or danger.

Your very true friend and servant

J. DONNE.

[*Letters*, 1651]

TO SIR ROBERT CARRE NOW EARLE OF ANKERUM, WITH MY BOOK BIATHANATOS AT MY GOING INTO GERMANY

SIR, [April 1619]

I HAD need do somewhat towards you above my promises; How weak are my performances, when even my promises are defective! I cannot promise, no not in mine own hopes, equally to your merit towards me. But besides the Poems, of which you took a promise, I send you another Book to which there belongs this History. It was written by me many years since; and because it is upon a misinterpretable subject, I have always gone so near suppressing it, as that it is onely not burnt: no hand hath passed upon it to copy it, nor many eyes to read it: onely to some particular friends in both Universities, then when I writ it, I did communicate it: And I remember, I had this answer, That certainly, there was a false thread in it, but not easily found: Keep it, I pray, with the same jealousie; let any that your discretion admits to the sight of it, know the date of it; and that it is a Book written by *Jack Donne*, and not by D. *Donne:* Reserve it for me, if I live, and if I die, I only forbid it the Presse, and the Fire: publish it not, but yet burn it

not; and between those, do what you will with it. Love me
still, thus farre, for your owne sake, that when you withdraw
your love from me, you will finde so many unworthinesses in
me, as you grow ashamed of having had so long, and so much,
such a thing as

Your poor servant in Christ Jesus.

J. DONNE
[*Letters*, 1651]

TO HIS MOTHER: COMFORTING HER AFTER
THE DEATH OF HER DAUGHTER

My most dear mother,   [1616]
WHEN I consider so much of your life, as can fall within
my memorie and observation, I find it to have been a Sea,
under a continuall Tempest, where one wave hath ever overtaken another. Our most wise and blessed Saviour chuseth what
way it pleaseth him, to conduct those which he loves, to his
Haven, and eternall Rest. The way which he hath chosen for
you, is strait, stormie, obscure, and full of sad apparitions of
death, and wants, and sundry discomforts; and it hath pleased
him, that one discomfort should still succeed, and touch another, that he might leave you no leasure, by anie pleasure or
abundance, to stay or step out of that way, or almost to take
breath in that way, by which he hath determined to bring you
home, which is his glorious Kingdom. One of the most certain
marks and assurances, that all these are his works, and to that
good end, is your inward feeling and apprehension of them,
and patience in them. As long as the Spirit of God distills and
dews his cheerfulnesse upon your heart; as long as he instructs
your understanding, to interpret his mercies and his judgments
aright; so long your comfort must needs be as much greater
than others, as your afflictions are greater than theirs. The happinesse which God afforded to your first young time, which
was the love and care of my most dear and provident Father,
whose soul, I hope, hath long since enjoyed the sight of our
blessed Saviour, and had compassion of all our miseries in this
world, God removed from you quickly. And hath since taken
from you all the comfort, that that Marriage produced. All those
children (for whose maintenance his industrie provided, and for
whose education you were so carefullie and so chargeablie diligent) he hath now taken from you. All that worth which he

left, God hath suffered to be gone from us all. So that God
hath seemed to repent, that he allowed any part of your life
any earthly happinesse, that he might keep your Soul in continuall exercise, and longing, and assurance, of comming immediately to him. I hope therefore, my most dear Mother, that
your experience of the calamities of this life, your continuall
acquaintance with the visitations of the holy Ghost, which gives
better inward comforts, than the world can outward discomforts,
your wisdom, to distinguish the value of this world from the
next, and your religious fear of offending our mercifull God, by
repining at any thing which he doth, will preserve you from
any inordinate and dangerous sorrow, for this losse of my most
beloved Sister. For my part, which am onely left now, to do
the office of a child; though the poornesse of my fortune, and
the greatnesse of my charge, hath not suffered me to expresse
my duty towards you, as became me; yet, I protest to you before Almighty God, and his Angells and Saints in Heaven,
that I do, and ever shall, esteem my self, to be as stronglie
bound to look to you, and provide for your relief, as for my
own poor wife and children. For, whatsoever I shall be able
to do, I acknowledge to be a debt to you, from whom I had
that education, which must make my fortune. This I speak not,
as though I feared my father *Rainsford's* care of you, or his
means to provide for you; for he hath been with me, and, as
I perceive in him, a loving and industrious care to give you
contentment; so, I see in his businesse, a happie and considerable forwardnesse. In the mean time, good Mother, take heed,
that no sorrow nor dejection in your heart, interrupt or disappoint God's purpose in you; his purpose is, to remove out of
your heart, all such love of this world's happinesse, as might
put Him out of possession of it. He will have you entirelie.
And, as God is comfort enough, so Hee is inheritance enough.
Joyne with God, and make his visitations and afflictions, as he
intended them, mercies and comforts. And, for God's sake, pardon those negligences, which I have heretofore used towards
you; and assist me, with your blessing to me, and all mine; and
with your prayers to our blessed Saviour, that thereby both my
mind and fortune may be apt to do all my duties, especially
those that belong to you.

God, whose omnipotent strength can change the nature of
any thing, by his raising-Spirit of comfort, make your Povertie
Riches, your Afflictions Pleasure, and all the Gall and Wormwood of your life, Hony and Manna to your taste, which he

hath wrought, whensoever you are willing to have it so. Which, because I cannot doubt in you, I will forbear more lines at this time, and most humblie deliver my self over to your devotions, and good opinion of me, which I desire no longer to live, than I may have.

[Sir Tobie Mathews Collection, 1660]

TO SIR H. [GOODYER?]

Octob. the 4th 1622. *almost at midnight*

SIR,

ALL our moralities are but our outworks, our Christianity is our Citadel; a man who considers duty but the dignity of his being a man, is not easily beat from his outworks, but from his Christianity never; and therefore I dare trust you, who contemplates them both. Every distemper of the body now, is complicated with the spleen, and when we were young men we scarce ever heard of the spleen. In our declinations now, every accident is accompanied with heavy clouds of melancholy; and in our youth we never admitted any. It is the spleen of the minde, and we are affected with vapors from thence; yet truly, even this sadnesse that overtakes us, and this yeelding to the sadnesse, is not so vehement a poison (though it be no Physick neither) as those false waies, in which we sought our comforts in our looser daies. You are able to make rules to your self, and our B. Saviour continue to you an ability to keep within those rules. And this particular occasion of your present sadnesse must be helped by the rule, for, examples you will scarce finde any, scarce any that is not encombred and distressed in his fortunes. I had locked my self, sealed and secured my self against all possibilities of falling into new debts, and in good faith, this year hath thrown me 400 l. lower than when I entred this house. I am a Father as well as you, and of children (I humbly thank God) of as good dispositions; and in saying so, I make account that I have taken my comparison as high as I could goe; for in good faith, I beleeve yours to be so: but as those my daughters (who are capable of such considerations) cannot but see my desire to accommodate them in this world, so I think they will not murmure if heaven must be their Nunnery, and they associated to the B. virgins there: I know they would be content to passe their lives in a Prison, rather than

should macerate my self for them, much more to suffer the
mediocrity of my house, and my means, though that cannot
preferre them: yours are such too, and it need not that patience, for your fortune doth not so farre exercise their patience. But to leave all in Gods hands, from whose hands nothing can be wrung by whining but by praying, nor by praying
without the *Fiat voluntas tua.* Sir, you are used to my hand,
and, I think have leisure to spend some time in picking out
sense, in ragges; else I had written lesse, and in longer time.
Here is room for an *Amen;* the prayer—so I am going to my
bedside to make for all you and all yours, with

Your true friend and servant in Christ Jesus

J. DONNE
[*Letters,* 1651]

TO THE R: HONORABLE SIR THOMAS ROE,
AMBASSADOR FOR HIS MAJESTIE OF GREAT BRITAINE
TO THE GRAND SEIGNOR

IF your lordships chapleine be as well shipd, as my letter is
shipd in him, they come both well to your lordship: Mine is
but a vessell for another weyther, for now when I begin to
write, I remember a commandment which my Lord of Carlile
layd upon me, to call for a letter from him, upon the first
commodity of sendinge; and before this letter be seald, I hope
he will returne from Court. If he do not, I may have leave to
say somethinge, both of that which he would, and that which
he would not have sayd in his own letter: He would not have
sayd, that which I may; That he is the directest man that ever
I knew, but he would have sayd, That he is as much directed
upon you, as any: for, in good fayth, he apprehends every
where, any occasion of testifienge well of your Lordship: To
speake in that language, which you know to be mine, that is
free inough, (at least), from flattery, he provides for his ease
and his thrift, in doinge so; for, truly, I have met no case any-
where where the delyveringe of a good opinion of you, or a
judgement upon any of your actions, costs any man anythinge,
or exercises him against an opposition . . . [Our] B: Savyor
give you the comfort of it all your way, and the reward of it,
at last. Many graines make up the bread that feeds us; and

many thornes make up the Crown that must glorifie us; and one of those thornes is, for the most part, the stinginge calumny of others tongues. This, (for any thinge that concernd the publique) you had not in your last employment, though then you had a domestique Satan, a viper, a tonguestinger, in your own house. In this employment, you have beene every way delyverd from it; I never heard your private, nor publique actions calumniated; so you have the lesse thorns to make up that Crowne. But, Sir, since that Crown is made of thorns, be not without them when you contemplate Christ Jesus crowned with thorns, remember that those thorns, which you see stand out, hurt him not; those which wounded him, were bent inward. Outward thorns of calumny, and mis-interpretation do us least harme; Innocency despises them; or friends and just examiners of the case blunt or breake them. Finde thorns within; a woundinge sense of sin; bringe you the thorns, and Christ will make it a Crown, or do you make it a Crowne, where two ends meet, and make a Circle, (consider your selfe, from one mother to another, from the wombe to the grave) and Christ will make it a Crown of glory. Add not you to my thorns, by givinge any ill interpretations of my silence or slacknes in writinge: you, who have so longe accustomed to assist me, with your good opinion, and testimonies, and benefits, will not easily do that; but if you have at any tyme declind towards it, I beseech you let this have some waight towards re-rectifienge you, that the assiduity of doinge the churche of God, that service, which, (in a poore measure) I ame thought to be able to do, possesses me, and fills me. You know, Sir, that the Astronomers of the world are not so much exercised, about all the Constellations, and their motions, formerly apprehended and beleeved, as when there arises a new, and irregular meteor. Many of these, this treaty of the Mariage of the prince hath produced, in our firmament, in our Divinity, and many men, measuringe publique actions, with private affections, have been scandalized and have admitted suspicions of a tepidnes in very high places. Some civill acts, in favor of the Papists, have been with some precipitation over-dangerously mis-applyed too. It is true, there is a Major proposition; but the Conclusion is so soone made, if there be not a minor too. I know to be sory for some things that are donne, (that is, sorry that our tymes are overtaken with a necessity to do them) proceeds of true zeale; but to conclude the worst upon the first degree of ill, is a distillinge with too hot a fire. One of these occurrences, gave the occasion to this

sermon, which by commandement I preached and which I send
your Lordship. Some few weekes after that, I preachd another
at the same place: upon the Gun-powder day. Therin I was
left more to mine owne liberty; and therfore I would I could
also send your Lordship a Copy of that; but that one, which,
also by commandement I did write after the preachinge, is as
yet in his Majesties hand, and, I know not whether he will in
it, as he did in the other, after his readinge thereof, command
it to be printed; and, whilst it is in that suspence, I know your
Lordship would call it Indiscretion, to send out any copy
thereof; neither truly, ame I able to committ that fault; for I
have no Copy. A few days after that, I preached, by invitation
of the Virginian Company, to an honorable auditory, and they
recompenced me with a new commandment, in their Service,
to printe that: and that, I hope, comes with this: for, with
papers of that kinde, I ame the apter to chardge your chapleyne in the Exercise of my Ministery. I have assisted in the
tyme of sicknes, and now attended at the funeralls, the first
night of my Lady Jacob, and the next of Sir Wm. Killegrew,
against whom the B: of Exeter my predecessor here, had com-
mencd a suite in Chancery of (as he layd it in his bill) 3000
l. in value. The case grew to a strange poynte; That which
was layd to him, was indirect dealinge in the execution of a
commission, about the value of that land, which was taken from
the Bishoprike. His sicknes made him unable to answer; without it, they could not proceed. There was propos'd a way, to
appointe him a Guardian, Ad hoc; but the defect beeinge not
in his understandinge, some of the Judges sayd, that if the case
were Treason, and he, by the hand of God, become unable to
awnswere, he could not be proceeded against. Whilst they were
in farther deliberation, the good Man is dead; and the chardge
beeinge personall, and of which, no other man can give an account, I hope the whole busines is dead too; though, if it be
pursued, I do not discerne that they are in any danger. I rec-
ommend myselfe to your Lordships prayers; and I enwrap you,
with mine own soule in mine: and our B: God enwrap in the
righteousnes of his sonne, both of you and

Your Lordships
humblest and thankfullest Servant in Christ Jesus

J. DONNE

at my poore house at
St. Pauls, London 1° Decemb. 1622

[Domestic State Papers]

THE MARQUIS OF BUCKINGHAM

MOST HONORED LORD,

I CAN thus far make myselfe beleeve, that I ame where you
Lordship is, in Spaine, that in my poore Library, where indeed
I ame, I can turne mine Ey towards no shelfe, in any profession, from the Mistresse of my youth, Poetry, to the wyfe of
mine age, Divinity, but that I meet more Autors of that nation, than of any other. Their autors in Divinity, though they
do not show us the best way to heaven, yet they thinke they
doe: And so, though they say not true, yet they do not ly, because they speake their Conscience. And since in charity, I beleeve so of them, for their Divinity, In Civility I beleeve it
too, for Civill matters, that therein also they meane as they say:
and by this tyme yor Lordship knowes what they say. I take
therfore this boldnes to congratulate thus with yor Lordship the
great honor which you receyve, in beeinge so great an instrument of that worke, in which the peace of christendome so
much consists. How to use a sword, when it is out, we know
you know: Thinke you that commandement of our Savyours to
be directed upon you, Put up the sword; study the ways of
peace. The hardest Autors in the world, are Kings; and yor
Lordship hath read over the hardest of them. Since you have
passed from the Text of the King of Kings, the booke of God,
by the Commentary of the wisest Kinge amongst Men, the
Counsayls of our Soveraigne, the knowledge of other states, and
other kings is down-hill, and obvious to yor Lordship and you
finde it in postinge. And for this blessed clearnesse in yor
Lordship all mighty God receyves every day, not the prayers
(their tyme [is] not when the thinge is given allready) but
the thanks [of]

Yor Lordships
humblest and devotedst and
thankfullest Servant in Christ Jesus

[PA]ULS   J. DONNE
[1]623

[Bodleian Tanner MS.]

TO THE HONOURABLE KNIGHT,
SIR ROBERT CARRE

SIR,   [1624]

THOUGH I have left my bed, I have not left my bedside; I sit there still, and as a Prisoner discharged, sits at the Prison doore, to beg Fees, so sit I here, to gather crummes. I have used this leisure, to put the meditations had in my sicknesse, into some such order, as may minister some holy delight. They arise to so many sheetes (perchance 20.) as that without staying for that furniture of an Epistle, That my Friends importun'd me to Print them, I importune my Friends to receive them Printed. That, being in hand, through this long Trunke, that reaches from Saint *Pauls,* to Saint *James,* I whisper into your eare this question, whether there be any uncomlinesse, or unseasonablenesse, in presenting matter of Devotion, or Mortification, to that Prince, whom I pray God nothing may ever Mortifie, but Holinesse. If you allow my purposes in generall, I pray cast your eye upon the Title and the Epistle, and rectifie me in them: I submit substance, and circumstance to you, and the poore Author of both,

Your very humble and very thankfull
Servant in Christ Jesus

J. DONNE
[*Letters,* 1651]

TO A LORD, UPON PRESENTING OF SOME OF
HIS WORK TO HIM

MY LORD,   [1624]

To make my self believe that our life is something, I use in my thoughts to compare it to something, if it be like any thing that is something. It is like a Sentence, so much as may be uttered in a breathing: and such a difference as is in Styles, is in our lives, contracted and dilated. And as in some Styles, there are open Parentheses, Sentences within Sentences; so there are lives, within our lives. I am in such a Parenthesis now, in a convalescence, when I thought my self verie near my period. God brought me into a low valley, and from thence shewed me high *Jerusalem,* upon so high a hill, as that he thought it fit to bid me stay, and gather more breath. This I do, by meditating.

by expostulating, by praying; for, since I am barred of my ordinarie diet, which is Reading, I make these my exercises, which
is another part of Physick. And these meditations, and expostulations, and prayers, I am bold to send to your Lordship; that
as this which I live now is a kind of second life, I may deliver
my self over to your Lordship in this life, with the same affection and devotion, as made me yours in all my former life; and
as long as any image of this world sticks in my soul, shall ever
remain your Lordships, &c.

[Sir Tobie Mathews Collection, 1660]

TO SIR ROBERT CARRE KNIGHT,
WHEN HE WAS IN SPAIN; ABOUT SEVERALL MATTERS

SIR,   [1624]
YOUR way into *Spain* was Eastward, and that is the way to
the land of Perfumes and Spices; their way hither is West-
ward, and that is the way to the land of Gold, and of Mynes.
The Wise men, who sought Christ, laid down both their Perfumes, and their Gold, at the feet of Christ, the Prince
of Peace. If All confer all to his glory, and to the peace of his
Church, *Amen*. But now I consider in Cosmography better; they
and we differ not in the East and West: we are much alike
Easterlie. But yet, *Oriens nomen ejus*, the East is one of Christ's
names, in one Prophet; and, *Filius Orientis est Lucifer*, the
East is one of the Devill's names, in another: and these two
differ diametrically. And so in things belonging to the worship
of God, I think we shall, *Amen*. But the difference of our
scituation is in North and South; and you know, that though
the labour of any ordinary Artificer in that Trade, will bring'
East and West together, (for if a flat Map be but pasted upon
a round Globe, the farthest East, and the farthest West meet,
and are all one) yet all this brings not North and South a
scruple of a degree the nearer. There are things in which we
may, and in that wherein we should not, my hope is in God,
and in Him, in whom God doth so evidently work, we shall
not meet, *Amen*. They have hotter daies in *Spain* than we have
here, but our daies are longer; and yet we are hotter in our
businesse here, and they longer stand it there. God is sometimes called a Gyant, running a race; and sometimes is so slow-
paced, as that a thousand years make but a day with God; and
yet still the same God. He hath his purposes upon our noble

and vehement affections, and upon their warie and sober discretions; and will use both to his glory. *Amen.*

Sir, I took up this Paper to write a Letter; but my imaginations were full of a Sermon before, for I write but a few hours before I am to preach, and so instead of a Letter, I send you a Homily. Let it have thus much of a Letter, That I am confident in your love, and deliver my self over to your service. And thus much of a Homily, That you and I shall accompanie one another to the possession of Heaven, in the same way wherein God put us at first, *Amen.*

> *Your very humble and very thankfull*
> *Servant in Christ,* &c.

[Sir Tobie Mathews Collection, 1660]

TO THE HONOURABLE LADY THE LADY
KINGSMEL *upon the death of her husband*

MADAM

THOSE things wch God dissolves at once, as he shall do the Sunne and Moone, and those bodyes at the last conflagration, he never intends to re-unite againe, but in those things wch he takes in pieces, as he doth Man and wyfe, in these divorces by death, and [*in*] single persons in the dyvorce of body and Soule, God hath another purpose, to make them up againe. That piece wch he takes to himselfe, ys [*presently*] cast in a mold, and in an instant made fitt for hys use; for Heaven ys not a place of proficiency, but of present perfection. That piece wch he leaves behinde in thys world, by the death of a part thereof, growes fitter and fitter for him, by the good use of his corrections, and the intire conformity to hys wyll. Nothinge disproportions us, nor makes us so uncapable of beinge re-united to those whom we loved here, as murmuringe, or not advauncinge the goodnes of him who hath remov'd them from hence. We would wonder, to see a Man, who in a wood, were left to hys liberty to fell what trees he would, take onely the crooked, and leave the straytest trees; but that man, hath perchance a ship to build, and not a house, and so hath use of that kinde of timber. Let not us, who know that in hys [*Gods*] house there are many Mansions, but yet have no Modell, no designe of [*the forme of*] y^t buildinge, wonder at hys takinge in [*of*] hys Materialls, why he takes the yonge, and leaves ye old, or why the sickly overlyve those that had better health. We are not

bound to thinke, that Souls departed have devested all affections towards them whom they left here; but we are bound to
thinke, that, for all theyr love, they would not be here againe.
Then ys the wyll of God donne in Earth, as yt ys in Heaven,
when we neyther pretermitt hys actions, nor resist them; neyther passe them over in an inconsideration, as though God had
no hand in them, nor go about to take them out of hys hands,
as though we could direct him to do them better. As Gods
Scriptures are hys wyll, so hys Actions are hys wyll; both are
Testaments, because they Testify hys Minde to us. It ys not
lawfull to add a Scedule to eyther of hys wylls; As they do yll,
who add to his written wyll, hys [the] Scriptures, a Scedule
of Apocryphall books, so do they also, who to hys other wyll,
his manifested Actions, add Apocryphall conditions, and a
Scedule of such limitations [as these], If God would have stayd
thus longe, or If God would have proceeded in thys, or thys
Manner, I could have borne it. To say, that our afflictions are
greater than we can bear, ys so near to despairinge, as that the
same words expresse both; for when we consider Cains words
in that Originalle tongue, in wch God spoke, we cannot tell,
whether the words be, My punishment ys greater than can be
borne or My Sinne ys greater then can be forgiven. But,
Madam, you who willingly sacrific'd yourselfe to God, in y^r
obedience to him, in y^r own sickness, cannot be doubted to dispute w^t him, about any part of you, wch he shall be pleas'd to
requier at y^r hands. The difference ys great, in the losse of an
arme, or a Head; of a child, or a Husband: But to them, who
are incorporated into Christ, theyr Head, there can be no be-
headinge; upon you, who are a Member of the spouse of Christ,
the Churche, there can fall no wydowhood, nor Orphanage upon
those children, to whom God ys father. I have not another office, by y^r husbands death; for I was y^r Chapleyne before in my dayly prayers; but I shall enlardge that office, w^t
other Collects then before, That God wyll continue to you, that
peace wch you have ever had in him, and send you quiet, and
peacable dispositions in all them, w^t whom you shall have any
thinge to doe, in y^r temperall estate. and matters of thys world.
Amen.

Y^r Laps
very humble and thankfull

At my poore house at S: Pauls   Servant in Chr: Jes:
    26 Octr: 1624.   J. DONNE

[Letters, 1651]

TO THE HONOURABLE KT AND MY MOST
HONOURED FRIEND SIR HENRY WOTTON,
PROVOST OF ETON

SIR,

THIS is your quietus est from me; it is your assurance that I
will never trouble you more about any place in your colledge.
But this quietus est must bear date from the end of the chapter; for in the letter, I must make a suite of that kinde to you,
in which I know you will give a good interpretation of mine
ingenuity, that I would not forbear even in the troublinge of
you, when I had a way presented to me, to do any service to
your noble family, to whom I owe even my posterity. Sir, at
your last election, Sir Robert More (to whom I have the honor
to be brother in law) had a sonne elected into your schools,
and his place is not falln, and so our hopes evacuated that way.
Because it was my worke at first, I would faine perfit it, and I
am in the right way of perfitinge it when I addresse myselfe
to you, who have a perfit power in the business, and have multiplied demonstrations of a perfit love to me. That which was
then donne, was donne by way of gratitude by Mr Woodford,
one of the then opposers, to whom I had given a church be-
longinge to our Pauls. And for the favor which you shall be
pleased to afford us herein, I offer your mother and daughters,
all the service I shall be able to doe to any servant of yours in
any place of any of our churches. Our most B. Savyor blesse
you with all his graces, and restore us to a confident meetinge
in wholesome place, and direct us all by good ways to good
ends. Amen.

Your very true frinde and humble
servant in Christ Jesus

J. DONNE

From Sir John Da[n]vers house at Chelsey (of which house
and my [Lord of C]arlils at Hanworth I make up my Tus-
culan) 12 Julli, 1625.

[Loseley MSS.–Kempe]

TO [SIR THOMAS ROE?]

Our blessed Savyour establish in you, and multiply to you, the seals of his eternall election, and testify his gracious purposes towards you in the next world for ever, by a continuall succession of his outward blessings here, and sweeten your age, by a rectified conscience of havinge spent your former tyme well and sweeten your transmigration by a modest but yet infallible assurance of a present union with him. Amen. Your Lordships letters of the 16 of August, were delyvered to me, 10 Novemb: in which, I ame first affected with that infection, which your Lordship told me, at that tyme, raigned in those parts. I make it another argument that our good God hath a holy and gracious purpose to enwrapp us in the same everlastinge communion of Joye, that enwrapps us now, in the same communion of Calamity: for your number of 2000 a day, was so far attempted by us, that in the city of London, and in a mile compas, I believe there dyed 1000 a day. But, by reason that these infections are not so frequent with us, the horror, I presume was greater here: for the Citezens fled away, as out of a house on fire, and stuffd theyr pockets with their best ware, and threw themselfs into the high-ways, and were not receyvd, so much as into barnes, and perishd so, some of them with more money about them, than would have bought the villadge where they died: A Justice of Peace, into whose Examination it fell, told me, of one that dyed so, with 1400 l. about him. I scattered my family; and, to be near as I could, to your inspection of our churche, I removd for a tyme to Chelssey, where within a few weeks, the infection multiplyed so fast, as that it was no good Manners, to go to any other place, and so I have been in a secular monastery, and so far, in a conformity to your Lordship too. Of those good things which God intends us in the next world, he affords us a sense, and an anticipation in this: So of those honors, and rewards, (which is a word that we may be bolder with, in matters of this nature, than when wee speake of heaven) which your noble and powerfull friends intend you here, I doubt not but you have good assurances from them. To me, it was a great comfort, both for your merit, and the states acknowledgement, (for, as S. Augustine says of Tentations, and Gods disposinge of them to our good, sometymes the Devyll is away, and sometymes the woman, so that God frustrates the tentation, so the Devyll counterfayts God so far, as that sometymes he corrupts publique instruments of state, with private vices, and then there is no merit, sometymes he corrupts great persons with a facility of admittinge Calumnityes, and so there is no acknowledgement, no reward of true meritt) but in this we had our comfort, that before the seale was removd from your B: of Lincoln, there beinge speeche of many removees, for ten days together, they were full of assurance, that your Lordship was Secretary. My Lord, in the poore low way that I have gone, in which I have not made many, nor wide stepps, since my first leape, which was my very entrance into this callinge, I have found, that missinge and faylinge of some places, have advancd my fortune, and that, though I were no great pretender, nor thruster myselfe, yet the promises in which some great persons had enlarged themselfs towards me, and even the voyce and rumor, which sometymes had invested me, in some vacant places, conduced to my future settlinge. Your Lordship is in the hands of a person, of whose lardgeness in doinge good, we abound with examples of particular persons advancd by him; but that exalts not my wonder, because he hath had it in his power to do so much: But havinge also the same power to do harme, and havinge conferd great favors upon persons that have proved very unthankfull, and practisinge to his prejudice, and so been put to a necessity of declaringe his power, by devestinge them, yet I cannot recover any Example of any, whom in such a just displeasure, he hath left worse, than he found him, but satisfyenge himselfe in havinge withdrawen those additions, which he pinnd upon him, hath left him to enjoye his former condition. By so good a hand, hath God made up mine, and is kneadinge and moldinge your Lordships fortune, though fortunes of that great kinde, be Elephants, and ly longe in the wombe, and not made up so soone, as ours that consist of peeces, and but a few, and but smalle. In the parturition and bringinge forth, of so great issues, God is the midwyfe, for he refuses no name, nor office, to do his servants good; Amongst your Men-midwyfes, I shall allways assist it, with my humble prayers, both for the birth of your Daughter, which is Honor in this world, and of your Sonne, which is Happines in the next. I will be bold to add this circumstance of gladnes, which we had, in this approche of yours to that place, that the opinion of Sir Dud: Carletons remove at that tyme (into whose place, our

worthy frinde Sir Rob: Kyllegrew is to goe) did not divert nor
retard your comminge into yours. I stay thus longe from givinge your Lordship an account, of some other parts of your
Lordships letter, because when I come to that, I ame swallowd,
and fall into the consideration of your Lordships continuall favors to me and my obligations from your Lordship. I owe no
man more, but ame happy in my Creditor, who is content to
take such payment as I can make, and to call my Gratitude the
sylver, and my Devotion the gold in which he is willinge to
be payd. Amongst those favors, this which your Lordship hath
donne now, is a great one, to take so expressly into your consideration the recommendation of that gentleman, of whom I
writt last to your Lordship. But I thinke, that by this letter, I
do absolutely restore your Lordship to your liberty; for since
that tyme, he hath embracd another employment, for Savoy;
And though he be not yet gone, yet, (I thinke,) he hath had
his privy seale some monethes. In this Generall Dispersion, I
know not where to seeke him; for the infection hath made this
vylladge so infamous as that I go not to Court, though it be at
Hampton. But except a letter of mine within a month after
this, refresh my request to yor Lordship, be pleased to take my
restoringe you to your full liberty, as a part of payment of my
debt, for that forward favor to me. Almighty God blesse you
where you are, and where you would be, when you are there,
and bringe you thether. Amen.

your Lordships humblest and thankfullest
servant in Christ Jesus

At Chelsey. 25 November   J. DONNE
1625.

YOUR LORDSHIP allways allowd me the freedome to communicate to you, whatsoever I writt, or meditated; therefore I continue it in tellinge your Lordship how I have spent this Summer in my close Emprisonment. I have reviewd as many of my
Sermons, as I had kept any notes of; and I have written out,
a great many, and hope to do more. I ame allready come to the
number of 80: of which my sonne who, I hope will take the
same profession, or some other in the world of middle understandinge, may hereafter make some use.

[Domestic State Papers]

TO THE RIGHT HONOURABLE SIR ROBERT
KARRE, AT COURT

SIR, [April 1627]

I WAS this morning at your door, somewhat early; and I am put in to such a distaste of my last Sermon, as that I dare not practise any part of it, and therefore though I said then, that we are bound to speake aloud, though we awaken men, and make them froward, yet after two or three modest knocks at the door, I went away. Yet I understood after, the King was gone abroad, and thought you might be gone with him. I came to give you an account of that, which this does as well. I have now put into my Lord of *Bath* and *Wells* hands the Sermon faithfully exs[cr]ibed. I beseech you be pleased to hearken farther after it; I am still upon my jealousie, that the King brought thither some disaffection towards me, grounded upon some other demerit of mine, and tooke it not from the Sermon. For, as Cardinal *Cusanus* writ a Book *Cribratio Alchorani,* I have cribrated, and re-cribrated and post-cribrated the Sermon, and must necessarily say, the King who hath let fall his eye upon some of my Poems, never saw, of mine, a hand, or an eye, or an affection, set down with so much study, and diligence, and labour of syllables, as in this Sermon I expressed those two points, which I take so much to conduce to his service, the imprinting of persuasibility and obedience in the subject, And the breaking of the bed of whisperers, by casting in a bone, of making them suspect and distrust one another. I remember I heard the old King say of a good Sermon, that he thought the Preacher never had thought of his Sermon, till he spoke it; it seemed to him negligently and extemporally spoken. And I knew that he had weighed every syllable, for halfe a year before, which made me conclude, that the King had before, some prejudice upon him. So, the best of my hope is, that some over bold allusions, or expressions in the way, might divert his Majesty, from vouchsafing to observe the frame, and purpose of the Sermon. When he sees the generall scope, I hope his goodnesse will pardon collaterall escapes. I intreated B. to aske his Majesty, whether his displeasure extended so farre, as that I should forbear waiting, and appearing in his presence; and I had a return, that I might come. Till I had that, I would not offer to put my self under your roof. To

day I come, for that purpose, to say prayers. And if, in any degree, my health suffer it, I shall do so, to morrow. If any thing
fall into your observation before that, (because the B. is likely
to speake to the King of it, perchance, this night) if it amount
to such an increase of displeasure, as that it might be unfit
for me to appear, I beseech you afford me the knowledge.
Otherwise, I am likely to inquire of you personally, to morrow
before nine in the morning, and to put into your presence
then

> *Your very humble and very true, and very*
>> *honest servant to God and the King and you*
>>> J. DONNE

I writ yesterday to my Lord Duke, by my Lord Carlile, who
assured me of a gracious acceptation of my putting my self in
his protection.

[Letters, 1651]

TO MRS. COCKAINE, OCCASIONED BY THE
REPORT OF HIS DEATH

MY NOBLE SISTER,   [1628]

THOUGH my Man, at *London*, might have made such a return to your Man's Letter, from himself, as might have given
satisfaction enough; yet, because there were so many hours, between his receipt of that Letter, and the return of the Carrier,
as might admit that delay, he thought best to acquaint me with
it. I am not sorrie he did so; for, I have found this rumour of
my death to have made so deep impressions, and to have been
so peremptorilie believed, that from very remote parts, I have
been entreated to signifie under my hand, that I am yet alive.
If you have believed the report, and mourned for me, I pray
let that that is done alreadie, serve at the time that it shall be
true. To mourn a second time, were to suspect, that I were
fallen into the second death, from which, I have abundant assurance, in the application of the superabundant Merits of my
Saviour. What gave the occasion of this rumour, I can make no
conjecture. And yet the hour of my death, and the day of my
buriall, were related in the highest place of this Kingdom. I
had at that time no kind of sicknesse, nor was otherwise, than
I had been ever since my feavour, and am yet; that is, too
weak at this time of the year to go forth, especiallie to *London*,
where the sicknesse is near my house, and where I must neces-

sarilie open my self to more businesse, than my present state
would bear. Yet, next tearm, by God's grace, I will be there:
at which time, I have understood from my Lord *Carlile's* house,
that the Dean of *Exeter* will be there: which hath made me
forbear to write, because I know how faintlie and lamelie businesses go on by Letters, in respect of Conferences. In the
mean time, my prayers for your happinesse shall fill all the
time of

> *Your true Friend, and Brother,*
> *and Servant.*

[Sir Tobie Mathews Collection, 1660]

[TO MRS. COKAIN]

My noblest and lovingest Sister,   [August 24, 1628]

NOTHING returns more oftner with more comfort to my
memorie, than that you nor I ever asked any thing of one another, which we might not safelie grant; and we can ask nothing safelie, that implies an offence to God, or injury to any
other person. I fall upon this consideration now, upon this occasion: Your Letter, upon the two and twentieth of *August,*
which I received this day, laies a commandment upon me, to
give you an account of my state in health; you do but ask me
how I do, and if your Letter had come yesterday, I could not
have told you that. At my return from *Kent* to my gate, I
found *Pegge* had the Pox; so I withdrew to *Peckham,* and spent
a fortnight there. And without comming home, when I could
with some justice hope that it would spread no farther amongst
them, (as, I humbly thank God, it hath not, nor much disfigured her that had it) I went into *Bedfordshire.* There, upon
my third *Sunday,* I was seized with a Feavour, which grew so
upon me, as forced me to a resolution, of seeking my Physitian
at *London.* Thither I came in a day, and a little piece; and
within four miles of home, I was surprised with an accident in
the Coach, which never befell me before, nor had been much
in my contemplation, and therefore affected me much. It was a
violent falling of the *Uvula.* Which when Doctor *Fox* (whom
I found at *London,* and who had not been there in ten daies
before) considered well, and perceived the feavour complicated
with a Squinancie; by way of prevention of both, he presentlie
took blood; and so with ten-daies starving in a close prison,
that is, my bed, I am (blessed be God) returned to a conven-

ient temper, and pulse, and appetite, and learn to eat, and this
day met the acceptablest guest in the acceptablest manner, your
Letter walking in my chamber. All which I tell you with these
particularities, lest my sicknesse might be presented by rumour
worse, than God hath been pleased to make it: For I humbly
thank him, now I feel no present ill, nor have reason to fear
worse. If I understand your Letter aright, much of your familie
is together; if it be so, entreat them, for your sake, to receive
my service, which, by your hand, I present to them all. If they
be otherwise severed, yet, in the ears of Almighty God, to
whom, I know, they all daily pray; my daily Praiers for them
all, shall also meet them all. And that's the onely service which
I can promise my self an ability to do to God's Church now,
since this infirmity in my mouth and voice, is likelie to take
me from any frequent exercise of my other duty of Preaching.
But, God will either enable me, or pardon me. His will be
done upon us all, as his goodnesse hath been overflowingly
poured out upon

> Your poor Friend, and lovingest
> Brother and Servant.
>
> [Sir Tobie Mathews Collection, 1660]

[TO MRS. COKAIN]

My noble and vertuous Sister,   [1629]

IF I had had such an occasion as this to have written to you,
in the first year of our acquaintance, I had been likelie to have
presented you with an Essay of Morall Comfort. Now my Letter may well be excused, if it amount to an Homilie. My profession and my willingnesse, to stay long upon so good an office, as to assist you, will bear it. Our Souls are trulie said to be
in everie part of our bodies; but yet, if any part of the bodie
be cut off, no part of the soul perishes, but is suckt in to that
soul that remains, in that that remains of the body. When any
limb or branch of a family is taken away, the vertue, the love,
and (for the most part) the patrimonie and fortune of him
that is gone, remaines with the Family. The family would not
think it self the lesse, if any little quillet of ground had been
evicted from it; nor must it, because a clod of earth, one person
of the family, is removed. In these cases, there is nothing lost;
one part, the soul, enjoyes a present gain; and the other, the
body, expects a future. We think it good husbandry to place

our childrens portions so, as that in so many years it may multiply to so much: Shall we not be as glad to lay their bodies there, where onely they can be mellowed and ripened for glorification. The perversnesse of the father put you to such a necessity of hiding your sons, as that this son is scarce more out of your sight, by being laid under ground, than he was before. And perchance you have been longer time, at some times, from meeting and seeing one another in this world, than you shall be now from meeting in the glory of the Resurrection. That may come sooner, than you looked he should come from the *Bath.* A man truly liberall, or truly charitable, will borrow monie to lend: For, if I be bound to assist another with my meat, or with my mony, I may be as much bound to assist him with my credit, and borrow tc lend. We do but borrow Children of God, to lend them to the world. And when I lend the world a daughter in marriage, or lend the world a son in a profession, the world does not alwaies pay me well again; my hopes are not alwaies answered in that daughter or that son. But, of all that I lend to, the Grave is my best pay-Master. The Grave shall restore me my child, where he and I shall have but one Father; and pay me my Earth, when that Earth shall be Amber, a sweet Perfume, in the nostrills of his and my Saviour. Since I am well content to send one sonne to the Church, the other to the Warrs; Why should I be loth to send one part of either sonne to Heaven, and the other to the Earth. Comfort your self in this, my noble Sister, that for those years he lived, you were answerable to God for him; for yet, he was so young, as a Mother's power might govern him; and so long he was under your charge, and you accountable for him. Now, when he was growing into those years, as needed a stronger hand, a Father's care, and had not that; God hath cancelled your Bonds, discharged you, and undertakes the office of a Father himself. But, above all, comfort your self in this, That it is the declared will of God. In sicknesses, and other worldlie crosses, there are anxieties, and perplexities; we wish one thing to day, in the behalf of a distressed child or friend, and another to morrow; because God hath not yet declared his will. But when he hath done that, in death, there is no room for anie anxietie, for anie perplexitie, no, not for a wish; for we may not so much as pray for the dead. You know, *David* made his child's Sicknesse his *Lent,* but his Death his *Easter:* he fasted till the Child's death, but then he returned to his repast, because then he had a declaration of God's will. I am farre from quenching in you, or discharging naturall affections; but, I know your easie apprehensions, and over-tendernesse in this kind. And, I know some persons in the world, that I wish may live, especially for this respect, because I know their death would over-affect you. In so noble and numerous a family as yours is, every year must necessarily present you some such occasion of sorrow, in the losse of some near friend, And therefore I, in the office of a Friend, and a Brother, and Priest of God, do not onelie look that you should take this patientlie, as a declaration of God's present will; but that you take it catechistically, as an instruction for the future; and that God, in this, tells you, That he will do so again, in some other your friends. For, to take any one crosse patiently, is but to forgive God for once; but to surrender one's self entirely to God, is to be ready for all that he shall be pleased to do. And, that his pleasure may be either to lessen your crosses, or multiply your strength, shall be the prayer of

Your Brother, and Friend, and
Servant, and Chaplain,

JOHN DONNE
[Sir Tobie Mathews Collection, 1660]

TO MY HONOURED FRIEND G[EORGE]. G[ARRARD]. ESQUIRE

SIR, [Dec. 1630 ?]

I SHOULD not only send you an account by my servant, but bring you an account often my self, (for our Letters are our selves, and in them absent friends meet) how I do, but that two things make me forbear that writing: first, because it is not for my gravity, to write of feathers, and strawes, and in good faith, I am no more, considered in my body, or fortune. And then because whensoever I tell you how I doe, by a Letter, before that Letter comes to you, I shall be otherwise, than when it left me. At this time, I humbly thank God, I am only not worse; for, I should as soon look for Roses at this time of the year, as look for increase of strength. And if I be no worse all spring, than now, I am much better, for, I make account that those Church services, which I would be very loth to decline, will spend somewhat; and, if I can gather so much as will bear my charges, recover so much strength at *London*, as I shall spend at *London*, I shall not be loth to be left in that state wherein I am now, after that's done; But I do but discourse, I do not wish; life, or health, or strength, (I thank God) enter not into my prayers for my self: for others they do; and amongst others, for your sick servant, for such a servant taken so young, and healed so long, is half a child to a master, and so truly I have observed that you have bred him, with the care of a father. Our blessed Saviour look graciously upon him, and glorifie himself in him, by his way of restitution to health; And by his way of peace of conscience in

Your very true friend and servant in Christ Jesus,

J. DONNE
[*Letters,* 1651]

[TO GEORGE GARRARD]

SIR,   [January 7, 1630/1]
THIS advantage you, and my other friends have, by my frequent Fevers, that I am so much the oftener at the gates of heaven, and this advantage by the solitude and close imprisonment that they reduce me to after, that I am thereby the oftener at my prayers; in which, I shall never leave out your happinesse; and, I doubt not, but amongst his many other blessings, God will adde to you some one for my prayers. A man would almost be content to dye, (if there were no other benefit in death) to hear of so much sorrow, and so much good testimony from good men, as I, (God be blessed for it) did upon the report of my death. Yet, I perceive it went not through all; for, one writ unto me, that some (and he said of my friends) conceived, that I was not so ill, as I pretended, but withdrew my self, to save charges, and to live at ease, discharged of preaching. It is an unfriendly, and God knows, an ill grounded interpretation: for in these times of necessity, and multitudes of poor there is no possibility of saving to him that hath any tendernesse in him; and for affecting my ease, I have been always more sorry when I could not preach, than any could be, that they could not hear me. It hath been my desire, (and God may be pleased to grant it me) that I might die in the Pulpit; if not that, yet that I might take my death in the Pulpit, that is, die, the sooner by occasion of my former labours. I thanke you, for keeping our *George* in your memory, I hope God reserves it for so good a friend as you are, to send me the first good newes of him. For the Diamond Lady, you

may safely deliver *Roper,* whatsoever belongs to me, and he will give you a discharge for the money. For my Lord *Percy,* we shall speake of it, when we meet at *London;* which, as I do not much hope before Christmas, so I do not much fear at beginning of Tearm; for I have intreated one of my fellowes to preach to my Lord Maior, at *Pauls* upon Christmas day, and reserved Candlemas day to my self for that service, about which time also, will fall my Lent Sermon, except my Lord Chamberlaine beleeve me to be dead, and leave me out; for as long as I live, and am not speechlesse, I would not decline that service. I have better leasure to write, than you to read, yet I will not oppresse you with too much letter. God blesse you, and your sonne, as

> *Your poor friend and humble servant in Christ Jesus*
>
> J. DONNE
> [*Letters,* 1651]

TO MY NOBLE FRIEND MISTRESS COKAIN AT ASHBURNE

My noblest sister,

BUT that it is sweetned by your command, nothing could trouble me more, than to write of my self. Yet, if I would have it known, I must write it my self; for, I neither tell children, nor servants, my state. I have never good temper, nor good pulse, nor good appetite, nor good sleep. Yet, I have so much leasure to recollect my self, as that I can thinke I have been long thus, or often thus. I am not alive, because I have not had enough upon me to kill me, but because it pleases God to passe me through many infirmities before he take me either by those particular remembrances, to bring me to particular repentances, or by them to give me hope of his particular mercies in heaven. Therefore have I been more affected with Coughs in vehemence, more with deafenesse, more with toothach, more with the [uvula], than heretofore. All this mellows me for heaven, and so ferments me in this world, as I shall need no long concoction in the grave, but hasten to the resurrection. Not onely to be nearer that grave, but to be nearer to the service of the Church, as long as I shall be able to do any, I purpose, God willing, to be at *London,* within a fortnight after your receit of this, as well because I am under the obligation of preaching at *Pauls* upon Candlemas day, as because I know nothing to the contrary, but that I may be called to Court, for Lent service; and my witnesse is in heaven, that I never left out S. *Dunstans*, when I was able to do them that service; nor will now; though they that know the state of that Church well, know that I am not so bound, as the world thinks, to preach there; for, I make not a shilling profit of S. *Dunstans* as a Church man, but as my Lord of *Dorset* gave me the lease of the Impropriation, for a certain rent, and a higher rent, than my predecessor had it at. This I am fain to say often, because they that know it not, have defamed me, of a defectiveness towards that Church; and even that mistaking of theirs I ever have, and ever shall endevour to rectifie, by as often preaching there, as my condition of body will admit. All our company here is well, but not at home now, when I write; for, lest I should not have another return to *London*, before the day of your Carrier, I write this, and rest

Your very affectionate servant,
and friend, and brother

J. DONNE

15 Jan. 1630 [/1]
Abrey-hatch.

[*Letters*, 1651]

[TO MRS. COKAIN]

My noble dear Sister,   [Jan. 1630/1]
   I AM come now, not onely to pay a Feavour every half year, as a Rent for my life; but I am called upon before the day, and they come sooner in the year than heretofore. This Feavour that I had now, I hoped, for divers daies, to have been but an exaltation of my damps and flashings, such as exercise me sometimes four or five daies, and passe away, without whining or complaint. But, I neglected this somewhat too long, which makes me (though, after I took it into consideration, the Feavour it self declined quickly) much weaker, than, perchance, otherwise I should have been. I had Doctor *Fox* and Doctor *Clement* with me, but, I thank God, was not much trouble to them. Ordinary means set me soon upon my leggs. And I have broke my close prison, and walk'd into the Garden; and (but that the weather hath continued so spitefully foul) make no doubt, but I might safely have done more. I eat, and digest well enough. And it is no strange thing, that I do not sleep

well; for, in my best health, I am not much used to do so. At
the same time, little *Betty* had a Feavour too; and, for her, we
used Doctor *Wright*, who, by occasion, lies within two miles of
us; and he was able to ease my sicknesse, with his report of
your good health, which, he told us, he had received from you.
But I found it not seconded in your own Letters, which I had
the honour to receive by Mr. *Hazard*. My noble sister, I am
afraid that Death will play with me so long, as he will forget
to kill me; and suffer me to live in a languishing and uselesse
age, A life, that is rather a forgetting that I am dead, than of
living. We dispute whether the dead shall pray for the living:
and because my life may be short, I pray with the most ear-
nestnesse for you now. By the advantage of sicknesse, I return the oftner to that holy exercise, and in it joyn yours with
mine own Soul. I would not have dignified my self, or my
sicknesse with saying so much of either, but that it is in obedience to your Command, that I should do so. And though there
lye upon me no Command, yet there lies a necessitie growing
out of my respect, and a nobler root, than that my love to you,
to enlarge my self, as farre as I have gone alreadie, in Mr.
Hazard's businesse. My noble Sister, when you carrie me up to
the beginning, which it pleases you to call a promise to your
self, and your noble Sister; I never slackned my purpose of
performing that promise. But if my promise, which was, that I
should be readie to assist him in any thing I could, were translated by you, or your noble Sister, or him, that I would give
him the next Living in my gift, certainlie we speak not one
language, or understand not one another, and I had thought we
had; This which he imagined to be vacant, (for it is not yet,
nor any way likely) is the first that fell to me, since I made
that promise. And, my noble Sister, if a person of my place,
from whom, one Scholler in each Universitie sucks something,
and must be weaned by me, and who hath otherwise a latitude
of importunate friends and verie many obligations, have a Living once in five or six yeares fall in his gift, (for it is so
long since I gave any) and may not make a good choice with
freedome then, it is hard; yet it is not my fortune to doe so
now: for, now there is a living fallen (though not that); I am
not left to my choice. For my Lords *Carlile*, and *Percy* have
chosen for me; but trulie such a man as I would have chosen;
and for him, they laid an obligation upon me three yeares
since, for the next that should fall: yet Mr. *Hazard* presses you
to write for that, because he to whom my promise belongs,

hath another before, but doth he or his Lord owe me any
thing for that? yet Mr. *Hazard* importunes me, to presse that
Chaplain of my Lord, that when he takes mine, he shall resign
the other to him, which, as it is an ignorant request, (for if it
be resign'd, it is not in his power to place it upon Mr. *Hazard*)
so it is an unjust request, that I that gave him fiftie pounds a
year, should take from him fortie. But amongst Mr. *Hazards*
manifold importunities, that that I took worst, was, that he
should write of domestique things, and what I said of my Son,
to you; and arme you with that plea, that my Son was not in
Orders. But, my noble Sister, though I am far from drawing
my Son immaturelie into Orders, or putting into his hands any
Church with cure; yet there are many Prebends and other helps
in the Church, which a man without taking Orders, may be
capable of, and for some such I might change a Living with
cure, and so begin to accomodate a Son in some Preparation.
But Mr. *Hazard* is too piercing. It is good counsell, (and as I
remember I gave it him) that if a man deny him any thing,
and accompany his deniall with a reason, he be not too searching, whether that be the true reason or no, but rest in the deniall: for many times it may be out of my power to doe a man
a courtesie which he desires, and yet I not tied to tell him the
true reason; Therefore out of his Letter to you, I continue my
opinion, that he medled too far herein. I cannot shut my Letter,
till (whilst we are upon this consideration or reasons of de-
nialls) I tell you one Answer of his, which perchance may
weaken your so great assurance of his modestie. I told him that
my often sicknesses, had brought me to an inability of Preaching, and that I was under a necessitie of Preaching twelve or
fourteen solemn Sermons every year, to great Auditories,
at *Paules,* and to the Judges, and at Court; and that therefore
I must think of conferring something upon such a man as may
supplie my place in these Solemnities: And surely, said I, I
will offer them no man in those cases which shall not be at
least equall to my selfe; and, Mr. *Hazard,* I do not know your
faculties. He gave me this answer, I will not make comparisons,
but I do not doubt but I should give them satisfaction in that
kind. Now, my noble Sister, whereas you repeat often, that you
and your sister rested upon my word, and my worth; and, but
for my word and my worth, you would not have proceeded so
far: I must necessarily make my protestation, that my word and
my worth is, herein, as chast, and untouch'd as the best Maidenhead in the world. For, my noble sister, Goes there no more to

the giving of a Scholler a Church in *London*, but that he was a young Gentleman's School-master? You know the ticklishnesse of *London*-Pulpits, and how ill it would become me, to place a man in a *London*-Church that were not both a strong and a sound man. And therefore, those things must come into consideration before he can have a Living from me; though there was no need of reflecting upon those things, when I made that generall promise, that I would assist his fortune in any thing. You end in a phrase of indignation and displeasure, rare in you towards me, therefore it affects me; which is, that he may part from me, as I received him at first, as though I were likely to hinder him. The heat that produced that word I know is past, and therefore, my most beloved Sister, give me leave to say to you, that he shall not part from me, but I shall keep him still in my care, and make you alwaies my judge of all omissions

Your faithfull Friend and Servant.
[Sir Tobie Mathews Collection, 1660]

From DEVOTIONS UPON EMERGENT OCCASIONS [1624]

THE EPISTLE DEDICATORIE TO THE MOST EXCELLENT PRINCE "PRINCE" CHARLES

MOST EXCELLENT PRINCE,

I have had three Births; *One*, Naturall, *when I came into the* World; *One*, Supernatural, *when I entred into the* Ministery; *and now, a* preter-naturall Birth, *in returning to* Life, *from this* Sicknes. *In my* second Birth, *your* Highnesse Royall Father *vouchsafed mee his Hand, not onely to sustaine mee* in it, *but to lead mee* to it. *In this* last Birth, *I my selfe am borne a* Father: *This* Child *of mine, this* Booke, *comes into the world,* from *mee, and* with *me. And therefore, I presume (as I did the* Father *to the* Father) *to present the* Sonne *to the* Sonne; *This* Image *of my* Humiliation, *to the lively* Image *of his* Majesty *your* Highnesse. *It might bee enough, that* God *hath seene my* Devotions: *But* Examples *of* Good Kings *are* Commandments; *And* Ezechiah *with the* Meditations *of his* Sicknesse, *after his* Sicknesse. *Besides, as I have liv'd to see (not as a* Witnesse *onely, but as a* Partaker) *the happinesses of a part of your* Royal Fathers *time, so shall I live* (in my way)

to see the happinesses of the times of your Highnesse *too,
if this* Child *of mine, inanimated by your gracious Acceptation,
may so long preserve alive the* Memory of
Your Highnesse
Humblest and
Devotedst

JOHN DONNE

Insultus Morbi   *The first alteration, The first
Primus ;*   *grudging of the sicknesse.*

I. MEDITATION

VARIABLE, and therfore miserable condition of Man; this minute I was well, and am ill, this minute. I am surpriz'd with a
sodaine change, and alteration to worse, and can impute it to
no cause, nor call it by any name. We study *Health,* and we
deliberate upon our *meats,* and *drink,* and *ayre,* and *exercises,*
and we hew, and wee polish every stone, that goes to
that building; and so our *Health* is a long and a regular work;
But in a minute a Canon batters all, overthrowes all, demolishes
all; a *Sicknes* unprevented for all our diligence, unsuspected for
all our curiositie; nay, undeserved, if we consider only *disorder,*
summons us, seizes us, possesses us, destroyes us in an instant.
O miserable condition of Man, which was not imprinted by
God, who as hee is *immortall* himselfe, had put a *coale,* a
beame of *Immortalitie* into us, which we might have blowen
into a *flame,* but blew it out, by our first sinne; wee beggard
our selves by hearkning after false riches, and infatuated our
selves by hearkning after false knowledge. So that now, we doe
not onely die, but die upon the Rack, die by the torment of
sicknesse; nor that onely, but are preafflicted, super-afflicted
with these jelousies and suspitions, and apprehensions of *Sicknes,* before we can cal it a sicknes; we are not sure we are ill;
one hand askes the other by the pulse, and our eye asks our
urine, how we do. O multiplied misery! we die, and cannot enjoy death, because wee die in this torment of sicknes; we are
tormented with sicknes, and cannot stay till the torment come,
but preapprehensions and presages, prophecy those torments,
which induce that *death* before either come; and our dissolution
is conceived in these *first changes, quickned* in the *sicknes* it
selfe, and *borne* in *death,* which beares date from these first

changes. Is this the honour which Man hath by being a *litle world,* That he hath these *earthquakes* in him selfe, sodaine shakings; these *lightnings,* sodaine flashes; these *thunders,* sodaine noises; these *Eclypses,* sodain offuscations, and darknings of his senses; these *Blazing stars,* sodaine fiery exhalations; these *Rivers of blood,* sodaine red waters? Is he a *world* to himselfe onely therefore, that he hath inough in himself, not only to destroy, and execute himselfe, but to presage that execution upon himselfe; to assist the sicknes, to antidate the sicknes, to make the sicknes the more irremediable, by sad apprehensions, and as if he would make a fire the more vehement, by sprinkling water upon the coales, so to wrap a hote fever in cold Melancholy, least the fever alone should not destroy fast enough, without this contribution nor perfit the work (which is *destruction*) except we joynd an artificiall sicknes, of our owne *melancholy,* to our natural, our unnaturall fever. O perplex'd discomposition, O ridling distemper, O miserable condition of Man!

Actio Laesa.   *The strength, and the function*
                                of the Senses, and other faculties
                                change and faile.

II. MEDITATION

THE *Heavens* are not the less constant, because they move continually, because they move continually one and the same way. The *Earth* is not the more constant, because it lyes stil continually, because continually it changes, and melts in al parts thereof. *Man,* who is the noblest part of the *Earth,* melts so away, as if he were a *statue,* not of *Earth,* but of *Snowe.* We see his owne *Envie* melts him, he growes leane with that; he will say, anothers *beautie* melts him; but he feeles that a *Fever* doth not melt him like *snow,* but powr him out like *lead,* like *iron,* like *brasse* melted in a furnace: It doth not only *melt* him, but *calcine* him, reduce him to *Atomes,* and to *ashes;* not to *water,* but to *lime.* And how quickly? Sooner than thou canst receive an answer, sooner than thou canst conceive the question; *Earth* is the *center* of my *Bodie, Heaven* is the *center* of my *Soule;* these two are the naturall places of those two; but those goe not to these two in an equall pace: My *body* falls downe without pushing, my *Soule* does not go up without pulling: *Ascension* is my *Soules* pace and measure, but *precipita-*

tion my *bodies:* And, even *Angells,* whose home is *Heaven,* and who are winged too, yet had a *Ladder* to goe to *Heaven,* by steps. The *Sunne* who goes so many miles in a minut, the *Starres* of the *Firmament,* which go so very many more, goe not so fast, as my *body* to the *earth.* In the same instant that I feele the first attempt of the disease, I feele the victory; In the twinckling of an eye, I can scarse see, instantly the tast is insipid, and fatuous; instantly the appetite is dull and desirelesse: instantly the knees are sinking and strengthlesse; and in an instant, sleepe, which is the *picture,* the *copie* of *death,* is taken away, that the *Originall, Death* it selfe may succeed, and that so I might have death to the life. It was part of *Adams* punishment, *In the sweat of thy browes thou shalt eate thy bread:* it is multiplied to me, I have earned bread in the sweat of my browes, in the labor of my calling, and I have it; and I sweat againe, and againe, from the brow, to the sole of the foot, but I eat no bread, I tast no sustenance: Miserable distribution of *Mankind,* where one halfe lackes meat, and the other stomacke.

Decubitus sequitur tandem.   *The Patient takes his bed.*

III. MEDITATION

WEE attribute but one priviledge and advantage to Mans body, above other moving creatures, that he is not as others, groveling, but of an erect, of an upright form, naturally built, and disposed to the contemplation of *Heaven.* Indeed it is a thankfull forme, and recompences that *soule,* which gives it, with carrying that soule so many foot higher, towards *heaven.* Other creatures look to the *earth;* and even that is no unfit object, no unfit contemplation for *Man;* for thither hee must come; but because, *Man* is not to stay there, as other creatures are, *Man* in his naturall forme, is carried to the contemplation of that place, which is his *home, Heaven.* This is *Mans* prerogative; but what state hath he in this *dignitie?* A fever can fillip him downe, a fever can depose him; a fever can bring that head, which yesterday caried a *crown* of gold, five foot towards a *crown* of glory, as low as his own foot, today. When *God* came to breath into *Man* the breath of life, he found him flat upon the ground; when he comes to withdraw that breath from him againe, hee prepares him to it, by laying him flat upon his bed. Scarse any prison so close, that affords not the prisoner two, or three steps. The *Anchorites* that barqu'd themselves up in hollowe trees, and immur'd themselves in hollow walls; that perverse man, that barrell'd himselfe in a Tubb, all could stand, or sit, and enjoy some change of posture. A sicke bed, is a grave; and all that the patient saies there, is but a varying of his owne *Epitaph.* Every nights bed is a *Type* of the *grave:* At night wee tell our servants at what houre wee will rise; here we cannot tell our selves, at what day, what week, what moneth. Here the head lies as low as the foot; the *Head* of the people, as lowe as they, whome those feete trod upon; And that hande that signed Pardons, is too weake to begge his owne, if he might have it for lifting up that hand: Strange fetters to the feete, strange Manacles to the hands, when the feete, and handes are bound so much the faster, by how much the coards are slacker; So much the lesse able to doe their Offices, by how much more the Sinewes and Ligaments are the looser. In the *Grave* I may speak through the stones, in the voice of my friends, and in the accents of those wordes, which their love may afford my memory; Here I am mine owne *Ghost,* and rather affright my beholders, than instruct them; they conceive the worst of me now, and yet feare worse; they give me for dead now, and yet wonder how I doe, when they wake at midnight, and aske how I doe to morrow. Miserable and, (though common to all) inhuman *posture,* where I must practise my lying in the *grave,* by lying still, and not practise my *Resurrection,* by rising any more.

Medicusque vocatur.   *The Phisician is sent for.*

IV. MEDITATION

It is too little to call *Man* a *little World;* Except *God,* Man is a *diminutive* to nothing. Man consistes of more pieces, more parts, than the world; than the world doeth, nay than the world is. And if those pieces were extended, and stretched out in Man, as they are in the world, Man would bee the *Gyant,* and the Worlde the *Dwarfe,* the World but the *Map,* and the Man the *World.* If all the *Veines* in our bodies, were extended to *Rivers,* and all the *Sinewes,* to *Vaines of Mines,* and all the *Muscles,* that lye upon one another, to *Hilles,* and all the *Bones* to *Quarries* of stones, and all the other pieces, to the proportion of those which correspond to them in the world, the *Aire* would be too litle for this *Orbe* of Man to move in, the firmament would bee but enough for this *Starre;* for, as the whole world hath nothing, to which something in man doth not answere, so hath man many pieces, of which the whole world hath no representation. Inlarge this Meditation upon this *great world, Man,* so farr, as to consider the immensitie of the creatures this world produces; our *creatures* are our *thoughts, creatures* that are borne *Gyants;* that reach from *East* to *West,* from *Earth* to *Heaven,* that doe not onely bestride all the *Sea,* and *Land,* but span the *Sunn and Firmament* at once; My thoughts reach all, comprehend all. Inexplicable mistery; I their *Creator* am in a close prison, in a sicke bed, any where, and any one of my *Creatures,* my *thoughts,* is with the *Sunne,* and beyond the *Sunne,* overtakes the *Sunne,* and overgoes the *Sunne* in one pace, one steppe, everywhere. And then as the other *world* produces *Serpents,* and *Vipers,* malignant, and venimous creatures, and *Wormes,* and *Caterpillars,* that endeavour to devoure that world which produces them, and *Monsters* compiled and complicated of divers parents, and kinds, so this world, our selves, produces all these in us, in producing *diseases,* and *sicknesses,* of all those sorts; venimous, and infectious diseases, feeding and consuming diseases, and manifold and entangled diseases, made up of many several ones. And can the other world name so many *venimous,* so many consuming, so many monstrous creatures, as we can diseases, of all these kindes? O miserable abundance, O beggarly riches! how much doe wee lacke of having *remedies* for everie disease, when as yet we have not *names* for them? But wee have a *Hercules* against these *Gyants,* these *Monsters;* that is, the *Phisician;* hee musters up al the forces of the other world, to succour this; all Nature to relieve Man. We *have* the *Phisician,* but we *are not* the *Phisician.* Heere we shrinke in our proportion, sink in our dignitie, in respect of verie meane creatures, who are *Phisicians* to themselves. The *Hart* that is pursued and wounded, they say, knowes an Herbe, which being eaten, throwes off the arrow: A strange kind of *vomit.* The *dog* that pursues it, though hee bee subject to sicknes, even *proverbially,* knowes his *grasse* that recovers him. And it may be true, that the *Drugger* is as neere to *Man,* as to other *creatures,* it may be that obvious and present *Simples,* easie to be had, would cure him; but the *Apothecary* is not so neere him, nor the *Phisician* so neere him, as they two are to other creatures; Man hath not that *innate instinct,* to apply these naturall medicines to his present danger, as those inferiour creatures have; he is not his owne *Apothecary*, his owne *Phisician*, as they are. Call back therefore thy Meditation again, and bring it downe; whats become of mans great extent and proportion, when himselfe shrinkes himselfe, and consumes himselfe to a handfull of dust? whats become of his soaring thoughts, his compassing thoughts, when himselfe brings himselfe to the ignorance, to the thoughtlessnesse of the *Grave?* His *diseases* are his owne, but the *Phisician* is not; hee hath them at home, but hee must send for the *Phisician.*

Solus adest.   *The Phisician comes.*

V. MEDITATION

As *Sicknes* is the greatest misery, so the greatest misery of sicknes, is *solitude;* when the infectiousnes of the disease deterrs them who should assist, from comming; even the *Phisician* dares scarse come. *Solitude* is a torment which is not threatned in *hell* it selfe. Meere *vacuitie,* the first *Agent, God,* the first *instrument* of *God, Nature,* will not admit; Nothing can be utterly *emptie,* but so neere a degree towards *Vacuitie,* as *Solitude,* to bee but one, they love not. When I am dead, and my body might infect, they have a remedy, they may bury me; but when I am but sick, and might infect, they have no remedy, but their absence, and my solitude. It is an *excuse* to them that are *great,* and pretend, and yet are loth to come; it is an *inhibition* to those who would truly come, because they may be made instruments, and pestiducts, to the infection of others, by their comming. And it is an *Outlawry,* an *Excommunication* upon the *Patient,* and seperats him from all offices not onely of *Civilitie,* but of *working Charitie.* A long sicknesse will weary friends at last, but a pestilentiall sicknes averts them from the beginning. God himself would admit a *figure* of *Society,* as there is a plurality of persons in *God,* though there bee but one *God;* and all his externall actions testifie a love of *Societie,* and *communion.* In *Heaven* there are *Orders* of *Angels,* and *Armies* of *Martyrs,* and *in that house, many mansions; in Earth, Families, Cities, Churches, Colleges,* all *plurall things;* and lest either of these should not be company enough alone, there is an association of both, a *Communion of Saints,* which makes the *Militant,* and *Triumphant Church,* one Parish; So that *Christ,* was not out of his *Dioces,* when hee was upon the

Earth, nor out of his *Temple,* when he was in our flesh. *God,* who sawe that all that hee made, was good, came not so neer seeing a *defect* in any of his works, as when he saw that it was not good, for man to bee *alone,* therefore *hee made him a helper;* and one that should helpe him so, as to increase the *number,* and give him *her owne,* and *more societie. Angels* who do not propagate, nor multiply, were made at the first in an abundant number; and so were starres: But for the things of this world, their blessing was, *Encrease;* for I think, I need not aske leave to think, that there is no *Phenix;* nothing singular, nothing alone: Men that inhere upon *Nature* only, are so far from thinking, that there is anything *singular* in this world, as that they will scarce thinke, that this world it selfe is *singular,* but that every *Planet,* and every *Starre,* is another *world* like this; They finde reason to conceive, not onely a *pluralitie* in every *Species* in the world, but a *pluralitie of worlds;* so that the abhorrers of *Solitude,* are not solitary; for *God,* and *Nature,* and *Reason* concurre against it. Now a man may counterfeyt the *Plague* in a *vowe,* and mistake a *Disease* for *Religion;* by such a retiring, and recluding of himselfe from all men, as to doe good to no man, to converse with no man. *God* hath two *Testaments,* two *Wils;* but this is a *Scedule,* and not of his, a *Codicill,* and not of his, not in the *body* of his *Testaments,* but *interlin'd,* and *postscrib'd* by others, that the way to the *Communion of Saints,* should be by such a *solitude,* as excludes all doing of good here. That is a *disease* of the *mind;* as the height of an infectious disease of the body, is *solitude,* to be left alone: for this makes an infectious bed, equall, nay worse than a *grave,* that thogh in both I be equally alone, in my bed I *know* it, and *feele* it, and shall not in my *grave:* and this too, that in my bedd, my soule is still in an infectious body, and shall not in my grave bee so.

Metuit.   *The Phisician is afraid.*

VI. MEDITATION

I OBSERVE the *Phisician,* with the same diligence, as hee the *disease;* I see hee *feares,* and I feare with him: I overtake him, I overrun him in his *feare,* and I go the faster, because he makes his pace slow; I feare the more, because he disguises his fear, and I see it with the more sharpnesse, because hee would not have me see it. He knowes that his *feare* shall not disorder the practise, and exercise of his *Art,* but he knows that my *fear* may disorder the effect, and working of his practise. As the ill affections of the *spleene,* complicate, and mingle themselves with every infirmitie of the body, so doth *feare* insinuat it self in every *action* or *passion* of the *mind;* and as the *wind* in the body will counterfet any disease, and seem the *stone* and seem the *Gout,* so feare will counterfet any disease of the *Mind;* It shall seeme *love,* a love of having, and it is but a *fear,* a jealous, and suspitious feare of loosing; It shall seem *valor* in despising, and undervaluing danger, and it is but *feare,* in an overvaluing of *opinion,* and *estimation,* and a feare of loosing that. A man that is not afraid of a *Lion* is afraid of a *Cat;* not afraid of *starving,* and yet is afraid of some *joynt of meat* at the table, presented to feed him; not afraid of the sound of *Drummes,* and *Trumpets,* and *Shot,* and those, which they seeke to drowne, the last cries of men, and is afraid of some particular *harmonious instrument;* so much afraid, as that with any of these the *enemy* might drive this man, otherwise valiant enough, out of the field. I know not, what fear is, nor I know not what it is that I fear now; I feare not the hastening of my *death,* and yet I do fear the increase of the *disease;* I should belie *Nature,* if I should deny that I feared this, and if I should say that I feared *death,* I should belye *God;* My weaknesse is from *Nature,* who hath but her *Measure,* my strength is from *God,* who possesses, and distributes infinitely. As then every cold ayre, is not a *dampe,* every *shivering* is not a *stupefaction,* so every *feare,* is not a *fearefulnes,* every declination is not a running away, every debating is not a resolving, every wish, that it were not thus, is not a murmuring, nor a dejection though it bee thus; but as my *Phisicians* fear puts not him from his *practise,* neither doth mine put me, from receiving from *God,* and *Man,* and *my selfe, spirituall* and *civill,* and *morall* assistances, and consolations.

Socios sibi jungier instat.   *The Phisician desires to have others joyned with him.*

VII. MEDITATION

THERE is *more feare,* therefore *more cause.* If the *Phisician* desire help, the burden grows great: There is a growth of the

Disease then: But there must bee an *Autumne* to; But whether an *Autumne* of the *disease* or *mee*, it is not my part to choose: but if it bee of *mee*, it is of *both;* My disease cannot *survive mee*, I may *overlive* it. Howsoever, his desiring of others, argues his *candor*, and his *ingenuitie;* if the danger be *great*, he *justifies* his proceedings, and he *disguises* nothing, that calls in *witnesses;* And if the danger bee not *great*, hee is not *ambitious*, that is so readie to divide the thankes, and the honour of that work, which he begun alone, with others. It diminishes not the dignitie of a *Monarch*, that hee derive part of his care upon others; *God* hath not made many *Suns*, but he hath made many *bodies*, that *receive*, and *give* light. The *Romanes* began with *one King;* they came to *two Consuls;* they returned in extremities, to *one Dictator:* whether in *one*, or *many*, the *Soveraigntie* is the same, in all *States*, and the danger is not the more, and the providence is the more, where there are more *Phisicians;* as the State is the happier, where businesses are carried by more counsels, than can bee in one breast, how large soever. *Diseases* themselves hold *Consultations*, and conspire how they may multiply, and joyn with one another, and *exalt* one anothers force, so; and shal we not call *Phisicians*, to con*sultations?* *Death* is in an olde mans dore, he appeares, and tels him so, and *death* is at a young mans *backe*, and saies nothing; *Age* is a *sicknesse*, and *Youth* is an *ambush;* and we need so many *Phisicians*, as may make up a *Watch*, and spie every inconvenience. There is scarce any thing, that hath not killed some body; a *haire*, a *feather* hath done it; Nay, that which is our best *Antidote* against it, hath donn it; the best *Cordiall* hath bene *deadly poyson;* Men have dyed of *Joy*, and allmost forbidden their friends to weepe for them, when they have seen them dye laughing. Even that Tiran *Dyonisius* (I thinke the same, that suffered so much after) who could not die of that sorrow, of that high fal, from a *King* to a *wretched private man*, dyed of so poore a *Joy*, as to be declard by the *people* at a *Theater*, that hee was a good *Poet*. We say often that a *Man may live of a litle;* but, alas, of how much lesse may a Man dye! And therfore the more assistants, the better; who comes to a day of hearing, in a cause of any importance, with one *Advocate?* In our *Funerals*, we our selves have no interest; there wee cannot *advise*, we cannot *direct:* And though some *Nations*, (the *Egiptians* in particular) built themselves better *tombs*, than *houses*, because they were to dwell *longer* in them; yet, amongst our selves, the greatest *Man of Stile*, whom we have had, *The Conqueror,* was left, as soone as his soule left him, not only without persons to assist at his *grave,* but without a *grave.* Who will keepe us then, we know not; As long as we can, let us admit as much *helpe* as wee can; Another, and another *Phisician,* is not another, and another *Indication,* and *Symptom* of *death,* but another, and another *Assistant,* and *Proctor* of *life:* Nor doe they so much feed the imagination with apprehension of *danger,* as the understanding with *comfort;* Let not one bring *Learning,* another *Diligence,* another *Religion,* but every one bring all, and, as many Ingredients enter into a Receit, so may many men make the Receit. But why doe I exercise my Meditation so long upon this, of having plentifull helpe in time of need? Is not my Meditation rather to be enclined another way, to condole, and commiserate their distresse, who have *none?* How many are sicker (perchance) than I, and laid on their wofull straw at home (if that corner be a home) and have no more hope of helpe, though they die, than of preferment, though they live? Nor doe no more expect to see a *Phisician* then, than to bee an *Officer* after; of whome, the first that takes knowledge, is the *Sexten* that buries them; who buries them in *oblivion* too? For they doe but fill up the number of the dead in the Bill, but we shall never heare their *Names,* till wee reade them in the Booke of life, with our owne. How many are sicker (perchance) than I, and thrown into *Hospitals,* where, (as a fish left upon the Sand, must stay the tide) they must stay the *Phisicians* houre of visiting, and then can bee but *visited?* How many are sicker (perchaunce) than all we, and have not this *Hospitall* to cover them, not this straw, to lie in, to die in, but have their *Grave-stone* under them, and breathe out then soules in the eares, and in the eies of passengers, harder than their bed, the flint of the street? That taste of no part of our *Phisick,* but a *sparing dyet;* to whom ordinary porridge would bee *Julip* enough, the refuse of our servants, *Bezar* enough, and the off-scouring of our Kitchen tables, *Cordiall* enough. O my *soule,* when thou art not enough awake, to blesse thy *God* enough for his plentifull mercy, in affoording thee many *Helpers,* remember how many lacke them, and helpe them to them, or to those other things, which they lacke as much as them.

Et Rex ipse
suum mittit.

The King sends his
owne Phisician.

VIII. MEDITATION

STIL when we return to that *Meditation,* that *Man* is a *World,* we find new *discoveries.* Let him be a *world,* and him self will be the *land,* and *misery* the *sea.* His misery (for misery is his, his own; of the happinesses of this world hee is but *Tenant,* but of misery the *Free-holder;* of happines he is but the *farmer,* but the *usufructuary,* but of misery, the *Lord,* the *proprietary*) his misery, as the *sea,* swells above all the hilles, and reaches to the remotest parts of this *earth, Man;* who of himselfe is but *dust,* and coagulated and kneaded into earth, by *teares;* his *matter* is *earth,* his *forme, misery.* In this *world,* that is *Mankinde,* the highest ground, the eminentest *hils,* are *Kings;* and have they line, and lead enough to fadome this *sea,* and say, My misery is but this deepe? Scarce any misery equal to *sicknesse;* and they are subject to that equally, with their lowest subject. A glasse is not the lesse brittle, because a *Kings* face is represented in it; nor a King the lesse brittle, because *God* is represented in him. They have *Phisicians* continually about them, and therfore *sicknesses,* or the worst of sicknesses, continuall feare of it. Are they *gods?* He that calld them so, cannot flatter. They are *Gods,* but *sicke gods;* and *God* is presented to us under many human affections, as far as *infirmities; God* is called *Angry,* and *Sorry,* and *Weary,* and *Heavy;* but never a *sicke God:* for then hee might *die* like men, as our *gods* do. The worst that they could say in reproch, and scorne of the *gods* of the *Heathen,* was, that perchance they were *asleepe;* but *Gods* that are so sicke, as that they cannot sleepe, are in an infirmer condition. A *God,* and need a *Phisician?* A *Jupiter* and need an *Æsculapius?* that must have *Rheubarbe* to purge his *choller,* lest he be too angry, and *Agarick* to purge his *flegme,* lest he be too drowsie; that as *Tertullian* saies of the *Ægyptian gods, plants* and *herbes, That God was beholden to Man, for growing in his garden,* so wee must say of these *gods, Their eternity,* (*an eternity* of three score and ten yeares) is in the *Apothecaryes* shop, and not in the *Metaphoricall Deity.* But their *Deitye* is better expressed in their *humility* than in their *heighth:* when abounding and overflowing, as *God,* in means of doing good, they descend, as *God,* to a communi-

cation of their abundances with men, according to their necessities, then they are *Gods*. No man is well, that understands
not, that values not his being well; that hath not a cheereful-
nesse, and a joy in it; and whosoever hath this *Joy*, hath a desire to communicate, to propagate that, which occasions his
happinesse, and his *Joy*, to others; for every man loves witnesses of his happinesse; and the best witnesses, are experi-
mentall witnesses; they who have tasted of that in themselves,
which makes us happie: It consummates therefore, it perfits
the happinesse of *Kings*, to confer, to transfer, honor, and
riches, and (as they can) health, upon those that need them.

Medicamina   *Upon their Consultation,*
scribunt.   *they prescribe.*

IX. MEDITATION

THEY have seene me, and heard mee, arraign'd mee in these
fetters, and receiv'd the *evidence;* I have cut up mine
Anatomy, dissected my selfe, and they are gon to *read* upon
me. O how manifold, and perplexed a thing, nay, how wanton
and various a thing is *ruine* and *destruction! God* presented to
David three kinds, *War, Famine,* and *Pestilence; Satan* left out
these, and brought in, *fires from heaven,* and *windes from the
wildernes*. [As] if there were no *ruine* but *sicknes*, wee see,
the Masters of that *Art,* can scarce *number,* nor *name* all sicknesses; every thing that *disorders* a faculty, and the function of
that is a sicknesse: The names wil not serve them which are
given from the *place affected,* the *Plurisie* is so; nor from the
effect which it works, the *falling sicknes* is so; they cannot
have names enow, from *what it does,* nor *where it is,* but they
must extort names from what *it is like,* what it *resembles,* and
but in some one thing, or els they would lack names; for the
Wolf, and the *Canker,* and the *Polypus* are so; and that question, *whether there be more names or things,* is as perplexd
in sicknesses, as in any thing else; except it be easily re-
solvd upon that side, that there are more *sicknesses* than
names. If *ruine* were reduc'd to that one way, that Man could
perish noway but by *sicknes*, yet his danger were infinit; and
if *sicknes* were reduc'd to that one way. that there were no
sicknes but a *fever,* yet the way were infinite still; for it would
overlode, and oppress any naturall, disorder and discompose any

artificiall *Memory,* to deliver the *names* of severall *fevers;* how intricate a worke then have they, who are gone to *consult,* which of these *sicknesses* mine is, and then which of these *fevers,* and then what it would do, and then how it may be countermind. But even in *ill,* it is a degree of *good,* when the *evil* wil admit *consultation.* In many *diseases,* that which is but an *accident,* but a *symptom* of the main *disease,* is so violent, that the *Phisician* must attend the cure of that, though hee pretermit (so far as to intermit) the cure of the *disease* it self. Is it not so in *States* too? somtimes the insolency of those that are *great,* put[s] the people into *commotions;* the great disease, and the greatest danger to the *Head,* is the *insolency of the great ones;* and yet, they execute *Martial law,* they come to present executions upon the *people,* whose commotion was indeed but a *symptom,* but an *accident* of the maine *disease;* but this *symptom,* grown so violent, would allow no time for a *consultation.* Is it not so in the accidents of the *diseases* of our *mind* too? Is it not evidently so in our *affections,* in our *passions?* If a *cholerick* man be ready to strike, must I goe about to purge his *choler,* or to breake the blow? But where there is room for *consultation,* things are not desperate. They *consult;* so there is nothing *rashly, inconsideratly* done; and then they *prescribe,* they *write,* so there is nothing *covertly, disguisedly, unavowedly* done. In *bodily diseases* it is not alwaies so; sometimes, as soon as the *Phisicians* foote is in the *chamber,* his *knife* is in the patients *arme;* the disease would not allow a *minutes* forbearing of *blood,* nor *prescribing* of other remedies. In States and matter of government it is so too; they are somtimes surprizd with such *accidents,* as that the *Magistrat* asks not what may be done by *law,* but does that, which must *necessarily* be don in that case. But it is a degree of *good,* in *evill,* a degree that carries hope and comfort in it, when we may have recourse to that which is *written,* and that the proceedings may be apert, and ingenuous, and candid, and avowable, for that gives satisfaction, and acquiescence. They who have received my *Anatomy* of my selfe, *consult,* and end their *consultation* in *prescribing,* and in prescribing *Phisick;* proper and convenient remedy: for if they should come in again, and chide mee, for some disorder, that had occasion'd, or inducd, or that had hastned and exalted this *sicknes,* or if they should begin to write now rules for my *dyet,* and *exercise* when I were well, this were to *antidate,* or to *postdate* their *Consultation,* not to give *Phisicke.* It were

rather a vexation, than a reliefe, to tell a condemnd prisoner,
you might have liv'd if you had done this; and if you can get
pardon, you shal do wel, to take this, or this course hereafter.
I am glad they know (I have hid nothing from them) glad
they consult, (they hide nothing from one another) glad they
write (they hide nothing from the world) glad that they write
and prescribe *Phisick*, that there are *remedies* for the present
case.

Lentè et Serpenti   *They find the Disease to steale*
satagunt occurrere   *on insensibly, and endeavour*
Morbo.   *to meet with it so.*

X. MEDITATION

THIS is *Natures nest of Boxes;* The Heavens containe the
Earth, the *Earth*, *Cities*, *Cities*, *Man*. And all these are *Concentrique;* the common *center* to them all, is *decay, ruine;*
only that is *Eccentrique,* which was never made; only that
place, or garment rather, which we can *imagine*, but not *dem-
onstrate*, That light, which is the very emanation of the light
of *God*, in which the *Saints* shall dwell, with which the *Saints*
shall be appareld, only that bends not to this *Center*, to *Ruine;*
that which was not made of *Nothing*, is not threatned with
this annihilation. All other things are; even *Angels*, even our
soules; they move upon the same *poles*, they bend to the same
Center; and if they were not made immortall by *preservation*,
their *Nature* could not keep them from sinking to this *center*,
Annihilation. In all these (the *frame of the heavens*, the
States upon earth, and *Men in them*, comprehend all). Those
are the greatest mischifs, which are least discerned; the most
insensible in their *wayes* come to bee the most sensible in
their *ends*. The *Heavens* have had their *Dropsie*, they drownd
the world, and they shall have their *Fever*, and burn the world.
Of the *dropsie*, the flood, the world had a foreknowledge 120
yeares before it came; and so some made provision against it,
and were saved; the *fever* shall break out in an instant, and
consume all; The *dropsie* did no harm to the *heavens*, from
whence it fell, it did not put out those *lights*, it did
not quench those *heates;* but the *fever*, the fire shall burne
the *furnace* it selfe, annihilate those *heavens*, that breath it
out; Though the *Dog-Starre* have a pestilent breath, an infectious exhalation, yet because we know when it wil rise, we

clothe our selves, and wee diet our selves, and we shadow our selves to a sufficient prevention; but *Comets* and *blazing starres*, whose effects, or significations no man can interrupt or frustrat, no man foresaw: no *Almanack* tells us, when a *blazing starre* will break out, the matter is carried up in secret; no *Astrologer* tels us when the effects will be accomplished, for thats a secret of a higher spheare, than the other; and that which is most *secret*, is most *dangerous*. It is so also here in the *societies* of men, in *States*, and *Commonwealths*. Twentie *rebellious drums* make not so dangerous a noise, as a few *whisperers*, and secret plotters in corners. The *Canon* doth not so much hurt against a wal, as a *Myne* under the wall; nor a thousand enemies that threaten, so much as a few that take an *oath* to say *nothing*. God knew many heavy sins of the people, in the wildernes and after, but still he charges them with that one, with *Murmuring, murmuring* in their *hearts*, secret disobediences, secret repugnances against his declar'd wil; and these are the most deadly, the most pernicious. And it is so too, with the *diseases* of the *body;* and that is my case. The *pulse*, the *urine*, the *sweat*, all have sworn to say nothing, to give no *Indication*, of any dangerous *sicknesse*. My forces are not enfeebled, I find no decay in my strength; my provisions are not cut off, I find no abhorring in mine appetite; my counsels are not corrupted or infatuated, I find no false apprehensions, to work upon mine understanding; and yet they see, that invisibly, and I feele, that insensibly the *disease* prevailes. The *disease* hath established a *Kingdome*, an *Empire* in mee, and will have certaine *Arcana Imperii, secrets of State*, by which it will proceed, and not be bound to *declare* them. But yet against those secret conspiracies in the State, the *Magistrate* hath the *rack;* and against the insensible diseases, *Phisicians* have their *examiners;* and those these employ now.

Nobilibusque trahunt, a cincto Corde, venenum, Succis et Gemmis, et quæ generosa, Ministrant Ars, et Natura, instillant.	*They use Cordials, to keep the venim and Malignitie of the disease from the Heart.*

XI. MEDITATION

WHENCE can wee take a better argument, a clearer demonstration, that all the *Greatnes* of this world, is built upon *opinion*

of others, and hath in itself no *reall being,* nor power of sub-
sistence, than from the *heart of man?* It is always in *action,*
and *motion,* still busie, still pretending to doe all, to furnish
all the powers, and faculties with all that they have; But if an
enemy dare rise up against it, it is the soonest endangered, the
soonest defeated of any part. The *Braine* will hold out longer
than it, and the *Liver* longer than that; They will endure a
Seige; but an unnatural heat, a rebellious heat, will blow up
the *heart,* like a *Myne,* in a *minute.* But howsoever, since the
Heart hath the *birthright* and *Primogeniture,* and that it is
Natures eldest Sonne in us, the part which is first borne to
life in man, and that the other parts, as *younger brethren,* and
servants in this family, have a dependance upon it, it is reason
that the principall care bee had of it, though it bee not the
strongest part; as the *eldest* is oftentimes not the strongest of
the family. And since the *Braine,* and *Liver,* and *Heart,* hold
not a *Triumvirate* in *Man,* a *Soveraigntie* equally shed upon
them all, for his *well-being,* as the foure *Elements* doe, for his
very *being,* but the *Heart* alone is in the *Principalitie,* and in
the *Throne,* as *King,* the rest as *Subjects,* though in eminent
Place and *Office,* must contribute to that, as *Children* to their
Parents, as all persons to all kinds of *Superiours,* though oftentimes, those *Parents,* or those *Superiours,* bee not of stronger
parts, than them selves, that serve and obey them that
are weaker; Neither doth this Obligation fall upon us, by second *Dictates* of *Nature,* by *Consequences* and *Conclusions* aris-
ing out of *Nature,* or deriv'd from *Nature,* by *Discourse,* (as
many things binde us even by the Law of *Nature,* and yet not
by the *primarie* Law of *Nature;* as all Lawes of *Proprietie* in
that which we possesse, are of the Law of *Nature,* which law
is, *To give every one his owne,* and yet in the *primarie* law of
Nature there was no *Proprietie,* no *Meum* and *Tuum,* but an
universall *Communitie* over all; So the Obedience of *Superiours,* is of the law of *Nature,* and yet in the *primarie* law of
Nature, there was no *Superioritie,* no *Magistracie;*) but this
contribution of assistance of all to the *Soveraigne,* of all parts
to the *Heart,* is from the very *first dictates of Nature;* which
is, in the first place, to have care of our owne *Preservation,* to
look first to ourselves; for therefore doth the *Phisician* intermit
the present care of *Braine,* or *Liver,* because there is a possibilitie that they may subsist, though there bee not a present
and a particular care had of them, but there is no possibilitie
that they can subsist, if the *Heart* perish: and so, when we

seem to begin with others, in such assistances, indeed wee doe beginne with ourselves, and wee ourselves are principally in our contemplation; and so all these officious, and mutual assistances are but *complements* towards others, and our true end is *ourselves*. And this is the reward of the paines of *Kings*; sometimes they neede the power of law, to be obey'd; and when they seeme to be obey'd *voluntarily*, they who doe it, doe it for their owne sakes. O how little a thing is all the *greatnes of man*, and through how false glasses doth he make shift to *multiply it*, and *magnifie* it to himselfe! And yet this is also another misery of this *King of man*, the *Heart*, which is also applyable to the *Kings of this world, great men*, that the venime and poyson of every pestilentiall disease directs itself to the *Heart*, affects that (pernicious affection,) and the *malignity* of ill men, is also directed upon the *greatest*, and the *best*; and not only *greatnesse*, but *goodnesse* looses the vigour of beeing an *Antidote*, or *Cordiall* against it. And as the noblest, and most generous *Cordialls* that *Nature* or *Art* afford, or can prepare, if they be often taken, and made *familiar*, become no *Cordialls*, nor have any extraordinary operation, so the greatest *Cordiall* of the *Heart*, patience, if it bee much exercis'd, exalts the *venim* and the *malignity* of the *Enemy*, and the more we suffer, the more wee are insulted upon. When God had made this *Earth* of *nothing*, it was but a little helpe, that he had, to make other things of this *Earth*: nothing can be neerer nothing, than this *Earth*; and yet how little of this *Earth* is the greatest *Man*! Hee thinkes he treads upon the *Earth*, that all is under his feete, and the *Braine* that thinkes so, is but *Earth*; his highest Region, the flesh that covers that, is but *earth*; and even the toppe of that, that, wherein so many *Absolons* take so much pride, is but a bush growing upon that *Turfe of Earth*. How litle of the world is the *Earth*! And yet that is all that *Man hath*, or *is*. How little of a *Man* is the *Heart*, and yet it is all, by which he *is*; and this continually subject, not only to forraine poysons, conveyed by others, but to intestine poysons, bred in ourselves by pestilentiall sicknesses. O who, if before hee had a beeing, he could have sense of this miserie, would buy a being here upon these conditions?

Spirante Columbâ
Suppositâ pedibus, Revocantur
ad ima vapores.

*They apply Pidgeons, to
draw the vapors from
the Head.*

XII. MEDITATION

WHAT will not kill a man if a *vapor* will? How great an *Ele-
phant,* how small a *Mouse* destroys! To dye by a *bullet* is the
Souldiers dayly bread; but few men dye by *haile-shot:* A man
is more worth, than to bee sold for *single money;* a *life* to be
valued above a *trifle.* If this were a violent shaking of the Ayre
by *Thunder,* or by *Canon,* in that case the *Ayre* is condensed
above the thicknesse of *water,* of *water* baked into *Ice,* almost
petrified, almost made stone, and no wonder that kills; but that
that which is but a *vapor,* and a *vapor* not forced, but breathed,
should kill, that our *Nourse* should overlay us, and *Ayre* that
nourishes us, should destroy us, but that it is a *halfe Atheisme*
to murmure against *Nature,* who is *Gods immediate commis-
sioner,* who would not think himselfe miserable to bee put into
the hands of *Nature,* who does not only set him up for a
marke for others to shoote at, but delights herselfe to blow
him up like a *glasse,* till shee see him breake, even with her
owne breath? nay, if this infectious *vapor* were sought for, or
travail'd to, as *Plinie* hunted after the *vapor* of *Ætna,* and
dared and challenged *Death,* in the forme of a vapor, to doe
his worst, and felt the worst, he dyed; or if this *vapor* were
met withall in an *ambush,* and we surprised with it, out of a
long shutt *Well,* or out of a new opened *Myne,* who would
lament, who would accuse, when we had nothing to accuse,
none to lament against but *Fortune,* who is lesse than a *vapor:*
But when our selves are the *Well,* that breaths out this ex-
halation, the *Oven* that spits out this fiery smoke, the *Myne*
that spues out this suffocating, and strangling *dampe,* who can
ever after this, aggravate his sorrow, by this *Circumstance,* That
it was his *Neighbor,* his *familiar Friend,* his *Brother,* that de-
stroyed him, and destroyed him with a whispering, and a ca-
lumniating breath, when wee our selves doe it to our selves by
the same meanes, kill our selves with our owne *vapors?* Or if
these occasions of this selfe-destruction, had any contribution
from our owne *Wils,* any assistance from our owne *intentions,*
nay from our own *errors,* we might divide the rebuke, and
chide our selves as much as them. *Fevers* upon wilful distem-

pers of drinke, and surfets, *Consumptions* upon intemperances, and licentiousnes, *Madnes* upon misplacing, or overbending our naturall faculties, proceed from our selves, and so, as that our selves are in the plot, and wee are not onely *passive*, but *active* too, to our owne destruction; But what have I done, either to *breed*, or to *breath* these *vapors?* They tell me it is my *Melancholy;* Did I infuse, did I drinke in *Melancholly* into my selfe? It is my *thoughtfulnesse;* was I not made to *thinke?* It is my *study;* doth not my *Calling* call for that? I have don nothing, wilfully, perversly toward it, yet must suffer in it, die by it; There are too many *Examples* of men, that have bir their own *executioners*, and that have made hard shift to bec so; some have alwayes had *poyson* about them, in a *hollow ring* upon their finger, and some in their *Pen* that they used to write with: some have beat out their *braines* at the wal of their prison, and some have eate the *fire* out of their chimneys: and one is said to have come neerer our case than so, to have strangled himself, though his hands were bound, by crushing his throat between his knees; But I doe nothing upon my selfe, and yet am mine owne *Executioner*. And we have heard of *death* upon small occasions, and by scornefull *instruments:* a *pinne*, a *combe*, a *haire*, pulled, hath gangred, and killd; But when I have said, a *vapour*, if I were asked again, what is a *vapour*, I could not tell, it is so insensible a thing; so neere *nothing* is that reduces us to *nothing*. But extend this *vapour*, rarefie it; from so narow a roome, as our *Naturall bodies*, to any *Politike body*, to a *State*. That which is *fume* in us, is in a *State*, *Rumor*, and these *vapours* in us, which wee consider here pestilent and infectious fumes, are in a State *infectious rumors*, detracting and dishonourable *Calumnies, Libels*. The *Heart* in that *body* is the *King;* and the *Braine*, his *Councell;* and the whole *Magistracie*, that ties all together, is the *Sinewes*, which proceed from thence; and the *life* of all is *Honour*, and just *respect*, and due *reverence;* and therfore, when these *vapors*, these venimous *rumors*, are directed against these *Noble parts*, the whole body suffers. But yet for all their priviledges, they are not priviledged from our *misery;* that as the *vapours* most pernitious to us, arise in our owne bodies, so do the most dishonorable *rumours*, and those that wound a *State* most, arise at home. What ill *ayre*, that I could have met in the street, what *Channell*, what *Shambles*, what *Dunghill*, what *vault*, could have hurt mee so much, as these home-bredd *vapours?* What *Fugitive*, what *Almes-man of any for-*

raine State, can doe so much harme as a *Detracter*, a *Libeller*, a scornefull *Jester* at home? For, as they that write of *poysons*, and of creatures naturally disposed to the ruine of Man, do as well mention the *Flea*, as the *Viper*, because the *Flea*, though hee kill none, hee does all the harme hee can; so even these libellous and licentious *Jesters* utter the venim they have, though sometimes *vertue*, and alwaies *power*, be a good *Pigeon* to draw this *vapor* from the *Head*, and from doing any deadly harme there.

Ingeniumque malum, numeroso stigmate, fassus Pellitur ad pectus, Morbique Suburbia, Morbus.	*The Sicknes declares the infection and malignity thereof by spots.*

XIII. MEDITATION

WEE say, that the world is made of *sea*, and *land*, as though they were equal; but we know that ther is more *sea* in the *Western*, than in the *Eastern Hemisphere:* We say that the *Firmament* is full of *starres*, as though it were equally full; but we know, that there are more *stars* under the *Northerne*, than under the *Southern Pole*. We say, the *Elements* of man are *misery*, and *happinesse*, as though he had an equal proportion of both, and the dayes of man vicissitudinary, as though he had as many *good* daies, as *ill*, and that he liv'd under a perpetuall *Equinoctial night*, and *day* equall, good and ill fortune in the same measure. But it is far from that; hee *drinkes misery*, and he *tastes happinesse;* he *mowes misery*, and he *gleanes happinesse;* he *journies in misery*, he does but *walke in happinesse;* and which is worst, his misery is *positive*, and *dogmaticall*, his happinesse is but *disputable*, and *problematicall;* All men call *Misery, Misery,* but *Happinesse* changes the name, by the taste of man. In this *accident* that befalls mee now, that this sicknesse declares itself by *Spots*, to be a malignant, and pestilentiall disease, if there be a *comfort* in the declaration, that therby the *Phisicians* see more cleerely what to doe, there may bee as much *discomfort* in this, That the malignitie may bee so great, as that all that they can doe, shall doe *nothing;* That an enemy *declares* himselfe, then, when he is able to subsist, and to pursue, and to atchive his ends, is no great comfort. In intestine Conspiracies, *voluntary Confessions*

doe more good, than Confessions upon the *Rack;* in these Infections, when *Nature* her selfe confesses, and cries out by
these outward declarations, which she is able to put forth of
her selfe, they minister *comfort;* but when all is by strength
of *Cordials,* it is but a *Confession upon the Racke,* by which
though wee come to knowe the malice of that man, yet wee
doe not knowe whether there be not as much malice in his
heart then, as before his confession; we are sure of his *Treason,* but not of his *Repentance;* sure of *him,* but not of his
Complices. It is a faint comfort to know the worst, when the
worst is *remedilesse;* and a weaker than that, to know *much
ill,* and not to know, that that is the worst. A woman is
comforted with the birth of her *Son,* her body is eased of a
burthen; but if shee could *prophetically* read his *History,* how
ill a man, perchance how *ill a sonne,* he would prove, shee
should receive a greater burthen into her *Mind.* Scarce any
purchase that is not clogged with secret *encumbrances;* scarce
any *happines* that hath not in it so much of the *nature* of
false and base money, as that the *Allay* is more than the *Metall.* Nay, is it not so, (at least much towards it) even in the
exercise of *Vertues?* I must bee poore, and want, before I can
exercise the vertue of *Gratitude;* miserable, and in torment,
before I can exercise the vertue of *patience;* How deepe do
we dig, and for how coarse gold? And what other *Touchstone*
have we of our *gold,* but *comparison?* Whether we be as
happy, as others, or as ourselves at other times; O poore
stepp toward being well, when these *spots* do only tell us,
that we are worse, than we were sure of before.

Idque notant Criticis, Medici   *The Phisicians observe these*
     evenisse Diebus.   *accidents to have fallen upon*
                                      the criticall dayes.

XIV. MEDITATION

I WOULD not make *Man* worse than hee is, Nor his Condition
more miserable than it is. But could I though I would? As a
man cannot *flatter God,* nor over prayse him, so a man cannot
injure Man, nor undervalue him. Thus much must necessarily
be presented to his remembrance, that those *false Happinesses,*
which he hath in this World, have their *times,* and their *seasons,* and their *critical dayes,* and they are *Judged,* and *De-*

nominated according to the times, when they befall us. What poore *Elements* are our *happinesses* made of, if *Tyme, Tyme* which wee can scarce consider to be *any thing*, be an essential part of our happines! All things are done in some *place;* but if we consider *Place* to be no more, but the next hollow *Superficies* of the *Ayre, Alas,* how thinne, and fluid a thing is *Ayre,* and how thinne a *filme* is a *Superficies,* and a *Superficies* of *Ayre!* All things are done in *time* too; but if we consider *Tyme* to be but the *Measure of Motion,* and howsoever it may seeme to have three *stations, past, present,* and *future,* yet the *first* and *last* of these *are* not (one is not, now, and the other is not yet) and that which you call *present,* is not *now* the same that it was, when you began to call it so in this *Line,* before you sound that word, *present,* or that *Monosyllable, now,* the present, and the *Now* is past), if this *Imaginary halfe-nothing, Tyme,* be of the Essence of our *Happinesses,* how can they be thought *durable? Tyme* is not so; How can they bee thought to be? *Tyme* is not so; not so, considered in any of the *parts* thereof. If we consider *Eternity,* into that, *Tyme* never entred; *Eternity* is not an everlasting flux of *Tyme;* but *Tyme* is a short *parenthesis* in a longe *period;* and *Eternity* had been the same, as it is, though time had never beene; If we consider, not *Eternity,* but *Perpetuity,* not that which had no *Tyme* to beginne in, but which shall outlive *Tyme* and be, when *Tyme shall bee no more,* what *A Minute* is the life of the Durablest *Creature,* compared to that! And what a Minute is Mans life in respect of the *Sunnes,* or of a Tree! and yet how little of our *life* is *Occasion, opportunity* to receyve good in; and how litle of that *occasion,* doe wee apprehend, and lay hold of! How busie and perplexed a *Cobweb,* is the *Happinesse* of Man here, that must bee made up with a *Watchfulnesse,* to lay hold upon *Occasion,* which is but a little peece of that, which is *Nothing, Tyme!* And yet the best things are *Nothing* without that. *Honors, Pleasures, Possessions,* presented to us, out of time, in our decrepit, and distasted, and unapprehensive *Age,* loose their *Office,* and loose their *Name;* They are not *Honors* to us, that shall never appeare, nor come abroad into the Eyes of the people, to receive *Honor,* from them who give it: Nor *pleasures* to us, who have lost our sense to taste them; nor *possessions* to us, who are departing from the possession of them. Youth is their *Criticall Day;* that *Judges* them, that *Denominates* them, that *inanimates,* and *informes* them, and makes them *Honors,* and

Pleasures, and *Possessions;* and when they come in an unapprehensive *Age,* they come as a *Cordial* when the bell rings out, as a *Pardon,* when the Head is off. We rejoyce in the Comfort of *fire,* but does any man cleave to it at *Midsomer;* Wee are glad of the freshnesse, and coolenes of a *Vault,* but does any man keepe his *Christmas* there; or are the pleasures of the *Spring* acceptable in *Autumne?* If happinesse be in the *season,* or in the *Clymate,* how much happier then are *Birdes* than *Men,* who can change the *Climate,* and accompanie, and enjoy the same season ever.

Intereà insomnes noctes Ego	*I sleepe not day*
duco, Diesque.	*nor night.*

XV. MEDITATION

NATURALL men have conceived a twofold use of *sleepe;* That it is a *refreshing* of the body in this life; That it is a *preparing* of the *soule* for the next; That it is a *feast,* and it is the *grace* at that *feast;* That it is our *recreation,* and cheeres us, and it is our *Catechisme* and instructs us; wee lie downe in a hope, that wee shall rise the stronger; and we lie downe in a knowledge, that wee may rise no more. *Sleepe* is an *Opiate* which gives us *rest,* but such an *Opiate,* as perchance, being under it, we shall wake no more. But though naturall men, who have induced secondary and figurative considerations, have found out this second, this *emblematicall* use of *sleepe,* that it should be a *representation of death,* God, who wrought and perfected his worke, before *Nature* began, (for *Nature* was but his *Apprentice,* to learne in the first *seven daies,* and now is his *foreman,* and works next under him) God, I say, intended *sleepe* onely for the *refreshing* of man by bodily rest, and not for a *figure of death,* for he intended not *death* it selfe then. But *Man* having induced *death* upon himselfe, God hath taken *Mans Creature,* death, into his hand, and mended it; and whereas it hath in itselfe a fearefull forme and aspect, so that Man is afraid of his own *Creature,* God presents it to him, in a *familiar,* in an *assiduous,* in an *agreeable* and *acceptable* forme, in *sleepe,* that so when hee awakes from *sleepe,* and saies to himselfe, shall I bee no otherwise when I am dead, than I was even now, when I was asleep, hee may bee ashamed of his waking *dreames,* and of his *Melancholique* fancying out

a horrid and an affrightfull figure of that *death* which is so
like sleepe. As then wee need *sleepe* to live out our *threescore
and ten yeeres,* so we need *death,* to live that *life* which we
cannot *out-live.* And as *death* being our *enemie,* God allowes
us to defend ourselves against it (for wee *victuall* ourselves
against *death, twice* every day, as often as we *eat*) so *God* having so sweetned *death* unto us as hee hath in *sleepe,* wee put
ourselves into our *enemies* hands *once* every day; so farre,
as *sleepe* is *death;* and *sleepe* is as much *death,* as *meat* is *life.*
This then is the *misery* of my *sicknesse,* That death as it is
produced from mee, and is mine owne *Creature,* is now before mine *Eyes,* but in that forme, in which *God* hath mollified it to us, and made it acceptable, in *sleepe,* I cannot see
it: how many *prisoners,* who have even hollowed themselves
their *graves* upon that *Earth,* on which they have lien long under heavie fetters, yet at this *houre* are *asleepe,* though they
bee yet working upon their owne *graves* by their owne *waight!*
Hee that hath seene his *friend* die to *day,* or knowes hee shall
see it to *morrow,* yet will sinke into a sleepe betweene. I cannot; and oh, if I be entring now into *Eternitie,* where there
shall bee no more distinction of *houres,* why is it al my businesse now *to tell Clocks?* why is none of the heavinesse of
my *heart,* dispensed into mine *Eye-lids,* that they might fall as
my heart doth? And why, since I have lost my delight in all
objects, cannot I discontinue the facultie of seeing them, by
closing mine *eyes* in *sleepe?* But why rather being entring
into that presence, where I shall wake continually and never
sleepe more, doe I not interpret my continuall waking here,
to bee a *parasceve,* and a *preparation* to that?

Et properare meum clamant,
   è Turre propinqua,
Obstreperæ Campanæ aliorum
   in funere, funus.
	*From the Bells of the Church
	adjoyning, I am daily remem-
	bred of my buriall in the
	funeralls of others.*

XVI. MEDITATION

WE HAVE a *Convenient Author,* who writ a *Discourse of Bells,*
when hee was prisoner in *Turky.* How would hee have enlarged himselfe if he had beene my *fellow-prisoner* in this
sicke bed, so neere to that *Steeple,* which never ceases, no
more than the *harmony of the spheres,* but is more heard.

When the *Turkes* took *Constantinople,* they melted the *Bells* into *Ordnance;* I have heard both *Bells* and *Ordnance,* but never been so much affected with those, as with these *Bells.* I have *lien* near a *Steeple,* in which there are said to be more than *thirty Bels;* And neere another, where there is one so bigge, as that the *Clapper* is said to weigh more than *six hundred pound,* yet never so affected as here. Here the *Bells* can scarse solemnise the funerall of any person, but that I knew him, or knew that he was my *Neighbour:* we dwelt in houses neere to one another before, but now hee is gone into that house, into which I must follow him. There is a way of correcting the *Children* of great persons, that other *Children* are corrected in their *behalfe,* and in their names, and this workes upon them, who indeed had more deserved it. And when these *Bells* tell me, that now one, and now another is buried, must not I acknowledge, that they have the *correction* due to me, and paid the *debt* that I owe? There is a story of a *Bell* in a *Monastery* which, when any of the house was sicke to death, rung alwaies *voluntarily,* and they knew the inevitablenesse of the danger by that. It rung once, when no man was sick; but the next day one of the house, fell from the *steeple,* and died, and the *Bell* held the reputation of a *Prophet* still. If these *Bells* that warne to a *Funerall* now, were appropriated to none, may not I, by the houre of the *Funerall,* supply? How many men that stand at an *execution,* if they would aske, for what dies that man should heare their owne faults condemned, and see themselves executed, by *Atturney?* We scarce heare of any man *preferred,* but wee thinke of our selves, that wee might very well have beene that *Man;* Why might not I have beene that *Man,* that is carried to his *grave* now? Could I fit my selfe, to *stand,* or *sit* in any mans *place,* and not to lie in any mans *grave?* I may lacke much of the *good parts* of the meanest, but I lacke nothing of the *mortality* of the weakest; They may have acquired better *abilities* than I, but I was borne to as many *infirmities* as they. To be an *Incumbent* by lying down in a *grave,* to be a *Doctor* by teaching *Mortification* by *Example,* by *dying,* though I may have *seniors,* others may be *elder* than I, yet I have proceeded apace in a good *University,* and gone a great way in a little time, by the furtherance of a vehement *Fever;* and whomsoever these *Bells* bring to the ground to day, if hee and I had beene compared yesterday, perchance I should have been thought likelier to come to this preferment, then, than he. *God* hath kept the power of *death* in his owne hands, lest any man should *bribe death*. If man knew the *gaine of death*, the *ease of death*, he would solicite, he would provoke *death* to assist him, by any hand, which he might use. But as when men see many of their owne *professions* preferd, it ministers a hope that that may light upon them; so when these hourely *Bells* tell me of so many *funerals* of men like me, it presents, if not a *desire* that it may, yet a *comfort* whensoever mine shall come.

Nunc lento sonitu dicunt,   *Now, this Bell tolling softly for*
    Morieris.   *another, saies to me, Thou must*
                                   die.

XVII. MEDITATION

PERCHANCE hee for whom this *Bell* tolls, may be so ill, as that he knowes not it tolls for him; And perchance I may thinke my selfe so much better than I am, as that they who are about mee, and see my state, may have caused it to toll for mee, and I know not that. The *Church* is *Catholike, universall,* so are all her *Actions; All* that she does, belongs to *all.* When she *baptizes a child,* that action concernes mee; for that child is thereby connected to that *Head* which is my *Head* too, and engraffed into that *body,* whereof I am a *member.* And when she *buries* a *Man,* that action concernes me: All *mankinde* is of one *Author,* and is one *volume;* when one Man dies, one *Chapter* is not *torne* out of the *booke,* but *translated* into a better *language;* and every *Chapter* must be so *translated; God* emploies several *translators;* some peeces are translated by *age,* some by *sicknesse,* some by *warre,* some by *justice;* but *Gods* hand is in every *translation;* and his hand shall binde up all our scattered leaves againe, for that *Librarie* where every *booke* shall lie open to one another: As therefore the *Bell* that rings to a *Sermon,* calls not upon the *Preacher* onely, but upon the *Congregation* to come; so this *Bell* calls us all: but how much more mee, who am brought so neere the *doore* by this *sicknesse.* There was a *contention* as farre as a *suite,* (in which both *pietie* and *dignitie, religion,* and *estimation,* were mingled) which of the religious *Orders* should ring to *praiers* first in the *Morning;* and it was *determined,* that *they should ring first that rose earliest.* If we understand aright the *dignitie* of this *Bell* that tolls for our *evening prayer,* wee would bee glad to make it ours, by rising early, in that *application,* that it might bee ours, as wel as his, whose indeed it is. The *Bell* doth toll for him that *thinkes* it doth; and though it *intermit* againe, yet from that *minute* that that occasion wrought upon him, hee is united to *God.* Who casts not up his *Eye* to the *Sunne* when it rises? but who takes off his *Eye* from a *Comet* when that breakes out? Who bends not his *eare* to any *bell,* which upon any occasion rings? but who can remove it from that *bell,* which is passing a *peece of himselfe* out of this *world?* No man is an *Iland,* intire of it selfe; every man is a peece of the *Continent,* a part of the *maine;* if a *Clod* bee washed away by the *Sea,* *Europe* is the lesse, as well as if a *Promontorie* were, as well as if a *Mannor* of thy *friends* or of *thine owne* were; any mans *death* diminishes *me,* because I am involved in *Man-kinde;* And therefore never send to know for whom the *bell* tolls; It tolls for *thee.* Neither can we call this a *begging* of *Miserie* or a *borrowing* of *Miserie,* as though we were not miserable enough of our selves, but must fetch in more from the next house, in taking upon us the *Miserie* of our *Neighbours.* Truly it were an excusable *covetousnesse* if wee did; for *affliction* is a *treasure,* and scarce any man hath *enough* of it. No man hath *affliction* enough that is not matured, and ripened by it, and made fit for *God* by that *affliction.* If a man carry *treasure* in *bullion,* or in a *wedge* of *gold,* and have none coined into *currant Monies,* his *treasure* will not defray him as he travells. *Tribulation* is *Treasure* in the *nature* of it, but it is not *currant money* in the *use* of it, except wee get nearer and nearer our *home, Heaven,* by it. Another man may be sicke too, and sick to *death,* and this *affliction* may lie in his *bowels,* as *gold* in a *Mine,* and be of no use to him; but this *bell,* that tells me of his *affliction,* digs out, and applies that *gold* to *mee;* if by this consideration of anothers danger, I take mine owne into contemplation, and so secure my selfe, by making my recourse to my *God,* who is our onely securitie.

At inde   *The Bell rings out, and tells*
Mortuus es, Sonitu celeri,   *me in him, that I am dead.*
    pulsuque agitato.

XVIII. MEDITATION

THE *Bell* rings out; the *pulse* thereof is changed; the *tolling*
was a *faint,* and *intermitting pulse,* upon one side; this
stronger, and argues *more* and *better life.* His *soule* is gone
out; and as a Man, who had a lease of 1000. *yeeres* after the
expiration of a short one, or an inheritance after the *life* of a
man in a *consumption,* he is now entred into the possession
of his *better estate.* His *soule* is gone; *whither?* Who saw it
come in, or who saw it *goe out? No body;* yet every body is
sure, he *had one,* and *hath none.* If I will aske meere *Philoso-*
phers, what the *soule* is, I shall finde amongst them, that will
tell me, it is nothing, but the *temperament* and *harmony,* and
just and equall composition of the Elements in the body, which
produces all those *faculties* which we ascribe to the *soule;* and
so, in it selfe is *nothing,* no *seperable substance,* that over-
lives the *body.* They see the *soule* is nothing else in other
Creatures, and they affect an *impious humilitie,* to think *as*
low of *Man.* But if my *soule* were no more than the soul of a
beast, I could not thinke so; that *soule* that can *reflect* upon
it selfe, *consider* it selfe, is *more* than so. If I will aske, not
meere *Philosophers,* but *mixt men, Philosophicall Divines, how*
the *soule,* being a *separate substance,* enters into *Man,* I shall
finde some that will tell me, that it is by *generation,* and
procreation from *parents,* because they thinke it hard, to
charge the *soule* with the guiltiness of *originall* sinne, if the
soule were infused into a *body,* in which it must necessarily
grow *foule,* and contract *originall sinne,* whether it *will* or
no; and I shall finde some that will tell mee, that it is by
immediate infusion from God, because they think it hard, to
maintaine an *immortality* in such a *soule,* as should be begot-
ten, and derived with the *body* from *mortall parents.* If I will
aske, not a *few men,* but almost *whole bodies, whole Churches,*
what becomes of the *soules* of the *righteous,* at the *departing*
thereof from the *body,* I shall bee told by some, *That they*
attend an expiation, a purification in a place of torment; By
some, that *they attend the fruition of the sight of God, in a*
place of rest; but yet, but of expectation; By some, that *they*

passe to an immediate possession of the presence of God. S. Augustine studied the *nature* of the *soule*, as much as anything, but the *salvation of the soule;* and he sent an expresse *Messenger* to Saint *Hierome*, to consult of some things concerning the *soule:* But he satisfies himselfe with this: *Let the departure of my soule to salvation be evident to my faith, and I care the lesse, how darke the entrance of my soule, into my body, bee to my reason.* It is the *going out,* more than the *comming in,* that concernes us. This *soule,* this *Bell* tells me, is *gone out; Whither?* Who shall tell mee that? I know not *who it is;* much less *what he was;* The condition of the man, and the course of his life, which should tell mee *whither* hee is gone, I know not. I was not there in his *sicknesse,* nor at his *death;* I saw not his *way,* nor his *end,* nor can aske them, who did, thereby to *conclude,* or *argue,* whither he is gone. But yet I have one neerer mee than all these; mine owne *Charity;* I aske that; and that tels me, *He is gone to everlasting rest,* and *joy,* and *glory:* I owe him a good *opinion;* it is but *thankfull charity* in mee, because I received *benefit* and *instruction* from him when his *Bell* told: and I, being made the fitter to *pray,* by that disposition, wherein I was assisted by his occasion, did *pray* for him; and I *pray* not without *faith;* so I doe *charitably,* so I do *faithfully* beleeve, that that *soule* is gone to everlasting *rest,* and *joy,* and *glory.* But for the *body,* how poore a wretched thing is *that?* wee cannot expresse it *so fast,* as it growes *worse* and *worse.* That *body* which scarce *three minutes* since was such a *house,* as that that *soule,* which made but one step from thence to *Heaven,* was scarse thorowly content, to leave that for *Heaven:* that *body* hath lost the *name* of a *dwelling house,* because none dwells in it, and is making haste to lose the name of a *body,* and dissolve to *putrefaction.* Who would not bee affected, to see a cleere and sweet *River* in the *Morning,* grow a *kennell* of muddy land water by *noone,* and condemned to the saltnesse of the *Sea* by *night?* And how lame a *picture,* how faint a *representation* is that, of the precipitation of mans body to *dissolution! Now* all the parts built up, and knit by a lovely *soule, now* but a *statue* of *clay,* and *now,* these limbs melted off, as if that *clay* were but *snow;* and now, the whole *house* is but a *handfull* of *sand,* so much *dust,* and but a *pecke* of *rubbidge,* so much *bone.* If *he,* who, as this *Bell* tells mee, is gone now, were some *excellent Artificer,* who comes to him for a *clocke,* or for a *garment* now? or for *counsaile,* if hee were a *Lawyer?*

If a *Magistrate*, for *Justice?* Man, before hee hath his *immortall soule*, hath a *soule* of *sense*, and a *soule* of *vegitation* before that: This *immortall soule* did not forbid other *soules*, to be in us before, but when this *soule* departs, it carries all with it; no more *vegetation*, no more *sense*: such a *Mother in law* is the *Earth*, in respect of our *naturall mother*; in her *wombe* we *grew*; and when she was delivered of us, wee were planted in some *place*, in some *calling* in the *world*; In the wombe of the *earth*, wee *diminish*, and when shee is *deliverd* of us, our *grave opened* for another, wee are not *transplanted*, but *transported*, our *dust* blowne away with *prophane dust*, with *every wind*.

Oceano tandem emenso, aspicienda resurgit Terra; vident, justis, medici, jam cocta mederi se posse, indiciis.	*At last, the Physitians, after a long and stormie voyage, see land; They have so good signes of the concoction of the disease, as that they may safely proceed to purge.*

XIX. MEDITATION

ALL this while the *Physitians* themselves have beene *patients*, patiently attending when they should see any *land* in this *Sea*, any *earth*, any *cloud*, any *indication* of *concoction* in these waters. Any *disorder* of mine, any *pretermission* of theirs, exalts the disease, accelerates the rages of it; no *diligence* accelerates the *concoction*, the *maturitie* of the *disease;* they must stay till the *season* of the sicknesse come, and till it be ripened of it selfe, and then they may put to their hand, to *gather* it before it *fall* off, but they cannot hasten the *ripening*. Why should wee looke for it in a *disease*, which is the *disorder*, the *discord*, the *irregularitie*, the *commotion*, and *rebellion* of the *body?* It were scarce a *disease*, if it could bee *ordered*, and made obedient to our *times*. Why should wee looke for that in *disorder*, in a *disease*, when we cannot have it in *Nature*, who is so *regular*, and so *pregnant*, so forward to bring her worke to perfection, and to light? Yet we cannot awake the *July-flowers* in *January*, nor retard the *flowers* of the *spring* to *autumne*. We cannot bid the *fruits* come in *May*, nor the *leaves* to sticke on in *December*. A *woman* that is weake cannot put off her *ninth moneth* to a *tenth*, for her *deliverie*, and say shee will stay till shee bee *stronger;* nor a *Queene* cannot hasten it to a *seventh,* that shee may bee ready for some other pleasure. *Nature* (if we looke for *durable* and *vigorous* effects) will not admit *preventions,* nor *anticipations,* nor *obligations* upon her; for they are *precontracts,* and she will bee left to her *libertie. Nature* would not be spurred, nor forced to mend her pace; nor power, the *power of man; greatnesse* loves not that kinde of *violence* neither. There are of *them* that will *give,* that will *do justice,* that will *pardon,* but they have their owne *seasons* for al these, and he that knowes not *them,* shall *starve* before that gift come, and *ruine,* before the Justice, and *dye* before the pardon save him: some *tree* beares no fruit, except much *dung* be laid about it; and *Justice* comes not from some, till they bee richly manured: some *trees* require much *visiting,* much *watring,* much *labour;* and some men give not their *fruits* but upon *importunitie;* some *trees* require *incision,* and *pruning,* and *lopping;* some men must bee *intimidated* and *syndicated* with *Commissions,* before they will deliver the fruits of *Justice;* some *trees* require the *early* and the *often* accesse of the *Sunne;* some men *open* not, but upon the *favours* and *letters* of *Court mediation;* some *trees* must bee *housd* and kept within doores; some men locke up, not onely their liberalitie, but their *Justice,* and their *compassion,* till the sollicitation of a *wife,* or a *sonne,* or a *friend,* or a *servant* turne the *key. Reward* is the *season* of one man, and *importunitie* of another; *feare* the *season* of one man, and *favour* of another; *friendship* the *season* of one man, and *naturall affection* of another; and hee that knowes not their *seasons,* nor cannot *stay* them, must lose the *fruits;* As *Nature* will not, so *power* and *greatnesse* will not bee put to change their *seasons;* and shall wee looke for this *Indulgence* in a *disease,* or thinke to shake it off before it bee *ripe?* All this while, therefore, we are but upon a *defensive warre,* and that is but a *doubtfull state;* especially where they who are *besieged* doe know the *best* of their *defenses,* and doe not know the *worst* of their *enemies power;* when they cannot mend their *works within,* and the *enemie* can increase his *numbers without.* O how many farre more miserable, and farre more worthy to be lesse miserable than I, are besieged with this *sicknesse,* and lacke their *Sentinels,* their *Physitians* to *watch,* and lacke their *munition,* their *cordials* to *defend,* and perish before the *enemies* weaknesse might invite them to *sally,* before the *disease* shew any *declination,* or admit any way of *working* upon it selfe! In me the *siege* is so farre slackned, as that we may come to *fight,* and so die in the *field,* if I *die,* and not in a *prison.*

XIX. EXPOSTULATION

MY *God,* my *God,* Thou art a *direct God,* may I not say a *literall God,* a *God* that wouldest bee understood *literally,* and according to the *plaine sense* of all that thou saiest? But thou art also (*Lord* I intend it to thy *glory,* and let no *prophane misinterpreter* abuse it to thy *diminution*) thou art a *figurative,* a *metaphoricall God too:* A *God* in whose words there is such a *height of figures,* such *voyages,* such *peregrinations* to fetch remote and precious *metaphors,* such *extentions,* such *spreadings,* such *Curtaines of Allegories,* such *third Heavens* of *Hyperboles,* so *harmonious eloquutions,* so *retired* and so *reserved expressions,* so *commanding perswasions,* so *perswading commandments,* such *sinewes* even in thy *milke,* and such *things* in thy *words,* as all *prophane Authors,* seeme of the seed of the *Serpent,* that *creepes,* thou art the *Dove,* that flies. O, what words but thine, can expresse the inexpressible *texture,* and *composition* of thy *word;* in which, to one man, that *argument* that binds his faith to beleeve that to bee the Word of *God,* is *the reverent simplicity* of the Word, and to another, the *majesty* of the Word; and in which two men, equally pious, may meet, and one wonder, that all should not understand it, and the other, as much, that any man should. So, *Lord,* thou givest us the same *earth,* to labour on and to lie in; a *house,* and a *grave,* of the same *earth;* so *Lord,* thou givest us the same *Word* for our *satisfaction,* and for our *Inquisition,* for our *instruction,* and for our *Admiration* too; for there are places, that thy servants *Hierom* and *Augustine* would scarce beleeve (when they grew warm by mutual letters) of one another, that they understood them, and yet both *Hierome* and *Augustine* call upon persons, whom they knew to bee farre weaker, than they thought one another (*old women and young maids*) to read thy *Scriptures,* without confining them, to these or those places. Neither art thou thus a *figurative,* a *metaphoricall God* in thy *word* only, but in thy *workes* too. The *stile* of thy *works,* the *phrase* of thine *actions,* is *metaphoricall.* The *institution* of thy whole *worship* in the *old Law,* was a continuall *Allegory; types* and *figures* overspread all; and *figures* flowed into *figures,* and powred themselves out into *farther figures; Circumcision* carried a *figure* of *Baptisme,* and *Baptisme* carries a *figure* of that *purity,* which we shall have in *perfection* in the *new Jerusalem.* Neither didst thou *speake* and *worke* in this *language,* onely in the time of thy *Prophets;* but since thou spokest in thy *Son,* it is so too. How often, how much more often doth **thy** *Sonne* call himselfe a *way,* and a *light,* and a *gate,* and a **Vine,** and *bread,* than the *Sonne of God,* or of *Man?* How much oftner doth he exhibit a *Metaphoricall Christ,* than a *reall,* a *literall?* This hath occasioned thine ancient *servants,* whose delight it was to write after thy *Copie,* to proceede the same way in their *expositions* of the *Scriptures,* and in their composing both of *publike liturgies,* and of *private prayers* to thee, to make their accesses to thee in such a kind of *language,* as thou wast pleased to speake to them, in a *figurative,* in a *Metaphoricall language;* in which manner I am bold to call the comfort which I receive now in this *sicknesse,* in the *indication* of the *concoction* and *maturity* thereof, in certaine *clouds,* and *recidences,* which the *Physitians* observe, a discovering of *land* from *Sea,* after a long, and tempestuous *voyage.* But wherefore, O my *God,* hast thou presented to us the *afflictions* and *calamities* of this life, in the *name* of *waters?* so often in the *name* of *waters,* and *deepe waters,* and *Seas* of *waters?* must we looke to bee *drowned?* are they *bottomlesse,* are they *boundles?* Thats not the *dialect* of thy *language;* thou hast given a *Remedy* against the deepest *water,* by *water;* against the *inundation* of sinne, by *Baptisme;* and the first *life,* that thou gavest to any *Creatures,* was in *waters;* therefore thou dost not threaten us, with an *irremediablenesse,* when our *affliction* is a *Sea.* It is so, if we consider *our selves;* so thou callest *Gennezareth,* which was but a Lake, and not *salt,* a *Sea;* so thou callest the *Mediterranean Sea,* still the *great Sea,* because the *inhabitants* saw no other *Sea;* they that dwelt there, thought a *Lake,* a *Sea,* and the others thought a *little Sea,* the *greatest,* and wee that know not the *afflictions* of others, call our owne the *heaviest.* But, O my *God,* that is *truly great,* that overflowes the *channell;* that is *really* a *great affliction,* which is above my *strength,* but thou, O *God,* art my *strength,* and then what can bee above it? *Mountaines shake with the swelling of thy Sea, secular mountaines,* men *strong in power, spirituall mountaines,* men *strong in grace,* are shaked with *afflictions;* but *thou laiest up thy sea in storehouses;* even thy *corrections* are of thy *treasure,* and thou wilt not waste thy *corrections;* when they have done their *service,* to humble thy *patient,* thou wilt call them in againe, for *thou givest the Sea thy decree, that the waters should not passe thy Commandement.* All our *waters* shal run into *Jordan,* and *thy servants passed Jordan dry foot;* they shall run into the red Sea (the Sea of thy *Sons bloud*) and the red Sea, that red Sea, drownes none of *thine.* But, *they that saile in the Sea, tell of the danger thereof;* I that am yet in this affliction, owe thee *glory* of *speaking* of it; But, as the *Wise man* bids me, I say, I may *speak much, and come short; wherefore in sum thou art all.* Since thou art so, O my *God,* and *affliction* is a *Sea,* too *deepe* for us, what is our *refuge?* thine *Arke,* thy *ship.* In all other *Seas,* in all other *afflictions,* those *meanes* which thou hast ordained; In this *Sea,* in *Sicknesse,* thy *Ship* is thy *Physitian. Thou hast made a way in the Sea, and a safe path in the waters, shewing that thou canst save from all dangers; yea, though a man went to Sea without art;* yet where I finde all that, I finde this added, *Neverthelesse thou wouldest not, that the worke of thy wisdome should be idle.* Thou canst save without *meanes;* but thou hast told no man that thou *wilt:* Thou hast told every man, that thou *wilt not.* When the *Centurion* beleeved the *Master* of the *ship* more than Saint *Paul,* they were all opened to a great danger; this was a *preferring* of thy *meanes,* before thee, the *Author* of the *meanes;* but, my *God,* though thou beest *every where,* I have no promise of *appearing* to me, but in thy *ship:* Thy blessed *Sonne preached out of a ship*: The *meanes* is preaching, he did that; and the *Ship* was a *type* of the *Church;* hee did it there. *Thou gavest S. Paul the lives of all of them, that saild with him;* If they had not beene in the *Ship* with him, the gift had not extended to them. *As soone as thy Son was come out of the ship, immediately there met him out of the tombes, a man with an uncleane spirit, and no man could hold him, no not with chaines.* Thy *Sonne* needed no use of *meanes;* yet there wee apprehend the *danger* to us; if we leave the *ship,* the *meanes;* in this case, the *Physitian.* But as they are *Ships* to us in those *Seas,* so is there a *Ship* to them too, in which they are to stay. Give mee leave, O my *God,* to assist my selfe with such a *construction* of these words of thy servant *Paul,* to the *Centurion,* when the *Mariners* would have left the *Ship, Except these abide in the Ship, you cannot be safe;* Except they who are our *Ships,* the *Physitians,* abide in that which is theirs, and our *ship,* the *truth,* and the *sincere* and *religious worship of thee,* and thy *Gospell,* we cannot promise our selves, so good *safety;* for though we have our *ship,* the *Physitian,* he hath not his *ship, Religion;* And meanes are not meanes, but in their *concatenation,* as they *depend,* and are *chained* together. *The ships are great,* saies thy *Apostle, but a helme turns them;* the *men* are *learned,* but their *Religion* turnes their *labours* to good: And therefore it was a heavy *curse, when the third part of the ships perished:* It is a heavy case, where either *all Religion,* or *true Religion* should forsake many of these *ships,* whom thou hast sent to convey us over these *Seas.* But, O my *God,* my *God,* since *I have my ship,* and *they theirs,* I have *them,* and they have *thee,* why are we yet no neerer land? As soone as thy *Sonnes disciple* had taken him into the *ship, immediatly the ship was at the land, whither they went.* Why have not *they* and *I* this dispatch? Every thing is *immediatly* done, which is done when *thou* wouldst have it done. Thy purpose *terminates* every action, and what was *done* before that, is *undone* yet. Shall that slacken my *hope?* Thy *Prophet* from *thee,* hath forbid it. *It is good that a man should both hope, and quietly wait for the salvation* of the Lord. Thou puttest off many *judgements,* till the *last* day, and many passe this life without any; and shall not I endure the putting off thy *mercy* for a day? and yet, O my *God,* thou puttest me not to that; for, the *assurance* of *future mercy,* is *present mercy.* But what is my *assurance* now? What is my *seale?* It is but a *cloud;* that which my *Physitians* call a *cloud,* is *that,* which gives them their *Indication.* But a *cloud?* Thy *great Seale* to all the world, the *Rainebow,* that secured the *world* for ever, from *drowning,* was but a *reflexion upon a cloud.* A *cloud* it selfe was a *pillar* which guided the *church,* and *the glory of God,* not only *was,* but *appeared in a cloud.* Let me returne, O my *God,* to the consideration of thy *servant Eliahs* proceeding, in a time of *desperate drought;* he bids them look towards the *Sea;* They looke, and see *nothing.* He bids them *againe* and *againe, seven times:* and at the *seventh time,* they saw a little *cloud* rising out of the *Sea;* and presently they had their desire of *raine. Seven dayes,* O my *God,* have we looked for this *cloud,* and now we have it; none of thy *Indications* are *frivolous;* thou makest thy *signes, seales;* and thy *seales, effects;* and thy *effects, consolation,* and *restitution,* wheresoever thou maiest receive *glory* by that way.

XIX. PRAYER

O Eternall and most gracious *God*, who though thou
passedst over infinite millions of generations, before thou
camest to a *Creation* of this *world*, yet when thou beganst,
didst never intermit that *worke*, but continuedst *day* to *day*,
till thou hadst perfited all the *worke*, and deposed it in the
hands and rest of a *Sabbath*, though thou have beene pleased
to *glorifie* thy selfe in a long exercise of my *patience*, with an
expectation of thy *declaration* of thy selfe in this my *sicknesse*,
yet since thou hast now of thy goodnesse afforded that, which
affords us some hope, if that bee still *the way* of thy *glory*,
proceed in *that way*, and perfit *that worke*, and establish me
in a *Sabbath*, and *rest* in *thee*, by this thy *seale* of *bodily restitution*. Thy *Priests* came up to thee, by *steps* in the *Temple*;
Thy *Angels* came *downe* to *Jaacob*, by *steps* upon the *ladder*;
we finde no *staire*, by which thou *thy selfe* camest to *Adam*
in *Paradise*, nor to *Sodome* in thine *anger*; for *thou*, and *thou
onely* art able to doe all at once. But, O *Lord*, I am not *wearie*
of thy *pace*, nor *wearie* of mine owne *patience*. I provoke
thee not with a *praier*, not with a *wish*, not with a *hope*, to
more haste than consists with thy *purpose*, nor looke that any
other thing should have entred into thy *purpose*, but thy *glory*.
To *heare* thy steps comming *towards* mee is the same comfort,
as to see thy face present with mee; whether thou doe the
worke of a *thousand yeeres* in a *day*, or extend the *worke of
a day* to a *thousand yeeres*, as long as *thou workest*, it is *light*,
and *comfort*. *Heaven* it selfe is but an *extention* of the same
joy; and an *extention* of this *mercie*, to proceed at thy *leisure*,
in the way of *restitution*, is a *manifestation* of *heaven* to me
here upon *earth*. From that *people*, to whom thou appearedst
in *signes* and in *Types*, the *Jewes*, thou art departed, because
they trusted in *them*; but from thy *Church*, to whom thou hast
appeared in *thy selfe*, in thy *Sonne*, thou wilt never depart;
because we cannot trust *too much* in *him*. Though thou have afforded me these *signes* of *restitution*, yet if I *confide* in
them, and beginne to say, all was but a *naturall accident*, and
nature begins to *discharge* her selfe, and shee will *perfit* the
whole *worke*, my *hope* shall vanish because it is not in *thee*.
If thou shouldest take thy *hand* utterly from me, and have
nothing to doe with me, *nature* alone were able to *destroy* me;
but if thou withdraw thy *helping hand*, alas how frivolous are

the helps of *Nature,* how impotent the assistances of *Art?* As
therefore the *morning dew,* is a *pawne* of the *evening fatnesse,*
so, O *Lord,* let *this daies* comfort be the *earnest* of to *mor-
rowes,* so far as may *conforme* me entirely to thee, to what
end, and by what *way* soever thy *mercie* have appointed mee.

Id agunt.   *Upon these Indications of digested
                             matter, they proceed to purge.*

XX. MEDITATION

THOUGH *counsel* seeme rather to consist of *spirituall parts,* than
action, yet *action* is the *spirit* and the *soule* of *counsell. Counsels*
are not alwaies determined in *Resolutions;* wee cannot alwaies
say, *this was concluded; actions* are alwaies determined in *effects;* wee can say *this was done.* Then have *Lawes* their *reverence,* and their *majestie,* when we see the *Judge* upon the
Bench executing them. Then have *counsels of warre* their *impressions,* and their *operations,* when we see the *seale* of an
Armie set to them. It was an ancient way of celebrating the
memorie of such as deserved well of the *State,* to afford them
that kinde of *statuarie representation,* which was then called
Hermes; which was, *the head and shoulders of a man, standing upon a Cube,* but those *shoulders* without *armes* and *hands.*
All together it figured a *constant supporter of the State,* by
his *counsell:* But in this *Hieroglyphique,* which they made
without *hands,* they passe their consideration no farther, but that
the *Counsellor* should bee without *hands,* so farre as *not to
reach out his hand to forraigne tentations of bribes, in matters
of Counsell,* and that it was not necessary, that the *head* should
employ *his owne hand;* that *the same men* should serve in
the *execution,* which assisted in the *Counsell;* but that there
should not belong *hands* to every *head, action* to every *counsell,* was never intended, so much as in *figure,* and *representation.* For, as *Matrimonie* is scarce to bee called *Matrimonie,*
where there is a *resolution* against the *fruits of matrimonie,*
against the having of *Children,* so counsels are not *counsels,*
but *illusions,* where there is from the beginning no purpose to
execute the determinations of those *counsels.* The *arts* and
sciences are most properly referred to the *head;* that is their
proper *Element* and *Spheare;* but yet the *art* of *proving,
Logique,* and the *art* of *perswading, Rhetorique,* are deduced

DEVOTIONS UPON EMERGENT OCCASIONS

to the *hand*, and *that* expressed by a *hand* contracted into a *fist*, and *this* by a *hand* enlarged, and expanded; and evermore the *power of man*, and the *power of God* himselfe is expressed so, *All things are in his hand;* neither is *God* so often presented to us, by names that carry our consideration upon *counsell*, as upon *execution of counsell;* he is oftner called the *Lord of Hosts*, than by all other *names*, that may be referred to the other signification. Hereby therefore wee take into our *meditation*, the slipperie condition of *man*, whose *happinesse*, in any kinde, the defect of *any one thing*, conducing to that *happinesse*, may *ruine;* but it must have *all the peeces* to make it up. Without *counsell*, I had not got thus farre; without *action* and *practise*, I should goe no farther towards *health*. But what is the present necessary *action?* purging: A *withdrawing*, a violating of *Nature, a farther weakening: O deare price*, and O *strange* way of *addition*, to doe it by *subtraction;* of *restoring* Nature, to *violate Nature;* of *providing strength*, by *increasing weaknesse!* Was I not *sicke* before? And is it a *question* of *comfort* to be asked now, Did *your Physicke make you sicke?* Was that it that my *Physicke* promised, to make me *sicke?* This is another *step*, upon which we may stand, and see farther into the *miserie of man*, the *time*, the *season* of his *Miserie*: It must bee done *now:* O *over-cunning, over-watchfull, over-diligent,* and *over-sociable misery of man*, that seldome comes alone, but then when it may accompanie other *miseries*, and so put one another into the higher *exaltation*, and better *heart!* I am ground even to an *attenuation*, and must proceed to *evacuation*, all waies to exinanition and annihilation.

Atque annuit Ille,
Qui, per eos, clamat, Linquas
jam, Lazare, lectum.

God prospers their practise, and he, by them, calls Lazarus out of his tombe, mee out of my bed.

XXI. MEDITATION

IF MAN had beene left *alone* in this *world*, at first, shall I thinke, that he would not have *fallen?* If there had beene no *Woman*, would not man have served, to have beene his own *Tempter?* When I see him now, subject to infinite weaknesses, fall into *infinite sinne*, without any *forraine tentations*, shall I

thinke, hee would have had *none*, if hee had beene *alone:*
God saw that Man needed a *Helper*, if hee should bee well;
but to make *Woman* ill, the *Devill* saw, that there needed no
third. When *God*, and *wee* were *alone*, in *Adam*, that was not
enough; when the *Devill* and wee were *alone*, in *Eve*, it was
enough. O what a *Giant* is *Man*, when he fights against himselfe, and what a *Dwarfe* when hee *needs*, or *exercises* his
owne assistance for himselfe! I cannot *rise* out of my bed, till
the *Physitian enable* mee, nay I cannot tel, that I am able to
rise, till *hee tell* me so. I *doe* nothing, I *know* nothing of myselfe: how little, and how impotent a peece of the *world*, is
any *Man* alone! and how much lesse a peece of *himselfe* is
that Man! So little, as that when it falls out, (as it falls out
in some cases) that more *misery*, and more *oppression*, would
be an *ease* to a *man*, he cannot give himselfe that *miserable
addition*, of *more misery*; a *man* that is *pressed to death*, and
might be eased by more *weights*, cannot lay those more
weights upon himselfe: Hee can sinne *alone*, and suffer *alone*,
but not *repent*, not bee *absolved*, without *another*. Another
tels mee, *I may rise*; and *I doe* so. But is every *raising* a *preferment?* or is every present *preferment* a *station?* I am
readier to fall to the *Earth*, now I am up, than I was when I
lay in the bed: O *perverse way, irregular motion* of *Man*; even
rising it selfe is the way to *Ruine*. How many *men* are raised,
and then doe not *fill* the place they are raised to? No *corner*
of any place can bee *empty*; there can be no *vacuity*; If that
Man doe not fill the place, *other men* will; complaints of his
insufficiency will *fill* it; Nay, such an abhorring is there in *Nature*, of *vacuity*, that if there be but an *imagination* of not *filling*, in any *man*, that which is but *imagination* neither, will
fill it, that is, *rumor* and *voice*, and it will be *given out*, (upon
no ground, but *Imagination*, and no man knowes *whose imagination*) that hee is *corrupt* in his place, or *insufficient* in his
place, and another prepared to *succeed* him in his place. A
man *rises*, sometimes, and *stands* not, because hee doth not, or
is not beleeved to *fill* his place; and sometimes he *stands* not,
because hee *overfills* his place: Hee may bring so much *vertue*,
so much *Justice*, so much *integrity* to the place, as shall *spoile*
the place, *burthen* the place; his *integrity* may bee a *Libell*
upon his *Predecessor*, and cast an *infamy* upon him, and a
burthen upon his *successor*, to proceede by *example*, and to
bring the place itselfe to an *under-value*, and the *market* to an
uncertainty. 1 am *up*, and I seeme to *stand*, and I go *round;*

and I am a new *Argument* of the *new Philosophie,* That the *Earth* moves round; why may I not beleeve, that the *whole earth* moves in a *round motion,* though that seeme to mee to *stand,* when as I seeme to *stand* to my *Company,* and yet am *carried,* in a giddy, and *circular motion,* as I *stand?* Man hath no *center* but *misery; there* and onely *there,* hee is *fixt,* and sure to finde himselfe. How little soever hee bee *raised,* he *moves,* and moves in a *circle,* giddily; and as in the *Heavens,* there are but a few *Circles,* that goe about the whole world, but man, *Epicircles,* and other lesser *Circles,* but yet *Circles,* so of those men, which are *raised,* and put into *Circles,* few of them move from *place* to *place,* and passe through many and beneficiall places, but fall into little *Circles,* and, within a step or two, are at their *end,* and not so well, as they were in the *Center,* from which they were *raised.* Every thing serves to *exemplifie,* to *illustrate* mans *misery.* But I need goe no farther, than *my selfe:* for a long time, I was not able to *rise;* At last, I must bee *raised* by others; and now I am *up,* I am ready to sinke *lower* than before.

Sit morbi fomes tibi cura ;   *The Physitians consider the root and occasion, the embers, and coales, and fuell of the disease, and seeke to purge or correct that.*

XXII. MEDITATION

How *ruinous* a *farme* hath *man* taken, in taking *himselfe!* How ready is the *house* every day to fall downe, and how is all the *ground* overspread with *weeds, all the* body with *diseases!* where not onely every *turfe,* but every *stone,* beares *weeds;* not onely every *muscle* of the *flesh,* but every *bone* of the *body,* hath some *infirmitie;* every little *flint* upon the *face* of this *soile,* hath some *infectious weede,* every *tooth* in our *head,* such a paine as a *constant man* is afraid of, and yet *ashamed* of that *feare,* of that sense of the paine. How *deare,* and how *often* a *rent* doth Man pay for this *farme!* hee paies *twice a day,* in *double meales,* and how little time he hath to *raise his rent!* How many *holy daies* to call him from his labour! Every day is *halfe-holy day,* halfe spent in *sleepe.* What *reparations,* and *subsidies,* and *contributions* he is put to, besides his *rent!* What *medicines*, besides his *diet!* and what *In-mates* he is *faine* to take in, besides his owne *familie*, what *in-fectious diseases*, from *other men!* Adam might have had *Para-dise* for *dressing* and *keeping* it; and *then* his rent was not *im-proved* to such a *labour*, as would have made his *brow sweat;* and yet he gave it over; how farre greater a *rent* doe wee pay for this farme, this *body*, who pay *our selves*, who pay the *farme it selfe*, and cannot *live* upon it! Neither is our *labour* at an end, when wee have cut downe some *weed*, as soone as it sprung up, corrected some *violent* and dangerous *accident* of a *disease*, which would have destroied *speedily;* nor when wee have pulled up that *weed*, from the very *root*, recovered *entirely* and *soundly*, from that *particular disease;* but the whole *ground* is of an *ill nature*, the whole soile *ill disposed;* there are inclinations, there is a propensenesse to *diseases* in the *body*, out of which without any other *disorder*, *diseases* will grow, and so wee are put to a continuall labour upon this *farme*, to a continuall studie of the whole *complexion* and *con-stitution* of our *body*. In the *distempers* and *diseases* of *soiles*, *sourenesse*, *drinesse*, *weeping*, any kinde of *barrennesse*, the *remedy* and the *physicke*, is, for a great part, sometimes in *themselves;* sometime[s] the very *situation* releeves them; the *hanger* of a *hill*, will purge and vent his owne *malignant mois-ture;* and the burning of the upper *turfe* of some ground (as *health* from *cauterizing*) puts a *new* and a *vigorous youth* into that *soile*, and there rises a kinde of *Phœnix* out of the *ashes*, a *fruitfulnesse* out of that which was *barren* before, and *by that*, which is the barrennest of all, *ashes*. And where the *ground* cannot give it selfe *Physicke*, yet it receives *Physicke* from other grounds, from other *soiles*, which are not the worse, for having contributed that helpe to them, from *Marle* in other *hils*, or from *slimie sand* in other *shoares: grounds* help *them-selves*, or hurt not other *grounds*, from whence they receive *helpe*. But I have taken a *farme* at this *hard rent*, and upon those *heavie covenants*, that it can afford it selfe no *helpe;* (no part of my *body*, if it were cut off, would *cure* another part; in some cases it might *preserve* a sound part, but in no case *recover* an infected) and, if my *body* may have any *Physicke*, any *Medicine* from another *body*, one *Man* from the flesh of another *Man* (as by Mummy, or any such *composition*,) it must bee from a man that is dead, and not, as in other *soiles*, which are never the worse for contributing their *Marle*, or their fat slime to my *ground*. There is nothing in the same

man, to helpe *man,* nothing in *mankind* to help *one another*
(in this sort, by way of *Physicke*) but that hee who *ministers*
the *helpe,* is in as ill case, as he that *receives* it would have
beene, if he had not had it; for hee from whose *body* the
Physicke comes, is *dead.* When therefore I tooke this *farme,*
undertooke this body, I undertooke to *draine,* not a *marish,* but
a *moat,* where there was, not water *mingled* to offend, but all
was *water;* I undertooke to *perfume dung,* where no one part,
but all was equally *unsavory;* I undertooke to make such a
thing *wholsome,* as was not *poison* by any manifest quality,
intense heat, or *cold,* but *poison* in the *whole substance,* and
in the *specifique forme* of it. To cure the *sharpe accidents* of
diseases, is a great worke; to cure the *disease it selfe* is a
greater; but to cure the *body,* the *root,* the *occasion* of *diseases,* is a worke reserved for the great *Phisitian,* which he
doth never any other way, but by *glorifying* these *bodies* in
the next world.

Metusque, relabi.   *They warne mee of the fearefull*
                                     danger of relapsing.

XXIII. MEDITATION

It is not in *mans body,* as it is in the *Citie,* that when the
Bell hath rung, to cover your *fire,* and rake up the *embers,* you
may lie downe and sleepe without feare. Though you have by
physicke and *diet,* raked up the *embers* of your *disease,* stil
there is a feare of a *relapse;* and the *greater* danger is in that.
Even in *pleasures,* and in *paines,* there is a *propriety,* a *Meum*
and *Tuum;* and a man is most affected with that *pleasure*
which is *his, his* by forme, enjoying and experience, and most
intimidated with those *paines* which are *his, his* by a wofull
sense of them, in former afflictions. A *covetous* person, who
hath preoccupated all his senses, filled all his capacities, with
the *delight* of *gathering,* wonders how any man can have *any
taste* of *any pleasure* in *any opennesse,* or *liberalitie;* So also
in *bodily paines,* in a fit of the *stone,* the Patient wonders why
any man should call the *Gout* a *paine:* And hee that hath felt
neither, but the *tooth-ach,* is as much afraid of a fit of that,
as either of the other, of either of the other. *Diseases,* which
we never *felt* in our selves, come but to a *compassion* of

others that have endured them; Nay, *compassion* it selfe comes to no great *degree*, if wee have not felt in some *proportion*, in *our selves*, that which wee lament and condole in another. But when wee have had those torments in their *exaltation*, *our selves*, wee tremble at a relapse. When wee must *pant* through all those *fierie heats*, and *saile* thorow all those *overflowing sweats*, when wee must *watch* through all those long *nights*, and *mourne* through all those long *daies*, (*daies* and *nights*, so *long*, as that *Nature* her selfe shall seeme to be *perverted*, and to have put the *longest day*, and the *longest night*, which should bee *six moneths* asunder, into one *naturall, unnaturall day*) when wee must stand at the same *barre*, expect the re-turne of *Physitians* from their *consultations*, and not bee sure of the same *verdict*, in any good *Indications*, when we must goe the same *way* over againe, and not see the same *issue*, this is a *state*, a *condition*, a *calamitie*, in respect of which, any other *sicknesse*, were a *convalescence*, and any *greater*, *lesse*. It addes to the *affliction*, that *relapses* are, (and for the most part justly) imputed to *our selves*, as occasioned by some *disorder* in us; and so we are not onely *passive*, but *active*, in our owne *ruine;* we doe not onely stand under a *falling house*, but *pull* it downe upon us; and wee are not onely *executed*, (that implies *guiltinesse*) but wee are *executioners*, (that implies *dishonor*) and *executioners* of *our selves*, (and that implies *impietie*.) And wee fall from that *comfort* which wee might have in our first *sicknesse*, from that *meditation, Alas, how generally miserable is Man, and how subject to diseases*, (for in that it is some degree of *comfort*, that wee are but in the state *common* to all) we fall, I say, to this *discomfort*, and *selfe accusing*, and *selfe condemning; Alas, how unprovident, and in that, how unthankfull to God and his instruments am I, in making so ill use of so great benefits, in destroying so soone, so long a worke, in relapsing, by my disorder, to that from which they had delivered mee;* and so my *meditation* is fearefully transferred from the *body* to the *minde*, and from the consideration of the *sicknesse* to that sinne, that *sinful carelessnes*, by which I have occasioned my *relapse*. And amongst the many *weights* that aggravate a *relapse*, this also is one, that a *relapse* proceeds with a more violent dispatch, and more *irremediably*, because it finds the *Countrie weakned*, and *depopulated* before. Upon a *sicknesse*, which as yet ap-peares not, wee can scarce fix a *feare*, because wee know not

what to feare; but as *feare* is the *busiest,* and *irksomest affection,* so is a *relapse* (which is still *ready to come*) into that,
which is but newly gone, the *nearest object,* the *most immediate* exercise of that *affection* of *feare.*

FROM THE SERMONS
AND *DEATH'S DUELL*

PREACHED ON ALL-SAINTS DAY

IF THE calamities of the world, or the heavy consideration of
thine own sins, have benummed and benighted thy soule in
the vale of darknesse, and in the shadow of death; If thou
thinke to wrastle and bustle through these strong stormes, and
thick clouds, with a strong hand; If thou thinke thy money, thy
bribes shall conjure thee up stronger spirits than those that oppose thee; If thou seek ease in thy calamities, that way to
shake and shipwrack thine enemies; In these crosse winds, in
these countermines, (to oppresse as thou art oppressed) all
this is but a turning to the North, to blow away and scatter
these sadnesses, with a false, an illusory, and a sinfull comfort.
If thou thinke to ease thy selfe in the contemplation of thine
honour, thine offices, thy favour, thy riches, thy health, this is
but a turning to the South, the Sun-shine of worldly prosperity. If thou sinke under thy afflictions, and canst not finde
nourishment (but poyson) in Gods corrections, nor justice
(but cruelty) in his judgements, nor mercy (but slacknesse)
in his forbearance till now; If thou suffer thy soule to set in
a cloud, a dark cloud of ignorance of Gods providence and
proceedings, or in a darker, of diffidence of his performance
towards thee, this is a turning to the West, and all these are
perverse and awry. But turne to the East, and to the Angel
that comes from thence, The Ministery of the Gospel of Christ
Jesus in his Church; It is true, thou mayst find some dark
places in the Scriptures; and, *Est silentii species obscuritas,*
To speake darkly and obscurely is a kinde of silence, I were
as good not be spoken to, as not be made to understand that
which is spoken, yet fixe thy selfe upon this Angel of the East,
the preaching of the Word, the Ordinance of God, and thine
understanding shall be enlightned, and thy beliefe established,

and thy conscience thus far unburthened, that though the sins which thou hast done, cannot be undone, yet neither shalt thou bee undone by them; There, where thou art afraid of them, in judgement, they shall never meet thee; but as in the round frame of the World, the farthest West is East, where the West ends, the East begins, So in thee (who art a World too) thy West and thy East shall joyne, and when thy Sun, thy soule comes to set in thy death-bed, the Son of Grace shall suck it up into glory.

[*LXXX. Sermons* (45), 1640]

PREACHED UPON THE PENITENTIALL PSALMES
(PS. XXXII)

The hand of God shall grow heavy upon a silent sinner, in his body, in his health; and if he conceive a comfort, that for all his sicknesse, he is rich, and therefore cannot fayle of helpe and attendance, there comes another worme, and devours that, faithlessnesse in persons trusted by him, oppressions in persons that have trusted him, facility in undertaking for others, corrupt Judges, heavy adversaries, tempests and Pirats at Sea, unseasonable or ill Markets at land, costly and expensive ambitions at Court, one worme or other shall devoure his riches, that he eased himselfe upon. If he take up another Comfort, that though health and wealth decay, though he be poore and weake, yet he hath learning, and philosophy, and morall constancy, and he can content himselfe with himselfe, he can make his study a Court, and a few Books shall supply to him the society and the conversation of many friends, there is another worme to devoure this too, the hand of divine Justice shall grow heavy upon him, in a sense of an unprofitable retirednesse, in a disconsolate melancholy, and at last, in a stupidity, tending to desperation.

[*LXXX. Sermons* (57), 1640]

PREACHED UPON THE PENITENTIALL PSALMES
(PS. XXXII)

Now the pride of the wicked is to conceale their sorrowes, that God might receive no glory by the discovery of them. And therefore if we should goe about to number their sor-

rowes, they would have their victory still, and still say to themselves, yet for all his cunning he hath mist; they would ever
have some bosome-sorrowes, which we could not light upon.
Yet we shall not easily misse, nor leave out any, if we remember those men, that even this false and imaginary joy, which
they take in concealing their sorrow and affliction, is a new
affliction, a new cause of sorrow. We shall make up the number apace, if we remember these men, that all their new sins,
and all their new shifts, to put away their sorrowes, are sorrow-
full things, and miserable comforters; if their conscience doe
present all their sins, the number growes great; And if their
own conscience have forgotten them, if God forget nothing
that they have thought, or said, or done, in all their lives, are
not their occasions of sorrow the more for their forgetting, the
more for Gods remembring? *Judgements are prepared for the
scorners,* sayes *Solomon,* God foresaw their wickednesse from
before all times, and even then set himselfe on work, *To prepare judgements for them;* And as they are *Prepared* before,
so *affliction followeth sinners,* sayes the same Wise King; It
followes them, and it knowes how to *overtake* them; eyther by
the sword of the Magistrate, or by that which is nearer them,
Diseases in their owne bodies, accelerated and complicated by
their sins. And then, as affliction is *Prepared,* and *Followes,*
and *Overtakes,* so sayes that wise King still, *There shall be no
end of plagues to the evill man;* We know the beginning of
their plagues; they are *Prepared* in Gods Decree, as soone as
God saw their sins; we know their continuance, they shall *Follow,* and they shall *Overtake;* Their end we doe not know, we
cannot know, for they have none. Thus they are *Many.*

And if we consider farther, the manifold Topiques, and
places, from which the sorrowes of the wicked arise, That every
inch of their ground is overgrown with that venomous weed,
that every place, and every part of time, and every person
buddes out a particular occasion of sorrow to him, that he can
come into no chamber, but he remembers, In such a place as
this, I sinned thus, That he cannot heare a Clock strike, but he
remembers At this hour I sinned thus, That he cannot converse
with few persons, but he remembers, With such a person I
sinned thus, And if he dare goe no farther than to himselfe,
he can look scarcely upon any limb of his body, but in that he
sees some infirmity, or some deformity, that he imputes to
some sin, and must say, By this sin, this is thus: When he can
open the Bible in no place, but if he meet a judgement, he

must say, *Vindicta mihi,* This vengeance belongs to me; and if he meet a mercy, he must say, *Quid mihi?* What have I to doe to take this mercy into my mouth? In this deluge of occasions of sorrow, I must not say with God to *Abraham,* Look up to heaven, and number the Starres, (for this man cannot look up to heaven) but I must say, Continue thy dejected look, and look downe to the earth, thy earth, and number the graines of dust there, and the sorrowes of the wicked are more than they. *Many are the sorrowes;* And as the word as naturally denotes, *Great; Great sorrowes are upon the wicked.*

That Pill will choak one man, which will slide down with another easily, and work well. That sorrow, that affliction would strangle the wicked, which would purge, and recover the godly. The coare of *Adams* apple is still in their throat, which the blood of the Messias hath washt away in the righteous; *Adams* disobedience works in them still, and therefore Gods Physick, the affliction, cannot work. So they are great to them, as *Cains* punishment was to him, greater than he could beare, because he could not ease himselfe upon the consideration of Gods purpose, in laying that punishment upon him. But it is not onely their indisposition, and impatience, that makes their sorrowes and afflictions great; They are truly so in themselves; as the Holy Ghost expresses it, *Is not destruction to the wicked, and strange punishment to the workers of iniquity?* A punishment, which we cannot tell how to measure, how to waigh, how to call, *A strange punishment;* Greater than former examples have presented. There the greatnesse is exprest in the Word; And in *Esay* it is exprest in the action; *When the scourge shall run over you, and passe thorow you, Eritis in con-culcationem, You shall be trodden to dust;* Which is, as the Prophet cals it there, *Flagellum inundans,* An affliction that overflowes, and surrounds all, as a deluge, a flood, that shall wash away from thee, even the water of thy Baptisme, and all the power of that, And wash away from thee the blood of thy Saviour, and all his offers of grace to worthy receivers; A flood that shall carry away the Ark it selfe out of thy sight, and leave thee no apprehension of reparation by Gods institution in his Church; A flood that shall dissolve, and wash thee thy selfe into water; Thy sorrowes shall scatter thee into drops, into teares, upon a carnall sense of thy torment, And into drops, into incoherent doubts, and perplexities, and scruples, in understanding, and conscience, and into desperation at last. And this is the Greatnesse: *Solutis doloribus inferni,* In another sense then *David* speaks that of Christ; There it is, that the sorrowes of hell were loosed, that is, were slacked, dissolved by him: But here it is that the sorrowes of hell are loosed, that is, let loose upon thee; and when thou shalt heare Christ say from the Crosse, *Behold and see, if ever there were any sorrow like my sorrow,* thou shalt finde thy sorrow like his in the Greatnesse, and nothing like his in the Goodnesse: Christ bore that sorrow, that every man might rejoyce, and thou wouldest be the more sorry, if every man had not as much cause of desperate sorrow, as thou hast.

Many, and great are the sor[r]owes of the wicked, and then *eternall* too, which is more than intimated, in that the Originall hath neither of those particles of supplement, which are in our Translations, no such (*shall come*) no such (*shall be*) nor no (*shall*) at all; but onely, *Many sorrowes to the wicked,* Many and great now, more and greater hereafter, All for ever, if they amend not.

It is not, They have had sorrowes, but they are overblown; nor that they have them, but patience shall outweare them; nor that they shall have them, but they have a breathing time to gather strength before hand, But as it was in the beginning, is now, and ever shall be; Sorrowes upon them, and upon them for ever. Whatsoever any man conceives for ease in this case, it is a false conception; *You shall conceive chaffe and bring forth stubble.* And this stubble is your vaine hope of a determination of this sorrow; But the wicked shall not be able to lodge such a hope, though this hope, if they could apprehend it, would be but an aggravating of their sorrowes in the end. It is eternall, no determination of time afforded to it. For, *They shall bee as the burning of lime, and as thornes cut up shall they bee burnt in the fire. Who amongst us shall dwell with the devouring fire? Who amongst us shall dwell with that everlasting burning?* It is a *devouring fire,* and yet it is an *everlasting burning.* The Prophet asks, *Who can dwell there?* In that intensenesse who can last? They that must, and that is, All the wicked. *Fire is kindled in my wrath,* saith God; Yet may not teares quench it? Teares might, if they could be had; But *It shall burne to the bottome of hell,* saith God there. And *Dives* that could not procure a drop of water to coole his tongue there, can much lesse procure a repentant teare in that place: There, as S. *John* speaks, *Plagues shall come in one day;* Death, and Sorrow, and Famine. But it is in a long day; Short for the suddennesse of comming, for that is come already, which for any thing we know, may come this minute, before we be at an end of this point, or at a period of this sentence: So it is sudden in comming, but long for the enduring. For it is that day, when *They shall be burnt with fire, for strong is the Lord God, that will condemne them.* That is argument enough of the vehemence of that fire, that the *Lord God,* who is called the *strong God,* makes it a Masterpiece of his strength, to make that fire.

Art thou able to dispute out this *Fire,* and to prove that there can be no reall, no materiall fire in Hell, after the dissolution of all materiall things created? If thou be not able to argue away the immortality of thine owne soule, but that that soule must last, nor to argue away the eternity of God himselfe, but that that must last, thou hast but little ease, in making shift to give a figurative interpretation to that fire, and to say, It may be a torment, but it cannot be a fire, since it must be an everlasting torment; nor to give a figurative signification to the *Worme,* and to say, It may bee a paine, a remorse, but it can bee no worme after the generall dissolution, since that Conscience, in which that remorse, and anguish shall ever live, must live ever: If there bee a figure in the names, and words, of *Fire* and *Wormes,* there is an indisputable reality in the sorrow, in the torment, and in the manifoldnesse, and in the weightinesse, and in the everlastingnesse thereof. For in the inchoation of these sorrowes, in this life, and in the consummation of them, in the life to come, *The sorrowes of the wicked are many,* and *great,* and *eternall.*

[*LXXX. Sermons* (63), 1640]

PREACHED AT ST. PAUL'S

AMONGST *naturall Creatures,* because howsoever they differ in bignesse, yet they have some proportion to one another, we consider that some very little creatures, contemptible in themselves, are yet called enemies to great creatures, as the Mouse is to the Elephant. (For the greatest Creature is not *Infinite,* nor the least is not *Nothing.*) But shall man, betweene whom and nothing, there went but a word, *Let us make Man,* That Nothing, which is infinitely lesse than a Mathematicall point, than an imaginary Atome, shall this Man, this yesterdayes Nothing, this to morrow worse than Nothing, be capable of that honour, that *dishonourable honour,* that confounding honour, to be the enemy of God, of God who is not onely a multiplied Elephant, millions of Elephants multiplied into one, but a multiplied World, a multiplied All, All that can be conceived by us, infinite many times over; Nay, (if we may dare to say so,) a multiplied God, a God that hath the Millions of the Heathens gods in himselfe alone, shall this man be an enemy to this God? Man cannot be allowed so high a sinne as enmity with God. The Devil himselfe is but a *slave* to God, and shall Man be called his enemy? It is true, if we consider the infinite disproportion between them, he cannot; but to many sad purposes, and in many heavy applications Man is an enemy to God. *Job* could goe no higher in expressing his misery, *Why hidest thou thy face, and holdest me for thine enemy?* and againe, *Behold, he findeth occasions against me, and counteth me for his enemy.* So Man is an enemy to God; And then to adhere to an enemy, is to become an enemy; for Man to adhere to Man, to ascribe any thing to the power of his *naturall faculties,* to thinke of any beame of clearnesse in his own understanding, or any line of rectitude in his owne will, this is to accumulate and multiply enmities against God, and to assemble and muster up more, and more m[e]n, to fight against God.

[*Fifty Sermons* (40), 1649]

PREACHED AT WHITEHALL. APRIL 21st, 1616

How desperate a state art thou in, if nothing will convert thee, but a speedie execution, after which, there is no possibility, no room left for a Conversion! God is *the Lord of hosts,* and he can proceed by Martial Law: he can hang thee upon the next tree; he can choak thee with a crum, with a drop, at a voluptuous feast; he can sink down the Stage and the Player, The bed of wantonness, and the wanton actor, into the jaws of the earth, into the mouth of hell: he can surprise thee, even in the act of sin; and dost thou long for such a speedy execution, for such an expedition? Thou canst not lack Examples, that he hath done so upon others, and will no proof serve thee, but a speedy judgement upon thy self? Scatter thy thoughts no farther then; contract them in thy self, and consider Gods speedy execution upon thy soul, and upon thy

body, and upon thy soul and body together. Was not Gods
judgement executed speedily enough upon thy soul, when in
the same instant that it was created, and conceiv'd, and infus'd, it was put to a necessity of contracting Original sin, and
so submitted to the penalty of *Adam's* disobedience, the first
minute? Was not Gods judgement speedily enough executed
upon thy body, if before it had any temporal life, it had a
spiritual death; a sinful conception, before any inanimation?
If hereditary diseases from thy parents, Gouts and Epilepsies,
were in thee, before the diseases of thine own purchase, the
effects of thy licentiousness and thy riot; and that from the
first minute that thou beganst to live, thou beganst to die too?
Are not the judgements of God speedily enough executed
upon thy soul and body together, every day, when as soon as
thou commitst a sin, thou ar[t] presently left to thine Impenitence, to thine Insensibleness, and Obduration? Nay, the
judgement is more speedy than so; for, that very sin it self,
was a punishment of thy former sins.

[*XXVI. Sermons* (6), 1660]

LINCOLNS INNE [Oct. 1616–Feb. 1621/2]

Corruption in the skin, says *Job;* In the outward beauty, These
be the Records of velim, these be the parchmins, the endict-
ments, and the evidences that shall condemn many of us, at
the last day, our *own skins;* we have the book of God, the
Law, written in our own hearts; we have the image of God
imprinted in our own souls; wee have the character, and seal
of God stamped in us, in our baptism; and, all this is bound
up in this velim, in this parchmin, in this skin of ours, and we
neglect book, and image, and character, and seal, and all for
the covering. It is not a clear case, if we consider the originall words properly, *That Jesabel did paint;* and yet all translators, and expositors have taken a just occasion, out of the
ambiguity of those words, to cry down that abomination of
painting. It is not a clear case, if we consider the propriety of
the words, That *Absolon was hanged by the hair of the head;*
and yet the Fathers and others have made use of that indifferency, and verisimilitude, to explode that abomination, of cherishing and curling haire, to the enveagling, and ensnaring, and
entangling of others; *Judicium patietur æternum,* says *Saint
Hierome,* Thou art guilty of a murder, though no body die;

Quia vinum attulisti, si fuisset qui bibisset; Thou hast poy-son'd a cup, if any would drink, thou hast prepar'd a tentation, if any would swallow it. *Tertullian* thought he had done enough, when he had writ his book *De Habitu muliebri,* against the excesse of women in clothes, but he was fain to adde another with more vehemence, *De cultu fœminarum,* that went beyond their clothes to their skin. And he concludes, *Illud ambitionis crimen,* there's vain-glory in their excesse of clothes, but, *Hoc prostitutionis,* there's prostitution in drawing the eye to the skin. *Pliny* says, that when their thin silke stuffes were first invented at Rome, *Excogitatum ad fœminas denudandas;* It was but an invention that women might go naked in clothes, for their skins might bee seen through those clothes, those thinne stuffes: Our women are not so carefull, but they expose their nakednesse professedly, and paint it, to cast bird-lime for the passengers eye. Beloved, good dyet makes the best Complexion, and a good Conscience is a continuall feast; A cheerfull heart makes the best blood, and peace with God is the true cheerfulnesse of heart. Thy Saviour neglected his skin so much, as that at last, he scarse had any; all was torn with the whips, and scourges; and thy skin shall come to that absolute corruption, as that, though a hundred years after thou art buryed, one may find thy bones, and say, this was a *tall* man, this was a *strong* man, yet we shall soon be past saying, upon any relique of thy skinne, This was a *fair* man; Corruption seises the skinne, all outward beauty quickly, and so it does the body, the whole frame and constitution, which is another consideration; *After my skinne, my body.*

If the whole body were an eye, or an ear, where were the body, says Saint *Paul;* but, when of the whole body there is neither eye nor ear, nor any member left, where is the body? And what should an eye do there, where there is nothing to be seen but loathsomnesse; or a nose there, where there is nothing to be smelt, but putrefaction; or an ear, where in the grave they doe not praise God? Doth not that body that boasted but yesterday of that priviledge above all creatures, that it onely could goe upright, lie to day as flat upon the earth as the body of a horse, or of a dogge? And doth it not to morrow lose his other priviledge, of looking up to heaven? Is it not farther remov'd from the eye of heaven, the Sunne, than any dogge, or horse, by being cover'd with the earth, which they are not? Painters have presented to us with some horrour, the *sceleton*, the frame of the bones of a mans body; but the state of a body, in the dissolution of the grave, no pencil can present to us. Between that excrementall jelly that thy body is made of at first, and that jelly which thy body dissolves to at last; there is not so noysome, so putrid a thing in nature. This skinne, (this outward beauty) this body, (this whole constitution) must be destroy'd, says *Job*, in the next place.

The word is well chosen, by which all this is expressed, in this text, *Nakaph*, which is a word of as heavy a signification, to expresse an utter abolition, and annihilation, as perchance can be found in all the Scriptures. *Tremellius* hath mollifyed it in his translation; there is but one *Confodere*, to pierce. And yet it is such a piercing, such a sapping, such an undermining, such a demolishing of a fort or Castle, as may justly remove us from any high valuation, or any great confidence, in that skinne, and in that body, upon which this *Confoderint* must fall. But, in the great Bible it is *Contriverint*, Thy *skinne*, and thy *body* shall be *ground* away, trod away upon the ground. Aske where that iron is that is ground off of a knife, or axe; Aske that marble that is worn off of the threshold in the Church-porch by continuall treading, and with that iron, and with that marble, thou mayst finde thy Fathers skinne, and body; *Contrita sunt*, The knife, the marble, the skinne, the body are ground away, trod away, they are destroy'd, who knows the revolutions of dust? Dust upon the Kings high-way, and dust upon the Kings grave, are both, or neither, Dust Royall, and may change places; who knows the revolutions of dust? Even in the dead body of Christ Jesus himself, one dram of the decree of his Father, one sheet, one sentence of the prediction of the Prophets preserv'd his body from corruption, and incineration, more than all *Josephs* new tombs, and fine linnen, and great proportion of spices could have done. O, who can expresse this inexpressible mystery? The soul of Christ Jesus, which took no harm by him, contracted no Originall sin, in coming to him, was guilty of no more sin, when it went out, than when it came from the breath and bosome of God; yet this soul left this body in death. And the Divinity, the Godhead, incomparably better than that soul, which soul was incomparably better than all the Saints, and Angels in heaven, that Divinity, that God-head did not forsake the body, though it were dead. If we might compare things infinite in themselves; it was nothing so much, that God did assume mans nature, as that God did still cleave to that man, then when he was no man, in the separation of body and soul, in the grave. But fall we from incomprehensible mysteries; for, there is mortification enough, (and mortification is vivification, and aedification) in this obvious consideration; *skinne and body,* beauty and substance must be destroy'd; And, *Destroyed by wormes,* which is another descent in this humiliation, and exinanition of man, in death; *After my skinne, wormes shall destroy this body.*

I will not insist long upon this, because it is not in the Originall; In the Originall there is no mention of *wormes.* But because in other places of *Job* there is, (*They shall lye down alike in the dust, and the* worms *shall cover them*) (*The* womb *shal forget them, and the* worm *shal feed sweetly on on them;* and because the word *Destroying* is presented in that form and number, *Contriverint,* when *they* shall destroy, *they* and no other persons, no other creatures named) both our later translations, (for indeed, our first translation hath no mention of *wormes*) and so very many others, even *Tremellius* that adheres most to the letter of the Hebrew, have filled up this place, with that addition, *Destroyed by worms.* It makes the destruction the more contemptible; Thou that wouldest not admit the beames of the Sunne upon thy skinne, and yet hast admitted the spirit of lust, and unchast solicitations to breath upon thee, in execrable oathes, and blasphemies, to vicious purposes; Thou, whose body hath (as farre as it can) putrefyed and corrupted even the body of thy Saviour, in an unworthy receiving thereof, in this *skinne,* in this *body,* must be the food of worms, the prey of destroying worms. After a low birth thou mayst passe an honourable life, after a sentence of an ignominious death, thou mayst have an honourable end; But, in the grave canst thou make these worms silke worms? They were bold and early worms that eat up *Herod* before he dyed; They are bold and everlasting worms, which after thy skinne and body is destroyed, shall remain as long as God remains, in an eternall gnawing of thy conscience; long, long after the destroying of skinne and body, by bodily worms.

[*Fifty Sermons* (14), 1649]

LINCOLNS INNE [Oct. 1616–Feb. 1621/2]

1

AFTER wee have parled with a tentation, debating whether we should embrace it or no, and entertain'd some discourse with it, though some tendernesse, some remorse, make us turn our back upon it, and depart a little from it, yet the arrow overtakes us; some *reclinations*, some *retrospects* we have, a little of *Lots wife* is in us, a little *sociablenesse*, and *conversation*, a little point of *honour*, not to be false to former promises, a little *false gratitude*, and thankfulnesse, in respect of former obligations, a little of the *compassion* and *charity* of Hell, that another should not be miserable, for want of *us*, a little of this, which is but the good nature of the *Devill*, arrests us, stops us, fixes us, till the arrow, the tentation shoot us in the back, even when wee had a purpose of departing from that sin, and kils us over again.

2

Every tentation, every tribulation is not *deadly*. But their multiplicity disorders us, discomposes us, unsettles us, and so hazards us. Not onely every *periodicall* variation of our years, *youth* and *age*, but every day hath a divers arrow, every houre of the day, a divers tentation. An old man wonders then, how an arrow from an eye could wound him, when he was young, and how *love* could make him doe those things which hee did *then;* And an arrow from the tongue of inferiour people, that which we make shift to call *honour*, wounds him deeper now; and *ambition* makes him doe as strange things now, as *love* did then; A fair day shoots arrows of *visits*, and come-dies, and *conversation*, and so wee goe abroad: and a foul day shoots arrows of *gaming*, or *chambering*, and *wantonnesse*, and so we stay at home.

[*Fifty Sermons* (19), 1649]

LINCOLNS INNE [Oct. 1616–Feb. 1621/2]

FOR, this plurality, this multiplicity of sin, hath found first a spunginesse in the soul, an aptnesse to receive any liquor, to

embrace any sin, that is offered to it; and after a while, a
hunger and thirst in the soul, to hunt, and pant and draw
after a tentation, and not to be able to endure any *vacuum*,
any discontinuance, or intermission of sinne: and hee will
come to think it a melancholique thing, still to stand in
fear of Hell; a sordid, a *yeomanly* thing, still to be plowing,
and weeding, and worming a conscience; a mechanicall thing,
still to be removing logs, or filing iron, still to be busied in
removing occasions of tentation, or filing and clearing particular actions: and, at last he will come to that case, which S.
Augustine out of an abundant ingenuity, and tendernesse, and
compunction, confesses of himself, *Ne vituperarer vitiosior
fiebam,* I was fain to sin, lest I should lose my credit, and be
under-valued; *Et ubi non suberat, quo admisso, aequarer per-
ditis,* when I had no means to doe some sins, whereby I might
be equall to my fellow, *Fingebam me fecisse quod non fec-
eram, ne viderer abjectior, quo innocentior,* I would bely myself, and say I had done that, which I never did, lest I should
be under-valued for not having done it. *Audiebam eos exal-
tantes flagitia,* sayes that tender blessed Father, I saw it was
thought wit, to make Sonnets of their own sinnes, *Et libebat
facere, non libidine facti, sed libidine laudis,* I sinn'd, not for
the pleasure I had in the sin, but for the pride that I had to
write feelingly of it. O what a *Leviathan* is sin, how vast, how
immense a body! And then, what a spawner, how numerous!
Between these two, the *denying* of sins, which we have done,
and the *bragging* of sins, which we have not done, what a space,
what a compasse is there, for millions of millions of sins!

[Fifty Sermons (21), 1649]

PREACHED TO THE NOBILITY *[Before Apr. 1619]*

In finem dilexit eos, saith S. *John, He loved them to the end,*
not for any particular end, for any use of his own, but to their
end *Qui erant in mundo,* saith *Cyril, ad distinctionem Angel-
orum;* he loved them in the world, and not Angels: he loved
not onely them who were in a confirmed estate of mutuall
loving of him too, but even them who were themselves conceived in sinne, and then conceived all their purposes in sinne
too; them who could have no cleansing but in his bloud, and
when they were cleansed in his bloud, their own clothes
would defile them again; them, who by nature are not able to

love him at all; and when by grace they are brought to love him, can expresse their love no other way, but to be glad that he was betrayed, and scourged, and scorned, and nailed, and crucified; and to be glad, that if all this were not alreadie done, it might be done yet; and to long and to wish, if Christ were not crucified, to have him crucified now (which is a strange manner of expressing love) those men he loved, and loved to the end; men, and not Angels; and then men, *Ad distinctionem mortuorum*, saith *Chrysostome*: not onely the Patriarchs who were departed out of the world, who had loved him so well as to take his word for their salvation, and had lived and died in a faithfull contemplation of a future promise, which they never saw performed; but those who were the partakers of the performance of all those promises; those, into the midst of whom he came in person; those, upon whom he wrought by his piercing doctrine and powerfull miracles; those, who for all this loved not him, he loved, *Et in finem*, he loved them to the end. It is much he should love them *in fine*, at their end; that he should look graciously on them at last; that when their sunne sets, their eyes faint, his sunne of grace should arise, and his East should be brought to their West; that then, in the shadow of death, the Lord of life should quicken and inanimate their hearts; that when their last bell tolls, and calls them to their first and last judgement, which to this purpose is all one; for the passing bell and the Angels trump sound but one note: *Surgite qui dormitis in pulvere, Arise ye that sleep in the dust*, which is the voice of the Angels; and, *Surgite qui vigilatis in plumis, Arise ye that cannot sleep in feathers*, for the pangs of death, which is the voice of the bell, is in effect but one voice: for God at the generall judgement shall never reverse any particular judgement formerly given: that God should then come to thy bedside *Ad sibilandum populum suum*, as the Prophet *Ezechiel* saith, to hisse softly for his childe, to speak comfortably in his eare, to whisper gently to his departing soul, and to drown and overcome with this soft musick of his all the clangour of the Angels trumpets, all the horrour of the ringing bell, all the cries and vociferations of a distressed, and distracted, and scattering family; yea, all the accusations of his own conscience, and all the triumphant acclamations of the devil himself: that God should love a man thus *in fine*, at his end, and return to him then though he had suffered him to go astray before, is a great testimonie of the inexpressible love. But this love is not *in fine, in the end;* but *in finem, to the end.* He leaves them not uncalled at the first, he leaves them not unaccompanied in the way, he leaves them not unrecompensed at the last. That God, who is Almighty, Alpha and Omega, First and Last, that God is also Love it self; and therefore this Love is Alpha and Omega, First and Last too. Consider Christs proceeding with *Peter* in the ship, in the storm: First he suffered him to be in some danger in the storm, but then he visits him with that strong assurance, *Noli timere, Be not afraid, it is I:* any testimonie of his presence rectifies all. This puts *Peter* into that spirituall confidence and courage, *Jube me venire, Lord bid me come to thee;* he hath a desire to be with Christ, but yet stayes his bidding: he puts not himself into an unnecessarie danger, without commandment: Christ bids him, and *Peter* comes: but yet, though Christ were in his sight, and even in the actuall exercise of his love to him, so soon as he saw a gust, a storm, *Timuit, He was afraid;* and Christ lets him fear, and lets him sink, and lets him crie, but he directs his fear and his crie to the right end: *Domine, salvum me fac; Lord, save me;* and thereupon he stretched forth his hand and saved him. God doth not raise his children to honour and great estate, and then leave them, and expose them to be subjects and exercises of the malice of others; neither doth he make them mightie and then leave them, *ut glorietur in malo qui potens est,* that he should think it a glorie to do harm: he doth not impoverish and dishonour his children, and then leave them unsensible of that doctrine, that patience is as great a blessing as abundance. God gives not his people health, and then leaves them to a boldnesse in surfeting; nor beautie, and then leaves them to a confidence, and opening themselves to all sollicitations; nor valour, and then leaves them to a spirituous quarrelsomnesse: God makes no patterns of his works, nor models of his houses; he makes whole pieces, and perfect houses: he puts his children into good wayes, and he directs and protects them in those wayes; for this is the constancie and perseverance of the love of Christ Jesus to us, as he is called in this Text *a stone.*

[*Six Sermons* (4), 1634]

PREACHED UPON THE PENITENTIALL PSALMES
[1615–1619?]

IT MAY well be inquired, why Death seemed so terrible to the good and godly men of those times, as that evermore we see them complaine of shortnesse of life, and of the neerenesse of death. Certainely the rule is true, in naturall, and in civill, and in divine things, as long as wee are in this World, *Nolle meliorem, est corruptio primæ habitudinis,* That man is not well, who desires not to be better; It is but our corruption here, that makes us loth to hasten to our incorruption there. And besides, many of the Ancients, and all the later Casuists of the other side, and amongst our owne men, *Peter Martyr,* and *Calvin,* assigne certain cases, in which it hath *Rationem boni,* The nature of Good, and therefore is to be embraced, to wish our dissolution and departure out of this world; and yet, many good and godly men have declared this lothnesse to dye. Beloved, waigh Life and Death one against another, and the balance will be even; Throw the glory of God into either balance, and that turnes the scale. S. *Paul* could not tell which to wish, Life or Death; There the balance was even; Then comes in the glory of God, the addition of his soule to that Quire, that spend all their time, eternity it selfe, only in glorifying God, and that turnes the scale, and then, he comes to his *Cupio dissolvi,* To *desire to be dissolved, and to be with Christ.* But then, he puts in more of the same waight in the other scale, he sees that it advances Gods glory more, for him to stay, and labour in the building of Gods Kingdome here, and so adde more soules than his owne to that state, than only to enjoy that Kingdome in himself, and that turnes the scale againe, and so he is content *to live.*

[*LXXX. Sermons* (53), 1640]

TO THE LORDS UPON EASTER DAY AT THE COMMUNION, THE KING BEING DANGEROUSLY SICK AT NEW-MARKET. MARCH 28, 1619

WEE are all conceived in close Prison; in our Mothers wombes, we are close Prisoners all; when we are borne, we are borne but to the liberty of the house; Prisoners still, though within larger walls; and then all our life is but a going out to the place of Execution, to death. Now was there ever any man seen to sleep in the Cart, between New-gate, and Tyborne? between the Prison, and the place of Execution, does any man sleep? And we sleep all the way; from the womb to the grave we are never throughly awake; but passe on with such dreames, and imaginations as these, I may live as well, as another, and why should I dye, rather than another? but awake, and tell me, sayes this Text, *Quis homo?* who is that other that thou talkest of? *What man is he that liveth, and shall not see death?*

[*LXXX. Sermons* (27), 1640]

THE HAGUE. "SINCE IN MY SICKNESSE AT ABREY-HATCHE IN ESSEX, 1630, REVISING MY SHORT NOTES OF THAT SERMON, I DIGESTED THEM INTO THESE TWO." DEC. 19TH, 1619

1

EVEN that murmuring at poverty, is a net; leave that. Leave thy superfluous desire of having the riches of this world; though thou mayest flatter thy selfe, that thou desirest to have onely that thou mightest leave it, that thou mightest employ it charitably, yet it might prove a net, and stick too close about thee to part with it. *Multa relinquitis, si desideriis renunciatis,* You leave your nets, if you leave your over-earnest greedinesse of catching; for, when you doe so, you doe not onely fish with a net, (that is, lay hold upon all you can compasse) but, (which is strange) you fish for a net, even that which you get proves a net to you, and hinders you in the following of Christ, and you are lesse disposed to follow him, when you have got your ends, than before. He that hath least, hath enough to waigh him down from heaven, by an inordinate love of that little which he hath, or in an inordinate and murmuring desire of more. And he that hath most, hath not too much to give for heaven; *Tantum valet regnum Dei, quantum tu vales,* Heaven is alwayes so much worth, as thou art worth. A poore man may have heaven for a penny, that hath no greater store; and, God lookes, that he to whom he hath given thousands, should lay out thousands upon the purchase of heaven. The market changes, as the plenty of money changes; Heaven

costs a rich man more than a poore, because he hath more to
give. But in this, rich and poore are both equall, that both
must leave themselves without nets, that is, without those
things, which, in their own Consciences they know, retard the
following of Christ. Whatsoever hinders my present following,
that I cannot follow to day, whatsoever may hinder my con·
stant following, that I cannot follow to morrow, and all my
life, is a net, and I am bound to leave that.

And these are the pieces that constitute our first part, the
circumstances that invest these persons, *Peter*, and *Andrew*, ir
their former condition, before, and when Christ called them.

2

So early, so primary a sin is pride, as that, out of every
mercy, and blessing, which God affords us, (and, *His mercies
are new every morning*) we gather Pride; we are not the
more thankfull for them, and yet we are the prouder of them.
Nay, we gather Pride, not onely out of those things, which
mend and improve us, (Gods blessings and mercies) but out
of those actions of our own, that destroy and ruine us, we
gather pride; sins overthrow us, demolish us, destroy and ruine
us, and yet we are proud of our sinnes. How many men have
we heard boast of their sinnes; and, (as S. *Augustine* confesses
of himselfe) belie themselves, and boast of more sinnes than
ever they committed? Out of every thing, out of nothing sin
grows. Therefore was this commandment in our text, *Sequere,
Follow*, come after, well placed first, for we are come to see
even children strive for place and precedency, and mothers are
ready to goe to the Heralds to know how Cradles shall be
ranked, which Cradle shall have the highest place; Nay, even
in the wombe, there was contention for precedency; *Jacob*
tooke hold of his brother *Esaus* heele, and would have been
borne before him.

And as our pride begins in our Cradle, it continues in our
graves and Monuments. It was a good while in the primitive
Church, before any were buried in the Church; The best contented themselves with the Churchyards. After, a holy ambition,
(may we call it so) a holy Pride brought them *ad Limina,* to
the Church-threshold, to the Church-doore, because some great
Martyrs were buried in the Porches, and devout men desired
to lie near them, as one Prophet did to lie neare another, (*Lay
my bones besides his bones.*) But now, persons whom the

Devill kept from Church all their lives, Separatists, Libertines, that never came to any Church, And persons, whom the Devill brought to Church all their lives, (for, such as come meerly out of the obligation of the Law, and to redeem that vexation, or out of custome, or company, or curiosity or a perverse and sinister affection to the particular Preacher, though they come to Gods house, come upon the Devils invitation) Such as one Devill, that is, worldly respect, brought to Church in their lives, another Devill, that is, Pride and vain-glory, brings to Church after their deaths, in an affectation of high places, and sumptuous Monuments in the Church. And such as have given nothing at all to any pious uses, or have determined their almes and their dole which they have given, in that one day of their funerall, and no farther, have given large annuities, perpetuities, for new painting their tombes, and for new flags, and scutcheons, every certaine number of yeares.

O the earlinesse! O the latenesse! how early a Spring, and no Autumne! how fast a growth, and no declination, of this branch of this sin Pride, against which, this first word of ours, *Sequere, Follow,* come after, is opposed! this love of place, and precedency, it rocks us in our Cradles, it lies down with us in our graves. There are diseases proper to certaine things, Rots to sheepe, Murrain to cattell. There are diseases proper to certaine places, as the Sweat was to us. There are diseases proper to certaine times, as the plague is in divers parts of the Eastern Countryes, where they know assuredly, when it will begin and end. But for this infectious disease of precedency, and love of place, it is run over all places, as well Cloysters as Courts, And over all men, as well spirituall as temporall, And over all times, as well the Apostles as ours.

3

Forraine crosses, other mens merits are not mine; spontaneous and voluntary crosses, contracted by mine owne sins, are not mine; neither are devious, and remote, and unnecessary crosses, my crosses. Since I am bound to take up my crosse, there must be a crosse that is mine to take up; that is, a crosse prepared for me by God, and laid in my way, which is tentations or tribulations in my calling; and I must not go out of my way to seeke a crosse; for, so it is not mine, nor laid for my taking up. I am not bound to hunt after a persecution, nor to stand it, and not flye, nor to affront a plague, and not remove, nor to open my selfe to any injury, and not defend. I am not bound to starve my selfe by inordinate fasting, nor to teare my flesh by inhumane whippings, and flagellations. I am bound to take up my Crosse; and that is onely mine which the hand of God hath laid for me, that is, in the way of my Calling, tentations and tribulations incident to that.

[LXXX. *Sermons* (71, 72), 1640]

PREACHED AT WHITEHALL. APRIL 30th, 1620

For the first temporall blessing of peace, we may consider the lovelinesse, the amiablenesse of that, if we looke upon the horror and gastlinesse of warre: either *in Effigie,* in that picture of warre, which is drawn in every leafe of our own Chronicles, in the blood of so many Princes, and noble families, or if we look upon warre it selfe, at that distance where it cannot hurt us, as God had formerly kindled it amongst our neighbours, and as he hath transferred it now to remoter Nations, whilest we enjoy yet a Goshen in the midst of all those Egypts. In all Cities, disorderly and facinorous men, covet to draw themselves into the skirts and suburbs of those Cities, that so they may be the nearer the spoyle, which they make upon passengers. In all Kingdomes that border upon other Kingdomes, and in Islands which have no other border but the Sea, particular men, who by dwelling in those skirts and borders, may make their profit of spoile, delight in hostility, and have an adversenesse and detestation of peace: but it is not so within: they who till the earth, and breed up cattell, and imploy their industry upon Gods creatures, according to Gods ordinance, feele the benefit and apprehend the sweetnesse, and pray for the continuance of peace.

[*LXXX. Sermons* (74), 1640]

WHITEHALL. BEFORE THE KING. Feb. 16th 1620/1

It is not enough to hear Sermons; it is not enough to live a morall honest life; but take it in the midst, and that extends to all; for there is no believing without hearing, nor working without believing. Be pleased to consider this great work of believing, in the matter, what it was that was to be believed: That that Jesus, whose age they knew, must be antidated so

far, as that they must believe· him to be elder than *Abraham:*
That that Jesus, whose Father and Mother, and Brothers and
Sisters, they knew, must be believed to be of another Family,
and to have a Father in another place; and yet he to be as old
as his Father; And to have another proceeding from him, and
yet he to be no older than that person who proceeded from
him: That that Jesus, whom they knew to be that Carpenters
Son, and knew his work, must be believ'd to have set up a
frame, that reached to heaven, out of which no man could, and
in which any man might be saved: was it not as easie to believe, that those teares which they saw upon his cheeks, were
Pearles; that those drops of Blood, which they saw upon his
back were Rubies; That that spittle, which they saw upon his
face, was ennamel: that those hands which they saw buffet him,
were reached out to place him in a Throne: And that that
Voyce which they heard cry, *Crucifige, Crucifie him,* was
a *Vivat Rex, Long live Jesus of Nazareth King of the Jewes;*
As to believe that from that man, that worm, and no man, ingloriously traduced as a Conjuror, ingloriously apprehended as
a Thief, ingloriously executed a Traytor; they should look for
glory, and all glory, and everlasting glory? And from that mel-
ancholick man, who was never seen to laugh in all his life, and
whose soul was heavy unto death; they should look for joy,
and all joy, and everlasting joy: And for salvation, and everlasting salvation from him, who could not save himself from
the Ignominy, from the Torment, from the Death of the
Crosse?

[XXVI. Sermons (4), 1660]

PREACHED AT WHITEHALL. APRIL 8th, 1621

1

WE NEED not quarrell the words of the Poet, *Tu quamcunque;
Deus tibi fortunaverit horam, Grata sume manu,* Thanke God
for any good fortune, since the Apostle sayes too, that *Godli-
nesse hath the promise of this life;* The godly man shall be
fortunate, God will blesse him with good fortune here; but
still it is fortune, and chance, in the sight and reason of man,
and therefore he hath but found, whatsoever he hath in that
kinde. It is intimated in the very word which we use for all
worldly things: It is *Inventarium,* an Inventory; we found them

here, and here our successors finde them, when we are gone from hence. *Jezabel* had an estimation of beauty, and she thought to have drawne the King with that beauty, but she found it, she found it in her box, and in her wardrope, she was not truly fayre. *Achitophel* had an estimation of wisedome in Counsell, I know not how he found it; he counselled by an example, which no man would follow, he hanged himselfe. Thou wilt not be drawne to confesse, that a man that hath an office is presently wiser than thou, or a man that is Knighted, presently valianter than thou. Men have preferment for those parts, which other men, equall to them in the same things, have not, and therefore they doe but finde them; And to things that are but found, what is our title? *Nisi reddantur, rapina est,* sayes the Law, If we restore not that which we finde, it is robbery. S. *Augustine* hath brought it nearer, *Qui alienum negat, si posset, tolleret,* He that confesseth not that which he hath found of another mans, if he durst, he would have taken it by force. For that which we have found in this world, our calling is the owner, our debts are the owner, our children are the owner; our lusts, our superfluities are no owners: of all the rest, God is the owner, and to this purpose, the poore is God.

2

We know the receipt, the capacity of the ventricle, the stomach of man, how much it can hold; and wee know the receipt of all the receptacles of blood, how much blood the body can have; so wee do of all the other conduits and cisterns of the body; But this infinite Hive of honey, this insatiable whirlpoole of the covetous mind, no Anatomy, no dissection hath discovered to us. When I looke into the larders, and cellars, and vaults, into the vessels of our body for drink, for blood, for urine, they are pottles, and gallons; when I looke into the furnaces of our spirits, the ventricles of the heart and of the braine, they are not thimbles; for spirituall things, the things of the next world, we have no roome; for temporall things, the things of this world, we have no bounds. How then shall this over-eater bee filled with his honey?

[*LXXX. Sermons* (70), 1640]

LINCOLN'S INN. SUNDAY AFTER TRINITY. [1612?]

THE Lord then, the Son of God, had a *Sitio* in heaven, as well as upon the Crosse; He thirsted our salvation there; and in the midst of the fellowship of the Father from whom he came, and of the Holy Ghost, who came from him and the Father, and all the Angels, who came (by a lower way) from them all, he desired the conversation of Man, for Mans sake; He that was God *The Lord* became *Christ*, a man, and he that was *Christ* became *Jesus*, no man, a dead man, to save man: To save man, all wayes, in all his parts, And to save all men, in all parts of the world: To save his soule from hell, where we should have felt pains, and yet been dead, then when we felt them; and seen horrid spectacles, and yet been in darknes and blindnes, then when we saw them; And suffered unsufferable torments, and yet have told over innumerable ages in suffering them: To save this soule from that hell, and to fill that capacity which it hath, and give it a capacity which it hath not, to comprehend the joyes and glory of Heaven, this *Christ* became *Jesus*. To save this body from the condemnation of everlasting corruption, where the wormes that we breed are our betters, because they have a life, where the dust of dead Kings is blowne into the street, and the dust of the street blowne into the River, and the muddy River tumbled into the Sea, and the Sea remaunded into all the veynes and channels of the earth; to save this body from everlasting dissolution, dispersion, dissipation, and to make it in a glorious Resurrection, not onely a Temple of the holy Ghost, but a Companion of the holy Ghost in the kingdome of heaven, This *Christ* became this *Jesus*. To save this man, body and soule together, from the punishments due to his former sinnes, and to save him from falling into future sinnes by the assistance of his Word preached, and his Sacraments administred in the Church, which he purchased by his bloud, is this person, The *Lord*, the *Christ*, become this *Jesus*, this Saviour. To save so, All wayes, In soule, in body, in both; And also to save all men. For, to exclude others from that Kingdome, is a tyrannie, an usurpation; and to exclude thy selfe, is a sinfull, and a rebellious melancholy. But as melancholy in the body is the hardest humour to be purged, so is the melancholy in the soule, the distrust of thy salvation too. Flashes of presumption a calamity will quench, but clouds of desperation calamities thicken upon us; But even in this inordinate dejection thou exaltest thy selfe above God, and makest thy worst better than his best, thy sins larger than his mercy.

[*LXXX. Sermons* (40), 1640]

ST. PAULS. CHRISTMAS-DAY. 1621

THE *reason* therefore of Man, must first be satisfied; but the way of such satisfaction must be *this*, to make him see, That this World, a frame of so much harmony, so much concin-nitie and conveniencie, and such a correspondence, and subordi-nation in the parts thereof, must necessarily have had a worke man, for nothing can make it selfe: That no such workemaṇ would deliver over a frame, and worke, of so much Majestie, to be governed by *Fortune*, casually, but would still retain the Administration thereof in his owne hands: That if he doe so, if he made the World, and *sustaine* it still by his watchfull Providence, there belongeth a worship and service to him, for doing so: That therefore he hath certainly revealed to man, what kinde of worship, and service, shall be acceptable to him: That this manifestation of his Will, must be permanent, it must be *written*, there must be a *Scripture*, which is his *Word* and his *Will:* And that therefore, from that Scripture, from that Word of God, all Articles of our Beliefe are to bee drawne.

If then his *Reason* confessing all this, aske farther proofe, how he shall know that *these Scriptures* accepted by the Chris-tian Church, are the true Scriptures, let him bring any other Booke which pretendeth to be the Word of God, into com-parison with these; It is true, we have not a *Demonstration;* not such an Evidence as that one and two, are three, to prove these to be Scriptures of God; God hath not proceeded in that manner, to drive our Reason into a pound, and to force it by a peremptory necessitie to accept these for Scriptures, for then, here had been no exercise of our *Will*, and our assent, if we could not have resisted. But yet these Scriptures have so or-derly, so sweet, and so powerfull a working upon the reason, and the understanding, as if any third man, who were utterly discharged of all preconceptions and anticipations in matter of Religion, one who were altogether neutrall, disinteressed, un-concerned in either party, nothing towards a *Turke*, and as lit-tle toward a *Christian*, should heare a *Christian* pleade for his

Bible, and a *Turke* for his Alcoran, and should weigh the evidence of both; the Majesty of the *Style,* the punctuall accomplishment of the *Prophecies,* the harmony and concurrence of
the *foure Evangelists,* the consent and unanimity of the *Christian Church* ever since, and many other such reasons, he would
be drawne to such an Historicall, such a Gramaticall, such a
Logicall beliefe of our Bible, as to preferre it before any other,
that could be pretended to be the Word of God. He would believe it, and he would know *why* he did so. For let no man
thinke that *God* hath given him so much ease here, as to save
him by believing he knoweth not what, or why. *Knowledge* cannot save us, but we cannot be saved without Knowledge; Faith
is not on this side Knowledge, but beyond it; we must necessarily come to *Knowledge* first, though we must not stay at it,
when we are come thither. For, a regenerate Christian, being
now a *new Creature,* hath also *a new facultie of Reason:* and
so believeth the Mysteries of Religion, out of another Reason,
than as a meere natural Man, he believed naturall and morall
things. He believeth them for their own sake, by *Faith,* though
he take *Knowledge* of them before, by that common Reason,
and by those humane Arguments, which worke upon other
men, in naturall or morall things. Divers men may walke by
the Sea side, and the same beames of the Sunne giving light
to them all, one gathereth by the benefit of that light pebles,
or speckled shells, for curious vanitie, and another gathers precious Pearle, or medicinall Ambar, by the same light. So the
common light of reason illumins us all; but one imployes this
light upon the searching of impertinent vanities, another by a
better use of the same light, finds out the Mysteries of Religion: and when he hath found them, loves them, not for the
lights sake, but for the naturall and true worth of the thing it
self. Some men by the benefit of this light of Reason, have
found out things profitable and usefull to the whole world; As
in particular, *Printing,* by which the learning of the whole
world is communicable to one another, and our minds and our
inventions, our wits and compositions may trade and have commerce together, and we may participate of one anothers understandings, as well as of our Clothes, and Wines, and Oyles, and
other Merchandize: So by the benefit of this light of reason,
they have found out *Artillery,* by which warres come to quicker
ends than heretofore, and the great expence of bloud is
avoyded: for the numbers of men slain now, since the invention of Artillery, are much lesse than before, when the sword

was the executioner. Others, by the benefit of this light have
searched and found the secret corners of gaine, and profit,
wheresoever they lie. They have found wherein the weakenesse
of another man consisteth, and made their profit of that, by
circumventing him in a bargain: They have found his riotous,
and wastefull inclination, and they have fed and fomented that
disorder, and kept open that leake, to their advantage, and the
others ruine. They have found where was the easiest, and the
most accessible way, to sollicite the Chastitie of a woman,
whether *Discourse, Musicke,* or *Presents,* and according to that
discovery, they have pursued *hers,* and *their* own eternall destruction. By the benefit of this light, men see through the
darkest, and most impervious places that are, that is, *Courts of
Princes,* and the greatest *Officers* in Courts; and can submit
themselves to second, and to advance the humours of men in
great place, and so make their profit of the weaknesses which
they have discovered in these great men. All the wayes, both
of *Wisdome,* and of *Craft* lie open to this light, this light of
naturall reason: But when they have gone all these wayes by
the benefit of this light, they have got no further, than to have
walked by a tempestuous Sea, and to have gathered pebles, and
speckled cockle shells. Their light seems to be great out of the
same reason, that a Torch in a misty night, seemeth greater
than in a clear, because it hath kindled and inflamed much
thicke and grosse Ayre round about it. So the light and wisedome of worldly men, seemeth great, because he hath kindled
an admiration, or an applause in Aiery flatterers, not because
it is so in deed.

But, if thou canst take this light of reason that is in thee,
this poore snuffe, that is almost out in thee, thy faint and
dimme knowledge of God, that riseth out of this light of nature, if thou canst in those embers, those cold ashes, finde out
one small coale, and wilt take the paines to kneell downe, and
blow that coale with thy devout *Prayers,* and light thee a *little
candle,* (a *desire* to reade that Booke, which they call the
Scriptures, and the Gospell, and the Word of God;) If with
that little candle thou canst creep humbly into low and poore
places, if thou canst finde thy Saviour in a *Manger,* and in his
swathing clouts, in his humiliation, and blesse God for that beginning, if thou canst finde him flying into Egypt, and finde
in thy selfe a disposition to accompany him in a persecution,
in a banishment, if not a bodily banishment, a locall banishment, yet a *reall, a spirituall banishment,* a banishment from

those sinnes, and that sinnefull conversation, which thou hast
loved more than thy *Parents,* or *Countrey,* or thine owne body,
which perchance thou hast consumed, and destroyed with that
sinne; if thou canst find him contenting and containing himselfe at home in his fathers house, and not breaking out, no
not about the worke of our salvation, till the due time was
come, when it was to be done. And if according to that example, thou canst contain thy selfe in that station and vocation
in which God hath planted thee, and not, through a hasty and
precipitate *zeale,* breake out to an imaginary, and intempes-
tive, and unseasonable *Reformation,* either in *Civill* or *Ecclesiasticall* businesse, which belong not to thee; if with this little
poore light, these *first degrees* of *Knowledge* and *Faith,* thou
canst follow him into the *Garden,* and gather up some of the
droppes of his precious Bloud and sweat, which he shed for
thy soule, if thou canst follow him to *Jerusalem,* and pick up
some of those *teares,* which he shed upon that City, and upon
thy soule; if thou canst follow him to the place of his scourging, and to his crucifying, and provide thee some of that
balme, which must cure thy soule; if after all this, thou canst
turne this little light inward, and canst thereby discerne where
thy diseases, and thy wounds, and thy corruptions are, and
canst apply those teares, and blood and balme to them, (all
this is, That if thou attend the light of naturall reason, and
cherish that, and exalt that, so that that bring thee to a *love of
the Scriptures,* and that *love to a beleefe* of the truth thereof,
and that *historicall faith* to a *faith of application, of appropria-
tion,* that as all those things were certainly done, so they were
certainly done *for thee*) thou shalt never envy the lustre and
glory of the great lights of worldly men, which are great by
the infirmity of others, or by their own opinion, great because
others think them great, or because they think themselves so,
but thou shalt finde, that howsoever they magnifie their lights,
their wit, their learning, their industry, their fortune, their favour, and *sacrifice to their owne nets,* yet thou shalt see, that
thou by thy small light hast gathered *Pearle* and *Amber,* and
they by their great lights nothing but shels and pebles; they
have determined the light of nature, upon the booke of nature,
this world, and thou hast carried the light of nature higher,
thy naturall reason, and even *humane arguments,* have brought
thee to reade the Scriptures, and to that *love,* God hath set to
the seale *of faith.* Their light shall set at noone; even in their
heighth, some heavy crosse shall cast a damp upon their soule,

and cut off all their succours, and devest them of all comforts, and thy light shall grow up, from a *faire hope*, to a modest assurance and *infallibility*, that that light shall never go out, nor the *works of darknesse*, nor the *Prince of darknesse* ever prevaile upon thee, but as thy light of *reason* is exalted by *faith* here, so thy light of *faith* shall be exalted into the light *of glory*, and fruition in the Kingdome of heaven. Before the sunne was made, there was *a light* which did that office of distinguishing night and day; but when the sunne was created, that did all the offices of the former light, and more. *Reason* is that first, and primogeniall light, and goes no farther in a naturall man; but in a man regenerate by faith, that light does all that reason did, *and more;* and all his *Morall*, and *Civill*, and *Domestique*, and indifferent actions, (though they be never done *without Reason*) yet their principall scope, and marke is the glory of God, and though they seeme but *Morall*, or *Civill*, or *domestique*, yet they have a deeper tincture, a heavenly nature, a relation *to God*, in them.

[*Fifty Sermons* (36), 1649]

AT WHITEHALL. 1ST FRIDAY IN LENT.
MARCH 8. 1621/2

1

DOTH not man die even in his birth? The breaking of prison is death, and what is our birth, but a breaking of prison? As soon as we were clothed by God, our very apparell was an Embleme of death. In the skins of dead beasts, he covered the skins of dying men. As soon as God set us on work, our very occupation was an Embleme of death; It was to digge the earth; not to digge pitfals for other men, but graves for our selves. Hath any man here forgot to day, that yesterday is dead? And the Bell tolls for to day, and will ring out anon; and for as much of every one of us, as appertaines to this day. *Quotidiè morimur, et tamen nos esse æternos putamus*, sayes S. *Hierome;* We die every day, and we die all the day long; and because we are not absolutely dead, we call that an eternity, an eternity of dying: And is there comfort in that state? why, that is the state of hell it self, Eternall dying, and not dead.

But for this there is enough said, by the Morall man; (that

we may respite divine proofes, for divine points anon, for our severall Resurrections) for this death is meerly naturall, and it is enough that the morall man sayes, *Mors lex, tributum, officium mortalium.* First it is *lex,* you were born under that law, upon that condition to die: so it is a rebellious thing not to be content to die, it opposes the Law. Then it is *Tributum,* an imposition which nature the Queen of this world layes upon us, and which she will take, when and where she list; here a yong man, there an old man, here a happy, there a miserable man; And so it is a seditious thing not to be content to die, it opposes the prerogative. And lastly, it is *officium,* men are to have their turnes, to take their time, and then to give way by death to successors; and so it is *Incivile, inofficiosum,* not to be content to die, it opposes the frame and form of government. It comes equally to us all, and makes us all equall when it comes. The ashes of an Oak in the Chimney, are no Epitaph of that Oak, to tell me how high or how large that was; It tels me not what flocks it sheltered while it stood, nor what men it hurt when it fell. The dust of great persons graves is speechlesse too, it sayes nothing, it distinguishes nothing: As soon the dust of a wretch whom thou wouldest not, as of a Prince whom thou couldest not look upon, will trouble thine eyes, if the winde blow it thither; and when a whirle-winde hath blowne the dust of the Church-yard into the Church, and the man sweeps out the dust of the Church into the Church-yard, who will undertake to sift those dusts again, and to pronounce, This is the Patrician, this is the noble flowre, and this the yeomanly, this the Plebeian bran.

2

Death hangs upon the edge of every persecutors sword; and upon the sting of every calumniators, and accusers tongue. In the Bull of Phalaris, in the Bulls of Basan, in the Bulls of Babylon, the shrewdest Bulls of all, in temporall, in spirituall persecutions, ever since God put an enmity between Man, and the Serpent, from the time of *Cain* who began in a murther, to the time of Antichrist, who proceeds in Massacres, Death hath adhered to the enemy, and so is an enemy.

Death hath a Commission, *Stipendium peccati mors est, The reward of sin is Death,* but where God gives a Supersedeas, upon that Commission, *Vivo Ego, nolo mortem, As I live saith the Lord, I would have no sinner dye,* not dye the second death, yet Death proceeds to that execution: And whereas the enemy, whom he adheres to, the Serpent himselfe, hath power but *In calcaneo*, upon the heele, the lower, the mortall part, the body of man, *Death is come up into our windowes*, saith the Prophet, into our best lights, our understandings, and be-nights us there, either with ignorance, before sin, or with senselesnesse after: And a Sheriffe that should burne him, who were condemned to be hanged, were a murderer, though that man must have dyed: To come in by the doore, by the way of sicknesse upon the body, is, but to come in at the window by the way of sin, is not deaths Commission; God opens not that window.

3

Death is the last, and in that respect the worst enemy. In an enemy, that appeares at first, when we are or may be provided against him, there is some of that, which we call Honour: but in the enemie that reserves himselfe unto the last, and attends our weake estate, there is more danger. Keepe it, where I in-tend it, in that which is my spheare, the Conscience: If mine enemie meet me betimes in my youth, in an object of tenta-tion, (so *Josephs* enemie met him in *Potifars* Wife) yet if I doe not adhere to this enemy, dwell upon a delightfull medi-tation of that sin, if I doe not fuell, and foment that sin, assist and encourage that sin, by high diet, wanton discourse, other provocation, I shall have reason on my side, and I shall have grace on my side, and I shall have the History of a thousand that have perished by that sin, on my side; Even Spittles will give me souldiers to fight for me, by their miserable example against that sin; nay perchance sometimes the vertue of that woman, whom I sollicite, will assist me. But when I lye under the hands of that enemie, that hath reserved himselfe to the last, to my last bed, then when I shall be able to stir no limbe in any other measure than a Feaver or a Palsie shall shake them, when everlasting darknesse shall have an inchoation in the present dimnesse of mine eyes, and the everlasting gnash-ing in the present chattering of my teeth, and the everlasting worme in the present gnawing of the Agonies of my body, and anguishes of my minde, when the last enemie shall watch my remedilesse body, and my disconsolate soule there, there, where not the Physitian, in his way, perchance not the Priest in his, shall be able to give any assistance, And when he hath

sported himselfe with my misery upon that stage, my death-
bed, shall shift the Scene, and throw me from that bed, into
the grave, and there triumph over me, God knowes, how many
generations, till the Redeemer, my Redeemer, the Redeemer of
all me, body, as well as soule, come againe; As death is *Novissi-
mus hostis,* the enemy which watches me, at my last weaknesse,
and shall hold me, when I shall be no more, till that Angel come,
Who shall say, and sweare that time shall be no more, in that
consideration, in that apprehension, he is the powerfullest, the
fearfullest enemy; and yet even there this enemy *Abolebitur,*
he shall be destroyed.

[*LXXX. Sermons* (15), 1640]

ST. PAUL'S. EASTER DAY. [1622]

How barren a thing is Arithmetique! (and yet Arithmetique
will tell you, how many single graines of sand, will fill this
hollow Vault to the Firmament) How empty a thing is Rhetorique! (and yet Rhetorique will make absent and remote
things present to your understanding) How weak a thing is
poetry! (and yet Poetry is a counterfait Creation, and makes
things that are not, as though they were) How infirme, how
impotent are all assistances, if they be put to expresse this
Eternity!

[*LXXX. Sermons* (26), 1640)]

PREACHED AT THE SPITAL. APRIL 22, 1622

1

OUR God is not out of breath, because he hath blown one
tempest, and swallowed a Navy: Our God hath not burnt out
his eyes, because he hath looked upon a Train of Powder: In
the light of Heaven, and in the darkness of hell, he sees alike;
he sees not onely all Machinations of hands, when things come
to action; but all Imaginations of hearts, when they are in
their first Consultations; past, and present, and future, distinguish not his *Quando;* all is one time to him: Mountains and
Vallies, Sea and Land, distinguish not his *Ubi;* all is one place
to him: *When I begin,* says God to *Eli, I will make an end;*
not onely that all Gods purposes shall have their certain end,

but that even then, when he begins, he makes an end: from the very beginning, imprints an infallible assurance, that whom he loves, he loves to the end: as a Circle is printed all at once, so his beginning and ending is all one.

2

The drowning of the first world, and the repairing that again; the burning of this world, and establishing another in heaven, do not so much strain a mans Reason, as the Creation, a Creation of all out of nothing. For, for the repairing of the world after the Flood, compared to the Creation, it was eight to nothing; eight persons to begin a world upon, then; but in the Creation, none. And for the glory which we receive in the next world, it is (in some sort) as the stamping of a print upon a Coyn; the metal is there already, a body and a soul to receive glory: but at the Creation, there was no soul to receive glory, no body to receive a soul, no stuff, no matter, to make a body of. The less any thing is, the less we know it: how invisible, how [un]intelligible a thing then, is this *Nothing!* We say in the School, *Deus cognoscibilior Angelis,* We have better means to know the nature of God, than of Angels, because God hath appeared and manifested himself more in actions, than Angels have done: we know what they are, by knowing what they have done; and it is very little that is related to us what Angels have done: what then is there that can bring this Nothing to our understanding? what hath that done? A Leviathan, a Whale, from a grain of Spawn; an Oke from a buried Akehorn, is a great; but a great world from nothing, is a strange improvement. We wonder to see a man rise from nothing to a great Estate; but that Nothing is but nothing in comparison; but absolutely nothing, meerly nothing, is more incomprehensible than any thing, than all things together. It is a state (if a man may call it a state) that the Devil himself in the midst of his torments, cannot wish.

3

The light of the knowledge of the glory of this world, is a good, and a great peece of learning. To know, that all the glory of man, is as the flower of grass: that even the glory, and all the glory, of man, of all mankind, is but a flower, and but as a flower; somewhat less than the Proto-type, than the

Original, than the flower it self; and all this but as the flower
of grass neither, no very beautiful flower to the eye, no very
fragrant flower to the smell: To know, that for the glory of
Moab, Auferetur, it shall be contemned, consumed; and for
the glory of *Jacob* it self, *Attenuabitur,* It shall be extenuated,
that the glory of Gods enemies shall be brought to nothing,
and the glory of his servants shall be brought low in this
word: To know how near nothing, how meer nothing, all the
glory of this world is, is a good, a great degree of learning.

<h1 style="text-align:center">4</h1>

Some things the Angels do know by the dignity of their
Nature, by their Creation, which we know not; as we know
many things which inferior Creatures do not; and such things
all the Angels, good and bad know. Some things they know by
the Grace of their confirmation, by which they have more
given them, than they had by Nature in their Creation; and
those things only the Angels that stood, but all they, do know.
Some things they know by Revelation, when God is pleased to
manifest them unto them; and so some of the Angels know
that, which the rest, though confirm'd, doe not know. By Creation, they know as his Subjects; by Confirmation, they know as
his servants; by Revelation, they know as his Councel. Now,
Erimus sicut Angeli, says Christ, *There we shall be as the Angels:* The knowledge which I have by Nature, shall have no
Clouds; here it hath: that which I have by Grace, shall have no
reluctation, no resistance; here it hath: That which I have by
Revelation, shall have no suspition, no jealousie; here it hath:
sometimes it is hard to distinguish between a respiration from
God, and a suggestion from the Devil. There our curiosity
shall have this noble satisfaction, we shall know how the Angels know, by knowing as they know. We shall not pass from
Author, to Author, as in a Grammar School, nor from Art to
Art, as in an University; but, as that General which Knighted
his whole Army, God shall Create us all Doctors in a minute.
That great Library, those infinite Volumes of the Books of
Creatures, shall be taken away, quite away, no more Nature; those reverend Manuscripts, written with Gods own hand,
the Scriptures themselves, shall be taken away, quite away; no
more preaching, no more reading of the Scriptures, and that
great School-Mistress, Experience, and Observation shall be remov'd, no new thing to be done, and in an instant, I shall know

more, than they all could reveal unto me. I shall know, not only as I know already, that a Bee-hive, that an Ant-hill is the same Book in *Decimo sexto,* as a Kingdom is in *Folio,* That a flower that lives but a day, is an abridgment of that King, that lives out his threescore and ten yeers; but I shall know too, that all these Ants, and Bees, and Flowers, and Kings, and Kingdoms, howsoever they may be Examples, and Comparisons to one another, yet they are all as nothing, altogether nothing, less than nothing, infinitely less than nothing, to that which shall then be the subject of my knowledge, for, *it is the knowledge of the glory of God.*

[*XXVI. Sermons* (25), 1660]

PREACHED "AT HANWORTH, TO MY LORD OF CAR-LILE, AND HIS COMPANY, BEING THE EARLES OF NORTHUMBERLAND, AND BUCKINGHAM, ETC." AUGUST 25th, 1622

1

How different are the wayes of God, from the ways of man! the eyes of God from the eyes of man! and the wayes and eyes of a godly man, from the eyes, and wayes of a man of this world! We looke still upon high persons, and after high places, and from those heights, we thinke, we see far; but he that will see this object, must lye low; it is best discerned in the dark, in a heavy, and a calamitous fortune. The naturall way is *upward;* I can better know a man upon the top of a steeple, than if he were halfe that depth in a well; but yet for higher objects, I can better see the stars of heaven, in the bottome of a well, than if I stood upon the highest steeple upon earth. If I twist a cable of infinite fadomes in length, if there be no ship to ride by it, nor anchor to hold by it, what use is there of it? If Mannor thrust Mannor, and title flow into title, and bags powre out into chests, if I have no anchor, (*faith in Christ*) if I have not a ship to carry to a haven, (a soule to save) what's my long cable to me? If I adde number to number, a span, a mile long, if at the end of all that long line of numbers, there be nothing that notes, *pounds,* or *crownes,* or *shillings;* what's that long number, but so many millions of millions of nothing? If my span of life become a mile of life.

my penny a pound, my pint a gallon, my acre a sheere; yet
if there be nothing of the next world at the end, so much
peace of conscience, so much joy, so much glory, still all is but
nothing multiplied, and that is still nothing at all. 'Tis the *end*
that qualifies all; and what kinde of man I shall be at my
end, upon my *death-bed,* what trembling hands, and what lost
legs, what deafe eares, and what gummy eyes, I shall have
then, I know; and the nearer I come to that disposition, in my
life, (the more *mortified* I am) the better I am disposed to
see this object, future glory. God made the Sun, and Moon,
and Stars, glorious lights for man to see by; but mans infirmity
requires *spectacles;* and affliction does that office. Gods meaning was, that by the sun-shine of prosperity, and by the beames
of honour, and temporall blessings, a man should see farre
into him; but I know not how he is come to need *spectacles;*
scarse any man sees much in this matter, till affliction shew it
him.

2

How many times go we to Comedies, to Masques, to places
of great and noble resort, nay even to Church onely to see the
company? If I had no other errand to heaven, but the *communion of Saints,* the fellowship of the faithfull, [T]o see
that flock of *Lambs,* Innocent, unbaptized *children,* recom-
pensed with the twice-baptized *Martyrs,* (baptized in *water,*
and baptized in their owne *blood*) and that middle sort, the
children baptized in blood, and not in the water, that rescued
Christ Jesus, by their death, under *Herod;* to see the *Prophets*
and the *Evangelists,* and not know one from the other, by their
writings, for they all write the same things (for *prophecy* is
but *antidated Gospell,* and *Gospell* but *postdated prophecy;*)
to see holy *Matrons* saved by the bearing, and bringing up of
children, and holy *Virgins,* saved by restoring their bodies in
the integrity, that they received them, sit all upon one seate;
to see *Princes,* and *Subjects* crowned all with one crowne, and
rich and *poore* inherit one portion; to see this scene, this
Court, this Church, this Catholique Church, not onely *Easterne* and *Westerne,* but *Militant* and *Triumphant* Church, all
in one roome together, to see this *Communion of Saints,* this
fellowship of the faithfull, is worth all the paynes, that that
sight costs us in this world.

[*Fifty Sermons* (31), 1649]

ST. PAULS. OCT. 13th, 1622

A PAINTER can hardly diminish or contract an Elephant into so little a forme, but that that Elephant, when it is at the least, will still be greater than an Ant at the life, and the greatest. Sinne hath diminished man shrowdly, and brought him into a narrower compasse; but yet, his *naturall immortality,* (his soule cannot dye) and his *spirituall possibility,* even to the last gaspe, of spending that immortality in the kingdome of glory, and living for ever with God, (for otherwise, our immortality were the heaviest part of our curse; exalt this valley, this clod of earth, to a noble heighth. How ill husbands then of this dignity are we by *sinne,* to forfeit it by submitting our selves to inferiour things! either to *gold,* than which every worme, (because a worme hath life, and gold hath none) is in nature, more estimable, and more precious: Or, to that which is lesse than gold, to *Beauty;* for there went neither labour, nor study, nor cost to the making of that; (the Father cannot diet himselfe so, nor the mother so, as to be sure of a faire child) but it is a thing that hapned by chance, wheresoever it is; and, as there are Diamonds of divers waters, so men enthrall themselves in one clime to a black, in another to a white beauty. To that which is lesse than *gold* or *Beauty, voice, opinion, fame, honour,* we sell our selves. And though the good opinion of good men, by good ways, be worth our study, yet popular applause, and the voice of inconsiderate men, is too cheape a price to set our selves at. And yet, it is hardly got too; for as a ship lies in harbour within land, sometimes needs most of the points of the Compasse, to bring her forth: so if a man surrender himselfe wholly to the opinion of other men, and have not his *Criterium,* his touchstone within him, he will need both *North* and *South,* all points of the Compasse, the breath of all men; because, as there are contrary Elements in every body, so there are contrary factions in every place, and when one side cries him up, the other will depresse him, and he shall, (if not *shipwrack*) lie *still.* But yet we doe forfeit our dignity, for that which is lesse than all, than *Gold,* than *Beauty,* than *Honour;* for *sinne;* sinne which is but a privation, (as darknesse is but a privation) and privations are nothing.

[Fifty Sermons (38), 1649]

PREACHED "TO THE EARLE OF CARLILE, AND HIS COMPANY, AT SION."

[AFTER SEPT. 1622]

THAT God should let my soule fall out of his hand, into a bottomlesse pit, and roll an unremoveable stone upon it, and leave it to that which it finds there, (and it shall finde that there, which it never imagined, till it came thither) and never thinke more of that soule, never have more to doe with it. That of that providence of God, that studies the life of every weed, and worme, and ant, and spider, and toad, and viper, there should never, never any beame flow out upon me; that that God, who looked upon me, when I was nothing, and called me when I was not, as though I had been, out of the womb and depth of darknesse, will not looke upon me now, when, though a miserable, and a banished, and a damned creature, yet I am his creature still, and contribute something to his glory, even in my damnation; that that God, who hath often looked upon me in my foulest uncleannesse, and when I had shut out the eye of the day, the Sunne, and the eye of the night, the Taper, and the eyes of all the world, with curtaines and windowes and doores, did yet see me, and see me in mercy, by making me see that he saw me, and sometimes brought me to a present remorse, and (for that time) to a forbearing of that sinne, should so turne himselfe from me, to his glorious Saints and Angels, as that no Saint nor Angel, nor Christ Jesus himselfe, should ever pray him to looke towards me, never remember him, that such a soule there is; that that God, who hath so often said to my soule, *Quare morieris?* Why wilt thou die? and so often sworne to my soule, *Vivit Dominus,* As the Lord liveth, I would not have thee dye, but live, will nether let me dye, nor let me live, but dye an everlasting life, and live an everlasting death; that that God, who, when he could not get into me, by standing, and knocking, by his ordinary meanes of entring, by his Word, his mercies, hath applied his judgements, and hath shaked the house, this body, with agues and palsies, and set this house on fire, with fevers and calentures, and frighted the Master of the house, my soule, with horrors, and heavy apprehensions, and so made an entrance into me; That that God should frustrate all his owne purposes and practises upon me, and leave me, and cast me away, as though I had cost him nothing, that this God at last, should let this soule goe away, as a smoake, as a vapour, as a bubble, and that then this soule cannot be a smoake, a vapour, nor a bubble, but must lie in darknesse, as long as the Lord of light is light it selfe, and never sparke of that light reach to my soule; What Tophet is not Paradise, what Brimstone is not Amber, what gnashing is not a comfort, what gnawing of the worme is not a tickling, what torment is not a marriage bed to this damnation, to be secluded eternally, eternally, eternally from the sight of God? Especially to us, for as the perpetuall losse of that is most heavy, with which we have been best acquainted, and to which wee have been most accustomed; so shall this damnation, which consists in the losse of the sight and presence of God, be heavier to us than others, because God hath so graciously, and so evidently, and so diversly appeared to us, in his pillar of fire, in the light of prosperity, and in the pillar of the Cloud, in hiding himselfe for a while from us; we that have seene him in all the parts of this Commission, in his Word, in his Sacraments, and in good example, and not beleeved, shall be further removed from his sight, in the next world, than they to whom he never appeared in this. But *Vincenti et credenti*, to him that beleeves aright, and overcomes all tentations to a wrong beliefe, God shall give the accomplishment of fulnesse, and fulnesse of joy, and joy rooted in glory, and glory established in eternity, and this eternity is God; To him that beleeves and overcomes, God shall give himselfe in an everlasting presence and fruition, *Amen.*

[*LXXX. Sermons* (76), 1640]

CANDLEMAS DAY. FEB. 2 [1616/7 or 1622/3]

1

THAT soule, that is accustomed to direct her selfe to God, upon every occasion, that, as a flowre at Sun-rising, conceives a sense of God, in every beame of his, and spreads and dilates it selfe towards him, in a thankfulnesse, in every small blessing that he sheds upon her; that soule, that as a flowre at the Suns declining, contracts and gathers in, and shuts up her selfe, as though she had received a blow, when soever she heares her Saviour wounded by a[n] oath, or blasphemy, or execration; that soule, who, whatsoever string be strucken in her, base or treble, her high or her low estate, is ever tun'd toward God, that soule prayes sometimes when it does not know that it prayes. I heare that man name God, and aske him what said you, and perchance he cannot tell; but I remember, that he casts forth some of those *ejaculationes animæ,* (as S. *Augustine:* calls them) some of those darts of a devout soule, which, though they have not particular deliberations, and be not formall prayers, yet they are the *indicia,* pregnant evidences and blessed fruits of a religious custome; much more it is true, which S. *Bernard* saies there, of them, *Deus audit,* God heares that voice of the heart, which the heart it selfe heares not, that is, at first considers not. Those occasionall and transitory prayers, and those fixed and stationary prayers, for which, many times, we binde our selves to private prayer at such a time, are payments of this debt, in such peeces, and in such summes, as God, no doubt, accepts at our hands. But yet the solemne dayes of payment, are the Sabbaths of the Lord, and the place of this payment, is the house of the Lord, where, as *Tertullian* expresses it, *Agmine facto,* we muster our forces together, and besiege God; that is, not taking up every tatter'd fellow, every sudden ragge or fragment of speech, that rises from our tongue, or our affections, but mustering up those words, which the Church hath levied for that service, in the Confessions, and Absolutions, and Collects, and Litanies of the Church, we pay this debt, and we receive our acquittance.

2

Begin therefore to pay these debts to thy selfe betimes; for, as we told you at beginning, some [of] you are too tender at noone, some at evening. Even at your noon and warmest Sunshine of prosperity, you owe your selves a true information, how you came by that prosperity, who gave it you, and why he gave it. Let not the Olive boast of her own fatnesse, nor the Figtree of her own sweetnesse, nor the Vine of her own fruitfulnesse, for we were all but Brambles. Let no man say, I could not misse a fortune, for I have studied all my youth; How many men have studied more nights, than he hath done hours, and studied themselves blinde, and mad in the Mathematiques, and yet withers in beggery in a corner? Let him never adde, But I studied in a usefull and gainfull profession; How many have

done so too, and yet never compassed the favour of a Judge?
And how many that have had all that, have struck upon a Rock,
even at full Sea, and perished there? In their Grandfathers and
great Grandfathers, in a few generations, whosoever is greatest
now, must say, With this Staffe came I over Jordan; nay, without any staffe came I over Jordan, for he had in them at first,
a beginning of nothing. As for spiritual happinesse, *Non vo-
lentis, nec currentis, sed miserentis Dei,* It is not in him that
would run, nor in him that doth, but only in God that prospers
his course; so for the things of this world, it is in vain to rise
early, and to lie down late, and to eat the bread of sorrow, for.
nisi Dominus ædificaverit, nisi Dominus custodierit, except the
Lord build the house, they labour in vaine; except the Lord keep
the City, the watchman waketh but in vain. Come not therefore
to say, I studied more than my fellows, and therefore am richer
than my fellows, but say, God that gave me my contemplations
at first, gave me my practice after, and hath given me his blessing now. How many men have worn their braines upon other
studies, and spent their time and themselves therein? how many
men have studied more in thine own profession, and yet, for
diffidence in themselves, or some disfavour from others, have
not had thy practice? How many men have been equall to thee,
in study, in practice, and in getting too, and yet upon a wanton
confidence, that that world would alwayes last, or upon the burden of many children, and an expensive breeding of them, or
for other reasons, which God hath found in his wayes, are left
upon the sand at last, in a low fortune? whilest the Sun shines
upon thee in all these   pay thy self the debt, of knowing
whence, and why all t' is came, for else thou canst not know
how much, or how little is thine, nor thou canst not come to
restore that which is none of thine, but unjustly wrung from
others. Pay therefore this debt of surveying thine estate, and
then pay thy selfe thine own too, by a chearfull enjoying and
using that which is truly thine, and doe not deny nor defraud
thy selfe of those things which are thine, and so become a
wretched debtor, to thy back, or to thy belly, as though the
world had not enough, or God knew not what were enough for
thee.

Pay this debt to thy selfe of looking into thy debts, of surveying, of severing, of serving thy selfe with that which is truly
thine, at thy noone, in the best of thy fortune, and in the
strength of thine understanding; that when thou commest to pay
thy other, thy last debt to thy self, which is, to open a doore out

of this world, by the dissolution of body and soule, thou have
not all thy money to tell over when the Sun is ready to set, all
the account to make of every bag of money, and of every quillet
of land, whose it is, and whether it be his that looks for it from
thee, or his from whom it was taken by thee; whether it belong
to thine heire, that weepes joyfull tears behinde the curtain, or
belong to him that weeps true, and bloody teares, in the hole in
a prison. There will come a time, when that land that thou
leavest shall not be his land, when it shall be no bodies land,
when it shall be no land, for the earth must perish; there will
be a time when there shall be no Mannors, no Acres in the
world, and yet there shall lie Mannors and Acres upon thy soul,
when land shall be no more, when time shall be no more, and
thou passe away, not into the land of the living, but of eternal
death. Then the Accuser will be ready to interline the schedules
of thy debts, thy sins, and insert false debts, by abusing an over-
tendernesse, which may be in thy conscience then, in thy last
sicknesse, in thy death-bed: Then he will be ready to adde a
cyphar more to thy debts, and make hundreds thousands, and
abuse the faintnesse which may be in thy conscience then, in thy
last sicknesse, in thy death-bed. Then he will be ready to abuse
even thy confidence in God, and bring thee to think, that as a
Pirate ventures boldly home, though all that he hath be stoln,
if he be rich enough to bribe for a pardon; so, howsoever those
families perish whom thou hast ruined, and those whole parishes
whom thou hast depopulated, thy soule may goe confidently
home too, if thou bribe God then, with an Hospitall or a Fellowship in a Colledge, or a Legacy to any pious use in appar-
ance, and in the eye of the world.

[*LXXX. Sermons* (9), 1640]

ST. PAUL'S. EASTER DAY IN THE EVENING. MARCH 28. 1624

1

BUT when the Church was newly conceived, and then lay like
the egge of a Dove, and a Gyants foot over it, like a worm, like
an ant, and hill upon hill whelmed upon it, nay, like a grain of
corn between the upper and lower Mill-stone, ground to dust
between Tyrans and Heretiques, when as she bled in her Cradle,
in those children whom *Herod* slew, so she bled upon her

crutches, in those decrepit men whom former persecutions and
tortures had creepled before, when East and West joyned hands
to crush her, and hands, and brains, joyned execution to consultation to annihilate her; in this wane of the Moon God gave
her an instant fulnesse; in this exinanition, instant glory; in this
grave, an instant Resurrection.

2

That soule, which being borne free, is made a slave to this
body, by comming to it; It must act, but what this body will
give it leave to act, according to the Organs, which this body
affords it; and if the body be lame in any limme, the soule must
be lame in her operation, in that limme too; It must doe, but
what the body will have it doe, and then it must suffer, whatsoever that body puts it to, or whatsoever any others will put that
body to: If the body oppresse it selfe with Melancholy, the soule
must be sad; and if other men oppresse the body with injury,
the soule must be sad too; Consider, (it is too immense a thing
to consider it) reflect but one thought, but upon this one thing
in the soule, here, and hereafter, In her grave, the body, and in
her Resurrection in Heaven; That is the knowledge of the soule.

Here saies S. *Augustine*, when the soule considers the things
of this world, *Non veritate certior, sed consuetudine securior;*
She rests upon such things as she is not sure are true, but such
as she sees, are ordinarily received and accepted for truth: so
that the end of her knowledge is not Truth, but opinion, and
the way, not Inquisition, but ease: But saies he, when she proceeds in this life, to search into heavenly things, *Verberatur luce
veritatis,* The beames of that light are too strong for her, and
they sink her, and cast her downe, *Et ad familiaritatem tene-
brarum suarum, non electione sed fatigatione convertitur;* and so
she returnes to her owne darknesse, because she is most familiar, and best acquainted with it; *Non electione,* not because she
loves ignorance, but because she is weary of the trouble of seeking out the truth, and so swallowes even any Religion to escape
the paine of debating, and disputing: and in this lazinesse she
sleeps out her lease, her terme of life, in this death, in this
grave, in this body.

But then in her Resurrection, her measure is enlarged, and
filled at once; There she reads without spelling, and knowes
without thinking, and concludes without arguing; she is at the
end of her race, without running; In her triumph, without fight-

ing; In her Haven, without sayling: A free-man, without any
prentiship; at full yeares, without any wardship; and a Doctor,
without any proceeding: She knowes truly, and easily, and immediately, and entirely, and everlastingly; Nothing left out at
first, nothing worne out at last, that conduces to her happinesse.
What a death is this life! what a resurrection in this death! For
though this world be a sea, yet (which is most strange) our
Harbour is larger than the sea; Heaven infinitely larger than this
world. For, though that be not true, which *Origen* is said to say,
That at last all shall be saved, nor that evident, which *Cyril* of
Alexandria saies, That without doubt the number of them that
are saved, is far greater than of them that perish, yet surely the
number of them, with whom we shall have communion in
Heaven, is greater than ever lived at once upon the face of the
earth: And of those who lived in our time, how few did we
know? and of those whom we did know, how few did we care
much for? In Heaven we shall have Communion of Joy and
Glory with all, alwaies; *Ubi non intrat inimicus, nec amicus exit,*
Where never any man shall come in that loves us not, nor go
from us that does.

[*LXXX. Sermons.* (19), 1640]

ST. PAUL'S. CHRISTMAS DAY IN THE EVENING. 1624

THE aire is not so full of Moats, of Atomes, as the Church is
of Mercies; and as we can suck in no part of aire, but we take
in those Moats, those Atomes; so here in the Congregation we
cannot suck in a word from the preacher, we cannot speak, we
cannot sigh a prayer to God, but that that whole breath and aire
is made of mercy. But we call not upon you from this Text, to
consider Gods ordinary mercy, that which he exhibites to all in
the ministery of his Church; nor his miraculous mercy, his extraordinary deliverances of States and Churches; but we call
upon particular Consciences, by occasion of this Text, to call to
minde Gods occasionall mercies to them; such mercies as a regenerate man will call mercies, though a naturall man would call
them accidents, or occurrences, or contingencies; A man wakes
at midnight full of unclean thoughts, and he heares a passing
Bell; this is an occasionall mercy, if he call that his own knell,
and consider how unfit he was to be called out of the world
then, how unready to receive that voice, *Foole, this night they
shall fetch away thy soule.* The adulterer, whose eye waites for

the twy-light, goes forth, and casts his eyes upon forbidden
houses, and would enter, and sees a *Lord have mercy upon us*
upon the doore; this is an occasionall mercy, if this bring him
to know that they who lie sick of the plague within, passe
through a furnace, but by Gods grace, to heaven; and hee without, carries his own furnace to hell, his lustfull loines to everlasting perdition. What an occasionall mercy had *Balaam*, when
his Asse Catechized him: What an occasionall mercy had one
Theefe, when the other catechized him so, *Art not thou afraid
being under the same condemnation?* What an occasionall mercy
had all they that saw that, when the Devil himself fought for
the name of Jesus, and wounded the sons of *Sceva* for exorcis-
ing in the name of Jesus, with that indignation, with that increpation, *Jesus we know, and Paul we know, but who are ye?*
If I should declare what God hath done (done occasionally) for
my soule, where he instructed me for feare of falling, where he
raised me when I was fallen, perchance you would rather fixe
your thoughts upon my illnesse, and wonder at that, than at
Gods goodnesse, and glorifie him in that; rather wonder at my
sins, than at his mercies, rather consider how ill a man I was,
than how good a God he is. If I should inquire upon what occasion God elected me, and writ my name in the book of Life,
I should sooner be afraid that it were not so, than finde a reason
why it should be so. God made Sun and Moon to distinguish
seasons, and day, and night, and we cannot have the fruits of
the earth but in their seasons: But God hath made no decree to
distinguish the seasons of his mercies; In paradise, the fruits
were ripe, the first minute, and in heaven it is alwaies Autumne,
his mercies are ever in their maturity. We ask *panem quo-
tidianum,* our daily bread, and God never sayes you should have
come yesterday, he never sayes you must againe to morrow, but
to day if you will heare his voice, to day he will heare you. If
some King of the earth have so large an extent of Dominion, in
North, and South, as that he hath Winter and Summer together
in his Dominions, so large an extent East and West, as that he
hath day and night together in his Dominions, much more hath
God mercy and judgement together: He brought light out of
darknesse, not out of a lesser light; he can bring thy Summer
out of Winter, though thou have no Spring; though in the
wayes of fortune, or understanding, or conscience, thou have
been benighted till now, wintred and frozen, clouded and
eclypsed, damped and benummed, smothered and stupefied till
now, now God comes to thee, not as in the dawning of the day,

not as in the bud of the spring, but as the Sun at noon to illustrate all shadowes, as the sheaves in harvest, to fill all penuries,
all occasions invite his mercies, and all times are his seasons.

[*LXXX. Sermons* (2), 1640]

ST. PAUL'S. THE SUNDAY AFTER THE CONVERSION OF S. PAUL. JANUARY 30th, 1624/5

I TAKE no farther occasion from this Circumstance, but to arme
you with consolation, how low soever God be pleased to cast
you, Though it be to the earth, yet he does not so much cast
you downe, in doing that, as bring you home. Death is not a
banishing of you out of this world; but it is a visitation of your
kindred that lie in the earth; neither are any nearer of kin to
you, than the earth it selfe, and the wormes of the earth. You
heap earth upon your soules, and encumber them with more and
more flesh, by a superfluous and luxuriant diet; You adde earth
to earth in new purchases, and measure not by Acres, but by
Manors, nor by Manors, but by Shires; And there is a little
Quillet, a little Close, worth all these, A quiet Grave. And
therefore, when thou readest, That God makes thy bed in thy
sicknesse, rejoyce in this, not onely that he makes that bed,
where thou dost lie, but that bed where thou shalt lie; That
that God, that made the whole earth, is now making thy bed in
the earth, a quiet grave, where thou shalt sleep in peace, till
the Angels Trumpet wake thee at the Resurrection, to that
Judgement where thy peace shall be made before thou
commest, and writ, and sealed, in the blood of the Lamb.

Saul falls to the earth; So farre; But he falls no lower.
God brings his servants to a great lownesse here; but he brings
upon no man a perverse sense, or a distrustfull suspition of
falling lower hereafter; His hand strikes us to the earth, by way
of humiliation; But it is not his hand, that strikes us into hell,
by way of desperation. Will you tell me, that you have observed
and studied Gods way upon you all your life, and out of that
can conclude what God meanes to doe with you after this life?
That God took away your Parents in your infancy, and left you
Orphanes then, That he hath crossed you in all your labours in
your calling, ever since, That he hath opened you to dishon-
ours, and calumnies, and mis-interpretations, in things well intended by you, That he hath multiplied sicknesses upon you,
and given you thereby an assurance of a miserable, and a short

life, of few, and evill dayes, nay, That he hath suffered you to fall into sins, that you your selves have hated, To continue in sins, that you your selves have been weary of, To relapse into sins, that you your selves have repented; And will you conclude out of this that God had no good purpose upon you, that if ever he had meant to doe you good, he would never have gone thus farre, in heaping of evills upon you? Upon what doest thou ground this? upon thy selfe? Because thou shouldest not deal thus with any man, whom thou mean'st well to? How poore, how narrow, how impious a measure of God, is this, that he must doe, as thou wouldest doe, if thou wert God! God hath not made a week without a Sabbath; no tentation, without an issue; God inflicts no calamity, no cloud, no eclipse, without light, to see ease in it, if the patient will look upon that which God hath done to him, in other cases, or to that which God hath done to others, at other times. *Saul fell to the ground,* but he fell no lower; God brings us to humiliation, but not to desperation.

He fell; he fell to the ground, And *he fell blinde;* for so it is evident in the story. Christ had said to the Pharisees, *I came into the world, that they which see, might be made blinde;* And the Pharisees ask him, *Have you been able to doe so upon us? Are we blinde?* Here Christ gives them an example: a reall, a literall, an actuall example; *Saul,* a Pharisee, is made blinde. He that will fill a vessell with wine, must take out the water; He that will fill a covetous mans hand with gold, must take out the silver that was there before, sayes S. *Chrysostome.* Christ, who is about to infuse new light into *Saul,* withdrawes that light that was in him before; That light, by which *Saul* thought he saw all before, and thought himselfe a competent Judge, which was the onely true Religion, and that all others were to be persecuted, even to death, that were not of his way. *Stultus factus est omnis homo à scientia,* sayes God in the Prophet, Every man that trusts in his owne wit, is a foole. But *let him become a foole, that he may be wise,* sayes the Apostle; Let him be so, in his own eyes, and God will give him better eyes, better light, better understanding. *Saul* was struck blinde, but it was a blindnesse contracted from light; It was a light that struck him blinde, as you see in his story. This blindnesse which we speak of, which is a sober and temperate abstinence from the immoderate study, and curious knowledges of this world, this holy simplicity of the soule, is not a darknesse, a dimnesse, a stupidity in the understanding, contracted by living in a corner, it is not an idle retiring into a

Monastery, or into a Village, or a Country solitude, it is not a lazy affectation of ignorance; not darknesse, but a greater light, must make us blinde.

The sight, and the Contemplation of God, and our present benefits by him, and our future interest in him, must make us blinde to the world so, as that we look upon no face, no pleasure, no knowledge, with such an Affection, such an Ambition, such a Devotion, as upon God, and the wayes to him. *Saul* had such a blindnesse, as came from light; we must affect no other simplicity, than arises from the knowledge of God, and his Religion. And then, *Saul* had such a blindnesse, as that he fell with it. There are birds, that when their eyes are cieled, still soare up, and up, till they have spent all their strength. Men blinded with the lights of this world, soare still into higher places, or higher knowledges, or higher opinions; but the light of heaven humbles us, and layes flat that soule, which the leaven of this world had puffed and swelled up. That powerfull light felled *Saul;* but after he was fallen, his owne sight was restored to him againe; *Ananias* saies to him, *Brother Saul, receive thy sight.* To those men, who imploy their naturall faculties to the glory of God, and their owne, and others edification, God shall afford an exaltation of those naturall faculties; In those, who use their learning, or their wealth, or their power, well, God shall increase that power, and that wealth, and that learning, even in this world.

[LXXX. Sermons (46), 1640]

PREACHED TO THE KING'S MAJESTIE AT WHITEHALL 24 FEBR. 1625.

1

For the first *generall sale* by *Adam,* wee complaine now that *Land* will not sell; that 20. is come to 15. yeares purchase; but doe wee not take too late a *Medium,* too low a time to reckon by? How cheape was *Land* at first, how cheape were *we?* what was *Paradise* sold for? What was *Heaven,* what was *Mankinde* sold for? *Immortalitie* was sold, and what yeares Purchase was that worth? *Immortalitie* is our *Eternitie; God* hath another manner of *eternitie* in *him;* He hath a *whole eternall day; an eternall afternoone,* and an *eternall forenoone* too; for as he shall have no *end,* so hee never had *beginning;* we have an *eternall afternoone* in our *immortalitie:* we shall no more see an *end,* than

God hath seene a *beginning;* and *Millions* of yeares, multiplied by *Millions,* make not up a *Minute* to this *Eternitie,* this *Immortalitie.* When *Dives* values a *droppe* of water at so high a price, what would he give for a *River?* How poore a *Clod* of Earth is a *Mannor!* how poore an *inch,* a *Shire!* how poore a *spanne,* a *Kingdome!* how poore a *pace,* the whole *world!* and yet how prodigally we sell *Paradise, Heaven, Soules, Consciences, Immortalitie, Eternitie,* for a *few Graines* of this *Dust!* What had *Eve* for *Heaven;* so little, as that the *Holy Ghost* will not let us know, what she had, not what kinde of *Fruite;* yet something *Eve* had. What had *Adam* for *Heaven?* but a satisfaction that hee had pleased an *Ill wife,* as St. *Hierome* states his fault, that he eate that Fruite, *Ne contristaretur Delicias suas,* least he should cast her, whom he lov'd so much, into an inordinate dejection; but if he *satisfied* her, and his owne *Uxoriousnesse,* any *satisfaction* is not *nothing.* But what had *I* for *Heaven? Adam* sinnd, and *I* suffer; I *forfeited* before I had any *Possession,* or could claime any *Interest;* I had a *Punishment,* before I had a *being,* And *God* was displeased with *me* before *I* was *I;* I was built up scarse 50. years ago, in my Mothers womb, and I was cast down, almost 6000. years agoe, in *Adams* loynes; I was *borne* in the last *Age* of the world, and *dyed* in the first. How and how justly do we cry out against a Man, that hath sold a *Towne,* or sold an *Army.* And *Adam* sold the *World.* He sold *Abraham,* and *Isaac* and *Jacob,* and all the *Patriarchs,* and all the *Prophets.* He sold *Peter,* and *Paul,* and both their *Regiments,* both the glorious *Hemispheres* of the World, The *Jewes,* and the *Gentiles.* He sold *Evangelists,* and *Apostles,* and *Disciples,* and the *Disciple whom the Lord loved,* and the *beloved Mother of the Lord, her selfe,* say what they will to the contrary. And if *Christ* had not provided for himselfe, by a *miraculous Generation, Adam* had sold *him:* If *Christ* had bene conceivd in *Originall sinne,* hee must have dyed for *himselfe,* nay, he could not have dyed for *himselfe,* but must have needed another *Saviour.* It is in that Contemplation, as hee was descended from *Adam,* that St. *Paul* sayes of himselfe, *Venundatus, I am carnall, sold under sinne.* For though St. *Augustine,* and some others of the *Fathers,* doe sometimes take the *Apostle,* in that place, to speake of himselfe, as in the person of a *naturall Man,* (that every Man considered in *nature, is sold under sinne,* but the *Supernaturall,* the *Sanctified* Man is not so) yet St. *Augustine,* himselfe, in his latest, and gravest Bookes, and particularly in his *Retractations,* returnes to this sense of these words,

That no man, in what measure soever *Sanctified*, can so eman-
cipate himselfe from that *Captivitie,* to which *Adam* hath en-
thralld him, but that, as hee is enwrapped in *Originall* sinne,
hee is *solde under sinne.* And both S. *Hierome,* and S. *Ambrose,* (both which, seeme in other places, to goe an other way,
That onely they are *sold under sinne,* which have abandond,
and prostituted themselves to particular sinnes,) doe yet returne to this sense, That because the *Embers,* the *Spaune,* the
leaven of *Originall sinne,* remaines, by *Adams* sale, in the best,
the best are sold under sinne.

So the *Jewes* were, and so were *we* sold by *Adam,* to
Originall sinne, very *cheape;* but in the *second sale,* as wee are
sold to *actuall,* and *habituall* sinnes, by *our selves, cheaper;* for
so, sayes this *Prophet, You have sold your selves for nothing:*
Our selves, that is *all our selves; o[u]r bodies* to intemperance,
and ryot, and licenciousnes, and our *soules* to a greedines of
sinne; and all this for *nothing,* for *sinne* it selfe, for which wee
sell our selves, is but a *privation,* and *privations* are *nothing.*
*What fruit had you of those things, whereof you are now
ashamed, sayes the Apostle;* here is *Barrennesse* and *shame; Barrennesse* is a *privation* of *fruit, shame* is a *privation* of that
confidence, which a good *Conscience* administers, and when the
Apostle tells them, they sold themselves for barrennesse and
shame, it was for *privation,* for *nothing.* The *Adulterer waits for
the twy-light,* sayes *Job.* The *Twy-light* comes, and serves his
turne; and *sin,* to night looks like a *Purchase,* like a *Treasure;*
but aske this *sinner* to *morrow,* and he hath sold *himselfe* for
nothing; for *debility* in his limnes, for *darknesse* in his understanding, for *emptinesse* in his purse, for *absence of grace* in
his Soule; and *Debilitie,* and *Darkenes,* and *emptinesse,* and
Absence, are *privations,* and *privations* are *nothing.* All the name
of *Substance* or *Treasure* that *sinne* takes, is that in the *Apostle,
Thesaurizastis Iram Dei, You have treasured up the wrath of
God, against the day of wrath:* And this is a fearefull *privation,*
of the *grace* of *God* here, and of the *Face* of *God* hereafter;
a *privation* so much worse than *nothing,* as that they upon
whom it falls, would faine be *nothing,* and cannot.

2

As some *Schoolemasters* have usd that *Discipline,* to correct
the Children of great Persons, whose personall correction they
finde reason to forbeare, by correcting other Children in their

names, and in their *sight,* and have wrought upon *good Natures,* that way, So did *Almightie God* correct the *Jewes* in the *Ægyptians;* for the *ten plagues of Ægypt,* were as *Moses Decem Verba,* as the *Ten Commandements to Israel,* that they should not provoke GOD. Every *Judgement* that falls upon another, should be a *Catechisme* to me. But when this *Discipline* prevaild not upon them, *God sold* them away, *gave* them away, *cast* them away, in the tempest, in the whirlewinde, in the inundation of his indignation, and scatterd them as so much dust in a windy day, as so many broken strawes upon a wrought Sea. With one *word, One Fiat,* (*Let there bee a world,*) nay with one *thought* of God cast toward it, (for *Gods* speaking in the *Creation,* was but a *thinking,*) *God* made all of *Nothing.* And is any one *rationall Ant,* (The wisest *Phylosopher* is no more) Is any *roaring Lyon,* (the most ambitious and devouring Prince is no more) Is any *hive of Bees,* (The wisest *Councels,* and *Parliaments* are no more) Is any of these so estab[l]ishd, as that, that *God* who by a *word,* by a *thought,* made them of *nothing,* cannot by recalling that *word,* and withdrawing that *thought,* in sequestring his *Providence,* reduce them to *nothing* againe? That *Man,* that *Prince,* that *State* thinks Past-board Canon-proofe, that thinkes Power, or Policy a Rampart, when the *Ordinance* of God is planted against it. *Navyes* will not keepe off *Navies,* if *God* be not the *Pilot,* Nor *Walles* keepe out *Men,* if *God* be not the *Sentinell.* If they could, if wee were walld with a *Sea* of fire and brimstone without, and walld with *Brasse* within, yet we cannot ciel the Heavens with a roofe of Brasse, but that *God* can come downe in *Thunder* that way, Nor pave the Earth with a floare of Brasse, but that God can come up in *Earthquakes* that way. God can call up *Damps,* and *Vapors* from below, and powre down putride *defluxions* from above, and bid them meet and condense into a *plague,* a *plague* that shall not be onely uncureable, uncontrollable, unexorable, but undisputable, unexaminable, unquestionable; A *plague* that shall not onely not admit a *remedy,* when it is come, but not give a *reason* how it did come. If God had not set a marke upon *Cain,* every Man, any Man, any thing might have killd him. Hee apprehended that of himselfe, and was afraid, when we know of none, by name, in the world, but his Father, and Mother: But, as Saint *Hierome* exalts this consideration, *Cains* owne Conscience tells him, *Catharma sum, Anathema sum,* I am the *plague* of the world, and I must dye, to deliver it, *Catharma sum.* I am a *separated Vagabond,* not an *Anachorit* shut up be-

tweene two walls, but shut out from all, *Anathema sum*. As long
as the *Cherubim*, and the fiery Sword is at the Gate, *Adam* cannot returne to *Paradise;* as long as the Testimonies of GODS
anger lye at the dore of the *Conscience*, no man can returne
to peace there. If *God* sell away a Man, give him away, give
way to him, by withdrawing his Providence, he shall but neede
(as the *Prophet* sayes) *Sibilare Muscam*, to hisse, to whisper for
the *Fly*, for the *Bee*, for the *Hornet*, for *Forraigne Incumbrances;* nay, hee shall not neede to hisse, to whisper for them:
for at home, *Locusts* shall swarme in his *Gardens*, and *Frogs in
his bedchamber*, and *hailstones, as big as talents*, (as they are
measured in the *Revelation*) shall breake, as well the coverd,
and the armd, as the bare, and naked head; as well the *Mytred*,
and the *Turband*, and the *crownd* head, that lifts it selfe up
against GOD, lyes open to him, as his that must not put on his
Hat, as his that hath no Hat to put on; when as that head,
which being exalted here, submits it selfe to that GOD, that
exalted it, GOD shall crowne, with multiplied crownes here, and
having so crownd that head with Crownes here, hee shall crowne
those crownes, with the Head of all, *Christ Jesus*, and all that is
his, hereafter.

[Published separately, 1626]

"DENMARK HOUSE, SOME FEW DAYS BEFORE THE BODY OF KING JAMES WAS REMOVED FROM THENCE, TO HIS BURIALL," APRIL 26, 1625

HERE, at your coming hither now, you have *two glasses*, wherein
you may see your selves from head to foot; One in the Text,
your *Head, Christ Jesus*, represented unto you, in the name and
person of *Solomon, Behold King Solomon crowned, &c*. And
another, under your feet, in the dissolution of this great *Monarch*, our *Royall Master*, now layd lower by death than any of us,
his Subjects and servants.

First then, behold your selves in that first glasse, *Behold King
Solomon; Solomon* the sonne of *David*, but not the Son of
Bathsheba, but of a better mother, the most blessed *Virgin Mary*.
For, *Solomon*, in this text, is not a *proper* Name, but an *Appel-
lative;* a significative word: *Solomon* is *pacificus*, the *Peace-
maker*, and our peace is made in, and by Christ Jesus: and he is
that *Solomon*, whom we are called upon to see here. Now, as

Saint *Paul* says, that *he would know nothing but Christ,* (that's
his first abridgement) and then he would know nothing of
Christ, but *him crucified,* (and that's the re-abridgement) so we
seek no other glasse, to see our selves in, but Christ, nor any
other thing in this glasse, but his *Humiliation.* What need we?
Even that, his lowest humiliation, his death, is expressed here,
in three words of exaltation, It is a *Crown,* it is a *Mariage,* it is
the *gladnesse of heart: Behold King Solomon crowned,* &c.

The Crown, which we are called to see him crowned with,
his mother put upon him; The Crown which his *Father gave
him,* was that glory, wherewith he was glorifyed, with the Father, *from all eternity,* in his *divine nature:* And the Crown
wherewith his Father crowned his *Humane nature,* was the glory
given to that, in his *Ascension. His Mother* could give him
no such Crown: she her selfe had no Crown, but that, which
he gave her. The Crown that *she* gave him, was that substance,
that he received from her, *our flesh,* our *nature,* our *humanity;*
and this, *Athanasius,* and this, Saint *Ambrose,* calls the *Crown,*
wherewith *his mother crowned him,* in this text, his infirm, his
humane nature. Or, *the Crown wherewith his Mother crowned
him,* was that Crown, to which, that infirme nature which he
tooke from her, submitted him, which was his *passion,* his *Crown
of thornes;* for so *Tertullian,* and divers others take this Crown
of his, from her, to be his *Crown of thorns: Woe to the Crown
of pride, whose beauty is a fading flower,* says the Prophet; But
blessed be this Crown of Humiliation, whose flower cannot fade.
Then was there truly a *Rose* amongst *Thorns,* when through his
Crown of *Thorns,* you might see his title, *Jesus Nazarenus:* for,
in that very name *Nazarenus,* is involved the signification of a
flower; the very word signifies *a flower. Esay's* flower in the
Crown of pride fades, and is removed; This flower in the Crown
of Thornes fades not, nor could be removed; for, for all the importunity of the Jews, *Pilate* would not suffer *that title* to be
removed, or to be changed; still *Nazarenus* remained, and still
a rose amongst thorns. You know the curse of the earth, *Thorns
and thistles shall it bring forth unto thee;* It did so to our *Solomon* here, it brought forth thornes to Christ, and he made a
Crown of those thorns, not onely for *himself,* but for us too,
*Omnes aculei mortis, in Dominici Corporis tolerantia, obtusi
sunt,* All the thorns of life and death, are broken, or blunted
upon the head of our *Solomon,* and now, even our *thorns,* make
up *our Crown,* our tribulation in life, our dissolution in death,
conduce to our glory: *Behold him crowned with his Mothers*

Crown, for even that brought him to his *Fathers Crown*, his humiliation to exaltation, his passion to glory.

Behold your *Solomon*, *your Saviour* again, and you shall see another *beam* of Comfort, in your tribulations from his; for even this *Humiliation* of his, is called his *Espousals*, his *marriage, Behold him crowned in the day of his Espousals.* His Spouse is the *Church*, His marriage is the *uniting* of himselfe to this Spouse, in his becomming *Head of the Church.* The great City, the heavenly Jerusalem, is called *The Bride*, and *The Lambs wife*, in the *Revelation:* And he is the *Head* of this body, the *Bridegroom* of this Bride, the Head of this Church, as he is *The firstborne of the Dead;* Death, that dissolves all ours, made up this marriage. His Death is his Marriage, and upon his Death flowed out from his side, those two *Elements of the Church, water* and *bloud;* The Sacraments of *Baptisme*, and of the *Communion* of himself. Behold then this *Solomon crowned* and *married;* both words of *Exaltation*, and *Exultation*, and both by *Death;* and trust him for working the same effects upon thee; That thou *(though by Death)* shalt be *crowned* with a Crown of Glory, and *married* to him, in whose right and merit thou shalt have that Crown.

And *Behold* him once again, and you shall see not a *beam*, but a *stream* of comfort; for this day, which is the day of death, he calls here *The day of the gladnesse of his heart. Behold him crowned in the day of the gladnesse of his heart.* The fulnesse, the compasse, the two *Hemispheres* of Heaven, are often designed to us, in these two names, *Joy* and *Glory:* If the *Crosse* of Christ, the *Death* of Christ, present us both these, how neare doth it bring, how fully doth it deliver Heaven it self to us in this life? And then we heare the Apostle say, *We see Jesus, for the suffering of Death, crowned with Honour and Glory:* There is *half* Heaven got by *Death, Glory.* And then, *for the joy that was set before him, he indured the Crosse;* There is the *other half, Joy;* All Heaven purchased by Death. And therefore, *if any man suffer as a Christian, let him not be ashamed,* saith the *Apostle;* but *let him glorifie God, In isto Nomine,* as the *vulgate* read it: *In that behalfe,* as *we translate it.* But, *In isto Nomine,* saith S. *Augustine:* Let us glorifie God, in that Name; *Non solum in nomine Christiani, sed Chri[sti]ani patientis,* not onely because he is a *Christian* in his *Baptisme,* but a Christian in a *second Baptisme,* a *Baptisme of bloud;* not onely as he hath received Christ, in accepting his *Institution,* but because he hath conformed himself to Christ, in fulfilling his *sufferings.* And therefore, though we admit *naturall* and *humane sorrow*, in the calamities which overtake us, and surround us in this life: (for as *all glasses* will gather drops and tears from externall causes, so this very glasse which we looke upon now, our *Solomon* in the Text, our *Saviour*, had those *sadnesses of heart* toward his Passion, and *Agonies* in his passion) yet *count it all Joy when you fall into tentations*, saith the Apostle: *All Joy*, that is, both the *interest*, and the *principall*, hath the *earnest* and the *bargain;* for if you can conceive joy in your tribulations in this world, how shall that joy be multiplied unto you, when no tribulations shall be mingled with it? There is not a better evidence, nor a more binding earnest of everlasting Joy in the next world, than to find *Joy of heart* in the *tribulations* of this; fixe thy self therefore upon this first glasse, this *Solomon*, thy Saviour, *Behold King Solomon crownd*, &c. and by conforming thy self to his *holy sadnesse*, and *humiliation*, thou shalt also become like him, in his Joy, and Glory.

But then the hand of God, hath *not set up*, but *laid down another Glasse*, wherein thou maist see thy self; a glasse that reflects thy self, and nothing but thy selfe. Christ, who was the other glasse, *is like thee in every thing*, but not absolutely, for *sinne* is *excepted;* but in this glasse presented now (*The Body of our Royall*, but *dead Master and Soveraigne*) we cannot, we doe not except sinne. Not onely the greatest man is subiect to *naturall infirmities*, (Christ himself was so) but the holiest man is subject to *Originall and Actuall sinne*, as thou art, and so a fit glasse for thee, to see thy self in. *Jeat* showes a man his face, as well as *Crystall;* nay, a Crystall glasse will not show a man his face, except it be steeled, except it be darkned on the backside: Christ as he was a pure *Crystall* glasse, as he was *God*, had not been a glasse for us, to have seen our selves in, except he had been *steeled, darkened with our humane nature;* Neither was he ever so throughly darkened, as that he could present us wholly to our selves, because he had no *sinne*, without seeing of which we do not see our selves. Those therefore that are like thee in all things, subject to humane *infirmities*, subject to *sinnes*, and yet are translated, and *translated by Death*, to everlasting *Joy*, and *Glory*, are nearest and clearest glasses for thee, to see thy self in; and such is this glasse, which God hath proposed to thee, in this house. And therefore, change the word of the Text, in a letter or two, from *Egredimini*, to *Ingredimini;* never goe forth to see, but *Go in and see a Solomon crowned with his mothers crown, &c.* And when you shall find that hand that has signed to one of you a *Patent* for *Title*, to another for *Pension*, to another for *Pardon*, to another for *Dispensation*, *Dead:* That hand that settled Possessions by his *Seale*, in the *Keeper*, and rectified *Honours* by the *sword*, in his *Marshall*, and distributed relief to the *Poore*, in his *Almoner*, and *Health* to the *Diseased*, by his *immediate Touch*, Dead: That Hand that ballanced his *own three Kingdomes* so equally, as that none of them complained of one another, nor of him; and carried the *Keyes* of all the Christian world, and locked up, and let out *Armies* in their due season, Dead; how poore, how faint, how pale, how momenta[r]y, how transitory, how empty, how frivolous, how Dead things, must you necessarily thinke *Titles*, and Possessions, and *Favours*, and all, when you see that Hand, which was the *hand of Destinie*, of *Christian Destinie*, of the *Almighty God*, lie dead! It was not so *hard* a hand when we touched it last, nor so *cold* a hand when we kissed it last: That hand which was wont to *wipe all teares from all our eyes*, doth now but presse and squeaze us as so many spunges, filled one with one, another with another cause of teares. Teares that can have no other banke to bound them, but the declared and manifested *will of God:* For, till our teares flow to that heighth, that they might be called a *murmuring* against the declared will of God, it is against our Allegiance, it is *Disloyaltie*, to give our teares any stop, any termination, any measure. It was a great part of *Anna's prayse, That she departed not from the Temple, day nor night;* visit Gods Temple often in the day, meet him in his owne House, and depart not from his *Temples*, (The *dead bodies* of his Saints are his Temples still) even at *midnight;* at midnight remember them, who resolve into dust, and make them thy glasses to see thy self in. Looke now especially upon him whom God hath presented to thee now, and with as much cheerfulnesse as ever thou heardst him say, *Remember my Favours, or remember my Commandements;* heare him say now with the wise man, *Remember my Judgement, for thine also shall be so; yesterday for me, and to day for thee;* He doth not say *to morrow*, but *to Day, for thee.* Looke upon him as a beame of that Sunne, as an abridgement of that *Solomon* in the Text; for every Christian truely reconciled to God, and *signed* with his hand in the *Absolution*, and *sealed* with his bloud in the *Sacrament*, (and this was his case) is a beame, and an abridgement of *Christ* himselfe. *Behold him* therefore, *Crowned with the Crown that his Mother gives him: His Mother, The Earth.* In antient times, when they used to reward Souldiers with particular kinds of *Crowns*, there was a great dignity *in Corona graminea*, in a Crown of Grasse: That denoted a Conquest, or a Defence of that land. He that hath but *Coronam Gramineam*, a turfe of grasse in *a Church yard*, hath a Crown from his *Mother*, and even in that buriall taketh *seisure* of the *Resurrection*, as by a turfe of grasse men give seisure of land. *He is crowned in the day of his Marriage*; for though it be a day of *Divorce* of us from him, and of *Divorce* of his body from his soul, yet neither of these Divorces breake the Marriage: His *soule* is married to him that made it, and his body and soul shall meet again, and all we, both then in that Glory where we shall acknowledge, that there is no way to this *Marriage*, but this *Divorce*, nor to *Life*, but by *Death*. And lastly, he is *Crowned in the day of the Gladnesse of his heart:* He leaveth that heart, which was accustomed to the halfe joyes of the earth, in the earth; and he hath enlarged his heart to a greater capacity of Joy, and Glory, and God hath filled it according to that new capacity. And therefore, to end all with the Apostles words, *I would not have you to be ignorant, Brethren, concerning them, which are asleepe, that ye sorrow not, as others that have no hope; for if ye beleeve that Jesus died, and rose again, even so them also, which sleepe in him, will God bring with him.* But when you have performed this *Ingredimini*, that you have gone in, and mourned upon him, and performed the *Egredimini*, you have gone forth, and laid his Sacred body, in Consecrated Dust, and come then to another *Egredimini*, to a going forth in many severall wayes: some to the service of their *new Master*, and some to the enjoying of their Fortunes conferred by their old; some to the raising of new *Hopes*, some to the burying of old, and all; some to new, and busie endeavours in Court, some to contented retirings in the Countrey; let none of us, goe so farre from him, or from one another, in any of our wayes, but that all we that have served him, may meet once a day, the first time we see the Sunne, in the eares of almighty God, with humble and hearty prayer, that he will be pleased to hasten that day, in which it shall be *an addition*, even to the joy of that place, as perfect as it is, and as infinite as it is, to see that face againe, and to see those eyes open there, which we have seen closed here. Amen.

[*Fifty Sermons* (33), 1649]

ST. PAUL'S. "THE FIRST OF THE PREBEND OF CHESWICK'S FIVE PSALMES." MAY 8, 1625

THE Applause of the people is vanity, Popularity is vanity. At how deare a rate doth that man buy the peoples affections, that payes his owne head for their hats! How cheaply doth he sell his Princes favour, that hath nothing for it, but the peoples breath! And what age doth not see some examples of so ill merchants of their owne honours and lives too! How many men, upon confidence of that flattering gale of winde, the breath and applause of the people, have taken in their anchors, (that is, departed from their true, and safe hold, The right of the Law, and the favour of the Prince) and as soone as they hoysed their sailes, (that is, entred into any by-action) have found the wind in their teeth, that is, Those people whom they trusted in, armed against them! And as it is in Civill, and Secular, so it is in Ecclesiasticall, and Spirituall things too. How many men, by a popular hunting after the applause of the people, in their manner of preaching, and humouring them in their distempers, have made themselves incapable of preferment in the Church where they tooke their Orders, and preached themselves into a necessity of running away into forraine parts, that are receptacles of seditious and schismaticall Separatists, and have been put there, to learne some trade, and become Artificers for their sustentation? The same people that welcommed Christ, from the Mount of Olives, into Jerusalem, upon Sunday, with their *Hosannaes to the Sonne of David,* upon Friday mocked him in Jerusalem, with their *Haile King of the Jews,* and blew him out of Jerusalem to Golgotha, with the pestilent breath, with the tempestuous whirlwind of their *Crucifiges.* And of them, who have called the Master Beelzebub, what shall any servant looke for? *Surely men of low degree are vanity.*

And then, under the same oath, and asseveration, *Surely,* as surely as the other, *men of high degree are a lie.* Doth *David* meane these men, whom he calls *a lie,* to be any lesse than those whom hee called *vanity?* Lesse than vanity, than emptinesse, than nothing, nothing can be; And low, and high are to this purpose, and in this consideration, (compared with God, or considered without God) equally nothing. He that hath the largest patrimony, and space of earth, in the earth, must heare me say, That all that was nothing; And if he ask, But what was

this whole Kingdom, what all Europe, what all the World? It
was all, not so much as another nothing, but all one and the
same nothing as thy dunghill was.

[*LXXX. Sermons* (65), 1640]

ST. PAUL'S. WHITSUNDAY. [1625?]

1

HEAVEN is Glory, and heaven is Joy; we cannot tell which
most; we cannot separate them; and this comfort is joy in the
Holy Ghost. This makes all *Jobs* states alike; as rich in the first
Chapter of his Booke, where all is suddenly lost, as in the last,
where all is abundantly restored. This consolation from the Holy
Ghost makes my mid-night noone, mine Executioner a Physitian,
a stake and pile of Fagots, a Bone-fire of triumph; this consolation makes a Satyr, and Slander, and Libell against me, a Panegyrique, and an Elogy in my praise; It makes a *Tolle* an *Ave*,
a *Væ* an *Euge*, a *Crucifige* an *Hosanna;* It makes my death-bed,
a mariage-bed, And my Passing-Bell, an Epithalamion.

2

As the world is the whole frame of the world, God hath put
into it a reproofe, a rebuke, lest it should seem eternall, which
is, a sensible decay and age in the whole frame of the world,
and every piece thereof. The seasons of the yeare irregular and
distempered; the Sun fainter, and languishing; men lesse in
stature, and shorter-lived. No addition, but only every yeare,
new sorts, new species of wormes, and flies, and sicknesses,
which argue more and more putrefaction of which they are en-
gendred. And the Angels of heaven, which did so familiarly
converse with men in the beginning of the world, though they
may not be doubted to perform to us still their ministeriall assistances, yet they seem so far to have deserted this world, as
that they do not appeare to us, as they did to those our Fathers.
S. *Cyprian* observed this in his time, when writing to *Demetri-
anus,* who imputed all those calamities which afflicted the
world then, to the impiety of the Christians who would not
joyne with them in the worship of their gods, *Cyprian* went
no farther for the cause of these calamities, but *Ad senescentem
mundum,* To the age and impotency of the whole world; And

therefore, sayes he, *Imputent senes Christianis, quòd minùs valeant in senectutem;* Old men were best accuse Christians, that they are more sickly in their age, than they were in their youth; Is the fault in our religion, or in their decay? *Canos in pueris videmus, nec ætas in senectute desinit, sed incipit à senectute;* We see gray haires in children, and we do not die old, and yet we are borne old. Lest the world (as the world signifies the whole frame of the world) should glorifie it selfe, or flatter, and abuse us with an opinion of eternity, we may admit usefully (though we do not conclude peremptorily) this observation to be true, that there is a reproofe, a rebuke born in it, a sensible decay and mortality of the whole world.

[*LXXX. Sermons* (36), 1640]

ST. DUNSTANS. "THE FIRST SERMON AFTER OUR DISPERSION BY THE SICKNESS." JAN. 15th, 1625/6

1

MEN whose lust carried them into the jaws of infection in lewd houses, and seeking one sore perished with another; men whose rapine and covetousness broke into houses, and seeking the Wardrobes of others, found their own winding-sheet, in the infection of that house where they stole their own death; men who sought no other way to divert sadness, but strong drink in riotous houses, and there drank up *Davids* cup of Malediction, the cup of Condemned men, of death, in the infection of that place. For these men that died in their sins, that sinned in their dying, that sought and hunted after death so sinfully, we have little comfort of such men, in the phrase of this Text, *They were dead;* for they are dead still: As *Moses* said of the *Egyptians,* I am afraid we may say of these men, *We shall see them no more for ever.*

2

As between two men of equal age, if one sleep, and the other wake all night, yet they rise both of an equal age in the morning; so they who shall have slept out a long night of many ages in the grave, and they who shall be caught up in the clouds, to meet the Lord Jesus in the aire, at the last day, shall enter all at once in their bodies into Heaven. No antiquity, no seniority for their bodies; neither can their souls who went before, be said to have been there a minute before ours, because we shall all be in a place that reckons not by minutes. Clocks and Sun-dials were but a late invention upon earth; but the Sun it self, and the earth it self, was but a late invention in heaven. God had been an infinite, a super-infinite, an unimaginable space, millions of millions of unimaginable spaces in heaven, before the Creation. And our afternoon shall be as long as Gods forenoon; for, as God never saw beginning, so we shall never see end; but they whom we tread upon now, and we whom others shall tread upon hereafter, shall meet at once, where, though we were dead, dead in our several houses, dead in a sinful *Egypt*, dead in our family, dead in our selves, dead in the Grave, yet we shall be received, with that consolation, and glorious consolation, you were dead, but are alive. *Enter ye blessed into the Kingdom, prepared for you, from the beginning. Amen.*

[*XXVI. Sermons* (21), 1660]

ST. PAUL'S. "THE SECOND OF MY PREBEND SERMONS UPON MY FIVE PSALMES." JAN. 29, 1625/6

1

ALL our life is a continuall burden, yet we must not groane; A continuall squeasing, yet we must not pant; And as in the tendernesse of our childhood, we suffer, and yet are whipt if we cry, so we are complained of, if we complaine, and made delinquents if we call the times ill. And that which adds waight to waight, and multiplies the sadnesse of this consideration, is this, That still the best men have had most laid upon them. As soone as I heare God say, that he hath found *an upright man, that fears God, and eschews evill,* in the next lines I finde a Commission to Satan, to bring in Sabeans and Chaldeans upon his cattell, and servants, and fire and tempest upon his children, and loathsome diseases upon himselfe. As soone as I heare God say, That he hath found *a man according to his own heart,* I see his sonnes ravish his daughters, and then murder one another, and then rebell against the Father, and put him into straites for his life. As soone as I heare God testifie of Christ at his Baptisme, *This is my beloved Sonne in whom I am well pleased,* I finde that Sonne of his *led up by the Spirit, to be tempted of*

the Devill. And after I heare God ratifie the same testimony
againe, at his Transfiguration, (*This is my beloved Sonne, in
whom I am well pleased*) I finde that beloved Sonne of his,
deserted, abandoned, and given over to Scribes, and Pharisees,
and Publicans, and Herodians, and Priests, and Souldiers, and
people, and Judges, and witnesses, and executioners, and he
that was called the beloved Sonne of God, and made partaker of
the glory of heaven, in this world, in his Transfiguration, is
made now the Sewer of all the corruption, of all the sinnes of
this world, as no Sonne of God, but a meere man, as no man,
but a contemptible worme. As though the greatest weaknesse in
this world, were man, and the greatest fault in man were to be
good, man is more miserable than other creatures, and good
men more miserable than any other men.

2

Let me wither and weare out mine age in a discomfortable,
in an unwholesome, in a penurious prison, and so pay my debts
with my bones, and recompence the wastfulnesse of my youth,
with the beggery of mine age; Let me wither in a spittle under
sharpe, and foule, and infamous diseases, and so recompence the
wantonnesse of my youth, with that loathsomnesse in mine age;
yet if God with-draw not his spirituall blessings, his Grace, his
Patience, If I can call my suffering his Doing, my passion his
Action, All this that is temporall, is but a caterpiller got into
one corner of my garden, but a mill-dew fallen upon one acre of
my Corne; The body of all, the substance of all is safe, as long
as the soule is safe. But when I shall trust to that, which wee
call a good spirit, and God shall deject, and empoverish, and
evacuate that spirit, when I shall rely upon a morall constancy,
and God shall shake, and enfeeble, and enervate, destroy and
demolish that constancy; when I shall think to refresh my
selfe in the serenity and sweet ayre of a good conscience, and
God shall call up the damps and vapours of hell it selfe, and
spread a cloud of diffidence, and an impenetrable crust of desperation upon my conscience; when health shall flie from me,
and I shall lay hold upon riches to succour me, and comfort me
in my sicknesse, and riches shall flie from me, and I shall snatch
after favour, and good opinion, to comfort me in my poverty;
when even this good opinion shall leave me, and calumnies and
misinformations shall prevaile against me; when I shall need
peace, because there is none but thou, O Lord, that should

stand for me, and then shall finde, that all the wounds that I have, come from thy hand, all the arrowes that stick in me, from thy quiver; when I shall see, that because I have given my selfe to my corrupt nature, thou hast changed thine; and because I am all evill towards thee, therefore thou hast given our being good towards me; When it comes to this height, that the fever is not in the humors, but in the spirits, that mine enemy is not an imaginary enemy, fortune, nor a transitory enemy, malice in great persons, but a reall, and an irresistible, and an inexorable, and an everlasting enemy, The Lord of Hosts himselfe, The Almighty God himselfe, the Almighty God himselfe onely knowes the waight of this affliction, and except hee put in that *pondus gloriæ*, that exceeding waight of an eternall glory, with his owne hand, into the other scale, we are waighed downe, we are swallowed up, irreparably, irrevocably, irrecoverably, irremediably.

[*LXXX. Sermons* (66), 1640]

ST. PAUL'S. EASTER DAY IN THE EVENING.
APRIL 9th, 1626

Thus it is, when a soule is scattered upon the daily practise of any one predominant, and habituall sin; but when it is indifferently scattered upon all, how much more is it so? In him, that swallowes sins in the world, as he would doe meats at a feast; passes through every dish, and never askes Physitian the nature, the quality, the danger, the offence of any dish: That baits at every sin that rises, and poures himselfe into every sinfull mold he meets: That knowes not when he began to spend his soule, nor where, nor upon what sin he laid it out; no, nor whether he have, whether ever he had any soule, or no; but hath lost his soule so long agoe, in rusty, and in incoherent sins, (not sins that produced one another, as in *Davids* case (and yet that is a fearfull state, that concatenation of sins, that pedigree of sins) but in sins which he embraces, meerely out of an easinesse to sin, and not out of a love, no, nor out of a tentation to that sin in particular) that in these incoherent sins hath so scattered his soule, as that he hath not soule enough left, to seek out the rest. And therefore *David* makes it the Title of the whole Psalme, *Domine ne disperdas, O Lord doe not scatter us:* And he begins to expresse his sense of Gods Judgements, in the next Psalme, so, *O Lord thou hast cast us out, thou hast scattered us, turn again unto us;* for even from this aversion, there may be conversion, and from this last and lowest fall, a resurrection. But how?

In the generall resurrection upon naturall death, God shall work upon this dispersion of our scattered dust, as in the first fall, which is the Divorce, by way of Re-union, and in the second, which is Putrifaction, by way of Re-efformation; so in this third, which is Dispersion, by way of Re-collection; where mans buried flesh hath brought forth grasse, and that grasse fed beasts, and those beasts fed men, and those men fed other men, God that knowes in which Boxe of his Cabinet all this seed Pearle lies, in what corner of the world every atome, every graine of every mans dust sleeps, shall re-collect that dust, and then re-compact that body, and then re-inanimate that man, and that is the accomplishment of all.

[*LXXX. Sermons* (21), 1640]

"PREACHED TO THE KING IN MY ORDINARY WAYTING AT WHITEHALL." APRIL 30th, 1626

GOD hath a progresse house, a removing house here upon earth, His house of prayer; At this houre, God enters into as many of these houses, as are opened for his service at this houre: But his standing house, his house of glory, is that in Heaven, and that he promises them. God himselfe dwelt in Tents in this world, and he gives them a House in Heaven. A House, in the designe and survay whereof, the Holy Ghost himselfe is figurative, the Fathers wanton, and the School-men wilde. The Holy Ghost, in describing this House, fills our contemplation with foundations, and walls, and gates, of gold, of precious stones, and all materialls, that we can call precious. The Holy Ghost is figurative; And the Fathers are wanton in their spirituall elegancies, such as that of S. *Augustins,* (if that booke be his) *Hiems horrens, Æstas torrens,* And, *Virent prata, vernant sata,* and such other harmonious, and melodious, and mellifluous cadences of these waters of life. But the School-men are wild; for as one Author, who is afraid of admitting too great a hollownesse in the Earth, lest then the Earth might not be said to be solid, pronounces that Hell cannot possibly be above three thousand miles in compasse, (and then one of the torments of Hell will be the throng, for their bodies must be there, in their dimensions, as well as their soules) so when the School-men come to measure this house in heaven, (as they will measure it, and

the Master, God, and all his Attributes, and tell us how Allmighty, and how Infinite he is) they pronounce, that every
soule in that house shall have more roome to it selfe, than all
this world is. We know not that; nor see we that the consolation lyes in that; we rest in this, that it is a House, It hath a
foundation, no Earth-quake shall shake it, It hath walls, no Artillery shall batter it, It hath a roofe, no tempest shall pierce it.
It is a house that affords security, and that is one beame; And it
is *Domus patris,* His Fathers house, a house in which he hath
interest, and that is another beame of his Consolation.

It was his Fathers, and so his: And his, and so ours; for we
are not joynt purchasers of Heaven with the Saints, but we are
co-heires with Christ Jesus. We have not a place there, because
they have done more than enough for themselves, but because
he hath done enough for them and us too. By death we are
gathered to our Fathers in nature; and by death, through his
mercy, gathered to his Father also. Where we shall have a full
satisfaction, in that wherein S. *Philip* placed all satisfaction,
*Ostende nobis patrem, Lord, shew us thy Father, and it is
enough.* We shall see his Father, and see him made ours in him.

And then a third beame of this Consolation is, That in this
house of his Fathers, thus by him made ours, there are *Mansions:* In which word, the Consolation is not placed, (I doe
not say, that there is not truth in it) but the Consolation is not
placed in this, That some of these Mansions are below, some
above staires, some better seated, better lighted, better vaulted,
better fretted, better furnished than others; but onely in this,
That they are *Mansions:* which word, in the Originall, and Latin,
and our Language, signifies a *Remaining,* and denotes the
perpetuity, the everlastingnesse of that state. A state but of one
Day, because no Night shall over-take, or determine it, but
such a Day, as is not of a thousand yeares, which is the longest
measure in the Scriptures, but of a thousand millions of millions
of generations: *Qui nec præceditur hesterno, nec excluditur
crastino,* A day that hath no *pridie,* nor *postridie,* yesterday doth
not usher it in, nor to morrow shall not drive it out. *Methusalem,* with all his hundreds of yeares, was but a Mushrome of a
nights growth, to this day, And all the foure Monarchies, with
all their thousands of yeares, And all the powerfull Kings,
and all the beautifull Queenes of this world, were but as a bed
of flowers, some gathered at six, some at seven, some at eight,
All in one Morning, in respect of this Day. In all the two
thousand yeares of Nature, before the Law given by *Moses,* And

the two thousand yeares of Law, before the Gospel given by Christ, And the two thousand of Grace, which are running now, (of which last houre we have heard three quarters strike, more than fifteen hundred of this last two thousand spent) In all this six thousand, and in all those which God may be pleased to adde, *In domo patris*, In this House of his Fathers, there was never heard quarter clock to strike, never seen minute glasse to turne. No time lesse than it selfe would serve to expresse this time, which is intended in this word *Mansions;* which is also exalted with another beame, that they are *Multa, In my Fathers House there are many Mansions.*

In this Circumstance, an Essentiall, a Substantiall Circumstance, we would consider the joy of our society, and conversation in heaven, since society and conversation is one great element and ingredient into the joy, which we have in this world. We shall have an association with Christ himselfe; for *where he is,* it is his promise, *that we also shall be.* We shall have an association with the Angels, and such a one, as we shall be such as they. We shall have an association with the Saints, and not onely so, to be such as they, but to be they: And with all *who come from the East, and from the West, and from the North, and from the South, and sit down with Abraham, and Isaac, and Jacob in the kingdome of heaven.* Where we shall be so far from being enemies to one another, as that we shall not be strangers to one another: And so far from envying one another, as that all that every one hath, shall be every others possession: where all soules shall be so intirely knit together, as if all were but one soule, and God so intirely knit to every soule, as if there were as many Gods as soules.

[*LXXX. Sermons* (73), 1640]

ST. PAUL'S. "IN VESPERIS." "THE THIRD OF MY PREBEND SERMONS UPON MY FIVE PSALMES." NOV. 5th, 1626

Upon this earth, a man cannot possibly make one step in a straight, and a direct line. The earth it selfe being round, every step wee make upon it, must necessarily bee a segment, an arch of a circle. But yet though no piece of a circle be a straight line, yet if we take any piece, nay if wee take the whole circle, there is no corner, no angle in any piece, in any intire circle. A perfect rectitude we cannot have in any wayes in this world; In every Calling there are some inevitable tentations. But, though wee cannot make up our circle of a straight line, (that is impossible to humane frailty) yet wee may passe on, without angles, and corners, that is, without disguises in our Religion, and without the love of craft, and falsehood, and circumvention in our civill actions. A Compasse is a necessary thing in a Ship, and the helpe of that Compasse brings the Ship home safe, and yet that Compasse hath some variations, it doth not looke directly North; Neither is that starre which we call the Northpole, or by which we know the North-pole, the very Pole it selfe; but we call it so, and we make our uses of it, and our conclusions by it, as if it were so, because it is the neerest starre to that Pole. He that comes as neere uprightnesse, as infirmities admit, is an upright man, though he have some obliquities. To God himselfe we may alwayes go in a direct line, a straight, a perpendicular line; For God is verticall to me, over my head now, and verticall now to them, that are in the East, and West-Indies; To our Antipodes, to them that are under our feet, God is verticall, over their heads, then when he is over ours.

[*LXXX. Sermons* (67), 1640]

"PREACHED AT THE FUNERAL OF SIR WILLIAM COKAYNE, KNIGHT, ALDERMAN OF LONDON."
DEC. 12th, 1626

1

JOH. II. 21

Lord, if thou hadst been here, my brother had not died.

GOD made the first Marriage, and man made the first Divorce; God married the Body and Soule in the Creation, and man divorced the Body and Soule by death through sinne, in his fall. God doth not admit, not justifie, not authorize such Superinductions upon such Divorces, as some have imagined; That the soule departing from one body, should become the soule of another body, in a perpetuall revolution and transmigration of soules through bodies, which hath been the giddinesse of some Philosophers to think; Or that the body of the dead should become the body of an evill spirit, that that spirit might at his will, and to his purposes informe, and inanimate that dead body; God allowes no such Super-inductions, no such second Marriages upon such divorces by death, no such disposition of soule or body, after their dissolution by death. But because God hath made the band of Marriage indissoluble but by death, farther than man can die, this divorce cannot fall upon man; As farre as man is immortall, man is a married man still, still in possession of a soule, and a body too; And man is for ever immortall in both; Immortall in his soule by Preservation, and immortall in his body by Reparation in the Resurrection. For, though they be separated *à Thoro et Mensa,* from Bed and Board, they are not divorced; Though the soule be at the *Table of the Lambe,* in Glory, and the body but at the table of *the Serpent, in dust;* Though the soule be *in lecto florido,* in that bed which is alwayes green, in an everlasting spring, in *Abrahams Bosome;* And the body but in that green-bed, whose covering is but a yard and a halfe of Turfe, and a Rugge of grasse, and the sheet but a winding sheet, yet they are not divorced; they shall returne to one another againe, in an inseparable re-union in the Resurrection.

2

How imperfect is all our knowledge! What one thing doe we know perfectly? Whether wee consider Arts, or Sciences, the servant knows but according to the proportion of his Masters knowledge in that Art, and the Scholar knows but according to the proportion of his Masters knowledge in that Science; Young men mend not their sight by using old mens Spectacles; and yet we looke upon Nature, but with *Aristotles* Spectacles, and upon the body of man, but with *Galens,* and upon the frame of the world, but with *Ptolomies* Spectacles. Almost all knowledge is rather like a child that is embalmed to make Mummy, than that is nursed to make a Man; rather conserved in the stature of the first age, than growne to be greater; And if there be any addition to knowledge, it is rather a new knowledge, than a greater knowledge; rather a singularity in a desire of proposing something that was not knowne at all before, than an emproving, an advancing, a multiplying of former inceptions; and by that meanes, no knowledge comes to be perfect. One Philosopher thinks he is dived to the bottome, when he sayes, he knows nothing but this, That he knows nothing; and yet another thinks, that he hath expressed more knowledge than he, in saying, That he knows not so much as that, That he knows nothing. S. *Paul* found that to be all knowledge, To know Christ; And Mahomet thinks himselfe wise therefore, because he knows not, acknowledges not Christ, as S. *Paul* does. Though a man knew not, that every sin casts another shovell of Brimstone upon him in Hell, yet if he knew that every riotous feast cuts off a year, and every wanton night seaven years of his seventy in this world, it were some degree towards perfection in knowledge. He that purchases a Mannor, will thinke to have an exact Survey of the Land: But who thinks of taking so exact a survey of his Conscience, how that money was got, that purchased that Mannor? We call that a mans meanes, which he hath; But that is truly his meanes, what way he came by it. And yet how few are there, (when a state comes to any great proportion) that know that; that know what they have, what they are worth? We have seen great Wills, dilated into glorious uses, and into pious uses, and then too narrow an estate to reach to it; And we have seen Wills, where the Testator thinks he hath bequeathed all, and he hath not knowne halfe of his own worth. When thou knowest a wife, a sonne, a servant, a friend no better, but that that wife betrayes thy bed, and that sonne thine estate, and that servant thy credit, and that friend thy secret, what canst thou say thou knowest? But we must not insist upon this Consideration of knowledge; for, though knowledge be of a spirituall nature, yet it is but as a terrestriall Spirit, conversant upon Earth; Spirituall things, of a more rarified nature than knowledge, even faith it selfe, and all that grows from that in us, falls within this Rule, which we have in hand, That even in spirituall things, nothing is perfect.

3

When we consider with a religious seriousnesse the manifold weaknesses of the strongest devotions in time of Prayer, it is a sad consideration. I throw my selfe downe in my Chamber, and I call in, and invite God, and his Angels thither, and when they are there, I neglect God and his Angels, for the noise of a Flie, for the ratling of a Coach, for the whining of a doore; I talke on, in the same posture of praying; Eyes lifted up; knees bowed downe; as though I prayed to God; and, if God, or his Angels should aske me, when I thought last of God in that prayer, I cannot tell: Sometimes I finde that I had forgot what I was about, but when I began to forget it, I cannot tell. A memory of yesterdays pleasures, a feare of to morrows dangers, a straw under my knee, a noise in mine eare, a light in mine eye, an any thing, a nothing, a fancy, a Chimera in my braine, troubles me in my prayer. So certainely is there nothing, nothing in spirituall things, perfect in this world.

4

I need not call in new Philosophy, that denies a settlednesse, an acquiescence in the very body of the Earth, but makes the Earth to move in that place, where we thought the Sunne had moved; I need not that helpe, that the Earth it selfe is in Motion, to prove this, That nothing upon Earth is permanent; The Assertion will stand of it selfe, till some man assigne me some instance, something that a man may relie upon, and find permanent. Consider the greatest Bodies upon Earth, The Monarchies; Objects, which one would thinke, Destiny might stand and stare at, but not shake; Consider the smallest bodies upon Earth, The haires of our head, Objects, which one would thinke, Destiny would not observe, or could not discerne; And yet, Destiny, (to speak to a naturall man) And God, (to speake to a Christian) is no more troubled to make a Monarchy ruinous, than to make a haire gray. Nay, nothing needs be done to either, by God, or Destiny; A Monarchy will ruine, as a haire will grow gray, of it selfe. In the Elements themselves, of which all sub-elementary things are composed, there is no acquiescence, but a vicissitudinary transmutation into one another; Ayre condensed becomes water, a more solid body, And Ayre rarified becomes fire, a body more disputable, and in-apparent. It is so in the Conditions of men too; A Merchant condensed, kneaded and packed up in a great estate, becomes a Lord; And a Merchant rarified, blown up by a perfidious Factor, or by a riotous Sonne, evaporates into ayre, into nothing, and is not seen. And if there were any thing permanent and durable in this world, yet we got nothing by it, because howsoever that might last in it selfe, yet we could not last to enjoy it; If our goods were not amongst Moveables, yet we our selves are; if they could stay with us, yet we cannot stay with them; which is another Consideration in this part.

The world is a great Volume, and man the Index of that Booke; Even in the body of man, you may turne to the whole world; This body is an Illustration of all Nature; Gods recapitulation of all that he had said before in his *Fiat lux,* and *Fiat firmamentum,* and in all the rest, said or done, in all the six

SERMONS 527

dayes. Propose this body to thy consideration in the highest exaltation thereof; as it is the *Temple of the Holy Ghost:* Nay, not in a Metaphor, or comparison of a Temple, or any other similitudinary thing, but as it was really and truly the very body of God, in the person of Christ, and yet this body must wither, must decay, must languish, must perish. When *Goliah* had armed and fortified this body, And *Jezabel* had painted and perfumed this body, And *Dives* had pampered and larded this body, As God said to *Ezekiel,* when he brought him to the *dry bones, Fili hominis, Sonne of Man doest thou thinke these bones can live?* They said in their hearts to all the world, Can these bodies die? And they are dead. *Jezabels* dust is not Ambar, nor *Goliahs* dust *Terra sigillata,* Medicinall; nor does the Serpent, whose meat they are both, finde any better relish in *Dives* dust, than in *Lazarus.* But as in our former part, where our foundation was, That in nothing, no spirituall thing, there was any perfectnesse, which we illustrated in the weaknesses of Knowledge, and Faith, and Hope, and Charity, yet we concluded, that for all those defects, God accepted those their religious services; So in this part, where our foundation is, That nothing in temporall things is permanent, as we have illustrated that, by the decay of that which is Gods noblest piece in Nature, The body of man; so we shall also conclude that, with this goodnesse of God, that for all this dissolution, and putrefaction, he affords this Body a Resurrection.

The Gentils, and their Poets, describe the sad state of Death so, *Nox una obeunda,* That it is one everlasting Night; To them, a Night; But to a Christian, it is *Dies Mortis,* and *Dies Resurrectionis,* The day of Death, and The day of Resurrection; We die in the light, in the sight of Gods presence, and we rise in the light, in the sight of his very Essence. Nay, Gods corrections, and judgements upon us in this life, are still expressed so, *Dies visitationis,* still it is a Day, though a *Day of visitation;* and still we may discerne God to be in the action. The *Lord of Life* was the first that named *Death; Morte morieris,* sayes God, Thou shalt die the Death. I doe the lesse feare, or abhorre Death, because I finde it in his mouth; Even a malediction hath a sweetnesse in his mouth; for there is a blessing wrapped up in it; a mercy in every correction, a Resurrection upon every Death. When *Jezabels* beauty, exalted to that height which it had by art, or higher than that, to that height which it had in her own opinion, shall be infinitely multiplied upon every Body; And as God shall know no man from his own Sonne, so as not to see the very righteousnesse of his own Sonne upon that man; So the Angels shall know no man from Christ, so as not to desire to looke upon that mans face, because the most deformed wretch that is there, shall have the very beauty of Christ himselfe; So shall *Goliahs* armour, and *Dives* fulnesse, be doubled, and redoubled upon us, And every thing that we can call good, shall first be infinitely exalted in the goodnesse, and then infinitely multiplied in the proportion, and againe infinitely extended in the duration. And since we are in an action of preparing this dead Brother of ours to that state, (for the Funerall is the Easter-eve, The Buriall is the depositing of that man for the Resurrection) As we have held you, with Doctrine of Mortification, by extending the Text, from *Martha* to this occasion; so shall we dismisse you with Consolation, by a like occasionall inverting the Text, from passion in *Martha's* mouth, *Lord, if thou hadst been here, my Brother had not dyed,* to joy in ours, *Lord, because thou wast here, our Brother is not dead.*

The Lord was with him in all these steps; with him in his life; with him in his death; He is with him in his funerals, and he shall be with him in his Resurrection; and therefore, because the Lord was with him, our Brother is not dead. He was with him in the beginning of his life, in this manifestation, That though he were of Parents of a good, of a great Estate, yet his possibilty and his expectation from them, did not slacken his own industry; which is a Canker that eats into, nay that hath eat up many a family in this City, that relying wholly upon what the Father hath done, the Sonne does nothing for himselfe. And truly, it falls out too often, that he that labours not for more, does not keepe his own. God imprinted in him an industrious disposition, though such hopes from such parents might have excused some slacknesse, and God prospered his industry so, as that when his Fathers estate came to a distribution by death, he needed it not. God was with him, as with *David* in a Dilatation, and then in a Repletion; God enlarged him, and then he filled him; He gave him a large and a comprehensive understanding, and with it, A publique heart; And such as perchance in his way of education, and in our narrow and contracted times, in which every man determines himselfe in himselfe, and scarce looks farther, it would be hard to finde many Examples of such largenesse. You have, I thinke, a phrase of Driving a Trade; And you have, I know, a practise of Driving away Trade, by other use of money; And you have lost a man, that drove a great Trade, the right way in making the best use of our home-commodity. To fetch in Wine, and Spice, and Silke, is but a drawing of Trade; The right driving of trade, is, to vent our owne outward; And yet, for the drawing in of that, which might justly seeme most behoofefull, that is, of Arts, and Manufactures, to be imployed upon our owne Commodity within the Kingdome, he did his part, diligently, at least, if not vehemently, if not passionately. This City is a great Theater, and he Acted great and various parts in it; And all well; And when he went higher, (as he was often heard in Parliaments, at Councell tables, and in more private accesses to the late King of ever blessed memory) as, for that comprehension of those businesses, which he pretended to understand, no man doubts, for no man lacks arguments and evidences of his ability therein, So for his manner of expressing his intentions, and digesting and uttering his purposes, I have sometimes heard the greatest Master of Language and Judgement, which these times, or any other did, or doe, or shall give, (that good and great King of ours) say of him, That he never heard any man of his breeding, handle businesses more rationally, more pertinently, more elegantly, more perswasively; And when his purpose was, to do a grace to a Preacher, of very good abilities, and good note in his owne Chappell, I have heard him say, that his language, and accent, and manner of delivering himselfe, was like this man. This man hath God accompanied all his life; and by performance thereof seemes to have made that Covenant with him, which he made to *Abraham, Multiplicabo te vehementer, I will multiply thee exceedingly.* He multiplied his estate so, as was fit to endow many and great Children; and he multiplied his Children so, both in their number, and in their quality, as they were fit to receive a great Estate. God was with him all the way, In *a Pillar of Fire,* in the brightnesse of prosperity, and in the *Pillar of Clouds* too, in many darke, and sad, and heavy crosses: So great a Ship, required a great Ballast, So many blessings, many crosses; And he had them, and sailed on his course the steadier for them; The *Cloud* as well as the *Fire,* was a *Pillar* to him; His crosses, as well as his blessings established his assurance in God; And so, in all the course of his life, *The Lord was here,* and therefore *our Brother is not dead;* not dead in the evidences and testimonies of life; for he, whom the world hath just cause to celebrate, for things done, when he was alive, is alive still in their celebration.

The Lord was here, that is, with him at his death too. He was served with the Processe here in the City, but his cause was heard in the Country; Here he sickned, There he languished, and dyed there. In his sicknesse there, those that assisted him, are witnesses, of his many expressings, of a religious and a constant heart towards God, and of his pious ioyning with them, even in the holy declaration of kneeling, then, when they, in favour of his weaknesse, would disswade him from kneeling. I must not defraud him of this testimony for my selfe, that into this place where we are now met, I have observed him to enter with much reverence, and compose himselfe in this place with much declaration of devotion. And truly it is that reverence, which those persons who are of the same ranke that he was in the City, that reverence that they use in this place, when they come hither, is that that makes us, who have now the administration of this Quire, glad, that our Predecessors, but a very few yeares before our time, (and not before all our times neither) admitted these Honourable and worshipfull Persons of this City, to sit in this Quire, so, as they do upon Sundayes: The Church receives an honour in it; But the honour is more in their reverence, than in their presence; though in that too: And they receive an honour, and an ease in it; and therefore they do piously towards God, and prudently for themselves, and gratefully towards us, in giving us, by their reverent comportment here, so just occasion of continuing that honour, and that ease to them here, which to lesse reverend, and unrespective persons, we should be lesse willing to doe. To returne to him in his sicknesse; He had but one dayes labour, and all the rest were Sabbaths, one day in his sicknesse he converted to businesse; Thus; He called his family, and friends together; Thankfully he acknowledged Gods manifold blessings, and his own sins as penitently: And then, to those who were to have the disposing of his estate, joyntly with his Children, he recommended his servants, and the poore, and the Hospitals, and the Prisons, which, according to his purpose, have beene all taken into consideration; And after this (which was his Valediction to the world) he seemed alwaies loath to returne to any worldly businesse, His last Commandement to Wife and Children was Christs last commandement to his Spouse the Church, in the Apostles, *To love one another.* He blest them, and the Estate devolved upon them, unto them: And by Gods grace shall prove as true a Prophet to them in that blessing, as he was to himselfe, when in entring his last bed, two dayes before his Death, he said, *Help me off with my earthly habit, and let me go to my last bed.* Where, in the second night after, he said, *Little know*

*ye what paine I feele this night, yet I know, I shall have joy in
the morning;* And in that morning he dyed. The forme in
which he implored his Saviour, was evermore, towards his end,
this, *Christ Jesus, which dyed on the Cross, forgive me my sins;
He have mercy upon me:* And his last and dying words were
the repetition of the name of Jesus; And when he had not
strength to utter that name distinctly and perfectly, they might
heare it from within him, as from a man a far off; even then,
when his hollow and remote naming of Jesus, was rather a cer-
tifying of them, that he was with his Jesus, than a prayer that
he might come to him. And so *The Lord was here,* here with
him in his Death; and because *the Lord was here, our Brother
is not dead;* not dead in the eyes and eares of God; for as the
blood of *Abel* speaks yet, so doth the zeale of Gods Saints; and
their last prayers (though we heare them not) God continues
still; and they pray in Heaven, as the Martyrs under the Altar,
even till the Resurrection.

He is with him now too; Here in his Funerals. Buriall, and
Christian Buriall, and Solemne Buriall are all evidences, and
testimonies of Gods presence. God forbid we should conclude,
or argue an absence of God, from the want of Solemne Buriall,
or Christian Buriall, or any Buriall; But neither must we deny it,
to be an evidence of his favour and presence, where he is
pleased to afford these. So God makes that the seale of all his
blessings to *Abraham, That he should be buried in a good age;*
God established *Jacob* with that promise, *That his Son Joseph
should have care of his Funerals:* And *Joseph* does cause his
servants, *The Physitians, to embalme him, when he was dead.*
Of Christ it was Prophecied, *That he should have a glorious
Buriall;* And therefore Christ interprets well that profuse, and
prodigall piety of the Woman that poured out the Oyntment
upon him, *That she did it to Bury him;* And so shall *Joseph* of
Arimathea be ever celebrated, for his care in celebrating Christs
Funerals. If we were to send a Son, or a friend, to take possession of any place in Court, or forraine parts, we would send him
out in the best equipage: Let us not grudge to set downe our
friends, in the Anti-chamber of Heaven, the Grave, in as good
manner, as without vaine-gloriousnesse, and wastfulnesse we
may; And, in inclining them, to whom that care belongs, to expresse that care as they doe this day, *The Lord is with him,* even
in this Funerall; And because *The Lord is here, our brother is
not dead;* Not dead in the memories and estimation of men.

And lastly, that we may have God present in all his Manifestations, *Hee that was, and is, and is to come,* was with him, in his life and death, and is with him in this holy Solemnity, and shall bee with him againe in the Resurrection. God sayes to *Jacob, I will goe downe with thee into Egypt, and I will also surely bring thee up againe.* God goes downe with a good man into the Grave, and will surely bring him up againe. When? The Angel promised to returne to *Abraham* and *Sarah,* for the assurance of the birth of *Isaac, according to the time of life;* that is, in such time, as by nature a woman may have a childe. God will returne to us in the Grave, *according to the time of life;* that is, in such time, as he, by his gracious Decree, hath fixed for the Resurrection. And in the meane time, no more than the God-head departed from the dead body of our Saviour, in the grave, doth his power, and his presence depart from our dead bodies in that darknesse; But that which *Moses* said to the whole Congregation, I say to you all, both to you that heare me, and to him that does not, *All ye that did cleave unto the Lord your God, are alive, every one of you, this day;* Even hee, whom wee call dead, is alive this day. In the presence of God, we lay him downe; In the power of God, he shall rise; In the person of Christ, he is risen already. And so into the same hands that have received his soule, we commend his body; beseeching his blessed Spirit, that as our charity enclines us to hope confidently of his good estate, our faith may assure us of the same happinesse, in our owne behalfe; And that for all our sakes, but especially for his own glory, he will be pleased to hasten the consummation of all, in that kingdome which that Son of God hath purchased for us, with the inestimable price of his incorruptible blood. *Amen.*

[*LXXX. Sermons* (80), 1640]

TO THE KING AT WHITE-HALL.
THE FIRST SUNDAY IN LENT [1626/7?]

1

WHAT can be certain in this world, if even the mercy of God admit a variation? what can be endlesse here, if even the mercy of God receive a determination? and *sin* doth vary the nature, *sin* doth determine even the infinitenesse of the mercy of God himself, for though *The childe shall die a hundred yeares old,* yet *the sinner being a hundred years old shall be accursed.* Disconsolate soul, dejected spirit, bruised and broken, ground and trodden, attenuated, evaporated, annihilated heart come back; heare thy *reprieve,* and sue for thy *pardon;* God will not take thee away in thy sins, thou shalt have time to repent, *The childe shall die a hundred years old.* But then lame and decrepit soul, gray and inveterate sinner, behold the full ears of corn blasted with a mildew, behold this long day shutting up in such a night, as shall never see light more, the night of death; in which, the deadliest pang of thy *Death* will be thine *Immortality:* In this especially shalt thou die, that thou canst not die, when thou art dead; but must live dead for ever: for *The sinner being a hundred yeers old, shall be accursed,* he shall be so for ever.

2

God antidates no malediction: Till there be a sinner, there is no malediction; nay not till there be an *inveterate* sinner; *A sinner of a hundred yeares,* at least, such a sinner, as would be so, if God would spare him a hundred yeares here. And upon such a sinner, God thunders out this Prosternation, this Consternation, in this one word of our Text, which involves and inwraps all kinds of miseries, feeblenesse in body, infatuation in mind, evacuation of power, dishonour in fame, eclipses in favour, ruine in fortune, dejection in spirit, *He shall be accursed.* Where, because in this second part we are in the Region and Sphear of maledictions, we cannot consider this future, *He shall be,* as a future of favour, a prorogation, a deferring of the malediction: *He shall be,* is not, he shall be hereafter, but not yet: but it is *a future of continuation; He shall be accursed,* that is, he shall be so *for ever.*

3

Long life is a blessing, as it is an image of eternity: as Kings are blessings, because they are Images of God. And as to speak properly, a King that possest the whole earth, hath no proportion at all to God, (he is not a dramme, not a grain, not an atome to God) so neither if a thousand *Methusalems* were put in one life, had that long life any proportion to eternity; for *Finite* and *Infinite* have no proportion to one another. But yet when we say so, That the King is *nothing* to *God,* we speak then between God and the King; and we say that, onely to assist the

Kings Religious humiliation of himself in the presence of God. But when we speak between the King and our selves his Subjects, there we raise our selves to a just reverence of him, by taking knowledge that he is the Image of God to us. So though *long life* be nothing to eternity, yet because we need such *Glasses* and such *Images,* as God shews us himself in the King, so he shewes us his eternitie in a long life.

4

How men do bear it, we know not; what passes between God and those men, upon whom the curse of God lieth, in their dark *horrours at midnight,* they would not have us know, because it is part of their curse, to envy God that glory. But we may consider in some part the insupportablenesse of that weight, if we proceed but so farre, as to accommodate to God, that which is ordinarily said of naturall things. *Corruptio optimi pessima*; when the best things change their nature, they become worst. When God, who is all sweetnesse, shall have learned frowardnesse from us, as *David* speaks; and being all rectitude, shall have learned perversenesse and crookednesse from us, as *Moses* speaks; and being all providence, shall have learned negligence from us: when God who is all Blessing, hath learned to curse of us, and being of himself spread as an universall Hony-combe over All, takes in an impression, a tincture, an infusion of gall from us, what extraction of Wormwood can be so bitter, what exaltation of fire can be so raging, what multiplying of talents can be so heavy, what stifnesse of destiny can be so inevitable, what confection of gnawing worms, of gnashing teeth, of howling cries, of scalding brimstone, of palpable darknesse, can be so, so insupportable, so inexpressible, so in-imaginable, as the curse and malediction of God? *And therefore* let not us by our works provoke, nor by our words teach God to curse.

5

This is the *Anathema Maran-atha,* accursed *till the Lord, come;* and when the Lord cometh, he cometh not to reverse, nor to alleviate, but to ratifie and aggravate that curse. As soon as Christ curst the *fig-tree,* it withered, and it never recovered: for saith that Gospell, he curst it *In æternum,* for ever. In the course of our sinne, the *Holy Ghost* hath put here a number of yeares, a hundred yeares: We sinne long, as long as we can, but yet sinne hath an end. But in this curse of God in the Text, there is no number; it is an *indefinite* future; *He shall be accursed:* A mile of cyphers or figures, added to the former hundred, would not make up a minute of this eternity. Men have calculated how many particular graines of sand, would fill up all the vast space between the Earth and the Firmament: and we find, that a few lines of cyphers will designe and expresse that number. But if every grain of sand were that number, and multiplied again by that number, yet all that, all that inexpressible, inconsiderable number, made not up one minute of this eternity; neither would this curse, be a minute the shorter for having been indured so many Generations, as there were grains of sand in that number.

6

But we are now in the work of an houre, and no more. If there be a minute of sand left, (There is not) If there be a minute of patience left, heare me say, This minute that is left, is that eternitie which we speake of; upon this minute dependeth that eternity: And this minute, God is in this Congregation, and puts his eare to every one of your hearts, and hearkens what you will bid him say to yourselves: whether he shall blesse you for your acceptation, or curse you for your refusall of him this minute: for this minute makes up your *Century,* your hundred yeares, your eternity, because it may be your last minute. We need not call that a *Fable,* but a *Parable,* where we heare, That a Mother to still her froward childe told him, she would cast him to the Wolf, the Wolf should have him; and the Wolf which was at the doore, and within hearing, waited, and hoped he should have the childe indeed: but the childe being still'd, and the Mother pleased, then she saith, so shall we kill the Wolf, the Wolf shall have none of my childe, and then the Wolf stole away. No metaphor, no comparison is too high, none too low, too triviall, to imprint in you a sense of Gods everlasting goodnesse towards you. God bids your Mother the Church, and us her Servants for your Souls, to denounce his judgements upon your sinnes, and we do it; and the executioner *Satan,* beleeves us, before you beleeve us, and is ready on his part. Be you also ready on your part, to lay hold upon those conditions, which are annext to all Gods maledictions, Repentance of former, *preclusion* against *future sinnes,* and we shall be alwayes ready, on our part to assist you with the *Power* of our *Intercession,* to deliver you with the *Keies* of our *Absolution,* and to establish you with the *seales* of *Reconciliation,* and so disappoint that *Wolf,* that roaring *Lion,* that seeks whom he may devour: Go in Peace, and be this your Peace, to know this, *Maledictus qui pendet in Cruce,* God hath laid the whole curse belonging to us upon him, that hangs upon the Crosse; But *Benedictus qui pendet in pendentem;* To all them that hang upon him, that hangeth there, God offereth now, all those blessings, which he that hangeth there hath purchased with the inestimable price of his Incorruptible blood; And to this glorious *Sonne* of God, who hath *suffered* all this, and to the most Almighty *Father,* who hath *done* all this, and to the *blessed Spirit of God,* who offereth now to *apply* all this, be ascribed by us, and by the whole Church, All power, praise, might, majesty, glory, and dominion, now and for evermore. *Amen.*

[*Fifty Sermons* (26), 1649]

ST. PAUL'S. EASTER DAY. MARCH 25th, 1627

1

THERE is nothing that God hath established in a constant course of nature, and which therefore is done every day, but would seeme a Miracle, and exercise our admiration, if it were done but once; Nay, the ordinary things in Nature, would be greater miracles, than the extraordinary, which we admire most, if they were done but once; The standing still of the Sun, for *Josuahs* use, was not, in it selfe, so wonderfull a thing, as that so vast and immense a body as the Sun, should run so many miles, in a minute; The motion of the Sun were a greater wonder than the standing still, if all were to begin againe; And onely the daily doing takes off the admiration. But then God having, as it were, concluded himself in a course of nature, and written downe in the booke of Creatures, Thus and thus all things shall be carried, though he glorifie himselfe sometimes, in doing a miracle, yet there is in every miracle, a silent chiding of the world, and a tacite reprehension of them, who require, or who need miracles.

2

Now what was this that they qualified and dignified by that addition, *The better Resurrection?* Is it called better, in that it is better than this life, and determined in that comparison, and degree of betternesse, and no more? Is it better than those honours, and preferments which that King offered them, and determined in that comparison, and no more? Or better than other men shall have at the last day, (for all men shall have a Resurrection) and determined in that? Or, as S. *Chrysostome* takes it, is it but a better Resurrection than that in the former part of this Text, where dead children are restored to their mothers alive again? Is it but a better Resurrection in some of these senses? Surely better in a higher sense than any of these. It is a supereminent degree of glory, a larger measure of glory, than every man, who in a generall happinesse, is made partaker of the Resurrection of the righteous, is made partaker of.

Beloved, There is nothing so little in heaven, as that we can expresse it; but if wee could tell you the fulnesse of a soul there, what that fulnesse is; the infinitenesse of that glory there, how far that infinitenesse goes; the Eternity of that happinesse there, how long that happinesse lasts; if we could make you know all this, yet this *Better Resurrection* is a heaping, even of that Fulnesse, and an enlarging, even of that Infinitenesse, and an extention, even of that eternity of happinesse; For, all these, this Fulnesse, this Infinitenesse, this Eternity are in all the Resurrections of the Righteous, and this is a *better Resurrection;* We may almost say, it is something more than Heaven; for, all that have any Resurrection to life, have all heaven; And something more than God; for, all that have any Resurrection to life, have all God; and yet these shall have a better Resurrection. Amorous soule, ambitious soule, covetous soule, voluptuous soule, what wouldest thou have in heaven? What doth thy holy amorousnesse, thy holy covetousnesse, thy holy ambition, and voluptuousnesse most carry thy desire upon? Call it what thou wilt; think it what thou canst; think it something that thou canst not think; and all this thou shalt have, if thou have any Resurrection unto life; and yet there is a *Better Resurrection.* When I consider what I was in my parents loynes (a substance unworthy of a word, unworthy of a thought) when I consider what I am now, (a Volume of diseases bound up together, a dry cynder, if I look for naturall, for radicall moisture, and yet a Spunge, a bottle of overflowing Rheumes, if I consider accidentall; an aged childe, a gray-headed Infant, and but the ghost of mine own youth) When I consider what I shall be at last, by the hand of death, in my grave, (first, but Putrifaction, and then, not so much as Putrifaction, I shall not be able to send forth so much as an ill ayre, not any ayre at all, but shall be all insipid, tastelesse, savourlesse dust; for a while, all wormes, and after a while, not so much as wormes, sordid, senselesse, namelesse dust) When I consider the past, and present, and future state of this body, in this world, I am able to conceive, able to expresse the worst that can befall it in nature, and the worst that can be inflicted upon it by man, or fortune; But the least degree of glory that God hath prepared for that body in heaven, I am not able to expresse, not able to conceive.

[*LXXX. Sermons* (22), 1640]

TO THE KING AT WHITEHALL, MAY 6th, 1627

1

THE first thing that God made, was *light;* The last thing, that he hath reserved to doe, is the manifestation of the light of his Essence in our Glorification. And for Publication of himselfe here, by the way, he hath constituted a *Church,* in a Visibility, in an eminency, *as a City upon a hill;* And in this Church, his Ordinance is Ordinance indeed; his Ordinance of preaching batters the soule, and by that breach, the Spirit enters; His Ministers are an *Earth-quake,* and shake an earthly soule; They are the *sonnes of thunder,* and scatter a cloudy conscience; They are as the fall of waters, and carry with them whole Congregations; 3000 at a Sermon, 5000 at a Sermon, a whole City, such a City as Nineveh at a Sermon; and they are as the roaring of a Lion, where the Lion of the tribe of Juda, cries down the Lion that seekes whom he may devour; that is, Orthodoxall and fundamentall truths, are established against clamorous, and vociferant innovations. Therefore what Christ tels us in the darke, he bids us speake in the light; and what he saies in our eare, he bids us preach on the house-top. Nothing is Gospell, not *Evangelium,* good message, if it be not put into a Messengers mouth, and delivered by him; nothing is conducible to his end, nor available to our salvation, except it be avowable doctrine, doctrine that may be spoke alowd, though it awake them, that sleep in their sinne, and make them the more froward, for being so awaked.

God hath made all things in a *Roundnesse,* from the round superficies of this earth, which we tread here, to the round convexity of those heavens, which (as long as they shal have

any beeing) shall be our footstool, when we come to heaven,
God hath wrapped up all things in Circles, and then a Circle
hath no *Angles;* there are no *Corners* in a Circle.

2

This whisperer wounds thee, and with a stilletta of gold, he
strangles thee with scarfes of silk, he smothers thee with the
down of Phœnixes, he stifles thee with a perfume of Ambar, he
destroys thee by praising thee, overthrows thee by exalting thee,
and undoes thee by trusting thee; By trusting thee with those
secrets that bring thee into a desperate perplexity, *Aut alium
accusare in subsidium tui,* (as the Patriarch, and Oracle of
Statesmen, *Tacitus,* says) Either to betray another, that pretends
to have trusted thee, or to perish thy selfe, for the saving of another, that plotted to betray thee. And therefore, if you can
heare a good Organ at Church, and have the musique of a domestique peace at home, peace in thy walls, peace in thy bosome,
never hearken after the musique of sphears, never hunt after the
knowledge of higher secrets, than appertaine to thee; But since
Christ hath made you *Regale Sacerdotium,* Kings and Priests, in
your proportion, *Take heed what you hear,* in derogation of either the State, or the Church.

[Fifty Sermons (27), 1649]

A SERMON OF COMMEMORATION OF
THE LADY DANVERS, LATE WIFE OF
SIR JOHN DANVERS.

JULY 1st, 1627

THE PRAYER BEFORE THE SERMON

O ETERNALL, *and most* Glorious God, *who sometimes in thy*
Justice, *dost* give the dead bodies of the Saints, to be meat unto
the Fowles of the Heaven, *and the* flesh of thy Saints unto the
beasts of the Earth, *so that* their bloud is shed like water, and
there is none to burie them, *Who sometimes,* sel'st thy People
for nought, *and dost* not increase thy wealth, by their price, *and
yet never leav'st us without that knowledge, That* precious in
thy sight is the death of thy Saints, *inable us, in life and death,
seriously to consider the value, the price of a* Soule. *It is pre-*

*cious, ô Lord, because thine Image is stampt, and imprinted
upon it; Precious, because the bloud of thy Sonne was paid for
it; Precious, because thy blessed Spirit, the Holy Ghost workes
upon it, and tries it, by his divers fires; And precious, because
it is enter'd into thy Revenue, and made a part of thy Treasure.
Suffer us not therefore, ô Lord, so to undervalue our selves, nay,
so to impoverish thee, as to give away those soules, thy soules,
thy deare and precious soules, for nothing, and all the world is
nothing, if the Soule must be given for it. We know, ô Lord, that
our Rent, due to thee, is our Soule; and the day of our death, is
the day, and our Death-bed the place, where this Rent is to bee
paid. And wee know too, that hee that hath sold his soule before,
for unjust gaine, or given away his soule before, in the society
and fellowship of sinne, or lent away his soule, for a time, by a
lukewarmnesse, and temporizing, to the dishonor of thy name, to
the weaking of thy cause, to the discouraging of thy Servants,
he comes to that day, and to that place, his Death, and Death-
bed, without any Rent in his hand, without any soule, to this
purpose, to surrender it unto thee. Let therefore ô Lord, the
same hand which is to receive them then, preserve these soules
till then; Let that mouth, that breath'd them into us, at first,
breath alwaies upon them, whilst they are in us, and sucke them
into it selfe, when they depart from us. Preserve our soules ô
Lord, because they belong to thee; and preserve our bodies,
because they belong to those soules. Thou alone, dost steere our
Boat, through all our Voyage, but hast a more especiall care of
it, a more watchfull eye upon it, when it comes to a narrow currant, or to a dangerous fall of waters. Thou hast a care of the
preservation of those bodies, in all the waies of our life; But in
the Straights of Death, open thine eyes wider, and enlarge thy
providence towards us, so farre, that no Fever in the body, may
shake the soule, no Apoplexie in the body, dampe or benumbe
the soule, nor any paine, or agonie of the body, presage future torments to the soule. But so make thou our bed in all our
sicknesse, that being us'd to thy hand, wee may be content with
any bed of thy making; Whether thou bee pleas'd to change our
feathers into flockes, by withdrawing the conveniences of this
life, or to change our flockes into dust, even the dust of the
Grave, by withdrawing us out of this life. And though thou
divide man and wife, mother and child, friend and friend, by
the hand of Death, yet stay them that stay, and send them away
that goe, with this consolation, that though we part at divers
daies, and by divers waies, here, yet wee shall all meet at one*

place, and at one day, a day that no night shall determine, the day of the glorious Resurrection. *Hasten that day, ô* Lord, *for their sakes, that beg it at thy hands, from under the* Altar *in* Heaven; *Hasten it for our sakes that groane under the manifold incombrances of these* mortall bodies; *Hasten it for her sake, whom wee have lately laid downe, in this thy* holy ground; *And hasten it for thy* Son Christ Jesus *sake, to whom then, and not till then, all things shall bee absolutely* subdu'd. *Seale to our* soules *now an assurance of thy gracious purpose towards us in that day, by accepting this daies service, at our hands. Accept our humble thankes, for all thy benefits, spirituall, and temporall, already bestowed upon us, and accept our humble prayers for the continuance and enlargement of them. Continue, and enlarge them, ô* God *upon thine* universall Church, *dispersed, etc.*

1

First then, to shake the constancy of a Christian, there will alwaies be *Scorners, Jesters, Scoffers,* and *Mockers at Religion;* The *Period* and Consummation of the *Christian Religion,* the *Judgement day,* the *second comming of Christ,* will alwaies be subject to *scornes.* And many times a *scorne* cuts deeper than a *sword. Lucian* wounded *Religion* more by making *Jests* at it, than *Arius,* or *Pelagius,* or *Nestorious,* with making *Arguments* against it. For, against those profest *Heretikes,* and against their studied *Arguments,* which might seeme to have some weight, it well beseem'd those grave and Reverend *Fathers* of the *Church,* to call their *Councels,* and to take into their serious consideration those *Arguments,* and solemnly to conclude, and determine, and decree in the point. But it would ill have become those reverend persons, to have cal'd their Councels, or taken into their so serious considerations, *Epigrams,* and *Satyres,* and *Libells,* and *scurrill* and *scornfull jests,* against any point of *Religion; Scornes* and *Jests* are easilier apprehended, and understood by vulgar and ordinary capacities, than *Arguments* are; and then, learned men are not so earnest, nor so diligent to overthrow, and confute a *Jest,* or *Scorne,* as they are, an Argument; and so they passe more uncontrol'd, and prevaile further, and live longer, than *Arguments* doe. It is the height of *Jobs* complaint, that contemptible persons made *Jests* upon him. And it is the depth of *Samsons* calamity, that when the *Philistins hearts were merry,* then they cald for *Samson, to make them*

sport. So to the *Israelites* in *Babylon,* when they were in that
heavinesse, that every breath they breath'd was a *sigh,* their enemies cal'd, *to sing them a song.* And so they proceeded with
him, who fulfil'd in himselfe alone, all *Types,* and *Images,* and
Prophesies of sorrowes, who was (as the *Prophet* calls him) *Vir
dolorum,* A man compos'd, and elemented of sorrowes, our *Lord*
and *Saviour Christ Jesus;* For, *They platted a crowne of thornes
upon his head, and they put a reed into his hand, and they
bowed the knee before him, and mockt him.* Truly, the conniv-
ing at several *Religions,* (as dangerous as it is) is not so *dishonourable* to *God,* as the suffering of *Jesters* at *Religion:*
That may induce *heresie;* but this does establish *Atheisme.*
And as that is the publike mischiefe, so, for the private, there
lies much danger in this, that hee that gives himselfe the liberty,
of *jesting* at *Religion,* shall finde it hard, to take up at last; as,
when *Julian* the *Apostate* had received his Deathes-wound, and
could not chuse but confesse, that that wound came from the
hand, and power of *Christ,* yet he confest it, in a Phrase of
Scorne, Vicisti Galilæe, The day is thine, O Galilean, and no
more; It is not, Thou hast accomplish't thy purpose, *O my God,
nor O my Maker, nor O my Redeemer,* but, in a stile of contempt, *Vicisti Galilæe,* and no more.

2

It is a fearefull thing to fall into the hands of the living God, if
I doe but fall into his hands, in a fever in my bed, or in a tempest
at Sea, or in a discontent at home; But, *to fall into the hands of
the living God,* so, as that, that *living God,* enters into *Judgement,*
with mee, and passes a finall, and irrevocable Judgement upon
mee, this is a Consternation of all my spirits, an Extermination
of all my succours. I consider, what *God* did with one word;
with one *Fiat* he made all; And, I know, he can doe as much
with another word; With one *Pereat,* he can destroy all; As hee
spake, and it was done, he commanded and all stood fast; so he
can *speak,* and all shall bee *undone; command,* and all shall *fall
in peeces.* I consider, that I may bee surpriz'd by *that day,* the
day of Judgement. Here Saint *Peter* saies, *The day of the Lord
wil come as a Thiefe.* And Saint *Paul* saies, we cannot be ignorant of it, *Your selves know perfectly, that the day of the Lord
so commeth as a Thiefe.* And, as the *Judgement* it selfe, so the
Judge himselfe saies of himselfe, *I will come upon thee as a
Thiefe.* He saies, *he will,* and he *does* it. For it is not, *Ecce*

veniam, but *Ecce venio, Behold I doe come upon thee as a Thiefe;* There, the *future,* which might imply a *dilatorinesse,* is reduc'd to an infallible *present;* It is so sure, that he *will* doe it, that he is said, to *have* done it already. I consider, *hee will come as a Thiefe,* and then, *as a Thiefe in the night;* And I doe not only not know *when* that night shall be, (For, himselfe, as he is the Son of man, knowes not that) but I doe not only not know *what* night, that is, *which* night, but not *what* night, that is, *what kinde* of night he meanes. It is said so often, so often repeated, that *he will come as a Thiefe in the night,* as that hee may meane all kinde of *nights.* In my night of *Ignorance* hee may come; and hee may come in my night of *Wantonnesse;* In my night of inordinate and sinfull *melancholy,* and *suspicion* of his *mercy,* hee may come; and he may come in the night of so *stupid,* or so *raging* a *sicknesse,* as that he shall not *come* by *comming;* Not come so, as that I shall receive him in the *absolution* of his *Minister,* or receive him in the participation of his *body* and his *bloud* in the *Sacrament.* So hee may come upon mee, as *such a Thiefe,* in *such a night;* nay, when all these nights of *Ignorance,* of *Wantonnesse,* of *Desperation,* of *Sicknesse,* of *Stupiditie,* of *Rage,* may bee upon mee all at once. I consider, that the *Holy Ghost* meant to make a deepe impression of a great *terror* in me, when he came to that expression, *That the Heavens should passe away,* Cum stridore, *with a great noise, and the Elements melt with fervent heat, and the earth, and the workes that are therein,* shall be burnt up; And when he adds in *Esay, The Lord will come with fire, and with his Chariots, like a whirlewind, to render his anger, with fury; for by fire, and by his sword will the Lord plead with all flesh.* So when hee proceeds in *Joel, a day of darknesse, and gloominesse; and yet a fire devoureth before them, and a flame burneth behind them.* And so in *Daniel* also, *His Throne a fiery flame, and his wheeles a burning fire, and a fiery streame issuing from him.* I consider too, that with this *streame* of *fire,* from him, there shall bee a *streame,* a deluge, a floud of teares, from us; and all that *floud,* and *deluge* of teares, shall not put out one coale, nor quench one sparke of that fire. *Behold, hee commeth with clouds, and every eye shall see him;* And, *plangent omnes, All the kindreds of the earth shall waile and lament,* and weepe and howle *because of him.* I consider, that I shall *looke* upon him then, and see all my *Sinnes, Substance,* and *Circumstance* of sin, *Waight,* and *measure* of sinne, *hainousnesse,* and *continuance* of sinne, all my sinnes imprinted in *his* wounds; and how shall I bee affected then, confounded then to see him so mangled with my sinnes? But then I consider againe, that I shall looke upon him againe, and not see all my sinnes in his wounds; My *forgotten* sinnes, mine *unconsidered, unconfest, unrepented* sinnes, I shall not see there; And how shall I bee affected then, when I shall stand in *Judgement,* under the guilt-inesse of some sins, not buried in the wounds, not drown'd in the bloud of my *Saviour? Many,* and *many,* and *very many, infinite,* and *infinitely infinite,* are the *terrours* of that day.

3

For, if we consider *God* in the *present,* to day, now, *God* hath had as long a *forenoone,* as he shall have an *afternoone; God* hath beene *God,* as many millions of millions of generations, already, as hee shall be hereafter; but if we consider *man* in the *present,* to day, now, how short a *forenoone* hath any man had; if 60. if 80. yeeres, yet, *few and evill have his daies beene.* Nay if we take man *collectively, entirely, altogether,* all mankind, how short a *forenoone* hath man had? It is not yet 6000. yeeres, since man had his first *being.* But if we consider him in his *Afternoone,* in his *future state,* in his *life* after *death,* if every minute of his 6000. yeeres, were multipli'd by so many millions of *Ages,* all would amount to nothing, meerely nothing, in respect of that *Eternity,* which hee is to dwell in. We can expresse mans *Afternoone,* his future Perpetuity, his Everlasting-nesse, but one way; But it is a faire way, a noble way; This; That how late a *Beginning* soever *God* gave Man, Man shall no more see an *end,* no more die, than *God* himselfe, that gave him life.

4

But as it is said of old *Cosmographers,* that when they had said all that they knew of a *Countrey,* and yet much more was to be said, they said that the rest of those countries were possest with *Giants,* or *Witches,* or *Spirits,* or *Wilde beasts,* so that they could pierce no farther into that Countrey, so when wee have travell'd as farre as wee can, with safetie, that is, as *farre* as *Ancient,* or *Moderne Expositors* lead us, in the *discoverie* of these *new Heavens,* and *new Earth,* yet wee must say at last, that it is a *Countrey* inhabited with *Angells,* and *Arch-angells,* with *Cherubins,* and *Seraphins,* and that wee can looke no far-

ther into it, with these eyes. Where it is *locally,* wee enquire
not; We rest in this, that it is the habitation prepar'd for the
blessed *Saints* of *God; Heavens,* where the *Moone* is more
glorious than our *Sunne,* and the *Sunne* as glorious as *Hee* that
made it; For it is he himselfe, the *Sonne* of *God,* the *Sunne* of
glorie. A new Earth, where all their *waters* are *milke,* and all
their *milke, honey;* where all their *grasse* is *corne,* and all
their *corne, Manna;* where all their *glebe,* all their *clods* of
earth are *gold,* and all their *gold* of innumerable *carats;* Where
all their *minutes* are *ages,* and all their *ages, Eternity;* Where
every thing, is every minute, in the highest exaltation, as good
as it can be, and yet super-exalted, and infinitely multiplied, by
every minutes addition; every minute, *infinitely* better, than
ever it was before. Of these *new heavens,* and this *new earth*
we must say at last, that wee can say nothing; For, the *eye of
Man hath not seene, nor eare heard, nor heart conceiv'd, the
State of this place.* We limit, and determine our consideration
with that *Horizon,* with which the *Holy Ghost* hath limited us,
that it is that *new Heavens,* and *new Earth, wherein dwelleth
Righteousnesse.*

Here then the *Holy Ghost* intends the same *new Heavens,*
and *new Earth,* which he does in the *Apocalyps,* and describes
there, by another name, the *new Jerusalem.* But here, the *Holy
Ghost* does not proceed, as there, to enamour us of the place, by
a promise of improvement of those things, which wee *have,* and
love here; but by a promise of that, which here wee have not at
all. There, and elsewhere, the *holy Ghost* applies himselfe, to
the natural affections of men. To those that are affected with
riches, he saies, that *that new City shall be all of gold,* and in
the *foundations, all manner of precious stones;* To those that are
affected with *beauty,* hee promises an everlasting association,
with that beautifull Couple, that faire Paire, which spend their
time, in that contemplation, and that protestation, *Ecce tu
pulchra dilecta mea; Ecce tu Pulcher; Behold thou art faire, my
Beloved,* saies he; and then, she replies, *Behold thou art faire
too;* noting the mutuall complacencie betweene *Christ* and his
Church there. To those which delight in *Musicke,* hee promises
continuall *singing,* and every minute, a *new song;* To those,
whose thoughts are exerciz'd upon *Honour,* and *Titles, Civill,* or
Ecclesiasticall, hee promises *Priesthood,* and if that be not honour enough, a *Royall Priesthood;* And to those, who looke after
military honor, Triumph after their *victory,* in the *Militant
Church;* And to those, that are carried with sumptuous, and

magnifique *feasts,* a *Mariage supper* of the *Lambe,* where, not onely all the rarities of the whole world, but the whole world it selfe shall be serv'd in; The whole world shall bee brought to that *fire,* and serv'd at that *Table.* But here, the *holy Ghost* proceeds not that way, by improvement of things, which wee *have,* and *love* here; *riches,* or *beauty,* or *musicke,* or *honour,* or *feasts;* but by an everlasting possession of that, which wee hunger, and thirst, and pant after, here, and cannot compasse, that is, *Justice,* or *Righteousnesse;* for, both those, our present word denotes, and both those wee want here, and shall have both, for ever, in these *new Heavens,* and *new Earth.*

5

And for her, some sicknesses, in the declination of her yeeres, had opened her to an overflowing of *Melancholie;* Not that she ever lay under that *water,* but yet, had sometimes, some high Tides of it; and, though this distemper would sometimes cast a cloud, and some halfe damps upon her naturall cheerfulnesse, and sociablenesse, and sometimes induce darke, and sad apprehensions, *Neverthelesse,* who ever heard, or saw in her, any such effect of *Melancholy* as to murmure, or repine, or dispute upon any of *Gods* proceedings, or to lodge a Jelousie, or Suspition of his mercy, and goodnesse towards her, and all hers? The *Wit* of our time is *Prophanesse; Neverthelesse,* shee, that lov'd *that,* hated *this;* Occasionall *Melancholy* had taken some hold in her; *Neverthelesse,* that never Ecclipst, never interrupted her cheerfull confidence, and assurance in *God.*

Our second word denotes the *person; We, Neverthelesse We;* And, here in this consideration, *Neverthelesse shee.* This may seeme to promise some picture, some Character of her *person.* But, shee was no stranger to them that heare me now; nor scarce to any that may heare of this hereafter, which you heare now, and therefore, much needes not, to that purpose. Yet, to that purpose, of her *person,* and *personall circumstances,* thus much I may *remember* some, and *informe* others, That from that *Worthy family,* whence she had her originall extraction, and birth, she suckt that love of *hospitality,* (*hospitality,* which hath celebrated that *family,* in many Generations, successively) which dwelt in her, to her end. But in that *ground,* her Fathers *family,* shee grew not many yeeres. Transplanted young from thence, by mariage, into another *family* of *Honour,* as a flower that doubles and multiplies by transplantation, she multiplied into *ten Children; Job's* number; and *Job's* distribution, (as shee, her selfe would very often remember) *seven sonnes,* and *three daughters.* And, in this ground, shee grew not many yeeres more, than were necessary, for the producing of so many plants. And being then left to chuse her owne ground in her *Widow-hood,* having at home establisht, and increast the estate, with a faire, and noble Addition, proposing to her selfe, as her principall care, the education of her *children,* to advance that, shee came with them, and dwelt with them, in the *Universitie;* and recompenc't to them, the losse of a *Father,* in giving them *two mothers;* her owne personal care, and the advantage of that place; where shee contracted a friendship, with divers reverend persons, of eminency, and estimation there; which continued to their ends. And as this was her greatest *businesse,* so she made this state, a large *Period;* for in this state of *widowhood,* shee continued *twelve yeeres.* And then, returning to a *second mariage,* that *second mariage* turnes us to the consideration of another *personall circumstance;* that is, the *naturall endowments of her person;* Which were such, as that, (though her *vertues* were his principall *object*) yet, even these her *personall,* and *natural endowments,* had their part, in drawing, and fixing the affections of such a person, as by his *birth,* and *youth,* and *interest in great favours in Court,* and *legall proximity* to great possessions in the world, might justly have promist him acceptance, in what *family* soever, or upon what *person* soever, hee had directed, and plac't his Affections. He plac't them here; neither *diverted* then, nor *repented* since. For, as the well tuning of an *Instrument,* makes *higher* and *lower* strings, of one sound, so the inequality of their yeeres, was thus reduc't to an evennesse, that shee had a *cheerfulnesse,* agreeable to his *youth,* and he a *sober staidnesse,* conformable to her *more yeeres.* So that, I would not consider her, at so much more than *forty,* nor him, at so much lesse than *thirty,* at that time, but, as their *persons* were made *one,* and their *fortunes* made one, by *mariage,* so I would put their *yeeres* into *one number,* and finding a *sixty* betweene them, thinke them *thirty* a peece; for, as twins of one houre, they liv'd. *God,* who joyn'd them, then, having also separated them now, may make their *yeres* even, this other way too; by giving him, as many yeeres after her going out of this World, as he had given her, before his comming into it; and then, as many more, as *God* may receive *Glory,* and the World, *Benefit* by that Addition; That so, as at their first meeting, she was, at their last meeting, he may bee the *elder person.*

To this consideration of her *person* then, belongs this, that *God* gave her such a *comelinesse*, as, though shee were not *proud* of it, yet she was so content with it, as not to goe about to mend it, by any *Art*. And for her *Attire*, (which is another *personall circumstance*) it was never *sumptuous*, never *sordid;* But alwayes agreeable to her *quality*, and agreeable to her *company;* Such as shee might, and such, as others, such as shee was, did weare. For, in such things of *indifferency* in themselves, many times, a *singularity* may be a little worse, than a fellowship in that, which is not altogether so good. It may be *worse*, nay, it may be a *worse pride*, to weare worse things, than others doe. Her *rule* was *mediocrity*.

And, as to the consideration of the *house*, belongs the consideration of the *furniture* too, so, in these *personall circumstances*, we consider her *fortune*, her *estate*. Which was in a faire, and noble proportion, deriv'd from her *first husband*, and fairely, and nobly dispenc'd, by her selfe, with the allowance of her *second*. In which shee was one of *Gods* true *Stewards*, and *Almoners* too. There are dispositions, which had rather *give presents*, than *pay debts;* and rather doe good to *strangers*, than to those, that are *neerer* to them. But *shee* always thought the care of her family, a *debt*, and upon that, for the *provision*, for the *order*, for the *proportions*, in a good largenesse, shee plac't her first thoughts, of that kinde. For, for our *families*, we are *Gods Stewards;* For those without, we are his *Almoners*. In which office, shee gave not at some *great dayes*, or some solemne goings abroad, but, as *Gods true Almoners*, the *Sunne*, and *Moone*, that passe on, in a continuall doing of good, as shee receiv'd her *daily bread* from God, so *daily*, she distributed, and imparted it, to others. In which office, though she never turn'd her face from those, who in a strict inquisition, might be call'd idle, and vagrant Beggers, yet shee ever look't first, upon them, who *labour'd*, and whose *labours* could not overcome the *difficulties*, nor bring in the *necessities* of this life; and to the *sweat* of *their browes*, shee contributed, even her *wine*, and her *oyle*, and any thing that was, and any thing, that might be, if it were not, prepar'd for her owne table. And as her house was a *Court*, in the conversation of the best, and an *Almeshouse*, in feeding the poore, so was it also an *Hospitall*, in ministring releefe to the *sicke*. And truly, the love of doing good in this kind, of *ministring to the sicke*, was the *hony*, that was spread over all her bread; the *Aire*, the *Perfume*, that breath'd over all her house; The disposition that dwelt in those her children, and

those her *kindred*, which dwelt with her, so bending this way,
that the *studies* and *knowledge* of *one*, the *hand* of another, and
purse of all, and a *joynt-facility*, and *opennesse*, and *accessible-nesse* to persons of the meanest quality, concur'd in this blessed
Act of *Charity*, to *minister releefe to the sicke*. Of which, my
selfe, who, at that time, had the favour to bee admitted into
that *family*, can, and must testifie this, that when the late heavy
visitation fell hotly upon this *Towne*, when every doore was
shut up, and, lest *Death* should enter into the house, every house
was made a *Sepulchre* of them that were in it, then, then, in
that time of *infection*, divers persons visited with that *infection*,
had their releefe, and releefe *appliable to that very infection*,
from this house.

Now when I have said thus much (rather thus little) of her
person, as of a *house*, That the *ground* upon which it was built,
was the *family* where she was *borne*, and then, where she was
married, and then, the time of her *widowhood*; and lastly, her
last mariage, And that the *house* it selfe, was those faire *bodily
endowments*, which *God* had bestow'd upon her, And the *furniture* of that *house*, the *fortune*, and the *use* of that *fortune*, of
which *God* had made her *Steward* and *Almoner*, when I shall
also have said, that the *Inhabitants* of this *house*, (rather the
servants, for they did but wait upon *Religion* in her) were those
married couples, of *morall vertues*, *Conversation* married with a
Retirednesse, *Facility* married with a *Reservednesse*, *Alacrity*
married with a *Thoughtfulnesse*, and *Largenesse* married with a
Providence, I may have leave to depart from this consideration
of her *person*, and *personall circumstances*, lest by insisting
longer upon them, I should seeme to pretend, to say all the
good, that might bee said of her; But that's not in my *purpose;*
yet, onely therefore, because it is not in my *power;* For I would
doe her all *right*, and all you that good, if I could, to say all.
But, I haste to an end, in consideration of some things, that appertaine more expresly to me, than these *personall*, or *civill*, or
morall things doe.

In those, the next is, the *Secundum promissa*, That shee govern'd her selfe, *according to his promises;* his promises, laid
downe in his *Scriptures*. For, as the *rule* of all her *civill Actions*, was *Religion*, so, the *rule* of her *Religion*, was the *Scripture;* And, her *rule*, for her particular understanding of the
Scripture, was the *Church*. Shee never diverted towards the
Papist, in undervaluing the *Scripture;* nor towards the *Separatist*,
in undervaluing the *Church*. But in the *doctrine*, and *discipline*

of that *Church,* in which, *God* seal'd her, to himselfe, in *Baptisme,* shee brought up her children, she assisted her family, she dedicated her soule to *God* in her life, and surrendered it to him in her death; And, in that forme of *Common Prayer,* which is ordain'd by that *Church,* and to which shee had accustom'd her selfe, with her family, twice every day, she joyn'd with that company, which was about her *death-bed,* in answering to every part thereof, which the Congregation is directed to answer to, with a *cleere understanding,* with a *constant memory,* with a *distinct voyce,* not two houres before she died.

According to this promise, that is, the will of *God* manifested in the *Scriptures,* She *expected;* She expected this, that she hath received; *Gods Physicke,* and *Gods Musicke;* a *Christianly death.* For, *death,* in the *old Testament* was a *Commination;* but in the *new Testament, death* is a *Promise;* When there was a *Superdying,* a *death* upon the *death,* a *Morte* upon the *Morieris,* a *Spirituall* death after the *bodily,* then wee died *according to Gods threatning;* Now, when by the *Gospell,* that *second death* is taken off, though wee die still, yet we die *according to his Promise;* That's a part of his *mercy,* and his *Promise,* which his *Apostle* gives us from him, That wee shall *all bee changed:* For, after that *promise,* that *change,* follows that triumphant *Acclamation, O death where is thy sting, O grave where is thy victory?* Consider us fallen in *Adam,* and wee are miserable, that wee must die; But consider us restor'd, and redintegrated in *Christ,* wee were more miserable if wee might not die; Wee lost the *earthly Paradise* by death then; but wee get not *Heaven,* but by *death,* now. This shee expected till it came, and embrac't it when it came. How may we thinke, shee was joy'd to see that face, that *Angels* delight to looke upon, the face of her *Saviour,* that did not abhor the face of his fearfullest *Messenger,* Death? Shee shew'd no feare of his face, in any change of her owne; but died without any change of *countenance,* or *posture;* without any *strugling,* any *disorder;* but her *Death-bed* was as quiet, as her *Grave.* To another *Magdalen, Christ* said upon earth, *Touch me not, for I am not ascended.* Being ascended now, to his glory, and she being gone up to him, after shee had awaited his leisure, so many yeeres, as that more, would soone have growne to bee *vexation,* and *sorrow,* as her last words here, were, *I submit my will to the will of God;* so wee doubt not, but the first word which she heard there, was that *Euge,* from her *Saviour, Well done good and faithfull servant; enter into thy masters joy.*

Shee expected that; dissolution of body, and soule; and rest in both, from the incumbrances, and tentations of this world. But yet, shee is in *expectation* still; Still a *Reversionarie;* And a *Reversionarie* upon a long life; The whole world must die, before she come to a *possession* of this *Reversion;* which is a *Glorified body in the Resurrection.* In which *expectation,* she returns to her former *charity;* shee will not have that, till *all wee* shall have it, as well as shee; She eat not her morsels alone, in her life, (as *Job* speakes); Shee lookes not for the *glory* of the *Resurrection* alone, after her death. But when *all wee,* shall have beene mellow'd in the earth, many yeeres, or chang'd in the *Aire,* in the twinkling of an eye, (*God* knowes which) That *body* upon which you tread now, That *body* which now, whilst I speake, is mouldring, and crumbling into lesse, and lesse dust, and so hath some *motion,* though no *life,* That *body,* which was the *Tabernacle* of a *holy Soule,* and a *Temple* of the *holy Ghost,* That *body* that was eyes to the blinde, and hands, and feet to the lame, whilst it liv'd, and being dead, is so still, by having beene so *lively* an example, to teach others, to be so, That *body* at last, shall have her last expectation satisfied, and dwell *bodily,* with that *Righteousnesse,* in these *new Heavens,* and *new Earth,* for *ever,* and *ever,* and *ever,* and *infinite,* and *super infinite evers.* Wee end all, with the *valediction* of the *Spouse* to *Christ: His left hand is under my head, and his right embraces mee,* was the *Spouses valediction,* and *goodnight* to *Christ* then, when she laide her selfe downe to sleepe in the strength of his *Mandrakes,* and in the power of his *Spices,* as it is exprest there; that is, in the *influence* of his *mercies.* Beloved, every good *Soule* is the *Spouse* of *Christ.* And this good *Soule,* being thus laid downe to sleepe in his peace, *His left hand under her head,* gathering, and composing, and preserving her *dust,* for *future Glory, His right hand embracing her,* assuming, and establishing her *soule* in present *Glory,* in his *name,* and in her *behalfe,* I say that, to *all you,* which *Christ* sayes there, in the behalfe of that *Spouse, Adjuro vos, I adjure you, I charge you, O daughters of Jerusalem, that yee wake her not, till she please.* The words are directed to the *daughters,* rather than to the *sons* of *Jerusalem,* because for the most part, the aspersions that women receive, either in *Morall* or *Religious* actions, proceed from women themselves. Therfore, *Adjuro vos,* I charge you, O ye daughters of *Jerusalem,* wake her not. Wake her not, with any *halfe calumnies,* with any *whisperings;* But if you wil wake her, wake her, and keepe her awake with an active imitation, of her

Morall, and her *Holy vertues.* That so her *example* working
upon you, and the number of *Gods Saints,* being, the sooner, by
this blessed *example,* fulfil'd, wee may all meet, and meet
quickly in that *kingdome,* which *hers,* and *our Saviour,* hath
purchac't for us all, with the inestimable price of his incorruptible bloud.

[Published separately, 1627]

AT THE EARL OF BRIDGEWATERS HOUSE IN LONDON AT THE MARRIAGE OF HIS DAUGHTER. NOV. 19th, 1627

THERE are so many evidences of the immortality of the soule,
even to a naturall mans *reason,* that it required not an Article
of the Creed, to fix this notion of the Immortality of the soule.
But the Resurrection of the *Body* is discernible by no other
light, but that of *Faith,* nor could be fixed by any lesse assurance
than an *Article* of the *Creed.* Where be all the splinters of that
Bone, which a shot hath shivered and scattered in the Ayre?
Where be all the Atoms of that flesh, which a *Corrasive* hath eat
away, or a *Consumption* hath breath'd, and exhal'd away from
our arms, and other Limbs? In what wrinkle, in what furrow, in
what bowel of the earth, ly all the graines of the ashes of a body
burnt a thousand years since? In what corner, in what ventricle
of the sea, lies all the jelly of a Body drowned in the *generall
flood?* What cohaerence, what sympathy, what dependence main-
taines any relation, any correspondence, between that arm that
was lost in Europe, and that legge that was lost in Afrique or
Asia, scores of yeers between? One humour of our dead body
produces worms, and those worms suck and exhaust all other
humour, and then all dies, and all dries, and molders into dust,
and that dust is blowen into the River, and that puddled water
tumbled into the sea, and that ebs and flows in infinite revolutions, and still, still God knows in what *Cabinet* every *seed-
Pearle* lies, in what part of the world every graine of every mans
dust lies; and, *sibilat populum suum,* (as his Prophet speaks in
another case) he whispers, he hisses, he beckens for the bodies
of his Saints, and in the twinckling of an eye, that body that
was scattered over all the elements, is sate down at the right
hand of God, in a glorious resurrection. A Dropsie hath extended me to an enormous corpulency, and unwieldinesse; a
Consumption hath attenuated me to a feeble macilency and

leannesse, and God raises me a body, such as it should have
been, if these infirmities had not interven'd and deformed it.

[*Fifty Sermons* (1), 1649]

ST. PAUL'S. "THE FIFTH OF MY PREBEND SERMONS UPON MY FIVE PSALMES." [1627]

1

WHEN I look upon God, as I am bid to doe in this Text, in
those terrible Judgements, which he hath executed upon some
men, and see that there is nothing between mee and the same
Judgement, (for I have sinned the same sinnes, and God is the
same God) I am not able of my selfe to dye that glasse, that
spectacle, thorow which I looke upon this God, in what colour I
will; whether this glasse shall be black, through my despaire,
and so I shall see God in the cloud of my sinnes, or red in the
blood of Christ Jesus, and I shall see God in a Bath of the blood
of his Sonne, whether I shall see God as a Dove with an Olive
branch, (peace to my soule) or as an Eagle, a vulture to prey,
and to prey everlastingly upon mee, whether in the deepe
floods of Tribulation, spirituall or temporall, I shall see God as
an Arke to take mee in, or as a Whale to swallow mee; and if
his Whale doe swallow mee, (the Tribulation devour me)
whether his purpose bee to restore mee, or to consume me, I, I
of my selfe cannot tell. I cannot look upon God, in what line I
will, nor take hold of God, by what handle I will; Hee is a terrible God, I take him so; And then I cannot discontinue, I cannot breake off this terriblenesse, and say, Hee hath beene terrible
to that man, and there is an end of his terror; it reaches not to
me. Why not to me? In me there is no merit, nor shadow of
merit; In God there is no change, nor shadow of change. I am
the same sinner, he is the same God; still the same desperate
sinner, still the same terrible God.

2

The true feare of God is true wisedome. It is true Joy; *Rejoice in trembling*, saith *David;* There is no rejoycing without
this feare; there is no Riches without it; *Reverentia Jehovæ*, The
feare of the Lord is his treasure, and that is the best treasure.
Thus farre we are to goe; *Let us serve God with reverence.
and godly feare*. (godly feare is but a Reverence, it is not a

Jealousie, a suspition of God.) And let us doe it upon the reason that followes in the same place, *For our God is a consuming fire,* There is all his terriblenesse; he is *a consuming fire*
to his enemies, but he is *our God;* and God is love: And
therefore to conceive a cruell God, a God that hated us, even to
damnation, before we were, (as some, who have departed from
the sense and modesty of the Ancients, have adventured to
say) or to conceive a God so cruell, as that at our death, or in
our way, he will afford us no assurance, that hee is ours, and we
his, but let us live and die in anxiety and torture of conscience,
in jealousie and suspition of his good purpose towards us in
the salvation of our soules, (as those of the Romane Heresie
teach) to conceive such a God as from all eternity meant to
damne me, or such a God as would never make me know, and
be sure that I should bee saved, this is not to professe God to
be terrible in his works; For, his Actions are his works, and his
Scriptures are his works, and God hath never done, or said any
thing to induce so terrible an opinion of him.

                                   [*LXXX. Sermons* (69), 1640]

ST. PAUL'S. CHRISTMAS DAY. 1627

MAN is but earth; Tis true; but earth is the center. That man
who dwels upon himself, who is alwaies conversant in himself,
rests in his true center. Man is a celestial creature too, a heavenly creature; and that man that dwels upon himselfe, that hath
his conversation in himselfe, hath his conversation in heaven. If
you weigh any thing in a scale, the greater it is, the lower it
sinkes; as you grow greater and greater in the eyes of the world,
sinke lower and lower in your owne. If thou ask thy self *Quis
ego,* what am I? and beest able to answer thy selfe, why now I
am a man of title, of honour, of place, of power, of possessions,
a man fit for a Chronicle, a man considerable in the Heralds
Office, goe to the Heralds Office, the spheare and element of
Honour, and thou shalt finde those men as busie there, about
the consideration of Funerals, as about the consideration of Crea-
tions; thou shalt finde that office to be as well the Grave, as the
Cradle of Honour; And thou shalt finde in that Office as many
Records of attainted families, and escheated families, and em-
poverished and forgotten, and obliterate families, as of families
newly erected and presently celebrated. In what heighth soever,
any of you that sit here, stand at home, there is some other in

some higher station than yours, that weighs you downe: And he
that stands in the highest of subordinate heighths, nay in the
highest supreme heighth in this world, is weighed downe, by
that, which is nothing; for what is any Monarch to the whole
world? and the whole world is but that; but what? but nothing.

[*LXXX. Sermons* (5), 1640]

PREACHED AT WHITEHALL. FEB. 29, 1627/8

1

HE THAT will dy the Christ upon Good-Friday, must hear his
own bell toll all Lent; he that will be partaker of his passion
at last, must conform himself to his discipline of prayer and
fasting before. Is there any man, that in his chamber hears a
bell toll for another man, and does not kneel down to pray for
that dying man? and then when his charity breaths out upon another man, does he not also reflect upon himself, and dispose
himself as if he were in the state of that dying man? We begin
to hear Christs bell toll now, and is not our bell in the chime?
We must be in his grave, before we come to his resurrection.
and we must be in his death-bed before we come to his grave:
we must do as he did, fast and pray, before we can say as he
said, that *In manus tuas*, Into thy hands O Lord I commend my
Spirit. You would not go into a Medicinal Bath without some
preparatives; presume not upon that Bath, the blood of Christ
Jesus, in the Sacrament then, without preparatives neither.
Neither say to your selves, we shall have preparatives enough,
warnings enough, many more Sermons before it come to that,
and so it is too soon yet; you are not sure you shall have more;
not sure you shall have all this; not sure you shall be affected
with any. If you be, when you are, remember that as in that
good Custome in these Cities, you hear cheerful street musick
in the winter mornings, but yet there was a sad and doleful bell-
man, that wak'd you, and call'd upon you two or three hours before that musick came; so for all that blessed musick which
the servants of God shall present to you in this place, it may be
of use, that a poor bell-man wak'd you before, and though but
by his noyse, prepared you for their musick.

2

Here I shall only present to you two Pictures, two pictures in
little: two pictures of dying men; and every man is like one of

these, and may know himself by it; he that dies in the Bath of a peaceable, and he that dies upon the wrack of a distracted conscience. When the devil imprints in a man, a *mortuum me esse non curo*, I care not though I were dead, it were but a candle blown out, and there were an end of it all, where the Devil imprints that imagination: God will imprint an *Emori nolo*, a loathness to die, and fearful apprehension at his transmigration: As God expresses the bitterness of death, in an ingemination, *morte morietur*, in a conduplication of deaths, he shall die, and die, die twice over; So *ægrotando ægrotabit*, in sicknesse he shall be sick, twice sick, body-sick and soul-sick too, sense-sick and conscience-sick together; when, as the sinnes of his body have cast sicknesses and death upon his Soule, so the inordinate sadnesse of his Soule, shall aggravate and actuate the sicknesse of his body. His Physitian ministers, and wonders it works not; He imputes that to flegme, and ministers against that, and wonders again that it works not: He goes over all the humors, and all his Medicines, and nothing works, for there lies at his Patients heart a dampe that hinders the concurrence of all his faculties, to the intention of the Physitian, or the virtue of the Physick. Loose not, O blessed Apostle, thy question upon this Man, *O Death where is thy Sting? O Grave where is thy victory?* for the sting of Death is in every limb of his body, and his very body, is a victorious grave upon his Soule: And as his Carcas and his Coffin shall lie equally insensible in his grave, so his Soule, which is but a Carcas, and his body, which is but a Coffin of that Carcas, shall be equally miserable upon his Deathbed; And Satan's Commissions upon him shall not be signed by Succession, as upon *Job*, first against his goods, and then his Servants, and then his children, and then himselfe; but not at all upon his life; but he shall apprehend all at once, Ruine upon himselfe and all his, ruine upon himselfe and all him, even upon his life; both his lives, the life of this, and the life of the next world too. Yet a drop would redeeme a shoure, and a Sigh now a Storme then: Yet a teare from the eye, would save the bleeding of the heart and a word from the mouth now, a roaring, or (which may be worse) a silence of consternation, of stupefaction, or obduration at that last houre. Truly, if the death of the wicked ended in Death, yet to scape that manner of death were worthy a Religious life. To see the house fall, and yet be afraid to goe out of it; To leave an injur'd world, and meet an incensed God; To see oppression and wrong in all thy professions, and to foresee ruine and wastefulnesse in all thy

Posterity; and Lands gotten by one sin in the Father, molder away by another in the Sonne; to see true figures of horror, and ly, and fancy worse; To begin to see thy sins but then, and finde every sin (at first sight) in the proportion of a Gyant, able to crush thee into despair; To see the Blood of Christ, imputed, not to thee, but to thy Sinnes; To see Christ crucified, and not crucifyed for thee, but crucified by thee; To heare this blood speake, not better things, than the blood of *Abel*, but lowder for vengeance than the blood of *Abel* did; This is his picture that hath been Nothing, that hath done nothing, that hath proposed no *Stephen*, No Law to regulate, No example to certifie his Conscience: But to him that hath done this, Death is but a Sleepe.

Many have wondred at that note of Saint *Chrysostom's,* That till Christ's time death was called death, plainly, literally death, but after Christ, death was called but sleepe; for, indeede, in the old-Testament before Christ, I thinke there is no one metaphor so often used, as Sleepe for Death, and that the Dead are said to Sleepe: Therefore wee wonder sometimes, that Saint *Chrysostome* should say so: But this may be that which that holy Father intended in that Note, that they in the old-Testament, who are said to have slept in Death, are such as then, by Faith, did apprehend, and were fixed upon Christ; such as were all the good men of the old-Testament, and so there will not bee many instances against Saint *Chrysostome's* note, That to those that die in Christ, Death is but a Sleepe; to all others, Death is Death, literally Death. Now of this dying Man, that dies in Christ, that dies the Death of the Righteous, that embraces Death as a Sleepe, must wee give you a Picture too.

There is not a minute left to do it; not a minutes sand; Is there a minutes patience? Bee pleased to remember that those Pictures which are deliver'd in a minute, from a print upon a paper, had many dayes, weeks, Moneths time for the graving of those Pictures in the Copper; So this Picture of that dying Man, that dies in Christ, that dies the death of the Righteous, that embraces Death as a Sleepe, was graving all his life; All his publique actions were the lights, and all his private the shadowes of this Picture. And when this Picture comes to the Presse, this Man to the streights and agonies of Death, thus he lies, thus he looks, this he is. His understanding and his will is all one faculty; He understands Gods purpose upon him, and he would not have God's purpose turned any other way; hee sees God will dissolve him, and he would faine be dissolved, to be with Christ;

His understanding and his will is all one faculty; His memory
and his foresight are fixt, and concentred upon one object, upon
goodnesse; Hee remembers that hee hath proceeded in the sin-
ceritie of a good Conscience in all the wayes of his calling, and
he foresees that his good name shall have the Testimony, and
his Posterity the support of the good men of this world; His
sicknesse shall be but a fomentation to supple and open his
Body for the issuing of his Soule; and his Soule shall goe forth,
not as one that gave over his house, but as one that travelled to
see and learne better Architecture, and meant to returne and
re-edifie that house, according to those better Rules: And as
those thoughts which possesse us most awake, meete us againe
when we are asleepe; So his holy-thoughts, having been alwaies
conversant upon the directing of his family, the education of his
Children, the discharge of his place, the safety of the State, the
happinesse of the King all his life; when he is faln asleepe in
Death, all his Dreames in that blessed Sleepe, all his devotions
in heaven shall be upon the same Subjects, and he shal solicite
him that sits upon the Throne, and the Lamb, God for Christ
Jesus sake, to blesse all these with his particular blessings: for,
so God giveth his beloved sleep, so as that they enjoy the next
world and assist this.

So then, the Death of the Righteous is a sleepe; first, as it
delivers them to a present rest. Now men sleepe not well fasting; Nor does a fasting Conscience, a Conscience that is not
nourish'd with a Testimony of having done well, come to this
Sleepe; but *dulcis somnus operanti,* The sleepe of a labouring
man is sweete. To him that laboureth in his calling, even this
sleepe of Death is welcome. *When thou lyest downe thou shalt
not be afraid,* saith *Salomon;* when thy Physician sayes, Sir, you
must keepe your bed, thou shalt not be afraid of that sick-bed;
And then it followes, *And thy sleepe shall be sweet unto thee;*
Thy sicknesse welcome, and thy death too; for, in those two
David seems to involve all, *I will both lay me downe in Peace,
and sleep;* imbrace patiently my death-bed and Death it selfe.

So then this death is a sleepe, as it delivers us to a present
Rest; And then, lastly, it is so also as it promises a future waiting in a glorious Resurrection. To the wicked it is far from
both: Of them God sayes, *I will make them drunke, and they
shall sleepe a perpetuall sleepe and not awake;* They shall have
no part in the *Second Resurrection.* But for them that have
slept in Christ, as Christ sayd of *Lazarus,* Lazarus *Sleepeth,
but I goe that I may wake him out of sleep,* he shall say to his fa-

ther; Let me goe that I may wake them who have slept so long
in expectation of my coming: And *Those that sleep in Jesus
Christ* (saith the Apostle) *will bring God with him;* not only
fetch them out of the dust when he comes, but bring them with
him, that is, declare that they have beene in his hands ever since
they departed out of this world. They shall awake as *Jacob* did,
and say as *Jacob* said, *Surely the Lord is in this place,* and *this
is no other but the house of God, and the gate of heaven,* And
into that gate they shall enter, and in that house they shall
dwell, where there shall be no Cloud nor Sun, no darknesse nor
dazling, but one equall light, no noyse nor silence, but one
equall musick, no fears nor hopes, but one equal possession, no
foes nor friends, but an equall communion and Identity, no ends
nor beginnings; but one equall eternity. Keepe us Lord so awake
in the duties of our Callings, that we may thus sleepe in thy
Peace, and wake in thy glory, and change that infallibility which
thou affordest us here, to an Actuall and undeterminable possession of that Kingdome which thy Sonne our Saviour Christ
Jesus hath purchased for us, with the inestimable price of his
incorruptible Blood. *Amen.*

[*XXVI. Sermons* (15), 1660]

ST. PAUL'S. EASTER DAY. APRIL 13th, 1628

1

THE whole frame of the world is the Theatre, and every creature the stage, the *medium,* the glasse in which we may see
God. *Moses made the Laver in the Tabernacle, of the looking
glasses of women:* Scarce can you imagine a vainer thing (except you will except the vaine lookers on, in that action) than
the looking glasses of women; and yet *Moses* brought the looking-glasses of women to a religious use, to shew them that came
in, the spots of dirt which they had taken by the way, that they
might wash themselves cleane before they passed any farther.

There is not so poore a creature but may be thy glasse to see
God in. The greatest flat glasse that can be made, cannot represent any thing greater than it is: If every gnat that flies were
an Arch-angell, all that could but tell me, that there is a God;
and the poorest worme that creeps, tells me that. If I should
aske the Basilisk, how camest thou by those killing eyes, he
would tell me, Thy God made me so; And if I should aske the

Slow-worme, how camest thou to be without eyes, he would tell
me, Thy God made me so. The Cedar is no better a glasse to
see God in, than the Hyssope upon the wall; all things that are,
are equally removed from being nothing; and whatsoever hath
any beeing, is by that very beeing, a glasse in which we see
God, who is the roote, and the fountaine of all beeing. The
whole frame of nature is the Theatre, the whole Volume of creatures is the glasse, and the light of nature, reason, is our light,
which is another Circumstance.

2

God affords no man the comfort, the false comfort of Athe-
ism: He will not allow a pretending Atheist the power to flatter himself, so far, as seriously to thinke there is no God. He
must pull out his own eyes, and see no creature, before he can
say, he sees no God; He must be no man, and quench his reasonable soule, before he can say to himselfe, there is no God.
The difference betweene the Reason of man, and the Instinct of
the beast is this, That the beast does but know, but the man
knows that he knows. The bestiall Atheist will pretend that he
knows there is no God; but he cannot say, that hee knows, that
he knows it; for, his knowledge will not stand the battery of an
argument from another, nor of a ratiocination from himselfe. He
dares not aske himselfe who is it that I pray to, in a sudden
danger, if there be no God? Nay he dares not aske, who it is
that I sweare by, in a sudden passion if there be no God?
Whom do I tremble at, and sweat under, at midnight, and
whom do I curse by next morning, if there be no God?

3

He that asks me what heaven is, meanes not to heare me, but
to silence me; He knows I cannot tell him; When I meet him
there, I shall be able to tell him, and then he will be as able to
tell me; yet then we shall be but able to tell one another, This,
this that we enjoy is heaven, but the tongues of Angels, the
tongues of glorified Saints, shall not be able to expresse what
that heaven is; for, even in heaven our faculties shall be finite.
Heaven is not a place that was created; for, all place that was
created, shall be dissolved. God did not plant a Paradise for
himself, and remove to that, as he planted a Paradise for *Adam,*
and removed him to that; But God is still where he was before

the world was made. And in that place, where there are more Suns than there are Stars in the Firmament, (for all the Saints are Suns) And more light in another Sun, The S[o]n of right-eousnesse, the Son of Glory, the Son of God, than in all them, in that illustration, that emanation, that effusion of beams of glory, which began not to shine 6000. yeares ago, but 6000. millions of millions ago, had been 6000. millions of millions before that, in those eternall, in those uncreated heavens, shall we see God.

[*LXXX. Sermons* (23), 1640]

PREACHED AT WHITEHALL. APRIL 15th 1628

But if the whole space to the Firmament were filled with sand, and we had before us *Clavius* his number, how many thousands would be; If all that space were filled with water, and so joyned the waters above with the waters below the Firmament, and we had the number of all those drops of water; And then had every single sand, and every single drop multiplied by the whole num-ber of both, we were still short of numbring the benefits of God, as God; But then, of God in Christ, infinitely, super-in-finitely short. To have been once nothing, and to be now co-heire with the Son of God, is such a Circle, such a Compasse, as that no revolutions in this world, to rise from the lowest to the highest, or to fall from the highest to the lowest, can be called or thought any Segment, any Arch, any Point in respect of this Circle; To have once been nothing, and now to be co-heires with the Son of God: That Son of God, who if there had been but one soule to have been saved, would have dyed for that; nay, if all soules had been to be saved, but one, and that that onely had sinned, he would not have contented himselfe with all the rest, but would have dyed for that. And there is the goodnesse, the liberality of our King, our God, our Christ, our Jesus.

[*LXXX. Sermons* (75), 1640]

ST. PAULS. IN THE EVENING. NOV. 23rd, 1628

He that oppresses the poor, digs in a dunghill for wormes; And he departs from that posture, which God, in nature gave him, that is, *erect*, to look upward; for his eye is always down, upon them, *that lie in the dust,* under his feet. Certainly, he that seares up himselfe, and makes himselfe insensible of the cries, and curses of the poor here in this world, does but prepare himselfe for the *howlings,* and *gnashings of teeth,* in the world to come. It is the Serpents taste, the Serpents diet, *Dust shalt thou eate all the days of thy life;* and he feeds but on dust, that oppresses the poor. And as there is evidently, more *inhumanity,* more violation of *nature,* in this oppression, than in emulation. so may there well seem to be more *impiety,* and more violation of *God* himselfe, by that word, which the holy Ghost chooses in the next place, which is *Reproach, He that oppresses the poor, reproaches his Maker.*

[Fifty Sermons (42), 1649]

ST. PAUL'S. IN THE EVENING. UPON THE DAY OF ST. PAUL'S CONVERSION. JANUARY 25, 1628/9

1

Alas, they, we, men of this world, wormes of this dunghil, whether Basilisks or blind wormes, whether Scarabs or Silk-wormes, whether high or low in the world, have no minds to change. The Platonique Philosophers did not only acknowledge *Animam in homine,* a soule in man, but *Mentem in anima,* a minde in the soul of man. They meant by the minde, the superior faculties of the soule, and we never come to exercise them. Men and women call one another inconstant, and accuse one another of having changed their minds, when, God knowes, they have but changed the object of their eye, and seene a better white or red. An old man loves not the same sports that he did when he was young, nor a sicke man the same meats that hee did when hee was well: But these men have not changed their mindes; The old man hath changed his fancy, and the sick man his taste; neither his minde.

2

Poore intricated soule! Riddling, perplexed, labyrinthicall soule! Thou couldest not say, that thou beleevest not in God, if there were no God; Thou couldest not beleeve in God, if there were no God; If there were no God, thou couldest not speake, thou couldest not thinke, not a word, not a thought, no not

against God; Thou couldest not blaspheme the Name of God,
thou couldest not sweare, if there were no God: For, all thy
faculties, how ever depraved, and perverted by thee, are from
him; and except thou canst seriously beleeve, that thou art nothing, thou canst not beleeve that there is no God. If I should
aske thee at a Tragedy, where thou shouldest see him that had
drawne blood, lie weltring, and surrounded in his owne blood,
Is there a God now? If thou couldst answer me, No, These are
but Inventions, and Representations of men, and I beleeve a
God never the more for this; If I should ask thee at a Sermon, where thou shouldest heare the Judgements of God formerly denounced, and executed, re-denounced, and applied to
present occasions, Is there a God now? If thou couldest answer
me, No, These are but Inventions of State, to souple and regulate Congregations, and keep people in order, and I beleeve a
God never the more for this; Bee as confident as thou canst, in
company; for company is the Atheists Sanctuary; I respit thee
not till the day of Judgement, when I may see thee upon thy
knees, upon thy face, begging of the hills, that they would fall
downe and cover thee from the fierce wrath of God, to aske
thee then, Is there a God now? I respit thee not till the day of
thine own death, when thou shalt have evidence enough, that
there is a God, though no other evidence, but to finde a Devill,
and evidence enough, that there is a Heaven, though no other
evidence, but to feele Hell; To aske thee then, Is there a God
now? I respit thee but a few houres, but six houres, but till
midnight. Wake then; and then darke, and alone, Heare God
aske thee then, remember that I asked thee now, Is there a
God? and if thou darest, say No.

                              [LXXX. Sermons (48), 1640]

PREACHED TO THE KING AT THE COURT [APRIL 1629]

1

GOD himself made all that he made, according to a pattern. God
had deposited and laid up in himself certain forms, patterns,
Ideas of every thing that he made. He made nothing, of which
he had not preconceived the form, and predetermined in himself, I will make it thus. And when he had made any thing, he
saw that it was good; Good, because it answered the pattern, the
image; Good, because it was like to that. And therefore though

of other creatures God pronounced they were good, because they
were presently like their pattern, that is, like that form which was
in him for them: yet of man, he forebore to say that he was good;
because his conformitie to his pattern was to appeare after in
his subsequent actions. Now as God made man after another
pattern, and therefore we have a dignitie above all, that we
had another manner of creation than the rest: so have we a comfort above all, that we have another manner of administration
than the rest. God exercises another manner of providence upon
man, than upon other creatures. *A sparrow falls not without God,*
sayes Christ: yet no doubt God works otherwise in the fall of
eminent persons, than in the fall of sparrows; *for ye are of more
value than many sparrows,* sayes Christ there of every man: and
some men single, are of more value than many men. God doth
not thank the ant, for her industrie and good husbandrie in
providing for her self. God doth not reward the foxes, for con-
curring with *Samson* in his revenge. God doth not fee the lion,
which was his executioner upon the Prophet which had disobeyed
his commandment; nor those two she-bears, which slew the petu-
lant children, who had calumniated and reproached *Elisha.* God
doth not fee them before, nor thank them after, nor take knowledge of their service: But for those men that served Gods execution upon the idolaters of the golden calf, it is pronounced in their
behalf, that therein they consecrated themselves unto God; and
for that service God made that Tribe, the Tribe of Levi, his portion, his clergie, his consecrated Tribe: So, *Quia fecisti hoc,* sayes
God to Abraham, *By my self I have sworn, because thou hast
done this thing, and hast not withheld thy sonne, thine onely
sonne: that in blessing I will blesse thee, and in multiplying I
will multiply thee.* So neither is God angrie with the dog that
turns to his vomit; nor with the sow, that after her washing wal-
lows in the mire. But of man in that case he says, *It is impossible
for those who were once enlightned, if they fall away, to renew
themselves again by repentance.* The creatures live under his
law, but a law imposed thus, This they shall do, this they must
do: Man lives under another manner of law, This you shall do,
that is, This you should do, This I would have you do. And, *Fac
hoc, Do this, and you shall live;* disobey, and you shall die: but
yet the choice is yours; choose you this day life or death. So that
this is Gods administration in the creature, that he hath imprinted
in them an instinct, and so he hath something to preserve in
them: In man, his administration is this, that he hath imprinted
in him a facultie of will and election, and hath something to

reward in him. That instinct in the creature God leaves to the naturall working thereof in it self: but the freewill of man God visits and assists with his grace, to do supernaturall things. When the creature doth an extraordinary action above the nature thereof (as when Balaams asse spake) the creature exercises no facultie, no will in it self; but God forced it to that it did. When man doth any thing conducing to supernaturall ends, though the work be Gods, the will of man is not meerly passive. The will of man is but Gods agent; but still an agent it is, and an agent in another manner than the tongue of the beast. For the will considered as a will (and grace never destroyes nature; nor, though it make a dead will a live will, or an ill will a good will, doth it make the will no will) might refuse or omit that it does. So that because we are created by another pattern, we are governed by another law, and another providence.

2

We should wonder to see a mother in the midst of many sweet children, passing her time in making babies and puppets for her own delight. We should wonder to see a man, whose chambers and galleries were full of curious master-pieces, thrust in a village-fayre, to look upon sixpenie pictures and three-farthing prints. We have all the image of God at home; and we all make babies, fancies of honour in our ambitions. The master-piece is our own, in our own bosome; and we thrust in coun-trey-fayres, that is, we endure the distempers of any unseason-able weather, in night-journeys and watchings; we endure the oppositions, and scorns, and triumphs of a rivall and competi-tour, that seeks with us, and shares with us. We endure the guiltinesse and reproach of having deceived the trust, which a confident friend reposes in us, and solicite his wife or daughter. We endure the decay of fortune, of bodie, of soul, of honour, to possesse lower pictures; pictures that are not originals, not made by that hand of God, Nature; but artificiall beauties: and for that bodie we give a soul; and for that drug which might have been bought where they bought it, for a shilling, we give an estate. The image of God is more worth than all substances; and we give it for colours, for dreams, for shadows.

[*Six Sermons* (2), 1634]

PREACHED AT ST. PAUL'S CROSSE. NOV. 22nd, 1629

1

BELOVED, there is an *inward Joy,* there is an *outward dignity* and reverence, that accompanies *Riches,* and the *Godly,* the righteous man is not incapable of these; Nay, they belong rather to him, than to the ungodly: *Non decent stultum divitæ,* (as the Vulgate reades that place) *Riches doe not become a fool.* But because, for all that, though Riches doe not *become* a fool, yet *fools doe become rich;* our Translations read that place thus: *joy, pleasure, delight, is not seemly for a fool;* Though the fool, the ungodly man, may bee rich, yet a right joy, a holy delight in riches, belongs onely to the wise, to the righteous. The Patriarchs in the Old Testament, many examples in the New, are testimonies to us of the compatibility of riches, and righteousnesse; that they may, that they have often met in one person. For, is fraud, and circumvention so sure a way, of attaining Gods blessings, as industry, and conscientiousnesse is? Or is God so likely to concurre with the fraudulent, the deceitfull man, as with the laborious, and religious? Was not *Ananias,* with his disguises, more suddenly destroyed, than *Job,* and more irrecoverably? And cannot a *Star-chamber,* or an *Exchequer,* leave an ungodly man as poor, as a *storm at sea,* in a ship-wracke, or a *fire at land,* in a lightning, can doe the godly? Murmure not, be not scandalized, nor offended in him, if God hath exposed the riches of this world, as well, rather to the godly, than the wicked.

2

Blessednesse it self, is God himselfe; our blessednesse is our possession; our union with God. In what consists this? A great limbe of the Schoole with their *Thomas,* place this blessednesse, this union with God, *In visione,* in this, That in heaven *I shall see God,* see God essentially, *God face to face,* God as he is. We do not see one another so, in this world; In this world we see but outsides; In heaven I shall see God, and God essentially. But then another great branch of the Schoole, with their *Scotus,* place this blessednesse, this union with God, *in Amore,* in this, that in heaven, I shall love God. Now love presumes knowledge; for *Amari nisi nota non possunt,* we can love nothing, but that which we do, or think we do understand. There, in heaven, I shall *know* God, so, as that I shall be admitted, not onely to an *Adoration* of God, to an *admiration* of God, to a *prosternation,* and reverence before God, but to an *affection,* to an office, of more familiarity towards God, of more equality with God, I shall *love* God. But even love it selfe, as noble a passion as it is, is but a paine, except we enjoy that we love; and therefore another branch of the Schoole, with their *Aureolus,* place this blessednesse, this union of our souls with God, *in Gaudio,* in our joy, that is, in our enjoying of God. In this world we enjoy nothing; enjoying presumes perpetuity; and here, all things are fluid, transitory: There I shall enjoy, and possesse for ever, God himself. But yet, every one of these, to *see* God, or to *love* God, or to *enjoy* God, have seemed to some too narrow to comprehend this blessednesse, beyond which, nothing can be proposed; and therefore another limbe of the Schoole, with their *Bonaventure,* place this blessednesse *in all these* together. And truly, if any of those did exclude any of these, so, as that I might *see* God, and not *love* him, or *love* God, and not *enjoy* him, it could not well be called *blessednesse;* but he that hath any one of these, hath every one, all: And therefore the greatest part concurre, ard safely, *In visione,* That vision is *beatification,* to see God, as he is, is that blessednesse.

There then, in heaven, I shall have *continuitatem Intuendi;* It is not onely *vision,* but *Intuition,* not onely a seeing, but a beholding, a contemplating of God, and that *in Continuitate,* I shall have an un-interrupted, an un-intermitted, an un-discontinued sight of God; I shall looke, and never looke off; not looke, and looke againe, as here, but looke, and looke still, for that is, *Continuitas intuendi.* There my soule shall have *Inconcussam quietem;* we need owe *Plato* nothing; but we may thank *Plato* for this expression, if he meant so much by this *Inconcussa quies,* That in heaven my soule shall sleep, not onely without trouble, and startling, but without rocking, without any other help, than that peace, which is in it selfe; My soule shall be thoroughly awake, and thoroughly asleep too; still busie, active, diligent, and yet still at rest. But the Apostle will exceed the Philosopher, St. *Paul* will exceed *Plato,* as he does when he sayes, *I shall be unus spiritus cum Deo,* I shall be still but the servant of my God, and yet I shall be *the same spirit with that God.* When? *Dies quem tanquam supremum reformidas, æterni natalis est,* sayes the Morall mans Oracle, *Seneca.* Our last day is our first day, our *Saturday* is our *Sunday,* our *Eve* is our *Holyday,* our *sun-setting* is our *morning,* the day of our death, is the first day of our eternall life. The next day after that, which is the day of judgement, *Veniet dies, quae me mihi revelabit,* comes that day that shall show me to my selfe; here I never saw my selfe, but in disguises: There, Then, I shall see my selfe, and see God too. *Totam lucem, et Totus lux aspiciam;* I shall see the whole light; Here I see some parts of the ayre enlightned by the Sunne, but I do not see the whole light of the Sunne; There I shal see God intirely, all God, *totam lucem,* and *totus lux,* I my self shal be al light to see that light by. Here, I have one faculty enlightned, and another left in darknesse: mine *understanding* sometimes cleared, my *will,* at the same time perverted. There, I shall be all light, no shadow upon me; my soule invested with the *light of joy,* and my body in the *light of glory.* How glorious is God, as he looks down upon us, through the Sunne! How glorious in that glasse of his! How glorious is God, as he looks out amongst us through *the King!* How glorious in that Image of his! How glorious is God, as he calls up our eyes to him, in the beauty, and splendor, and service of the Church! How glorious in that spouse of his! But how glorious shall I conceive this light to be, *cum suo loco viderim,* when I shall see it, in his owne place. In that Spheare, which though a Spheare, is a Center too; In that place, which, though a place, is all, and every where. I shall see it, in the face of that God, who is all face, all manifestation, all Innotescence to me, (for, *facies Dei est, qua Deus nobis innotescit,* that's Gods face to us, by which God manifests himselfe to us) I shall see this light in his face, who is all face, and yet all hand, all application, and communication, and delivery of all himselfe to all his Saints. This is *Beatitudo in Auge,* blessednesse in the Meridionall height, blessednesse in the South point, in a perpetuall Summer solstice, beyond which nothing can be proposed, to see God so, Then, There. And yet the farmers of heaven and hell, the merchants of soules, *the Romane Church,* make this blessednesse, but an under degree, but a kinde of apprentiship; after they have beatified, declared a man to be blessed in the fruition of God in heaven, if that man, in that inferiour state doe good service to that Church, that they see much profit will rise, by the devotion, and concurrence of men, to the worship of that person, then they will proceed to a *Canonization;* and so, he that in his *Novitiat,* and years of probation was but blessed

Ignatius, and blessed *Xavier*, is lately become Saint *Xavier*, and Saint *Ignatius*. And so they pervert the right order, and method, which is first to come to *Sanctification*, and then to *Beatification*, first to holinesse, and then to blessednesse. And in this method, our blessed God bee pleased to proceed with us, by the operation of his holy Spirit, to bring us to *Sanctification* here, and by the merits and intercession of his glorious Sonne, to *Beatification* hereafter. That so not being offended in him, but resting in those meanes and seales, of reconciliation, which thou hast instituted in thy Church, wee may have life, and life more abundantly, life of grace here, and life of glory there, in that kingdome, which thy Sonne, our Saviour Christ Jesus hath purchased for us, with the inestimable price of his incorruptible bloud. *Amen.*

[*Fifty Sermons* (44), 1649]

ST. PAUL'S. CHRISTMAS DAY [1629]

1

GOD, who vouchsafed to be made Man for man, for man vouchsafes also to doe all the offices of man towards man. He is our Father, for he made us: Of what? Of clay; So God is *Figulus*, so in the Prophet; so in the Apostle, God is our Potter. God stamped his Image upon us, and so God is *Statuarius*, our Minter, our Statuary. God clothed us, and so is *vestiarius;* he hath opened his wardrobe unto us. God gave us all the fruits of the earth to eate, and so is *œconom[ic]us* our Steward. God poures his oyle, and his wine into our wounds, and so is *Medicus*, and *Vicinus*, that Physitian, that Neighbour, that Samaritan intended in the Parable. God plants us, and waters and weeds us, and gives the increase; and so God is *Hortulanus*, our Gardiner. God builds us up into a Church, and so God is *Architectus*, our Architect, our Builder; God watches the City when it is built; and so God is *Speculator*, our Sentinell. God fishes for men, (for all his *Johns*, and his *Andrews*, and his *Peters*, are but the nets that he fishes withall) God is the fisher of men: And here, in this Chapter, God in Christ is our Shepheard. The book of *Job* is a representation of God, in a Tragique-Comedy, lamentable beginnings comfortably ended: The book of the Canticles is a representation of God in Christ, as a Bridegroom in a Marriage-song, in an Epithalamion: God in Christ is represented to us, in divers formes, in divers places, and this Chapter is his Pastorall. The Lord is our Shepheard, and so called, in more places, than by any other name; and in this Chapter, exhibits some of the offices of a good Shepheard. Be pleased to taste a few of them. First, he sayes, *The good Shepheard comes in at the doore,* the right way. If he come in at the window, that is, alwayes clamber after preferment; If he come in at vaults, and cellars, that is, by clandestin, and secret contracts with his Patron, he comes not the right way: When he is in the right way, *His sheep heare his voyce:* first there is a voyce, He is heard; Ignorance doth not silence him, nor lazinesse, nor abundance of preferment; nor indiscreet, and distempered zeale does not silence him; (for to induce, or occasion a silencing upon our selves, is as ill as the ignorant, or the lazie silence). There is a voyce, and (sayes that Text) [it] is his voyce, not alwayes another in his roome; for (as it is added in the next verse) *The sheep know his voyce,* which they could not doe, if they heard it not often, if they were not used to it. And then, for the best testimony, and consummation of all, he sayes, *The good Shepheard gives his life for his sheep.* Every good Shepheard gives his life, that is, spends his life, weares out his life for his sheep: of which this may be one good argument, That there are not so many crazie, so many sickly men, men that so soon grow old in any profession, as in ours.

2

What eye can fixe it self upon East and West at once? And he must see more than East and West, that sees God, for God spreads infinitely beyond both: God alone is all; not onely all that is, but all that is not, all that might be, if he would have it be. God is too large, too immense, and then man is too narrow, too little to be considered; for, who can fixe his eye upon an Atome? and he must see a lesse thing than an Atome, that sees man, for man is nothing. First, for the incomprehensiblenesse of God, the understanding of man, hath a limited, a determined latitude; it is an intelligence able to move that Spheare which it is fixed to, but could not move a greater: I can comprehend *naturam naturatam,* created nature, but for that *natura naturans,* God himselfe, the understanding of man cannot comprehend. I can see the Sun in a looking-glasse, but the nature, and the whole working of the Sun I cannot see in that glasse. I can see God in the creature, but the nature, the essence, the secret purposes of God, I cannot see there. There is *defatigatio in in-tellectualibus*, sayes the saddest and soundest of the Hebrew Rabbins, the soule may be tired, as well as the body, and the understanding dazeled, as well as the eye.

3

Let man be something; how poore, and inconsiderable a ragge of this world, is man! Man, whom *Paracelsus* would have undertaken to have made, in a Limbeck, in a Furnace: Man, who, if they were altogether, all the men, that ever were, and are, and shall be, would not have the power of one Angel in them all, whereas all the Angels, (who, in the Schoole are conceived to be more in number, than, not onely all the Species, but all the individualls of this lower world) have not in them all, the power of one finger of Gods hand: Man, of whom when *David* had said, (as the lowest diminution that he could put upon him) *I am a worme and no man*, He might have gone lower, and said, I am a man and no worm; for man is so much lesse than a worm, as that wormes of his own production, shall feed upon his dead body in the grave, and an immortall worm gnaw his conscience in the torments of hell.

4

There is Ayre enough in the world, to give breath to every thing, though everything doe not breathe. If a tree, or a stone doe not breathe, it is not because it wants ayre, but because it wants meanes to receive it, or to returne it. All egges are not hatched that the hen sits upon; neither could Christ himselfe get all the chickens that were hatched, to come, and to stay under his wings. That man that is blinde, or that will winke, shall see no more sunne upon S. *Barnabies* day, than upon S. *Lucies;* no more in the summer, than in the winter solstice. And therefore as there is *copiosa redemptio*, a plentifull redemption brought into the world by the death of Christ, so (as S. *Paul* found it in his particular conversion) there is *copiosa lux*, a great and a powerfull light exhibited to us, that we might see, and lay hold of this life, in the Ordinances of the Church, in the Confessions, and Absolutions, and Services, and Sermons, and Sacraments of the Church; Christ came *ut daret*, that he might bring life into the world, by his death, and then he instituted his Church: *ut haberent*, that by the meanes thereof this life might be infused into us, and infused so, as the last word of our Text delivers it, *Abundantiùs, I came, that they might have life more abundantly.*

Dignaris Domine, ut eis, quibus debita dimittis, te, promissionibus tuis, debitorem facias; This, O Lord, is thine abundant proceeding; First thou forgivest me my debt to thee, and then thou makest thy selfe a debter to me by thy large promises; and after all, performest those promises more largely than thou madest them. Indeed, God can doe nothing scantly, penuriously, singly. Even his maledictions, (to which God is ever loth to come) his first commination was plurall, it was death, and death upon death, *Morte morieris.* Death may be plurall; but this benediction of life cannot admit a singular; *Chajim,* which is the word for *life,* hath no singular number. This is the difference betweene Gods Mercy, and his Judgements, that sometimes his Judgements may be plurall, complicated, enwrapped in one another, but his Mercies are alwayes so, and cannot be otherwise; he gives them *abundantiùs, more abundantly.*

5

Humiliation is the beginning of sanctification; and as without this, without holinesse, no man shall see God, though he pore whole nights upon the Bible; so without that, without humility, no man shall heare God speake to his soule, though hee heare three two-houres Sermons every day. But if God bring thee to that humiliation of soule and body here, hee will emprove, and advance thy sanctification *abundantiùs,* more abundantly, and when he hath brought it to the best perfection, that this life is capable of, he will provide another *abundantiùs,* another man[n]er of abundance in the life to come; which is the last beating of the pulse of this text, the last panting of the breath thereof, our anhelation, and panting after the joyes, and glory, and eternity of the kingdome of Heaven; of which, though, for the most part, I use to dismisse you, with saying something, yet it is alwaies little that I can say thereof; at this time, but this, that if all the joyes of all the Martyrs, from *Abel* to him that groanes now in the Inquisition, were condensed into one body of joy, (and certainly the joyes that the Martyrs felt at their deaths, would make up a far greater body, than their sorrowes would doe), (for though it bee said of our great Martyr, or great Witnesse, (as S. *John* calls Christ Jesus) to whom, all other Martyrs are but sub-martyrs, witnesses that tes-

tifie his testimony, *Non dolor sicut dolor ejus,* there was never
sorrow like unto his sorrow, it is also true, *Non gaudium sicut
gaudium ejus,* There was never joy like unto that joy which
was set before him, when he endured the crosse;) If I had all
this joy of all these Martyrs, (which would, no doubt, be such
a joy, as would worke a liquefaction, a melting of my bowels)
yet I shall have it *abundantiùs,* a joy more abundant, than even
this superlative joy, in the world to come. What a dimme ves-
pers of a glorious festivall, what a poore halfe-holyday, is
Methusalems nine hundred yeares, to eternity! what a poore
account hath that man made, that saies, this land hath beene in
my name, and in my Ancestors from the Conquest! what a yesterday is that? not six hundred yeares. If I could beleeve the
transmigration of soules, and thinke that my soule had beene
successively in some creature or other, since the Creation, what
a yesterday is that? not six thousand yeares. What a yesterday
for the past, what a to morrow for the future, is any terme, that
can be comprehendred in Cyphar or Counters! But as, how
abundant a life soever any man hath in this world for temporall
abundances, I have life more abundantly than hee, if I have
the spirituall life of grace, so what measure soever I have of this
spirituall life of grace, in this world, I shall have that more
abundantly in Heaven, for there, my terme shall bee a terme for
three lives; for those three, that as long as the Father, and the
Son, and the holy Ghost live, I shall not dye.

[LXXX. Sermons (7), 1640]

ST. PAUL'S. CONVERSION OF ST. PAUL.
JANUARY 25[?], 1629/30

BUT stop we the floodgates of this consideration; it would melt
us into teares. End we all with this, That we have all, all these,
Sadduces and Pharisees in our owne bosomes: Sadduces that
deny spirits; carnall apprehensions that are apt to say, Is your
God all Spirit, and hath bodily eyes to see sin? All Spirit, and
hath bodily hands to strike for a sinne? Is your soule all spirit,
and hath a fleshly heart to feare? All spirit, and hath sensible
sinews to feele a materiall fire? Was your God, who is all Spirit,
wounded when you quarrelled? or did your soule, which is all
spirit, drink when you were drunk? Sins of presumption, and
carnall confidence are our Sadduces; and then our Pharisees are
our sins of separation, of division, of diffidence and distrust

in the mercies of our God; when we are apt to say, after a sin, Cares God, who is all Spirit, for my eloquent prayers, or for my passionate teares? Is the giving of my goods to the poore, or of my body to the fire, any thing to God who is all Spirit? My spirit, and nothing but my spirit, my soule, and nothing but my soule, must satisfie the justice, the anger of God, and be separated from him for ever. My Sadduce, my Presumption suggests, that there is no spirit, no soule to suffer for sin; and my Pharisee, my Desperation suggests, That my soule must perish irremediably, irrecoverably, for every sinne that my body commits.

Now if I go S. *Pauls* way, to put a dissention between these my *Sadduces,* and my *Pharisees,* to put a jealousie between my presumption and my desperation, to make my presumption see, that my desperation lies in wait for her; and to consider seriously, that my presumption will end in desperation, I may, as S. *Paul* did in the Text, scape the better for that. But if, without farther troubling these *Sadduces* and these *Pharisees,* I be content to let them agree, and to divide my life between them, so as that my presumption shall possesse all my youth, and desperation mine age, I have heard my sentence already, *The end of this man will be worse than his beginning,* How much soever God be incensed with me, for my presumption at first, he will be much more inexorable for my desperation at last. And therefore interrupt the prescription of sin; break off the correspondence of Sin; unjoynt the dependency of sin upon sin. Bring every single sin, as soon as thou committest it, into the presence of thy God, upon those two legs, Confession, and Detestation, and thou shalt see, that, as, though an intire Iland stand firme in the Sea, yet a single clod of earth cast into the Sea, is quickly washt into nothing; so, howsoever thine habituall, and customary, and concatenated sins, sin enwrapped and complicated in sin, sin entrenched and barricadoed in sin, sin screwed up, and riveted with sin, may stand out, and wrastle even with the mercies of God, in the blood of Christ Jesus; yet if thou bring every single sin into the sight of God, it will be but as a clod of earth, but as a graine of dust in the Ocean. Keep thy sins then from mutuall intelligence; That they doe not second one another, induce occasion, and then support and disguise one another, and then, neither shall the body of sin ever oppresse thee, nor the exhalations, and damps, and vapors of thy sad soule, hang between thee, and the mercies of thy God; But thou shalt live in the light and serenity of a peaceable conscience here, and die in a faire possibility of a present melioration and improvement of that light. All thy life thou shalt be preserved, in an Orientall light, an Easterne light, a rising and a growing light, the light of grace; and at thy death thou shalt be super-illustrated, with a Meridionall light, a South light, the light of glory. And be this enough for the explication, and application of these words, and their complication with the day; for the justifying of S. *Pauls* Stratagem in himselfe, and the exemplifying, and imitation thereof in us. *Amen.*

[*LXXX. Sermons* (49), 1640]

WHITEHALL. TO THE KING. FEB. 12th, 1629/30

I HAVE seen Minute-glasses; Glasses so short-liv'd. If I were to preach upon this Texte, to such a glass, it were enough for half the Sermon; enough to show the worldly man his Treasure, and the Object of his heart (*for, where your Treasure is, there will your Heart be also*) to call his eye to that Minute-glass, and to tell him, There flows, there flies your Treasure, and your Heart with it. But if I had a Secular Glass, a Glass that would run an age; if the two Hemispheres of the World were composed in the form of such a Glass, and all the World calcin'd and burnt to ashes, and all the ashes, and sands, and atoms of the World put into that Glass, it would not be enough to tell the godly man what his Treasure, and the Object of his Heart is. A Parrot, or a Stare, docile Birds, and of pregnant imitation, will sooner be brought to relate to us the wisdom of a Council Table, than any *Ambrose*, or any *Chrysostome*, Men that have Gold and Honey in their Names, shall tell us what the Sweetness, what the Treasure of Heaven is, and what that mans peace, that hath set his Heart upon that Treasure.

[*XXVI. Sermons* (5), 1660]

DEATH'S DUELL
OR, A CONSOLATION TO THE SOULE, AGAINST THE DYING LIFE, AND LIVING DEATH OF THE BODY

Delivered in a Sermon at White-Hall, before the Kings Majesty, in the beginning of Lent [Feb. 25], 1630. Being his last Sermon, and called by his Majesties household THE DOCTORS OWNE FUNERALL SERMON

TO THE READER
[Preface to the 1st edition (1632) by Richard Redmer, the publisher.]

This Sermon was, by Sacred Authoritie, stiled the Authors owne funeral Sermon. Most fitly: whether wee respect the time, or the matter. It was preached not many dayes before his death; as if, having done this, there remained nothing for him to doe, but to die: And the matter is, of Death; the occasion and subject of all funerall Sermons. It hath beene observed of this Reverent Man, That his Faculty in Preaching continually encreased: and, That as hee exceeded others at first; so, at last hee exceeded himselfe. This is his last Sermon; I will not say, it is therefore his best; because, all his were excellent. Yet thus much: A dying Mans words, if they concerne our selves, doe usually make the deepest impression, as being spoken most feelingly, and with least affectation. Now, whom doth it not concerne to learn, both the danger, and benefit of death? Death is every mans enemy, and intends hurt to all; though to many, hee be occasion of greatest goods. This enemy wee must all combate dying; whom hee living did almost conquer; having discovered the utmost of his power, the utmost of his crueltie. May wee make such use of this and other the like preparatives, That neither death, whensoever it shall come, may seeme terrible; nor life tedious, how long soever it shall last.

R.

PSALME 68. VERS. 20. *In finè.*

And unto God the (LORD) *belong the issues of death*
i.e. *From death.*

BUILDINGS stand by the benefit of their *foundations* that sus-
teine and *support* them, and of their *butteresses* that comprehend and *embrace* them, and of their *contignations* that knit
and *unite* them: The *foundations* suffer them not to *sinke,* the
butteresses suffer them not to *swerve,* and the *contignation* and
knitting suffers them not to *cleave;* The body of our building
is in the former part of this verse: It is this; hee that *is our
God* is the *God of salvation; ad salutes,* of salvations in the
plurall, so it is in the originall; the *God* that gives us spirituall
and temporall salvation too. But of this *building,* the *foundation,* the *butteresses,* the *contignations* are in this part of the
verse, which constitutes *our text,* and in the three divers *accepta-
tions* of the words amongst our expositors. *Unto God the Lord
belong the issues from death.* For *first* the *foundation* of this
building, (that our *God* is the *God of all salvations*) is laid in
this; That *unto* this *God the Lord belong the issues of death,*
that is, it is in his power to give us an *issue* and deliverance,
even then when wee are brought to the jawes and teeth of
death, and to the lippes of that whirlepoole, the grave. And so
in this acceptation, this *exitus mortis,* this *issue of death* is *liberatio à morte, a deliverance from death,* and this is the most obvious and most ordinary acceptation of these words, and that
upon which our *translation* laies hold, *The issues from death.*
And then *secondly* the butteresses that comprehend and settle
this building, That hee that is *our God,* is the *God of* all *salvations,* are thus raised; *Unto God the Lord belong the issues of
death,* that is, the disposition and *manner of our death:* what
kinde of *issue* and *transmigration* wee shall have out of this
world, whether prepared or sudden, whether violent or naturall,
whether in our perfect senses or shaken and disordered by
sicknes, there is no condemnation to bee argued out of that, no
Judgement to bee made upon that, for howsoever they dye,
precious in his sight is the death of his saints, and with him
are *the issues of death,* the *wayes* of our *departing* out of this
life are in his *hands.* And so in this *sense* of the *words,* this
exitus mortis, the *issue of death,* is *liberatio in morte, A deliver-*

ance in death; Not that *God* will *deliver* us *from dying,* but that hee will *have a care* of us in the *houre of death,* of what kinde soever our passage be. And in this *sense* and acceptation of the *words,* the naturall frame and contexture doth well and pregnantly administer unto us; And then *lastly* the *contignation* and knitting of this building, that hee that is *our God* is the *God of all salvations,* consists in this, *Unto this God the Lord belong the issues of death,* that is, that this *God* the *Lord* having *united* and knit *both natures in one,* and being *God,* having also *come* into this *world,* in our *flesh,* he could have no other meanes to save us, he could have no other *issue* out of this world, nor *returne* to his former *glory,* but by *death;* And so in this sense, this *exitus mortis,* this *issue of death,* is *liberatio per mortem,* a *deliverance by death,* by the death of this *God* our *Lord Christ Jesus.* And this is Saint *Augustines* acceptation of the words, and those many and great persons that have adhered to him. In all these three lines then, we shall looke upon these words; *First,* as the *God* of *power,* the *Almighty Father* rescues his servants from the jawes of death: *And then* as the *God* of *mercy,* the glorious *Sonne* rescued us, by taking upon himselfe this *issue of death: And then* betweene these two, as the *God* of *comfort,* the *holy Ghost* rescues us from all discomfort by his blessed impressions before hand, that what manner of death soever be ordeined for us, yet this *exitus mortis* shall bee *introitus in vitam,* our *issue in death* shall be an *entrance into everlasting life.* And these three considerations, our deliverance *à morte, in morte, per mortem, from death, in death, and by death,* will abundantly doe all the offices of the *foundations,* of the *butteresses,* of the *contignation* of this our *building;* That he that is our *God,* is the *God of all salvations,* because *unto* this *God the Lord belong the issues of death.*

First, then, we consider this *exitus mortis,* to bee *liberatio à morte,* that with *God* the *Lord* are the *issues of death,* and therefore in all our deaths, and deadly calamities of this life, wee may justly *hope* of a good *issue* from him. And all our *periods* and *transitions* in this life, are so many passages *from death* to *death;* our very *birth* and entrance into this life, is *exitus à morte,* an *issue from death,* for in our mothers *wombe* wee are *dead so,* as that wee doe *not know* wee *live,* not so much as wee doe in our *sleepe,* neither is there any *grave* so close, or so *putrid* a *prison,* as the *wombe* would be unto us, if we stayed in it *beyond* our time, or dyed there *before* our time. In the *grave* the *wormes* doe not kill us, wee *breed* and *feed,* and then *kill* those wormes which wee our selves produc'd. In the *wombe* the dead *child* kills the *Mother* that conceived it, and is a murtherer, nay a *parricide,* even after it is dead. And if wee bee not dead so in the *wombe,* so as that being dead wee kill her that gave us our first life, our life of *vegetation,* yet wee are dead so, as *Davids Idols* are dead. In the *wombe* wee have *eyes and see not, eares and heare not;* There in the wombe wee are fitted for *workes of darknes,* all the while deprived of light: And there in the *wombe* wee are taught *cruelty,* by being *fed with blood,* and may be *damned,* though we be *never borne.* Of our very making in the *wombe, David* says, *I am wonderfully and fearefully made,* and, *Such knowledge is too excellent for me,* for even that *is the Lords doing,* and it *is wonderfull in our eyes; Ipse fecit nos,* it is *hee that hath made us, and not wee our selves* nor our parents neither; *Thy hands have made me and fashioned me round about,* saith *Job,* and (as the *originall word is*) *thou hast taken paines about me,* and yet, sayes he, *thou doest destroy me.* Though I bee the *Master-peece* of the greatest *Master* (*man is* so), yet if thou doe no more for me, if thou leave me where thou madest mee, destruction will follow. The *wombe* which should be the *house of life,* becomes *death* it selfe, if *God* leave us there. That which God threatens so often, the *shutting of the womb,* is not so *heavy,* nor so discomfortable a *curse* in the *first,* as in the *latter* shutting, nor in the shutting of *barrennes,* as in the shutting of *weakenes,* when *children are come to the birth,* and there is not *strength to bring forth.*

It is the *exaltation of misery,* to *fall* from a *neare hope* of *happines.* And in that vehement imprecation, the *Prophet* expresses the highest of *Gods* anger, *give them ô Lord, what wilt thou give them?* give them a *miscarying wombe.* Therefore as soone as wee are men, (that is, *inanimated,* quickned in the *womb*) thogh we cannot our selves, our parents have reason to say in our behalf, *wretched man that he is, who shall deliver him from this body of death?* for even the *wombe* is a *body of death,* if there bee no deliverer. It must be he that said to *Jeremy,* Before *I formed thee I knew thee,* and *before thou camest out of the wombe I sanctified thee.* Wee are not sure that there was no kinde of shippe nor boate to fish in, nor to passe by, till *God* prescribed *Noah* that absolute *form* of the *Arke.* That word which the *holy Ghost* by *Moses* useth for the *Arke,* is common to all kinde of *boates, Thebah,* and is the same word that *Moses* useth for the *boate* that he was *exposed in, That his mother layed him in an arke of bulrushes.* But we are sure that *Eve* had no *Midwife* when she was *delivered* of *Cain,* therefore shee might well say, *possedi virum à Domino,* I *have gotten a man from the Lord,* wholly, entirely from the Lord; It is the *Lord* that *enabled* me to *conceive,* The *Lord* that *infus'd* a *quickening soule* into that conception, the *Lord* that *brought into the world* that which himself *had quickened,* without all this might *Eve* say, My *body had bene* but *the house of death,* and *Domini Domini sunt exitus mortis,* to God the Lord *belong the issues of death.*

But then this *exitus à morte,* is but *introitus in mortem,* this *issue,* this deliverance *from* that *death,* the death of the *wombe,* is an *entrance,* a delivering over to *another death,* the manifold deathes of this *world.* Wee have a winding sheete in our Mothers wombe, which growes with us from our conception, and wee come into the world, wound up in that *winding sheet,* for wee come to *seeke a grave;* And as prisoners discharg'd of actions may lie for fees, so when the *wombe* hath discharg'd us, yet we are bound to it by *cordes* of flesh by such a *string,* as that wee cannot goe thence, nor stay there; wee celebrate our owne funeralls with cries, even at our birth; as though our *threescore and ten years life* were spent in our mothers labour, and our circle made up in the first point thereof, we begge our *Baptisme,* with another *Sacrament,* with *teares:* And we come into a world that lasts many ages, but wee last not; *in domo Patris,* says our *Saviour,* speaking of *heaven, multæ mansiones,* there *are many mansions,* divers and durable, so that if a man cannot possesse a *martyrs* house, (he hath shed no blood for *Christ*) yet hee may have a *Confessors,* he hath bene ready to glorifie *God* in the *shedding of his blood.* And if a woman cannot possesse a *virgins* house (she hath embrac'd the *holy state* of *mariage*) yet she may have a *matrons* house, she hath brought forth and brought up *children in the feare of God. In domo patris, in my fathers house,* in heaven there *are many mansions;* but here upon earth the *sonne of man hath not where to lay his head,* sayes he himselfe. *Nonne terram dedit filiis hominum?* how then hath *God given this earth* to the *sonnes of men?* hee hath *given them earth* for their *materialls* to bee made of earth, and hee hath given them *earth* for their *grave* and sepulture, to *returne* and resolve to *earth,* but not for their *possession: Here wee have no continuing citty,* nay no *cottage* that continues, nay no persons, no bodies that continue. Whatsoever moved Saint *Jerome* to call the journies of the *Israelites,* in the *wildernes,* mansions; The *word* (the word is

Nasang) signifies but a *journey,* but a peregrination. Even the
Israel of God hath no mansions; but journies, pilgrimages in
this life. By that measure did *Jacob* measure his life to *Pharaoh;*
the dayes of the years *of my pilgrimage.* And though the
Apostle would not say *morimur,* that, whilest wee *are in the*
body wee *are dead,* yet hee sayes, *Peregrinamur,* whilest wee
are *in the body,* wee are but in *a pilgrimage,* and wee are *ab-*
sent from the Lord; hee might have said *dead,* for this whole
world is but an *universall churchyard,* but one *common grave,*
and the life and motion that the greatest persons have in it, is
but as the shaking of buried bodies in the grave, by an *earth-*
quake. That which we call life, is but *Hebdomada mortium,* a
weeke of deaths, seaven dayes, seaven periods of our life spent
in dying, *a dying seaven times over;* and there is an end. *Our*
birth dies in *infancy,* and our *infancy* dies in *youth,* and *youth*
and the rest die in *age,* and *age* also dies, and *determines all.*
Nor doe all these, youth out of infancy, or age out of youth
arise so, as a *Phœnix* out of the *ashes* of another *Phœnix* formerly *dead,* but as a *waspe* or a *serpent* out of a *caryon,* or as a
Snake out of *dung.* Our *youth* is *worse* than our *infancy,* and
our *age worse* than our *youth.* Our *youth* is *hungry and thirsty,*
after those *sinnes,* which our *infancy knew not;* And our *age* is
sory and *angry,* that it *cannot pursue* those *sinnes* which our
youth did; and besides, all the way, so many deaths, that is, so
many deadly calamities accompany every condition, and every
period of this life, as that death it selfe would bee an ease to
them that suffer them: Upon this sense doth *Job* wish that
God had not given him an *issue* from the *first death,* from the
wombe, Wherefore hast thou brought me forth *out of the*
wombe? O *that I had given up the Ghost, and no eye seene*
me! I should have beene as though I had not beene. And not
only the impatient *Israelites* in their murmuring (*would to God*
wee had died by the hand of the Lord in the land of Egypt)
but *Eliah* himselfe, when he *fled* from *Jesabell,* and went for
his life, as that text sayes, under the *Juniper tree,* requested that
hee might die, and said, *it is enough now, O Lord, take away my*
life. So *Jonah* justifies his impatience, nay his anger towards
God himselfe. *Now ô Lord take, I beseech thee, my life from*
mee, for it is better to die than to live. And when *God* asked
him, *doest thou well to be angry for this,* he replies, *I doe well*
to be angry, even unto death. How much worse a death than
death, is this life, which so good men would so often change for
death! But if my case bee as Saint *Paules* case, *quotidiè morior,*

that *I die dayly*, that something heavier than death falls upon
me every day; If my case be *Davids* case, *tota die mortificamur;
all the day long wee are killed*, that not onely every day, but
every houre of the day some thing heavier than death falls
upon me, though that bee true of me, *Conceptus in peccatis*, I
was shapen in *iniquity, and in sinne did my mother conceive
me*, (there I dyed one death), though that be true of me
(*Natus filius iræ*) I *was borne* not onely the child of sinne, but
the child of wrath, of the wrath of *God* for sinne, which is a
heavier death; Yet *Domini Domini sunt exitus mortis*, with *God
the Lord are the issues of death*, and after a *Job*, and a *Joseph*,
and a *Jeremie*, and a *Daniel*, I cannot doubt of a deliverance.
And if no other deliverance conduce more to his glory and my
good, yet he hath the *keys of death*, and hee can let me out at
that dore, that is, deliver me from the manifold deaths of this
world, the *omni die* and the *tota die*, the *every days death* and
every houres death, by that *one death*, the *finall dissolution* of
body and soule, the end of all. But then is that the end of all?
Is that dissolution of body and soule, the last death that the
body shall suffer? (for of spirituall death wee speake not now)
It is not. Though this be *exitus à morte*, It is *introitus in mortem;* though it bee an *issue from* the manifold *deaths* of this
world, yet it is an *entrance* into the *death of corruption* and
putrefaction and *vermiculation* and *incineration*, and dispersion
in and from the *grave*, in which every dead man dies over
againe. It was a *prerogative* peculiar to *Christ*, not to die this
death, *not to see corruption:* what gave him this priviledge?
Not *Josephs* great proportion of *gummes and spices*, that
might have preserved his body from corruption and *incineration*
longer than he needed it, longer than *three dayes*, but would not
have done it for ever: what preserved him then? did his exemption and *freedome from originall sinne* preserve him from
this corruption and *incineration?* 'tis true that original sinne
hath induced this corruption and *incineration* upon us; If wee
had not sinned in *Adam, mortality had not put on immortality*,
(as the *Apostle* speakes) nor, *corruption had not put on incorruption*, but we had had our *transmigration* from this to the
other world, without any *mortality*, any *corruption at all*. But
yet since Christ tooke *sinne* upon him, so farre as made him
mortall, he had it so farre too, as might have made him see this
corruption and *incineration*, though he had no *originall sinne* in
himself; what preserv'd him then? Did the *hypostaticall union*
of both *natures*, *God* and *Man*, preserve him from this corrup-

tion and *incineration?* 'tis true that this was a most powerfull *embalming*, to be embalmd with the *divine nature* itselfe, to bee embalmd with *eternity*, was able to preserve him from corruption and *incineration* for ever. And he was embalmd so, embalmd with the *divine nature* it selfe, even in his *body* as well as in his *soule;* for the *Godhead*, the *divine nature* did not depart, but remained still *united* to his *dead body* in the *grave;* But yet for al this powerful *embalming*, this *hypostaticall union* of both natures, we see *Christ* did *die;* and for all this *union* which made him *God* and *Man,* hee became no man (for the *union* of the *body* and *soule* makes the man, and hee whose soule and body are separated by *death* as long as that state lasts is properly no man.) And therefore as in him the dissolution of *body* and *soule* was no *dissolution* of the *hypostaticall union;* so is there nothing that constraines us to say, that though the *flesh* of *Christ* had *seene corruption* and *incineration* in the grave, this had bene any *dissolution* of the *hyposticall union,* for the divine *nature,* the Godhead might have remained with all the *Elements* and *principles* of *Christs* body, as well as it did with the two *constitutive* parts of his *person,* his *body* and his *soul.* This *incorruption* then was not in *Josephs gummes* and *spices,* nor was it in *Christs* innocency, and *exemption* from *originall sin,* nor was it (that is, it is not necessary to say it was) in the *hypostaticall union.* But this *incorruptiblenes* of his *flesh* is most conveniently plac'd in that, *Non dabis, thou wilt not suffer thy holy one to see curruption.* Wee looke no further for *causes* or *reasons* in the *mysteries of religion,* but to the *will* and pleasure of *God: Christ* himselfe limited his *inquisition* in that *ita est, even so Father, for so it seemeth good in thy sight. Christs* body did *not see corruption,* therefore, because *God* had *decreed* it s#old not. The humble soule (and onely the humble soule is the religious soule) rests himselfe upon *Gods* purposes and the decrees of *God,* which he hath declared and manifested not such as are *conceived* and imagined in our selves, though upon some probability, some *veresimilitude.* So in our present case *Peter* proceeds in his *Sermon* at *Jerusalem,* and so *Paul* in his at *Antioch.* They preached *Christ* to have *bene risen* without seeing *corruption* not onely because *God* had *decreed* it, but because he had *manifested* that *decree* in his *Prophet.* Therefore doth Saint *Paul* cite by speciall number the *second Psalme* for that *decree;* And therefore both Saint *Peter* and S. *Paul* cite for it that place in the 16. *Psalme,* for when *God* declares his *decree* and purpose in the expresse words of his *Prophet,* or when he declares it in the reall execution of the decree, then he makes it ours, then he manifests it to us. And therfore as the *Mysteries* of our *Religion,* are *not* the *objects* of *our reason,* but *by faith we rest* on *Gods decree* and purpose, (It is so *ô God,* because it is *thy will,* it should be so) so *Gods decrees* are ever to be considered in the *manifestation* thereof. All *manifestation* is either in the *word* of God, or in the *execution* of the *decree;* And when these two concur and meete, it is the strongest *demonstration* that can be: when therefore I finde those *markes* of *adoption* and *spiritual filiation,* which are delivered in the *word* of God to be upon me, when I finde that reall *execution* of his *good purpose* upon me, as that *actually* I doe *live* under the *obedience,* and under the *conditions* which are *evidences* of *adoption* and *spiritual filiation;* Then so long as I see these *markes* and live so; I may safely comfort my selfe in a *holy certitude* and a *modest infallibility* of my *adoption. Christ* determines himself in that, the purpose of *God* was manifest to him: S. *Peter* and S. *Paul* determine themselves in those two wayes of knowing the *purpose* of *God,* the *word* of God before, the *execution* of the *decree* in the *fulnes of time.* It was *prophecyed before,* say they, and it *is performed now, Christ is risen* without seeing corruption. Now this which is so singularly peculiar to him, that *his flesh should not see corruption,* at his *second coming,* his coming to *Judgement,* shall extend to all that are then alive, their flesh shall not *see corruption,* because as th' *Apostle* sayes, and sayes as *a secret,* as *a mystery; Behold I shew you a mistery, we shall not all sleepe,* (that is, not continue in the state of the dead in the grave,) *but wee shall all be changed in an instant,* we shall have a *dissolution,* and in the *same instant* a *redintegration,* a *recompacting* of *body* and *soule,* and that shall be truely a death and truely a resurrection, but no sleeping in corruption; But for us that die now and sleepe in the state of the dead, we must al passe this *posthume* death, this *death* after *death,* nay this death after buriall, this *dissolution* after *dissolution,* this *death* of *corruption* and *putrifaction,* of *vermiculation* and *incineration,* of *dissolution* and *dispersion* in and *from* the *grave,* when these bodies that have beene the *children* of *royall parents,* and the *parents* of *royall children,* must say with *Job, Corruption thou art my father,* and *to the Worme thou art my mother and my sister. Miserable riddle,* when the *same worme* must bee *my mother,* and *my sister,* and *my selfe. Miserable incest,* when I must bee *maried* to my *mother* and my *sister,* and bee both *father* and *mother* to my *owne mother* and *sister, beget* and *beare* that *worme* which is all that *miserable penury;* when my *mouth* shall be *filled* with *dust,* and the *worme* shall *feed,* and *feed sweetely* upon me, when the *ambitious* man shall have *no* satisfaction, *if* the *poorest alive* tread upon him, nor the *poorest* receive any *contentment* in being made *equall* to *Princes,* for they *shall bee equall* but *in dust.* One dyeth at his full strength, being wholly at ease and in quiet, and another dies in the *bitternes of his soul,* and never *eates* with *pleasure,* but they lye downe *alike* in *the dust,* and the *worme covers them;* In *Job* and in *Esay,* it *covers them and is spred under them,* the worme is spred *under thee,* and the worme *covers thee,* There's the *Mats* and the *Carpets* that *lie under,* and there's the *State* and the *Canapye,* that *hangs over* the greatest of the sons of men; Even those bodies that were *the temples of the holy Ghost,* come to this *dilapidation,* to ruine, to rubbidge, to dust, even the *Israel of the Lord,* and *Jacob* himselfe hath no other specification, no other denomination, but that *vermis Jacob,* thou *worme of Jacob.* Truely the consideration of this *post-hume death,* this death after buriall, that after *God,* (with whom are the *issues of death*) hath delivered me from the *death* of the *wombe,* by bringing mee into the *world,* and from the manifold *deaths* of the *world,* by laying me in the *grave,* I must die againe in an *Incineration* of this *flesh,* and in a dispersion of that dust. That that *Monarch,* who spred over many nations alive, must in his dust lie in a corner of that *sheete of lead,* and there, but so long as that lead will laste, and that privat and *retir'd man,* that thought himselfe his owne for ever, and never came forth, must in his dust of the grave bee published, and (such are the *revolutions* of the *graves*) bee mingled with the dust of every high way, and of every dunghill, and swallowed in every puddle and pond: This is the most inglorious and contemptible *vilification,* the most deadly and peremptory *nullification* of man, that wee can consider; *God* seemes to have caried the declaration of his *power* to a great height, when hee sets the *Prophet Ezechiel* in the *valley of drye bones,* and says, *Sonne of man can these bones live?* as though it had bene impossible, and yet they did; The *Lord* layed *Sinewes upon them, and flesh,* and *breathed into them,* and *they did live:* But in that case there were *bones* to bee *seene,* something visible, of which it might be said can this thing live? But in this death of *incineration,* and dispersion of dust, wee see *nothing* that wee call *that mans;* If we say, can this dust live?

perchance it *cannot,* it may bee the meere *dust* of the *earth,* which never did live, never shall. It may be the dust of that mans *worme,* which did live, but shall no more. It may bee the dust of *another* man, that concernes not him of whom it is askt. This death of *incineration* and dispersion, is, to naturall *reason,* the most *irrecoverable death* of all, and yet *Domini Domini sunt exitus mortis, unto God the Lord belong the issues of death,* and by *recompacting* this *dust* into the *same body,* and *reinanimating* the *same body* with the *same soule,* hee shall in a blessed and glorious *resurrection* give mee such an *issue from* this *death,* as shal never passe into any other *death,* but establish me into a life that shall last as long as the *Lord of life* himself.

And so have you that that belongs to the *first acceptation* of these words, (*unto God the Lord belong the issues of death*) That though from the *wombe* to the *grave* and in the grave it selfe wee passe from *death* to *death,* yet, as *Daniel* speakes, the *Lord our God is able to deliver us, and hee will deliver us.*

And so wee passe unto our *second accommodation* of *these words* (*unto God the Lord belong the issues of death*) That it *belongs* to God, and *not* to *man* to *passe a judgement* upon us at our death, or to conclude a dereliction on *Gods* part upon the manner thereof.

Those *indications* which the *Physitians* receive, and those *presagitions* which they give for *death* or *recovery* in the *patient,* they receive and they give out of the grounds and the *rules of their art:* But we have no such rule or art to give a *presagition* of *spirituall death* and damnation upon any such *indication* as wee see in any *dying man;* wee see often enough to be sory, but not to despaire; wee may bee deceived both wayes; wee use to comfort our selfe in the death of *a friend,* if it be testified that he went away like a *Lambe,* that is, without any *reluctation.* But, *God* knowes, that [he] may bee accompanied with a *dangerous damp* and *stupefaction,* and *insensibility* of his *present state.* Our blessed *Saviour* suffered *coluctations* with *death,* and a *sadnes even in his soule to death,* and an *agony* even to a *bloody sweate* in his *body,* and *expostulations* with *God,* and *exclamations* upon the crosse. He was a *devout man,* who said upon his death bed, or dead turfe (for hee was an *Heremit) septuaginta annis Domino servivisti, et mori times? hast thou served a good Master threescore and ten yeares,* and *now art thou loath to goe into his presence?* yet *Hilarion* was loath; *Barlaam* was a *devout* man (an *Heremit* too) that

said that day hee died, *Cogita te hodie cœpisse servire Domino,
et hodie finiturum. Consider this to be the first days service that
ever thou didst thy Master,* to glorifie him in a Christianly and a
constant death, *and if thy first day be thy last day too, how
soone dost thou come to receive thy wages?* yet *Barlaam* could
have beene content to have staid longer for it: Make no *ill
conclusions* upon any mans *loathnes* to *die,* for the *mercies* of
God worke *momentarily* in minutes, and many times *insensibly*
to *bystanders* or any other than the party departing. And then
upon *violent deaths* inflicted, as upon malefactors, *Christ* himselfe hath forbidden us by his owne death to make any *ill conclusion;* for his owne *death* had those impressions in it; He
was *reputed,* he was *executed* as a *malefactor,* and no doubt
many of them who concurred to his death, did beleeve him to
bee so; Of *sudden death* there are scarce examples to be found
in the *scriptures* upon *good men,* for *death* in *battaile* cannot
be called *sudden death;* But God governes not by *examples,*
but by *rules,* and therefore make no *ill conclusion* upon *sudden death* nor upon *distempers* neither, though perchance
accompanied with some *words of diffidence* and distrust in the
mercies of God: The *tree lies as it falles* its true, but it is *not*
the *last stroake* that *fells* the *tree,* nor the *last word* nor *gaspe*
that *qualifies* the *soule.* Stil *pray* wee for a *peaceable life* against
violent death, and for *time* of *repentance* against *sudden death,*
and for *sober* and *modest assurance* against *distemperd* and
diffident death, but never make *ill conclusions* upon persons
overtaken with such deaths; *Domini Domini sunt exitus mortis,
to God the Lord belong the issues of death.* And *he* received
Sampson, who went out of this world in *such* a *manner* (consider it *actively,* consider it *passively* in his *owne death,* and in
those whom he *slew* with himselfe) as was subject to interpretation hard enough. Yet the *holy Ghost* hath moved S. *Paul* to
celebrate *Sampson* in his *great Catalogue,* and so doth all the
Church: Our *criticall* day is *not* the *very day* of our *death:* but
the whole course of our life. I thanke him that *prayes* for me
when the *Bell* tolles, but I thank him much more that *Catechises*
mee, or *preaches* to mee, or *instructs mee how to live. Fac hoc
et vives, there's* my securitie, the mouth of the *Lord hath said it,
doe this and thou shalt live:* But *though I doe it, yet I shall die
too,* die a bodily, a naturall death. But God never mentions,
never seems to consider that death, the bodily, the naturall
death. God doth not say, live well and thou shalt die well, that
is, an easie, a quiet death; But *live well here,* and thou shalt

live well for ever. As the first part of a sentence peeces wel
with the last, and never respects, never hearkens after the
parenthesis that comes betweene, so doth a *good life* here flowe
into an *eternall life,* without any consideration, what *manner*
of *death* wee dye: But whether the *gate* of *my prison* be *opened*
with an *oyld key* (by a gentle and *preparing sicknes*), *or* the
gate bee *hewen downe* by a *violent death, or* the gate bee *burnt
downe* by a *raging* and *frantique feaver, a gate into heaven* I
shall have, for *from* the *Lord is the cause* of *my life,* and *with*
God *the Lord* are the *issues of death.* And further wee cary not
this *second acceptation* of the *words,* as this *issue of death is
liberatio in morte, Gods care* that the *soule* be *safe,* what *agonies*
soever the *body suffers* in the *houre* of *death.*

But passe to our *third part* and last part; as this *issue of
death* is *liberatio per mortem,* a *deliverance by the death* of another, by the death of Christ. *Sufferentiam Job audiisti, et vidisti
finem Domini,* sayes Saint *James* 5. 11. *You have heard of the
patience of Job,* says he, All this while you have done that, for
in every man, calamitous, miserable man, a *Job* speakes; Now
see the end of the Lord, saith that *Apostle,* which is not that
end that the *Lord* propos'd to himselfe *(salvation to us)* nor
the end which he proposes to us *(conformitie to him)* but *see
the end of the Lord,* sayes he, The end, *that the Lord* himselfe
came to, Death and a painefull and a shamefull death. But why
did he die? and why die so? *Quia Domini Domini sunt exitus
mortis* (as Saint *Augustine* interpreting this *text* answeres that
question) because *to* this *God our Lord belong'd the issues of
death. Quid apertius diceretur?* sayes hee there, what can bee
more obvious, more manifest than this sense of these words. In
the former part of this verse, it is said; *He that is our God, is
the God of salvation, Deus salvos faciendi,* so hee reads it, the
God that must save us. Who can that be, sayes he, but *Jesus?*
for *therefore* that *name* was *given him,* because he was to *save
us.* And to this *Jesus,* sayes he, this *Saviour, belong the issues of
death; Nec oportuit eum de hac vita alios exitus habere quam
mortis.* Being come into this life in our mortal nature, *He could
not goe out of it* any other way *but by death. Ideo dictum,*
sayes he, *therefore it is said,* To *God the Lord belong the issues
of death; ut ostenderetur moriendo nos salvos facturum,* to *shew
that his way to save us was to die.* And from this *text* doth
Saint *Isodore* prove, that *Christ* was *truely Man,* (which as
many *sects* of *heretiques denied,* as that he was *truely God*) because to him, though he were *Dominus Dominus* (as the *text*

doubles it) *God* the *Lord,* yet to *him,* to *God the Lord belong'd the issues of death, oportuit eum pati* more can not be said, than *Christ* himselfe sayes of himselfe; *These things Christ ought to suffer,* hee had no other way but by death: So then *this* part of our *Sermon* must needes be a *passion Sermon;* since all his *life* was a *continuall passion,* all *our Lent* may well bee a *continuall good Friday. Christs* painefull life tooke off none of the paines of his death, hee felt not the lesse then for having felt so much before. Nor will any thing that shall be said before, lessen, but rather inlarge the devotion, to that which shall be said of his passion at the time of due *solemnization* thereof. *Christ* bled not a droppe the lesse at the last, for having bled at his *Circumcision* before, nor wil you shed a teare the lesse then, if you shed some now. And therefore bee now content to consider with mee how to *this God the Lord belong'd the issues of death.* That *God,* this *Lord,* the *Lord* of *life could die,* is a strange contemplation; That the *red Sea* could bee drie, That the *Sun* could *stand still,* That an *Oven* could be *seaven times heat* and *not burne,* That *Lions* could be *hungry* and *not bite,* is strange, *miraculously strange,* but *supermiraculous* that *God could die;* but that *God would die* is an *exaltation* of that. But even of that also it is a *superexaltation,* that *God shold die, must die,* and *non exitus* (said S. *Augustin, God* the *Lord had no issue but by death,* and *oportuit pati* (says *Christ* himself, all this *Christ ought to suffer,* was bound to suffer; *Deus ultionum Deus* says *David, God* is the *God of revenges,* he wold *not passe* over the *sinne of man* unrevenged, unpunished. But then *Deus ultionum liberè egit* (sayes *that place*) The *God of revenges workes freely,* he *punishes,* he *spares whome he will.* And wold he *not spare himselfe?* he would not: *Dilectio fortis ut mors, love is strong as death,* stronger, it drew in death that naturally is not welcom. *Si possibile,* says *Christ, If it be possible, let this Cup passe,* when his *love expressed in a former decree* with his *Father,* had *made it impossible.* Many *waters quench not love, Christ* tried many; He was *Baptized* out of his *love,* and his love determined not there. He *mingled blood* with *water* in his *agony* and that determined not his love; hee *wept pure blood,* all his blood at all his eyes, at all his pores, in his *flagellation* and *thornes* (*to the Lord our God belong'd the issues of blood*) and these *expressed,* but these did *not quench his love.* Hee *would not* spare, nay he *could not spare himselfe.* There was nothing more free, more voluntary, more spontaneous than the death of *Christ.* 'Tis true, *libere egit,* he *died voluntarily,* but yet when we consider the *contract* that had passed betweene his *Father* and *him,* there was an *oportuit,* a kind of *necessity* upon him. All this *Christ ought to suffer.* And when shall we *date* this *obligation,* this *oportuit,* this *necessity?* when shall wee say *that begun?* Certainly this *decree* by which *Christ was to suffer* all this, was an *eternall decree,* and was there any thing before that, that was eternall? *Infinite love, eternall love;* be pleased to follow this home, and to consider it seriously, that what liberty soever wee can *conceive* in *Christ,* to die or not to die; this *necessity of dying,* this *decree* is as *eternall* as that *liberty;* and yet how small a matter made hee of this *necessity* and this *dying?* His *Father* cals it but a *bruise,* and but a *bruising of his heele (the serpent shall bruise his heele)* and yet that was that, the *serpent* should *practise* and *compasse* his *death.* Himselfe calls it but a *Baptisme,* as though he were to bee the better for it. *I have a Baptisme to be Baptized with,* and he was in paine till it was accomplished, and yet this *Baptisme* was *his death.* The *holy Ghost* calls it *Joy (for the Joy which was set before him hee indured the Crosse)* which was not a *joy* of his reward after his passion, but a joy that filled him even in the middest of those torments, and arose from him; when *Christ* calls his *Calicem, a Cuppe,* and no worse *(can ye drink of my Cuppe)* he speakes not odiously, not with detestation of it: Indeed it was a *Cup, salus mundo, a health to all the world.* And *quid retribuam,* says *David,* what shall I render to the Lord? answere you with *David, accipiam Calicem,* I *will take the Cup of salvation,* take it, that *Cup* is *salvation,* his *passion,* if not into your *present imitation,* yet into your *present contemplation.* And behold how that *Lord* that was *God,* yet *could die, would die, must die,* for your *salvation.* That *Moses* and *Elias talkt with Christ* in the *transfiguration,* both Saint *Mathew* and Saint *Marke* tell us, but what they talkt of onely S. *Luke, Dicebant excessum ejus,* says he, *they talkt of his decease,* of *his death* which *was to be accomplished* at *Jerusalem,* The *word* is of his *Exodus,* the very word of our *text, exitus,* his *issue by death. Moses* who in his *Exodus* had *prefigured* this *issue of our Lord,* and in passing *Israel* out of *Egypt* through the *red Sea,* had foretold in that actuall *prophesie, Christ passing of mankind through* the *sea* of his *blood.* And *Elias,* whose *Exodus* and *issue out of* this *world* was a *figure* of *Christs ascension,* had no doubt a great satisfaction in *talking* with our *blessed Lord de excessu ejus,* of the *full consummation of all this* in *his death,* which was to bee *accomplished* at *Jerusalem.* Our *meditation* of his *death* should be more *viscerall* and affect us more because it is of a thing already done. The ancient *Romans* had a certain tendernesse and detestation of the name of death, they could not name death, no, not in their wills. There they could not say *Si mori contigerit,* but *si quid humanitus contingat,* not if, or when I die, but when the course of nature is accomplished upon me. To us that speake daily of the *death* of *Christ,* (he was *crucified, dead* and *buried*) can the memory or the mention of our owne *death* bee irkesome or bitter? There are in these latter times amongst us, that name death freely enough, and the death of *God,* but in *blasphemous oathes* and *execrations.* Miserable men, who shall therefore bee said never to have named *Jesus,* because they have named him *too often.* And therefore heare *Jesus* say, *Nescivi vos,* I *never knew you,* because they made themselves *too familiar* with him. *Moses* and *Elias* talkt with *Christ* of his *death,* only, in *a holy* and *joyfull sense* of the *benefit* which *they* and *all* the world were to *receive by that. Discourses* of *Religion* should not be *out* of *curiosity,* but to *edification.* And then they talkt with *Christ* of his *death* at that time, when he was in the greatest *height of glory* that ever he admitted in this world, that is, his *transfiguration.* And wee are afraid to speake to the *great men* of this world of their *death,* but nourish in them a *vaine imagination* of *immortality,* and *immutability.* But *bonum est nobis esse hic* (as Saint *Peter* said there) It *is good to dwell here,* in this *consideration* of his *death,* and therefore *transferre* wee our *tabernacle* (our *devotions*) through some of those *steps* which *God* the Lord made to his *issue of death* that *day.* Take in the *whole day* from the *houre* that *Christ received* the *passeover* upon *Thursday, unto* the *houre* in which hee *died* the *next day.* Make *this* present *day* that *day* in thy *devotion,* and consider what *hee did,* and remember what *you have done.* Before hee *instituted* and *celebrated* the *Sacrament,* (which was *after* the *eating of the passeover*) hee proceeded to that *act* of *humility,* to *wash his disciples feete,* even *Peters, who* for a while re*sisted* him; In thy *preparation* to the holy and blessed *Sacrament,* hast thou with a sincere *humility* sought a *reconciliation* with all the *world,* even with those that have beene *averse* from it, and *refused* that *reconciliation* from thee? If so and not else thou hast spent that *first part* of his *last day,* in a *conformity* with him. After the *Sacrament* hee spent the time till night in *prayer,* in *preaching,* in *Psalmes;* Hast thou considered that a *worthy receaving* of the *Sacrament* consists in a *continuation* of *holinesse after*, as wel as in a *preparation* before? If so, thou hast therein also *conformed* thy selfe to him, so *Christ* spent his time till night; *At night* hee *went into the garden* to *pray*, and he prayed *prolixius*, he spent *much time* in *prayer*. How much? Because it is literally expressed, that he *prayed there three severall times*, and that *returning to his Disciples* after his *first prayer*, and *finding them asleepe* said, *could ye not watch with me one houre*, it is collected that he *spent three houres* in *prayer*. I dare scarce aske thee *whither* thou *wentest*, or *how* thou *disposedst of thy self*, when it *grew darke* and after *last night:* If that time were spent in a *holy recommendation* of thy selfe to *God*, and a *submission* of *thy will* to *his*, It was spent in a *conformity* to him. In that *time* and in those *prayers* was *his agony* and *bloody sweat*. I will *hope* that thou didst *pray*, but not *every ordinary* and *customary prayer*, but *prayer actually* accompanied with *shedding of teares*, and *dispositively* in a readines to *shed blood* for *his glory* in *necessary cases*, puts thee into a *conformity* with him; About midnight he was *taken* and *bound with a kisse*. Art thou not *too conformable* to him in that? Is not that *too literally*, too exactly *thy case?* at *midnight* to have *bene taken and bound with a kisse?* from thence he was *caried back* to *Jerusalem*, first to *Annas*, then to *Caiphas*, and (as late as it was) then hee was *examined* and *buffeted*, and *delivered over* to the custody of those *officers*, from whome he received all those *irrisions*, and *violences*, the *covering of his face*, the *spitting upon his face*, the *blasphemies of words*, and the *smartnes of blowes* which that *Gospell* mentions. In which compasse fell that *Gallicinium*, that *crowing of the Cock* which *called up Peter* to his *repentance*. How thou passedst all that time last night thou knowest. If thou didst any thing that needed *Peters teares*, and hast *not shed them*, let me be thy *Cock*, doe it now, Now thy *Master* (in the unworthiest of his servants) *lookes back upon thee*, doe it now; *Betimes*, in the morning, so soone as it was day, the *Jewes held a counsell* in the *high Priests hall*, and *agreed upon their evidence* against him, and then caried him to *Pilate*, who was to be his *Judge;* diddest thou *accuse* thy selfe when thou *wakedst this morning*, and wast thou content even with *false accusations* (that is) rather to *suspect actions* to have beene sin, which were not, than to *smother* and *justify* such as were *truly sins?* then thou spentst that *houre* in *conformity* to him: *Pilate* found *no evidence against him*, and therefore to ease himselfe, and to passe a *complement* upon *Herod, Tetrarch* of *Galilee,* who was at that time at *Jerusalem* (because *Christ* being a *Galilean* was of *Herods jurisdiction*) *Pilat sent him* to *Herod,* and rather as a *madman* than a *malefactor, Herod* remaunded him (*with scornes*) to *Pilat* to proceed against him; And this was about *eight* of the *clock.* Hast thou been content to come to this *Inquisition,* this examination, this agitation, this cribration, this pursuit of thy *conscience,* to *sift* it, to follow it from the *sinnes* of thy *youth* to thy *present sinnes,* from the *sinnes* of thy *bed,* to the *sinnes* of thy *boorde,* and from the *substance* to the *circumstance* of thy *sinnes?* That's *time spent* like thy *Saviours. Pilat* wold have *saved Christ,* by using the *priviledge of the day* in his behalfe, because that *day* one *prisoner was to be delivered,* but they *choose Barrabas.* Hee would have *saved* him *from death,* by *satisfying their fury,* with *inflicting* other *torments* upon him, *scourging* and *crowning with thornes,* and *loading* him with many *scornefull* and *ignominious contumelies;* But they regarded him not, they pressed a *crucifying.* Hast thou gone about to *redeeme thy sinne,* by *fasting,* by *Almes,* by *disciplines* and *mortifications,* in way of *satisfaction* to the *Justice* of *God?* that will not serve, that's not the right way, *wee presse* an utter *Crucifying* of that *sinne* that governes thee; and that *conformes* thee to *Christ.* Towards *noone Pilat* gave *judgement,* and they made such *hast* to execution, as that *by noone* hee was *upon the Crosse.* There now hangs that *sacred Body* upon the *Crosse, rebaptized* in his owne *teares* and *sweat,* and *embalmed* in his *owne blood alive.* There are those *bowells of compassion,* which are so conspicuous, so manifested, as that you may *see them through his wounds.* There those *glorious eyes* grew faint in their light: so as the *Sun ashamed* to survive them, *departed with his light too.* And then that *Sonne of God,* who was *never from us,* and yet had now come a *new way unto* us in *assuming our nature,* delivers that *soule* (which was *never out* of his *Fathers hands*) by a *new way,* a *voluntary emission* of it into his Fathers hands; For though to this *God our Lord, belong'd these issues of death,* so that considered in his owne contract, he *must* necessarily *die,* yet at *no breach* or *battery,* which they had made upon his *sacred Body,* issued his *soule,* but *emisit,* hee *gave up the Ghost,* and as *God breathed a soule into* the *first Adam,* so this *second Adam breathed his soule into God, into the hands of God.* There wee leave you in that blessed dependancy, to *hang* upon *him* that *hangs* upon the *Crosse,* there *bath* in his *teares,* there *suck* at his *woundes,* and *lie downe in peace* in his *grave*, till hee vouchsafe you a *resur-rection*, and an *ascension* into that *Kingdome*, which hee *hath purchas'd for you*, with the *inestimable price* of his *incorruptible blood*. Amen.

[Published separately, 1632, etc.]